Introduction to Counseling

Fifth Edition

To Laura and Aja,

Whose amazing mother-daughter relationship transcends time and space . . . and the love and laughter that bring joy to our days.

⊛SAGE | 50 YEARS

SAGE was founded in 1965 by Sara Miller McCune to support the dissemination of usable knowledge by publishing innovative and high-quality research and teaching content. Today, we publish more than 850 journals, including those of more than 300 learned societies, more than 800 new books per year, and a growing range of library products including archives, data, case studies, reports, and video. SAGE remains majority-owned by our founder, and after Sara's lifetime will become owned by a charitable trust that secures our continued independence.

Los Angeles | London | New Delhi | Singapore | Washington DC

Introduction to Counseling

An Art and Science Perspective

Fifth Edition

Michael Scott Nystul

New Mexico State University

Los Angeles | London | New Delhi
Singapore | Washington DC

Los Angeles | London | New Delhi
Singapore | Washington DC

FOR INFORMATION:

SAGE Publications, Inc.
2455 Teller Road
Thousand Oaks, California 91320
E-mail: order@sagepub.com

SAGE Publications Ltd.
1 Oliver's Yard
55 City Road
London EC1Y 1SP
United Kingdom

SAGE Publications India Pvt. Ltd.
B 1/I 1 Mohan Cooperative Industrial Area
Mathura Road, New Delhi 110 044
India

SAGE Publications Asia-Pacific Pte. Ltd.
3 Church Street
#10-04 Samsung Hub
Singapore 049483

Printed in the United States of America

ISBN 978-1-4833-1661-1

Acquisitions Editor: Kassie Graves
Associate Editor: Abbie Rickard
Editorial Assistant: Carrie Montoya
eLearning Editor: Lucy Berbeo
Production Editor: Laura Barrett
Copy Editor: Paula L. Fleming
Typesetter: C&M Digitals (P) Ltd.
Proofreader: Catherine Forrest
Indexer: Sheila Bodell
Cover Designer: Janet Kiesel
Marketing Manager: Shari Countryman

This book is printed on acid-free paper.

15 16 17 18 19 10 9 8 7 6 5 4 3 2 1

Brief Contents

Detailed Contents

PART 2 MULTICULTURAL COUNSELING AND COUNSELING THEORIES 167

Chapter 6 Developing a Personal Approach to Counseling From a Multicultural Perspective 168

Preface

Features of this Book

Why I Wrote the Book

Introduction to Counseling: An Art and Science Perspective is designed for undergraduate and graduate courses such as Introduction to Counseling and Professional Issues in Counseling. My experience with the book has been that it can be used successfully with students who are majoring in the helping professions and with nonmajors. I wrote this book from the perspective that counseling concepts can be useful to address daily challenges of living (e.g., attempting to understand and appreciate individual differences and not overreact to life events). I get excited when I share these ideas with students, because I am convinced they can make a significant difference in terms of expanding worldviews and finding personal meaning in life.

Encouraging Feedback and Uses of Book

Introduction to Counseling: An Art and Science Perspective has been used in a variety of settings and formats with overall positive feedback (e.g., "very readable and personal, like the book is talking to me, not lecturing to me"). The book has been used in colleges and universities across the United States and in other countries and has been translated into Chinese. There is also a sound version for people who are blind or dyslexic, and a Braille version.

I have used this book with large undergraduate classes (around 100 students) and with smaller graduate-level classes (e.g., professional issues courses associated with our CACREP-accredited mental health counseling program at New Mexico State University). The book has been used in different formats—WebCT and on-campus classroom. I have been pleased with the positive feedback instructors have given me regarding WebCT use (they tell me students really like the book). This feedback is especially important to me, because in WebCT the textbook provides a major role in the class (e.g., it covers information normally presented to students in lecture format).

New to this Edition

Emerging Trends

The fifth edition has addressed a number of emerging trends in the field of counseling. Highlights of these trends are as follows:

- Professional identity of counselors is explored from a number of perspectives, including a recent definition of counseling (endorsed by all but two of the counseling professional organizations) that can be shared with the public.

- Wellness and positive psychology are addressed as important means to promote optimal development (as contrasted with the medical model's focus on mental illness and pathology).

- An awareness of social justice issues and willingness to advocate for them are described as important dimensions of multicultural counseling that can be used to help clients overcome oppressive forces that undermine their ability to obtain equal rights and opportunities (e.g., by ensuring that all clients, regardless of issues of diversity, have access to quality mental health services).

- Research methodologies are presented from a variety of perspectives, including their utility for analyzing large numbers of research studies (e.g., meta-analytical methods), how action research can be used to enhance the lives of participants, and the use of research to identify evidence-based treatment modalities.

- Cybercounseling and other technology-assisted methods of counseling are explored in terms of potential gains and challenges regarding delivery of mental health services.

- Discussions of counseling and neuroscience explore the neurobiological basis of behavior and how professional counselors can expand their role to include a neuroscience perspective for understanding and treating mental disorders.

Updated Information

Updated information regarding professional counseling codes of ethics and the recently published 5th edition of the *Diagnostic Statistical Manual of Mental Disorders* (DSM-5; American Psychiatric Association, 2013) are provided in this fifth edition of this text.

Changes to Codes of Ethics and Professional Conduct

This edition was updated throughout to reflect the American Counseling Association's 2014 code of ethics and the American Psychological Association's 2010 code of conduct. Information is provided regarding client welfare, informed consent, confidentiality, and dual relations. Other ethical codes updated include the American School Counseling Association's ethical standards for school counselors, the code of ethics of the American Mental Health Counselors Association, and the American Association for Marriage and Family Therapy's code of ethics.

The *DSM-5*

Updated information provided about the *DSM-5* (American Psychiatric Association, 2013) includes:

- History of the *DSM*

- Definition of mental disorders

- Neuroscience perspectives on diagnosis

- Elements of a diagnosis

- Multicultural considerations in diagnosis

- Categorical versus dimensional approaches to *DSM-5* diagnosis

- Personal note regarding categorical and dimensional diagnosis

- New table differentiating categorical and dimensional diagnosis

- Controversies regarding the *DSM-5* (e.g., potential for overdiagnosing, changes to diagnostic criteria for some disorders, and disorders that were added and deleted).

Pedagogical Aids

Pedagogical aids added to the 5th edition include a glossary of terms for each chapter, expanded lists of questions for personal exploration, and inclusion of learning activities to encourage students to apply ideas they are learning in the classroom to situations in everyday life.

Instructor's Manual and Student Resources

The Instructor's Manual was updated regarding chapter summary, key concepts, learning objectives, lecture organization, discussion questions, class activities, and test questions. Hopefully these materials will be a useful supplement for instructors and students. The manual, along with a complete test bank, PowerPoints, practice quizzes and flashcards, can be accessed on the companion website at **study.sagepub.com/nystul**.

Overview of Book

Introduction to Counseling: An Art and Science Perspective provides an overview of the counseling profession. It is written from the perspective of counseling and psychotherapy as both art and science, a theme extended throughout the book in an effort to highlight the balance between the subjective and objective dimensions of counseling. I have also included *Personal Notes* that provide candid remarks and insights based on more than 45 years of clinical experience.

The first part of the book presents an overview of counseling and the counseling process. It attempts to provide a conceptual framework for understanding what counseling and the counseling process are. Chapter 1 presents several models that can be used to conceptualize counseling, including counseling and psychotherapy as art and science, formal versus informal helping, counseling as storytelling, postmodernism, counseling from a historical perspective, and emerging trends in counseling. Chapter 2 provides information about professional preparation and legal-ethical issues, including information on the recently updated ACA (2014) code of ethics. Chapter 3 gives an overview of the counseling process and provides a description of the skills involved in the art of listening. Chapters 4 and 5 cover the art and science of assessment, diagnosis, research, and evaluation.

The second part of the book provides information on multicultural counseling and counseling theories. Chapter 6 offers specific guidelines for developing a counseling approach from a multicultural perspective. Chapters 7, 8, and 9 address major counseling theories that can be utilized in one's counseling approach. Special attention is paid to the importance of applying a multicultural perspective to the development and use of counseling theories and procedures (i.e., considering diversity issues such as age, gender, sexual orientation, culture, spirituality, and socioeconomic status).

The third part of the book comprises of Chapters 10 through 15, which address special approaches and settings for counselors. After counselors have gained fundamental knowledge and skills in counseling, it is common to begin to develop expertise in working with special populations and settings, such as counseling children and adolescents in a school setting or working with mental health issues in clinics, hospitals, and private practice. Special approaches to counseling, such as marriage and family, child and adolescent, group, and career counseling, can be useful modalities for counselors seeking to promote clients' optimal development across the life span. Numerous challenges and rewards are associated with developing these special skills and practices associated with the counseling profession.

For the 5th edition, I have attempted to incorporate emerging trends, changes in ethical codes, and the guidelines for diagnosis in the *DSM-5*. Together, these trends and changes in the profession offer opportunities for major paradigm shifts that can redefine important elements of the theory, research, and practice of counseling. The ultimate goal of these changes appears to be developing models of helping that are more inclusive and adaptive, as opposed to culturally encapsulated, and that can be translated into effective, efficient methods of helping in an environment of decreasing resources. It is indeed an exciting and rewarding time to be exploring the field of counseling.

Acknowledgments

I would like to recognize a number of individuals who have provided valuable input, ideas, and encouragement regarding this book: Eve Adams, Gerald Becker, Jon Carlson, Gerald Corey, Martin Greer, Michael Waldo, and Richard Watts. I would also like to thank the reviewers of the fifth edition who provided excellent suggestions for the revision process: Chad Luke, Tennesse Tech; Darren H. Iwamoto, Chaminade University of Honolulu; Julie M. Koch, Oklahoma State University; and Maria Cuddy-Casey, Immaculata University.

Special thanks are extended to Kassie Graves, Publisher, and Carrie Montoya, Senior Editorial Assistant, whose expertise, encouragement, and assistance made this edition possible! I would also like to express my gratitude to the other people at SAGE who truly make SAGE "the natural home of authors," including production editor Laura Barrett and copy editor Paula Fleming, whose input and expertise were invaluable, as well as senior graphic designer Janet Kiesel, whose cover art design was truly amazing!

I would like to recognize Professor Peter Sheehan and Dr. Frank Zeran—two amazing individuals who provided me with opportunities when I was just beginning my career as a student and professional. They truly made my academic career possible. I also want to express my appreciation to the students and instructors who have used *Introduction to Counseling: An Art and Science Perspective*. I appreciate your encouragement and have learned so much from you!

Last, but certainly not least, I would like to thank my wife, Laura, for her encouragement, love, and support in writing this book. Her beautiful smiles inspired me to reach for the stars and beyond.

About the Author

 Michael Scott Nystul received his PhD in counseling from Oregon State University in 1974. He holds the position of Professor Emeritus in the Department of Counseling and Educational Psychology at New Mexico State University. Professor Nystul has worked as a professor for 30 years and as a mental health counselor, school counselor, and psychologist in a variety of clinical settings such as schools, hospitals, community mental health centers, university counseling centers, and private practice. His first position was as an elementary and middle school counselor with the Bureau of Indian Affairs in 1970. He continues to be active in the counseling field. Professor Nystul has more than 100 publications, including journal articles, book chapters, and books, to his credit. He has three daughters, five grandchildren, and one great-grandchild and relies on his wife, Laura, to maintain a sense of balance in life.

An Overview of Counseling and the Counseling Process

Part 1 provides a conceptual framework for understanding counseling and the counseling process. The following five chapters are covered in Part 1:

An Overview of Counseling

Welcome to the Field of Counseling

The field of counseling can be of interest to you even if you do not want to become a professional counselor. It offers tools for understanding, connecting, and helping that can be used to promote self-awareness and self-improvement and to enhance all aspects of life, including interpersonal relations, coping with stress, and problem solving.

Moreover, counseling as a career can be exciting and rewarding, and there are many reasons for becoming a counselor. You may expect that helping a client work through a crisis or develop a more effective and meaningful lifestyle will be personally gratifying. Perhaps you simply find people interesting, or you are curious about how the mind functions, or even fascinated by abnormal conditions such as schizophrenia. In addition, you may find appealing the challenge of working in a relatively new profession. Counseling offers numerous opportunities for its practitioners to make a significant contribution to the field. For example, you can develop new approaches to counseling or become involved in professional issues such as licensure. Indeed, there are many ways to involve yourself in the counseling profession, and this book seeks to help you identify those facets of counseling that you would like to explore.

What Is Counseling?

No simple answer addresses the question "What is counseling?" **Counseling** can most appropriately be understood as a dynamic process associated with an emerging profession. It involves a professionally trained counselor assisting a client with particular concerns. In this process, the counselor can use a variety of counseling strategies, such

Chapter Overview

This chapter provides several models that can be used to conceptualize counseling. Highlights of the chapter include the following:

- **The art and science of counseling and psychotherapy**
- **Counseling as storytelling**
- **Counseling versus psychotherapy**
- **Formal versus informal helping**
- **Personal qualities of effective helpers**
- **The helping profession**
- **Counseling from a historical perspective**
- **Future trends in counseling**

as individual, group, or family counseling, to assist the client with bringing about beneficial changes and generating a variety of outcomes—facilitating behavior change, enhancing coping skills, promoting decision making, and improving relationships.

This chapter presents several conceptual models for understanding the different facets of counseling. Counseling is described first as an art and a science, then from the perspective of narrative psychology or storytelling. The chapter also differentiates counseling from **psychotherapy** and formal from informal helping, describes the personal qualities of effective helpers, identifies members of the helping profession, and provides information on past and future trends in counseling.

The Art and Science of Counseling and Psychotherapy

Counseling is essentially both an art and a science. The art-and-science model promoted throughout the book suggests that counseling is an attempt to balance the subjective and objective dimensions of the counseling process. From this perspective, the counselor, like an artist, can sensitively reach into the world of the client yet on some level maintain a sense of professional and scientific objectivity.

The theoretical origins of the art and science of counseling and psychotherapy can be traced to the scientist-practitioner model set forth in Boulder, Colorado, in 1949. The scientist-practitioner, or Boulder, model (Raimy, 1950) suggests that science should provide a foundation for clinical practice. The Boulder model continues to have a major influence over the structure of university programs for the education of those in the helping profession (Baker & Benjamin, 2000; Peterson, 2000). However, Beutler, Williams, Wakefield, and Entwistle (1995) noted that practitioners have become increasingly dissatisfied with traditional research methodologies, instead becoming interested in alternative approaches to research that are more directly linked to everyday clinical practice. Single-case research design (see Chapter 5), for example, is receiving attention as a viable tool for helping counselors bridge the gap between research and practice (Murray, 2009; Sharpley, 2007).

The art-and-science model of counseling and psychotherapy represents an extension of the scientist-practitioner model. From this perspective, the **science of counseling** generates a base of knowledge that promotes competency and efficacy in counseling. The **art of counseling** involves using this knowledge base to develop skills that can be applied sensitively to clients in a multicultural society. The art of counseling relates to the subjective dimension, and the science of counseling reflects the objective dimension. The focus of counseling can shift back and forth between these two dimensions as one proceeds through the counseling process. For example, during initial sessions, the counselor may function more like an artist, using listening skills to understand the client. Later, the focus might shift to the science dimension as the counselor uses psychological tests to obtain an objective understanding of the client. Together, the art and science can create a balanced approach to counseling. A more detailed description of these two dimensions follows.

THE ART OF COUNSELING To a large degree, counseling is an art. To call counseling an art suggests it is a *flexible, creative process* whereby the counselor adjusts the approach to the unique and emerging needs of the client. The first *Personal Note* that follows illustrates how a counselor can be flexible and creative in working with a client.

A Personal Note

As a psychologist working for the Public Health Service on a Navajo Indian Reservation, I was asked to work with a child with autism as part of my consultation with the public schools. School personnel had placed the young girl in a classroom for the mentally retarded, not knowing she was autistic. The child was referred to me for counseling and self-concept development. When she came into my office, I had some puppets ready to use with her. These puppets were part of a self-concept program called Developing an Understanding of Self and Others (DUSO; Dinkmeyer & Dinkmeyer, 1982). I soon realized that she seemed oblivious to me and the puppets. My counseling plans appeared to be useless.

I wanted to make contact with the child and find a way to reach into her world and develop a special relationship with her. I decided to let her be the guide, and I would follow. She walked over and threw the puppets into a neat pile. If she missed the pile with a puppet, she threw it over again until it landed right on top of the others. She was very good at throwing puppets into a pile, and she seemed to enjoy doing it. I had identified one of her assets— something she felt good about, something she felt secure with. It was an extension of her world, her way of doing things. It made sense to her.

I wanted to become part of her world by reaching into it. I walked over and put my arms around her pile of puppets, becoming a puppet-basketball net. She continued to throw her puppets through my net onto the pile. For the next 20 minutes, the child threw the puppets into a pile. When she ran out of puppets, she would gather them up and start over, throwing them into a new pile. I would move the "net" as necessary. During this time, she never made eye contact with me or said a word. I became discouraged and walked back to my seat. As I did, I noticed that her eyes followed my movement. At that instant, I knew I had made contact. I had found a way into her world.

Over the next year, she let me further into her world. For the most part, she was the guide and I the follower—a guest in her home. As the relationship grew stronger, she became willing to explore my world. Through our relationship, I helped her reach out into the world of others. For example, I helped her with language development and encouraged her to move away from her ritualistic behavioral patterns. (A more detailed description of this case can be found by referring to Nystul, 1986.)

Another aspect of the art of counseling is the giving of oneself in counseling. This concept, derived from humanistic psychology, emphasizes the importance of counselors being authentic and human in their approach. Counselors can give of themselves on many levels. They can give concern and support as they empathize with their client or, at a more intense level, engage in an existential encounter, which involves the process of self-transcendence. In this experience, the counselor moves beyond the self and feels at one with the client (Nystul, 1987a). The experience can help a client overcome feelings of aloneness and alienation.

Giving of oneself in counseling may be especially appropriate in situations that involve working with neglected and abused children. These children may be wards of a court, without parents or significant others. They may feel unloved and lost, lacking a reason to live. In these cases, the counselor may attempt to communicate compassion, kindness, tenderness, and perhaps even love. The second *Personal Note* that follows illustrates the concept of giving of oneself in counseling.

Counselors must use safeguards when expressing intense feelings to a client. They must, for example, clearly establish their role as a counselor and not a parent. They must also avoid becoming overly involved to the point where they lose professional objectivity. In addition, counselors must be aware that excessive concern or worry about a child could lead to burnout. Giving of oneself in counseling is a very delicate process: Though it can be enriching and rewarding for the counselor and the child, it can also be exhausting. Communicating intense emotion may not be practical for some counselors. For others, it is an art that can be developed over time.

A Personal Note

A 5-year-old child was abandoned by her parents and placed in a residential facility for neglected and abused children. On one occasion, the caretakers of the institution became concerned because the child had stayed up all night crying and vomiting. They brought her to a hospital the next morning. A pediatrician found nothing physically wrong with the child and referred her to me for mental health services.

After introducing myself to the child, I asked her how she was feeling. She sat down, put her face between her legs, and began to cry. It was the most deep-sorrowful sobbing I had ever heard. I leaned forward and gently touched her head, trying to comfort her. I could feel her pain. She looked up at me and appeared frightened and alone. I reached over and held her hand and told her I wanted to help her feel better. My heart reached out to her. I looked at her and said I thought she was a beautiful person and I wanted to work with her every day. She nodded in agreement. I worked with her in play therapy for several weeks. During that time, her depression gradually lifted.

THE SCIENCE OF COUNSELING The science of counseling provides a balance to the art of counseling by supplying an objective dimension to the counseling process. Claiborn (1987) noted that science is an important aspect of counselors' identity in that the scientific perspective differentiates professional counselors from nonprofessional helpers. He suggested that counselors should strive to be counselors-as-scientists (i.e., to function as a counselor and think as a scientist). Thinking as a scientist requires the counselor to have the skills to formulate objective observations and inferences, test hypotheses, and build theories (Claiborn). Claiborn also suggested that the scientist-practitioner model, set forth by Pepinsky and Pepinsky (1954), could provide useful guidelines for contemporary counselors. This model conceptualizes science and practice as integrated, mutually dependent, and overlapping activities. The interrelationship of theory, research, and practice illustrates the complementary nature of science and practice. A counseling theory, for example, can be tested in practice and can then, in turn, be evaluated by research.

The science aspect of counseling also encourages counselors to develop skills that can promote professional objectivity in the counseling process. These skills include observation, inference, hypothesis testing, and theory building, which Claiborn (1987) suggested are necessary for counselors to think as scientists. The use of psychological tests, a systematic approach to diagnosis, a consideration of neuroscience, and research methods to establish counseling accountability and efficacy are other aspects of the scientific model. We should not view these as entities apart from counseling. Instead, counselors should integrate these skills and strategies into the counselor's overall role and function.

POSTMODERNISM Postmodernism is based on theoretical perspectives such as constructivism and social constructionism that can be used to conceptualize counseling. Constructivism (Mahoney, 1988) emphasizes the role of cognition in interpreting external events, whereas social constructionism (Gergen, 1994b) stresses the impact of social forces on constructing reality. Both theories recognize the role that narratives play in creating stories that individuals utilize to define personal meaning in life. Postmodernism offers multiple opportunities for theory building, especially in terms of incorporating diversity issues into counseling.

Postmodernism recognizes that truth, knowledge, and reality are reflected contextually in terms of social, political, cultural, and other forces that can affect personal experience. Postmodernism offers opportunities for integrating multicultural issues, such as the role of culture and economic forces, into mental health and counseling. Postmodernism is associated with an evolving view of the self that suggests a movement away from the autonomous, integral self to a social-community self that extends beyond the individual to all aspects of society (Gergen, 1994b; M. B. Smith, 1994). Continued research regarding postmodernism appears warranted.

Counseling as Storytelling

Counseling as storytelling, also referred to a narrative counseling, suggests that people live "storied lives" (lives based on the stories they tell and hear about themselves) and that they can re-story their lives to create new meanings and opportunities (Nafziger & DeKruyf, 2013; Winslade & Monk, 2007). Howard (1991) and Sexton and Whiston (1994) suggested that narrative (or storytelling) methods for understanding human behavior have become increasingly popular in psychology. For example, identity development can represent life-story construction, and psychopathology can be related to dysfunctional life stories and can involve story repair (Howard).

Narrative psychology and its application to counseling as a form of storytelling are related to two emerging and complementary trends in counseling—the theories associated with **postmodernism** and **brief-solution-focused counseling** approaches (additional information regarding these trends is provided throughout the text). Narrative approaches to counseling attempt to simplify and demystify counseling by focusing on the client's own language as opposed to psychological jargon (Eron & Lund, 1993). The role of the counselor is to engage in a collaborative, nonimpositional relationship with the client (Eron & Lund). In this process, the counselor and client work together to create new narratives (or alternative stories) as a means of enhancing the client's well-being.

Howard (1991) provided a detailed description of the role of storytelling in counseling:

> In the course of telling the story of his or her problem, the client provides the therapist with a rough idea of his or her orientation toward life, his or her plans, goals, ambitions, and some idea of the events and pressures surrounding the particular presenting problem. Over time, the therapist must decide whether this problem represents a minor deviation from an otherwise healthy life story. Is this a normal, developmentally appropriate adjustment issue? Or does the therapist detect signs of more thoroughgoing problems in the client's life story? Will therapy play a minor, supportive role to an individual experiencing a low point in his or her life course? If so, the orientation and major themes of the life will be largely unchanged in the therapy experience. But if the trajectory of the life story is problematic in some fundamental way, then more serious, long-term story repair (or rebiographing) might be indicated. So, from this perspective, part of the work between client and therapist can be seen as life-story elaboration, adjustments, or repair. (p. 194)

Meichenbaum and Fitzpatrick (1992) provided additional information on storytelling in terms of how people cope with stress:

- People organize information in terms of stories about themselves.

- Negative, stressful life events affect people's belief systems, thereby altering the nature of their stories.

- How people rescript their stories (i.e., engage in narrative repair) will influence how well they cope with stress.

- The literature is beginning to identify what are adaptive and maladaptive narratives and how stress-inoculation training can be used to help clients construct adaptive narratives to stressful life events.

Counseling as storytelling is an intriguing concept that appears to offer much promise for understanding counseling. As Russell and Lucariello (1992) have noted, there is a great need for empirical research to investigate the impact of storytelling on the counseling process. The following *Personal Note* provides an illustration of the role of storytelling in counseling.

A Personal Note

It seems as if everyone has a story to tell if one is willing to listen. I remember a mail carrier (whom I did not even know) once stopping me when I was walking around in my backyard. He was visibly angry and proceeded to tell me how a police officer had blocked his way on the road while the officer was writing a ticket. The mail carrier said, "I asked him to let me by, so I could do my job. But he wouldn't, so I went by anyway, driving onto the shoulder. Good grief, some people only think of themselves."

As he talked on, I thought, *This is a story that this man must tell someone, anyone, to ventilate and to feel understood.* I can think of many other examples of times (such as on some plane and bus trips I've had) when people have expressed their desire to tell their stories. I have also been in need of telling my own stories from time to time.

Lately I have become more aware of the role of storytelling in counseling. It has been my experience that most clients have stories to tell. Many of these clients have told their stories to others (such as friends or family members) with disappointing results. In counseling, the clients' stories will hopefully be shown the respect and care they deserve.

One client's story that stands out for me is one of pain, struggle, and courage. Pat was a 40-year-old Anglo single parent of four children. She had been in a serious car accident a year before I had my first counseling session with her. Much of our first sessions involved Pat sharing her story of the accident and her anger at the drunk driver who had hit her and the lack of support she was feeling from her insurance company.

Pat's story was also one of fighting for her physical and emotional survival. She had endured numerous operations for her physical injuries; was unable to go back to work due to physical limitations; and had multiple psychological problems that included insomnia, depression, and anxiety. It was therefore necessary to work closely with a psychiatrist to include medication in conjunction with counseling in her treatment program.

Fortunately, Pat had a very strong support system, including friends and family members who helped her feel safe and encouraged, and this helped her overcome some of her feelings of anxiety and depression. Gradually, Pat was able to work her way out of her depression and see some hope and possibilities for a better tomorrow. As she struggled to regain control of her life, she appeared to be engaging in a process of narrative repair, replacing words of gloom with those of hope.

Counseling and Psychotherapy

In order to understand what counseling is, it is important to understand key terms and concepts such as *counseling* and *psychotherapy*. The counseling literature has not made a clear distinction between these concepts (Corsini & Wedding, 2000), perhaps because the two processes are more similar than different. A counselor may do both counseling and psychotherapy in one session. The two processes can therefore blend. We can probably best understand their relationship on a continuum, with counseling at one end and psychotherapy at the other.

One subtle difference between the two is that counseling addresses the conscious mental state, whereas psychotherapy also ventures into the client's unconscious processes—providing insight to a client. Several other differences between counseling and psychotherapy, listed in Table 1.1, address focus, clients' problems, goals, treatment, and setting.

As depicted in Table 1.1, the focus of counseling tends to be developmental in nature, whereas psychotherapy has a remediative emphasis. Counseling attempts to empower clients with tools they can use to meet the normal developmental challenges of progressing through the life span. Counseling is therefore preventative in nature and

Table 1.1 Comparison of Counseling and Psychotherapy

	Counseling	Psychotherapy
Focus	Developmental—fosters coping skills to facilitate development and prevent problems.	Remediative—aims at helping clients overcome existing problems, such as anxiety and depression.
Clients' Problems	Clients tend to have "problems of living," such as relationship difficulties, or need assistance with specific problems, such as career choice.	Clients' problems are more complex and may require formal diagnostic procedures to determine whether there is a mental disorder.
Goals	The focus is on short-term goals (resolution of immediate concerns).	The focus is on short- and long-term goals. Long-term goals can involve processes such as helping the client overcome a particular mental disorder.
Treatment Approaches	The treatment program can include preventative approaches and various counseling strategies to assist with the client's concerns.	Psychotherapeutic approaches are complex. They utilize strategies that relate to conscious and unconscious processes.
Setting	Counseling services can be provided in a variety of settings, such as schools, churches, and mental health clinics.	Psychotherapy is typically offered in settings such as private practice, mental health centers, and hospitals.

growth facilitating. Counseling is used with clients whose problems do not stem from a serious mental disorder, such as a major depression. Instead, it is more appropriate for clients who have "problems of living," such as parent-child conflicts or marital difficulties. The goals of counseling tend to focus on resolving immediate concerns, such as helping clients work through a relationship difficulty or make a career decision.

Treatment programs in counseling vary according to the client's concern. For example, counseling might involve a parent education program to help parents learn how to establish a positive relationship with their child. Other counseling strategies might help a client work through marital difficulties. Counseling approaches are usually short-term, involving one session each week for 3 to 12 weeks, and counseling services may take place in a variety of settings, such as schools, churches, and mental health clinics.

Psychotherapy, on the other hand, is directed at helping clients overcome the pain and suffering associated with existing problems, such as anxiety and depression. The problems addressed by psychotherapy tend to be more complex, and treatment can involve both short- and long-term goals: The short-term goals may focus on problems similar to those addressed in counseling, for example, dealing with marital problems; long-term goals relate to more deep-seated or involved problems, such as depression or schizophrenia. Psychotherapy itself is complex and requires expertise in several areas, such as personality theory and abnormal psychology. It also relates to both conscious and unconscious processes; for example, the process may involve hypnosis, projective tests, and dream analysis techniques to examine unconscious processes. Psychotherapeutic approaches are usually long-term, involving sessions once each week for 3 to 6 months and sometimes even longer. Typical settings for psychotherapy are private practice, mental health centers, and hospitals.

Differentiating Formal From Informal Helping

Another way to answer the question "What is counseling?" is to differentiate counseling from the informal helping that can take place between friends. Some individuals who have had no formal training in counseling can provide valuable assistance. These informal helpers usually have some of the personal qualities associated with effective counselors, such as being caring and nonjudgmental and having good listening skills. However, professional counselors may differ from informal helpers in a number of ways.

First, counselors can maintain a degree of objectivity because they are not directly involved in the client's life. Though there are exceptions, informal helpers usually have a personal relationship with the individual, so the assistance they provide is likely to reflect a personal bias. A related fact is that counselors usually do not have a preconceived idea of how a client should behave. Thus, having had no previous experience with the counselor, the client is free to try new modes of behaving and relating. This often does not occur with informal helpers, who may expect the person they are trying to help to act in a certain way; the person being helped might easily fall into the habits established in the relationship, which can create a restrictive environment.

Second, counselors are guided by a code of ethics, the American Counseling Association (ACA) *Code of Ethics and Standards of Practice* (2014), which is designed to protect the rights of clients. For example, the information that a client presents to a counselor must be held in confidence, except in extreme circumstances, such as when the client plans to do serious harm to self or others. Knowing this, a client might feel more free to share thoughts and feelings with a professional counselor than with an informal helper.

Third, formal counseling can be an intense and emotionally exhausting experience. After establishing rapport, the counselor may find it necessary to confront the client with painful issues. Informal helpers may avoid confrontation to avoid jeopardizing the friendship. They often play a more supportive and reassuring role, at times even attempting to rescue the person they are helping. In doing so, the helper, despite good intentions, does not communicate the all-important belief that the client is a capable person. In this way, the helper may deprive the individual of an opportunity to get in touch with feelings.

A final difference lies in the repertoire of counseling strategies and techniques available to professional counselors and their ability to systematically utilize these strategies and techniques to promote client growth. For example, a client may have a phobia about heights. The counselor may use a behavioral technique called systematic desensitization, which helps the client replace an anxiety response to heights with a relaxation response. Some clients may not be able to stand up for their rights or state their opinions and could therefore benefit from assertiveness training. Other clients may have marriage or family problems; the professional counselor may draw upon various marriage and family therapies to assist these clients. Lacking formal training as a counselor, informal helpers are unfamiliar with and thereby unable to utilize these strategies. Instead, they typically rely on advice giving as their main method of helping.

Personal Qualities of Effective Helpers

The following *helping formula* developed by Brammer (1999) provides yet another conceptual model for answering the question "What is counseling?"

Personality of the Helper	+	Helping Skills	=	Growth-Facilitating Conditions	→	Specific Outcomes

This formula suggests that taking the personality of the helper and adding some helping skills like counseling techniques can generate growth-facilitating conditions. A feeling of mutual trust, respect, and freedom between the counselor and client characterizes these conditions (Brammer, 2002), and when they exist, desirable outcomes tend to emerge from the counseling process.

The helping formula emphasizes the importance of the personality of the helper (Brammer, 2002). Evidence is emerging that suggests the personal characteristics of the counselor play a critical role in the efficacy of counseling (Corey, Corey, Corey, & Callanan, 2015; Herman, 1993). As early as 1969, Combs et al. (1969) suggested that the central technique of counseling is to use the "self as an instrument" of change. In other words, counselors use their personality to create a presence that conveys encouragement for, belief in, and support of the client. Rogers (1981) also commented on the importance of the counselor's personal qualities. He noted that the client's perception of the counselor's attitude is more important than the counselor's theories and methods. Rogers's point underscores the fact that clients are interested in and influenced by the personal style of the counselor.

A number of attempts have been made to identify the personal characteristics that promote positive outcomes in counseling. Strong (1968) suggested that counselors be perceived as expert, attractive, and trustworthy. Corey et al. (2015) contended that effective counselors present a positive model for their clients by being actively involved in their own self-development, expanding their self-awareness as they look honestly at their lives and the choices associated with personal growth and development. Beutler, Machado, and Neufeldt (1994) found some empirical support for other counselor characteristics, such as emotional well-being, self-disclosure, and optimism.

It would not be realistic to imply that an effective counselor must be a certain type of person. At the same time, the literature does suggest certain basic qualities tend to be important to the counseling process. I have incorporated these basic qualities into what I believe are the 14 personal characteristics of an effective counselor.

1. *Encouraging.* Being encouraging may be the most important quality of an effective counselor. Encouragement helps clients learn to believe in their potential for growth and development. A number of Adlerian counselors have written about the power of encouragement (e.g., Dinkmeyer & Losoncy, 1980).

2. *Artistic.* As mentioned, effective counselors tend to be sensitive and responsive to their clients. Being artistic implies being creative and flexible and adjusting counseling techniques to the unique needs of the client. Just as true artists give something of themselves to each thing they create, counselors must give of themselves to the counseling process. Effective counselors cannot insist on maintaining an emotional distance from the client if such a distance inhibits client growth. If necessary, counselors must allow themselves to experience the client's world directly and be personally affected by the counseling process, as they bring their humanness and vulnerability to the moment. Counselors who allow themselves to be human may also promote authenticity and genuineness in the counseling process.

3. **Emotionally stable.** An emotionally unbalanced counselor will probably do more harm than good for the client. Unfortunately, some counselors enter the counseling profession in order to work through their own serious mental health problems. These counselors may attempt to meet their own needs at the expense of their clients. Langs (1985) went so far as to suggest that a substantial number of clients spend much of their energy adjusting to the mood swings of their counselor. In some instances, clients might even believe they have to provide temporary counseling for the counselor (Langs, 1985). Role reversals of this type are obviously not in the best interest of the client. An inconsistent counselor will not only waste valuable time but create confusion and insecurity within the client.

4. **Empathic and caring.** Effective counselors care about people and have the desire to help those in need. They are sensitive to the emotional states of others and can communicate an understanding of their struggles with life. Clients experience a sense of support and kindness from these counselors. This can help the client have the courage to face life realistically and explore new directions and possibilities.

5. **Self-aware.** Being self-aware enables counselors to become aware of their limitations. Self-awareness can also help counselors monitor their needs so that they can gratify those needs in a manner that does not interfere with the counseling process. Self-awareness requires an ongoing effort by the counselor. The various ways in which counselors can promote their self-awareness include using meditation techniques and taking time for personal reflection.

   Self-awareness appears to be related to a number of other concepts related to the "self," such as self-acceptance, self-esteem, and self-realization. In this regard, as people become more aware of themselves, they are in a better position to accept themselves. Self-acceptance (see the next characteristic) can then lead to enhancement of one's self-image or self-esteem, which in turn can free a person to move toward self-realization.

6. **Self-acceptance.** Self-acceptance suggests that counselors are comfortable with themselves. Although ideally they are working on enhancing their personal growth and development, the discrepancy between the real self and the ideal self is not be so great as to cause undue anxiety.

7. **Positive self-esteem.** Positive self-esteem can help counselors cope with their personal and professional lives and maintain the emotional stability that is central to their job. Also, counselors who do not feel positive about themselves may look for the negative in their clients. Even worse, such counselors may attempt to degrade the client to enhance their own self-image.

8. **Self-realization.** Self-realization is the process of actualizing one's potential. It represents a journey into personal growth and discovery. Effective helpers reach out in new directions and explore new horizons. As they do, they realize that growth requires commitment, risk, and suffering. In this process, they model for their clients that one must stretch to grow. Counselors welcome life experiences and learn from them. They develop a broad outlook on life that can help their clients put their problems in perspective. Counselors' enthusiasm for life can create energy and optimism that can energize and create hope for a client.

9. **Self-disclosure.** Effective counselors are constructively open with their thoughts and feelings. When counselors model openness, they encourage their clients to be open. The resulting candidness can be critical to the counseling process.

10. **Courageous.** Although it is important for clients to perceive their counselors as competent, counselors are not perfect and should not be viewed as perfect. Instead, they should try to model the courage to be imperfect (Nystul, 1979a). Counselors with the courage to communicate their weaknesses as well as their strengths are disclosing an authentic picture of themselves. They are also presenting a realistic view of the human condition and can help clients avoid self-defeating, perfectionist tendencies. Another facet of the courage to be imperfect is the willingness of counselors to seek out counseling services for themselves if the need arises. Counselors should not feel that they are so "complete" or "perfect" they have no need for counseling; otherwise, they may develop a condescending attitude about counseling that could result in regarding their clients as "inferior." Obtaining counseling can also help counselors understand what it feels like to be in the role of client, contributing to a better understanding of the counseling process.

11. **Patient.** Being patient can be valuable in the counseling process. Helping someone change is a complex process and requires significant effort. Clients may make some progress and then regress to old habits. Counselors must be patient and recognize the goal of achieving overall positive therapeutic movement.

12. **Nonjudgmental.** Counselors must be careful not to impose their values or beliefs on the client, even though they may wish at times to expose clients to new ideas. Being nonjudgmental communicates respect for clients and allows them to actualize their unique potential.

13. **Tolerance for ambiguity.** Ambiguity can be associated with the art of counseling. For example, the counselor never knows for sure what the best technique is to use with a client or exactly what was accomplished during a session. Although the science of counseling can contribute to the objective understanding of the counseling process, counselors must be able to tolerate some ambiguity.

14. **Spirituality.** Spirituality recognizes the value of addressing the spiritual-religious dimension in the helping process. Characteristics of spirituality include being sensitive to religious-spiritual issues in oneself and others (such as concepts of morality and the soul) and being able to function from and relate to the spiritual world as distinct from the material world.

The Helping Profession

Counseling can also be understood within the general context of the helping profession. The term *helping profession* encompasses several professional disciplines, including psychology, counseling, and psychiatry, each of which is distinguished by its unique training programs and resulting specialties. Many individuals from these various groups provide similar services, such as counseling and psychotherapy.

Members of the helping profession often work together on multidisciplinary teams. For example, school counselors and school psychologists join forces to provide counseling services in school settings. Psychiatrists, psychiatric nurses, psychiatric social workers, psychologists, and mental health counselors blend their specialized skills to provide a comprehensive treatment plan in mental health settings. An overview of the degree requirements, specialized skills, and work settings for the members of the helping profession is provided in Table 1.2.

Table 1.2 Types of Professional Helpers

Type of Helper	Licensure and Degree Requirements	Skills and Responsibilities	Work Setting
Mental health counselor	Master's degree in counseling or related field. Most states require licensure.	Use of counseling and psychotherapeutic strategies	Community mental health centers, hospitals, and private practice
Marriage, child, and family counselors	Usually a master's degree in marriage, child, and family counseling or related field. An increasing number of states require licensure.	Marriage, child, and family counseling	Private practice
Psychiatric social worker	Usually a master's degree in social work. Most states require licensure.	Counseling and psychotherapy, usually from a family perspective; knowledge about psychiatric service; ability to assist with social services (food, shelter, child abuse and neglect, foster and nursing care)	Most work in hospitals and social service agencies. Some have their own private practice.
Pastoral counselor	Master's degree in counseling or related field. Some states require certification or licensure.	Counseling and psychotherapy from a religious perspective. Some focus on issues pertaining to marriage and the family (e.g., marital enrichment).	Churches or agencies with church affiliation
Clinical and counseling psychologist	PsyD, PhD, or EdD (doctor of psychology, philosophy, or education). All states require licensure or certification.	Counseling and psychotherapy, psychological testing, and mental health specialist. Some states grant prescription privileges.	University counseling centers, community mental health centers, hospitals, and private practice

Type of Helper	Licensure and Degree Requirements	Skills and Responsibilities	Work Setting
Psychiatrist	MD (medical degree) and 3–4 years specialized training in psychiatry in a full residency program. All states require licensure.	Treatment of serious mental disorders, usually involving the use of medications; some counseling and psychotherapy; and consultation. Supervision of other mental health workers is usually involved.	Hospitals, community mental health centers, and private practice
Psychiatric nurse	RN (registered nurse degree). All states require licensure.	Assist in the psychiatric treatment of mental disorders by monitoring medication and providing counseling and psychotherapy.	Hospitals and community mental health centers
School counselor	Many states require a master's degree in counseling. All states require certification or licensure in school counseling.	Personal and career counseling and consultation with school staff and parents	Elementary, middle, and high schools
School psychologist	Many states require at least a master's degree in school psychology or a related field. All states require certification or licensure as a school psychologist.	Psychological testing, counseling, and consulting	Elementary, middle, and high schools

Counseling: Past, Present, and Future

The counseling profession has undergone a dynamic evolution. This section provides information on the key individuals and events in the history of the profession, the current professional identity of counselors, and future trends in counseling.

Counseling From a Historical Perspective

Kottler and Brown (2000, 2004) have traced the origins of counseling to noted individuals in our ancestral past who provided insights into the human condition that continue to influence the evolution of counseling and modern clinical practice.

- Hippocrates (400 BCE) developed a classification system for mental illness and personality types.

- Socrates (400 BC) posited that self-awareness was the purest state of knowledge.

- Plato (350 BC) described human behavior as an internal state.

- Aristotle (350 BC) provided a psychological perspective on emotions, including anger.

- St. Augustine (AD 400) suggested that introspection was necessary to control emotions.

- Leonardo da Vinci (1500) described the human condition in terms of art and science.

- Shakespeare (1600) created psychologically complex characters in his literary works.

- Phillippe Pinel (1800) described abnormal conditions in terms of neurosis and psychosis.

- Anton Mesmer (1800) used hypnosis to treat psychological conditions.

- Charles Darwin (1850) proposed that individual differences are shaped by evolutionary events relating to the survival of the species.

- Søren Kierkegaard (1850) related existential thought to personal meaning in life.

A number of other prominent individuals have made unique and lasting contributions to the counseling profession. The pioneering work of Freud, Adler, and Jung (see

Chapter 7) can be credited with establishing the foundation for modern clinical practice. These three men, colleagues in Vienna in the early 1900s, each went on to develop a unique school of counseling and psychotherapy. Freud developed *psychoanalysis*, which emphasizes the role of sexuality in personality development. Adler developed his own school of psychology called *individual psychology*, which emphasizes the importance of social interest in mental health. Jung is credited with originating the school of psychology called *analytic psychology*. Jung's work was influenced by various disciplines, including theology, philosophy, and anthropology. His theory is probably best known for its recognition of a collective unconscious, an idea that suggests that all people share some common memories.

Numerous other schools of counseling have emerged since the pioneering work of Freud, Adler, and Jung. Perhaps more than any other theorist, Rogers has influenced the development of contemporary counseling approaches. His person-centered approach was founded on a belief in the dignity and worth of the individual (Rogers, 1981) and has gained wide support among individuals in the helping profession. Rogers was particularly influential in the development of the third-force, or humanistic, school of counseling and psychotherapy. Becoming increasingly popular are the cognitive-behavioral theories of counseling, such as those developed by Albert Ellis (1994) and Aaron Beck (1993). These approaches have been welcomed by managed-care health organizations because they tend to focus on relief of symptoms (such as anxiety or depression) and can be accomplished in a time-limited format.

Recent trends in counseling are reflected in the postmodern theories of constructivism (Mahoney, 1995a) and social constructionism (Gergen, 1994b), brief-solution-focused approaches to counseling (de Shazer, 1994), and empirically supported treatments (Norcross & Hill, 2003). Postmodern theories have created an opportunity for a paradigm shift in counseling by recognizing the roles that cognition, language, and narratives play in defining truth, knowledge, and reality. Similarly, brief-solution-focused approaches have also created potential for a paradigm shift through their focus on strengths and solutions as opposed to problems, weakness, and pathology.

KEY HISTORIC EVENTS Several events have been important in the history and evolution of counseling. Among these are the vocational guidance movement, the standardized testing movement, the mental health movement, and key legislative acts.

The vocational guidance movement had its inception in the efforts of Frank Parsons, a Boston educator who started the Vocational Bureau in 1908. Parsons contended that an individual who took the time to choose a vocation, as opposed to a job, would be more likely to experience success and work satisfaction (Brown & Brooks, 2002). Career counseling, which focuses on helping clients explore their unique potential in relation to the world of work, evolved from the vocational movement.

The standardized testing movement can be traced to Sir Francis Galton, an English biologist, and his study of heredity. Galton developed simple tests to differentiate characteristics of genetically related and unrelated people (Anastasi & Urbina, 1997). Many others have made significant contributions to the testing movement. For example, James Cattel set forth the concept of mental testing in 1890 (Anastasi & Urbani), and Alfred Binet developed the first intelligence scale in 1905.

World Wars I and II played important roles in the testing movement. The military's need to classify new recruits for training programs resulted in the development of mass intelligence and ability testing. Examples are World War I's Army Alpha and Army Beta tests and World War II's Army General Classification test. After World War II, the use of tests proliferated throughout American society and soon became an integral part of the public school system. Tests were also used in a variety of other settings, including mental health services and employment agencies. During the 1960s, the testing movement declined to some extent when it became apparent that many standardized tests reflected a cultural bias (Minton & Schneider, 1981). Since that time, the construction and use of tests appear to incorporate an increased sensitivity to multicultural issues.

The mental health movement arose as a result of several forces. In 1908, Clifford Beers wrote *A Mind That Found Itself* describing the horrors of his 3 years as a patient in a mental hospital. Beers's efforts resulted in an increased public awareness of the issues relating to mental disorders. Beers later formed the Society for Mental Hygiene, which promoted comprehensive treatment programs for the mentally ill (Baruth & Robinson, 1987).

Another major factor in the mental health movement was the development in 1952 of medications that could treat serious disorders such as schizophrenia (Rosenhan & Seligman, 1995). Today, it is uncommon for psychiatric patients to remain in a hospital for more than a couple of weeks. Although medications do not cure mental disorders, they often can control symptoms to the degree that a person can function in society. Unfortunately, it has been difficult to develop effective follow-up programs for psychiatric patients after their discharge, which has resulted in an alarming number of mentally disturbed people wandering the streets as homeless "street people." Several studies have estimated that 25%–50% of homeless people are mentally ill (Ball & Harassy, 1984; Frazier, 1985). Many mental health professionals are attempting to develop more effective follow-up and outreach services for the chronically mentally ill.

Key legislative acts have also contributed to the evolution of the counseling profession, in particular, the National Defense Education Act (NDEA) of 1958. This act, designed to improve the teaching of science in public schools, was motivated by a popular belief that the United States was lagging behind Russia's achievements in science, which developed after Americans learned of the Soviet Union's success in launching the first space satellite, *Sputnik*. The NDEA had a major impact on the counseling profession by providing funds to train school counselors, resulting in a marked increase in the number of counselors employed in US schools.

PROFESSIONAL IDENTITY Mellin, Hunt, and Nichols (2011) noted that the counseling profession has historically struggled to establish a clear identity distinct from other members of the helping profession (e.g., psychologist, social workers, and psychiatrists). In an effort to clarify the role of professional counselors, Mellin et al. surveyed 238 practicing counselors regarding professional identity to determine the underlying philosophical orientation that characterized the counseling profession. Results of the survey were consistent with previous research that suggested that the counseling profession emphasized human development, prevention, and wellness.

Mellin et al. (2011) reported that professional counselors embraced having a unified professional identity across counseling specialities (e.g., mental health counseling and school counseling). The authors suggested that professional counselors appeared to take this position because of common training within Council for Accreditation of Counseling and Related Educational Programs (CACREP) programs, which shared standards and promoted licensure, and the ethical code of the American Counseling Association. Mellin et al. suggested there has been an ongoing debate among counseling faculty and professional organizations regarding the merits of having a unified professional identity. Kaplan & Gladding (2011) addressed these issues by noting that the American School Counseling Association contends there are several counseling professions (not one) and professional identity definitions should reflect the different counseling specialties.

More recently, representatives of the American Counseling Association put forth a definition of counseling that could be used to inform the public about what characterizes professional counseling: "Counseling is a professional relationship that empowers diverse individuals, families, and group to accomplish mental health, wellness, education, and career goals" (Kaplan, Tarvydas, & Gladding, 2014, p. 366). The definition of counseling evolved from a process referred to as "20/20: A Vision for the Future of Counseling: The New Consensus Definition of Counseling," which included representatives from throughout the counseling profession, including all major counseling organizations. All but 2 of the 31 counseling organizations endorsed the definition. The American School Counselor Association refused to endorse the definition because that organization believed the definition did not differentiate professional counselors from other mental health practitioners; it preferred to use its own definition of counseling; and the definition lacked research support. The Association for Social Justice also did not endorse the definition, because that organization contended that the definition failed to recognize the importance of multicultural competencies, social justice, and advocacy issues.

Reiner, Dobmeier, and Hernandez (2013) noted that professional identity of counselors continues to be associated with promoting human development, prevention, and wellness. The authors suggested that a unified (single) professional identity is necessary for the counseling profession to promote professional goals of obtaining third-party insurance reimbursement, such as from Medicare, and for licensure portability between states. Reiner et al. believed that professional counselors are in the best position to promote a unified professional identity with professional organizations, CACREP, and counselor educators also playing important roles in this regard.

The counseling profession appears to be making significant gains regarding addressing and clarifying professional identity issues. Additional dialogue and action will be necessary to ensure that the public understands the merits of professional counseling and supports the professional goals of licensure portability and access to third-party insurance.

Emerging Trends

Emerging trends that may impact the future of counseling include mindfulness-based approaches, research, multicultural counseling, managed mental health services, evidenced-based (empirically supported) treatment, wellness, positive psychology, mental disorders, spirituality, cybercounseling, technology, problematic-impaired counseling students, self-care for counselors, and neuroscience.

MINDFULNESS-BASED APPROACHES Mindfulness-based approaches integrate Eastern philosophies, such as Zen Buddhism, and psychotherapy. Kabat-Zinn (2003) suggested that mindfulness is an awareness that results from nonjudgmentally paying attention in the moment. Emerging trends associated with mindfulness approaches include the following:

- Integrating mindfulness approaches with positive psychology (e.g., well-being and optimal functioning) and character strengths (universal qualities associated with human goodness, such as wisdom and knowledge, courage, humanity, justice, temperance, and transcendence; Niemiec, Rashid, & Spinella, 2012).

- Loving-kindness meditation strategies that focus on love, acceptance, and satisfaction with oneself and others to promote self-care, inner peace and bliss, positive interpersonal relationships, empathy, compassion, and altruism (Kristeller & Johnson, 2005; Leppma, 2012).

- Use of mindfulness approaches to treat trauma. For example, dialetical behavior therapy and acceptance commitment therapy have been effective in treating posttraumatic stress disorder (Goodman & Calderon, 2012).

Pickert (2014) reported that there has been a surge of interest in mindfulness strategies, such as meditation, as a way of empowering clients to cope with the stress of daily living; enhancing health, wellness, and happiness; and increasing the quality of life. Mindfulness-based approaches have also been integrated into a number of psychotherapeutic perspectives such as cognitive-behavioral, humanistic, and psychodynamic therapy to treat mental disorders and promote health and wellness (Germer, 2013).

Pickert (2014) suggested that mindfulness strategies are being utilized by a cross section of people in a variety of settings. Examples of mindfulness strategies going mainstream are educators teaching students meditation techniques to improve concentration and deal with stress; Steve Jobs, co-founder of Apple, and other entrepreneurs using mindfulness strategies to get into a "zone" of enhanced concentration, freeing up mental space for creativity and innovative ideas; and US Marines using mindfulness training to foster soldiers' resiliency during combat. There appears to be much potential for the use of mindfulness-based approaches to foster health and wellness (see Chapter 9 for additional information on mindfulness-based approaches).

RESEARCH Historically, professional counselors have experienced a disconnect between research and practice due to research's perceived lack of relevance to daily practice (Edelson, 1994; Havens, 1994; Wester & Borders, 2014). The current emphasis on "best practices" associated with evidence-based, empirically supported interventions (which are recognized by third-party insurers) has contributed to a resurgence of interest regarding the role of research in practice (Marquis, Douthit, & Elliot, 2011).

Marquis et al. (2011) reported that there has been vigorous debate within the counseling profession regarding whether best-practice research is in the best interest of clients. Advocates believe there is a need for evidence-based, empirically supported research to promote accountability, reliability, and quality of counseling services (Marquis et al.). Critics contend that research methodology often cited as the best way to determine best practices (e.g., quantitative experimental design) appears to be driven by third-party insurers and the medical model and is not consistent with the philosophical foundations of the counseling profession relating to human development, preventation, and wellness (Marquis et al.).

Marquis et al. (2011) noted that research with fewer participants (e.g., single-subject case designs and qualitative research methodologies) may be more appropriate to address clinically sensitive issues such as the counseling relationship, multiculturalism, and advocacy. Qualitative methods are similar to counseling in that they utilize a variety of research strategies, such as interviews, to discover with participants clinically relevant information. Hays and Wood (2011) identified six emerging qualitative methodologies and their research goals as follows: *Grounded theory* can be used for theory development and validation; *phenomenology* provides an understanding of events from the participant's perspective; *consensual qualitative research* is based on the consensus opinions of participants and researchers; *ethnography* explores issues from the perspective of a cultural group or setting; *narratology* provides an understanding of phenomenon based on the stories shared by others; and *participatory action research* promotes participant empowerment and transformation through advocacy and real-world change.

Mixed-methods research designs have emerged as an attempt to integrate quantitative and qualitative research methodologies (Hanson, Creswell, Plano Clark, Petska, & Creswell, 2005). Mixed-methods designs allow data to be gathered and analyzed from a variety of perspectives, expanding the horizons of scientific inquiry. Mixed-methods designs recognize the value of both the objective and subjective dimensions, thereby reflecting the concept of counseling as an art and a science that is advocated in this text.

Wester and Borders (2014) identified 159 counseling research competencies based on input from a panel of counseling research experts. Wester and Borders suggested that the advancement of the counseling profession depends on rigorous research methodology and that research competencies can be used to promote quality research.

MULTICULTURAL COUNSELING Multicultural counseling can be considered the fourth force in psychology, following the psychodynamic, existential-humanistic, and cognitive-behavioral perspectives (Pedersen, 1991a; Sue, Ivey, & Pedersen, 2007). D'Andrea and Foster Heckman (2008a) noted that multicultural counseling has become the centerpiece of the counseling profession. The multicultural counseling movement is directed at reconceptualizing traditional counseling theory and practice to address diversity issues such as culture, race, ethnicity, gender, age, sexual orientation, and advocacy.

Advocacy, which has become an increasingly important piece of a multicultural approach, involves taking action to overcome oppressive forces that undermine human rights and opportunity. Kohn-Wood & Hooper (2014) noted that mental health counselors need to increase their advocacy efforts to help clients from racial and ethnic minorities and of low socioeconomic status overcome inequities regarding access, utilization, and quality of mental health services. Nilsson, Schale, & Khamphakdy-Brown (2011) found that advocacy skills can be promoted by providing counseling students opportunities to work directly with refugees and other immigrants (e.g., making home visits and advocating for necessary social services and legal aid).

Multicultural competencies have been identified that are associated with a wide range of counselor-client variables, including the counselor's self-awareness and cultural knowledge and culturally sensitive counselor interventions (Arredondo, Tovar-Blank, & Parham, 2008). Multicultural competencies are beginning to attract research interest. Chao (2012, 2013) conducted research that explored the complex relationships among factors that influence the development of multicultural competencies (e.g., multicultural training, racial/ethnic identity, and color-blind racial attitudes such as (denial of the existence of racism). Additional research on how multicultural competencies can be promoted appears warranted.

MANAGED MENTAL HEALTH SERVICES Managed care, which contrasts with managing benefits, began for mental health services in the late 1980s (Freeman, 1995) and continues to be a major part of contemporary health care. Managed care typically involves health maintenance organizations (HMOs), managed mental health care organizations (MMHCOs), independent provider organizations (IPOs), and employer assistance programs (EAPs). It is becoming increasingly important for mental health practitioners to affiliate themselves with these organizations in order to become part of the health care system and be able to provide services. Some major concerns about the managed-care movement include a reduced number of visits (usually three to seven sessions), problems with confidentiality, depersonalization, the questionable training of those screening for mental health problems, and restrictions on the choice of mental health providers (Solomon, 1996). Rupert and Baird's (2004) study of the impact of managed care on the independent practice of psychology shows that managed care is a source of stress for practitioners, especially in terms of paperwork and external constraints, such as reimbursement issues. The degree of involvement with managed care is also related to stress and burnout, with those highly involved in managed care being at risk for stress-related burnout.

The Affordable Care Act was signed into law March 23, 2010, with the goal of improving health care coverage for all Americans. The intent of this law was to increase Americans's opportunity to access high-quality medical coverage, including mental health services. Further monitoring and research regarding these issues is needed.

EVIDENCE-BASED (EMPIRICALLY SUPPORTED) TREATMENT Marquis, Douthit, and Elliot (2011) noted that *evidence-based practice* and *best practices* are used interchangeably to describe the use of empirically supported research to identify optimal counseling interventions. Norcross and Hill (2003) have noted an international movement in the health care professions toward empirically supported treatments (EST). Managed-care organizations have recognized the merits of empirically supported interventions as a means of identifying approved treatment protocols associated with specific diagnostic conditions (Wampold, Lichtenberg, & Waehler, 2002).

The APA Division of Clinical Psychology (Task Force, 1995) attempted to identify ESTs that are effective with certain mental health disorders and to communicate this information to the public and members of the helping profession, but there has been considerable debate regarding what constitutes evidence of effective treatment (Wampold et al., 2002). As a result, numerous models have evolved to evaluate treatment modalities. Wampold et al. identified seven principles that could be used to review evidence of empirically supported interventions. Chwalisz (2003) suggested that evaluation of EST should be expanded to include consideration of philosophical, political, and social issues. And Marquis et al. (2011) recommended that EST should include consideration of multicultural issues and clinical expertise. Norcross and Hill (2003) and Marquis et al. noted that the EST movement does not consider personal factors such as client characteristics and the nature of the therapeutic relationship that can have an important influence on therapeutic outcomes. Murray (2009) suggested that information regarding EST needs to be communicated to clinicians in a manner that is more clinician friendly (e.g., easy to access, understand, and apply). Murray also suggested that applied research be given greater emphasis within counselor education programs.

Karlin and Cross (2014) reported that, although there has been significant progress in identifying evidence-based practices, dissemination of this information to practitioners often takes years. In addition, when the information does reach practitioners, it is often inaccurate, resulting in clients not receiving the true **evidence-based treatment**.

Considering these problems, it is not surprising that only 10% of practitioners treating clients with posttraumatic stress disorder (PTSD) utilize evidence-based practices (Rosen et al. 2004). Karlin & Cross (2014) noted that the US Department of Veterans Affairs has implemented a multidimensional model to address these issues so that veterans can receive accurate evidence-based treatments in a timely manner. EST appears to hold much promise for mental health services. It can promote accountability and provide a recognized protocol for research and the development of mental health treatments. Future research strategies regarding EST could include consideration of human factors, such as the counseling relationship, and multicultural factors in determining counseling efficacy.

WELLNESS The concept of wellness, along with an emphasis on promoting human development and prevention of illness, has been central to the identity of professional counselors and counseling psychologists (Raque-Bogdan, Torrey, Lewis, & Borges, 2012; Reiner, Dobmeier, & Hernandez, 2013). Wellness was also included in a recent definition of counseling that stated counseling is a professional relationship that promotes "mental health, wellness, education, and career goals" (Kaplan, Tarvydas, & Gladding, 2014, p. 366). Meyers (2014) described wellness within the framework of holistic health noting that "the essence of wellness is the integration of mind, body, and spirit" (p. 33). Meyers also suggested that wellness and holistic health can be promoted by mindfulness strategies, the creative arts, nutritionists, and trainers.

Myers and Sweeney's (2004, 2008) Indivisible Self Model of Wellness (IS-Wel) provides "an evidence-based paradigm for understanding the multidimensional nature of holistic well-being" (Lawson & Myers, 2011, p. 163). IS-Wel, which is based on Adlerian psychology, includes the Five Factor Wellness Inventory relating to five dimensions of the self (the creative self, the coping self, the social self, the essential self, and the physical self). Myers, Willse, and Villalba (2011) conducted research to determine whether wellness factors (as measured by the Five Factor Wellness Inventory) were predictive of self-esteem in adolescents. Results of the study showed that strength of the coping self (ability to self-regulate and transcend negative events) was consistently related to all aspects of self-esteem, as measured by the Coopersmith Self-Esteem Inventory. These findings suggest that counselors should include interventions that promote coping mechanisms when addressing adolescents' self-esteem issues.

Lawson and Myers (2011) utilized the IS-Wel model and the Five Factor Wellness Inventory in a study that investigated the relationships among wellness, professional quality of life, and career-sustaining behaviors. Results of the study suggested that counselors who had high wellness scores were less prone to experience burnout because they engaged in more career-sustaining behaviors (e.g., spending time with family and sense of humor) and because they reported higher levels of professional quality of life (e.g., were able to find pleasure in helping others). Additional research regarding the concept of wellness appears warranted.

POSITIVE PSYCHOLOGY **Positive psychology** emphasizes the role of strengths and positive emotions such as happiness, hope, motivation, flow, and forgiveness on health and well-being (Harris, Thoresen, & Lopez, 2007; Scheel, Davis, & Henderson 2012). It represents a shift in emphasis from pathology to wellness, from problems to solutions. Waterman (2013) noted that the historical roots of positive psychology can be traced to the theories of humanistic psychologists, such as Carl Rogers's person-centered therapy that described the fully functioning person and Abraham Maslow's theory of motivation relating to self-actualization. Waterman reported that Martin Seligman's research on optimisim, optimal development, and flourishing has also played a significant role in the evolution of positive psychology.

Harris et al. (2007) recommended that counselors consider positive psychology and the language of strengths and solutions when formulating counseling goals and interventions (e.g., asking a child "What will your teacher say about you when you turn in your assignments on time?"). In addition, postmodern perspectives such as narrative psychology can be used to promote self-fulfilling prophecies of success (e.g., parental encouragement messages can instill a can-do spirit in a child).

Rashid and Seligman (2014) provided evidence of increased interest in positive psychology by noting that between 2000 and 2010, there have been more than a thousand publications on positive psychology and health and wellness. Sin and Lyubomirsky (2009) conducted a metaanalysis of 51 studies that showed positive interventions were effective in the treatment of depression and promotion of well-being. There appears to be much promise in the role that positive psychology can play in counseling to promote physical health, mental health, and well-being.

MENTAL DISORDERS Yager (1989) and Pincus et al. (1989) made projections about the impact of advances in science on the diagnosis and treatment of mental disorders that continue to accurately predict trends in this area. Following is a summary of their predictions:

- Genetics will play an increasingly important role in the diagnosis and treatment of mental disorders. For example, scientists could use genetic engineering to alter the gene structure to prevent or treat mental disorders, and clinicians will be able to identify children who are at risk of developing mental disorders.

- Neurobiologists will gain a more complete understanding of the role of neurotransmitters, or agents that facilitate communication between neurons, in the development and treatment of mental disorders.

- Psychopharmacology researchers will develop more effective medications with fewer unwanted side effects. Scientists will also develop new medications that will successfully treat mental disorders previously unresponsive to medication (e.g., substance use disorders, personality disorders, and sexual disorders).

- Sociobiologists will identify factors that trigger the onset of mental disorders.

- Advances in computer technology and software will enable clinicians to make better use of computers in the diagnosis and treatment of mental disorders.

The American Psychiatric Association initially intended that the Diagnostic Statistical Manual, Fifth Edition (DSM-5; American Psychiatric Association, 2013) would represent a paradigm shift reflecting an emphasis on neuroscience (Paris, 2013b). Paris noted that the APA backed away from this position when it was unable to identify clear biological markers associated with mental disorders (e.g., genetics, neuroscience). The APA addressed these issues in the DSM-5 by noting:

> Until incontrovertible etiological or pathophysiological mechanisms are identified to fully validate specific disorders or disorder spectra, the most important standard of the DSM-5 disorder criteria will be their clinical utility for the assessment of clinical course and treatment response of individuals grouped by a given set of diagnostic criteria." (p. 20)

It appears that the importance of biological markers in diagnosing mental disorders will be an important part of future DSMs.

SPIRITUALITY The recognition of spirituality in counseling offers opportunities and challenges for professional counselors (Richards & Bergin, 1997, 2004). Spirituality can be conceptualized as a universal human quality reflected in the search for meaning in existence (Haase, Britt, Coward, Kline, & Penn, 1992; Ingersoll, 1995). Spirituality and religion are interrelated, with religion providing the structure within which spirituality can be expressed. Given that spirituality is a widespread phenomenon with 90% of US residents believing in God (Kroll & Sheehan, 1989), counselors are recognizing its potential importance to the counseling process (Miranti & Burke, 1995).

Spirituality can be an important force in all phases of the counseling process, from establishing a relationship through assessment, goal setting, and treatment (Richards & Bergin, 1997). The spiritual perspective is also consistent with the movement toward brief-solution-focused counseling from the point of view of utilizing strengths. For example, it is common for people to turn to prayer and other forms of spirituality during times of great need to gain strength and support to promote recovery and healing (Miranti & Burke, 1995).

Fowler's (1981) faith development theory (FDT) "offers a nonsectarian model of spiritual growth that permits assessment of spiritual development apart from the specific contents of various faith traditions" (Parker, 2011, p. 112). FDT can be used by counselors to provide a development framework for conceptualizing spiritual change and transitions, identify and address adaptive and problematic modes of spiritual expression, and offer a growth-facilitating model for spiritual development (Parker).

Snodgrass, McCreight, and McFee (2014) suggested that when counselors have difficulty understanding and addressing clients' spiritual-religious issues, they should consider referring them to mental health practitioners who have theological training (e.g., pastoral counselors). Snodgrass et al. provided guidelines for the referral process and information regarding the unique services that such counselors can provide. Furthermore, the counseling literature provides empirical support for considering the spiritual domain in counseling. For example, many clients indicate that they cannot be effectively helped unless their spiritual issues are addressed sensitively and capably (Richards & Bergin, 1997, 2004; Shafranske, 1996). In addition, increasing evidence suggests that spiritual health plays an important role in physical and psychological health and well-being (Bergin, 1991; Richards & Bergin, 1997, 2004). Studies such as these appear to be giving spirituality the scientific credibility that will help propel it into the mainstream of counseling.

CYBERCOUNSELING Cybercounseling (also referred to as online or distance counseling) is becoming an increasingly popular means of providing counseling services (Wiggins-Frame, 1998). Cybercounseling can take many forms but often involves counselors using the Internet to create websites like Psych Central (Hannon, 1996). Counseling on these sites is done via email; clients typically submit questions of up to 200 words to the counselor, and the counselor responds to the client in 1 to 3 days (Wiggins-Frame).

Haley and Vazquez (2009), Sude (2013), and Warren (2012) identified a number of emerging forms of cybercounseling, including the following:

- *Email counseling.* The counselor and client use email as a forum for counseling.

- *Bulletin board counseling.* Clients post questions on a bulletin board, typically using pseudonyms to ensure confidentiality. A mental health professional then posts a response that is visible to all users.

- *Chat room counseling.* Clients and counselors engage in real-time (synchronous) communication over the Internet in a chat room.

- *Web-telephony counseling.* The client and counselor use a microphone and speakers to talk over the Internet (e.g., while in a video chat room).

- *Computer-assisted or stimulated counseling.* Computer-generated counseling answers clients' concerns.

- *E-coaching.* Counselors provide guided activities for clients regarding specific problems such as how to cope with anxiety or depression. Clients are often given information and tasks designed to address these issues and then receive feedback from the counselor.

- *Text messaging.* Text messaging can be used to send messages that may include pictures and videos relating to clinical and administrative issues (e.g., to provide support regarding interventions and scheduling appointments).

- *Mind mapping.* Clients download mind-mapping applications to provide visual aids and information they can use as an adjunct to therapy (e.g., SimpleMind and Thinking Space provide clients with a list of rational statements they can assess when implementing rational emotive behavior therapy).

Counselors appear to be expressing guarded interest in participating in cybercounseling. Kirk (1997) conducted a survey of professional counselors that showed 30% would never engage in cybercounseling, 25% would consider using it, and 45% would use it as an adjunct to face-to-face counseling. Finn (2006) found that social workers also had concerns regarding the use of technology, with 87.7% reporting that email was not appropriate for providing clinical services to clients.

Wiggins-Frame (1998) and Sude (2013) identified potential benefits and hazards of cybercounseling. Benefits include providing counseling services to individuals who otherwise might not be able to receive services (such as those who live in rural areas) and efficiently handling administrative functions such as scheduling appointments. Cybercounseling may also be more attractive to individuals with disabilities, such as those with hearing impairments. Hazards include a number of potential ethical problems, such as difficulty ensuring confidentiality, promoting client welfare, and providing adequate informed consent. Sude also noted possible problems with service delivery, such as difficulty establishing rapport without face-to-face interactions and responding appropriately to certain clinical issues, including crises.

Heinlen, Welfel, Richmond, and Rak (2003) provided additional information regarding cybercounseling. They surveyed 136 websites offering counseling services via chat rooms and email. Results of their study showed a wide range of services, fee schedules, and provider credentials. For example, credentialed providers maintained significantly higher levels of compliance with ethical standards than did noncredentialed providers. Cybercounseling was also found to be an unstable source of counseling, with more than a third of the websites surveyed no longer in existence 8 months after the study was initiated. Heinlen et al., expressed concern over the quality and scope of services provided, the instability of the websites, and what appeared to be widespread ethical violations (especially among noncredentialed providers). Additional research regarding the merits and concerns of cybercounseling appears warranted.

TECHNOLOGY Haley and Vazquez (2009) provided an overview of technology and counseling. They noted that in addition to cybercounseling, technology is being used in a wide variety of counseling tasks, including the following:

- *Computers as counselors.* The earliest example of computers as counselors occurred over 45 years ago when Joseph Weizenbaum developed a computer program called ELIZA. ELIZA was a nondirective Rogerian type of counselor that responded to clients' concerns.

- *Voice-activated computer systems.* This exciting new form of counseling uses such state-of-the-art technology as virtual reality to systematically desensitize phobic clients.

- *Online testing.* Online testing (including test interpretation and scoring) is widely used for virtually all types of standardized testing (e.g., interest inventories, personality assessment, and career assessment).

- *Databases.* Databases can assess clients on a variety of topics such as degree of risk for homicidal or suicidal behavior. These databases typically require responses to approximately a thousand questions relating to variables associated with specific areas of assessment. For example, databases relating to predicting violence could include questions on history of violence, family background, and personality tendencies.

- *Client intervention aides.* Counselors can turn to the Internet to obtain materials for therapy. For example, http://www .therapistaid.com was developed to help child trauma victims create a virtual world in which they could safely address difficult life situations.

- *Information services and forums.* Numerous sites on the Internet provide information on all aspects of counseling, including the latest treatment regimens for specific mental disorders (such as empirically supported treatments for childhood depression). Forums can allow for joint communication between researchers and practitioners regarding clinical issues, for example, the role of informed consent in legal-ethical decision making.

- *Virtual self-help groups.* Internet self-help groups that communicate via email, chat rooms, and other forums are becoming increasingly popular. Self-help groups find the Internet a convenient way to address a wide range of problems (e.g., attention deficit hyperactivity disorder). These groups often provide guidance and other forms of support for the participants.

- *Client-therapist referrals.* Many websites provide information on what counseling is (e.g., the American Psychological Association's Help Center at http://helping.apa.org) and how to receive assistance with obtaining counseling services (e.g., E. G. Aletta's World of Psychology blog post at http://psychcentral.com/blog/archives/2010/01/26/10-ways-to-find-a-good-therapist/).

- *Counselor supervision.* Sophisticated forms of technology are being quickly integrated into the process of supervision. Some examples include online supervision of student counselors (e.g., group chat room supervision sessions). Another form of technology used in supervision is electromyography (EMG), which helps supervisors monitor student counselors' emotional state via changes in skin temperature and skin conductance levels and process this information during videotaped replay or live supervision.

PROBLEMATIC-IMPAIRED COUNSELING STUDENTS Interest in "gatekeeping" issues relating to counseling students who demonstrate professional deficiencies such as emotional problems, inappropriate interpersonal relation skills, and unethical behavior—that is, **problematic-impaired counseling students**—appears to be growing (Johnson & Campbell, 2004). Other professions, such as law, have an established history of considering issues like character and fitness, but the same rigor has not been applied in the helping profession (Johnson & Campbell, 2004). Vacha-Haase, Davenport, and Kerewsky (2004) provided an overview of terms used to describe the personal issues of students in training programs, such as **problematic** and **impaired**. *Impairment* relates to mental illness, emotional distress, and other personal conflict that can undermine professional function. *Problematic* relates to behaviors that are unacceptable, such as inappropriate interpersonal behavior during academic training or clinical practice.

Vacha-Haase et al. (2004) recommended that training programs provide guidelines for what could be considered acceptable and problematic (unacceptable) behavior and what should be done when students engage in unacceptable behavior. Issues regarding what is developmentally normal (such as counselors in training experiencing anxiety when they first see clients) should be differentiated from abnormal emotional responses. Problematic student behavior must also be differentiated from impairment relating to disabilities as defined by the Americans with Disabilities Act of 1990. Elman and Forrest (2004) have provided guidelines for psychotherapeutic remediation for students in training programs. They noted a number of challenges, including balancing the need to protect confidentiality in therapy with the need to keep informed of the student's progress on issues that needed to be addressed.

SELF-CARE FOR COUNSELORS Counseling can be a stressful profession as counselors attempt to deal with a wide array of challenging issues such as large caseloads, low salaries, clients who present with serious emotional issues that may include harm to self and others, and clients with chronic mental health problems

(Lee, Cho, Kissinger, & Ogle, 2010). These challenges can be overwhelming for counselors, especially if they are not receiving the support from supervisors and others and/or lack self-care coping strategies (Lee et al). When these problems are not resolved, burnout can occur. Burnout has been described as feelings of hopelessness (nothing will get better), emotional and physical exhaustion, and not feeling appreciated for one's contribution.When counselors experience burnout, it can undermine psychological and physiological well-being and their ability to provide counseling services (Lee et al.).

Lawson and Myers (2011) and Lent and Schwartz (2012) provided evidence that community mental health practitioners and school counselors experienced significantly more burnout than those in private practice. Lent and Schwartz also reported that burnout was associated with demographic factors such as sex, race, and years of experience (e.g., experience helps reduce burnout). In addition, personal characteristics that promote job satisfaction and mental health included being outgoing, agreeable, and commited to doing a good job (Lawson & Meyers).

Richards, Campenni, and Muse-Burke (2010) noted that professional counselors can use self-care strategies to promote well-being that include exercising; receiving personal counseling; addressing spiritual issues; and obtaining support from friends, family, and colleagues. Richards et al. also found that mindfulness (awareness of self and surroundings) can play an important role in enhancing well-being. In addition, Wolf, Thompson, Thompson, and Smith-Adcock (2014) reported that Myers and Sweeney's *Indivisible Self Model of Wellness* (2004, 2008) promoted self-care strategies for graduate students in counseling fields. Additional research regarding counselor burnout and self-care strategies for counselors appears warranted.

COUNSELING AND NEUROSCIENCE The field of neuroscience explores the neurobiological basis of behavior. By combining **counseling and neuroscience**, professional counselors can expand their role to include using a neuroscience perspective for the diagnosis and treatment of mental disorders. Interest in the role of neuroscience in counseling has increased (Montes, 2013). Advocates of this approach suggest that counselors must know what is occurring in the client's brain to be effective, whereas critics are concerned that the neuroscience movement will take counseling away from its humanistic roots (Montes).

Myers and Young (2012) noted that CACREP's *2009 Standards* recognized the importance of neuroscience in counselor education by requiring coursework that promotes an understanding of the neurobiology of behavior: "the relationship among brain anatomy, function, biochemistry, and learning and behavior" (p. 60). Myers and Young suggested that the intent of CACREP was not to require separate coursework in neuroscience but to require counselors to get the training necessary to integrate neuroscience into their clinical work.

Montes (2013) reported that an increasing number of counselors are utilizing newer counseling approaches that incorporate a neuroscience perspective (e.g., cognitive enhancement therapy and eye movement desensitization and reprocessing therapy). Researchers are beginning to examine the efficacy of neurobiologically based counseling practices. For example, Myers and Young (2012) noted that neurofeedback, a subtype of biofeedback, can be used to help clients monitor, regulate, and change their brain wave patterns to promote wellness. Myers and Young cited metaanalyses and outcome studies that support the efficacy of neurofeedback for the treatment of a wide range of conditions and disorders (e.g., attention deficit hyperactivity disorder, autism spectrum disorder, drug addiction, and epilepsy).

Makinson and Young (2012) provided an in-depth description of neurobiological factors associated with posttraumatic stress disorder (e.g., the role of the prefrontal cortex and amygdala in processing traumatic events and in emotional self-regulation). Makinson and Young suggested that an understanding of the neurobiology of mental disorders can help counselors determine the most appropriate counseling interventions. They went on to identify how cognitive behavior therapies (e.g., trauma-focused cognitive behavior therapy, eye movement desensitization and reprocessing therapy, and mindfulness-based cognitive therapy) can be used to treat posttraumatic stress disorder from a neuroscience perspective.

The neuroscience perspective appears to offer much promise as it provides an objective scientific basis for counseling. Counselors can maintain a balanced counseling approach by recognizing how the art of counseling has arisen from the field's humanistic origins.

SUMMARY

Counseling is a complex process that does not afford a simple definition. For example, counseling is both an art and science, and thus both the subjective and objective dimensions are important. Counseling also has a basis in narrative psychology, or counseling as a form of storytelling.

Counseling is differentiated from psychotherapy in terms of clients, goals, treatment, and settings. It is also a helping profession, a category that includes psychiatrists, psychologists, mental health counselors, and school counselors.

Emerging trends in counseling encompass mindfulness-based approaches, research, multicultural counseling, managed mental health services, evidenced-based (empirically supported) treatment, wellness, positive psychology, mental disorders, spirituality, cybercounseling, technology, problematic-impaired counseling students, self-care for counselors, and the incorporation of neuroscience.

PERSONAL EXPLORATION

1. What interests you about counseling?

2. Do you think you would ever want to be a counselor. If so, why?

3. What are good and bad reasons for wanting to be a counselor?

4. Have you ever been to a counselor? If so, what did you like or dislike about the experience?

5. Who are the people associated with the evolution of counseling that intrigue you, and what fascinates you about these people?

6. What are some personal qualities you have that you believe would help make you an effective counselor, and why are these qualities important?

7. What are some future trends in counseling that interest you?

8. What is narrative psychology or counseling as storytelling?

9. What is the difference between postmodernism and modernism?

10. Do you think counseling should be both an art and science. If so, why?

LEARNING ACTIVITIES

1. Talk with someone who is in the helping profession (e.g., a school counselor or a professor) and explore why that person went into this profession and what he or she believes are the rewards and challenges of working in this field.

2. Wellness is considering an emerging trend in counseling. What actions can you take to promote wellness for yourself and others?

WEBSITES

American Counseling Association. (2015). *What is professional counseling?* Retrieved from http://www.counseling.org/aca-community/learn-about-counseling/what-is-counseling/. *Defines counseling and provides other resources for consumers.*

Eder, A. (n.d.). *What is the difference between counseling and psychotherapy?* Retrieved from http://www.ashleyeder.com/counseling-psychotherapy/. *Discusses the distinctions between these two disciplines.*

Hevern, V. W. (2004). *Narrative psychology: Basics.* Retrieved from http://web.lemoyne.edu/~hevern/narpsych/nr-basic.html. *Provides background information on narrative psychology.*

Metanoia. (2004). *ABC's of Internet therapy.* Retrieved from http://www.metanoia.org/imhs/. *Provides a brief overview of Internet therapy.*

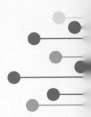

CHAPTER 2

Professional Preparation and Ethical and Legal Issues

Becoming a Professional Counselor

Becoming a professional counselor is a complex process that involves many challenges and opportunities. Moss, Gibson, and Dollarhide (2014) identified factors associated with professional identity development. One of the first challenges a beginning counselor faces is the need to establish realistic expectations regarding salary, work conditions, and the rewards and challenges of clinical practice. A second challenge is dealing with feelings of self-doubt, which are common during the first 2 years of clinical practice. Moss et al. noted that self-confidence tends to increase with clinical experience; supervision and guidance from experienced counselors; continuing education; and positive feedback from colleagues and clients. With increased confidence, counselors are better able to learn from their mistakes and move forward with their professional development.

The counseling profession also faces challenges such as gaining parity with other mental health disciplines regarding third-party insurance reimbursements and portability of licensure between states. Reiner, Dobmeier, and Hernandez (2013) surveyed counselor educators to determine the best course of action to address these challenges. Results of the study indicate that counselors and professional organizations are primarily responsible for advocating for the profession and that advocacy can best be served by communicating a single, clear message regarding the professional identity of counselors (those engaged in a profession based on wellness, human development, and prevention).

Being a professional counselor is an ongoing process that involves work, study, and commitment. This section describes four building blocks that characterize this

Chapter Overview

This chapter provides an overview of professional issues in counseling. It covers important aspects of becoming a professional counselor and major ethical and legal issues. Highlights of the chapter include the following:

- **Becoming a professional counselor, including formal study and professional affiliation, certification, and licensure; continuing education; and professional involvement**

- **Ethical issues, including client welfare, informed consent, confidentiality, and dual relationships**

- **Legal issues, including privileged communication and malpractice**

- **Special ethical and legal issues relating to marriage and family counseling, child counseling, group counseling, and AIDS**

- **Ethical-legal decision making, including clinical examples**

- **Diversity issues**

Some of the major issues associated with becoming a professional counselor include certification and licensure, professional organizations, and ethical and legal issues. Guidelines for ethical decision making and clinical examples can illustrate some applications of ethical and legal principles.

process, as shown in Figure 2.1. Deciding to undertake formal study in counseling constitutes the first step toward becoming a professional counselor.

Formal Study and Professional Affiliation

Formal study in counseling usually involves working toward a master's or doctoral degree in the counseling field. Pressure has been increasing for graduate programs offering these degrees to obtain accreditation from one or more organizations: the Council for the Accreditation of Counseling and Related Educational Programs (CACREP); the American Counseling Association (ACA) of the American Psychological Association (APA); and, in some instances, the American Association of Marriage and Family Therapy (AAMFT). Accreditation helps ensure that the programs meet acceptable standards. In addition, some certification processes in counseling or psychology require a degree from an accredited program. A current list of graduate programs approved by the ACA, APA, and AAMFT can be obtained by writing directly to each organization at the following addresses:

ACA: 5999 Stevenson Ave., Alexandria, VA 22304-3300

APA: 750 First Street NE, Washington, DC 20002-4242

AAMFT: 112 S. Alfred St., Alexandria, VA 22314-3061

Master's degree programs provide the necessary foundation for a career as a professional counselor. Students can also benefit from joining a professional organization such as the ACA or APA as a student member. Student members can attend conventions and involve themselves in professional issues facing counselors and psychologists. They also receive journals and newsletters that address important counseling issues and receive a copy of the code of ethics that guides clinical practice.

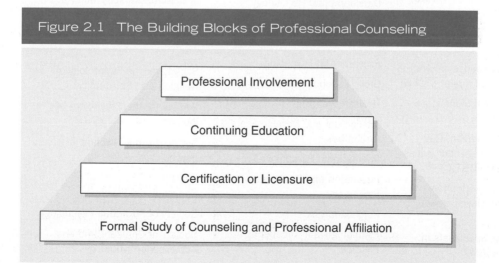

Figure 2.1   The Building Blocks of Professional Counseling

Professional Involvement

Continuing Education

Certification or Licensure

Formal Study of Counseling and Professional Affiliation

The ACA and APA each have numerous divisions that may be of interest to counselors and psychologists. Selected divisions are listed in Table 2.1.

Certification and Licensure

Certification and licensure are important to all professions, including counseling. They provide professional recognition as well as enable members of the helping profession to utilize third-party insurance to help clients pay for counseling services. Licensed counselors can access some form of third-party insurance for their clients in all states requiring counseling licensure.

Table 2.1   Selected Divisions of the ACA and APA

ACA	APA	
American College Counseling Association (ACCA)	Adult Development and Aging	Society for Industrial and Organizational Psychology
American Mental Health Counselors Association (AMHCA)	American Psychology-Law Society	Society for Personality and Social Psychology
American Rehabilitation Counseling Association (ARCA)	American Society for the Advancement of Pharmacotherapy	Society for Media Psychology and Technology
American School Counselor Association (ASCA)	Applied Experimental and Engineering Psychology	Society for the Advancement of Psychotherapy
Association for Adult Development and Aging (AADA)	Behavior Analysis	Society for the History of Psychology
Association for Assessment and Research in Counseling (AARC)	Behavioral Neuroscience and Comparative Psychology	Society for the Psychological Study of Culture, Ethnicity, and Race
Association for Counselor Education and Supervision (ACES)	Developmental Psychology	Society for the Psychology of Aesthetics, Creativity, and the Arts
	Educational Psychology	
Association for Counselors and Educators in Government (ACEG)	Exercise and Sport Psychology	Society for the Psychology of Religion and Spirituality
	Experimental Psychology	
Association for Humanistic Counseling (AHC)	Group Psychotherapy	Society for the Psychology of Women
	Health Psychology	
Association for Lesbian, Gay, Bisexual and Transgender Issues in Counseling (ALGBTIC)	Intellectual and Developmental Disabilities	Society for the Teaching of Psychology
	International Psychology	
Association for Multicultural Counseling and Development (AMCD)	Population and Environmental Psychology	Society for Theoretical and Philosophical Psychology
	Psychoanalysis	Society of Addiction Psychology
Association for Specialists in Group Work (ASGW)	Psychologists in Independent Practice	Society of Clinical Child and Adolescent Psychology

ACA	APA	
Association for Spiritual, Ethical, and Religious Values in Counseling (ASERVIC)	Psychologists in Public Service	Society of Clinical Psychology
	Psychopharmacology and Substance Abuse	Society of Consulting Psychology
Counselors for Social Justice (CSJ)		Society of Counseling Psychology
	Quantitative and Qualitative Methods	Society of Group Psychology and Military Psychology
International Association of Addictions and Offender Counselors (IAAOC)	Rehabilitation Psychology	Society of Pediatric Psychology
	Research and Action: Division of Community Psychology	Society of Psychological Hypnosis
International Association of Marriage and Family Counselors (IAMFC)	School Psychology	State, Provincial and Territorial Psychological Association Affairs
	Society for Child and Family Policy and Practice	Study of Lesbian, Gay, Bisexual and Transgender Issues
National Career Development Association (NCDA)	Society for Clinical Neuropsychology	Study of Men and Masculinity
National Employment Counseling Association (NECA)		Study of Social Issues
	Society for Community	
	Society for Consumer Psychology	
	Society for Family Psychology	
	Society for General Psychology	
	Society for Humanistic Psychology	

Although certification and licensure are similar processes in that the applicant must meet certain requirements in education, training, experience, and clinical competence, Forester (1977) identified several differences between them. **Certification** recognizes the competence of practitioners by authorizing them to use the title adopted by the profession. **Licensure**, on the other hand, is authorized by state legislation that regulates the practice and title of the profession. Since licensure is a legal process, legal sanctions can be imposed on an individual who is licensed. Licensure also has more specific and comprehensive regulations, necessitating greater training and preparation than the certification process (George & Cristiani, 1995).

Historically, most states have offered school counselors opportunities to become certified or licensed. Along with other school personnel, school counselors have traditionally been certified or licensed by a state board of education. Most states also require counselors to be certified or licensed as teachers. Since 1977, all states have required that psychologists be either certified or licensed by a state board of psychologist examiners (Cummings, 1990). More recently, the trend has been toward requiring certification or licensure for counselors who wish to practice outside the school setting, for example, in mental health clinics, hospitals, or private practice. The counseling profession has made progress in getting legislation passed at the state level requiring such certification or licensure. As of 2009, all 50 states as well as the District of Columbia, Guam, and Puerto Rico have passed certification or licensure laws for counselors (see Table 2.2).

Table 2.2	States That Have Passed Certification or Licensure Laws for Counselors		
State	Law Passed (Year)	State	Law Passed (Year)
Alabama	1979	Montana	1985
Alaska	1999	Nebraska	1988
Arizona	1988	Nevada	2007
Arkansas	1979	New Hampshire	1992
California	2009	New Jersey	1993
Colorado	1988	New Mexico	1993
Connecticut	1997	New York	2003
Delaware	1987	North Carolina	1983
District of Columbia*	1994	North Dakota	1989
Florida	1981	Ohio	1989
Guam**	1989	Oklahoma	1985
Georgia	1987	Oregon	1989
Hawaii	2004	Puerto Rico**	2002
Idaho	1982	Pennsylvania	1998
Illinois	1993	Rhode Island	1987
Indiana	1997	South Carolina	1985
Iowa	1991	South Dakota	1990
Kansas	1987	Tennessee	1987
Kentucky	1996	Texas	1981
Louisiana	1987	Utah	1994
Maine	1989	Vermont	1988
Maryland	1985	Virginia	1976
Massachusetts	1987	Washington	1987
Michigan	1988	West Virginia	1986
Minnesota	2003	Wisconsin	1992
Mississippi	1985	Wyoming	1987
Missouri	1985		

*Federal *district*

**US *territory*

Certification or licensure in counseling requires 30 to 60 graduate school class hours, depending on the state; a master's degree in counseling or a closely related field; 2 to 4 hours per week of supervised counseling experience, depending on the state; and passing an examination. Counselors may also pursue certification in a specialty field, for example, becoming a certified member of the National Certified Career Counselors, Certified Clinical Mental Health Counselors, or Certified Rehabilitation Counselors (Brooks & Gerstein, 1990). There is some concern that current examination practices do not assess an applicant's clinical skills and are therefore in need of modification (Brooks & Gerstein, 1990).

The ACA has taken an active role in certification and licensure for counselors at both the state and national levels (Brooks & Gerstein, 1990). For example, the ACA helped create the National Board for Certified Counselors (NBCC) in an attempt to establish national standards for professional counselors. Individuals wishing to obtain recognition as an NBCC counselor must have a master's or doctoral degree in counseling or a closely related field, have at least 2 years of supervised professional counseling experience, and successfully complete a certification exam. Some feel that the ACA may be focusing too much on promoting licensure to the detriment of its other activities. Heppner, Casas, Carter, and Stone (2000) noted that the ACA appears to have shifted from being a learned society to being more of a trade association focusing on issues of professional credentialing and accreditation.

To some extent, the members of various helping professions disagree about what are proper qualifications. The members of specialties such as psychiatry, psychology, and counseling emphasize the merits and requirements of their respective fields. Psychiatrists, for example, promote the need for medical training. Unfortunately, the real point of contention among the various specialties appears to be how to gain dominance and control. Psychiatry, for example, does not support psychology, psychology displays contempt for mental health counselors, and the counseling profession (represented by the ACA) refuses to recognize the standards of the AAMFT as a requirement for the practice of marriage and family counseling (Cummings, 1990; Everett, 1990). Clearly, there is a need for more cooperation among the helping professions and less concern with special interests (Brooks & Gerstein, 1990; Cummings).

Continuing Education

Some form of continuing education is essential for the ongoing development of professional counselors. Most certification and licensure regulations require counselors to take continuing education courses to maintain their professional credentials. This usually involves attending workshops or presentations at conferences or taking courses that have been approved for continuing education credits.

Other professional development activities can help counselors remain current and refine their clinical skills. Some of these are reading professional journals and books, attending in-service training programs, co-counseling with an experienced clinician, seeking ongoing supervision, and attending institutes for advanced training in a counseling specialty.

Professional Involvement

As mentioned, being a professional counselor requires ongoing work and effort. As individuals embark on a career in counseling, they initially draw help and guidance from the profession. As they advance in the profession, they find themselves in a position to make a contribution. Some ways that counselors can contribute include taking an active role in professional organizations, supporting efforts to establish requirements for certification and licensure, and writing in professional journals. Professional involvement not only helps support and maintain the profession but enriches the counselor as well. As counselors become professionally involved, they develop a network of friends who can often become an important support system. The experience can also diversify their interests and professional activities, which can be stimulating and professionally rewarding. The following *Personal Note* speaks to the importance of professional involvement in counseling.

A Personal Note

I've noticed that colleagues of mine who are active in professional organizations tend to be happier, more productive, and less prone to burnout than those who don't take an active role in professional organizations. It seems as if those who aren't as active tend to get frustrated more easily, have a more negative view of their jobs, and get tired and give up more easily than those who are professionally active. Perhaps one reason for these differences between the professionally active and inactive counselor is that professional organizations provide counselors with a broader sense of the counseling community and help them keep things in perspective.

I've made a lot of friends through my involvement in professional organizations and activities. These friends have formed an important network and been helpful in many ways. I've felt a sense of support and encouragement from these people. I've also experienced a number of career opportunities, such as reviewing one of my colleague's books for a publishing company and, due to that experience, obtaining my own book contract. Moreover, professional involvement has been a way for me to contribute to the profession. Giving of my time and energy has been personally rewarding as I have participated on committees and editorial boards and with other aspects of the various professional organizations with which I've been affiliated.

Ethical-Legal Issues

The Art and Science of Ethical-Legal Issues

Ethical-legal issues reflect both the art and the science of counseling. To a large degree, ethical codes and legal statutes are not written as hard-and-fast rules but serve rather as principles to guide one's clinical practice. The art of counseling suggests that practitioners engage in creative approaches to **ethical-legal decision making** that are sensitive to multicultural issues. The science of counseling recognizes that ethical codes and legal statutes also provide clear standards of practice regarding ethical-legal behavior, such as legal reporting duties when child abuse or neglect is suspected.

Meara, Schmidt, and Day (1996) envisioned ethics in a manner that complements the concept of counseling as art and science. They suggested that there are two dimensions to ethical decision making: principle ethics and virtue ethics. Principle ethics (akin to the science of counseling) are the overt ethical obligations that must be addressed in clinical situations, such as the duty to warn and protect when a client becomes homicidal. Virtue ethics (akin to the art of counseling) suggest that practitioners go beyond the *obligatory* and strive toward the *ideals* to which professionals aspire. Central to this task is the development of virtuous character traits, such as sensitivity to the cultural milieu, which can have an impact on ethical decision making. Meara et al. also suggested that principle ethics and virtue ethics be integrated to achieve ethical decision making that is not only ethically and legally correct but also in the best interest of society as a whole.

Ethical-legal issues are becoming increasingly revelant to the day-to-day practice of the professional counselor. This is as true for school counselors as it is for mental health counselors and other practitioners in the helping profession. The issues have emerged in response to the increased risk of malpractice suits (Corey, Corey, Corey, & Callanan, 2015) and to the ACA's (2014) position "that the primary responsibility of counselors is to respect the dignity and promote the welfare of clients" (A.1.a). It is therefore imperative that counselors have the necessary knowledge and skills to integrate legal and ethical issues into every aspect of their practice. The following *Personal Note* illustrates the importance of considering ethical-legal issues.

A Personal Note

For the past 44 years, I've worked as a school counselor, clinical mental health counselor, psychologist, and school psychologist in a variety of settings. Over the years, clinical practice has become increasingly challenging in terms of ethical-legal issues. An error in ethical-legal decision making can have disastrous effects for the students, staff, and parents whom I serve, as well as the school district and myself. For example, if I (as a school psychologist) tell a parent that his or her child needs to be hospitalized for treatment of a mental disorder, the school district may have to pay for it. To avoid this dilemma, I work closely with the student's parents to arrange to have students assessed by health care providers in the community to determine if the student needs to be hospitalized or receive other mental health services that go beyond the scope of the school setting.

Ethical Issues

Ethical codes and standards of practice have been formulated by the American Counseling Association (2014) and the American Psychological Association (2010). The ACA code of ethics covers topics such as the counseling relationship; confidentiality and privacy; professional responsibility; relationships with other professionals; evaluation, assessment, and interpretation; supervision, training, and teaching; research and publication; distance counseling, technology, and social media; and resolving ethical issues. The various ethical standards are guidelines for what a counselor can or cannot do. Of course, each clinical situation is unique and may require an interpretation of the particular code of ethics. The standards can therefore be viewed as guiding principles that counselors can use to formulate their clinical judgment. Mabe and Rollin (1986) noted that the codes of ethics provide a framework for professional behavior and responsibility and serve as a means for establishing professional identity.

Baruth and Huber (1985) have identified three major ethical issues that influence clinical practice: client welfare, informed consent, and confidentiality. An additional major ethical issue concerns dual relationships. An overview of these four ethical issues follows.

CLIENT WELFARE The counselor's primary responsibility is the welfare of the client. In this regard, the ACA's and the APA's codes of ethics indicate that the client's needs come before the counselor's needs, counselors should practice within their area of competence, and counselors should terminate or refer a client who is no longer benefiting from the service. Table 2.3 provides excerpts from the ACA's (2014) and the APA's (2010) codes of ethics regarding **client welfare** and conditions relating to client referral.

INFORMED CONSENT The ethical guidelines relating to **informed consent** require counselors to provide each client with an overview of what counseling will entail so that the client can decide whether to participate. Table 2.4 lists excerpts on this topic from the ACA's (2014) and the APA's (2010) codes of ethics. Mardirosian, McGuire, Abbott, and Blau (1990) noted that counselors can assist a client in giving informed consent by providing information on policies, goals, and procedures. For controversial issues such as pregnancy counseling, the authors suggested that counselors inform the client of their moral-value position.

One way of helping a client give informed consent is by providing a professional disclosure statement. McFadden and Brooks (1983) suggested using a professional disclosure statement that includes such helpful information as limits to confidentiality, type of licensure, and theoretical orientation. For example, school counselors might mention that their approach includes consultation with parents and teachers and counseling with students individually and in small and large groups. In terms of theoretical orientation, school counselors might explain the importance of a developmental perspective in addressing the developmental tasks of children at different grade levels.

Table 2.3	Ethical Considerations Relating to Client Welfare and Referral
Client Welfare	**Client Referral**
ACA (2014)	**ACA (2014)**
A.1.a: The primary responsibility of counselors is to respect the dignity and promote the welfare of clients.	A.11.b: Counselors refrain from referring prospective and current clients based solely on the counselor's personally held values, attitudes, beliefs, and behaviors. Counselors respect the diversity of clients and seek training in areas in which they are at risk of imposing their values onto clients, especially when the counselor's values are inconsistent with the client's goals or are discriminatory in nature.
APA (2010)	**APA (2010)**
Principle A: Psychologists strive to benefit those with whom they work and take care to do no harm. In their professional actions, psychologists seek to safeguard the welfare and rights of those with whom they interact professionally.	2.01: Psychologists provide services, teach, and conduct research with populations and in areas only within the boundaries of their competence, based on their education, training, supervised experience, consultation, study or professional experience. . . . Psychologists have or obtain the training, experience, consultation or supervision necessary to ensure the competence of their services, or they make the appropriate referrals.

Source: 2014 American Counseling Association Code of Ethics. Reprinted with permission from American Counseling Association.

CONFIDENTIALITY Confidentiality is a critical condition in counseling and psychotherapy (Paradise & Kirby, 1990). The client must feel safe in disclosing information to the counselor for the counseling process to be effective (Reynolds, 1976). Denkowski and Denkowski (1982) identified two purposes of confidentiality in counseling: (a) protecting the client from the social stigma often associated with being in therapy and (b) promoting the client's vital rights that are integral to the client's welfare. The ACA's (2014) and the APA's (2010) codes of ethics provide guidelines relating to confidentiality, as shown in Table 2.5. The major exception to the principle of confidentiality is when clients pose a clear and imminent danger to themselves or others, such as a client who threatens to commit suicide or kill someone

Table 2.4   Ethical Considerations Relating to Informed Consent

Informed Consent

ACA (2014)

A.2.a: Clients have the freedom to choose whether to enter into or remain in a counseling relationship and need adequate information about the counseling process and the counselor. Counselors have an obligation to review in writing and verbally with clients the rights and responsibilities of both counselors and clients. Informed consent is an ongoing part of the counseling process, and counselors appropriately document discussions of informed consent throughout the counseling relationship.

APA (2010)

3.10: When psychologists conduct research or provide assessment, therapy, counseling or consulting . . . , they obtain the informed consent of the individual or individuals using language that is reasonably understandable to that person or persons.

10.01: When obtaining informed consent to therapy . . . , psychologists inform clients/patients as early as is feasible in the therapeutic relationship about the nature and anticipated course of therapy, fees, involvement of third parties and limits of confidentiality and provide sufficient opportunity for the client/patient to ask questions and receive answers.

Source: 2014 American Counseling Association Code of Ethics. Reprinted with permission from American Counseling Association.

Table 2.5   Ethical Considerations Relating to Confidentiality

Confidentiality

ACA (2014)

B.1.c: Counselors protect the confidential information of prospective and current clients. Counselors disclose information only with appropriate consent or with sound legal or ethical justification.

APA (2010)

4.01: Psychologists have a primary obligation and take reasonable precautions to protect confidential information.

4.02: Psychologists discuss with persons . . . the relevant limits of confidentiality.

Source: 2014 American Counseling Association Code of Ethics. Reprinted with permission from American Counseling Association.

(Gross & Robinson, 1987). It is important to ensure that clients are aware of the limits regarding confidentiality before they begin counseling. This can be accomplished in several ways, including the use of a professional disclosure statement.

DUAL RELATIONSHIPS **Dual relationships** (or multiple relationships) involve counselors engaging in more than one relationship with a client (Corey et al., 2015), for example, a professor also being a student's counselor. Dual relationships can be problematic and violate ethical and legal standards when professional roles conflict (e.g., a counselor dating a client). Table 2.6 provides excerpts from the ACA's (2014) and APA's (2010) codes of ethics regarding dual relationships.

Lamb, Catanzaro, and Moorman (2004) provided information on how psychologists identify, assess, and respond to potential dual relationships with clients, supervisees, and students. Their research finds that relationships with supervisees in social situations is the most commonly discussed area of concern regarding nonsexual dual relationships. These researchers also noted that the main reasons cited by psychologists for not engaging in sexual dual relationships are concerns regarding ethics, values, and morals.

Sexual Relationships Sexual relationships between counselors and clients have become an important ethical-legal issue. Kitchener and Anderson's (2000) recent surveys of the issues associated with sexual relations in counseling suggest that 1% to 9% of male therapists and 0.04% to 2.5% of female therapists have sex with their clients. Professional organizations have issued strong prohibitions against sexual relationships between counselors and clients or even counselors' implying that they are a possibility. Approximately 87% of psychologists have sexual feelings toward clients; it is not considered unethical for a counselor to have sexual feelings, but acting on them can result in ethical and legal problems.

The power differential associated with the counseling relationship can result in clients being sexually exploited by counselors. Similar to the way in which ethical issues can arise from dual relations, sexual relations with clients can have adverse effects on the clients' welfare in that counselors may compromise their ability to keep the clients' best interests uppermost because counselors are concurrently attempting to meet their own needs. Furthermore, clients' trust in the counseling process can be undermined if the postcounseling relationship does not work out. Ethical codes (such as the APA's 2010 ethics code) prohibit psychologists from entering into a sexual relationship with clients for at least 2 years following termination of the counseling relationship. In addition, it is incumbent on the psychologist to prove that there has been no sexual exploitation as a result of the sexual relationship.

Emerging Issues in Dual Relationships Corey et al. (2015) suggested that dual relationships can best be understood within the context of boundary and role issues. These scholars noted an emerging controversy regarding how roles and boundaries

Table 2.6 Ethical Considerations Relating to Dual Relationships

ACA (2014)

A.5.a: Sexual and/or romantic counselor-client interactions or relationships with current clients, their romantic partners, or their family members are prohibited. This prohibition applies to both in-person and electronic interactions or relationships.

A.5.b: Counselors are prohibited from engaging in counseling relationships with persons with whom they have had a previous sexual and/or romantic relationship.

A.5.c: Sexual and/or romantic counselor-client interactions or relationships with former clients, their romantic partners, or their family members are prohibited for a period of 5 years following the last professional contact.

A.5.d: Counselors are prohibited from engaging in counseling relationships with friends or family members with whom they have an inability to remain objective.

A.5.e: Counselors are prohibited from engaging in a personal virtual relationship with individuals with whom they have a current counseling relationship (e.g., through social and other media).

A.6.a: Counselors consider the risks and benefits of accepting as clients those with whom they have had a previous relationship.

A.6.b: Counselors consider the risks and benefits of extending current counseling relationships beyond conventional parameters. Examples include attending a client's formal ceremony (e.g., a wedding).

Note: the ACA 2014 code of ethics provides additional information regarding dual relationships, including on the topics of documenting boundary extensions (A.6.c), role changes in the professional relationship (A.6.d), and nonprofessional interactions or relationships (other than sexual or romantic interactions or relationships; A.6.e).

APA (2010)

3.05: (a) A multiple relationship occurs when a psychologist is in a professional role with a person and (1) at the same time is in another role with the same person, (2) at the same time is in a relationship with a person closely associated with or related to the person with whom the psychologist has the professional relationship, or (3) promises to enter into another relationship in the future with the person or a person closely associated with or related to the person. A psychologist refrains from entering into a multiple relationship if the multiple relationship could reasonably be expected to impair the psychologist's objectivity, competence, or effectiveness in performing his or her functions as a psychologist, or otherwise risks exploitation or harm to the person with whom the professional relationship exists. Multiple relationships that would not reasonably be expected to cause impairment or risk exploitation or harm are not unethical. (b) If a psychologist finds that, due to unforeseen factors, a potentially harmful multiple relationship has arisen, the psychologist takes reasonable steps to resolve it with due regard for the best interests of the affected person and maximal compliance with the Ethics Code.

Source: 2014 American Counseling Association Code of Ethics. Reprinted with permission from American Counseling Association.

between practitioners and clients are defined. Lazarus (1998, 2001) contended that practitioners should take a reasonable, nondogmatic approach regarding boundary and role issues. He believed that under some conditions, nonsexual dual relationships can have therapeutic value and that rigid interpretation of ethical standards can undermine clinical decision making. Borys (1994) disagreed with Lazarus, stating that refraining from dual relationships does not imply rigidity in clinical decision making; Gabbard (1994) went further, noting that failure to establish and maintain clear boundaries is a recipe for disaster.

Younggren and Gottlieb (2004) stated that some dual relationships cannot be avoided and in fact can be obligatory, such as in the military. They outlined a risk management plan that can be used to assess the appropriateness of entering into a dual relationship. According to this plan, one asks the following questions:

- Is it necessary to enter into a dual relationship with the client?

- To what degree can a dual relationship cause harm or benefit to the client?

- Would the dual relationship undermine the counseling relationship?

- Can the practitioner maintain objectivity after entering into a dual relationship?

- Is there informed consent from the client regarding entering into a dual relationship (including identifying potential risks)?

- Has decision making regarding entering into a dual relationship been documented in the treatment records?

- Is there documented evidence of ongoing consultation?

- Is the decision making based on the client's welfare, including consideration of issues relating to diagnostic and treatment issues?

Addressing dual relationships in counseling is a challenging and complex process. Clearly, entering into a dual relationship should occur only after careful consideration of risk management questions and careful ethical-legal decision making.

Legal Issues

Legal problems can result when counselors engage in sexual relationships with clients. For example, many states consider it a felony for professional helpers to have a concurrent sexual relationship with a client. All things considered, it is not surprising that professional organizations strongly discourage counselors from ever engaging in sexual relationships with clients.

Confidentiality is another aspect of counseling that gives rise to several legal issues. As mentioned, counselors are ethically obligated to maintain confidentiality unless clients pose a clear and imminent danger to themselves or others. A legal precedent for counselors to take decisive action to protect human life was set in the landmark case *Tarasoff v. The Board of Regents of the University of California* (1974, 1976). The case involved a psychologist at the University of California at Berkeley who provided counseling services to a student. After the student threatened to kill his girlfriend, Tatiana Tarasoff, the psychologist failed to warn her of the threat. Two months later, the client killed the girl. Her parents filed suit against the university and won on the basis that the psychologist had been irresponsible. The California Supreme Court determined that there in cases similar to *Tarasoff*, there is a duty to protect, which typically involves arranging for clients to be hospitalized when they become homicidal.

Monahan (1993) provided additional guidelines regarding the duty to warn and the duty to protect. Monahan emphasized that the single best predictor of violence is a past history of violence. It is therefore imperative that an in-depth history be taken, including reviewing past hospitalizations and other forms of treatment as well as gathering information from significant others if necessary. Follow-up is also important to ensure that a homicidal client receives the necessary treatment to prevent harm to self or others. In addition, Monahan stressed the importance of documentation and consultation. Corey et al (2015) identified three other situations in which counselors are legally required to report information: (a) when the counselor believes that a client under the age of 16 is the victim of child abuse, sexual abuse, or some other crime; (b) if the counselor determines that a client is in need of hospitalization; and (c) if information is being made an issue in a court action.

The following *Personal Note* describes some of the stressors associated with the duty to warn and the duty to protect.

As society becomes increasingly violent, it is not surprising that counselors are dealing with an increased number of potentially violent situations. I therefore find myself in numerous clinical situations that require implementing the *Tarasoff* ruling by warning and protecting my client's intended victim. One method that I've used to help determine whether a client presents a serious threat to others is MMPI (not the test but an acronym for *means, motive, plan,* and *intent*). Other factors to consider are past histories of violence, abuse of alcohol and drugs, mental stability, and overall mental status. Consultation with a supervisor or colleague such as a psychologist or psychiatrist can also be helpful in determining whether someone represents a homicidal threat.

I have found the process of implementing *Tarasoff* in a clinical situation to be very stressful for all involved. These situations typically place one or more lives at risk and involve my client's welfare (including the client's mental health, career, family, and legal status). I find it very stressful to contact the intended victims and inform them that my client appears to be planning to kill them. It is also stressful to attempt to protect the client by taking the necessary steps, which often include arranging for hospitalization. Having a client admitted voluntarily or involuntarily to a hospital is often a very difficult and time-consuming process. I'm also amazed at how quickly some hospitals discharge these patients back into the community, often creating additional legal-ethical dilemmas and stress for all involved.

PRIVILEGED COMMUNICATION Another legal issue that pertains to confidentiality is the notion of **privileged communication**. This term refers to a legal protection for clients: A counselor is prevented from disclosing confidential communication in court without their permission (Herlihy & Sheeley, 1987). The privilege exists to protect the rights of the client, not the counselor. The client owns and controls the privilege (Herlihy & Sheeley) and can therefore determine whether a counselor may disclose confidential information in a court of law. There are exceptions, however. Corey et al. (2015), citing research from Remley and Herlihy (2014) and Welfel (2013), identified a number of legally mandated exceptions to priviledged communication, summarized as follows:

- Court orders disclosure of confidential information (e.g., during commitment proceedings).

- Client initiates a complaint or lawsuit against counselor.

- Client represents a risk of harm to self or others.

- There is reasonable suspicion of child or elder abuse or neglect.

Laws relating to privileged communication between a client and a member of the helping profession vary considerably from state to state (Herlihy & Sheeley, 1987).

For example, some states recognize privileged communication between psychologists and their clients but not between licensed counselors and their clients. Practitioners must therefore be aware of their state's laws regarding privileged communication.

LEGAL ISSUES IN MANAGED CARE Managed care is currently present in some form in every health care system (Appelbaum, 1993). Appelbaum has identified a number of legal issues that have emerged in conjunction with the movement toward managed care. Specifically, practitioners have several legal responsibilities associated with managed care. Some of these are the duty to appeal adverse decisions, the duty to disclose and to maintain confidentiality, and the duty to continue treatment.

Fulfilling the duty to appeal adverse decisions requires submitting a written request to the managed care provider to change the provider's decision to limit or decline services, if the counselor believes that doing so would not be in the best interest of the client (e.g., the client is suicidal or homicidal).

The duty to disclose involves informing clients about the financial limitations of managed care (payment for therapy may be stopped before the counselor or client believes that the goals of therapy have been reached). Problems associated with confidentiality concern the insurance provider having access to personal information that the client has disclosed during counseling.

There are also legal and ethical issues relating to the duty to continue treatment. It is not considered ethical or legal to "abandon" clients who no longer have the financial means for counseling (e.g., when the managed care insurer refuses to pay). Counselors should attempt to refer the client to free or affordable services, see the client for free, or move toward an appropriate termination (Appelbaum).

Managed care insurers also have legal responsibilities, including the duty to review appeals and other pertinent information regarding the care of clients, the duty to disclose to clients the limits of coverage, and the duty to select qualified providers (Appelbaum, 1993). Practitioners and insurers must work closely together to ensure that clients receive appropriate care and services.

MALPRACTICE Counselors are at increased risk of being sued for malpractice (Corey et al., 2015). It is therefore important for counselors to understand what malpractice is and what they can do to prevent legal difficulties.

Knapp (1980) defined *malpractice* as an act or omission by a counselor that is inconsistent with reasonable care and skill used by other reputable counselors and that results in injury to the client. Knapp noted that courts do not assume that malpractice exists if a counselor has made a mistake in judgment, since it is possible to make such a mistake and still exercise reasonable care. Keeton (1984) identified four conditions that must exist for malpractice to have occurred in a counseling situation: (1) the counselor had a duty to a client, (2) the duty of care was not met, (3) the client sustained an injury, and (4) there was a close causal relationship between the counselor's failure to provide reasonable care and the resulting injury.

DePauw (1986) has provided guidelines for avoiding ethical violations at each phase of the counseling process. These guidelines can minimize the risk of harm to clients and the incidence of malpractice suits for counselors.

Precounseling. Precounseling issues include accurately advertising services, making advance financial arrangements that are clearly understood and serve the best interest of the client, providing services within the counselor's parameters of competency, facilitating the client's informed choice of services, avoiding dual relationships, clearly indicating experimental treatment approaches and taking appropriate safety precautions, and identifying the limits to confidentiality.

Ongoing counseling. Ongoing counseling issues include maintaining confidentiality, seeking consultation as necessary, maintaining adequate client records, taking necessary action regarding clients who pose a clear and imminent danger to themselves or others, and complying with laws that relate to reporting child abuse and neglect.

Termination phase. Termination issues include being sensitive to the client's termination and posttermination concerns, initiating termination or referral if the client is no longer benefiting from services, and evaluating the efficacy of counseling services.

Special Ethical and Legal Issues

This section addresses some of the special ethical and legal issues relating to values of counselors, acquired immunodeficiency syndrome (AIDS), and online counseling.

ISSUES RELATING TO COUNSELOR'S VALUES *Ward v. Wilbanks* (2009, 2011) is considered one of the most important legal cases relating to the profession of counseling in the past 25 years (Kaplan, 2014). The case involved Julea Ward, who was a counseling student working on her graduate degree in the school counseling program at Eastern Michigan University. While taking a practicum class in counseling, she was randomly assigned a client who self-reported that he was gay. She refused to provide counseling to the student based on her religious beliefs and wanted assistance in reassigning the client to another counselor. Ms. Ward was informed by her practicum supervisor that falure to provide counseling services due to issues of sexual orientation was a violation of the American Counseling Association (ACA) code of ethics.

When the supervisor determined they were unable to resolve the issue, Ms. Ward's academic adviser was contacted. Her case was reviewed by faculty, who utilized the counseling program's disciplinary policy and procedure document regarding inappropriate student behavior, including consideration of due process issues. It was determined that she would participate in a remediation plan to address these issues. Ms. Ward refused to participate in the plan, contending that doing so would violate her basic rights.

She subsequently was dismissed from the school counseling program, and she sued the university in the US District Court claiming her dismissal was a violation of her civil rights. The district court ruled in favor of the university, noting that Ms. Ward's behavior was not consistent with the ACA code of ethics regarding not discriminating against individuals based on diversity issues such as race, ethnicity, and sexual orientation. Ms. Ward appealed the district court decision. The case was reviewed by Sixth Circuit Court of Appeals, which sent the case back to the district court for a trial jury. The case was settled out of court before it went to trial to the satisfaction of all parties.

Dugger and Francis (2014), who were faculty members at Eastern Michigan University at the time of the lawsuit, noted that having to respond to a lawsuit was a very disconcerting and challenging experience. They identified a number of lessons learned from the experience, which are summarized here:

- First and foremost, it is important to have and disseminate to students and others a disciplinary policy and procedure statement that includes information regading due process, expectations regarding behavior and performance, and consequences of unethical/inappropriate behavior.

- Second, the disciplinary statement should be followed carefully throughout the entire process of responding to student issues. Not following the policy and procedures would be a critical mistake in terms of being able to successfully respond to a lawsuit.

- University programs should identify procedures for how to respond to a lawsuit (before they are served one) so they will be prepared to respond appropriately.

- Realize that all communication (e.g., documents, email) can be subpoenaed during a lawsuit.

- Be aware that plaintiffs may use the "court of public opinion" to promote their views, which may be inappropriate and inaccurate. If this occurs, it is best to avoid responding in like manner. Instead, consult with the university's legal team.

- Consider requesting support from professional organizations, such as the ACA, if a lawsuit is brought. In addition, university staff responsible for managing the response to a lawsuit may require personal counseling and other support to cope with the associated emotional challenges.

Corey and Corey (2016) reviewed the case of *Ward v. Wilbanks* and noted that it is important for prospective students to be aware of program expectations from the onset of program enrollment (e.g., adhering to codes of ethics, including not discriminating against clients regardless of the student's values or religious beliefs). Kaplan's (2014) review of the case focused on issues associated with denying counseling services and referral. He noted that professional counselors can not deny clients right to counseling when the counselors' values are in conflict with clients' diversity status (e.g., sexual orientation). Referral can be considered when counselors lack necessary skill-based competencies. However, decisions regading referral should relate to clients' needs, not the counselor's belief system.

ISSUES RELATING TO AIDS Many authors have addressed ethical issues surrounding counseling services provided to clients infected by the AIDS virus (HIV; Cohen, 1990; Gray & Harding, 1988; Melton, 1988). The main ethical question that emerges from the literature concerns what a counselor should do when a sexually active client has tested positive for HIV and has not informed partners of the illness. In these instances, the counselor's ethical dilemma is whether to maintain confidentiality or inform the client's sexual partners that they have been exposed to HIV.

Gray and Harding (1988) believed that there are both ethical and legal precedents for breaking confidentiality in these cases. In terms of ethics, the ACA code of ethics (2014) states:

> The general requirement that counselors keep information confidential does not apply when disclosure is required to protect clients or identified others from serious and foreseeable harm or when legal requirements demand that confidential information must be revealed. Counselors consult with other professionals when in doubt as to the validity of an exception. Additional considerations apply when addressing end-of-life issues. (B.2.a)

The ACA's (2014) code of ethics also states:

> When clients disclose that they have a disease commonly known to be both communicable and life threatening, counselors may be justified in disclosing information to identifiable third parties, if the parties are known to be at serious and foreseeable risk of contracting the disease. Prior to making a disclosure, counselors assess the intent of clients to inform the third parties about their disease or to engage in any behaviors that may be harmful to an identifiable third party. (B.2.c)

The *Tarasoff* case also set a legal precedent regarding "duty to warn" (*Tarasoff v. Board of Regents of the University of California*, 1974, 1976). As a result of this case, professional counselors have a legal duty to warn a person if their client poses a serious threat.

Naturally, counselors should not arbitrarily break confidentiality in cases involving clients who have tested positive for HIV; they should do so only as a last resort. Gray and Harding (1988) and Cohen (1990) provided several guidelines, summarized here, that can assist counselors in dealing with these sensitive ethical dilemmas:

- Clients should be made aware of the limits to confidentiality before they begin counseling.

- Clients who have contracted the AIDS virus should be informed how the virus is spread and what precautions they can take to prevent its spreading.

- Clients should be encouraged to inform any sexual partner that they may have been exposed to the virus.

- If a client is unwilling to inform any partner who may be at risk, the counselor should first alert the client of the need to break confidentiality and then inform the sexual partner in a timely fashion.

- Counselors should limit disclosure of information to general medical information regarding the client's disease.

- Disclosures should only be made to the party at risk or to a guardian in the case of a minor.

- Disclosures should communicate willingness to provide counseling services to the client.

- Medical consultation and referral should be arranged as necessary.

Stanard and Hazler (1995) provided additional information regarding the implications of *Tarasoff* in cases involving a client with HIV/AIDS. They suggested that each case needs to be carefully evaluated in terms of its unique circumstances. When the case presents medical evidence of the AIDS virus, when there is a high-risk relationship, and when there is little likelihood of the client's self-disclosure, "counselors are directed to seek consultation, to make sure no reasonable alternative can be utilized, and even then to release only information that is necessary, relevant, and verifiable" (Stanard & Hazler, p. 97). In addition, the authors stress the importance of working with clients to prevent the infection of individuals both in the present and in the future.

Ethical Issues Relating to Online and Technology-Assisted Counseling

As an increasing number of individuals utilize the Internet for health-related services, online counseling has become an increasingly popular option (Mallen, Vogel, & Rochlen, 2005). There has also been an increase in other technology-assisted counseling, such as using mobile phones for text messaging, to broaden the communication options for practitioners and clients (Sude, 2013). Sude (2013) also noted that professional organizations such as the American Counseling Association and the American Mental Health Counselors Association have incorporated the special issues associated with online counseling and other forms of technology-assisted counseling into their ethical codes.

Shaw and Shaw (2006) have identified a number of ethical issues arising from online counseling that appear to create special challenges. They have also surveyed online counselors to identify rates of compliance with ethical guidelines.

- *Professional qualifications.* Online counselors have an ethical responsibility to provide information regarding professional qualification, including training, degrees and majors, licensure, theoretical orientation, specialties, and population served. Survey results indicated that online counselors tend not to provide comprehensive information about their professional qualifications. For example, 62% of online counselors did not provide information regarding their degree, major, or name of college granting the degree. In addition, 38% did not inform clients of their address and phone number.

- *Client abandonment.* Online counselors have an ethical obligation to ensure that clients are not unilaterally terminated from counseling services and, when necessary, to refer clients to other services. Client abandonment may occur in online counseling when a client attempts to contact the online counseling service and the site has disappeared. Survey results suggested that online counseling services are transitory in nature (e.g., 20% of online counseling websites disappeared, turned into another form of website, or were put up for sale within a 2-month period). In addition, survey results suggested 41% of online counselors did not assist clients with referrals when counseling services were not appropriate.

- *Confidentiality.* Online counselors have an ethical mandate to provide confidential counseling services. This may be a particular challenge when utilizing technologies that are not secure, such as email, or when encryption is not utilized. Survey results indicated that 74% percent of online counselors did not use encryption. In addition, 65% did not have statements on their websites informing users that the Internet is not secure.

- *Informed consent.* Online counselors have an ethical responsibility to inform clients regarding counseling services (such as how online counseling is different from face-to-face counseling and the limits to confidentiality) and obtain consent for services. Survey results showed that 39% of online counselors did not have a statement on their website that online counseling is not the same as face-to-face counseling. In addition, 67% did not obtain informed consent statements that described the limits of confidentiality.

- *Duty to warn and protect.* Online counselors have legal and ethical obligations to obtain clients' contact information to address mental health emergencies (including duty to warn and protect if a client becomes homicidal or suicidal). Survey results showed that 55% of online counselors did not obtain the contact information necessary to address mental health emergencies, such as a client's full name and address.

- *Client welfare.* Online counselors have an ethical responsibility to do what they can to promote the welfare of the client (i.e., doing what is in the client's best interest). Client welfare begins with an initial assessment to determine whether clients are appropriate for counseling services or they are in need of a referral. Survey results showed that 62% of online counselors did not conduct intake interviews, and 41% did not assist clients with referrals when counseling services were not appropriate.

- *Minors.* Online counselors have ethical and legal mandates to ensure that minors are eligible to receive counseling services. Survey results showed that 57% of online counselors did not obtain the age and date of birth of clients. In addition, 67% did not post a clear statement on their website that clients must be 18 or over or have permission from a legal guardian to receive counseling services.

Sude (2013) identified ethical and clinical concerns regarding text messaging such as problems maintaining confidentiality, difficulty establishing rapport with clients outside of a face-to-face relationship, and inability to respond to crises. Shaw and Shaw (2006) concluded that overall, online counselors appeared to be in need of additional knowledge about and to assume a stronger commitment to ethical codes and standards of practice. This was especially true of online counselors who were not licensed (33%) and who did not affiliate with professional organizations (60%). Additional training for and regulation of online counseling and other technology-assisted counseling appears warranted.

Ethical-Legal Decision Making

Ethical-legal issues in counseling require a structure for decision making. Throughout the decision-making process, it is critical to consult when necessary and to document all significant activities and events, such as consultation and treatment efforts (e.g., phone calls to a suicidal client). The following four-step process can be useful in establishing a process for ethical-legal decision making.

STEP 1: DETERMINE WHETHER AN ETHICAL–LEGAL ISSUE NEEDS TO BE ADDRESSED

Wilcoxon, Remley, and Gladding (2012) suggested that the first step in ethical-legal decision making is to determine whether an ethical-legal decision needs to be made. The four ethical "guiding principles" discussed in this chapter (client welfare, informed consent, confidentiality, and dual relationships) can be used to alert the counselor to potential ethical issues. Important legal issues that may also need to be addressed in ethical-legal decision making include counseling minors, complying with *Tarasoff* and associated legislation, engaging in privileged communication, and obeying laws relating to reporting child abuse and neglect.

STEP 2: ADDRESS CONTEXTUAL ISSUES SUCH AS CULTURE AND PERSONAL BIAS

Kelly (1999) suggested that the contextual perspective represents two basic assumptions: First, change is inevitable and ongoing. Second, change is systemic; that is, change in one context influences change in another.

Postmodern theories such as social constructivism emphasize the contextual nature of human experience. Social constructivism recognizes the contextual nature of decision making and the role that social-cultural forces play in constructing reality (Cottone, 2001). These social-cultural forces—racism, prejudice, stereotyping, and oppression—may undermine ethical-legal decision making. For example, if counselors believe that a particular culture is prone to the problems of alcoholism and child neglect, they may inadvertently make false charges of neglect when dealing with this population. Oppression can also interfere with ethical-legal decision making by contributing to overly zealous ethical-legal action toward individuals who are targets of prejudice and racism (e.g., professionals keeping other professionals "in their place" by filing unwarranted ethics charges).

Meara, Schmidt, and Day (1996) provided another perspective for integrating social constructivism into ethical-legal decision making. They noted that virtue ethics attempt to broaden ethical decision making beyond the self to reflect the interest of the community and culture. They suggested that "virtue ethics, rooted in the narratives and aspirations of specific communities, can be particularly helpful to professionals in discerning appropriate ethical conduct in multicultural settings and interactions" (p. 4). Virtue ethics thus appear to parallel social constructionism in terms of broadening the self to include sensitivity to the cultures reflected in the stories that clients tell. Meara et al. also noted that ethical-legal decision making evolved from a European-American perspective and that therefore a number of biases associated with ethnocentrism must be addressed. These authors cited Carol Gilligan's (1982, 1993) seminal work on the role of gender in moral development to support their argument about the importance of considering diversity issues in ethical-legal decision making.

The need to address issues of personal bias during ethical-legal decision making has also been discussed by Wilcoxon et al. (2012), who pointed out that ethical-legal decisions are not made in a vacuum, and Cottone (2001), who stated that decisions are better understood contextually in terms of relationships with others and within the context of where one works. Wilcoxon, Remley, and Gladding suggested that the relational aspects of ethical-legal decision making can create personal bias that undermines professional objectivity; a counselor's personal and professional values may be in conflict, thereby inhibiting appropriate action. For example, a counselor may have a colleague who is also a close friend. The counselor may become aware of unethical behavior on the part of the colleague but may not want to take action because of their friendship. Another example of personal bias is a reluctance to report ethical-legal problems where one works for fear of the adverse consequences of being considered a whistle-blower. One way for counselors to overcome this personal bias is to remember that they will be acting unethically if they do not take constructive action.

STEP 3: FORMULATING AN ETHICAL–LEGAL COURSE OF ACTION

Once counselors establish that an ethical-legal dilemma exists, they must determine what action to take. Consultation with a legal adviser and/or one's supervisor can be an important first step. Legal consultation can be useful in identifying potential legal issues and what action would be appropriate. Supervisors can also play a vital role.

Kitchener (1984, 1985) has identified two levels of ethics that can be used to formulate a course of action: intuitive and critical-evaluative. The intuitive level addresses immediate feelings in response to the situation. An intuitive reaction can be useful in situations that require immediate action, such as crisis intervention.

The critical-evaluative level of ethical reasoning can be used in situations that do not require immediate action. Most situations requiring an ethical decision are complex, with no clear right or wrong way to proceed. Kitchener (1984, 1985) suggested a three-tiered approach to critically evaluate a particular situation. The first tier relates to principle ethics, whereas the second and third tiers relate to virtue ethics. The first tier involves referring to the code of ethics for guidelines pertaining to the ethical situation. If the guidelines are insufficient, counselors can move on to the second tier and determine the philosophical foundations on which the ethical guidelines were based, such as the right to privacy or the right to make free choices. When counselors are still uncertain, they can proceed to the third tier and apply the principles of ethical theory. There are several noted ethical theorists whose work can help provide a rationale for ethical action. For example, Wilcoxon et al. (2012) suggested that counselors should do what they would want for themselves or significant others in a similar situation, or they should do what would result in the least amount of harm.

STEP 4: IMPLEMENTING AN ACTION PLAN

Once counselors have determined a course of action and have overcome possible personal-professional conflicts, they are in a position to implement an action plan. Taking action will require courage and the willingness to accept personal responsibility for their actions. After implementing a plan of action, counselors may wish to follow up and evaluate their professional functioning. Van Hoose (1980) has provided guidelines that counselors can use to determine whether their actions are ethically responsible: Counselors have probably acted ethically if they maintained personal and professional honesty, had the client's best interest in mind, acted without malice or personal gain, and can justify their action as following from the best judgment according to the current state of the profession.

Clinical Examples

The following clinical examples provide an opportunity to practice ethical decision making. The four ethical dilemmas presented relate to a variety of clinical situations. There is no right or wrong way to respond to these examples; counselors should simply attempt to develop a response that reflects sound clinical judgment. Each example is followed by a description of the way I would respond.

CLINICAL EXAMPLE #1 You are a counselor at a community mental health center. A young woman was convicted of drunk driving and told by the judge that she must attend your alcohol treatment program to keep her driver's license. You are concerned about the issue of informed consent. What would you do in this situation if you were the counselor?

Response Any situation that involves a client who has been ordered by the court to undergo counseling creates an ethical dilemma. The ethical code regarding informed consent requires that this client must not be forced to attend counseling. In addition, the client should feel free to terminate counseling whenever she chooses. At the same time, the counselor must inform the judge if the client does not complete the alcohol program. Technically, the client is free to choose counseling and keep her driver's license or choose no counseling and lose her license. At the very least, if the client chooses counseling, she may be doing so under duress.

As the counselor, I would first discuss with the client what the alcohol treatment program would entail and give her a professional disclosure statement. The statement would provide information such as my background, my definition of counseling, and the limits to confidentiality. I would then explore with her the available options— she may either lose her license or attend the alcohol program. If she did decide to participate in the alcohol program, I would acknowledge the duress she must be feeling and suggest that we both try to make the best of a difficult situation. I would tell her that she is free to terminate her participation in the program at any time. I would also emphasize that if she decided to do so, I would unfortunately be obligated to inform the judge that she did not complete the program successfully.

CLINICAL EXAMPLE #2 You are an elementary school counselor. After working at the school for a month, you identify several policies that conflict with your ethical code: (1) You are told you must provide counseling services for certain students even if they don't want them, and (2) you are not allowed to maintain confidentiality because you must inform the principal of what certain students tell you during their sessions.

Response The ACA's (2014) code of ethics states that when an institution functions in a manner that conflicts with the counselor's code of ethics, the counselor should attempt to resolve the differences with the institution. In this process, counselors can note that following recognized standards of practice (such as promoting the client's welfare) would be in the best interests of the institutions, the clients, and the staff. Counselors should also note that not following standards of practice can create opportunities for litigation that could adversely affect the institution. If the institution in this example is not willing to make the necessary changes, the counselor can consult with the personnel department and, if necessary, file charges against the organization (e.g., for promoting a hostile work environment). At no point in this process should a counselor engage in unethical acts. It is important to consider that even when an institution asks you to act unethically, you cannot defend your action later by saying, "My supervisor told me to do it." In extreme instances, a counselor may be forced to seek employment elsewhere.

CLINICAL EXAMPLE #3 You are a mental health counselor in a community mental health center. After the second session with a male client, you decide he may be suffering from a serious mental disorder. You don't feel comfortable providing counseling services because you think the client requires help beyond your area of competence. You decide to refer the client to a psychiatrist or other mental health professional. The client refuses to accept your suggestion and insists instead that you continue seeing him. What would you do if you were the counselor?

Response The ACA's (2014) and APA's (2010) codes of ethics regarding client welfare state that a counselor has an ethical responsibility to refer a client who requires help beyond the counselor's level of competency. If the client is reluctant to pursue a referral, the counselor can help the client overcome this impasse. The counselor may also wish to consult with a supervisor to gain ideas for facilitating the referral process. In addition, the counselor should document all attempts to assist with the referral to provide a "paper trail." This could be useful for documenting that the counselor did not commit the ethical violation of abandoning the client.

CLINICAL EXAMPLE #4 You have a private practice specializing in marriage, family, and child counseling. You are seeing a married couple, Dan and Mary. Your approach to marriage counseling is to see the marital partners individually for 15 minutes each and then together for 30 minutes.

During the initial session, you first talk with Dan. He informs you that he and Mary have been married for 2 years. Before the marriage, he was an intravenous drug user, shooting up heroin at least twice a day for several years. During this time, he tested positive for HIV. Dan says that Mary does not know that he tested positive for HIV, and he does not want to tell her because he is convinced that she would leave him. What would you do in this situation if you were the counselor?

Response This case has several ethical issues (client welfare and confidentiality) and one legal issue (relating to the *Tarasoff* ruling). In terms of client welfare, I would be concerned for Dan regarding his drug problem, for Mary regarding the potential of her contracting HIV, and for the two of them regarding their marriage. I would also have some ethical and legal concerns regarding confidentiality. Ethically, I need to do whatever I can to ensure my clients' safety when they are in imminent danger (including breaking confidentiality). In addition, as noted earlier, the ACA's (2014) code of ethics (Section B.2.c) states, "When clients disclose that they have a disease commonly known to be both communicable and life threatening, counselors may be justified in disclosing information to identifiable third parties." The *Tarasoff* ruling concerning the duty to warn and protect also may require me to break confidentiality and take the necessary steps to ensure Mary's safety.

Due to my paramount concern about the possibility that Dan could infect Mary with HIV, I would insist, before the end of the counseling session, that Dan tell Mary he had tested positive for HIV so she could take steps to minimize her risk for contracting the virus. If Dan refused to inform Mary, I would breach confidentiality on the basis that his illness presents a clear and imminent danger to Mary. At this time, I would also review with Mary and Dan the risk of having sexual intercourse so that she could make an informed decision as to what behaviors she would engage in with Dan. I would also encourage Dan to obtain necessary medical treatment, to enter a drug rehabilitation program, and to continue marital therapy as necessary.

DIVERSITY ISSUES Diversity issues such as sexual orientation, gender, socioeconomic status, race, ethnicity, culture, age, and spirituality affect all phases of the counseling process, including ethical-legal decision making. D'Andrea and Foster Heckman (2008) noted that the multicultural counseling movement has taken center stage in the counseling profession. In this regard, multicultural issues are addressed in professional organizations' codes of ethics, such as those of the ACA (2014), the APA (2010), and the National Association of Social Workers (NASW; 2008). The ACA's ethical code provides several examples of this multicultural focus:

> *Preamble:* Core professional values in the counseling profession include "honoring diversity and embracing a multicultural approach in support of the worth, dignity, potential, and uniqueness of people within their social and cultural contexts" (p. 3).

> *Section A: The Counseling Relationship (A.2.c.):* Counselors communicate information in ways that are both developmentally and culturally appropriate.

> *Section B: Confidentiality and Privacy (B.1.a):* Counselors maintain awareness and sensitivity regarding cultural meanings of confidentiality and privacy.

> *Section E: Evaluation, Assessment, and Interpretation (E.5.b.):* Counselors recognize that culture affects the manner in which clients' problems are defined and experienced. Clients' socioeconomic and cultural experiences are considerd when diagnosing mental disorders.

> *Section G: Research and Publication (Introduction):* Counselors minimize bias and respect diversity in designing and implementing research.

> *Section H: Distance Counseling, Technology, and Social Media (H.5.d):* Counselors who maintain websites provide accessability to persons with disabilities. They provide translation capabilities for clients who have a different primary lanague, when feasible.

Spirituality is a diversity issue that has also been incorporated into the multicultural perspective (Bishop, 1995). In counseling, acknowledging spiritual issues means recognizing the role that values and morality play in ethical-legal decision making and the need to address these issues from a multicultural perspective (Grant, 1992; Schulte, 1992). The literature suggests that counseling, by its very nature, is a value-laden process (Grant) whereby clients are aware of their counselors' value systems and counselors help clients explore value-laden issues (Patterson, 1992). Ethical-legal decision making must therefore take into consideration the multiple voices that define moral-ethical behavior. In this process, counselors can attempt to understand a client's values (including morality) in terms of the client's worldview and guard against imposing unidimensional definitions of morality (Pedersen, 1997).

SUMMARY

Counselors face many professional issues. An exploration of the four building blocks of professional counseling—formal study of counseling and professional affiliation, certification or licensure, continuing education, and professional involvement—demonstrates why it is important for students to become involved in professional issues as soon as possible.

Counselors and psychologists have codes of ethics, such as those provided by the ACA, APA, and AAMFT, to guide their clinical practice. These ethical codes must be interpreted and applied to each particular clinical situation. Major ethical issues for counselors include client welfare, informed consent, confidentiality, and dual relationships. Special ethical issues concern counselors' values, AIDS, and online and technology-assisted counseling.

Members of the helping profession also are faced with special legal issues, such as laws regarding the reporting of child abuse and neglect and the duty to warn and protect when serious threats of violence exist. Clinical examples provide opportunities to apply various ethical and legal principles. Counselors must also be aware of diversity when seeking to make decisions in an ethical-legal manner.

PERSONAL EXPLORATION

1. How can involvement in professional organizations be important to your career?

2. What intrigues you about legal-ethical issues in counseling?

3. What is malpractice, and what steps can be taken to avoid a lawsuit?

4. Do you think a parent should be legally responsible for his or her child's behavior? If so, why?

5. What did you think about the information on dual relationships in counseling?

6. What is the role of licensure and certification in counseling?

7. What is the *Tarasoff* ruling, and how does it impact counseling?

8. What steps do you believe are important in ethical-legal decision making?

9. How is confidentiality impacted by a client who may commit harm to self or others?

10. What is the most important guiding principle for ethical-legal decision making: informed consent, confidentiality, dual relationships, or client welfare? What are your reasons for your choice?

LEARNING ACTIVITIES

1. Read the ethical code of one of the professional organizations (e.g., ACA, 2014) and explore with your supervisors or instructor how it could be used to help in ethical-legal decision making.

2. Investigate how involvement in professional organizations could be important to your career. To carry out this investigation, you may wish to attend a professional organization's meeting.

WEBSITES

American Association for Marriage and Family Therapy. (2015). Code of ethics. Retrieved from http://www.aamft.org/iMIS15/AAMFT/Content/legal_ethics/code_of_ethics.aspx.

American Counseling Association (ACA). (2014). Code of ethics. Retrieved from http://www.counseling.org/resources/aca-code-of-ethics.pdf.

American Psychological Association (APA). (2010). Ethical principles of psychologists and code of conduct. Retrieved from http://www.apa.org/ethics/code/.

Buckner, F., & Firestone, M. (2000). "Where the public peril begins": 25 years after *Tarasoff*. *Journal of Legal Medicine, 21*(2). Retrieved from http://cyber.law.harvard.edu/torts01/syllabus/readings/buckner.html. *This comprehensive article by two medical doctors discusses the ramifications of the Tarasoff rulings.*

Thomas, R. V., & Pender, D. A. (2007). *Association for Specialists in Group Work: Best practice guidelines 2007 revisions.* Retrieved from http://asgw.org/pdf/Best_Practices.pdf.

CHAPTER 3

The Counseling Process

The Art and Science of the Counseling Process

As discussed in Chapter 1, the counseling process is both an art and a science. For example, it is an art to really listen to a client and to communicate caring and compassion. Through the art of listening, a counselor attempts to enter into the client's world and see things from the client's perspective. The art of counseling requires the counselor to reach sensitively into the world of clients and help them become aware of their strengths and hidden beauty. The art of counseling also recognizes the importance of tuning into and reacting appropriately to diversity issues such as culture, gender, and spirituality. All these aspects of the art of counseling play important roles in addressing the theory, research, and practice of the profession.

The science of counseling acts as an important balance to the subjective art of counseling, providing an objective dimension. Counselors must be able to utilize scientific tools to gain an objective understanding of what is occurring during the various stages of the counseling process, from formulating a counseling relationship to termination, follow-up, and research and evaluation. For example, the counseling literature has identified a number of factors associated with establishing a positive counseling relationship, such as core conditions (e.g., empathy, respect, genuineness, and immediacy). There are numerous other examples of the role of science in counseling, from the use of standardized tests in assessment to research methodology for evaluating efficacy.

Counseling is not a fixed entity but a fluid process in which the counselor continually tries to adjust course to accommodate the unique and emerging needs of clients. The art and science of counseling should provide a point of reference for charting an effective course through the counseling process.

Chapter Overview

This chapter provides an overview of the counseling process as well as a description of some of the common problems that beginning counselors experience. It explores what can occur in a counseling session and some of the special skills utilized in counseling. Highlights of the chapter include the following:

- **The art and science of the counseling process**

- **The six stages of the counseling process**

- **Listening skills**

- **Recent trends in the counseling process**

- **Brief-counseling approaches**

- **Common problems for beginning counselors**

- **Diversity issues**

The Six Stages of the Counseling Process

Most counseling sessions last approximately 50 minutes (Linder, 1954). A counseling session is therefore sometimes referred to as "the 50-minute hour." What takes place in a session depends on the client's needs and the counselor's personal approach to counseling. Although there is some variation during a session, most counseling approaches have a basic structure in common. As described by Cormier and Hackney (1993), counseling is a five-stage process: relationship building, assessment, goal setting, interventions, and termination and follow-up. These stages have been expanded into the following six-stage model of the counseling process:

Stage 1: Relationship building

Stage 2: Assessment and diagnosis

Stage 3: Formulation of counseling goals

Stage 4: Intervention and problem solving

Stage 5: Termination and follow-up

Stage 6: Research and evaluation

The focus of counseling may shift as the counseling process progresses over time. Initially, a counselor may place the primary emphasis on building a positive counseling relationship, assessment and diagnosis, formulating counseling goals, and intervention and problem solving. During the later phase of the counseling process, the counselor may shift the emphasis to termination and follow-up as well as research and evaluation. A more complete description of these six stages follows.

Stage 1: Relationship Building

The counseling relationship is the heart of the counseling process. It supplies the vitality and the support necessary for counseling to work, and it is the critical factor associated with successful outcomes in counseling (Kokotovic & Tracey, 1990; Lambert, 2011). Sexton and Whiston (1994) commented, "The quality of the counseling relationship has consistently been found to have the most significant impact on successful client outcome" (p. 6).

Although there appears to be a general consensus that the counseling relationship is important, it is less clear to what degree and in what way (Gelso & Carter, 1985). Research efforts on these issues can be grouped into two general categories: counselor-offered conditions and counselor- and client-offered conditions. Counselor-offered conditions relate to how the counselor influences the counseling process. The majority of the literature on the counseling relationship has focused on the core conditions for effective counseling and the social influence model. An overview of the issues associated with these two important topics follows.

CORE CONDITIONS Rogers (1957) identified what he believed were **core conditions** for successful counseling: empathic understanding, unconditional positive regard, and congruence. Rogers suggested that these core conditions were necessary and sufficient for constructive personality change to occur and that no other conditions were necessary. Later, Carkhuff (1969, 1971) expanded the core conditions to include respect, immediacy, confrontation, concreteness, and self-disclosure. Carkhuff also pioneered the development of listening skills that could be used to promote these core conditions. Following is a description of each of the conditions, and Table 3.1 presents an overview.

Table 3.1	Core Conditions	
Core Conditions	**Description**	**Purpose**
Empathy	Communicating a sense of caring and understanding	To establish rapport, gain an understanding of the client, and encourage self-exploration in the client
Unconditional positive regard	Communicating to clients that they have value and worth as individuals	To promote acceptance of the client as a person of worth as distinct from accepting the client's behavior
Congruence	Behaving in a manner consistent with how one thinks and feels	To be genuine (not phony) in interactions with the client
Respect	Focusing on the positive attributes of the client	To focus on the client's strengths (not weaknesses)
Immediacy	Communicating in the here and now about what is occurring in the counseling session	To promote direct mutual communication between the counselor and client
Confrontation	Pointing out discrepancies in what the client is saying and doing (between statements and nonverbal behavior) and how the client is viewed by the counselor and client	To help clients clearly and accurately understand themselves and the world around them
Concreteness	Helping clients discuss themselves in specific terms	To help clients focus on pertinent issues
Self-disclosure	Making the self known to others	To increase counseling-relevant communication from the client, enhance the client's evaluation of the counselor, and increase the client's willingness to seek counseling

Empathy **Empathy** is considered the most important core condition in terms of promoting positive outcomes (Orlando & Howard, 1986). Gelso and Fretz (2001) observed that virtually all major schools of counseling recognize the importance of empathy in the counseling process. Egan (2002) described empathic understanding as a process that involves listening, understanding, *and* communicating that understanding to the client. Rogers emphasized the experiential nature of empathy. He vigorously rejected mechanistic explanations of empathy that focus on techniques such as reflection of feeling (Raskin & Rogers, 2000, 2005). According to Rogers, empathy involves entering into and experiencing the client's phenomenological world. It is an active, immediate, and ongoing process in which the counselor becomes aware of the client's feelings, experiences those feelings, and creates a mirror through which clients can explore and discover deeper meanings associated with their feelings (Raskin & Rogers).

Empathic understanding can be understood as a multistage process (Barrett-Lennard, 1981, 1997; Gladstein, 1983) consisting of different types of empathy. Gladstein identified the following stages of empathy: the counselor has an emotional reaction to the client's situation, the counselor attempts to understand the client's situation from the client's perspective, the counselor communicates empathy to the client, and the client feels a sense of caring and understanding from the counselor.

Several kinds of empathy have also been identified, for example, primary and advanced empathy (Egan, 2002). Egan described primary empathy as a process that involves the counselor attending, listening, and communicating accurate perceptions of the client's messages. Advanced empathy involves employing the process of primary empathy as well as utilizing the skills of self-disclosure, directives, or interpretations.

The following *Personal Note* provides additional information on empathy.

A Personal Note

I believe an important point regarding empathy is that it involves not only actually caring about someone but being perceived as being caring. For example, a father who never tells his children he loves them can feel love toward his children but may not be perceived as being loving. Children often need to hear the words of love to feel loved.

As a counselor educator, I have conceptualized empathy in terms of three levels of intensity.

Level 1 involves using listening skills to phenomenologically understand the client's feelings and reflect the feelings back to the client in a manner that is perceived as caring.

Level 2 involves advanced empathy, which I define as "listening with a third ear" or "listening between the lines of communication." This type of listening can trigger a "journey into self," whereby the client experiences a deeper level of

(Continued)

emotional understanding. For example, when a client says to the counselor, "I am picking up a contradiction" [in terms of what you are telling me], the counselor can respond to the client by saying, "Perhaps you are feeling a contradiction on some level also." Something similar to this occurred during Shostrom's *Three Approaches to Psychotherapy* film series (1965) when "Gloria" asks Carl Rogers for advice regarding being honest with her daughter about sex.

The third level of empathy is what I refer to as "self-transcendence and the existential encounter." The existential encounter involves moving beyond the subject-object dichotomy, feeling at one with the client, and directly experiencing the client's innermost emotional state. Counselors can use the four stages of multimodality creative arts therapy, such as music therapy, to move beyond hearing about the client's blues to directly experiencing the client's emotional expression (see Chapter 8).

Unconditional Positive Regard **Unconditional positive regard** involves the counselor communicating to clients that they are of value and worthy as individuals. This concept has been referred to by several other terms, including *nonpossessive warmth, acceptance, prizing, respect,* and *regard*. Some controversy has arisen regarding the core condition of unconditional positive regard. Gelso and Fretz (2001), for example, contended that this concept is neither desirable nor obtainable. Martin (1989), on the other hand, suggested that the concept has been misunderstood. According to Martin, unconditional positive regard does not imply that the counselor reacts permissively, accepting all the client's behavior. Instead, it means that the counselor accepts the client while setting limits on certain behaviors. (See Rogers, Gendlin, Kiesler, and Truax [1967] for additional information on unconditional positive regard.)

Congruence **Congruence** involves counselors behaving in a manner consistent with how they think and feel. This condition has also been referred to as *genuineness*. An example of not functioning congruently is a counselor who says, "I'm glad to see you," when a client arrives for an appointment, even though the counselor does not like the client.

Respect Respect is similar to unconditional positive regard in that it focuses on the positive attributes of the client. Counselors can communicate respect by making positive statements about the client and openly and honestly acknowledging, appreciating, and tolerating individual differences (Okun, 2002).

Immediacy Carkhuff (1969, 1971) developed the concept of immediacy, which is similar to Ivey's (1971) notion of direct, mutual communication. Immediacy involves communication between the counselor and client that focuses on the here-and-now. It allows the counselor to directly address issues of importance to the counseling relationship. Immediacy can involve counselors describing how they feel in relation to the client in the moment. For example, if a client does not appear interested in counseling, the counselor might say, "I'm becoming concerned that you're not finding our sessions meaningful. How are you feeling about what is going on in counseling now?"

Confrontation The core condition of confrontation involves the counselor pointing out discrepancies in what a client is saying. There can be discrepancies between what the client is saying and doing (Gazda, Asbury, Blazer, Childress, & Walters, 1979), between statements and nonverbal behavior (Ivey, Ivey, & Zalaquett, 2010), and between how clients see themselves and how the counselor sees them (Egan, 2002).

Confrontation is a difficult and risky counseling technique that is used most effectively by high-functioning counselors (Berenson & Mitchell, 1968). A negative effect on the counseling process can occur when, for example, a client misreads the confrontation and feels attacked or rejected by the counselor (Egan, 2002).

Concreteness Concreteness refers to the counselor helping clients discuss their concerns in specific terms. Clients can feel overwhelmed by their problems and have difficulty putting things into perspective. When this occurs, concreteness can help the counselor create a focus for the client in the counseling process.

Self-Disclosure Jourard (1958) developed the concept of self-disclosure, which involves making the self known to another. Danish, D'Augelli, and Brock (1976) differentiated two types of self-disclosure statements: self-disclosing and self-involving. In self-disclosing statements, counselors disclose factual information about themselves. In self-involving statements, counselors describe what they are experiencing in relation to the client in the counseling process.

A review of the literature suggests support for both types of self-disclosure, with some studies favoring the merits of self-disclosing statements and other studies recognizing the value of self-involving statements in the counseling process (Sexton & Whiston, 1994). In addition, Collins and Miller (1994), in their meta-analytic review of the literature on self-disclosure and liking, found that people are liked more when they engage in intimate self-disclosure (as compared to people who self-disclose at less intimate levels of self-disclosure), self-disclosure increases when people like each other, and people like each other more when they engage in self-disclosure.

Current research trends on the various facets of self-disclosure show it to be a complex process subject to influence from mediating variables such as gender, culture, and disability (Collins & Miller, 1994; Sexton & Whiston, 1994). For example, Mallinckrodt and Helms (1986) found that counselors are perceived as being more attractive when they disclosed having a disability that is not apparent to the client. Regarding culture, African American clients favor counselor self-disclosure more than Caucasians do when disclosure concerns information relating to sex, personal and professional information, and success and failure in counseling (Cashwell, Shcherbakova, & Cashwell, 2003). Another study found that Asian American clients prefer self-disclosure that provides structure to the counseling session over disclosures that relate to approval/reassurance, facts/credentials, and feelings (Kim, B.S., et al., 2003).

RESEARCH ON CORE CONDITIONS Many researchers have conducted studies to evaluate Rogers's (1957) premise that the core conditions are all that is necessary or sufficient for constructive personality change. The early research of Truax and Carkhuff (1967) and Truax and Mitchell (1971) provided support for Rogers's theory, but during the 1970s researchers began to report negative results and criticize earlier studies for methodological flaws or failure to test the efficacy of core conditions in non-Rogerian approaches (Garfield & Bergin, 1971; Mintz, Luborsky, & Auerbach, 1971; Sloane, Staples, Cristol, Yorkston, & Whipple, 1975). However, more recent research has corrected many of the early methodological flaws and has shown overall support for the importance of the core conditions for enhancing the counseling relationship and fostering positive outcomes in counseling (Beutler, Machado, & Neufeldt, 1994; Sexton & Whiston, 1994).

Gelso and Fretz's (2001) review of the literature on core conditions concluded that core conditions are not, as Rogers suggested, necessary and sufficient but do facilitate positive outcomes in counseling. Recent research also suggests that the relationship between the core conditions and the counseling process is more complex than previously believed. The core conditions appear to be not so much counselor-offered conditions but a set of variables (such as empathy and respect) that are dependent on both the counselor and the client (Beutler et al., 1994).

The reductionist approach utilized by counselor educators regarding core conditions (e.g., microtraining methods that equate reflection of feeling with empathy) was rejected by Rogers and Wood (1974). From their perspective, core conditions are not discrete entities but are interrelated within the flow of the counseling session. How Rogers implemented core conditions in his counseling session with "Gloria" (see Shostrom's *Three Approaches to Psychotherapy* film series, 1965) was analyzed by Wickman and Campbell (2003). They concluded that Rogers's conversational style incorporated his core conditions in a manner consistent with his client-centered theory.

SOCIAL INFLUENCE MODEL Strong's (1968) **social influence model** also emphasizes the importance of counselor-offered conditions in the counseling process. The model has two stages, representing an integration of social psychology into counseling theory. During the first stage, the counselor attempts to be perceived by the client as expert, attractive, and trustworthy. When this occurs, the counselor establishes a power base. In the second stage of Strong's model, the counselor uses the power base to exert positive influence on the client within the counseling process.

Extensive research has been conducted to test both stages of Strong's model. (For literature reviews, see Corrigan, Dell, Lewis, & Schmidt [1980]; Heppner & Dixon [1981]; and Heppner & Claiborn [1989]; Heppner and Claiborn, for example, provided an overview of studies that have evaluated each stage of Strong's model.) Studies evaluating the first stage of the model have attempted to identify the factors that promote the client's perception of the counselor as expert, attractive, and trustworthy. Counselors tend to be perceived as *expert* when they have objective evidence of training and utilize prestigious cues (Angle & Goodyear, 1984; Littrell, Caffrey, & Hopper, 1987); use frequent, consistent, and responsive nonverbal behavior such as touch, smiling, and body leans (Roll, Crowley, & Rappl, 1985; Strohmer & Biggs, 1983; Tyson & Wall, 1983); and use narrative analogies and empathic responses (Suit & Paradise, 1985). Counselors are perceived as *attractive* when they have objective evidence of training (Angle & Goodyear; Paradise, Conway, & Zweig, 1986), have status (McCarthy, 1982), and are self-disclosing (Andersen & Andersen, 1985; Curran & Loganbell, 1985). Counselors appear more *trustworthy* when they use credible introductions and reputational cues (Bernstein & Figioli, 1983; Littrell et al.), responsive nonverbal behavior (Hackman & Claiborn, 1982), and verbal and nonverbal cues associated with confidentiality (La Fromboise & Dixon, 1981; Merluzzi & Brischetto, 1983).

As noted, the second stage of Strong's model suggests that once counselors establish a power base by appearing expert, attractive, and trustworthy, they can exert a positive influence on the client. The majority of the studies reviewed by Heppner and Claiborn (1989) provide support for the second stage of Strong's model. For example, expertness, attractiveness, and trustworthiness are related to client satisfaction (Heppner & Heesacker, 1983; McNeill, May, & Lee, 1987), changes in the client's self-concept (Dorn & Day, 1985), favorable counseling outcomes (La Crosse, 1980), and less-premature terminators (McNeill et al.).

COUNSELOR- AND CLIENT-OFFERED CONDITIONS The concept of a working alliance is another way to describe the counseling relationship. This idea goes beyond focusing on counselor-offered conditions to include both counselor- and client-offered conditions. Several models of the working alliance have emerged from the literature (Bordin, 1979; Gelso & Carter, 1985; Greenson, 1967), with Bordin's model receiving considerable attention (Kokotovic & Tracey, 1990). Bordin suggested that the working alliance is composed of three parts: agreement between the counselor and client about the goals of counseling, agreement between the counselor and client about the tasks of counseling, and the emotional bond between the counselor and client.

Research has suggested that positive outcomes in counseling are enhanced if the working alliance is established early in counseling (Kivlighan, 1990). The literature suggests (Al-Darmaki & Kivlighan, 1993) that the working alliance is dependent on four factors: client precounseling characteristics such as motivation and interpersonal skills, the counselor's personal characteristics, the counselor's skills, and the match between the client's needs and the counselor's skills and resources. With respect to the fourth factor (the importance of the counselor-client fit), Gelso and Fretz (2001) suggested that the strength of the working alliance depends on the degree of agreement relating to the goals and tasks of counseling and the level of emotional attachment between the counselor and client. Lazarus (1993) went on to note that the counseling relationship should be characterized by counselors functioning like "authentic chameleons," adjusting their therapeutic style to the unique and emerging needs of clients.

Stage 2: Assessment and Diagnosis

Assessment and diagnosis contribute to several important aspects of the counseling process. They can help a counselor develop an in-depth understanding of a client and identify mental disorders that require attention. This understanding can facilitate goal setting and suggest types of intervention strategies.

Assessment procedures can be divided into standardized and nonstandardized measures (Kottler, 2004). Standardized measures include psychological tests that have a standardized norm group. Nonstandardized measures do not have a standardized norm group and include strategies such as the clinical interview and assessment of life history.

Diagnosis is a medical term that means "identification of the disease-causing pathogens responsible for a physical illness" (Nathan & Harris, 1980, p. 110). Rosenhan and Seligman (1995) identified four reasons for making a diagnosis: facilitating communication shorthand, indicating possible treatment strategies, communicating etiology, and aiding in scientific investigation. Additional information regarding assessment and diagnosis can be found in Chapter 4.

Stage 3: Formulation of Counseling Goals

Goals serve three functions in the counseling process (Cormier & Hackney, 1993): motivational, educational, and evaluative. First, goals can have a motivational function, especially when clients are involved in establishing the goals. Clients appear to work harder on goals they help create (Cormier & Hackney). They may also be more motivated when they have specific, concrete goals to work toward, which can help clients focus their energy on specific issues. It is also important for counselors to encourage clients to make a verbal commitment to work on a specific counseling goal. Clients tend to be more motivated to work when they have made a commitment to do so (Strong & Claiborn, 1982).

The second function of a counseling goal is educational. From this perspective, clients can learn new skills and behaviors that they can use to enhance their functioning. For example, a counseling goal might be to become more assertive. During assertiveness training, clients can learn skills to enhance their functioning in interpersonal situations.

The third function of a counseling goal is evaluative. Clear goals give the counselor and client an opportunity to evaluate progress. Goals can also be useful in implementing research strategies, and they provide a means to assess counselor accountability.

We can also conceptualize counseling goals as either process or outcome goals (Cormier & Hackney, 1993). *Process goals* establish the conditions necessary to make the counseling process work. These goals relate to the issues of formulating a positive relationship by promoting the core conditions, as described earlier in this chapter. Process goals are primarily the counselor's responsibility. *Outcome goals* specify what the client hopes to accomplish in counseling. The counselor and client should agree on these goals and modify them as necessary. George and Cristiani (1995) identified five types of outcome goals: facilitating behavior change, enhancing coping skills, promoting decision making, improving relationships, and facilitating the client's potential. The following overview expands on these five outcome goals.

1. *Facilitating behavior change.* Some form of behavior change is usually necessary for clients to resolve their concerns. The amount of change necessary varies from client to client. For example, one client might need counseling to learn how to deal effectively with a child, whereas another might require psychotherapy to change an unhealthy, stressful lifestyle.

2. *Enhancing coping skills.* Erikson (1968) identified several developmental tasks and associated coping mechanisms unique to the various stages of development. Blocher (1974) later created a developmental counseling approach that identified coping skills necessary to proceed through the life span. For example, intimacy and commitment are developmental tasks of young adulthood. Coping behaviors necessary to meet these developmental tasks include appropriate sexual behavior, risk-taking behavior, and value-consistent behavior such as giving and helping. In more general terms, many clients may require help coping with life. They may have problems dealing with stress, anxiety, or a dysfunctional lifestyle. In these situations, clients may benefit from a stress management program that includes relaxation, meditation, and exercise.

3. *Promoting decision making.* Some clients have difficulty making decisions. They may feel that no matter what they decide, it will be wrong. They may even think they are "going crazy." Difficulty making decisions is often a normal reaction to a stressful life situation such as a recent divorce. In these situations, the counselor may want to reassure clients that they are not going crazy. Helping clients feel normal can encourage them and alleviate unnecessary worry. For clients who need help developing decision-making skills, the counselor may wish to take a more active role. It may be appropriate to involve family members if the client is suffering from a serious mental disorder, such as an organic brain syndrome.

4. *Improving relationships.* Adler (1930/1964) once suggested that the barometer of mental health is social interest. He believed that a person who did not have a close relationship with anyone was at risk for mental problems. Glasser (1965) noted that all people need one or more reciprocal relationships in which they feel loved and understood and experience a sense of caring. Counselors can use a variety of counseling strategies to help clients improve their interpersonal relations. These strategies include social-skill training programs (Argyle, 1981), group counseling that focuses on interpersonal relations (Rogers, 1970), couples therapy (Sager, 1976), and marital therapy (Humphrey, 1983).

5. ***Facilitating the client's potential.*** Goals in this category are more abstract and relate to the concepts of self-realization and self-actualization. Self-realization implies helping clients become all they can be as they maximize their creative potential. Roadblocks to self-realization require the counselor's attention. For example, clients may become discouraged and want to quit at the first sign of failure. In these instances, the counselor can help clients gain a more realistic understanding of what is required to be successful. Self-actualization, a concept developed by Abraham Maslow (1968), relates to the need to fulfill one's potential. He believed that as people's basic needs are met, they will move toward self-actualization. Rogers (1981) incorporated the concept of self-actualization into his person-centered counseling approach. He believed that if the counselor establishes certain conditions, such as communicating nonpossessive warmth, unconditional positive regard, and empathy, then the client can move toward self-actualization and become a healthy, integrated person.

Stage 4: Intervention and Problem Solving

Once the counselor and client have formulated a counseling goal, they can determine what intervention strategy to implement. They may choose from a variety of interventions, including individual, group, couples, and family counseling. It may be best to begin with individual counseling for clients with problems of an intrapersonal nature. As clients become more secure, they may be able to benefit from the open dialogue that often characterizes group counseling. Couples or family counseling may be more appropriate for clients with difficulties of an interpersonal nature, as in a marital or parent-child conflict.

Involving clients in the process of selecting intervention strategies has some advantages. For example, Devine and Fernald (1973) noted that this approach can help counselors avoid using strategies that a client has already tried without apparent success. Instead, the counselor and client together can select a strategy that seems realistic in terms of its strengths and weaknesses. The following guidelines, derived by Cormier and Cormier (1998), encourage client involvement in selecting the appropriate intervention strategy: The counselor should provide an overview of the different treatment approaches available, describe the role of the counselor and client for each procedure, identify possible risks and benefits that may result, and estimate the time and cost of each procedure. In addition, it is important for the counselor to be sensitive to client characteristics, such as values, beliefs, and multicultural issues, when selecting an intervention strategy (Cormier & Hackney, 1993).

Counselors should also be aware of a client's personal strengths and weaknesses in selecting a counseling approach. For example, counselors should determine whether a client has the necessary self-control or ego strength to utilize a counseling strategy (Cormier & Hackney, 1993). Smith's (2006) strengths-based counseling model suggests that instilling hope and optimism is believed to be a vital aspect of the counseling process as these attitudes can act as a buffer to mental illness. In addition, counselors can promote strengths by fostering resilience, encouragement, and empowerment.

PROBLEM-SOLVING STRATEGIES One way to conceptualize intervention is within the framework of problem solving. Dixon and Glover (1984) suggested that all counseling or psychotherapy is a problem-solving process, whether it involves individual, group, marriage, or family counseling. They noted that since the counseling process is focused on helping a client resolve problems, counselors should develop a systematic approach to problem solving. Dixon and Glover also believed that counselors should attempt to teach clients how to use problem-solving skills in their daily lives in order to enable clients to learn skills that could contribute to their personal autonomy.

Several problem-solving approaches can be used in the counseling process (e.g., Heppner & Krauskopf, 1987; Kanfer & Busemeyer, 1982). Kanfer and Busemeyer's six-stage model includes problem detection, problem definition, identification of alternative solutions, decision making, execution, and verification. This model is a behaviorally oriented approach that involves describing a particular problem in behavioral terms, identifying possible solutions associated with the problem, deciding on a course of action relative to the various alternative solutions, implementing the decision, and verifying whether the outcome is consistent with the expected outcome.

Heppner, Witty, and Dixon (2004) have identified the following variables associated with problem solving and adjustment:

- Effective counseling is associated with resolving clients' problems and enhancing problem-solving abilities (e.g., the number of alternatives generated in problem solving is positively associated with adjustment).

- Effective problem solvers are flexible and adaptive and can handle stress. They can also develop strategies to reach their goals and satisfy their needs.

- Ineffective problem solvers have difficulty solving problems and coping with environmental stressors.

- Problem-solving appraisal is related to how well clients are able to address a wide array of life's challenges.

Heppner et al. (2004) contended that problem-solving appraisal—clients' perceptions of their problem-solving ability (e.g., how and whether the person can solve the problem)—has become an increasingly important aspect of the problem-solving process in counseling. Butler and Meichenbaum (1981) suggested that appraisal of problem-solving skills influences problem-solving performance and outcomes of the problem-solving process. Bandura's (1997) self-efficacy theory provides support for the notion that belief in one's ability is related to performance outcomes.

Heppner and Petersen (1982) developed the Problem Solving Inventory (PSI) as a means of investigating the role of appraisal in problem solving. In a review of more than 120 studies that investigated problem-solving appraisal and human adjustment, Heppner et al. (2004) concluded that the PSI is a robust instrument useful in investigating a wide variety of areas, such as mental and physical health, coping with stress, and educational and vocational issues. They suggested that the PSI be used in clinical practice to assess problem-solving styles, to create goals associated with problem-solving deficits (including issues relating to appraisal), and to identify appropriate problem-solving interventions to address these goals. For example, clients with negative problem-solving appraisal and hopelessness and depression tend to be at higher risk for suicide than are clients who are depressed but who have more positive appraisals of their problem-solving skills.

Problem-solving strategies can also be used in conjunction with counseling theories. Nystul (1995, 1999), for example, developed a four-step problem-solving model based on Adler's and Glasser's theories. This model can be used with children, adolescents, or adults and has a built-in mechanism to enhance clients' involvement in counseling and to minimize client resistance. The model can be especially useful in brief-counseling approaches. An overview of the Nystul problem-solving model follows.

1. Step 1 is based on Glasser's theory (Glasser, 1989, 1998, 2000). It explores what the client is doing that is problematic and adding an "ing" to it to help the client realize the control he or she has over what he or she is doing (e.g., "angering").

2. Step 2, based on Adlerian psychology (Adler, 1969), involves exploring the purpose or psychology of use of the client's behavior. This process involves asking the client, "I'm sure your angering [or whatever it is that is problematic] has served some purpose and has been useful to you or you would not be doing it. I wonder when it all began—when do you first remember using angering?" Together, the counselor and client can then explore some early memories in terms of what needs the client may have met while engaging in the problematic behavior. Maslow's hierarchy of needs can be used to help identify possible needs that were being met.

   Step 2 is the most important phase of the problem-solving approach. It is respectful in that it recognizes that the problematic behavior must be useful or the client would not be doing the angering (or other behavior). This is in contrast to many approaches that simply say something like, "I hear a lot of *shoulds* and *musts* in your statements. These sound irrational and can be the cause of your problems." By showing respect for the psychology of use of the client's inefficient approach, the counselor can minimize resistance to the change process and maximize motivation for change.

3. Step 3 involves helping the client realize the cost of not changing. It is based on Homans's (1962) social exchange theory (from social psychology), which suggests that people will change when they realize that the behavior they are engaged in is costing more than it is getting them. During this step, the counselor can help clients realize that what they did to meet their needs as children is not working to meet their needs as adults. This realization can be a paradoxical point in therapy, shifting the client's motivation toward increased involvement in the change process.

4. Step 4 involves helping the client develop a new approach that meets the needs identified in step 2 without the costs associated with step 3. This may involve helping the client learn new coping skills and other strategies necessary to be successful in his or her new approach.

A CASE EXAMPLE A brief case example can be used to illustrate the four steps of the Nystul problem-solving method. Tom, a 45-year-old physician, had lost two jobs because of angry outbursts in front of his supervisors, and he had recently been given an ultimatum from his fiancée that he either get his anger under control or their relationship "will be history." During step 1 of the problem-solving approach, the counselor and Tom identified angering as the problem that he needed help with. Tom liked the idea of adding the *-ing* to *anger* because the resulting word gave him a feeling of control over his problematic behavior.

In step 2, the counselor and Tom explored the psychology of how Tom used his angering. Tom recalled several memories related to his early use of angering. His first early memory was of just having moved to a new city and having no friends. On the first day of school, he got into a fight and broke another boy's nose. Blood was everywhere, and people gathered around and said he was "one tough guy."

After the fight, several other boys wanted to be his friend. Tom's initial experience with angering enhanced his self-esteem and met his belonging needs.

Step 3 involved helping Tom become aware of the cost of his angering. In this process, Tom and his counselor did a cost-benefit analysis (what he gets from it versus what it is costing him). Quickly, it became clear that Tom's angering had worked for him when he was a child to meet his basic needs of self-esteem and belonging, but it was not working for him as an adult. In fact, angering was having an opposite effect in that it was driving people away and making them think he was immature and "infantile" in his behavior. Recognition of the paradoxical effect of angering helped Tom increase his motivation for letting go of his angering and developing more efficient means of meeting his needs.

The counselor then provided Tom with insight into his problematic behavior by noting that what works for people as children often does not work for adults (i.e., the primitive tools children use, such as angering, are not acceptable in adult relationships). However, people continue to use these primitive tools because their private logic (which is primarily unconscious) tricks them into thinking that they must use these tools in order to meet their needs. Providing Tom with this insight seemed to help normalize his angering and minimize his resistance to working through his problem.

Step 4 involved helping Tom learn a new approach to meeting his needs without the cost associated with angering. Tom saw angering as reactive to conflict situations, and he wanted to be more proactive. Together, the counselor and he decided that he could use encouragement as an approach to avoid conflict and to work through conflict from a more positive perspective. Encouragement was also seen as an excellent tool to meet needs such as self-esteem and belonging. The counselor and Tom then spent two sessions helping him develop and implement his new approach, which they called *encouraging*, to help him realize the control he would possess with this approach.

Stage 5: Termination and Follow-Up

Perhaps the ultimate goal in counseling is counselors becoming obsolete or unnecessary to their clients, which can occur when clients have worked through their concerns and are able to move forward in their lives without the counselor's assistance. At this point, counseling can be terminated. It is usually best for the counselor and client to agree on a termination date, reducing the chance of premature termination or feelings of ambivalence.

Research has identified four components of termination that are associated with positive outcomes in the counseling process (Quintana & Holahan, 1992, p. 299). These components are discussion of the end of counseling, review of the course of counseling, closure of the counselor-client relationship, and discussion of the client's future postcounseling plans. Based on the literature, it is clear that counselors should attempt to address all four components to prepare clients appropriately for termination (Lamb, 1985). In this process, clients can explore what they have learned in counseling and identify how they will apply that knowledge to enhance their psychological functioning. In addition, clients and counselors can process their feelings regarding the counseling relationship and work toward closure regarding potential affective issues. Counselors can also arrange a brief follow-up counseling session (e.g., several weeks after the last formal session) to see how the client is doing and provide additional counseling services as necessary.

Stage 6: Research and Evaluation

Research and evaluation can occur at any time during the counseling process or after termination. Some behavioral approaches utilize single-case or small-group research designs that require counselors to evaluate counseling whenever they implement an intervention strategy. These research procedures involve face-to-face interaction between the counselor and client. Other research procedures, which may or may not involve direct interaction between counselor and client, are empirical research involving hypothesis testing and alternative methodologies, such as the discovery approach. These procedures may be used before or after a client has terminated counseling (see Chapter 5 for a description of research methods).

Research and evaluation are an integral part of the counseling process. They contribute to the science dimension of counseling by promoting an objective understanding of what is occurring. Counselors can also use research and evaluation to communicate accountability.

Listening Skills

Listening skills play a vital role in virtually all aspects of counseling. Listening is a procedure that helps clients tell *their* story and feel connected to and understood by a caring and interested person. It is a complex process that involves a number of strategies. Some of these strategies include attending to (or tuning into) the verbal and nonverbal messages of clients, encouraging clients to freely express themselves, developing a phenomenological understanding of clients, and responding in an appropriate manner.

Listening skills can play an important role in all stages of the counseling process. Listening is especially important in terms of establishing a positive counseling relationship because the counselor can communicate care and understanding through listening-skill responses. Listening skills can be used in assessment, diagnosis, and goal setting as the counselor attempts to gain a phenomenological understanding of the client (seeing the client's concern from the client's perspective). They are useful interventions in the sense that talking in and of itself can have a healing power. This can occur when clients have their thoughts and feelings validated or normalized or can simply result from the letting go of feelings in the process of catharsis. Listening can also be an important tool for counselors during termination and follow-up and research and evaluation to determine how clients conceptualize their progress and the efficacy of counseling.

Listening skills can be conceptualized in terms of primary and secondary skills. **Primary listening skills** focus on generating the phenomenological understanding of the client and include open-ended questions, paraphrasing, reflection of feeling, minimal encouragers, clarifying remarks, summarizing, and perception checks. **Secondary listening skills** do not promote a phenomenological perspective but can be facilitative (in terms of the counseling process) while the counselor is utilizing listening skills. Secondary skills include normalizing, structuring, and probing. An overview of listening skills follows, along with a brief counseling vignette to illustrate these skills.

Primary Listening Skills

OPEN-ENDED QUESTIONS These are questions such as "What would you like to talk about?" or "How does this affect you?" These questions cannot be answered with a simple yes or no but instead encourage the client to elaborate on responses.

PARAPHRASING This can be useful after a client has talked at some length about a particular situation or problem. Paraphrasing allows the counselor to communicate that he or she has not only heard the client but understands what has been said. A paraphrase should be "tentatively" worded so the client can correct the counselor if necessary. Paraphrasing, like so many things, takes practice. A key to good paraphrasing is to keep it simple.

Paraphrasing often involves taking one or two key words that the client has said and finding analogous words. For example, if the client says, "I enjoy going on a run with my dog after work," a possible paraphrase is "You like to jog with your dog." In this example, the counselor has found analogous words for enjoy (*like*) and run (*jog*). Another way to paraphrase is to repeat the client's overall message using slightly different words. For example, the client may say, "I like to go jogging after a stressful day because it helps me unwind." A possible paraphrase would be "Jogging is a good stress release for you."

REFLECTION OF FEELING This involves the counselor reflecting what he or she senses the client is feeling. It communicates that the counselor not only understands how the client is feeling but also empathizes with the client. For example, if a client tells the counselor that her husband insults her in public, the counselor could respond by saying, "This seems to make you mad." Again, as in paraphrasing, it is important to phrase the reflection of feeling statement tentatively so the client can correct the counselor if necessary.

It is also important to be specific when attempting to reflect the client's feelings. For example, the word *upset* is usually too general and may not communicate a clear understanding of the client's feelings. It is therefore useful for counselors to develop a broad repertoire of words associated with various emotional states. (See Adler, Proctor, & Towne [2005] for a comprehensive list of words depicting various emotions.)

MINIMAL ENCOURAGERS This technique allows the counselor to facilitate what the client is saying without changing the client's line of thought. Minimal encouragers include such words of acknowledgment as *yes, yeah, oh, ah-ha,* and so forth.

CLARIFYING REMARKS This technique can be used when the counselor either did not hear or does not understand what the client has said. For example, the counselor could say, "I didn't understand that," or "Could you go through that again?" Through the use of clarifying statements, the counselor communicates that he or she genuinely wants to understand what the client is saying.

SUMMARIZING This involves restating some of the major concerns the client has mentioned during a particular session. Obviously, this helps identify the client's areas of concern. Summarizing can also lead to a "perception check" and to the development of problem-solving strategies.

PERCEPTION CHECK This technique helps the counselor determine what the client wants to work on. It follows the summary statement, as illustrated in the following example: "You seem to be worried about your performance at school, your relationship with your wife, and your lack of money [the summary statement]. I know all these problems concern you. I was wondering if you would like to focus on one of these areas, or is there something else that you haven't mentioned that you would like to talk about?"

Secondary Listening Skills

NORMALIZING Normalizing involves helping clients understand that what they are going through is a normal reaction to life (Nystul, 1994b). Normalizing can alleviate unnecessary stress and anxiety so that clients can focus their energy on recovery. The opposite of normalizing could be called *pathologicalizing*, which involves overdiagnosing or engaging in other activities with clients that make them feel sicker or discouraged. An example of normalizing is to tell someone whose husband just died and is very sad and indecisive that it is normal to have intense feelings of depression and to have difficulty making decisions after a loved one has died.

STRUCTURING Structuring, which involves describing the role and function of the counselor and client, provides a rationale for what the counselor is doing in counseling (Nystul, 1994b). It helps clients understand what is going on in counseling, increasing their motivation and enabling them to take an active role in the counseling process. Structuring can also help clients learn how to be their own self-therapist since they are helped to understand some of the dynamics of the counseling process.

PROBING Probing involves asking for specific information, such as when the counselor asks questions relating to a suicidal assessment. Probing may be necessary during the use of listening skills to obtain specific information that is critical to understanding the client. It is important to minimize the use of probing while using listening skills because it takes the perspective away from the client's phenomenological field and forces the client to respond to the counselor's frame of reference.

Counseling Vignette

The following counseling vignette provides an illustration of how the primary and secondary listening skills can be used.

COUNSELOR: What would you like to talk about today? (open-ended)

CLIENT: My daughter has me really worried.

COUNSELOR: About what? (open-ended)

CLIENT:	She's dating someone who is 15 years older than her.
COUNSELOR:	That could worry anybody. (normalizing)
CLIENT:	I just feel that in some ways he seems old enough to be her father.
COUNSELOR:	This really does bother you. (reflection of feeling)
CLIENT:	Yes, it does.
COUNSELOR:	Could you tell me more how you feel about this? (open-ended)
CLIENT:	I really don't know where to begin.
COUNSELOR:	Perhaps you could start by telling me the age of your daughter. (probing)
CLIENT:	Sure, she's 17 years old.
COUNSELOR:	How does it make you feel for your 17-year-old daughter to be dating this 32-year-old man? (open-ended)
CLIENT:	I feel like he's taking advantage of her and there is something immoral about it.
COUNSELOR:	You are really worried about her. (reflection of feeling)
CLIENT:	The whole thing just doesn't make sense to me.
COUNSELOR:	Things don't add up. (paraphrase)
CLIENT:	It's a crazy world.
COUNSELOR:	I don't quite understand what you mean. Could you run that one by me again? (clarifying)
CLIENT:	Sometimes I think she's just looking for a father figure.
COUNSELOR:	Searching for something she is missing? (paraphrase)
CLIENT:	I guess I just feel inadequate.
COUNSELOR:	Ah-ha. (minimal encourager)
CLIENT:	Yeah, like I'm one big zero.
COUNSELOR:	You really do have some strong negative feelings about yourself. (reflection of feeling)
CLIENT:	Yes, I could write a book on that one. My ex-wife said I had a *big* inferiority complex.
COUNSELOR:	There really is a lot going on there. (paraphrase)
CLIENT:	I guess my life is one big mess. I'm probably only supposed to talk about one problem at a time.

COUNSELOR: No, in counseling we want to get an overview of your concerns—especially during the initial stages of counseling. (structuring)

CLIENT: So what do we do now?

COUNSELOR: Well, so far we have identified some concerns about your daughter and her older boyfriend and your feelings about yourself. (summary)

CLIENT: Right.

COUNSELOR: Is there anything else you would like to tell me that you think I should know, or would you like to focus in on one of these concerns? (perception check)

Effective Listening "Don'ts"

This section provides some helpful guidelines for effective listening. Dinkmeyer and McKay's (1997) "roadblocks to effective listening" have been incorporated into the following list of actions to avoid.

AVOID MORALIZING OR BEING JUDGMENTAL Imposing one's belief system onto the client can cause defensive reactions and produce a demoralizing, dehumanizing experience for the client.

AVOID PREMATURE ANALYSIS Premature analysis involves identifying meaning behind the message, such as motivational forces associated with a particular action. It can occur when the counselor uses the word *because* in his or her paraphrase. For example, if the client says, "No matter what I do, nothing seems to go right," a counselor engaging in premature analysis might respond with "Nothing is going right because you lack confidence in yourself." When a counselor responds in this manner, the client may respond to the counselor's hunches (e.g., wondering "Is nothing going right because I lack confidence?"). This may result in redirecting the line of thought from the client to the counselor.

Once a counselor has gained a phenomenological understanding of the client, he or she may find it appropriate to analyze the content of the client's message and provide insights to the client (e.g., suggest that a lack of self-confidence may be a problem for the client).

AVOID "PARROTING" Parroting means repeating exactly what the client has said, just changing the order of the words. This communicates that the counselor has *heard* but may not understand the client (like a parrot). For example, if the client says, "I really like to jog after work," the counselor responding like a parrot might say, "After work, you really like to jog."

AVOID "GIMMICKY" PHRASES Some counselors get into the habit of using a "lead-in" phrase such as "Did I hear you say . . ." each time they paraphrase. This often sounds "gimmicky" to a client.

Effective Listening "Dos"

DECIDE TO BE IN THE ROLE OF THE LISTENER Effective listening is a skill the counselor must *decide* to take on. This larger skill incorporates a series of skills: attending and focusing on the client, encouraging the client to freely express him- or herself, attempting to develop a phenomenological understanding of the client, and implementing an appropriate response.

TRY TO SENSE THE CLIENT'S INNER MESSAGE Communication is a complex process. It is important to learn to listen with a "third ear." The counselor needs to learn to go beyond the spoken word and try to listen to what is really being communicated.

BE AWARE OF NONVERBAL COMMUNICATION A large percentage of communication is nonverbal. It often provides the most authentic indicator of the client's emotional state.

ALLOW YOURSELF TO CORRECT IMPRESSIONS Being in the role of listener is a tentative process. It is a joint effort in which the counselor works with the client until he or she gains a clear understanding of the client's situation.

A Final Thought Regarding Listening Skills

Becoming an effective listener is an art that takes time to develop. One of the best ways to learn listening skills is to obtain a videotape critique of one's work from an experienced counselor. It can also be helpful to do co-counseling with an experienced counselor and obtain feedback from the counselor regarding one's counseling approach.

Developing listening skills can be discouraging. At times, a counselor may even feel he or she is becoming a less effective communicator. During these times, the counselor could consider that he or she is in the process of becoming a more effective communicator. With practice, these new skills will become integrated into the counselor's natural mode of responding.

Recent Trends in the Counseling Process

This section addresses three emerging trends that constitute paradigm shifts in conceptualizing the counseling process. The first trend concerns the role of emotions in the counseling process. For instance, emerging theories of emotions, such as emotional balancing, can provide clients with a "road map" to their emotions and guidelines for obtaining emotional balance in interpersonal relationships. Postmodernism and brief-counseling approaches are two other emerging trends in counseling. These trends appear to be complementary in that they recognize the role that narratives and storytelling can play in the counseling process. An overview of these three emerging trends follows.

Role of Emotions

To a large degree, counseling is a process that focuses on helping clients with feelings such as shame, guilt, and anger. Unfortunately, there has been little emphasis on the role of emotions in counseling. Historically, emotions have taken a back seat in the conceptual bases of major schools of counseling. For example, Ellis & Ellis's (2008) rational-emotive behavior therapy emphasizes cognitions and behavior over emotions (i.e., emotions can be changed by focusing on changing cognitions and behaviors). The pendulum may be swinging toward emotions, however. For instance, there is some evidence that Beck (1996) has elevated the importance of emotions in cognitive therapy.

Warwar and Greenberg (2000) have provided an overview of the role of emotions in counseling. They suggest that emotions serve an adaptive-survival function, enabling people to meet basic needs and derive personal meaning in life. They contend that adaptive emotions should be developed and utilized in counseling to facilitate problem solving and maximize positive change. Dysfunctional emotions should be addressed to help clients overcome impasses to change. For example, clients may experience problems with emotional processing, such as an inability to consider and integrate emotional experiences.

Greenberg and Paivio (1997) described three phases associated with the use of emotions in the counseling process. The first phase is the *bonding* phase, in which emotional validation enables clients to assess their emotions. *Evoking*, the second phase, involves activating emotional expressions associated with counseling issues. The evoking phase explores and differentiates emotional expressions, such as the relationship among primary emotions, needs, and thoughts. The third phase is referred to as *restructuring*. Restructuring involves working through dysfunctional emotions and faulty self-perceptions to create adaptive emotions and a positive self-concept. For example, an adult who was sexually abused may have problems with feelings of shame and thoughts of worthlessness. Restructuring could involve helping the client work through the shame by unleashing unresolved anger and restructuring self-perceptions to "I'm worthwhile regardless of what others do."

Emotional balancing (Nystul, 2002a, 2002b) represents a theory of emotions based on the earlier work of Minuchin (1974). This theory of emotions can be used in counseling or as a self-help method to create a road map to the emotions and to facilitate emotional balance in interpersonal relationships. Emotional balancing conceptualizes emotions on a continuum with emotional disengagement at one end, emotional balance in the middle, and emotional enmeshment at the other end of the continuum.

Emotional disengagement is characterized by high levels of independence and separateness. It represents an extreme emotional position in which a person no longer attempts to maintain any form of a relationship with another person. An example of emotional disengagement could be a parent who disowns an adolescent for repeated acts of belligerence. Emotional enmeshment, on the other hand, is characterized by diffuse boundaries and a lack of individualization between people. It represents an emotional extreme whereby emotions interfere with one's ability to effectively relate to others. It can occur when a parent's emotions undermine choice and responsibility during disciplining. For example, when a father attempts to discipline his daughter for staying out late and drinking and driving, he loses his temper, yells at the teen, and grounds her for 6 months. The parent's emotional enmeshment allows the teen to shift her focus from taking responsibility for her bad choices (drinking and driving) and instead focus on how "crazy" and unreasonably she believes her parent is behaving.

Emotional balance is characterized by clear boundaries, autonomy, intimacy, and a moderate degree of connection and cohesion between people. Emotional balance represents a healthy emotional state whereby a person is able to maintain some degree of emotional contact with others in a manner that maximizes psychological functioning. An example of emotional balance would be a parent maintaining a line of communication versus utilizing ultimatums with a troubled teen. Guidelines for promoting emotional balance include the following:

- Maintain emotional balance on different levels of emotional intensity by using appropriate communication strategies, such as *I* messages versus *You* messages. (See Dinkmeyer and McKay [1997] for a description of *I* messages.)

- Consider systemic issues to identify impasses to emotional balance (e.g., when one parent becomes emotionally enmeshed, the other parent may become emotionally disengaged).

- Utilize the core counseling conditions of empathy, respect, concreteness, and self-disclosure developed by Rogers (1961) and others to promote healthy, functional relationships and emotional balance.

- Develop a plan of action by utilizing the emotions continuum to determine where one is emotionally, where one would like to go, and how to get there.

Enhancing the role of emotions in counseling appears to hold much promise. Additional research and development are required to integrate theories of emotions into the counseling process.

Postmodernism

As noted in Chapter 1, postmodernism is an emerging force in counseling that may constitute a paradigm shift in conceptualizing the counseling process. Bitter and Corey (1996) differentiated modern from postmodern in terms of different ways of viewing reality. Modernists believe in an objective reality that is independent from the observer, whereas postmodernists contend there is a subjective reality that varies contextually in relation to the observer. The modernist position is similar to behaviorist theory, which focuses on overt measurable behavior. An example would be recognizing a state of depression when a person has problems with sleep and appetite, loses interest in things that used to be fun, and so forth. The postmodernist position parallels experiential theories, contending that people are depressed when they experience depression as defined within the context of social-cultural forces such as language and narratives internalized by the individual.

Constructivism and social constructionism are two psychological perspectives that have evolved from postmodernism. Constructivism is primarily associated with cognitive behavioral approaches (see Neimeyer & Mahoney, 1995), and social constructionism has become an important dimension of marriage and family counseling (see Anderson & Goolishian, 1992). Gutterman (1996) contrasted constructivism and social constructionism by noting that constructivists contend that knowledge is based on the subjective cognitions of the individual, whereas social constructionists hold that reality is constructed from the conversations of people.

The postmodern theoretical perspectives of constructivism and social constructionism appear to have more similarities than differences. Both are concerned with issues relating to epistemology, "the theory of knowledge, or how we know what we think and what we think we think" (Durrant, 1995, p. 3). The theories appear to suggest that human experience is a highly individualized process based contextually on the interactions of cognition, social-cultural forces, language, and narratives. Knowledge and the concept of "truth" are therefore subjective and generate the possibility of multiple realities best understood from a phenomenological perspective. Postmodernists also emphasize the role that narratives and storytelling play in psychological functioning. According to this theory, people are constantly constructing stories about their lives, creating "storied lives" (Bitter & Corey, 1996).

The process of counseling and psychotherapy is therefore one of exploring life stories to gain insight into how clients generate personal meaning. When necessary, counselors can help clients engage in narrative repair, reauthoring life stories to help clients create opportunities to cope effectively and generate new meaning for life. Other goals of counseling include helping clients generate solution-focused approaches to problem solving and enhancing awareness of the effects of the dominant culture on human life (Bitter & Corey, 1996).

Bitter and Corey (1996) and Carlsen (1995) have identified techniques associated with postmodern counseling theories. These are summarized as follows.

LISTENING WITH AN OPEN MIND The counseling relationship is characterized as one of equality. Counselors avoid preconceived ideas or taking a judgmental position. The counselor attempts to empower clients by conveying optimism and encouragement and respecting and giving voice to the client's stories. The process is similar to qualitative research, in which the counselor and client are coinvestigators attempting to discover the meanings reflected in their stories and narratives. An example of listening with an open mind is using listening skills to obtain a phenomenological understanding of the client. In this process, the counselor can convey a nonjudgmental position, encouraging clients to tell their story from their perspective.

QUESTIONS THAT MAKE A DIFFERENCE The counselor engages clients in dialogues or conversations that help them address questions that can make a difference in terms of positive change. Questions tend to be circular or relational, as reflected in the systemic concept of circular causality (e.g., exploring the interrelationship between current and past problems). An example of a question that could make a difference is a counselor asking the client, "Describe what it's like when you don't have this problem?" This type of question can make a difference by getting the client to focus on what works as opposed to what does not work, thus replacing a cycle of defeatism with one of hope.

DECONSTRUCTION AND EXTERNALIZATION Externalization can be used to help clients deconstruct problems associated with their storied lives in two ways. Counselors can help clients gain valuable insights and minimize resistance by having them remove themselves from the problems associated with their storied lives. In the role of external observer, clients may be more open to engaging in an adversarial relationship with their problems (deconstruction) and developing new methods for problem resolution (reconstruction). Another deconstruction technique is similar to that used by feminists. It involves scientifically examining problematic narratives from the dominant culture (such as patriarchy) to provide evidence that refutes (deconstructs) the dominant culture's position. An example of externalizing could be to ask a client named Sam, "How does this affect Sam?" This process can minimize resistance by providing an indirect voice for Sam to express his concerns. Externalizing techniques such as this also facilitate story deconstruction, since Sam may feel more free to be critical of his story when "Sam" is referred to in the third person.

ALTERNATIVE STORIES, REAUTHORING, AND NARRATIVE REPAIR Clients are encouraged to rewrite their storied lives, creating alternative stories that are more consistent with their goals and aspirations. Reauthoring and narrative repair can be reflected in numerous ways, such as by clients beginning to focus on solutions rather than problems. *Alternative stories, reauthoring,* and *narrative repair* mean essentially the same thing: These approaches help clients develop more functional or meaningful life stories. For example, a client's story may be one of sorrow, loss, and despair owing to the death of a family member. In time, the client can learn to engage in narrative repair, reauthoring an alternative story that reflects purpose and hope in life. The following *Personal Note* describes the "Columbo" technique as a method of helping clients with the process of narrative repair and reauthoring.

I find the postmodern theories of constructivism and social constructionism very interesting. They offer exciting opportunities for developing creative counseling techniques. The "Columbo" technique and the use of metaphors in counseling are two examples of approaches that I have found useful. I developed the Columbo technique as a means of helping clients engage in narrative repair, or coauthoring more meaningful stories. The technique involves having the counselor act like the TV detective Columbo, who appears to lose track of a thought or need help from the suspect to clarify a point that he is confused about. In this process, the counselor can do such things as stop in midsentence and let the client finish the thought. For example, the counselor might say, "You are really trying to . . . ." The client may respond by saying, "Get my act together," and in doing so take responsibility for reauthoring his or her story in a more positive manner.

In an example of another Columbo technique, the counselor would say to the client, "I got the part about how you are convinced you are such a terrible parent. I'm just a bit confused about how a terrible parent is someone who has always been there for his children financially and emotionally and seems to care so much for his children's welfare. Perhaps you can help me understand that a bit better." As the parent offers his or her explanation, doing so will help him or her construct cognitions that foster more realistic, healthy narratives.

Metaphors are another counseling technique that is generating increased interest. I find metaphors to be especially useful in working with children and adolescents. Metaphors involve the use of similes, or implied comparisons, to symbolically represent an idea or a concept. An example of a metaphor that I am currently using with some of my students in special education is "going with the flow." In this metaphor, I suggest that life is like a river. I have the student visualize a river that he or she has seen, such as when going fishing. I have the student try to remember what the river was like and what the student saw floating down the river (such as leaves and so forth). I ask if the leaf had a motor to move it down the river, and the student says, "No." I say, "You're right, leaves don't need motors to go down the river; they use the current of the river and 'go with the flow.'" I tell my students that they, too, can go with the flow when they listen to their teacher, follow instructions, get their work done, and try to get along with others in a polite and caring manner. Students who do not follow the rules will see their problems mount up, and life for them will be like swimming against a current. I then have them imagine how it would feel to swim upriver against a current—against the flow of life.

USE OF METAPHORS A metaphor is a figure of speech that suggests one idea is similar or analogous to another idea or concept. Metaphors can be client generated or counselor generated. An example of a client-generated metaphor would be an individual saying his marriage is like a "leaky boat." Wickman, Daniels, White, and Fesmire (1999) suggested that it is important to be aware of the metaphors that clients use during counseling. For example, the "leaky boat" metaphor could tell the counselor that the client feels that no matter what is addressed in marriage counseling, other problems will emerge. Counselor-generated metaphors can be used to help clients look at their problems from a different perspective. For example, as described in the previous *Personal Note*, I use the metaphor of "going with the flow" to help children understand that cooperating with their teacher can be like going with the current of a river.

Metaphors are especially useful in overcoming resistance because they provide an indirect means of exploring painful issues and identifying alternative means of overcoming problems. In this regard, clients may not even be aware of the salient messages conveyed by metaphors, as they "have a way of dropping below the surface of awareness to influence us in ways that we may not fully acknowledge or understand" (Carlsen, 1995, p. 131).

EVALUATION OF POSTMODERN THEORIES Postmodern theories such as constructivism and social constructionism have been used to conceptualize the counseling process. They create opportunities to recognize the role that narrative psychology and diversity issues, such as language and culture, play in counseling. The postmodern perspective could provide another dimension to the multicultural counseling evolution.

Sexton and Whiston (1994) identified some concerns about postmodern theories like social constructivism. For example, they noted that social constructivism appears to be a theory that does not connect to any specific research methodology. Sexton and Whiston also suggested that social constructivism may be nothing more than "a call for relativism in which anything goes" (p. 69). Additional research is necessary to evaluate postmodern theories in terms of how they can generate evidence-based practice.

Brief-Counseling Approaches

Brief-counseling approaches are becoming increasingly popular, and it appears they will characterize the counseling wave of the future. Koss and Shiang (1994) identified some of the factors that have contributed to the popularity of brief-counseling approaches, summarized as follows.

1. People seek counseling for help with specific problems and are only willing to commit to a few counseling sessions to resolve their problems. The mean number of sessions (regardless of theoretical orientation or whether counseling is considered brief or nonbrief) is six to eight sessions, and 75% of those who are helped by counseling are helped during the first 6 months.

2. Research has shown that brief counseling has efficacy rates similar to those of traditional approaches to counseling, especially when treating certain types of clients with certain types of disorders. Brief counseling is particularly effective for clients who relate well,

are motivated, desire symptom relief, and suffer from a minor problem (e.g., a mild depression) or a severe stress reaction (e.g., to experiencing a natural disaster).

3. The popularity of brief counseling has to some degree evolved in response to managed care and its emphasis on time-limited, solution-focused counseling. Brief counseling is perceived to be a cost-effective alternative to traditional methods of counseling.

The origins of brief-counseling models can be traced to Milton Erickson (1954), who was one of its most influential pioneers. Erickson was a genius at using paradoxical techniques and hypnosis (sometimes in just one session) to generate solutions to clients' problems. A number of other individuals have contributed to the movement. Some of these are Haley (1984), de Shazer with his solution-focused brief therapy (1985, 1991), O'Hanlon and Weiner-Davis (1989), and the Brief Therapy Project at the Mental Research Institute (Fisch, Weakland, & Segal, 1982). Forms of brief counseling have also been adapted to most of the major traditional schools of counseling (see Koss & Shiang, 1994; Steenbarger, 1992).

Littrell, Malia, and Vanderwood (1995) identified three main assumptions associated with brief approaches to counseling. The first is that the problem clients present in counseling is the real problem. Although the problem can be related to some unknown deep-seated issues, simple, straightforward methods are used whenever possible. The second assumption is that clients are capable of solving their own problems. Counselors need to help clients become aware of their strengths and how they can use them effectively. The third assumption is that change does not need to be large to make a significant difference. Small steps toward change may be all that is necessary to break self-defeating cycles and contribute to problem resolution. Durrant (1995) has identified a number of other assumptions associated with brief-counseling models, which are summarized as follows.

1. All problems have examples of exceptions, such as a person who has a problem with heights but on one occasion was able to climb a historic landmark with friends.

2. Problems can be reframed in solution-focused terms.

3. If it's not broken, don't fix it. Do more of what is working and stop doing what is not working.

4. It's not important to know what the problem is. Instead, understand what things will be like when the problem is solved.

These assumptions taken collectively suggest that brief counseling utilizes a strengths perspective that aims to help clients solve their problems as quickly and directly as possible.

Brief-Solution-Focused Counseling

The brief-solution-focused counseling movement appears to be gaining significant momentum. The pressures of budgetary and time constraints and the shift toward managed care have contributed to increased interest. Many of the major counseling theories are being reinterpreted from a brief-counseling perspective (Friedman, 1997). In addition, some brief-counseling models have focused on problem solving (Nystul, 1995), while others are solution focused (de Shazer, 1994). Brief-counseling models provide opportunities to reconceptualize counseling theories from a strengths perspective. There is little doubt that the trends toward brief-solution-focused counseling and positive psychology will play a major role in the future of counseling.

The brief-solution-focused counseling model proposed in this text has four stages and is based primarily on brief-counseling models described by Durrant (1995), Koss and Shiang (1994), and Thompson (1996), as well as some of the techniques and procedures associated with postmodern theories of counseling.

STAGE 1: ESTABLISHING THE RELATIONSHIP AND DEFINING THE PROBLEM The counselor and client enter into a collaborative relationship. The counselor offers encouragement and hope and attempts to gain a phenomenological understanding of the client's life. Clients are encouraged to function as co-counselors and are empowered to take an active role in the counseling process, from assessment through intervention and follow-up.

Problems are defined in simple, direct terms without complicated psychological jargon. When possible, counselors normalize the client's problems and experience and communicate "wellness" as opposed to using psychological labels that communicate "sickness." Expectations for change and positive action are communicated to foster a positive self-fulfilling prophecy. In addition, most brief counseling is practiced within a time-limited framework. This usually requires that the counselor and client determine as quickly as possible how many sessions will be required (or authorized by managed care) to resolve the problems.

STAGE 2: ASSESSMENT AND ESTABLISHING TREATMENT GOALS Rapid and early assessment is crucial in brief counseling. Assessment procedures serve a number of purposes, such as determining whether a client is appropriate for brief counseling (e.g., it is contraindicated for people with severe problems, such as personality disorders, substance abuse, and psychosis), and it can also be used to obtain an overall understanding of clients and the nature of their problems. Assessment procedures can be directed at intrapsychic perspectives (within the person) as well as ecological perspectives (outside of the person). Assessment tends to focus on the here and now and avoid exploration of early life events. Another key aspect of assessment in brief-solution-focused counseling is assessing for strengths and resources and how clients can use these assets to resolve problems.

Standard, traditional assessment procedures can be used in conjunction with assessment procedures unique to brief-solution-focused counseling. One commonly used assessment method in brief counseling is the scaling technique. This procedure involves having a client rate his or her problems on a 1 to 10 scale, with 10 representing resolution of the problem. Scaling questions are used that emphasize change, exceptions to the problem, and future aspirations. For example, a counselor could ask, "So you're a 3 now in terms of your anger management. When were you more than a 3, what was that like, what were you doing then, and how were things different?"

Counseling goals are established that are concrete, observable, and measurable. They allow for ongoing evaluation of the counseling process and establish a point of termination. Goals must be flexible and interface effectively with intervention strategies. Thompson (1996, p. 19) identified the following key questions associated with counseling goals:

- What will be the very first sign that things are moving in the right direction?

- Who will be the first to notice?

- Are there small pieces of this that are already happening?

- What do you need to do to make it happen more?

- What else will you be doing differently when you no longer have this particular problem?

De Shazer's (1991) "miracle question" can be useful in generating counseling goals. The miracle question involves asking the client to imagine that a miracle occurred while he or she was asleep that solved the client's problem. What would be different in the client's life, and how would he or she know that the miracle had happened?

STAGE 3: DESIGNING AND IMPLEMENTING INTERVENTIONS
Interventions are designed to disrupt patterns of problematic behavior by introducing alternative ways of reacting to the problem. Some form of change (no matter how small) is a central component of intervention strategies. A focus on strengths or assets is another key concept associated with interventions used in brief-solution-focused counseling. Using this concept, counselors help clients discover what is working for them and how to use their strengths to overcome their problems.

The four interventions that are commonly used during the intervention stage are reframing, utilization, encouragement, and narrative repair. *Reframing* is a cognitive process that involves helping clients "frame" their problems in terms of what is right with their situation as opposed to what is wrong. *Utilization* involves helping clients find solutions within their problems. Solutions can be developed from the exceptions to the problem (e.g., times when the client did not get anxious with heights) or from developing alternative methods of problem solving. *Encouragement* helps clients to believe in themselves, thus promoting self-efficacy and the "can-do" spirit. Encouragement helps overcome self-doubt and fosters a self-fulfilling prophecy for positive change. *Narrative repair* involves helping clients reauthor their stories to reflect a positive-strength perspective as opposed to a pathological-defeatist perspective.

Brief-solution-focused counseling is a process oriented toward tasks, actions, and results whereby counselors and clients perceive their role as "doers" and not just "talkers." Clients are provided opportunities to learn solution-focused strategies and are encouraged to apply these strategies to their problems between sessions. Adjustments are made as necessary at the start of each session to ensure that clients can effectively make progress toward positive change

Lewis and Osborn (2004) suggested that motivational interviewing (MI) can be used in conjunction with solution-focused counseling to facilitate the change process. MI is designed to instill hope, increase intrinsic motivation, enhance self-efficacy, and minimize resistance to change. The use of empathy is considered a key aspect of the MI approach. Two MI techniques are "change talk" and "roll with the resistance." *Change talk* involves encouraging clients to engage in self-motivational statements associated with change. *Roll with the resistance* avoids an adversarial response to resistance. This technique recognizes that not all resistance is negative and may in fact be a client's self-protective response to avoid unwanted change.

Young, Winburn, and Hagedorn (2013) investigated the effects of MI training on client adherence for a university counseling center. Results of the study showed that clients who received MI training had lower rates of premature termination and participated in more therapy sessions than clients who did not have MI training. MI appears to hold much promise in terms of increasing clients' motivation for change. Additional research on MI appears warranted.

STAGE 4: TERMINATION, FOLLOW-UP, AND EVALUATION Once clients' problems have been resolved satisfactorily, they can terminate formal counseling. Brief-solution-focused counseling also encourages clients to become their own self-counselor and apply their problem-solving skills to new and emerging problems. The science of counseling suggests that research procedures can be used to evaluate the efficacy of the counseling experience. Moreover, during the counseling process, clients can be given opportunities to take an active role in the research process. In this way, they can function as coinvestigators with counselors in an ongoing journey of discovery. Clients should be encouraged to continue to take an active role in self-evaluation after termination through processes such as self-monitoring and self-reflection.

RESEARCH ON BRIEF COUNSELING Koss and Shiang (1994) provided a comprehensive overview of the research that has been conducted on brief counseling. Results of their findings can be summarized as follows:

- Brief-counseling approaches are being successfully applied to individual, group, and marriage and family counseling.

- Initial research efforts suggested that brief counseling was suitable only for less severe problems, such as adjustment reactions. However, more recent research indicates that brief counseling can be used successfully with a wide range of problems, including severe and chronic problems, if the treatment goals are reasonable.

- Some of the problems that brief counseling has been able to successfully treat are depression (Dobson, 1989), panic disorders (Beck, Sokol, Clark, Berchick, & Wright, 1992), and posttraumatic stress disorder (Foa, Rothbaum, Riggs, & Murdock, 1991).

Research has also been conducted to determine the client characteristics best suited to brief counseling. Koss and Shiang's (1994) review of this literature indicated that individuals who appear to benefit most from brief counseling are those whose problem had a sudden or acute onset, were previously reasonably well adjusted, could relate well to others, and had high initial motivation when entering counseling. Research suggests that brief counseling may be contraindicated for individuals whose personal characteristics are opposite to those noted above and, as mentioned previously, for some types of psychological disturbances, such as substance abuse, psychosis, and personality disorders (Koss & Shiang). Additional research is necessary to gain a clearer understanding of how brief counseling can be effectively integrated with various traditional and nontraditional counseling theories and techniques.

Common Problems for Beginning Counselors

Beginning counselors tend to experience similar problems in counseling. These problems can manifest themselves as roadblocks to the counseling process. This section discusses 15 typical roadblocks identified by the author that can impede counseling effectiveness and includes suggestions for overcoming each problem.

Focusing on the First Issue in a Session

Some beginning counselors tend to focus on the first problem the client presents in a session, even though a client may not want to work on this problem or be capable of working on it. The counselor may then spend the rest of the session trying futilely to help the client resolve this particular problem. Counselors can overcome this roadblock by first obtaining an overview of the client's concerns and then selecting a counseling goal with the client.

Overlooking Physical or Medical Issues

Beginning counselors may assume that when a client seeks their services for counseling, counseling is all the client needs (Nystul, 1981). For example, a client may seek counseling to learn stress management to help alleviate migraine headaches. In this instance, it would be important for the counselor to ensure the client has had a recent physical examination. This will rule out possible organic causes of the headache such as a brain tumor. A substance abuse problem may be another medical issue that counselors may overlook by assuming clients do not have substance abuse problems when they do not raise the issue. Counselors can avoid this problem by obtaining a history of alcohol and drug use when they gather other important background information.

Wanting to Rescue Clients From Their Unhappiness

Some beginning counselors have a naive notion that counseling is a process that makes clients feel happier. It is true that a major goal of counseling can be self-realization and inner peace. The road to that goal, however, will undoubtedly have ups and downs and emotional highs and lows.

Counseling is a process that requires the client to take risks and have the courage to face difficult issues. For example, a client may need to become aware of personal inadequacies or self-defeating patterns of behavior. This can make a client feel uncomfortable or sad and may even result in the client crying. Counselors may falsely conclude that since their client cried, they must have done something wrong. When this occurs, the counselor should consider that helping a client get in touch with inner feelings, including distressing feelings, is an important part of the counseling process.

There are several ways in which a counselor may "rescue" a client. The following are three common ones:

- *Reassuring clients.* When clients feel bad about their situation, the counselor may be tempted to say, "Don't worry—things will get better." It is important, however, for the counselor and client to have a realistic view of the counseling process. If the client does not make necessary changes, things probably will not get better. In fact, the client's situation may worsen.

- *Offering instant advice.* When clients are uncomfortable with their situation, the counselor may attempt to rescue the client by offering advice. In counseling, giving advice is usually unproductive, can foster dependency, and can be a superficial solution to a complex problem.

- *Rescuing clients from intense emotions.* Some beginning counselors tend not to allow clients to experience any intense emotions. When clients express intense emotions such as anger or grief, the counselor may want to calm them or get them to think about something else. This type of rescuing prevents clients from getting in touch with and working through their feelings.

Having Perfectionist Tendencies

Some beginning counselors may have perfectionist tendencies. They may fear making mistakes or looking bad. These tendencies may cause several problems, including counselors being reluctant to explore a new idea or technique for fear of not learning or using it correctly, avoiding supervision because they believe seeking assistance might reflect their inadequacy, and being hesitant to refer a client because they think a referral might imply they could not handle the situation. The following *Personal Note* provides some suggestions for helping beginning counselors overcome perfectionist tendencies.

A Personal Note

I have found several ways to help counselors overcome perfectionist tendencies. First, counselors should avoid absolutistic, or right-versus-wrong, views of the counseling process. Once counselors realize there is no right or wrong way of doing counseling, they can stop worrying about making mistakes. The counseling-as-an-art model maintains a realistic, pragmatic view of counseling. It suggests that when the client seems to be making progress, the counselor and client should continue using that counseling approach. When the client does not appear to be making gains, the counselor and client should make the necessary adjustments to the counseling process.

I identified the "monkey on the back" phenomenon as another way to help student counselors overcome perfectionist tendencies. It is not productive to try to look perfect while carrying a monkey on one's back. I explain to students that a counselor-training program is in some ways like having a "monkey" put on

their back. The monkey—instructions from the professor—may tell students to do some things differently than how they would ordinarily do them. For example, the instructions might be to use open rather than closed questions during active listening.

When the monkey suggests that students stop to consider different ways of responding, they may feel the monkey is interfering with their spontaneity. If they focus on having their professor perceive them as spontaneous, they may avoid trying new behaviors. Unfortunately, these students will also not learn much from their counseling program. I tell students that feeling as though the monkey is interfering with their spontaneity is a good sign. It indicates that they are trying some new skills and are in the process of becoming a more effective counselor. In time, the new skills will become integrated into their natural way of working with clients, and their spontaneity will be restored.

Having Unrealistic Expectations

Some beginning counselors have unrealistic expectations for their clients. They may therefore become frustrated when the client does not make steady progress. When a client has a setback and regresses to old, negative patterns of behavior, counselors may feel they have failed the client. In time, the counselor may project these negative feelings onto the client (Nystul, 1979c). The art-of-counseling model suggests that counselors develop a balanced set of expectations, blending optimism with realism. These expectations include believing that clients can improve and realizing that change can take time.

Getting Carried Away With the Latest Technique

Some beginning counselors tend to get carried away after learning a new technique, wanting to use it with all clients (Nystul, 1981). For example, after attending an extensive training program in hypnosis, a counselor may believe that every client could benefit from hypnosis. This enthusiasm may continue for a period of time until the counselor gets excited about another new technique. It is important for counselors to be enthusiastic about their education. At the same time, they must learn to channel this energy in a positive direction rather than imposing their current interest on clients.

Getting Lost in the Counseling Process

Clients often feel overwhelmed by issues when they begin counseling. Each time they come to a counseling session, they may talk about many different concerns. They may describe these concerns in a very interesting manner, and the concerns may begin to seem like an ongoing television soap opera.

As counselors hear these stories, they may find themselves taking a passive role. I call this the *popcorn syndrome* (Nystul, 1981). It is as if counselors are eating popcorn at the movies, listening to their client's latest struggle with life. Counselors who find themselves with the popcorn syndrome usually enjoy the counseling sessions, but they often have the feeling they are not accomplishing much. When this occurs, counselors may be lost in the ongoing storytelling. To overcome this problem, the counselor can focus the counseling process by exploring with the client what has happened in counseling—where they have been, what they are currently working on, and where they seem to be headed. Together they can make the necessary adjustments for future sessions. If the popcorn syndrome is occurring, the counselor may also want to create more of a sense of shared responsibility in the counseling process and work toward clearer counseling goals.

Using Inappropriate Phrases

Although I contend there are no right or wrong ways to approach counseling, I believe that certain phrases are usually inappropriate and unproductive in counseling. The following are three examples:

- **"Why" questions.** "Why" questions usually provoke a defensive response, causing people to believe they need to justify their behavior. Instead of asking, "Why did you and Tim break up?" the counselor might ask, "Could you tell me what happened regarding your breakup with Tim?"

- ***I know how you feel.*** Counselors may use this phrase to show
  that they have been through a similar situation and can therefore
  understand the client. Actually, no two people have exactly
  the same reaction to a situation. For example, take the varied
  reactions to a house burning down. One person might feel relief
  at the prospect of insurance money, whereas another might be
  heartbroken because of losing priceless family mementos. A
  client may have negative reactions to a counselor saying, "I know
  how you feel." The client may think, "No, she doesn't. She's
  not me. Who does she think she is?" Another client might react
  by thinking, "If this counselor knows how I feel, why bother
  exploring my feelings with him?"

- ***Let me tell you what I would do.*** This phrase can lead to instant
  advice. As mentioned earlier, advice giving usually does not
  promote positive outcomes in counseling.

Having an Excessive Desire to Help

Many students are drawn to counseling because they truly want to help others. Wanting
to help can be beneficial to the counseling process because it communicates enthusiasm,
desire, and caring. Some counselors can have an excessive need to help, however, to the
point of being overly invested in the counseling process. A useful indicator that counselors
may have gone too far in wanting to help is feeling they are working harder than the
client. Students should also explore their motives for wanting to become counselors. A
positive motive would be to enjoy helping a client overcome self-defeating forces to move
toward self-realization. A negative motive would be an excessive desire to feel needed by
someone. This desire could foster unnecessary dependency in the counseling relationship.
Another negative motive would be a need to feel power or control over others. This
need could lead to intimidating clients, undermining their self-esteem, and fostering
dependency. When counselors discover they have inappropriate motives for providing
counseling services, they should refer the client and seek counseling for themselves.

Having an Excessive Need to Be Liked

Most people, including counselors, enjoy being liked. At times, however, the counselor
may need to do things that could make the client angry or unhappy, such as confronting
the client. It is therefore not necessary for the client always to like the counselor.
Instead, it is essential to establish mutual respect to maintain a rapport throughout the
counseling process.

Getting Too Emotionally Involved

Some beginning counselors tend to get too emotionally involved with the counseling
process. There can be many reasons for developing this tendency. One is what I call
the *stray cat syndrome*, which involves counselors wanting to take responsibility for
the client's welfare. Counselors with this syndrome may go out of their way to help

all living creatures—including stray cats—that appear to need assistance. As a result, whenever they see a client suffering, they want to find a way to take away the pain and fix things, leading to the rescuing process described earlier.

Counselors can become so emotionally invested in their clients that they lose professional objectivity. They can also become emotionally exhausted and burn out. The art-of-counseling model suggests that for counseling to be effective, the counselor must be affected. At the same time, counselors should not assume ownership of the client's problems. They should instead help clients become capable of resolving their own problems.

Taking Things Too Personally

Beginning counselors may take things too personally when a client expresses intense emotions. For example, a client may react as if the counselor were another person with whom the client has had a close relationship, for example, a father or mother figure. During this process of transference, the client may become angry with the counselor. It would be inappropriate for the counselor to take this personally and retaliate against the client. Instead, the counselor should view the transference as an important part of therapy. Freudian psychoanalysis, for example, contends that transference is therapeutic in that it allows the client to work through unresolved emotional trauma (Freud, 1969).

Having Difficulty Differentiating Between Normal and Abnormal

Beginning counselors often have a difficult time deciding whether clients suffer from some form of psychopathology. For example, a counselor may wonder whether a client is acutely suicidal and needs hospitalization or mildly suicidal and only requires monitoring. Another dilemma may be differentiating a clinical depression, such as a major depression, from a normal depressive reaction to a life event relating to the death of a loved one.

The reason some beginning counselors have trouble differentiating between normal and abnormal may be their lack of exposure to psychopathology. Student counselors may overcome this obstacle by taking advantage of internships and other clinical placements during their education to obtain experience working with clients who suffer from mental disorders.

Being Uncertain About Self-Disclosure

Another problem that beginning counselors commonly experience is determining how much they should self-disclose. Although there are no hard-and-fast rules on this issue, the following suggestions may be useful:

- Answer questions about yourself that you feel comfortable with— just answer the questions without elaborating. Feel free to offer information about your professional qualifications. Be willing to share immediate reactions to what is taking place in the session.

- Don't tell your life story to your clients—they are there to tell you their story, not listen to yours. Don't say, "This is how I handled it." It could lead to ineffective advice giving.

Being Uncertain About Confidentiality

Many beginning counselors are unclear about the limits of confidentiality. One of the most common sources of confusion relates to the question "With whom can I discuss a client, and what information can I disclose?" Following are some suggestions: A counselor may discuss a case with a supervisor or when required by law, such as reporting child abuse or neglect. It is also permissible to break confidentiality when clients pose a serious threat of harm to themselves or others. It is not appropriate to discuss a case with an assistant, friends, or family members, even if you change the name of the client.

Diversity Issues

A number of diversity issues such as sexual orientation, gender, socioeconomic status, race, ethnicity, culture, age, and spirituality should be considered within the counseling process. Day-Vines et al. (2007) suggested that counselors take an active role in exploring issues of diversity with clients. They referred to this process as "broaching," implying that counselors should bring up the subjects of race, ethnicity, and culture to ensure they are considered and addressed appropriately in counseling. Day-Vines et al. believed this position is consistent with the multicultural competency, which suggests that counselors acknowledge cultural factors in the counseling relationship.

Liberation psychology (Duran, Firehammer, & Gonzalez, 2008) is an example of a counseling approach that requires counselors to actively explore multicultural issues with clients. This theory suggests that psychological distress is the result of oppressive forces that wound the very soul of a people and culture. Liberation psychology involves identifying these wounds and metaphorically transforming and liberating clients through soul healing. Counselors and clients explore the historical roots of oppression and how factors such as privilege reflected in the worldview of counselors and the counseling profession can contribute to social injustice. Counselor awareness of these multicultural issues can result in liberation of the oppressor and soul healing of the client. An aspect of cultural diversity with great potential for integration into counseling is spirituality, including religion (Bishop, 1995). Spirituality can be broadly defined as "attunement with God, the Spirit of Truth, or the divine intelligence that governs or harmonizes the universe" (Richards & Bergin, 1997, p. 77). This perspective considers that all people recognize the spiritual (but not necessarily religious) realm of existence (Ingersoll, 1995). Richards and Bergin referred to spiritual trends in counseling as the "new Zeitgeist" (spirit of our times), which is reflected in the increased interest in the healing power associated with spirituality and holistic health (Richards & Bergin, 2004; Witmer & Sweeney, 1995).

Historically, counseling and spirituality have to a large degree been kept separate. More recently, the counseling literature has suggested that spirituality is another form of diversity that should be carefully and sensitively addressed to obtain an accurate understanding of a client's worldview (Bishop, 1995). Many people turn to spirituality and religion for strength and support during times of crisis to derive meaning from life. This is especially true for people as they get older (Smith, 1993). Miranti and Burke (1995) suggested that recognition of the spiritual domain in counseling enables counselors to relate to the core essence of a client's being.

A number of individuals are beginning to provide a structure for how spirituality and religion can be integrated into the counseling process (Ingersoll, 1995; Richards & Bergin, 1997). Ingersoll suggested that counselors attempt to recognize and affirm clients' concepts of spirituality, enter the clients' spiritual worldviews to gain a phenomenological perspective, and consult with other "healers" in clients' lives as necessary. Richards and Bergin provided extensive guidelines, such as assessment and intervention, for addressing spiritual issues throughout the various phases of the counseling process. For example, spiritual forms of intervention can require special training and may include such strategies as cognitive restructuring of irrational religious beliefs, methods of fostering forgiveness, and meditation and prayer. The spiritual domain appears to possess a large but mostly untapped potential in counseling. Additional theory, research, and practice will be necessary to facilitate a meaningful incorporation of this important dimension into the counseling process.

SUMMARY

A six-stage approach to counseling involves relationship building, assessment and diagnosis, goal setting, intervention and problem solving, termination and follow-up, and research and evaluation.

Current trends in counseling, such as postmodernism and brief counseling, offer new ways of conceptualizing the counseling process in terms of narrative psychology, counseling as storytelling, and brief-solution-focused approaches. These counseling trends appear to offer special promise for addressing issues involved in multicultural counseling and managed care. A focus on addressing diversity issues and some emerging trends, such as taking into account spirituality

and religion, offer much hope for enriching the counseling process.

Problems that beginning counselors experience include focusing only on the first issue that arises in a session; overlooking medical issues; wanting to rescue clients; having perfectionist tendencies or unrealistic expectations; getting carried away with the latest technique learned; getting lost in the counseling process; using inappropriate phrases; having an excessive desire to help or to be liked; getting too emotionally involved or taking things too personally; and being uncertain about psychopathology issues, self-disclosure, or confidentiality.

Counseling is a process that varies in length and content according to the concerns of the client.

In this process, the client may appear to make some progress and then regress to self-defeating habits. When things appear to be going wrong, the counselor, like a navigator on a ship, can adjust course. Counseling may be considered successful when the overall direction of therapy is positive.

PERSONAL EXPLORATION

1. How would you assess your listening skills, and how can the skills described in this chapter facilitate your ability to listen?

2. Why is the phenomenological perspective important in listening?

3. How can you use Strong's social influence model to enhance your ability to influence others?

4. What problems that beginning counselors commonly experience you can identify with, and why might these be issues for you?

5. What are the strengths of solution-focused counseling, and how can you apply this approach in your life (e.g., looking for exceptions to your problems)?

6. How might you apply the four-step problem-solving method (that integrated Adler's and Glasser's theories) to problems you encounter?

7. Which listening skills do you like best, and how might you use them?

8. How can you use the theory of emotions (including information on emotional balancing) as a road map to your emotions?

9. What do you think of liberation psychology, and how could it be used to address oppressive forces in a person's life?

10. What factors do you believe are important in establishing a counseling relationship?

11. What did you learn about the different types of empathy, and how can you communicate empathy to others?

LEARNING ACTIVITIES

1. Try some of the listening skills described in this chapter and see how they influence your interactions with others in various contexts.

2. Try using social influence theory to develop aspects of yourself that might enhance the way you are viewed by others. Evaluate through self-reflection or discussion with others whether this self-development increases others' interest in your ideas and contributions.

WEBSITES

Narrative Therapy Centre of Toronto. (n.d.). *About narrative therapy.* Retrieved from http://www.narrative therapycentre.com/narrative.html. *Provides a variety of materials and resources for those interested in narrative therapy.*

White, M. (n.d.). *Narrative therapy.* Retrieved from http://www.massey.ac.nz/~alock/virtual/white.htm. *Provides a brief and accessible point-by-point overview of Michael White's narrative therapy.*

CHAPTER 4

Assessment and Diagnosis

The Art and Science of Assessment and Diagnosis

The art of assessment and diagnosis is an important dimension to the counseling process. The counselor-as-artist recognizes there are an infinite number of methods and procedures for discovering the overt and salient aspects of clients. Counselors adjust assessment and diagnostic procedures to accommodate the unique and emerging needs of the client. For example, they can use projective techniques to help a resistant client engage in a less threatening means of self-disclosure and adjust test procedures to accommodate issues arising from diversity.

Assessment and diagnosis are an important dimension of the science of counseling and psychotherapy as well. Standardized methods like intelligence and personality tests are used to obtain an objective understanding of the client's overall psychological functioning. The counselor-as-scientist recognizes the necessity of comprehensive, ongoing education in psychological testing for accurately administering, scoring, and interpreting tests. In addition, continuing education is necessary to keep up with the revisions in tests and the complete revamping of the procedures used in testing (such as the Exner system for the Rorschach inkblot test; for more information on the Rorschach and the Exner system, see http://en.wikipedia.org/wiki/Rorschach_test).

Virtually all aspects of assessment and diagnosis relate to both the art and science of counseling. For example, treatment planning is an art that requires the counselor to creatively integrate vast amounts of information from different sources into a meaningful composite of the client. At the same time, treatment planning is also a science, as the counselor must organize this information into a cohesive, effective program that provides structure and direction to the counseling process. Together, the art and science of assessment and diagnosis create a balance, bridging the subjective and objective underpinnings of this important aspect of the counseling process.

Chapter Overview

This chapter provides an overview of assessment and diagnosis. Highlights of the chapter include the following:

- **The art and science of assessment and diagnosis**
- **Evaluation of tests**
- **Administration and interpretation of tests**
- **Test bias**
- **Types of tests**
- **Historical perspective of diagnosis**
- **Uses of diagnosis**
- **The *DSM-5***
- **Treatment planning**
- **Diversity and postmodern issues in assessment and diagnosis**

Assessment and Diagnosis

Hohenshil (1996) noted that assessment and diagnosis tend to be interrelated processes, with assessment providing the necessary information for making a diagnosis. All counselors use some form of assessment to obtain an overall understanding of clients. Most counselors also incorporate diagnosis in their counseling process. Some theoretical perspectives, such as reality therapy and person-centered counseling, tend to abstain from the diagnostic process out of a belief that it may promote inaccurate and harmful labels. Most counselors, however, find diagnosis essential to formulating treatment strategies and as a means of shorthand communication (Hohenshil, 1996). Key publications dealing with diagnosis attempt to be sensitive to the issue of labeling by referring to someone as a "person with mental retardation" or as a "person with schizophrenia" and so on instead of saying that someone is mentally retarded or schizophrenic (Hohenshil, 1996). This certainly makes sense, as no one would be referred to as "a cancer" or "a broken bone" but as someone with cancer or with a broken bone.

In reality, as Hohenshil (1996) suggested, all counselors, regardless of their theoretical orientation, engage in some form of diagnosis. When a person-centered counselor, for example, decides that a client has psychopathology that requires the attention of a psychologist or psychiatrist, the counselor is making a diagnosis (Hohenshil). Hamann (1994) noted that most counselors are actively involved in making diagnoses so that they can communicate effectively with other professional helpers and provide necessary information to insurance companies and other parties.

Assessment

Assessment first appeared as a psychological term in *Assessment of Men* (Office of Strategic Services, 1948; Sundberg, 1977). The term was used to describe the process of selecting men to serve on special missions in World War II. Since that time, its meaning has broadened to include a wide range of techniques and processes, including standardized psychological tests, interviewing and observation strategies, sociocultural assessment, behavioral assessment, and environmental assessment. This section describes these assessment procedures as well as providing information on evaluating tests and the administration and interpretation of test results.

Evaluation of Tests

Anastasi and Urbina (1997) identified several sources of information that are valuable means of evaluating tests, which have been updated and incorporated into the following:

- *Mental Measurement Yearbook* (Carlson, Geisinger, & Jonson 2014), published every 2 to 4 years by The Buros Center for Testing, contains information on most tests as well as a critique of each test.

- Educational Testing Service (ETS) provides information on more than 25,000 tests and research instruments. The Test Collection at ETS is available at https://www.ets.org/test_link/about/.

- The *Standards for Educational and Psychological Testing*, developed by the American Educational Research Association, American Psychological Association, and the National Council on Measurement in Education provide guidelines for the proper test use and interpretation of test results. For more information, see http://en.wikipedia.org/wiki/Standards_for_Educational_and_Psychological_Testing and http://www.teststandards.org.

Three concepts are especially important in evaluating tests: validity, reliability, and norms.

VALIDITY **Validity** is the degree to which a test measures what it is intended to measure (Anastasi & Urbina, 1997). According to Anastasi and Urbina, validity, which provides a check on how well the test fulfills its intended function, is the most important characteristic of a test. For example, the Graduate Record Examination (GRE) could be used to help select students for PhD programs in counseling psychology, but the test would have a high validity only if the students who scored high were also successful in their graduate programs.

The three major types of validity, described by Anastasi and Urbina (1997), are content, construct, and criterion-related:

1. *Content validity* involves the examination of a test's content to determine whether it covers a representative sample of the behavior to be measured. Content validity is often used to determine whether the content in achievement tests is representative of the information to which an individual was exposed (e.g., biology concepts in a biology course).

2. *Construct validity* refers to the degree to which a test measures a theoretical construct or trait, such as neuroticism or anxiety.

3. *Criterion-related validity* is an indication of how well a test predicts an individual's performance on a particular criterion. For example, a mechanical aptitude test might be used to predict how well a person will perform as a machinist. There are two types of criterion-related validity. *Concurrent validity* is determined when the criterion used to measure performance is available at the time of testing. *Predictive validity* can be assessed when the criterion is available only after the testing has occurred.

RELIABILITY **Reliability** is another important factor that should be considered in test evaluation. It refers to the "consistency of scores obtained by the same persons when they are reexamined with the same test on different occasions, or with different sets of equivalent items, or under variable examining conditions" (Anastasi & Urbina, 1997, p. 84). Reliability can be determined by the following three methods:

1. *Test-retest reliability* involves administering the same test again to an individual.

2. *Alternate-forms reliability* refers to administering equivalent forms to the individual on separate occasions.

3. *Split-half reliability* involves dividing a test into two equivalent halves and administering each half to the individual. It provides a measure of the test's internal consistency.

NORMS To understand an individual's score on a test, it is necessary to have information on the scores of other people who have taken the test (i.e., the norm group; Sundberg, 1977). In evaluating the norms used in a test, it is important to determine whether the norm group is representative of the population for whom the test was designed (Sundberg). For example, a test with norms derived from an upper-class group of whites may be inappropriate to use with minority clients or clients of lower socioeconomic status.

Administration and Interpretation of Tests

Only qualified individuals should administer and interpret tests. Many tests, such as the Wechsler intelligence test, require specialized training in test administration and interpretation. In addition, counselors should carefully review the test manual to determine procedures to use in test interpretation. For example, it is important to determine the strengths and limitations of the test and whether the norm group is representative of the individual being tested.

Miller (1982) provided the following guidelines for interpreting test results to clients:

- The counselor should explore how the client felt about taking the test.

- The counselor should review the purpose of taking the test and provide information necessary for test interpretation (e.g., norms and percentiles).

- The counselor and client should examine the test results and discuss what the results mean to the client.

- The counselor should help the client integrate the test scores into other aspects of the client's self-knowledge.

- The counselor should encourage the client to develop a plan to utilize the test results.

Goodyear (1990) suggested that counselors should introduce test materials and interpretations in response to specific concerns raised by the client throughout the counseling process rather than at one particular point in counseling. Goodyear contended that a client will better assimilate information when interpretation occurs at various phases of the counseling process.

Several research studies provide useful information regarding interpretation. Jones and Gelso (1988) have found that clients perceive tentative interpretations as more helpful than absolute interpretations. Clients are also more willing to work with counselors who use tentative interpretations. Goodyear (1990) cited a study by Taylor and Brown (1988) that found mentally healthy individuals were more likely to harbor unrealistically positive self-perceptions. Based on these findings, Goodyear warned that clients may be prone to distort test interpretations in an unrealistically positive manner. Other studies have shown that clients prefer individual test interpretations over group interpretations for their clarity (Miller & Cochran, 1979), favorability (Oliver, 1977), and helpfulness (Wilkerson, 1967).

Rawlins, Eberly, and Rawlins (1991) noted that counselors are often ill-prepared to deal with the wide array of potential problems in testing and are in need of better training in measurement. The authors suggested that counselors could overcome some of these problems by using counseling skills when interpreting tests for the client. For example, Rawlins et al. suggested that neurolinguistic programming (NLP) can be integrated with counseling technique and theory to facilitate test interpretation. Counselors can use aspects of NLP technique, such as pacing, to gain insight into what the client is experiencing regarding the test interpretation. Pacing involves staying with the client's experience by using counseling techniques (such as listening skills) to determine what sensory modality the client is functioning from (e.g., visual, auditory, or tactile). The counselor then matches predicates (such as "I see your point," with a visual learner) and mirrors bodily states (such as breathing rates) to facilitate rapport and understanding. The use of NLP and other counseling strategies facilitates the art of counseling and test interpretation specifically by helping counselors adjust to the unique and emerging needs of clients.

Computer-based test interpretation (CBTI) has become an increasingly popular resource in testing and assessment (Sampson, 1990). A variety of computer software programs have been designed to assist counselors in interpreting the most commonly used tests, such as the Minnesota Multiphasic Personality Inventory (2nd ed.; MMPI-II) and the Wechsler intelligence scales. CBTI systems are not intended to replace the counselor's role in the assessment process. Instead, counselors should view CBTI as a tool to aid with assessment, diagnosis, and treatment planning (Sampson).

Test Bias

The literature reflects increasing concern over the fairness of tests and assessment methods with clients of culturally diverse backgrounds (Watkins & Campbell, 1990). Evidence of cultural bias has been found in numerous assessment procedures—projective techniques, intelligence tests, and self-report measures (Jewell, 1989). Reynolds (1982) identified the following factors often associated with **test bias**:

- *Inappropriate content.* Test content is biased toward the values and experiences of white, middle-class individuals.

- *Inappropriate standardization samples.* Most norm groups tend to underrepresent ethnic minorities and thus are not realistic reference groups for minorities.

- *Examiner and language bias.* Psychologists tend to be white and speak only standard English. When they act as test examiners, therefore, communication barriers can result. Furthermore, they may therefore intimidate ethnic minorities. Both conditions can account for lower performance on tests.

- *Inequitable social consequences.* When ethnic minorities receive unfair labels from tests (e.g., low intelligence), these individuals are relegated to dead-end educational tracks.

- *Measurement of different constructs.* Tests measure significantly different attributes than intended or claimed when used with ethnic minorities (e.g., the degree of adherence to the value system of the dominant culture).

- *Differential predictive validity.* Although tests can accurately predict outcomes, such as academic attainment, for whites, they are much less effective at predicting outcomes for ethnic minorities.

Anastasi and Urbina (1997) suggested that the potential problems in assessment should be addressed by adopting a multicultural perspective. Culture-fair tests, beginning with Penrose and Raven's (1936) Raven Progressive Matrices Test, have been developed in an attempt to overcome the problems associated with test bias. The Raven test, which was one of the first culture-fair intelligence tests, has three versions to allow for the evaluation of people ranging from mentally retarded to normal. Each version consists of a nonverbal test in which the examinee must choose a matrix that completes a particular pattern. Another nonverbal culture-fair intelligence test, the Cattell Culture-Fair Intelligence Test, was developed by Cattell (1949). The Cattell can be used with individuals from age 4 years through adult to assess fluid intelligence (e.g., the ability to use reasoning to identify complex relationships between between numbers and letters).

The System of Multicultural Pluralistic Assessment (SOMPA), developed by Mercer (1977), can be used to promote culture-fair assessment of children from 5 to 11 years of age. The SOMPA approach has several unique qualities. The child is first administered several tests, including the Wechsler Intelligence Scale for Children—Fourth Edition (WISC-IV). The child's primary caregiver is then interviewed to obtain information on how the child functions in various activities and settings (McMillan, 1984). After consideration of other test scores and the interview, the WISC-IV score is then "corrected." Mercer contended that the "uncorrected" test scores can be useful in making educational and instructional decisions, but the "corrected" score more accurately reflects the child's intellectual aptitude (McMillan).

Ridley, Li, and Hill (1998) developed the Multicultural Assessment Procedure (MAP) as a means of addressing the challenges associated with multicultural assessment and diagnosis. The four phases of MAP can be used to create a multicultural framework for assessment and diagnosis:

1. *Identifying cultural data.* Objective and subjective assessment procedures are used to identify cultural data. Listening skills, encouraging clients to tell their story, and the clinical interview can be used as a starting point to obtain this information. For example, clients may report cultural data that appear to be related to their depression, such as experiencing racism at work.

2. *Interpreting cultural data to formulate a working hypothesis.* MAP contends that assessment and diagnosis require creating a working hypothesis that can be used to interpret cultural data. A central task in this process is differentiating cultural data from idiosyncratic data (i.e., determining to what degree the information is specific to the client's culture or unique to the client). For example, a working hypothesis could be that a client's depression may be due in part to racism at work and conflicts between the culture there and his or her identity development (cultural-specific data) and may also be associated with alcoholism (idiosyncratic or specific to the individual).

3. *Incorporating cultural data to test the working hypothesis.* The third phase of MAP involves utilizing a comprehensive assessment and diagnostic approach to test the working hypothesis. This involves integrating culturally relevant information with such commonly used clinical procedures as medical examinations, psychological testing, and use of the *Diagnostic and Statistical Manual of Mental Disorders* (*DSM*). For example, counselors can make use of the explanations of cultural considerations in the *DSM* to strive for cultural sensitivity in the diagnostic process.

4. *Arriving at a sound assessment decision.* In the final phase of MAP the counselor creates a comprehensive, culture-inclusive assessment profile of clients from which clinical decisions can be made. Diagnostic decisions are finalized (in terms of the *DSM*), and culturally relevant treatment programs can be formulated.

Testing can provide counselors with objective information regarding the client's psychological functioning.

Types of Tests

Assessment procedures can be divided into two major categories: standardized and nonstandardized measures (Kottler, 2004). **Standardized measures**, tests that have a standardized norm group, include a wide variety of psychological tests, such as intelligence tests, personality tests, interest tests, aptitude tests, achievement tests, and neuropsychological tests. **Nonstandardized measures** do not have a standardized norm group; these include procedures such as observations, behavioral assessment, and environmental assessment.

Each type has advantages and disadvantages. Standardized assessment procedures provide the counselor with objective information regarding the client. In addition, information on validity and reliability, which can be used to evaluate test results, is available. Disadvantages include potential cultural bias, promotion of harmful labels, and scores that may be oversimplified or misleading.

Nonstandardized assessment procedures also have inherent strengths and weaknesses. One strength of these measures is their flexible and individualized approach, which yields information unique to the individual. They can also be easily modified to accommodate individual differences, thereby minimizing cultural bias. Weaknesses include a lack of information on reliability and validity with which to evaluate the assessment procedures and a lack of objectivity in terms of test results. The advantages and disadvantages of standardized and nonstandardized assessment procedures are summarized in Table 4.1.

STANDARDIZED MEASURES Standardized measures include a wide range of psychological tests. Anastasi and Urbina (1997) defined a psychological test as "an objective and standardized measure of a sample behavior" (p. 4). They went on to say that "standardization implies *uniformity of procedure* in administering and scoring the test" (p. 6). Psychological tests can be administered to an individual or a group to assess a wide range of traits and attributes such as intelligence, achievement, aptitude, interest, personality, and neuropsychological impairment.

Intelligence tests provide information regarding the client's intellectual functioning. The most common individually administered intelligence tests are the Stanford Binet and three Wechsler scales: the Wechsler Pre-School and Primary Scale of Intelligence—Third Edition (WPPSI-III), the Wechsler Intelligence Scale for Children—Fourth Edition (WISC-IV), and the Wechsler Adult Intelligence Scale—Fourth Edition (WAIS-IV). Two of the more commonly used group-administered intelligence tests are the Otis-Lennon Mental Ability Test and the California Tests of Mental Maturity. Nonverbal intelligence tests are also available, such as the Raven Progressive Matrices and the Test of Nonverbal Intelligence (TONI). These are especially useful to overcome language barriers in multicultural contexts. They can also be used if the counselor has limited time and needs only a rough estimate of the client's intellectual level (Anastasi & Urbina, 1997).

Achievement tests are used primarily in school settings. They provide information on what a person has learned. Three of the more popular achievement tests are the Iowa Test of Basic Skills, Wide Range Achievement Test, and Woodcock-Johnson Psycho-Educational Battery (Anastasi & Urbina, 1997).

Table 4.1 Comparison of Standardized and Nonstandardized Measures

Type of Test	Advantages	Disadvantages
Standardized	1. Provides objective information regarding the client	1. Is prone to cultural bias
	2. Provides specific information about a client relative to a norm group	2. Often results in "labels"
	3. Contains information on validity and reliability that can be used to evaluate the test	3. Can lead to oversimplified and misleading test results (e.g., IQ scores)
Nonstandardized	1. Provides a flexible, individualized approach that yields information unique to the individual client	1. Lacks information on validity and reliability
	2. Fosters an active role for the client in the assessment process	2. Lacks objectivity and ability to generalize to a reference group
	3. Can be easily modified to accommodate individual differences	3. Lacks specific scores and reference groups, which may make assessment results appear confusing to clients

Aptitude tests focus on the client's potential for success. As mentioned, the GRE is an example of an aptitude test designed to predict whether a person will be able to successfully complete graduate study. Another example is the Differential Aptitude Test, which counselors use frequently in educational and vocational counseling of students in Grades 8 through 12 (Anastasi & Urbina, 1997).

Interest inventories help the counselor determine where the client's interests lie. This information can be especially useful to career counselors. Three of the most commonly used interest inventories are the Kuder Preference Record, Career Assessment Inventory, and Strong Interest Inventory.

Personality tests provide information about personality dynamics and can also be part of the diagnostic process to determine whether a client has a mental disorder. Objective personality tests require more rigid responses, such as true-false or multiple-choice responses, than do the subjective tests. The most widely used objective personality test is the MMPI-II and the more recent MMPI-2 Restructured Form (MMPI-2 RF), which has 388 of the 567 items from the MMPI-II. These two versions of the MMPI are especially useful in identifying certain mental disorders, such as depression or schizophrenia. An overview of the personality is provided by two other popular objective personality tests, the California Psychological Inventory (CPI) and the 16 Personality Factors Questionnaire (16 PF).

Subjective tests make use of projective techniques that require clients to project their thoughts and feelings into a variety of ambiguous stimuli, such as the inkblots of the Rorschach test or pictures in the Thematic Apperception Test. Projective tests are sometimes more appropriate in multicultural settings since they minimize the use of words, thereby decreasing the potential for cultural bias. Two other commonly used subjective tests are the Draw-a-Person and House-Tree-Person tests. Projective tests are underutilized by counselors, Clark (1995) suggested, although they can be valuable in enhancing the counseling process by helping to overcome resistance, obtain a phenomenological understanding of the client, identify goals, and establish a treatment plan.

Neuropsychological tests "are used to evaluate the neurologically impaired patients' cognitive, behavioral, and psychological strengths and weaknesses and to determine their relationship to cerebral functioning" (Newmark, 1985, p. 383). Among the several popular neuropsychological tests and test batteries in use is the Bender-Gestalt Test, which involves having the client copy nine separate designs. This test can be scored by subjective, intuitive means or by an objective scoring procedure (Anastasi & Urbina, 1997). Another neuropsychological test is the Benton Visual Retention Test, which requires the client to reproduce 10 different geometric figures. Both of these tests can provide an indication of brain damage, but they should not be used as the sole means of making a diagnosis. Bigler and Ehrfurth (1981) even suggested that the Bender should be banned as a single neuropsychological technique.

In an attempt to arrive at a more comprehensive approach to assessment and diagnosis, researchers have developed several neuropsychological test batteries. The two most popular are the Halstead-Reitan Neuropsychological Test Battery and the Luria Nebraska Neuropsychological Battery. The Halstead-Reitan test, which can be used with individuals aged 15 and older, technically comprises 10 tests, 2 of which are considered allied procedures (Newmark, 1985). The main battery includes the Category Test, Speech-Sounds Perception, Seashore Rhythm, Tactual Performance Test (TPT), Finger Oscillation, Trail Making A and B, Aphasia Screening, and Sensory Perceptual Examination. The allied procedures are the WAIS-IV and the MMPI-II and MMPI-2 RF. Compared to the Halstead-Reitan, the Luria Nebraska Battery requires less time to administer (2.5 hours as opposed to 6 or more hours), is more highly standardized, and provides a fuller coverage of neurological deficits (Anastasi & Urbina, 1997).

NONSTANDARDIZED MEASURES Goldman (1990) referred to nonstandardized measures as qualitative assessment, noting that for the most part, these forms of assessment do not yield quantitative raw scores as standardized measures do. However, Goldman suggested that qualitative assessment has a number of advantages over standardized approaches, including the following:

- It fosters an "active role for the client in the process of collecting and teasing meaning out of data, rather than the role of a passive responder who is being measured, predicted, placed, or diagnosed" (p. 205).

- It emphasizes "the *holistic study* of the individual rather than the isolation and precise measurement of narrowly defined discrete elements of ability, interest, or personality" (p. 205).

- It encourages clients to learn about themselves within a developmental framework.

- It is especially effective in group work, in which clients can learn about individual differences as well as gain an understanding about themselves in relation to others in the group.

- It reduces the distinction between assessment and counseling by stimulating rather than hampering counseling methods, as can be the case with standardized assessment.

- It can be easily modified to accommodate individual differences, such as cultural diversity and gender, since nonstandardized measures do not attempt precise measurements from normative samples.

A variety of nonstandardized measures can be used in the counseling process, including observation, behavioral assessment, and environmental assessment. A description of each of these procedures follows.

Observation The power of observation can be a very revealing aspect of clinical assessment. Freud (1953) attested to the power of observation when he said, "He that has eyes to see and ears to hear may convince himself that no mortal can keep a secret. If his lips are silent, he chatters with his fingertips; betrayal oozes out of him at every pore" (pp. 77–78). As Freud noted, the skilled clinician can learn much from observing what occurs during the counseling session.

Ivey, Ivey, and Zalaquett (2010) and Baruth and Huber (1985) have described how nonverbal behavior can provide valuable information about clients, and these authors' observations have been incorporated into the following overview. In reviewing various facets of nonverbal behavior, it is important to consider how diversity issues such as culture and gender can contribute to variation in communication.

- *Touch.* The amount and nature of the physical contact (in terms of touch) can provide information on such things as interpersonal comfort and closeness, capacity for empathic responding, and so forth.

- *Proxemics.* Proxemics is the study of physical space or distance between people. For example, people who seek close physical proximity could be seeking intimacy, and those who desire more space could be seeking to meet needs such as solace or safety.

- *Kinesics.* Kinesics relates to how body movements contribute to communication. Much can be learned from a client's body language. For example, crossing the arms can suggest reluctance or resistance, leaning forward can imply interest, and leaning away can imply fear or boredom.

- *Autonomic physiological behavior.* Autonomic responses are very expressive and provide uncensored information about the client. For example, rapid breathing can suggest anxiety or nervousness, and blushing can indicate embarrassment.

- *Vocal qualities.* A client's voice quality can provide important information to the counselor. Changes in rate, volume, or pitch can communicate different messages. For example, hesitations and breaks can suggest confusion or stress.

- *Facial expressions.* Grimaces, frowns, smiles, and raised eyebrows all communicate something important about the client's emotional state.

- *Eye contact.* Pupils tend to dilate when clients are discussing an interesting topic and contract when they are bored or uncomfortable. In addition, clients tend to look away when discussing something that is depressing or disturbing.

Counselors can also learn from observing clients in their natural habitat. Goldman (1990) referred to this process as *shadowing*, which he defined as "following someone through a day or part of a day to observe how the person acts and reacts in various places and in various interactions" (p. 210). Thus, shadowing can provide information on how the client functions in a real-life situation. Numerous possibilities exist for making observations in the field. Examples include observing a student in a classroom, on a school bus, or on a playground to assess the child's interpersonal skills; observing a mother or father with a newborn to determine the degree of bonding; conducting a marriage or family session in a client's home to observe the family in their natural habitat; and observing a manager role-playing administrative functions in an organizational setting.

For observing and recording behavior in organizational settings, Sundberg (1977) listed the following systematic methods: the situational test, the in-basket test, and the critical incident technique.

- The *situational test* involves a contrived situation in which the subject is given a task to accomplish, for example, attempting to find a person who has mysteriously vanished. Specific measures of observation facilitate accurate recording of information.

- The *in-basket test* is a method used to select and train managers and executives (Bray, Campbell, & Grant, 1974; Lopez, 1966; Vernon & Parry, 1949). This test entails observing an individual role-playing various administrative tasks. Systematic procedures are then used to observe and record behavior.

- The *critical incident technique* involves an observer recording instances of behavior that indicate good or poor performance. From this information, procedures are identified to chart performance or plan training.

Behavioral Assessment Behavioral assessment, which evolved from behavioral psychology, involves the systematic measurement of behaviors, broadly defined to include attitudes, feelings, and cognitions (Sundberg, 1977). In behavioral assessment, counselors may use a wide variety of procedures, including direct observation in the natural environment, problem checklists, self-reports, and record keeping (Anastasi & Urbina, 1997; Sundberg).

Behavioral assessment can be related directly to treatment through the use of single-subject designs, such as A-B and A-B-A designs. The A phase involves obtaining a baseline of a problem behavior before treatment. The B phase assesses behavior after treatment. The behaviors recorded during the A and B phases are usually graphed to provide a measure of behavior change before and after treatment. Chapter 5 includes additional information on single-subject designs.

Environmental/Ecological Assessment Environmental assessment (also referred to as ecological assessment) involves considering environmental factors such as sociocultural forces in the assessment of psychological functioning. The theory has characteristics in common with other theories, such as family therapy, interpersonal psychotherapy, and postmodern theories. Family therapy recognizes the need to assess people from a systemic or systems perspective. Interpersonal psychotherapy is similar to family therapy in that it emphasizes the role of interpersonal relationships in mental health. Postmodern theories like social constructionism also emphasize the role of sociocultural forces in assessment. Central to this position is a redefining of the autonomous self as a social self that extends beyond the individual to all aspects of society (Gergen, 1994a). Adler's concept of social interest as the barometer of mental health is an excellent example of how the relationship between social embeddedness and psychological functioning can be considered (Jones, 1995).

Walsh (1990) observed that any assessment is incomplete without some assessment of the environment and suggested that counselors perform an environmental assessment to determine how clients perceive their environment and how these perceptions influence their behavior. Environmental assessment can be particularly important when determining the etiology, or cause, of psychopathology. A counselor who does not consider environmental factors may attribute a mental disorder to intrapsychic forces—that is, forces within the person—instead of considering environmental factors, such as living in poverty.

As the counseling profession becomes increasingly aware of the multicultural dimension to its work, the need to include an assessment of sociocultural factors when conducting an environmental assessment has become particularly apparent. Environments represent numerous tasks of life—such as work, marriage and family—and include the social and spiritual environment. They are influenced by various forces such as war and peace, poverty and affluence, and oppression and mutual respect.

These environmental forces can be reinforcing to an individual and contribute to need fulfillment or be a source of stress and discontent. Moreover, individual perceptions of the environment play a key role in what is actually experienced. For example, some perceive a disorganized work setting as a challenge, others as a major source of stress. Social forces that may warrant attention include how clients feel about where they live and with whom they live and their attitudes toward their job, family, and friends.

Topper (1985) has identified cultural factors that counselors should address during the assessment process. He noted that it is particularly important to evaluate the client's level of acculturation to determine whether traditional Western counseling approaches would be appropriate. In addition, he suggested that it would be advantageous to determine how the client's condition might be viewed by members of the client's culture and then evaluate the client in terms of patterns of psychological development that are normative to that culture.

Hershenson, Power, and Waldo (1996) provided additional information regarding environmental assessment. They noted the field's increased interest in the role of the environment in psychological functioning and contended that in many instances, the environment is both the primary source of a client's problem and a potential target for counseling intervention. Hershenson et al. described theories and strategies for environmental assessment, which include the behavior-setting approach (the environment shapes behavior), the need-press theory (the relationship between needs and environmental presses), the human aggregate model (the match between the individual and the environment), and the social climate model (a systems perspective that also considers the person's perception of environmental events). These theories describe a complex interaction between each individual and the environment.

Strategies for environmental assessment are directed at identifying the ultimate client-environment fit. In this process, it is important to assess how various environmental forces, such as stresses at work and functioning at home, affect each other. It is also critical to obtain an accurate reading of an individual's perceptions of these forces. Hershenson et al. (1996) adapted information from Huebner (1980) in developing the following guidelines for environmental assessment:

1. All aspects of the environment must be assessed independently and in relation to each other.

2. Instruments used in assessment should provide information on the sources of pressure within the environment.

3. Multiple strategies and procedures should be utilized when assessing complex person-environment relationships.

4. The relationship between the objective and perceived environment should be differentiated.

5. Assessment instruments should be reliable and valid for the purpose for which they are to be used.

Environmental assessment appears to add another important dimension to the assessment process. It expands the horizons of assessment beyond the individual to include the assessment of people within the context of the social milieu and appears to offer much promise in terms of generating information on the role of sociocultural forces in psychological functioning.

Diagnosis

Historical Perspective

The process of **diagnosis** can be traced to the preclassical period in Greece (Nathan & Harris, 1980). The Greeks were able to identify the behavioral consequences of the aging process and the mental health consequences of alcoholism. Somewhat later, during classical times, the Greeks identified and described psychological disorders that are still recognized today, such as mania, melancholia, and paranoia.

It was not until much later that a formal classification of psychological disorders was developed. Rosenhan and Seligman (1995) identified several key individuals who contributed to this process. Philippe Pinel (1745–1826), the psychiatric reformer, divided psychological disorders into melancholia, mania (with and without delirium), dementia, and idiotism. Emil Kraepelin (1856–1926) developed the first comprehensive system of classifying psychological disorders based on a medical model. In this regard, Krapelin believed that all medical disorders had a physical origin and that diagnosis required a careful assessment of symptoms.

Rosenhan and Seligman (1995) identified several other individuals, such as Eugen Bleuler and Adolf Meyer, who had proposed their own systems of diagnosis. Although each of these various diagnostic systems has merit, the need for one coherent system of diagnosis became apparent. This led to the American Psychiatric Association's (APA) development of the *Diagnostic and Statistical Manual of Mental Disorders* (DSM) in 1952.

The *DSM* has undergone several revisions since 1952. *DSM-I* and *DSM-II* were similar in that they were based on Freudian psychology (e.g., used terms such as *neurosis* to describe psychopathology). The *DSM-III* (APA, 1980) represented a major paradigm shift from the psychodynamic perspective to a more objective-scientific approach. In this process, clinicians utilized diagnositic criteria that they could observe and agree upon rather than using abstract theories, thereby increasing diagnostic reliability (Paris, 2013b). Pomerantz (2014) identified additional characteristics that differentiated the *DSM-III* from its predecessors and were incorporated into the *DSM-III-R* (APA, 1987), *DSM-IV* (APA, 1994), *DSM-IV-TR* (APA, 2000), and to some degree the *DSM-5* (APA, 2013).

- *DSM-III* was atheoretical, relying on empirical data to identify and define disorders.

- Specific criteria were provided (in the form of a checklist) to determine what symptoms must be present for a diagnosis (see Table 4.2 for an example from the *DSM-5*).

Table 4.2 DSM-5 Diagnostic Criteria for Reactive Attachment Disorder

Diagnostic Criteria 313.89 (F94.1)

A. A consistent pattern of inhibited, emotionally withdrawn behavior toward adult caregivers, manifested by both of the following:

1. The child rarely or minimally seeks comfort when distressed.

2. The child rarely or minimally responds to comfort when distressed.

B. A persistent social and emotional disturbance characterized by at least two of the following:

1. Minimal social and emotional responsiveness to others.

2. Limited positive affect.

3. Episodes of unexplained irritability, sadness, or fearfulness that are evident even during nonthreatening interactions with adult caregivers.

C. The child has experienced a pattern of extremes of insufficient care as evidenced by at least one of the following:

1. Social neglect or deprivation in the form of persistent lack of having basic emotional needs for comfort, stimulation, and affection met by caregiving adults.

2. Repeated changes of primary caregivers that limit opportunities to form stable attachments (e.g., frequent changes in foster care).

3. Rearing in unusual settings that severely limit opportunities to form selective attachments (e.g., institutions with high child-to-caregiver ratios).

D. The care in Criterion C is preseumed to be responsible for the disturbed behavior in Criterion A (e.g., the disturbances in Criterion A began following the lack of adequate care in Criterion C).

E. The criteria are not met for autism spectrum disorder.

F. The disturbance is evident before age 5 years.

G. The child has a developmental age of at least 9 months.

Specify if:

Persistent: The disorder has been present for more than 12 months.

Specify current severity: Reactive attachment disorder is specified as **severe** when a child exhibits all symptoms of the disorder, with each symptom manifesting at relatively high levels.

Source: Reprinted with permission from the Diagnostic and Statistical Manual of Mental Disorders, Fifth Edition, (Copyright ©2013). American Psychiatric Association. All Rights Reserved.

- A multiaxial assessment system addressed diagnostic issues on five separate axes. Axis I included problems of living (often given "V-codes" for billing and insurance purposes) and episodic disorders (disorders that have a specific beginning and end). Axis II was used for two disorders that begin early in life and endure throughout the life span (i.e., personality disorders and mental retardation). Axis III related to medical conditions that could impact mental disorders. Axis IV provided information on psychosocial/environmental stressors. Axis V was an assessment of overall level of functioning based on the Global Assessment of Functioning scale.

The APA had hoped that the *DSM-5* would represent another major paradigm shift: Now the diagnosis of mental disorders would be based primarily on neuroscience (Paris, 2013c). Paris (2013a) noted, however, that the *DSM-5* task force backed off from this position when it became apparent that there was insufficient supporting data from biological markers such as neurochemistry and imaging procedures. Paris (2013c) went on to say that "diagnostic systems need to adopt a broader model that does not reduce all of psychopathology to neuroscience. These developments could eventually lead to a better system for *DSM-6*" (p. vi).

USES OF DIAGNOSIS Diagnosis is an important aspect of the counseling process. Rosenhan and Seligman (1995) described four reasons for making a diagnosis:

1. *It allows communication shorthand among clinicians.* Diagnosis enables the clinician to incorporate the various symptoms of a client into a single diagnosis that other clinicians can easily understand.

2. *It suggests treatment possibilities.* Diagnosis can help clinicians select from among the various treatment possibilities. For example, a paranoid schizophrenic will usually not respond well to verbal therapies.

3. *It can communicate information about etiology.* Mental disorders are associated with different types of etiology. For example, one of the major causative factors associated with schizophrenia is an excess of the neurotransmitter dopamine in the brain.

4. *It aids scientific investigation.* Diagnosis helps group symptoms together so that they can be systematically studied to determine etiology and treatment strategies.

Woody, Hansen, and Rossberg (1989) noted that some counselors shy away from diagnosis because they believe it is a judgmental process that labels clients. These authors contended, however, that diagnosis is more than a process of labeling. It also provides an analysis of the client's functioning in order to determine the most appropriate treatment.

The *DSM-5*

The *DSM-5* represents the first major revision of the *DSM* in the last 30 years (Paris, 2013b). The development of the *DSM-5* was a massive undertaking incorporating research from a wide range of disciplines such as neurology, psychology, and genetics (Reichenberg, 2014). Reichenberg noted that "thousands of experts participated in more than 160 task forces, work groups, and study groups over a 12-year period to research, measure, and conduct field trials of diagnostic criteria for the mental health disorders" (p. 1). The intent of the task force was to make only changes that were supported by research, would improve diagnosing and treatment, and could be incorporated into clinical practice (Reichenberg).

The *DSM-5* is organized into three sections (APA, 2013). Section 1 provides information on the organizational structure of the *DSM-5*, identifies some of the changes that were made and a rationale for the changes, defines *mental disorder*, and identifies elements of a diagnosis that should be considered when making a diagnosis. Section 2 organizes all mental disorders within 20 categories (e.g., neurodevelopmental disorders, schizophrenia spectrum and other psychotic disorders). Categories are sequenced from a life span–developmental perspective, beginning with disorders that originate in childhood and ending with disorders that tend to occur in adulthood and later life. Section 3 includes supplemental information on a number of topics such as assessment measures, cultural considerations, models for conceptualizing personality disorders, and conditions that warrant further study.

DEFINITION OF *MENTAL DISORDER* The American Psychiatric Association (2013) noted that all disorders included in the *DSM-5* (with the exception of those relating to adverse effects of medication) met the definition of **mental disorder** as follows:

> A mental disorder is a syndrome characterized by clinically significant disturbance in an individual's cognition, emotion regulation, or behavior that reflects a dysfunction in the psychological, biological, or developmental processes underlying mental functioning. Mental disorders are usually associated with significant distress or disability in social, occupational, or other important activities. An expectable or culturally approved response to a common stressor or loss, such as death of a loved one, is not a mental disorder. Socially deviant behavior (e.g., political, religious, or sexual) and conflicts that are primarily between the individual and society are not mental disorders unless the deviance or conflict results from a dysfunction in the individual, as described above. (p. 20)

Frances (2013) noted that it is very difficult to formulate a definitive definition of *mental disorder*, especially when disorders are so different from each other (e.g., some relate to inner misery, while others are associated with cognitive impairment). Frances suggested that because symptom distress and degree of disability are common themes shared by all disorders, they are important factors to include in a definition of *mental disorder*.

Changes in the DSM-5. A number of changes were made in the *DSM-5*. The following overview provides information regarding the *DSM-5* as a "living document," the cross-referencing of the DSM with the World Health Organization's International Classification of Diseases Clinical Modifications (WHO-ICD-CM; Centers for Disease Control and Prevention [CDC], 2011), the multiaxial and nonaxial systems of diagnosis, the elements of a diagnosis, and the categorical/dimensional approaches to diagnosis.

"A living document." The *DSM-5* task force utilized the Arabic numeral 5 in the title of the *DSM* (*DSM-5*) and not Roman numeral V in parallel with previous editions (e.g., *DSM-III*). The *DSM-5* task force made this change because it wanted the *DSM-5* to function as a "living document" that could be updated easily (e.g., *DSM-5.1*) when new empirical data warrant a change in coding or another aspect of the *DSM*. The "Conditions for Future Study" section at the end of the *DSM-5* recognizes the evolving nature of the *DSM*.

Cross-referencing the DSM-5 with the WHO-ICD-CM. The *DSM-5* cross-referenced its diagnostic codes with the diagnostic codes of the WHO-ICD-CM (9th and 10th editions). The American Psychiatric Association (2013) noted that harmonizing the two diagnositic systems would facilitate global communication between clinicians and researchers and between clinicians and their clients.

The mutiaxial and nonaxial systems. The multiaxial system, a hallmark of *DSM-III*, *DSM-III-R*, *DSM-IV*, and *DSM-IV-TR*, was replaced in the *DSM-5* by a nonaxial system. The American Psychiatric Association (2013) amended the multiaxial system in the new *DSM-5* nonaxial format as follows:

- *Axes I, II, and III.* All recognized mental disorders and medical conditions were combined in the *DSM-5*, with the first condition listed being the primary diagnosis. The APA (2013) noted that this approach recognizes the interrelationship between mental disorders and medical conditions and is consistent with the WHO-ICD-CM.

- *Axis IV.* Psychosocial/environmental stressors are addressed in the *DSM-5* by utilizing WHO-ICD-CM (9th ed.) V-codes and WHO-ICD-CM (10th ed.) Z-codes (e.g., V61.20 and Z code 62.820, respectively, to designate "parent-child relational problem").

- *Axis V.* The General Adaptive Functioning scale was not utilized in the *DSM-5* because it lacked conceptual clarity regarding symptoms, degree of disability, and suicide risk (APA, 2013). The APA provided information in section 3 of the *DSM-5* on assessment instruments (including the WHO Disability Assessment Schedule) that can be used to determine level of disability.

Elements of a diagnosis. APA (2013) noted that diagnosis is a complex process involving a clinical interview, consideration of diagnostic criteria and text descriptions for each disorder (provided in section 2 of the *DSM-5*), and informed clinical judgement. Section 1 of the *DSM-5* addresses other diagnostic considerations, including the following:

- Subtypes and specifiers can increase diagnostic specificity regarding onset, severity, and duration of symptoms and treatment planning.

- Provisional diagnosis can be used to communicate degree of diagnostic certainty. This is important when it appears that the full criteria for a disorder will be met but not enough information is available at the time to make a definitive decision.

- Cultural factors should be considered when diagnosing and treating mental disorders (e.g., see the cultural concepts of distress given in Section 3 of the *DSM-5* and cultural and gender considerations provided in the text descriptions of Section 2).

- Diagnosis of a mental disorder is not required to provide treatment. Clinical judgment based on factors such as symptom severity, safety issues (e.g., harm to self or others), and degree of disability should also be considered in determining the need for treatment.

CATEGORICAL VERSUS DIMENSIONAL APPROACHES TO DIAGNOSIS

Paris (2013b) noted that the categorical approach has been the basis for making a differential diagnosis, fostering communicating between clinicians, and contributing to treatment planning. This approach is similar to the medical model, in which illness is classified according to discrete criteria into qualitatively different categories of diseases or medical conditions (Paris).

Critics of the categorical approach suggest it may be overly simplified, with arbitrary cutoff points for diagnostic criteria (Paris, 2013b). Reichenberg (2014) also noted that

> this system of categorization had many shortcomings, as many diagnoses are not discrete entities that fit neatly into categories. The result was excessive comorbidity, fuzzy boundaries between disorders, and excessive reliance by clinicians on the NOS (not otherwise specified) category used in past *DSMs*. (p. 3)

In respose to the perceived limitations of the categorical system, a dimensional model for diagnosis emerged. The dimensional approach is based on a quantitative perspective of psychopathology (Paris, 2013b). This data-driven model provides a realistic ("real-world") perspective on mental health issues, emphasizing such characteristics as symptom severity and degree of impairment.

The dimensional approach conceptualizes mental disorders on a spectrum of overlapping disorders. In this regard, Reichenberg (2014) noted that "separate disorders are not really separate at all but are actually related conditions on a continuum of behavior, with some conditions refecting mild symptoms, whereas others conditions are much more severe" (p. 4).

Although the dimensional approach has promise, especially in terms of attempting to provide a "real-world" perspective on mental disorders, it also appears to have shortcomings. For example, Paris (2013b) noted that the dimensional model is based on observations and self-reports that can be problematic, as the data generated may not provide clues to underlying psychopathology. In addition, it is not clear how the dimensional approach can be used to promote a differential diagnosis. Table 4.3 summarizes the differences between the categorical and dimensional approach.

Table 4.3 The Categorical and Dimensional Approaches to Diagnosis	
Categorical Approach	**Dimensional Approach**
1. *Strength.* Is central to differential diagnosis.	1. *Strength.* Attempts to provide realistic ("real-world") description of mental health issues and their impact on functioning.
2. *Diagnosis.* Is based on discrete criteria associated with qualitatively different disorders.	2. *Diagnosis.* Is based on quantifiable information regarding continuous/overlapping spectrums of disorders or conditions.
3. *Model.* Is similar to the medical model that classifies illness according to categories.	3. *Model.* Is data driven, based primarily on observations and self-reports regarding symptom severity and degree of impairment.

Paris (2013c) stated that the "*DSM-5* accepts categories provisionally but views them as artificial, proposing scoring procedures, whenever possible, to turn names into numbers. These scores are described as 'dimensions,' a geometrical metaphor that reflects a quantitative approach to psychopathology" (p. 68). Paris went on to note that dimensionality has not been consistently incorporated throughout the *DSM-5*, and to a large degree the system continues to be categorical. For example, the *DSM-5* task force attempted to utilize a dimensional classification system for personality disorders but discontinued the effort when it became apparent that too many issues could not be resolved (Paris). Although there have been obstacles to implementing the dimensional approach, the American Psychiatric Association (2013) contended that "the dimensional approach to diagnosis . . . will likely supplement or supersede current categorical approaches in coming years" (p. 13).

There appears to be merit in both the categorical and dimensional perspectives of diagnosing. The *DSM-5* has apparently incorporated this perspective for a number of disorders (e.g., the autism spectrum disorder, which conceptualizes autism in terms of diagnostic criteria along a spectrum). Additional research regarding these issues appears warranted.

The following *Personal Note* describes some of my concerns about using the categorical model when working with children and adolescents.

A Personal Note

While providing mental health services in schools, I was often impressed by the severity of the emotional and behavioral problems of many of the students I served (e.g., some were loners with no friends; had oppositional/defiant tendencies; and did not follow the directives of teachers, parents, or staff). These students were often evaluated by psychiatrists and other mental health professionals to determine whether they had a mental disorder. When they were diagnosed with a *DSM* disorder, such as attention deficit hyperactivity disorder (ADHD), they were often prescribed medication to treat it.

Not uncommonly, a student would almost meet the criteria for several disorders (e.g., conduct disorder, oppositonal defiant disorder, and reactive attachment disorder) but did not reach the criteria theshold for any one disorder. In these instances, the categorical approach in the *DSM* seemed to fall short in terms of providing a realistic description of these students. Indeed, I found that these students often had more serious problems than the student who had met the criteria for one disorder but who did not have significant issues beyond that disorder. Fortunately, school psychologists can conduct psychological evaluations for students with significant emotional/behavioral problems (regardless of whether they have a *DSM* disorder) to determine if they qualify for additional services.

CONTROVERSIES The publication of the *DSM-5* was met with more controversy than that of any past *DSM*. The strong, often emotionally charged negative reactions are in part associated with the increased importance of the *DSM* in everyday life (e.g., whether or not an insurance company will pay for mental health services, whether a person will receive disability assistance due to a mental disorder). Much of the controversy regarding the *DSM-5* relates to the proliferation of new disorders, apprehension about overdiagnosis, and the medicalization of mental disorders. Another source of disagreement arises from changes made to previous *DSM* disorders.

Proliferation of Disorders, Overdiagnosis, and Medicalization of Mental Disorders

Allen Frances, chair of the *DSM-IV-TR* task force, has been the most vocal critic regarding the *DSM-5*. Frances noted that the number of mental disorders has been increasing over the years, resulting in overdiagnoses and unnecessary and potentially harmful treatments. For example, only 5 disorders were reported in a mental health census of patients during the mid-19th century, 106 disorders were listed in the *DSM-1*, and 357 were included in the *DSM-IV* (Frances, 2013; Pierre, 2013). Frances suggested that a number of factors have contributed to this increase in mental disorders, including societal pressures (e.g., individuals who want treatment for everyday life stressors and pharmaceutical companies that are eager to sell more drugs).

Frances (2013) was also concerned that the new disorders included in the *DSM-5* (e.g., mild cognitive disorder and binge eating disorder) have made it possible for virtually all individuals to be diagnosed with a mental disorder, thereby undermining the definition of normalcy. In this regard, Frances stated:

> Were *DSM-5* to have its way we would have a wholesale medicalization of everyday incapacity (mild memory loss with aging); distress (grief, mixed anxiety, depression); defects in self-control (binge eating); eccentricity (psychotic risk); irresponsibility (hypersexuality); and even criminality (rape, statutory rape). (p. 99)

If these trends continue, it is estimated that half of the population of Americans will have a mental disorder at some time in their lives (Pierre, 2013).

T. L. Murray (2009) noted that the medicalization of mental disorders has become big business in the United States, with dramatic increases in the amount of money spent on antipsychotics and antidepressants ($24 billion was spent in 2008, 48 times the amount spent in 1986). In addition, Sadler (2013) reported that 5 pharmaceutical companies were in *Fortune* magazine's 2011 top 50 most profitable list. These companies profit from the increasing number of *DSM* mental disorders and the tendency for managed care to promote psychiatric medication over therapy as a means to control mental health care costs. Evidence of the medicalization of mental disorders is reflected in a dramatic increase in the use of mood stabilizers and antipsychotic medications (Frances, 2013) and the fact that 11% of adults in the United States take antidepressants (Paris, 2013a).

Changes From the DSM-IV-TR Pomerantz (2014) noted that there has been controversy regarding some of the changes the *DSM-5* made to *DSM-IV-TR* disorders. One change that has attracted attention was dropping the "bereavement exclusion" relating to major depression. In the *DSM-IV-TR*, a person would not be diagnosed with a major depression if the symptoms of depression occurred during the first 2 months after the death of a loved one, as these could be considered a normative reaction to loss. The *DSM-5*, on the other hand, allows a diagnosis of major depression within the 2-month period following the loss, if the clinician believes the symptoms of depression extend beyond what would be expected based on the client history and culture. The *DSM-5* contends that this change was made to ensure that necessary treatment for depression would occur regardless of the circumstances (APA, 2013).

Another controversial issue in the *DSM-5* related to how autism was conceptualized and how changes could impact future diagnosis. The *DSM-5* combined *DSM-IV-TR's* disorders relating to autism (Autistic disorder, Asperger's disorder, and Pervasive Developmental Disorders Not Otherwise Specified) into one disorder—autism spectrum disorder. The *DSM-5* made this change because it contended that previous forms of autism were really different versions of the same disorder (all had problems with communication, social interaction, and repetitive patterns of behavior or interest) which varied within a spectrum from high to low functioning (APA, 2013).

DSM-5: A Summary Paris (2013b) noted that the "*DSM-5* is a noble attempt at a revision in line with current research and can be considered a draft for future editons that will be based on more data" (p. xv). Highlights of changes in the *DSM-5* include the following:

- It includes dimensional as well as categorical perspectives on diagnoses.

- Mental disorders are organized into 20 developmentally sequenced categories.

- New mental disorders were added, and existing disorders were revised.

- The role of neuroscience in the development of mental disorders is given consideration.

- The multiaxial system of diagnosis was replaced by a nonaxial system of diagnosis.

- The *DSM-5* is a "living document" that will allow for ongoing revisions based on current research findings.

Changes in the *DSM-5* have been associated with controversies and concerns, including these:

- A proliferation of new diagnoses that may undermine the differentiation between normalcy and psychopathology.

- The overdiagnosis and medicalization of mental disorders has the potential to support harmful and unnecessary treatment.

- Criteria for mental disorders may not take into account multicultural concerns (e.g., gender bias), as may research methodology (e.g., minorities underrepresented as research participants).

These and other issues provide opportunities and challenges that will impact future editions of the *DSM*.

The Clinical Interview

The **clinical interview** provides a structure for assimilating information pertaining to assessment and diagnosis. May (1990) noted that the clinical interview is one of the most widely used assessment procedures. It serves a variety of purposes: providing information on the client's presenting problem and concerns; enabling the counselor to gain necessary historical information, including organic factors that could contribute to the client's condition; and aiding in the process of making a differential diagnosis to determine whether a client suffers from a particular mental disorder. The clinical interview normally is conducted early in the counseling process, during the first or second session. The clinical interview allows the counselor to gain important background information and determine whether the client suffers from a mental disorder or is in a state of crisis that requires immediate attention. The interview can be structured according to the counselor's theoretical orientation and the client's unique issues and concerns.

I have developed a four-stage model for the clinical interview: using listening skills, taking the client's history, conducting a mental status exam, and using standardized and nonstandardized measures. These four stages serve overlapping functions and should not be perceived as discrete entities. For example, a counselor may gain useful information about the client's history and mental status while using listening skills. An overview of these four stages follows.

STAGE 1: USING LISTENING SKILLS Counselors can begin the clinical interview by using listening skills to obtain a phenomenological understanding of the client. For example, a counselor can use an open-ended question such as "What brought you in today?" to determine what prompted the appointment and whether the client is self-referred. Listening skills can also be used to obtain a description of the presenting problem, any underlying concerns, and other pertinent information.

STAGE 2: TAKING THE CLIENT'S HISTORY The counselor may take an in-depth history after clients have had a chance to discuss their situation. The history can be divided into two parts. The first part involves the client providing background information regarding work, family, social relationships, health, and other areas of interest, such as important turning points in the client's life. In addition, it is important to identify clients' strengths and assets that can be used to address mental health issues and promote wellness. Counselors may use forms as an efficient method of gathering this part of the history. The second part of taking a history involves exploring the client's symptoms and concerns—such as difficulty sleeping, loss of appetite, or marital problems—in terms of onset, duration, and severity. This information can help the counselor gain a better overall understanding of the client's condition. It can also be particularly useful in diagnosis, since major systems of diagnosis such as the *DSM-5* require this information to make a differential diagnosis.

It is particularly important when conducting a history to explore possible organic factors that could contribute to mental disorders. These factors include the use of alcohol or drugs, including street drugs and prescription medications, and existing or past medical conditions. For example, excessive use of alcohol can cause hallucinations, a mental disorder called alcohol hallucinosis. In addition, many prescription drugs have been known to contribute to the symptoms associated with mental disorders (Othmer & Othmer, 1989). For example, estrogen can cause anxiety and depression; diuretics can produce irritability, restlessness, insomnia, and delirium; and insulin can induce psychosis and confusion. Medical conditions may also be accompanied by symptoms of psychological distress. For example, gout or brain tumors can produce depression; head injury can cause anxiety; and multiple sclerosis can foster anxiety, depression, and episodic psychiatric symptoms. Othmer and Othmer provided a more complete list of prescription drugs and medical conditions and their associated psychiatric symptoms.

STAGE 3: CONDUCTING A MENTAL STATUS EXAM A mental status exam can help counselors make a differential diagnosis. For a client who reports hearing voices, a counselor may consider schizophrenia as a possible diagnosis. The counselor could then use the mental status exam to explore whether the client has other symptoms associated with schizophrenia, such as delusions, flat or inappropriate affect, and evidence of a thought disorder. Trzepacz and Baker (1993) described six components that should be addressed in a mental status exam:

1. *Appearance, attitude, and activity level.* Much can be learned from *appearance*. Bizarre dress and overall appearance can suggest disorientation and a mental disorder. Physical appearance can also provide some information regarding the person's physical health (e.g., a runny nose can suggest a cold or other upper respiratory illness). *Attitude* relates to the individual's demeanor during the interview. This can range from cooperative to hostile and can indicate the person's interpersonal style and reaction to the counselor. *Activity level* relates to the quality and degree of physical and motor movement. Some clients are constantly pacing, suggesting possible explosive tendencies, whereas others are listless with little movement, which may suggest depression.

2. *Mood and affect.* *Mood* is the person's *internal* emotional state, such as happy, sad, or anxious. *Affect* is the *external* manifestation of how emotions are expressed. Affect is communicated verbally and nonverbally in numerous ways—facial expressions, tone of voice, laughter, and crying. Mood and affect can be congruent and appropriate (indicating mental health), such as laughing when one feels happy, or incongruent (indicating a possible mental disorder), such as laughing when one is sad.

3. *Speech and language.* *Speech* and *language* relate to verbal and written communication of words, concepts, and ideas. Assessment of speech and language can help identify problems with fluency (such as stuttering), communication disorders (relating to information processing), and learning disabilities.

4. ***Thought process, thought content, and perception.*** *Thought processes* have to do with *how* we are thinking, whereas *thought content* concerns *what* we are thinking. Normal thought processes tend to be connected (or linear), with one idea contributing to the next idea. Problems with thought processes (such as a thought disorder) can occur in schizophrenia, when the individual has difficulty staying with one line of thought and instead jumps from one topic to another, unrelated topic. Thought content and *perceptions* can also suggest mental health or illness. For example, it is common in psychosis for clients to have problems with thought content in terms of delusions and with perceptions associated with hallucinations.

5. ***Cognition.*** *Cognition* comprises a wide array of intellectual functions, including memory, the ability to think and reason, problem-solving skills, and creativity. Assessing cognition involves evaluating a variety of skills and abilities, such as a person's degree of orientation (e.g., who they are and where they are) and a person's ability to attend, concentrate, remember, and use abstract thinking to solve complex problems. Failure to use basic mental facilities can suggest brain damage like that found in Alzheimer's dementia.

6. ***Insight and judgment.*** *Insight* and *judgment* involve the use of a variety of higher-order functions that can be referred to as "emotional intelligence," or EQ. EQ can include such faculties as self-awareness, ability to "read social situations" to determine appropriate interpersonal behavior, and decision-making skills necessary for sound judgment.

STAGE 4: USING STANDARDIZED AND NONSTANDARDIZED MEASURES Counselors can use standardized and nonstandardized measures to refine diagnostic considerations and plan treatment. For example, a client's MMPI-II profile might include elevated scales on 2 (depression) and 9 (mania), which could contribute to a diagnosis of manic depression. In terms of nonstandardized measures, environmental assessment might show that the client feels depressed about living on the East Coast, hates working in a retail job, and wants to go back to school. Information from the environmental assessment can be useful in terms of understanding the etiology, or cause, of the mental disorder as well as in planning treatment. The depressed client in the example could consider moving and going to school.

Treatment Planning

Treatment planning can be defined as "an organized conceptual effort to design a program *outlining in advance* the specific steps by which the therapist will help the patient recover from his or her presenting dysfunctional state" (Makover, 1992, p. 338). Linda Seligman (1998) conceptualized treatment planning as an hourglass. Initially, the counselor generates a large amount of information during the assessment phases (such as psychosocial and medical history). This information gets narrowed down, generating one or more diagnoses. The diagnoses then broaden into consideration of treatment goals and associated counseling techniques and strategies.

It is important to consider counselor and client variables, including client's strengths and assets, when formulating a treatment plan for client problems and disorders and when selecting treatment modalities (Seligman & Reichenberg, 2012). For example, there is some evidence to suggest that depressed individuals with low social dysfunction respond well to interpersonal therapy and those with low cognitive dysfunction respond well to cognitive-behavioral therapy (Shea, et al., 1990). The literature provides additional information on treatment planning through a rich description of client variables (Garfield, 1994) and counselor variables (Beutler, Machado, & Neufeldt, 1994) on counseling outcomes.

Treatment planning can be approached from several perspectives: managed care, brief-solution-focused counseling, use of treatment planners, and curative factors. To a large degree, treatment planning must address the criteria acceptable to managed-care organizations. For example, Kelly (1999) notes that managed care will continue to require empirically validated treatment models. Managed care also subscribes to the idea that quicker is better.

Brief-solution-focused treatment planning has therefore become the rule and not the exception. In brief-solution-focused counseling, treatment planning tends to be narrow in nature focusing on symptom relief and returning the individual to a functional state as quickly as possible. Traditional treatment planning is more comprehensive, with the goal of addressing as many clinical issues and client modalities as necessary to move the client toward optimal development.

All treatment planning perspectives do share some common elements. Young (1992) identifies two aspects of treatment planning that would seem to be useful from most theoretical perspectives. First, the counselor and client formulate mutually agreed-on treatment goals, which are prioritized and associated with counseling strategies. Counselors have available a number of useful treatment planners with which to identify treatment goals and their associated counseling strategies for common counseling problems (such as anger management) and mental disorders (see Jongsma & Petersen, 1995). Second, the counselor utilizes common factors that are perceived to be curative and promote success in the treatment planning process. Maintaining a positive counseling relationship is believed to be the most important common factor, along with clients experiencing hope and positive expectations; practicing behaviors; and engaging in new learning experiences. Several comprehensive treatment planning models are described in the literature. Seligman and Reichenberg's (2012) model is based on the acronym DO A CLIENT MAP. Their model is a comprehensive treatment plan that addresses a number of clinical components, such as the overall diagnosis and treatment goals, nature of assessment procedures required, counselor characteristics that would be facilitative, types of interventions, and the prognosis regarding recovery. Table 4.4 describes each of the elements of Seligman and Reichenberg's approach.

Table 4.4	Overview of Seligman and Reichenberg's DO A CLIENT MAP	
Elements of the Model	**Description**
D Diagnosis	The overall diagnosis
O Objective	Treatment goals
A Assessments	Nature of assessment procedures required
C Clinician	Counselor characteristics that would be facilitative
L Location of treatment	Setting of treatment (e.g., school or hospital)
I Interventions	Types of counseling strategies utilized
E Emphasis of treatment	Behavioral, cognitive, affective, supportive, directive, and so forth
N Nature of treatment	Individual, group, marriage and family, and so forth
T Timing	Frequency, duration, and number of counseling sessions
M Medications	Nature of medication needs
A Adjunct services	Types of additional services needed, such as human services
P Prognosis	Amount of improvement that is expected

Lazarus's (1997, 2000) multimodal therapy (MMT) is both an approach to counseling and a treatment-planning method. The counseling approach is based on social-learning theory, general systems theory, and group and communication theory. Lazarus noted that MMT has always been a brief form of therapy that incorporates problem-centered, solution-focused, and active-directive modalities. Brief MMT is characterized by the following:

- Active-directive strategies that include advice giving and homework assignments

- A didactic-educational focus (such as direct teaching and bibliotherapy) to help clients learn effective coping responses

- Use of the BASIC I.D. modalities (as described in Table 4.5) in assessment, diagnosis, and treatment planning and to quickly identify key problems and counseling goals

- Use of "elegant solutions" (from such sources as Ellis's 1996 brief rational-emotive behavior therapy) to provide brief yet comprehensive approaches to problem resolution

Lazarus (1993) described MMT as a form of technical eclecticism that blends a recognized theory with counseling strategies from other theories, thus having an advantage over other approaches, because eclectic theories like MMT provide specific decision-making criteria for treatment planning. The core of MMT is summed up by the acronym BASIC I.D., which addresses seven modalities that provide a basis for treatment planning (see Table 4.5 for an overview).

An assessment of all seven modalities provides an overview of the client's physical and psychological functioning (Lazarus, 1997). Additional assessment can be conducted in each modality as necessary to obtain a more in-depth understanding. For example, an exploration of the nature and content of a client's cognition could suggest a pattern of self-destructive behavior (statements like "I'm no good. My wife would be better off without me"). Once the modalities have been evaluated, the counselor is in a position to formulate treatment goals with the client.

Another model of treatment planning is called *hierarchical treatment planning* (Makover, 1992). In this very practical, easy-to-understand approach, counselors and clients work together on formulating a treatment plan. Makover noted that agreement on a plan can be facilitated if clinicians generate answers to three questions by the end of the first session: "Why did the client come here?" "Why did the client come now?" and "What does the client want?" The answers can help identify what precipitated the request for counseling, current stressors, and the overall aim of receiving counseling.

The four-tier hierarchy of Makover's (1992) model provides a mechanism for understanding the interrelationship between the counseling process and treatment planning. It begins with identifying the final outcome or overall aim of counseling (e.g., an enhanced marital relationship). The second tier is the counseling goals (e.g., improved communication skills) associated with the overall aim. The third tier is the strategies (e.g., listening skills) that can be used to meet the goals. The fourth tier is the techniques (e.g., use of paraphrasing) that are associated with the counseling

Table 4.5   Lazarus's BASIC I.D.

Elements of Model	Description
B Behavior	Actions that people do (such as withdraw or avoid)
A Affect	Emotional states (such as depression and anxiety)
S Sensation	Feelings derived from the bodily senses (such as emptiness)
I Imagery	Visualizations (such as daydreaming and fantasizing)
C Cognition	Thoughts and ideas (such as *I wish I were dead*)
I Interpersonal relations	How people relate to each other (such as encouraging)
D Drugs	Biophysiological states (such as use of medication)

strategies. Hierarchical treatment planning thus begins by identifying the overall aim of counseling and works downward to goals, strategies, and techniques. Counselors who emphasize techniques in counseling can essentially do treatment planning "backward" according to this model, using a technique-oriented approach to generate what the final outcomes will be.

The three treatment planning models just described can be used together to form a comprehensive approach to treatment planning. Used in this way, they provide useful information for assessment, diagnosis, and treatment and on the interrelationships of aims, goals, strategies, and techniques. They also provide information on client modalities like affect, cognitions, and interpersonal relations. Treatment planning according to these models provides an organizational structure that promotes a sense of direction for the counseling process.

Diversity and Postmodern Issues in Assessment and Diagnosis

A multicultural perspective helps counselors gain an accurate understanding of clients in terms of race, ethnicity, culture, gender, spirituality, sexual orientation, age, and other aspects of diversity. Pomerantz (2014) noted that the *DSM* has made significant strides incorporating a cultural perspective, beginning with the *DSM-IV-TR* and continuing with the *DSM-5*. The *DSM-5* addresses cultural issues in Sections 2 and 3. Section 2 provides diagnostic criteria for each disorder, followed by text descriptions that include information on gender and culture that can facilitate diagnostic decision making. For example, the text description for acute stress disorder suggests that Latinos may experience *ataque de nervios* ("attack of nerves") following an acute stress event, such as loss of loved one. The "Glossary of Cultural Concepts and Distress" (located in Section 3 of the *DSM-5*) notes that *ataque de nervios* is "characterized by symptoms of intense emotional upset, including acute anxiety, anger, or grief; screaming and shouting uncontrollably; attacks of crying; trembling; heat in the chest rising into the head; and becoming verbally and physically aggressive" (APA, 2013, p. 833). Section 3 also includes "The Outline for Cultural Formulation and Cultural Formulation Interview," which clinicians can use to promote a cultural context for diagnosing mental disorders.

Pomerantz (2014) contended that although significant improvements regarding culture and gender have been made, there continue to be areas of concern such as gender bias and inadequate research models. Regarding gender bias, Pomerantz noted that some disorders are diagnosed disproportionally more in males (e.g., antisocial personality disorder, alcohol use disorder, and conduct disorder) and other disorders are diagnosed much more frequently in females (e.g., disorders relating to anxiety and depression, eating disorders, and borderline personality disorder). Pomerantz also suggested that research utilized in the *DSM-5* lacks representation of ethnic minorities as participants in the studies. In addition, the *DSM* could enhance its multicultural perspective by addressing diversity issues such as age and sexual orientation.

Although the *DSM* is beginning to make advances in terms of addressing diversity issues, additional work is needed to establish a realistic base for diagnosing and describing mental disorders from a multicultural perspective (Smart & Smart, 1997). Zalaquett, Fuerth, Stein, Ivey, and Ivey (2008) suggested reframing *DSM*-based diagnosis in terms of case conceptualization in order to incorporate a multicultural perspective. Using the developmental counseling and therapy theory of counseling, the authors described how to formulate culturally sensitive interventions (e.g., addressing social justice issues through psychological liberation).

Postmodern theories like social constructionism emphasize the role of diversity in assessment and diagnosis and stress the importance of considering the effects of culture, gender, age, environment, language, and the multiple realities that can be generated from each individual's unique worldview. Assessment and diagnosis must therefore involve processes that move beyond the intrapsychic or self-analysis to include a consideration of diversity issues. The importance of being aware of possible cultural bias is described earlier in this chapter. Environmental assessment and assessments of worldview are good examples of how a counselor can look beyond intrapsychic forces to gain a broader picture of the client's world.

Spirituality can also be considered during the assessment process (Richards & Bergin, 1997). There are few formal spiritual assessment instruments available. Richards and Bergin therefore recommended that spiritual assessment be done primarily during the initial history taking and the clinical interview. Spiritual assessment can be used with all clients to obtain an understanding of their worldview (which may or may not include religious beliefs). It may be particularly useful to determine whether clients perceive spirituality as a source of strength and guidance and whether they turn to spiritual processes during times of personal difficulty. In these instances, spirituality can be used to support a strengths perspective in counseling.

The following *Personal Note* illustrates the importance of a multicultural perspective in assessment and diagnosis.

A Personal Note

The importance of considering issues such as religion/spirituality and culture in assessment and diagnosis became very clear to me in a recent clinical case. The case involved "Jim," a 10th-grade Navajo student. Jim began experiencing anxiety and depression shortly after he witnessed his brother being killed by a shark during a family vacation in Australia a year earlier. He had also been in the water but was able to get out and back on the boat. Since the accident, Jim's personality began to change. He was no longer the fun-loving, outdoorsy person who seemed to

(Continued)

(Continued)

be full of self-confidence and was interested in playing sports and hanging out with his friends. Instead, Jim became solemn and isolated himself from others. He also developed paranoia shortly after the accident, contending that others were out to get him. When Jim returned to the United States, he had panic attacks at school several times a week, interfering with his ability to attend class. On several occasions he lost consciousness during the panic attack, resulting in the school calling for an ambulance.

Jim had several evaluations and received diagnoses associated with anxiety and depression, such as posttraumatic stress disorder, panic disorder, and so forth. Several medications had been used along with cognitive-behavioral therapy. When he did not respond to treatment, I was asked to provide consultation. In my clinical interview, I asked him several questions related to culture and religion/spirituality that turned out to be quite helpful in terms of assessment, diagnosis, and treatment. These questions were as follows: From the perspective of the Navajo culture, how are mental health and mental illness conceptualized? How can your culture, religion, and spirituality be used to explain how you developed your mental health problems? How can your culture, religion, and spirituality be used to help you get better?

Jim's responses to these questions were quite interesting. He said that Navajo culture did not separate mental from physical health—they were interrelated. In addition, when a person had health problems, it was often associated with being out of sync with one's culture or "traditional ways." Jim noted that he had a warning that this was the case for him before his family went to Australia—a coyote ran in front of his parents' car on the way to the airport. According to Navajo culture, this is a sign that his family was "not right" with their culture and that they would need a ceremony as soon as possible. In addition, Jim said an Aboriginal man in Australia gave him "the evil eye" a week after the shark attack and put a "hex" on him. From that point, he began to feel others were out to get him. Jim went on to say that for him to get better, he would need a ceremony to make his family "right" with their culture, and he would need a ceremony to help him get rid of his "hex." Shortly after the two ceremonies were arranged, Jim was able to overcome the paranoia and panic attacks and regain some self-confidence. At that point, he was able to benefit from counseling to address the posttraumatic stress disorder and anxiety and depression associated with the loss of his brother. After 6 months of weekly counseling, he was able to work through most of the issues that were undermining his health and well-being.

In some instances, counselors may also wish to determine whether clients' spiritual beliefs and values are healthy or unhealthy in terms of promoting mental health (Richards & Bergin, 1997). For example, Allport and Ross (1967) differentiated unhealthy and healthy religious practice in terms of extrinsic versus intrinsic motivation. Unhealthy religious practice is characterized by an extrinsic religious orientation; people may use religion as a way of impressing others with status and self-righteousness. Healthy religious orientation tends to be intrinsically motivated and is characterized by personal spiritual journeys with individualized goals and aspirations. Clients who have potentially unhealthy spiritual beliefs and values can address these issues in counseling or be referred to specialists for assistance.

In addition to its application in assessment, sensitivity to issues in diversity is required for accurate diagnosis. Counselors must especially be aware of the cultural context of language when differentiating mental health from mental illness. What might be considered normal can vary dramatically from one culture to the next. Gergen (1994a) has pointed out the role of language and culture in the etiology of mental disorders, noting that some cultures have survived for centuries without any word or concept for depression, yet cultures that have a term for depression seem to find this mental state virtually everywhere.

Diagnosis can also be affected by where the client is in the life span. The field of developmental psychopathology has identified how problems such as anxiety and depression manifest themselves differently according to age. For example, it is not uncommon for a child's or adolescent's depression to be "masked" by anger. Gender can also impact the process of diagnosis. For example, a woman who has just had a baby and becomes depressed could be experiencing a postpartum depression. Gender bias can undermine accurate assessment and diagnosis as well (Eriksen & Kress, 2008). To illustrate, sex-role stereotyping can lead clinicians to overdiagnose males with antisocial personality disorders and females with dependent personality disorders. Faulty assumptions regarding the female gender and mental health (e.g., women are more prone to mental health problems because they are more emotional than men) can be corrected by adopting a feminist perspective.

SUMMARY

Assessment and diagnosis are important parts of the counseling process. They provide critical background information that is necessary before the counselor and client can establish counseling goals. Assessment and diagnosis also contribute to the science dimension of counseling by providing objective information regarding the counseling process.

Standardized assessment procedures include psychological tests that have a standardized norm group, such as the MMPI-II. Nonstandardized tests do not have standardized norm groups, are more subjective in nature, and include a variety of procedures, such as observation and environmental assessment. Standardized and nonstandardized assessment procedures have inherent strengths and weaknesses. For example,

the major strength of nonstandardized measures lies in the ease of adapting these procedures to the unique characteristics of the individual, thereby reducing the risk of test bias.

The clinical interview, another valuable tool for both diagnosis and assessment, can be used along with the *DSM-5* to formulate a diagnosis. Counselors can use the interview to establish positive relationships and provide a structure for assessment and diagnosis. The interview can also help the counselor address such important issues as medical condition, past history of alcohol or drug abuse, and symptoms associated with a mental disorder. Diversity issues—such as culture, gender, age, sexual orientation, and spirituality— should also be considered in assessment and diagnosis.

PERSONAL EXPLORATION

1. What assessment procedures do you find interesting, and what intrigues you about them?

2. What is your opinion regarding the nature of mental disorders and what causes them?

3. How do issues of diversity—such as age, gender, culture, race, ethnicity, and sexual orientation—influence the way mental disorders are diagnosed and treated?

4. What is your opinion of using drugs to treat mental disorders in children and adolescents?

5. What concerns do you have about using psychological tests such as intelligence or personality tests?

6. What do you think about the *DSM-5* (e.g., what are its strengths and potential weaknesses)?

7. What do you believe is important in diagnosing mental disorders?

8. What do you think should be considered in treatment planning?

9. What are your thoughts regarding mental status exams?

LEARNING ACTIVITIES

1. Research what information is contained in the *DSM-5* (e.g., criteria for specific mental disorders) and consider how this information can help you better understand mental disorders.

2. Consider reviewing case studies of people with mental disorders (your professor may be able to assist you). What insights does this information provide you regarding what its like to have a mental disorder?

WEBSITES

Franklin, D. J. (2000). *Psychological evaluations.* Retrieved from http://psychologyinfo.com/treatment/evaluations.html. *Describes the interview process in counselor assessment.*

Franklin, D. J. (2000). *Psychological testing.* Retrieved from http://psychologyinfo.com/treatment/testing.html. *Describes psychological tests and various forms of testing used in the assessment process.*

Counseling Research and Evaluation

The Art and Science of Research and Evaluation

Counseling research, reflected in both the art and science of counseling, provides subjective and objective means for understanding and evaluating counseling. Traditionally, counseling research has emphasized the science dimension by utilizing experimental/quantitative research methodology that involves hypothesis testing and statistical analysis. Experimental/quantitative research continues to be important, for it provides counselors with an objective tool for understanding and evaluating techniques and procedures. Unfortunately, few practitioners use experimental/quantitative research methods, thus creating an ever-widening gap between practice and research (Murray, 2009; Reisetter et al. 2004). Goldfried and Wolfe (1996) have noted that the changes in health care delivery brought about by managed care make it increasingly important for clinicians to utilize some form of research to demonstrate accountability.

Recent trends have explored how the art of research can be used to bridge this gap between practice and research. Qualitative approaches have emerged that provide practitioners with methodologies that are less rigid and involve more clinical skills than are used in traditional, quantitative methodologies (Reisetter et al., 2004). For example, qualitative approaches may focus on the researcher/ evaluator and participant functioning as co-investigators who are attempting to discover important information relating to a particular subject. More emphasis is placed on awareness and sensitivity to diversity and other social forces and less emphasis on data gathering and statistical analysis.

Both quantitative and qualitative approaches to research and evaluation have their place in counseling. In time, they may become integrated, creating a balance between the art and science of this important work in the profession.

Chapter Overview

This chapter provides an overview of the issues relating to counseling research and evaluation. In addition to discussing traditional research methodologies, it addresses field-based methodologies such as action research, qualitative methods, and single-subject designs. These newer methodologies are attracting considerable attention in the literature, because they are particularly relevant to clinicians. Highlights of the chapter include the following:

- **The art and science of research and evaluation**

- **The purpose of research and evaluation, including the interrelationship of theory, research, and practice**

- **An overview of types of research, including qualitative research methodologies and single-subject designs**

- **Diversity and postmodern issues in research and evaluation**

The Purpose of Research and Evaluation

Counseling research serves many functions. This section reviews several of these: evaluating the efficacy of a counseling approach through the interaction of theory, practice, and research; providing a means for communicating counselor accountability; and contributing to the body of knowledge in the counseling field.

Theory, Research, and Practice

The art and science of counseling and psychotherapy work in a similar way as the scientist-practitioner model, which emphasizes the role that science plays in shaping clinical practice. Unfortunately, the science of counseling has not kept up with the art of counseling. Hill and Corbett (1993) noted that practitioners tend to rely on clinical judgment rather than research to formulate which theories and techniques to use.

The art and science of counseling emphasize the interrelationship of theory, research, and practice. Postmodern theories, such as social constructionism, stress the role of theory in scientific investigation. In this regard, Gergen (1994a) suggested that theories are representations of language and culture and provide a paradigm with which to understand reality.

Figure 5.1 provides an illustration of the interrelationship of theory, research, and practice. It shows theory at the apex of a triangle, thus placing it in the uppermost position. Arrows in the figure extend in both directions to depict the reciprocal influences of theory, research, and practice. For example, knowledge can flow up from practice to theory, and vice versa, in a circular, rather than linear, fashion. This model also recognizes the postmodern position regarding "action research," which suggests that practitioners and researchers are partners in the search for knowledge.

The interrelationship of these three factors can be illustrated by this example. The counseling theory of behavior therapy develops techniques such as assertiveness training. A counselor may use this technique in clinical practice and later implement

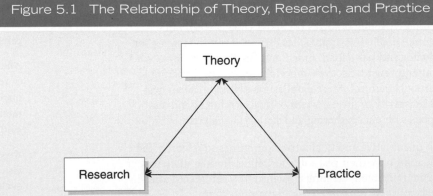

Figure 5.1   The Relationship of Theory, Research, and Practice

research strategies to evaluate its effectiveness. The results of this research can provide useful information to refine the theoretical origins of assertiveness training.

Research, Evaluation, and Counselor Accountability

Research and evaluation can also be used to communicate counselor accountability. One way to conceptualize how this occurs is through the interaction of research, evaluation, and accountability, as shown in Figure 5.2. From this perspective, counselors can use research strategies to evaluate their individual clinical skills or an entire counseling program. The information obtained from the evaluation process can then serve as a basis for establishing professional accountability. However, even once accountability has been established, the process is still incomplete. The counselor should set up an ongoing accountability program, which may require additional research strategies to evaluate the various facets of one's professional activities.

Gibson (1977) and Hershenson, Power, and Waldo (1996) have provided the following guidelines for evaluation research:

- *Determine the purpose of the evaluation.* It is necessary to identify what type of information needs to be generated from the evaluation. Should the evaluation focus on cost-effectiveness or other issues, such as quality control?

- *Effective evaluation uses valid measurement criteria.* Once goals have been identified, criteria for measuring these goals must be established. For example, a goal in a mental health center might be to have all counselors initiate a follow-up contact with each client within 1 to 2 months after termination of counseling services. The measurement criterion might be the percentage of clients for whom follow-up activities were initiated.

- *Effective program evaluation depends on accurate application of the measurement criteria.* Appropriate research strategies should be used to collect and analyze the data.

- *Program evaluation should obtain input from all people involved in the program.* Opportunities for input from all levels of the organization should be provided. In a mental health center, for example, the evaluation might include information from administrators, clerical staff, counselors, and clients.

- *The evaluation should include feedback and follow-through.* Once the evaluation is complete, the results may be communicated, in a clear and concise fashion, to the staff. They should include recommendations to facilitate future program planning and development.

- *Evaluation should be a planned and continuous process.* A program should include an ongoing evaluation component. This enables the staff to monitor strengths and weaknesses. Accountability does not imply that a program has only strengths; rather, it implies becoming aware of weaknesses and attempting to rectify them.

- *Program evaluations should be sensitive to the politics of the organization.* All organizational systems have unique political structures that impact their functioning. It is therefore important to take these political influences into consideration throughout the evaluation process.

Hershenson et al. (1996) also identified the knowledge and skills necessary for effective evaluation: familiarity with the particular program—its needs and resources, the population it serves, and how the evaluation process can be of use or benefit; how to create the best fit between program needs and evaluation procedures; and facilitative skills, such as communication, interpersonal, organizational, and advocacy skills.

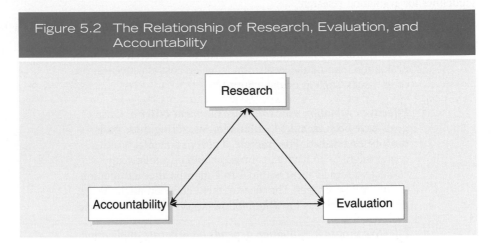

Figure 5.2 The Relationship of Research, Evaluation, and Accountability

The Contribution of Research to the Counseling Field

Another purpose of research is to contribute to the body of knowledge in the counseling field through the testing of theories and conducting outcome research to promote evidenced-based (empirically supported) treatment approaches. Hill and Corbett (1993) recommended that process and outcome research should be based on the following principles:

- "The overall goals of process and outcome research should be to develop new theories of therapy, to provide information for practitioners about how to intervene with clients at different points in therapy, and to develop training programs based on the empirical results of what works in therapy" (p. 16).

- Research should be directed at analyzing an entire model of the counseling process, such as the one proposed by Hill (1992), which includes therapist intentions, therapist response modes, client reactions, and client behaviors.

- Research should explore issues relating to competence in counseling (i.e., what it means to be a good counselor).

- Research priorities should focus on first determining what the effective process components of counseling are, then on developing and evaluating treatment models that emerge from this basic research.

- Additional research is necessary to determine similarities and differences between career and personal counseling.

- Measures need to be developed that can be used to evaluate the content of counseling (e.g., interpersonal relations and cultural conflicts) and to measure the strength and healthy functioning of clients as opposed to their psychopathology.

- And finally, researchers across disciplines need to increase efforts to work together to communicate methods and results.

Counselors can play a vital role in contributing to the evolution of their profession by engaging in research. Guidelines for formulating a research program follow.

1. Conduct research on topics that interest you and that you believe have significance to the counseling profession.

2. Develop some tenacity when doing research. Once you believe in a project, stick with it and follow it through. There will always be someone to tell you what you can't do. Your job is to tell yourself what you can do and will do.

3. Make a detailed outline before starting to write the research report. This will help you organize your ideas and make your paper easier to read and understand.

4. Don't get discouraged with the publishing process. Once you submit a paper to a journal, it may be accepted, accepted provisionally, rejected with suggestions for resubmission, or rejected outright. Don't give up if you are requested to revise and resubmit your paper. Only 4% of the articles submitted to American Counseling Association journals are accepted without requests for revisions (Seligman, 1986).

5. Finally, never assume your idea is so simple that someone must have published it already. There is a good chance that your idea has not been published, and your contribution might be valuable to the counseling profession.

In the following *Personal Note,* I share some of my personal rewards and struggles with the publishing process.

A Personal Note

I've had my share of ups and downs in conducting research. Some highs include having my first paper accepted for publication and feeling excited about contributing to an area of investigation. I was particularly pleased because this was a theoretical paper about a new dimension of social interest. I remember thinking, "Wow, now I'm part of the evolution of Adlerian theory development." I've also had my share of lows in conducting research. Rejection letters and critical reviews of articles are still painful to receive today.

To survive the research and publication process, I've had to develop a lot of resilience, patience, perseverance, and self-discipline. But it's been worth it. I've been able to gain a better understanding of a wide range of topics, from stuttering to why some children soil their pants. Research has also helped me continually develop my personal approach to counseling, as I carefully examine what has occurred through case studies. In addition, research has been a helpful tool for communicating accountability. For example, I have used a single-subject design, a topic discussed later in this chapter, to assess an approach I'm using to treat encopresis (soiling the pants).

Overview of the Types of Research

Research can be classified in several ways. One classification system differentiates basic research from applied research. **Basic research** is usually conducted under controlled conditions in a laboratory setting, often in a university, and usually involves university students as subjects. Although basic research studies tend to use rigorous research designs, it may be risky to generalize the results to the real world. **Applied research** typically tests theories in a field setting and is therefore reflective of people in their natural habitat. Unfortunately, field studies are not always easy to control and may provide misleading results. Regardless of these limitations, applied research may be a more realistic alternative for clinicians.

Types of Research Methodologies

Research can also be classified by its design. Some of the more common types of research are described in this section.

ACTION RESEARCH The historical roots of **action research** can be traced to Kurt Lewin, a social psychologist known for his study of group dynamics, who used research results as a tool to influence social change (Guiffrida, Douthit, Lynch, &

Mackie, 2011). Guiffrida et al. noted that action research is conducted collaboratively with participants (e.g., practitioners or clients) in real-world settings with the aim of providing results that have a beneficial impact on the lives of participants.

Hays and Wood (2011) reported that participatory action research (PAR) is an emerging form of qualitative research based on constructivist/feminist theory. The goals of PAR are empowering participants to transform settings and apply findings to issues that impact their lives (Hays & Wood). Hays and Wood contended that PAR is ideal for counselors to use to promote social change through advocacy.

Guiffrida et al. (2011) and Hays and Wood (2011) maintained that action research is consistent with the philosophical base of professional counselors (e.g., ecological-systemic, postmodern-constuctivist, and multicultural-social advocacy) with an overall goal of promoting positive change in the lives of others. Guiffrida et al. identified several ethical issues associated with action research that should be monitored and addressed as necessary (e.g., the dual role of practitioner/researcher, ensuring confidentiality of participants, and utilizing data gathering processes that do not interfere with the counseling process).

SURVEY STUDIES **Survey research** typically describes a variable in terms of its frequency in a population (Wilkinson & McNeil, 1996). For example, an investigator might survey a representative sample of professional counselors to determine which counseling approaches are used most often. An influential survey published by *Consumer Reports* (1995) was reviewed by Seligman (1995). He concluded that the study showed long-term therapy is superior to short-term therapy; therapy is as effective as medication and therapy; and psychologists, psychiatrists, and social workers are equally as effective as therapists and are more effective than marriage counselors and long-term family counseling. In addition, Seligman noted that clients whose length or choice of therapy was determined by managed care insurance do worse than those who were not so restricted. More recent research suggests that the *Consumer Reports* findings may be too optimistic and too general (e.g., longer, more intensive therapy is superior to short-term therapy; Nielsen et al. 2004).

Seligman noted that although the *Consumer Reports* study had several methodological shortcomings, it should be taken seriously because it provides valuable information regarding counseling efficacy. In terms of need and efficacy, it provided encouraging information on the public's perception of psychotherapy as a valuable form of mental health treatment (VandenBos, 1996). In addition, the survey was to a large degree supportive of previous empirical research. However, additional research appears necessary to address the issues posed by the *Consumer Reports* survey.

CORRELATIONAL STUDIES **Correlational studies** are used to determine whether two factors are related. For example, a counselor may want to determine whether there is a relationship between gender and age of clients. A review of the counselor's clients over a 2-year period may show that clients over 40 years of age tend to be female and those under 15 tend to be male.

EXPERIMENTAL METHODS **Experimental methods**, also referred to as *quantitative research,* involve evaluating a particular treatment under controlled conditions to determine whether a cause-and-effect relationship exists. For example, an investigator may wish to evaluate the effects of a parent education program on parental attitudes and parent-child behavioral interactions. Traditional experimental designs involve randomly assigning a group of subjects to a treatment group (subjects receiving parent education) and a control group (subjects who do not receive parent education). The two groups can then be compared before and after the program on attitudes, behaviors, or other measures. Statistical analysis is used to evaluate the degree of change on particular measures to determine the effects of the parent education program.

LONGITUDINAL STUDIES **Longitudinal studies** are designed to evaluate a particular group of subjects over an extended period of time. For example, a counselor may want to analyze how well a group of immigrants adjusts to American society. Under this research design, the counselor might check periodically on variables such as the percentage who graduate from high school and college or who have tendencies toward physical or mental health problems.

LARGE-SCALE REVIEW (META-ANALYSIS) **Large-scale reviews** provide a method for synthesizing counseling research (Whiston & Li, 2011). This methodology involves reviewing many published research studies using a sophisticated form of statistical analysis called *meta-analysis* to overcome the methodological problems that can result from grouping numerous studies together for analysis. Large-scale reviews originally were conducted in an attempt to assess the efficacy of counseling. Some of the early work of this type did much to challenge notions that counseling was effective. This was especially true for Eysenck (1965), who claimed that counseling was not effective and that people tended to get better regardless of whether they received counseling. Levitt (1957) also challenged the efficacy of counseling in a large-scale review of studies that evaluated the effectiveness of child counseling, concluding that Eysenck's findings were essentially correct.

However, several large-scale reviews of outcome research do support the effectiveness of counseling and psychotherapy (Elkin et al., 1989; Garfield, 1983; Lambert, 1991; McNeilly & Howard, 1991; Smith & Glass, 1977; Smith, Glass, & Miller, 1980). Smith and Glass conducted the first large-scale review that demonstrated strong empirical support for the effectiveness of counseling. Their investigation of 400 studies showed that treated individuals were better off than 75% of those who did not receive counseling. Smith et al. reviewed 475 studies and found that treated individuals were better off than 80% of those who did not receive counseling. (See Lambert & Bergin [1994] for additional information regarding the efficacy of counseling.)

More recently, Whiston and Li (2011) noted that there has been an increased use of meta-analysis to evaluate counseling issues such as multiculturalism, counseling interventions, and other factors that impact counseling theory and practice. In addition, Whiston and Li provided guidelines that could be used in conducting meta-analysis of quantitative and qualitative research.

QUALITATIVE METHODS Qualitative research designs attempt to understand people and events in their natural setting and are therefore referred to as a *naturalistic approach*. **Qualitative methods** are concerned with understanding the individual's point of view and the lived experience and perspective of the people under study (Silverman, 2004). Such methods typically employ nonstandardized measures, such as interviews and observations, as a means of collecting data. Qualitative methods are oriented to the discovery of insights rather than confirmation of hypotheses. Qualitative methods are also associated with postmodern concepts such as narrative psychology and social constructionism (Northcutt & McCoy, 2004; Reisetter et al., 2004).

CASE STUDIES AND SINGLE-SUBJECT DESIGNS **Case studies**, sometimes referred to as *single-subject designs,* are the intensive study of one individual or a group of individuals in which the researcher gathers information from interviews, observations, and client self-reports (Wilkinson & McNeil, 1996). Case studies can also incorporate some of the principles of experimental design, thereby increasing the counselor's ability to evaluate counseling outcomes objectively.

Shortcomings of Traditional Counseling Research

The scientist-practitioner model appears to be the goal in the counseling profession, but it is not yet a reality. Historically, university programs have advocated the merits of this model, yet clinicians have failed to integrate the two approaches in practice (Peterson, 1995). They have essentially taken the position that research is concerned with statistical abstractions, not the average person, and therefore has little relevance to the challenges of clinical practice (Beutler, Williams, Wakefield, & Entwistle, 1995). Several recommendations have been made about how to bridge the gap between science and practice: (1) Scientists need to become more knowledgeable about clinical issues by maintaining ongoing relationships with clinicians; (2) the role of science in practice needs to be reevaluated; (3) new research methods must be developed to make research more relevant to clinicians; and (4) new vehicles are needed to communicate research findings to practitioners (Beutler et al.).

It is obvious that changes are required to make research more relevant to the needs of practitioners. The emerging qualitative research methodologies offer much promise for practitioners and other researchers in the social sciences (Garfield & Bergin, 1994; Reisetter et al., 2004; Silverman, 2004). Reisetter et al. described several positive attributes of qualitative research described by graduate students in counseling:

- *Worldview congruence.* Students noted that the underlying philosophy of qualitative research and their worldviews were congruent (i.e., both adhered to postmodern concepts such as the social construction of knowledge, the rejection of absolutes, and the phenomenological perspective).

- *Counseling theory and skills.* Students contended that the principles of qualitative research were consistent with the theories and skills of counseling (e.g., an open-ended, "not-knowing" posture can generate personal meaning and opportunities for discovery).

- *Research identity and professional viability.* Students believed that the qualitative paradigm provided an opportunity to make research an ongoing dimension of their professional identity.

- *Holistic experience.* Students found that the qualitative perspective provided a useful structure for them to organize and conceptualize various roles in their lives (personal, counselor, and researcher).

Qualitative Research Methodologies

As mentioned, qualitative research methods have evolved in response to disillusionment with traditional basic research methodologies, their use of restrictive experimental designs such as subject and control groups, and results that have little relevance to practitioners (Mahrer, 1988; Reisetter et al., 2004). An extensive overview of qualitative methodologies is provided in Hoshmand (1989) and Hill, Thompson, and Willams (1997), including the following information relating to the purpose of qualitative methods, the roles of the researcher and participants, the process of inquiry, data-gathering procedures, and data analysis:

- *Purpose.* The purpose of qualitative research designs is to develop an understanding of the essence of human experience. These designs emphasize description and discovery rather than hypothesis testing. Qualitative research can also be used for theory construction and testing; see, for example, Glaser and Strauss's (1967) grounded theory.

- *Roles of the researcher and participants.* The researcher takes a more active role in the research process than simply observing and recording data. This may involve engaging in dialogue and interacting with the participants as a means of exploring and discovering significant events that the client has experienced. Participants also take a more active role, becoming co-investigators in a collaborative and reciprocal relationship with the researcher. Research activity, therefore, is not controlled by the researcher. In addition, participants are consulted as to what research questions they consider meaningful and relevant and whether the interpretations and conclusions are valid for them. In this context, reality can be defined from the perspective of the participants.

- **The process of inquiry.** Inquiry is characterized as an emergent, ongoing process that includes responsiveness to feedback from the participants. The course of inquiry is therefore determined by collaboration between the researcher and participant. In addition, the emphasis is on process and outcome rather than outcome alone.

- **Data gathering.** Data-gathering procedures vary according to the methodology employed. Typical methods include observation in the client's natural setting for extended periods of time; in-depth interviews from a phenomenological perspective; and collecting oral histories, such as by recording myths and legends.

- **Data analysis.** The methods of data analysis can be described as interpretive, with the goal of recognizing meaningful patterns. There are a number of differences between qualitative and quantitative data analysis. In qualitative analysis, phenomena are described rather than manipulated; the emphasis is on descriptions rather than explanations; the focus is on the emergence of concepts as opposed to relating findings to existing theories; results are expressed linguistically rather than numerically; scientific knowledge is viewed as tentative, not fixed; and data are conceptualized contextually, not as isolated, controlled entities.

TYPES OF QUALITATIVE RESEARCH METHODOLOGIES

Qualitative research methodologies can be classified into the following seven types: naturalistic-ethnographic, discovery-oriented, representative-case research, interactive qualitative analysis, grounded theory, consensual qualitative research, and mixed-methods designs.

Naturalistic-Ethnographic

Naturalistic-ethnographic methodologies involve the observation of participants in their natural context to obtain an understanding of the factors that influence human behavior (Hoshmand, 1989). This approach requires prolonged contact and immersion in a particular setting to enable the researcher to obtain an understanding of the members in that setting. Data gathering may incorporate observation, interviews, oral histories, reviews of existing research documents and literature, and the use of critical incidence (see Hays & Wood, 2011; Kidder, Judd, & Smith, 1986; and Lincoln & Guba, 1985, for detailed descriptions of these procedures). Selecting a particular data-gathering procedure requires a consideration of how to relate effectively to the population under study. For example, one investigation used "rap" groups as a data-gathering method with mentally retarded adults (Hoshmand, 1985). Data analysis entails constant recording, categorizing, sorting, and re-sorting in an attempt to create emergent core categories of meaning. Field notes are transcribed verbatim and analyzed during repeated readings of the data to identify key phrases and concepts. Independent judges identify categories of meaning and sort them into themes to check for reliability. The researcher then collaborates with the participants to gather their opinions on the data that were generated.

A naturalistic-ethnographic study that investigated the attitudes of West Indian American youths toward counseling is described by McKenzie (1986). In the first phase of the study, a counselor spent 6 months immersing himself in the schools, homes, peer groups, and other activities of the students under study, spending an average of 40 hours with each student. During the second phase, the researcher conducted in-depth interviews with the students and counseling staff, exploring issues such as development and attitudes toward counseling and toward seeking help. The data were then analyzed to identify meaningful patterns. Results of the study showed that West Indian Americans had strong taboos against seeking counseling, their cultural background affected their career choices, and biculturalism induced conflict within their families.

Discovery-Oriented Psychotherapy Research Another type of qualitative methodology is discovery-oriented psychotherapy research (Mahrer, 1988). The purpose of this approach is to discover important aspects of what is occurring in counseling, such as what prompted a personality change in a client, by taking an in-depth look at the process of psychotherapy. Mahrer described the following steps in this approach:

1. *Select the target of investigation.* Start by identifying some aspect of interest in the counseling process, no matter how large or insignificant it may seem. Avoid getting sidetracked by technical jargon such as *transference* or *locus of control.*

2. *Obtain instances of the target being investigated.* Obtain as many instances as possible of the target under investigation. For example, a researcher interested in what can be discovered about early childhood memories can attempt to obtain examples of these memories in a variety of ways, such as video recordings of sessions and narratives provided by clients.

3. *Obtain an instrument to take a closer look.* Once incidences of target behavior are obtained (e.g., early memories), the researcher can develop an instrument for taking a closer look at the target being investigated. In this process, judges can review videotapes of participants narrating their early memories until meaningful themes or categories of data emerge. The themes and categories obtained can then be used as an instrument for systematically evaluating the target of investigation.

4. *Gather data.* This step involves obtaining the necessary data for the study and applying the instrument to the data. This may involve analyzing the original data obtained during step 2 or obtaining new examples of the target under investigation (e.g., additional early memories).

5. *Make discovery-oriented sense of the data.* The data must be interpreted to determine what can be learned from the study. This process requires characteristics associated with the art of counseling. The investigator must be sensitive to the discoverable by being open to what appears new, unexpected, challenging, or disconcerting in the data.

Representative-Case Research Represenative-case research (Gordon & Shontz, 1990) is a case-study type of qualitative methodology that can be used to gain an in-depth understanding of people with various problems, such as children who are terminally ill. Gordon and Shontz described representative-case research as a process that involves carefully examining "chosen persons one at a time, in depth, to learn how each experiences and manages an event, situation, or set of circumstances or conditions that is important in human life" (p. 62). Representative-case research is considered a qualitative methodology because it requires the active involvement of the client, who is considered to be an expert on the problem under study and a co-investigator. The process attempts to discover what a client has learned about a particular experience or set of circumstances. Supervisors or advisers can promote objectivity; monitor different aspects of the research process; and help with various activities, such as data analysis and interpretation. They can also assist with the relationship between the counselor and client—the investigator and co-investigator.

Interactive Qualitative Analysis Interactive qualitative analysis (Northcutt & McCoy, 2004) has been influenced by postmodernism, grounded theory, action research, concept mapping, systems theory, and Kurt Lewin's field theory. It integrates a number of concepts and theories associated with qualitative research and establishes a set of procedures to facilitate data collection and analysis. Northcutt and McCoy noted that

> there appears to be no other single work in the field of qualitative research methods that integrates a theory of epistemology with systems theory to produce an explicit set of protocols by which qualitative studies can be conducted and documented. (p. xxiv)

Interactive qualitative analysis is concerned with scientific rigor, or "truth value," in research (Lincoln & Guba, 1985). From this perspective, it addresses the relationship among the following questions:

- The ontological: What is real?

- The epistemological: How do we know?

- The ethical/moral: What is good?

- The systemic: What is reliable and valid?

Interactive qualitative analysis provides a protocol for unraveling the mysteries of data collection, observation, interpreting, analysis, and coding and integrates a number of theoretical perspectives associated with qualitative research.

Grounded Theory The origins of grounded theory can be traced to the early work of Glaser and Strauss, two sociologists who investigated a variety of topics, including the process of dying (see Glaser & Strauss, 1965). The name comes from the idea that theories should evolve from data taken from the field and therefore be "grounded" in scientific evidence (Creswell, Hanson, Plano Clark, & Morales, 2007). Grounded theory has evolved over the years into one of the most respected and well-established methods in qualitative research (Ponterotto, 2005).

Most grounded theories currently adhere to a constructivist/interpretive perspective of reality and truth as socially constructed and influenced by the interpretive lenses of researchers (Fassinger, 2005). The constructivist perspective of grounded theories is consistent with "the interpretative tradition of qualitative research with flexible guidelines, a focus on theory that depends on the researcher's view; learning about the experience within embedded, hidden communication, and opportunity" (Charmaz, 2006, p. 250).

Consensual Qualitative Research Consensual qualitative research (Hill, Thompson, & Williams, 1997; Hill et al., 2005) provides structure and objectivity to qualitative research, enabling researchers to replicate studies. It advocates the use of three to five investigators during the data analysis stage who engage in consensual decision making so that a diversity of opinions is encouraged. One or two auditors are also employed to ensure that the investigators do not overlook important data. The three general steps used in consensual qualitative research are these:

1. Responses to open-ended questions from questionnaires or interviews for each individual case are divided into domains (i.e., topic areas).

2. Core ideas (i.e., abstracts or brief summaries) are constructed for all the material within each domain for each individual case.

3. A cross-analysis is conducted, which involves developing categories to describe consistencies in the core ideas within domains across cases (Hill et al., p. 523).

Consensual qualitative research appears to be a step toward the integration of qualitative and quantitative research in terms of attempting to standardize some of the highly subjective procedures associated with qualitative research. This integrative, "middle-ground" form of research methodology provides another valuable research alternative for supporting the art and science of counseling.

Mixed-Methods Designs Mixed-methods research designs can be defined as research that involves "the collection, analysis, and integration of quantitative and qualitative data into a single or multiphase study" (Hanson, Creswell, Plano Clark, Petska, & Creswell, 2005, p. 224). Mixed-methods designs incorporate the objective and subjective dimensions reflected in quantitative and qualitative research, thereby capturing the spirit of the art and science of counseling and psychotherapy advocated by this text. Mixed-method designs are either sequential or concurrent (Hanson et al.). *Sequential designs* relate to the order or sequencing of the research methodologies (whether the research begins with qualitative or quantitative design). Sequential designs include sequential explanatory (quantitative followed by qualitative), sequential exploratory (qualitative followed by quantitative), and sequential transformative (either sequential explanatory or exploratory from the perspective of advocacy). *Concurrent designs* involve quantitative and qualitative research in which data are collected and analyzed simultaneously. There are three types of concurrent designs: concurrent triangulation (priority of data is equal for quantitative and qualitative); concurrent nested (priority of data is equal or favors of one or the other method); and concurrent transformative (priority of data is interpreted through the lens of advocacy).

Mixed-methods designs provide opportunities to evaluate data from a variety of perspectives, expanding the horizons of scientific investigation. Clearly, this approach will play a major role in future research methodologies.

Evaluation of Qualitative Methodologies

Qualitative methods appear to hold much promise for practioners as viable research methods, but they also pose some potential problems. One way to assess this new form of research is to relate it to nonstandardized measures, as described in Chapter 4, since qualitative research methods typically utilize nonstandardized measures, such as observation and environmental assessment.

In terms of weaknesses, both nonstandardized assessment and qualitative research methods lack objectivity and the ability to generalize to a reference group, and they can create confusing results and often lack acceptable levels of validity and reliability. The advantages shared by nonstandardized measures and qualitative research methods are that they provide a flexible, individualized approach; this generates information unique to the individual, can be easily modified to accommodate individual differences, and fosters an active role for both the counselor (researcher) and the client (participant). Their advantages make qualitative research methods particularly attractive for research in multicultural counseling (Helms, 1989). Another advantage is that the methods require some of the same skills associated with effective counseling:

> These new methods are not for the faint of heart. They demand imagination, courage to face the unknown, flexibility, some creativeness, and a good deal of personal skill in observation, interviewing, and self-examination—some of the same skills, in fact, required for effective counseling, but now systematically directed toward the education of principles and generalizations, rather than effective change in individuals. (Goldman, 1989, pp. 83–84)

Although qualitative research has established its place among research methodologies, it continues to be subject to misconceptions and other challenges. For example, clinicians may have the impression that qualitative research methods require a lengthy investigative process that includes living in the particular setting under study. Active clinicians under this misapprehension would understandably be discouraged from considering this form of research. In addition, clearer guidelines for data gathering and analysis are needed. At present, many of the procedures appear vague, lack structure, and seem confusing. New approaches, such as integrative qualitative analysis, may prove useful in overcoming these challenges, including by clarifying the protocols associated with data gathering and analysis. Silverman (2001, 2011) addressed the challenges associated with maintaining scientific rigor in qualitative research, contending that qualitative research, like quantitative research, should be assessed by evaluating the quality of methods, data, and data analysis. "Silverman (2001) stresses the importance of adhering to sensible and rigorous methods for making sense of data even as we acknowledge that social phenomena are locally and socially constructed through the activities of participants" (Markham, 2004, p. 120).

Single-Subject Designs[1]

Single-subject designs constitute another emerging form of research that offers much promise to the practitioner. These designs may be used with one client or a single group of clients. In single-subject designs, subjects serve as their own controls; the controls are not other individuals or groups as in group designs. Since subjects serve as their own controls, research or evaluation using single-subject designs is considered a single-subject study, even with large numbers of participants (Cooper, Heron, & Heward, 2007). Despite the promise of these designs, Sharpley (2007) has observed that, as had been noted earlier by Lundervold and Belwood (2000), $N = 1$ is still a *secret* to counselors and counselor researchers. To correct this situation, Sharpley has urged counselor educators to adopt a training curriculum such as one outlined by Lundervold and Belwood to prepare their students to apply principles of $N = 1$ research to their everyday clinical practice.

Single-subject designs are classified into three distinct families or groups (Stile, 1993): ABA or "withdrawal" designs, multiple-baseline designs, and comparative treatment designs. This section describes the withdrawal and multiple-baseline designs and their application to counseling research and evaluation. Analysis of effects is delimited to *visual analysis,* as illustrated in Figures 5.3 and 5.4; statistical analysis with single-subject designs is also possible but is beyond the scope of this book. Table 5.1 summarizes the eight major steps involved in applying single-subject design strategies to counseling research or evaluation.

ABA DESIGNS This family of designs gets its name from the simplest single-subject experimental design, which requires *withdrawal* of a treatment in order to measure its effects when it is introduced and again when it is removed. The five

Table 5.1 Steps in Applying Single-Subject Strategies

Step	Procedure
1. Identification	Identify which skills or behaviors will be targeted for change (e.g., "irresponsibility").
2. Definition	Define the targeted skill or behavior in such a way that it can be observed and measured (e.g., "staying out late" provides a more adequate unit of measurement than "irresponsibility").
3. Selection of dependent variable or measure	Select the characteristic of the behavior to be measured and the counseling objective. For example, the *number* of occurrences of staying out late can be measured in relation to a particular treatment. Zero occurrences may be established as the outcome.
4. Identification of independent variable or treatment	Identify the treatment (e.g., counseling technique) to be applied to the dependent variable. For example, logical consequences may be applied to occurrences of staying out late.
5. Completion of planning	Complete all related planning. Decisions made at this step should include who will record the occurrence of the behavior (e.g., staying out late) and how the occurrence of the behavior will be recorded (e.g., tally marks on a simple recording instrument).
6. Training	Train (if appropriate) all other participants to consistently carry out data collection/treatment procedures. For example, all observers should practice collecting data until they reach close agreement on the recording of the dependent variable.
7. Intervention and data collection	Intervene by withholding, applying, or withdrawing the treatment while continuously collecting data on the dependent variable (e.g., number of occurrences).
8. Graphing	Graph the results of the treatment by plotting data points on graph paper and connecting the points to represent trends or by other methods such as entering the data into a spreadsheet software (e.g., Excel) and using the software's graphing functionality.

Source: © Stephen Stile.

most common ABA designs are the A, the B, the A-B, the A-B-A, and the A-B-A-B. The first three designs have been termed *preexperimental* (the A and B designs) and *quasi-experimental* (the A-B design) in relation to their inability to establish cause-and-effect relationships. The A-B-A and A-B-A-B designs are classified as *experimental* designs because they can be used to establish cause and effect with single subjects or groups.

The A Design This design has also been referred to as *case study research,* which is defined as "(a) the in-depth study of (b) one or more instances of a phenomenon (c) in its real-life context that (d) reflects the perspective of the participants involved in the phenomenon" (Gall, Gall, & Borg, 2007, p. 447). In the A design, data are collected on the dependent variable—the behavior you hope to change—over an extended period while treatment is withheld.

The B Design The B design is closely related to the A design. In this design, no baseline observations are made, but dependent variables are monitored throughout the course of a treatment. The B design is generally considered an improvement over the uncontrolled case study method.

The A-B Design The A-B design corrects for some of the weaknesses of the A and B designs. The inquirer begins by selecting a subject or subjects, pinpointing a problem, selecting a dependent variable, and choosing a treatment. Next, the dependent variable is measured during a minimum of three to five baseline (A) observations (Alberto & Troutman, 2006). In the second and final phase of this design, the investigator applies the treatment (B) and measures its effect on the dependent variable. In this design, the baseline can be thought of as a control because it predicts future behavior without intervention. The major objection to this design is the possibility that some other variable may be operating simultaneously with the treatment to bring about change in skills or behavior.

The A-B-A Design The A-B-A design addresses objections to the A-B design by employing a second baseline (A2) as a control. If withdrawal of treatment results in trends in A2 that approximate A1, arguments for a cause-and-effect relationship between the independent and dependent variables gain considerable support. The major shortcoming of the A-B-A design is that it often ends on a "negative note," since a presumably effective treatment is withdrawn (Gall, Gall, & Borg, 2007).

The A-B-A-B Design The A-B-A-B design addresses the major shortcoming of the ABA design because it ends in a second treatment condition, or B2. For this reason, the A-B-A design is rarely the original design of choice anymore. In fact, it is usually used only when attrition prevents the final phase of the A-B-A-B design. Since no limitation exists regarding the length of B2, a successful treatment may be left in place for a lengthy period to help ensure maintenance of change.

The following case illustrates the steps in the application of a member of the ABA family of single-subject designs (the A-B) to evaluate the efficiency of a counseling program. The steps refer to those listed in Table 5.1. The A-B design was chosen because it is easy to apply. Beginning counselors may wish to use this design in a pilot study of a new counseling technique.

Ann was a 17-year-old girl enrolled in a large urban high school. The target behavior identified (step 1 in Table 5.1) in this case was "school phobia." The school principal defined Ann's behavior (step 2) as often refusing to go to school or failing to remain there once she arrived. Ann was referred to the school counselor for assistance with this problem. Before seeing Ann, the school counselor examined her attendance records, which showed she had attended school for the entire day only 40%, 60%, and 20% of the time during the first, second, and third weeks of school, respectively. At this point, the counselor identified percent of attendance as the dependent variable and established the therapeutic objective (step 3) that Ann would attend school 95% of the time every week unless she had a legitimate excuse, such as a family emergency. Next, the counselor identified as the independent variable a treatment package consisting of individual and group counseling sessions and completed all necessary planning (steps 4 and 5). Since training (step 6) was not necessary in this case, the next step was to begin the intervention and data collection (step 7).

A behaviorally oriented approach was used in individual sessions. In these sessions, Ann was helped to understand how school had become threatening to her and how certain physical symptoms—including nausea, diarrhea, and dizziness—were related to her anxiety. After four sessions, Ann was able to enter the counselor's office and attend one class independently. She was then invited to attend weekly group sessions with the school's five other school-phobic students to discuss feelings toward school and related issues.

Over a 4-month period, the counselor observed that Ann developed a caring attitude toward other group members. She met with them before school, and they often walked home together. Beginning with the first group session, Ann was asked to monitor her own school attendance. By the beginning of Christmas vacation (week 15), she reported to the group that her attendance (i.e., the dependent variable) had increased to 100%. Periodic checks at monthly intervals revealed that her attendance remained at this level. The graph developed by Ann and her counselor (step 8) is shown as Figure 5.3.

MULTIPLE-BASELINE DESIGNS A variation of the A-B design is the multiple-baseline design. Frequently, withdrawal designs such as A-B-A or A-B-A-B are inappropriate for a given behavior. For example, a counselor might be viewed as unethical for beginning a second baseline phase when it appears that treatment (e.g., self-monitoring) is associated with a significant reduction of aggressive behavior in the client. As Carr (2005) has explained it, "One of the reasons for the MB design's popularity is that it does not require withdrawal of the independent variable, which may sometimes be impractical or impossible (e.g., a self-management strategy)" (p. 219).

The three major multiple-baseline designs are multiple baseline across behaviors, multiple baseline across settings, and multiple baseline across subjects. All three may be thought of as extensions of the A-B design illustrated by the case of Ann.

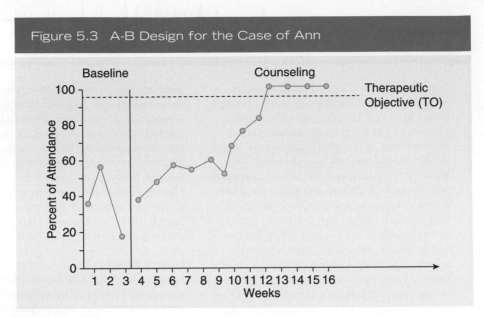

Figure 5.3   A-B Design for the Case of Ann

Source: © Stephen Stile.

Multiple Baseline Across Behaviors This design is intended for use with single subjects or groups. When used with groups, arithmetic means are calculated, and the group is treated as a single subject. When using the across-behaviors design, the inquirer is cautioned to select behaviors that are independent of one another. Borg and Gall (1989) explained this need for caution as follows:

> Independence is demonstrated by a change in the target behavior to which the treatment is being applied while other target behaviors (or controls) maintain a stable baseline rate. If other behaviors change reliably from baseline, the multiple-baseline design is invalid. (p. 585)

Multiple Baseline Across Settings The across-settings design is also intended for use with single groups or subjects. In this design, the effect of a treatment on a dependent variable is studied in independent temporal and/or physical settings.

Multiple Baseline Across Subjects The across-subjects design is used for inquiry with matched groups. For example, Gardill and Browder (1995) used this methodology to examine the effectiveness of training students with severe behavior disorders and developmental disabilities to use money independently.

The following case illustrates the steps in implementing the design of multiple baseline across behaviors in a counseling situation. As shown in Figure 5.4, the design requires that the counselor apply a treatment (B) to a *succession* of behaviors that are being baselined (A). The steps refer to those shown in Table 5.1.

Drew was an 18-year-old college freshman living at home with his mother and father. The target behavior identified (step 1) by counselor and parents was "irresponsibility." Irresponsible behavior was defined as (a) staying out too late on school nights, (b) not parking the car in the garage, and (c) not putting his father's tools away after use (step 2). After closely observing these behaviors for 5 days, Drew's father established the number of occurrences of irresponsible behavior as the dependent variable and set zero occurrences of the behavior as the therapeutic objective (step 3). After a lengthy discussion, the counselor and family decided that *logical consequences* (Dreikurs & Soltz, 1964) would be the treatment approach used in response to Drew's irresponsible behaviors (step 4). That is, Drew would experience the consequences of his behavior. Planning was completed (step 5) when it was decided that Drew would experience a logical consequence immediately upon occurrence of an irresponsible behavior. In addition, application of the logical consequences would be applied sequentially as follows: (a) first, only to staying out late; (b) second, to inappropriate car parking; and (c) finally, to all three behaviors (staying out late, inappropriately parking the car,

and not putting away the tools). Drew's father and mother were then trained by the counselor to tally occurrences of the three behaviors using a simple record-keeping instrument (step 6).

The treatment began (step 7) with Drew being told that he would lose the privilege of going out on school nights (Sunday through Thursday) if he came home after 11:00 p.m. After 5 more days, the logical consequence treatment was also applied to his parking the car: If he did not park the car in the garage, he would be unable to use it. Finally, after an additional 5 days (day 16), the logical consequence strategy was applied to putting his father's tools away: If Drew failed to put his father's tools away after using them, he would be unable to borrow them. Thus beginning on day 16, the treatment was applied to all three behaviors, with Drew's mother and father continuing observations and data collection. His father charted Drew's progress on a graph (step 8), as shown in Figure 5.4. The use of logical consequences appears to have resulted in the elimination of each of the problem behaviors targeted for change. In addition, the zero rate of occurrence was maintained until the treatment and monitoring were withdrawn after 40 days.

EVALUATION OF SINGLE-SUBJECT DESIGNS Single-case designs offer much potential for the active clinician. They provide an objective means to evaluate what is occurring in the counseling process with one client or one group of clients over time. Unfortunately, however, counselors rarely apply single-subject designs to report their findings. Sharpley (2007) has urged the use of $N = 1$ designs by counselors to show their clients that the services provided are having a favorable impact and to demonstrate to funding agencies that counseling is cost-effective. An additional benefit is that use of single-subject designs can give counselors feedback regarding their treatment programs and what adjustments may be needed. When applied in counseling, single-subject designs have been used primarily in conjunction with behavioral approaches. Additional research and development are necessary to expand their use to accommodate other schools of counseling.

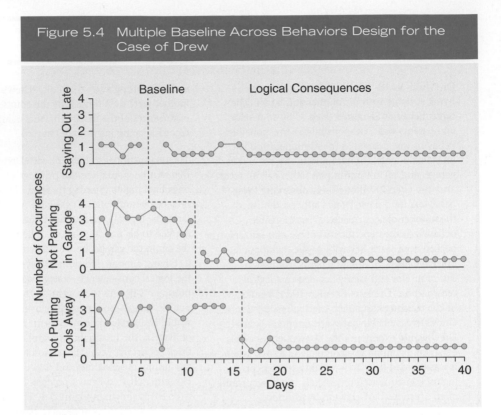

Figure 5.4 Multiple Baseline Across Behaviors Design for the Case of Drew

Source: © Stpehen Stile.

Diversity and Postmodern Issues in Research and Evaluation

A multicultural counseling perspective must be applied to all aspects of the counseling process (including research and evaluation). The multicultural perspective enables counselors, like artists, to sensitively navigate diversity issues that may have an impact on scientific investigations. For example, it is common to consider issues of age, gender, sexual orientation, socioeconomic status, race, ethnicity, culture, and spirituality when designing a research study.

Another issue relating to diversity and multicultural research is the role of white researchers. Some are concerned that the field of multicultural counseling has been dominated by white researchers at the expense of minority researchers (Mio &

Iwamasa, 1993). Atkinson (1993) contended that the major issues in this debate relate to ethics and turf. Ethical concerns center on determining who is in the best position to realistically evaluate multicultural counseling. The answer to this question will no doubt impact issues of turf. Pedersen (1993) maintained that a central problem in the debate relates to an oversimplification and polarization of categories, such as majority-minority, and that there is a need for all researchers to work toward a common ground characterized by shared interests.

Postmodernism, based on a subjective view of reality, appears to parallel characteristics of qualitative research and the art of counseling. Examples of postmodern research, case studies and in-depth interviews, provide opportunities to discover meanings from a participant's stories. Modernism adheres to an objective view of reality and therefore has more in common with quantitative research and the science of counseling. The modernists' fixed view of reality fits with quantitative research, which is characterized by statistically focused hypothesis testing that attempts to seek out "the truth" in definitive black-and-white terms.

Gergen (1994a) made a case for postmodern research and its subjective view of truth, contending that research that adheres to universal assumptions regarding reality and knowledge may convey inaccurate, misleading, and potentially harmful information about what is to be regarded as the truth. Gergen suggested that researchers should be aware of how sociocultural forces and language create multiple realities. For example, many Western cultures recognize depression and treat millions with antidepressant medications, whereas individuals from other cultures have survived for centuries without the concept of depression reflected in their language.

According to D'Andrea and Foster Heckman (2008b), the multicultural movement is characterized by faith and hope—faith that research will result in increased awareness and understanding of multicultural issues and hope that these insights will contribute to human dignity and mental health. These authors made a number of recommendations for future multicultural research (e.g., investigate the efficacy of multicultural competencies and alternative helping strategies). Research initiatives are underway to develop research instruments that can be used to assess multicultural competencies. Kim, Cartwright, Asay, and D'Andrea (2003) developed the Multicultural Knowledge Skills Survey–Counselor Edition Revised (MAKSS-CE-R) as a self-report instrument that could be used to assess multicultural competency. Cartwright, Daniels, and Zhang (2008) compared self-report ratings on the MAKSS-CE-R with independent observer ratings of videotaped counseling sessions. They found that self-reported assessments of students in training were inflated compared to the ratings of independent observers. The researchers concluded that multicultural competency research should not rely solely on self-reports but should also include the assessment of independent observers.

SUMMARY

Research and evaluation are an ongoing facet of the counseling process. Research strategies serve several functions, such as offering a means of evaluating the efficacy of a counseling approach, communicating accountability, and contributing to the body of knowledge relating to the counseling profession. Research and evaluation can also contribute to the science-of-counseling model by providing objective information regarding the counseling process. The practice of research and evaluation is both an art and a science, with approaches such as qualitative methodologies, action research, and single-subject designs encouraging clinicians to develop flexible, creative strategies of evaluation.

PERSONAL EXPLORATION

1. How is qualitative research similar to postmodern theory?

2. How do theory, research, and practice influence each other?

3. What are the strengths and weaknesses of single-subject research designs?

4. How can issues of diversity such as culture, ethnicity, gender, sexual orientation, socioeconomic status, and age be addressed by research?

5. What would be some rewards and challenges of conducting research?

6. What are mixed-methods research methodologies, and what are potential strengths of this approach?

7. What are some potential benefits of action research?

8. What factors should be considered in program evaluation, and how does program evaluation promote accountability?

9. What are examples of research methodologies that you find interesting, and what intrigues you about them?

10. If you could publish something on a topic, what would that topic be, and why would it be important to you?

LEARNING ACTIVITIES

1. Interview one or more individuals who have conducted research or evaluations to explore what they believe are challenges and rewards regarding these endeavors.

2. Develop a research question and obtain feedback regarding your question and ideas about how to answer it from a professor or another source.

NOTE

1. The section on single-subject designs was written by Dr. Stephen W. Stile.

WEBSITES

Boeree, C. G. (1997). *Qualitative methods workbook.* Retrieved from http://www.ship.edu/~cgboeree/ qualmeth.html. *Provides an interesting but lengthy description ("workbook") of qualitative research methods.*

Borgatti, S. (2009). *An overview of grounded theory.* http://www.analytictech.com/mb870/introtoGT.htm. *Provides an overview of the goals of grounded theory and the methods used to implement it in research.*

PART 2

Multicultural Counseling and Counseling Theories

Part Two provides guidelines for formulating a personal approach to counseling within a multicultural perspective, and it offers an overview of counseling theories. Part Two comprises the following four chapters.

Developing a Personal Approach to Counseling From a Multicultural Perspective

The Art and Science of Developing a Personal Approach to Counseling From a Multicultural Perspective

Developing a personal approach to counseling from a multicultural perspective is both an art and a science. It is an art to draw together multiple factors, such as personal preferences, **diversity issues**, and client characteristics, to develop and implement a counseling approach. The art of counseling begins with self-assessment to identify strengths, weaknesses, attitudes, and beliefs that can promote or inhibit the counseling process. Counselors are then encouraged to work toward developing personal characteristics that promote optimal development in the client. The science of developing a personal approach involves using research to determine the efficacy of theories and procedures so as to maximize the use of proven approaches throughout the counseling process.

The multicultural perspective contributes a critical dimension to the development of a personal approach to counseling. It can be thought of as a lens through which multicultural issues can be brought into focus during the counseling process. The art of multicultural counseling lies in the counselor's skill in adjusting this lens to accurately assess and respond to issues of diversity such as socioeconomic status, culture, gender, and sexual orientation. A related challenge in the art of counseling is learning how to adjust traditional counseling theories and procedures from a multicultural perspective to meet the unique and emerging needs of clients. This can involve recognizing the value of alternative methods of helping, such as traditional healers like the medicine men of American Indians. The art of counseling also offers counselors opportunities to experience and be enriched by multiculturalism. For example, they can take an interest

Chapter Overview

This chapter provides guidelines for formulating a personal approach to counseling and addresses issues relating to multicultural counseling. Highlights of the chapter include the following:

- **Developing a personal approach to counseling from a multicultural perspective**

- **An eight-stage model for developing a personal approach to counseling**

- **Terms and concepts used in multicultural counseling**

- **Potential challenges in multicultural counseling and guidelines for navigating these challenges** in the traditional art of a culture (such as Navajo weaving) to explore such issues as acculturation, worldview, and identity development, thereby gaining an awareness of individual differences and relational-contextual issues that can affect clients.

The science of multicultural counseling is entering an exciting phase. Competencies have been identified that promote awareness, knowledge, and skills associated with multicultural counseling. Traditional schools of counseling and research methodology are being reassessed from a multicultural perspective to overcome such problems as bias toward the white, middle-class, male model of counseling. Theories basic to counseling (e.g., developmental theories) are being modified to accommodate diversity issues such as gender and culture. Carol Gilligan's (1982, 1993) seminal work on female moral development is an excellent example of these exciting trends.

Hansen (2002) has identified postmodern implications for the art and science of counseling. He suggested that traditional counseling approaches are grounded in science, which can promote a career-long adherence to a particular approach. Hansen contended that when "approaches are conceptualized as narrative explanatory structures, beginning counselors can create less rigid professional identities that will naturally translate into more flexible, client-centered practice" (p. 321). The counselor can then help clients view their world from a creative new vantage point (a hallmark of the arts), which coincides with Hansen's view of counseling as a persuasive art that helps clients transition from despair to hope and from helplessness to personal autonomy.

Developing a Personal Approach to Counseling

All counselors and counselors in training have their own approach to counseling. Some put a considerable amount of time and effort into developing their approach, whereas others simply "do counseling." Using a personal approach that is the result of careful planning enhances the complex process of counseling.

Over the years, approaches to counseling have proliferated. Lynn and Garske (1985) noted more than 130, many of which they say were far from the mainstream and of questionable value. They also noted that a shift in emphasis appears to have taken place from more to fewer theories, creating an optimal climate for the integration of theories. Norcross and Beutler (2014) and Lazarus and Beutler (1993) supported the view that there is a trend toward integration and eclecticism. Several factors appear to be contributing to this trend (Norcross & Newman, 1992): (1) No one theory can possibly address the diversified needs of clients, (2) research has shown similar efficacy rates for the various counseling theories, and (3) the movement toward short-term counseling has required modification in the implementation of theories. With so many forces at work, it is not surprising that 30% to 50% of clinical and counseling psychologists surveyed consider themselves to be eclectic or integrative (Norcross & Newman), and 64% of counselors claim to be eclectic (Norcross, Prochaska, & Gallagher, 1989).

Historically, some have considered eclecticism to be a disjointed approach, whereby a counselor employs various theories and techniques without the benefit of an internally consistent psychological frame of reference (Wachtel, 1991). Adherents of the eclectic approach often lack a clear sense of structure or direction in the counseling process and struggle with such problems as how to shift from one therapeutic modality to another (Wachtel). Lazarus and Beutler (1993) referred to this type of eclecticism as *unsystematic eclecticism*, contending that the smorgasbord approach to counseling lacks clinical precision and contributes to confusion in counseling.

Lazarus and Beutler (1993) described *technical eclecticism*, one of the many models of eclecticism and integration that have emerged, as a practical and effective method of conceptualizing a personal approach to counseling. They summarized the basic tenets of technical eclecticism as follows:

> Technical eclectics select procedures from different sources without necessarily subscribing to the theories that spawned them; they work within a preferred theory (Dryden, 1987) but recognize that few techniques are inevitably wedded to any theory. Hence, they borrow techniques from other orientations, based on the proven worth of these procedures. (p. 384)

Technical eclecticism favors restricting the theories and techniques used to those that have proven their efficacy through research and those that contribute to systematic decision making in treatment planning. For example, the school of counseling called *multimodal therapy* developed by Lazarus (2000) is based on social learning theory, general systems theory, and group and communication theory. Central to this approach is the concept of the BASIC I.D., which provides a conceptual model for treatment planning (see Chapter 4).

Theoretical integration is another recognized model for formulating a personal approach to counseling. It involves the synthesis of two or more counseling theories (Norcross & Beutler, 2014), for example, the recent trend toward integrating cognitive and behavioral counseling. The complete integration of one school of counseling with another would be a daunting task, however, as Warwar and Greenberg (2000) pointed out. They suggested instead that the future will see an integration of elements of two or more theories, such as the assimilation of cognitions into humanistic approaches and emotions into cognitive therapy.

Assimilative integration, a form of integrative psychotherapy that is grounded in a central theory of psychotherapy, also assimilates aspects of other theories (Norcross & Beutler, 2014). Several others have suggested that theoretical integration should be based on a core counseling theory, such as Adlerian or existential, to promote internal consistency and a sense of structure and direction for counseling (Ginter, 1988; McBride & Martin, 1990; Wachtel, 1991; Watts, 1993).

A Personal Note

As a professor, I would help my counseling students prepare for their final "exit" exam for their counseling program. They often needed help articulating their personal approach to counseling and applying it to a case during their oral exam. I told them a simple way to do this was by using the analogy of the onion. The onion model encourages integration of theories from the various schools of counseling as well as the use of a multicultural perspective.

- The center of the onion can be considered one's philosophical foundation of counseling, which should be consistent with one's professional identity. Historically, the counseling profession has embraced a preventative-developmental-strengths perspective. In contrast, psychiatry, clinical psychology, and social work have their historical roots in the medical model and symptom reduction. In the future, counseling may be a balance of both (e.g., focus on developmental-preventative approaches and symptom reduction).

- The first layer of the onion from the center is the theory of personality. It provides the tools necessary for understanding human behavior, such as psychological constructs to help generalize and predict behavior (see Chapter 7).

- The second layer of the onion from the center incorporates theories of counseling and their associated counseling techniques for addressing counseling goals.

- The final, outermost layer of the onion addresses the unique and emerging needs of clients from a multicultural perspective.

Research and evaluation should be ongoing and allow for updating and modifying one's approach as necessary.

My students really appreciated this simple, yet comprehensive, model of counseling. They all did really well on their final oral exam and commented that the onion model helped them conceptualize and implement their "personal counseling theory."

Using the core approach to theory integration, one combines technical eclecticism with theoretical integration to develop a personal counseling approach. Doing so requires an in-depth understanding of at least one counseling theory to establish a core theory. The classic theories of Freud, Adler, and Jung, described in Chapter 7, are ideal for this purpose, since they include a comprehensive theory of personality to complement their theory of counseling. The core theory will help establish a degree of internal consistency, and the counselor can then select components from other counseling theories to meet the unique and emerging needs of clients. The techniques and procedures used should be supported by research and lead to appropriate treatment planning.

The **common factors** approach is another method of integrating psychotherapies. The common factors approach attempts to identify counseling strategies that different schools of psychotherapy share that are perceived to be curative and associated with positive therapeutic outcomes. Norcross and Beutler (2014) noted that the common factors most often cited are a positive therapeutic relationship (the most important one), the experience of catharsis or closure regarding a problem, the acquisition and utilization of new behaviors, and the client's positive expectations and hope regarding counseling.

Raskin, Rogers, and Witty (2014) provided an overview of common factors research and counseling outcomes. They found that approximately 30% of counseling efficacy could be attributed to therapeutic factors such as the counseling relationship, 15% was associated with counseling techniques, 15% related to the client's expectations of counseling, and 40% related to client variables and contextual-environmental issues (e.g., client's support system, resiliency, nature of client problems, and client's life experiences). Results of these studies suggest that the counseling relationship and client variables appear to be significantly more important to counseling efficacy than are counseling techniques.

An Eight-Stage Model for Developing a Personal Approach

The following eight-stage model can be used to develop a personal approach to counseling. The eight stages are self-assessment, a survey of supportive disciplines, an overview of major counseling theories, intensive study of one counseling theory, sensitivity to individual differences, integration of techniques from counseling theories, implementation, and research and evaluation.

Stage 1: Self-Assessment

Self-assessment helps counselors understand their values, beliefs, strengths, and weaknesses. With self-awareness, counselors can avoid overreacting in counseling and can use their strengths to maximize their effectiveness. Vontress (1988) has noted that self-knowledge may be the best predictor of effective living because it provides a clear direction in life and is necessary to making meaningful decisions. Richardson and Molinaro (1996) noted that multicultural sensitivity can be enhanced by counselors engaging in self-awareness exercises that explore their values, cultural identity, and worldview. McWhirter (1994) expanded on the need for multicultural self-awareness, noting that counselors should pay more attention to the *person of the counselor* in terms of how counselors can be vehicles of cultural oppression.

Counselors can undertake a self-assessment in numerous ways. Perhaps the most comprehensive approach is to obtain formal counseling. Through the use of tests and other counseling strategies, counselors can gain information about their self-concept, personality, interests, values, aptitudes, and other important aspects of the self. Many training programs—for example, in psychiatry—require students to undertake analysis by a psychotherapist for 1 year or longer in the belief that the experience can help provide students with personal insights necessary to becoming effective helpers.

Self-assessment through personal counseling or other procedures can generate an understanding of personal characteristics that may or may not be helpful in counseling. These were outlined in Chapter 1 and include being encouraging, empathic and caring, patient, nonjudgmental, and flexible. Such characteristics can enable counselors to use the "self as an instrument of change." With these characteristics, counselors can facilitate the counseling process by fostering the core conditions of unconditional positive regard, self-disclosure, empathy, and respect.

Stage 2: Survey of Supportive Disciplines

A variety of disciplines can contribute to the development of a personal approach to counseling, but psychology and medicine are perhaps the most relevant. Other useful disciplines may be philosophy, theology, anthropology, sociology, and literature. A brief description of each of these disciplines follows.

PSYCHOLOGY   Psychology is a vital discipline for counselors to draw from since it encompasses the major schools of counseling and psychotherapy, which are the topics of Chapters 7, 8, and 9. Psychology also has a number of specialties that can contribute to a counselor's personal theory. The following list summarizes the relevant aspects of some of these specialties:

- *Clinical and counseling psychology* investigates how psychological tests and other helping skills can be used in the counseling process.

- *Developmental psychology* helps counselors gain an understanding of how human growth and development take place over the life span. The counseling profession emphasizes the importance of a developmental perspective, which enables counselors to adapt their approaches to the unique needs of clients at different stages in their lives.

- *Experimental psychology* provides an important link to the science-of-counseling model by identifying research strategies for evaluating counseling approaches and processes.

- *Abnormal psychology* provides an overview of mental disorders and helps counselors learn how to use this information in the process of assessment and diagnosis.

- *Multicultural psychology* explores how psychology varies across cultures. This knowledge can be particularly important in developing a counseling perspective that addresses the needs of diverse clients.

- *School psychology* focuses on the use of psychological tests in the school setting to assess personality, intelligence, aptitude, and achievement.

- *Physiological psychology* explores the physiological foundations of psychology. It can contribute a frame of reference for understanding physiological factors associated with behavior, cognition, and emotions.

- *Social psychology* explores psychology from a social perspective. It is a promising approach to counseling research because it identifies paradigms relating to the social forces that influence the counseling process.

MEDICINE   Medicine is another important discipline for study to develop some theoretical grounding. The mind and body are not separate entities but an interrelated whole. To understand one, it is essential to have some knowledge of the other. The following *Personal Note* illustrates how some physical illnesses can cause psychiatric symptoms, such as hallucinations.

A Personal Note

A doctor suspected that a female patient had a schizophrenic disorder because she was having auditory hallucinations (was hearing voices) and referred the woman to me. My psychological evaluation of the patient did not suggest that she was suffering from schizophrenia. In reviewing her hospital chart, however, I noticed that she had been diagnosed as having syphilis more than 10 years earlier and that there was no record of her successfully completing treatment for the condition. I knew that syphilis could cause hallucinations, so I referred the patient back to the physician to begin medical treatment for syphilis. I also arranged for the patient to see a consulting psychiatrist, who gave her medication for the auditory hallucinations.

Psychiatry is a medical specialty that has direct relevance to counseling. The three "classic" theorists, who will be discussed in Chapter 7, were all psychiatrists. Psychiatry is the study of human behavior from a medical perspective. Psychiatrists have a special interest in how pathology, or abnormality, in the brain and nervous system can cause mental disorders such as schizophrenia and major depression. They also have special training in the use of medications to treat these mental disorders. A basic background in psychiatry can help counselors differentiate between a medical problem and a psychological problem so that the client can receive the appropriate treatment. It can also assist counselors in understanding physiological factors associated with mental disorders.

PHILOSOPHY Philosophy can provide a valuable foundation for counselors as they develop a personal approach. It can help them broaden and enrich how they see life and clarify their beliefs, attitudes, and values. The following issues may be useful to explore in undertaking a study of philosophy:

1. Do people have free will?

2. What is the purpose of anxiety in life? Is it something to be avoided at all cost?

3. In order to experience love and joy, must one also be able to bear pain and sorrow?

4. Are people inherently good or bad, or is their nature primarily determined by environmental forces?

The study of philosophy can help counselors explore these and other relevant issues. It can also help counselors become aware of personal biases so that they can avoid imposing their biases on clients.

A major school of philosophy that may be particularly interesting to counselors is existentialism. Existentialism contends that people are self-determined and have free will, which they can use to make choices in life. William Shakespeare (1603/1938) summed up the spirit of existentialism when he wrote, "To be or not to be—that is the question." The writings of several noted philosophers can be used to develop a philosophical perspective (a list of recommended reading is provided at the end of this chapter). Kahlil Gibran's (1965) popular book *The Prophet* expresses philosophical views that are easy to understand. It covers a wide variety of topics, from children to love; the following is an excerpt from the section on children:

ON CHILDREN

And a woman who held a babe against her bosom said, Speak to us of children. And he said: Your children are not your children. They are the sons and daughters of life's longing for itself. They come through you but not from you. You may give them your love but not your thoughts, for they have their own thoughts. You may house their bodies but not their souls, for their souls dwell in the house of tomorrow, which you cannot visit, not even in your dreams. You may strive to be like them, but seek not to make them like you. For life goes not backward nor tarries with yesterday. You are the bows from which your children as living arrows are sent forth. The archer sees the mark upon the path of the infinite, and he bends you with his might that his arrows may go swift and far. Let your bending in the archer's hand be for gladness; for even as he loves the arrow that flies, so he loves also the bow that is stable. (pp. 17–18)

THEOLOGY Theology is the study of spirituality and religion and incorporates various schools of philosophy. Traditionally, theological concepts have not played a significant role in counseling. Most counselors have viewed religion as a personal, private matter that is not necessary or appropriate to explore with a client. An exception to this viewpoint is found in pastoral counseling, in which counselors practice from a particular religious perspective. In those situations, the client often seeks counseling from a religious orientation. Many churches employ counselors for this purpose.

Spirituality can be used as a theological foundation for a personal approach to counseling, and it represents an important consideration in multicultural counseling (Bishop, 1995; Richards & Bergin, 1997). Spirituality is considered endemic to all people, whereas religion serves as a structure and focus for the spiritual realm (Ingersoll, 1995). Recognition of the strength and support people draw from spirituality is contributing to its acceptance as an important dimension of the counseling process (Miranti & Burke, 1995). When religious issues do come up in counseling, clients tend to expect counselors to be supportive of their religion or attend to psychological issues and not challenge their religious beliefs (Morrow, Worthington, & McCullough, 1993).

Worthington (1989) identified five reasons why counselors should make more of an effort to include spiritual and religious considerations in formulating their approach to counseling:

1. A high percentage of people in the United States are religious.

2. People often turn to religion during an emotional crisis.

3. Clients (especially religious clients) are reluctant to mention religious issues during secular therapy.

4. Counselors do not tend to be as religiously oriented as their clients.

5. Since many counselors are not as religiously oriented as their clients, they tend to be less informed about religion and are therefore less helpful to these clients.

Worthington (1989) has provided guidelines for incorporating spiritual and religious issues into the counseling process, including information on spiritual and religious faith across the life span and its implications for counseling and research.

Four of the helping orientations to religious and spiritual issues in counseling are rejectionist, exclusivist, constructivist, and pluralist (Zinnbauer & Pargament, 2000). Rejectionist and exclusivist represent rigid, extreme positions and are not considered useful perspectives for counselors. Rejectionists are essentially atheists; because they reject the notion of God and religion, they restrict opportunities for addressing spirituality and religion in counseling. Exclusivists on the other hand take an "orthodox" religious position, embracing a rigid definition of God and religion. Exclusivists contend that counselors and clients must share the same religion or spiritual worldview to be able to effectively work together in counseling.

In contrast, constructivism and pluralism are believed to be flexible, useful approaches for addressing religious/spiritual issues in counseling (Zinnbauer & Pargament, 2000). Constructivists do not believe in one ultimate reality, contending instead that individuals construct their own personal meanings and reality. They take a phenomenological perspective and attempt to communicate respect and understanding for whatever realities (including atheism) clients construct. However, unconditional acceptance of clients' values and beliefs can be counterproductive when those values and beliefs support self-defeating or destructive worldviews (e.g., when parents use religion to justify excessive punishment of children). Pluralists, unlike constructivists, believe that there is an ultimate spiritual reality and that God does exist. Although pluralists have a well-thought-out religious orientation, they (unlike exclusivists) can also appreciate the value and merits of other religions.

Theological issues can have an impact on virtually all aspects of the counseling process. Smith (1993) suggested that it is especially important to explore the religious-spiritual needs of the dying, noting that 79% of people surveyed believed that spiritual issues would play an important role in attaining a "healthy" death. Smith described the theological counseling tools that can be used with dying clients. For example, the client can be asked to write a "healthy death story" describing the ideal death. Smith recommends that counselors use these tools to explore clients' theological concerns, struggles, and resources.

Another impetus for incorporating a theological perspective is multicultural counseling (Pate & Bondi, 1992). According to Pate and Bondi, spiritual and religious beliefs are part of clients' cultural backgrounds and should therefore be taken into account. Multicultural counseling and therapy (MCT; Sue, Ivey, & Pedersen, 1996/2007) provide evidence of the need to address religious and spiritual issues. According to MCT (Sue, Ivey, & Pedersen), counselors need to modify conventional helping roles to accommodate various cultural groups, especially those from non-Western cultures. In a 16-country survey, Lee, Oh, and Mountcastle (1992) found the three main sources of healing to be communal groups and family, spiritualism and religion, and traditional healers. Counselors can effectively broaden their helping role by including these important sources of healing through using interventions (such as family counseling and support groups), addressing theological issues, and recognizing the value of culturally relevant healers.

The holistic health movement also recognizes the value of addressing all aspects of the mind and body (including spiritual issues) to foster health and wellness. Dealing with spiritual issues can be part of a holistic approach to the prevention and treatment of depression (Westgate, 1996). A spiritual void is associated with depressive symptomology such as meaninglessness, emptiness, alienation, and hopelessness (Westgate). The spiritually well person is able to draw strength from religion to gain meaning and a sense of direction in life. The four spiritual dimensions that counselors can use to overcome problems with depression are "a sense of meaning in life, a transcendent perspective, an intrinsic value system, and a sense of belonging to a spiritual community of shared values and support" (Westgate, p. 26).

Spirituality as a dimension of counseling offers many opportunities and challenges. It appears to fit the emerging strengths perspective in counseling, such as that used in brief-solution-focused counseling. Counselors can encourage clients to use their faith (including, if appropriate, prayer) as a strength to help them deal with the challenges they face. Unfortunately, many counselors appear to be unprepared to relate effectively to spiritual issues in counseling (Genia, 1994). According to Genia, counselor educators can play an important role in educating future counselors about the spiritual dimension by providing training on spirituality, for example, coursework on religion (e.g., the psychology of religion) and supervised experience in counseling religious clients. Additional research on counseling and spirituality seems warranted.

ANTHROPOLOGY Mental health cultural anthropology, a specialty within cultural anthropology (the study of cultures), investigates mental health issues unique to a particular culture. The mental health–cultural anthropology perspective can be particularly useful in addressing cross-cultural issues in counseling. For example, Topper (1985) has investigated Navajo alcoholism and treatment in terms of a changing cultural environment.

SOCIOLOGY A basic premise of sociology, the study of social group behavior, is that a person's behavior is primarily determined by social interaction. For example, during the socialization process, a person is encouraged to conform to the norms and laws of society. Many different groups and institutions can exert a significant influence on personality development—family, friends, church, the workplace, and school. A counselor may be interested in discovering how these factors have affected the client.

LITERATURE The paths of literature and psychology have often crossed, creating new perspectives for understanding the psychology of people and exploring the counseling process. Adler emphasized the importance of literature in the development of individual psychology:

> Some day soon it will be realized that the artist is the leader of mankind on the path to the absolute truth. Among poetic works of art which have led me to the insights of Individual Psychology, the following stand out as pinnacles: fairy tales, the Bible, Shakespeare, and Goethe. (Ansbacher & Ansbacher, 1956, p. 291)

Numerous possibilities exist in literature for exploring its implications for counseling. For example, Adlerian psychotherapy and lifestyle analysis have been related to the investigative strategies employed by Sherlock Holmes (Nystul, 1978a). In his (1971) analysis of *The Wizard of Oz,* Kopp noted that Dorothy is similar to a client in search of herself and the Wizard can be perceived as her counselor. As Dorothy journeys through the Land of Oz, she encounters the Scarecrow, the Tin Man, and the Cowardly Lion. These characters become her support system, and each develops insights into life:

> Acquiring wisdom involves risking being wrong or foolish; being loving and tender requires a willingness to bear unhappiness; courage is the confidence to face danger, though afraid; gaining freedom and power requires only a willingness to recognize their existence and to face their consequences. We can find ourselves only when we are willing to risk losing ourselves to another, to the moment, to a quest, and love is the bridge. (Kopp, p. 98)

Bibliotherapy is another connection between literature and counseling (see Chapter 8). Bibliotherapy involves having clients read books or other literary works in order to promote certain outcomes, such as anxiety reduction and stress management. Gelso and Fassinger (1990) suggested that counselors should take client characteristics into account when determining whether self-help literature is appropriate.

Stage 3: Overview of Major Counseling Theories

An overview of the major schools of counseling theories (see Chapters 7, 8, and 9) alerts counselors to the various theoretical perspectives available to use with different clients. One central theory can then be selected as the foundation of an integrative approach.

Stage 4: Intensive Study of One Counseling Theory

A solid foundation in theory is necessary for developing a personal approach to counseling. Indeed, the importance of a theoretical foundation is evident in all disciplines. For example, music students usually benefit from studying music theory and learning to read music before creating their own musical compositions. The same is true of counseling. After students have established an in-depth theoretical foundation, they are ready to develop their own personal style and approach. The theory selected for in-depth study should include a comprehensive theory of personality so that the student acquires an understanding of the dynamics of behavior. The theory should be well thought out and include an understanding of the counseling process. In this way, it can provide internal consistency in terms of how counselors understand and work with a client.

Counselors who do not have a well-thought-out theory are prone to superficial and fragmented personality assessment. They are likely to have a technique-oriented approach to counseling, thinking, for example, "With this client, I'll use this theory's suggested technique." It is important for counselors to read books and articles written by the originator of the theory they have selected; reading about an approach in a textbook will not provide an in-depth understanding. Training in an institute associated with the theory, such as the Gestalt Institute in Arizona, can also help counselors develop expertise in a particular school of counseling. In addition, it may be useful to join a professional organization associated with the chosen theory, like the North American Society of Individual Psychology for counselors interested in Adlerian psychology.

Stage 5: Sensitivity to Individual Differences

Recent trends in counseling have emphasized that counseling interventions must be matched with client characteristics and particularly with client needs, plans, and goals (Warwar & Greenberg, 2000). Counselors should not force a client to fit into their personal approach. I refer to this as "forcing square pegs into round holes" (Nystul, 1981). On the contrary, a counselor's approach should be adjusted to the unique and emerging needs of the client, and the counselor should be sensitive to individual differences. Multicultural issues are particularly important in making the counseling process relevant to the needs of the client. The next section of this chapter describes how these issues can be used to formulate one's personal approach to counseling.

Another way of matching interventions with client characteristics is in terms of how clients engage in problem solving regarding "spaces of perception." This theory suggests there are three spaces of perception: near-, mid-, and far-spaced (Nystul, 1981). *Near-spaced* clients tend to want a lot of detail in problem solving. For example, they want to know exactly what and how they are supposed to do something. These clients may be better able to utilize behavioral approaches that incorporate the monitoring of behavior with graphs and other objective procedures. At the other extreme are *far-spaced* clients. These are people who hate to be pinned down by a lot of details. They do not want to be locked into a preconceived method of problem solving. An existential or humanistically oriented approach may be more in keeping with their mode of problem solving. *Mid-spaced* clients have difficulty making decisions. They tend to want others to make decisions and resolve problems for them. Reality therapy or Gestalt therapy may help these clients become aware of choices and accept responsibility for their behavior.

Garfield (1994) provided an extensive review of the literature on client variables in terms of continuation and outcome in counseling and psychotherapy. For example, clients from an upper socioeconomic status tend to stay longer in counseling and have less tendency to engage in premature termination. Among other variables, some evidence suggests degree of disturbance is related to outcome, with extreme disturbance being negatively correlated with positive outcomes in counseling.

Stage 6: Integration of Techniques From Counseling Theories

In an integrative counseling approach, counselors may draw from different counseling theories to add to their repertoire of counseling techniques. In doing so, students may find more commonalities than differences among these theories. Subtle differences do exist, however, and these enable counselors to adjust their approach to the particular problems that present themselves in the counseling session.

Stage 7: Implementation

As counselors make the transition from theory to practice, they begin to implement their approach. The application of one's approach is an art—a creative process that varies according to the particular clinical situation.

Stage 8: Research and Evaluation

Research and evaluation enable counselors and counselors in training to determine the efficacy of their approach, use the literature to refine their approach, and contribute to the literature. Chapter 5 provides information pertaining to this important topic.

Multicultural Counseling

The preceding discussion suggests that a personal approach to counseling should incorporate a multicultural perspective that is sensitive to the individual differences reflected in contemporary society. Pedersen (1991a) contended that **multicultural counseling** has become a fourth force—after psychodynamic, behavioral, and humanistic counseling—and is relevant to all aspects of counseling as a generic rather than as an exotic perspective. More recently, social justice has been described as the fifth force in counseling (Sandage, Crabtree, & Schweer, 2014). Corey and Corey (2016) noted that "the social justice perspective is based on the premise that oppression, privilege, and social inequities do exist and have a negative impact on the lives of many persons from diverse cultural groups" and that advocacy strategies are necessary to overcome these oppressive forces.

The next section describes key terms and concepts associated with some of the major multicultural counseling issues. Then the two following sections provide an overview of multicultural counseling and therapy (MCT), identify potential problems associated with multicultural counseling, and provide guidelines for developing a multicultural perspective.

Terms and Concepts

The following explanations are intended to help clarify the many terms and concepts relating to multicultural counseling, which can be difficult to differentiate and can therefore obscure meaning:

- *Culture,* an ambiguous concept that defies definition, can in a broad sense be thought of as "things a stranger needs to know to behave appropriately in a particular setting" (Pedersen, 1988, p. viii).

- *Race* "refers to a pseudobiological system of classifying persons by a shared genetic history or physical characteristics such as skin color" (Pedersen, p. viii).

- *Minority* "generally refers to a group receiving differential and unequal treatment because of collective discrimination" (Pedersen, p. viii).

- *Ethnicity* "includes a shared sociocultural heritage that includes similarities of religion, history, and common ancestry" (Pedersen, p. viii).

- *Cross-cultural counseling* is "any counseling relationship in which two or more of the participants differ with respect to cultural background, values, and lifestyle" (Sue et al., 1982, p. 47).

- *Multicultural counseling* includes a broader definition of *culture* than is implied in cross-cultural counseling. Pedersen defined multicultural counseling as "a situation in which two or more persons with different ways of perceiving their social environment are brought together in a helping relationship" (p. viii) and preferred the broader definition of *culture* associated with multicultural counseling because it "helps counselors become more aware of the complexity in cultural identity patterns, which may or may not include the obvious indicators of ethnicity and nationality" (1991b, p. 11).

- *Diversity* refers to variables such as sexual orientation, age, gender, culture, ethnicity, race, socioeconomic status, and spirituality that are addressed within the context of multicultural counseling.

- *Social justice* recognizes the need for advocacy strategies to address social-political forces, such as oppression and discrimination, that undermine human rights and opportunity for full participation in society.

Theoretical Perspectives for Multicultural Counseling

Multicultural counseling and therapy (MCT) was the first comprehensive theory of multicultural counseling (Sue et al., 2007). It was developed in an attempt to overcome multicultural limitations associated with contemporary counseling theory, research, and practice. According to Sue et al., the major problem with existing schools of counseling is that they are culture bound and do not provide adequate conceptual tools with which to incorporate a multicultural perspective. *Culture-centered theory,* according to Sue et al., is necessary to broaden the theoretical foundations of counseling to make it relevant to the needs of a multicultural society. MCT can be used to provide a perspective, or lens, for conceptualizing such diversity issues as gender, culture, age, and sexual orientation in all phases of counseling. Throughout the process, the lens must be continuously adjusted in order to promote a clear understanding of emerging multicultural issues. Once these issues are identified, counseling theories and procedures can be modified to reflect an MCT perspective.

Sue et al. (2007) identified six MCT propositions that provide an overview of the basic assumptions upon which this theory is based.

Proposition 1. MCT can be used to provide an organizational framework for understanding Western and non-Western theories and methods of helping.

Proposition 2. Counselors' and clients' identities are reflected in various levels of human experience (individual, group, system, and universal). Contextual issues in treatment must therefore be addressed as necessary.

Proposition 3. Cultural identity development affects how the counselor and client view the self and others and how they formulate counseling goals and interventions. It is therefore important to be cognizant of how cultural identity development is affecting the counseling process, including being aware of the influence of different sociocultural forces.

Proposition 4. The efficacy of MCT is enhanced when counselors use procedures congruent with the values and experiences of the client. Counselors are encouraged to broaden their helping responses so that they demonstrate multicultural sensitivity throughout the counseling process.

Proposition 5. MCT encourages counselors to expand their helping roles to include conventional and alternative methods of helping as necessary to meet the cultural needs of clients.

Proposition 6. A fundamental goal of MCT theory is the liberation of consciousness from a relational-contextual perspective. In this regard, MCT attempts to provide opportunities for promoting an awareness of how cultural and relational issues (such as self in relation to family) affect present concerns.

Potential Challenges in Multicultural Counseling

Many studies have identified a wide range of potential challenges in multicultural counseling, including counseling as a white, middle-class activity, social class, gender, the intrapsychic perspective, sexual orientation, stereotyping, communication problems, faulty assumptions, test bias, prejudice, racism, and the efficacy of multicultural counseling.

Counseling as a White, Middle-Class Activity

A major criticism of contemporary counseling is that its theories and techniques have been developed primarily by people from a white, middle-class culture. As a result, contemporary counseling is not directly applicable to ethnic minorities because its theories and techniques do not address their specific issues and concerns

(Sue et al., 2007). In addition, traditionally trained counselors are encapsulated in a culturally biased framework and consequently tend to engage in culturally conflicting and oppressive counseling approaches (Ponterotto & Casas, 1991). It is therefore not surprising that counseling services are not utilized as much by minorities as by whites (Sue & Sue, 1999). In addition, the dropout rate after attending one counseling session is 50% for ethnic minorities versus 30% for whites (Sue & Sue).

Social Class

Differences in social class may be more profound than differences in culture (Baruth & Manning, 1999). For example, whites in the lower socioeconomic class may have more in common with Hispanics in the same class than with whites in the middle or upper class. Diagnostic and treatment bias is one concern that has been associated with social class. In one of the earliest studies on this subject, Lee (1968) found that clients from a lower socioeconomic class received a diagnosis of mental illness at a higher rate than did clients from an upper socioeconomic class. Some evidence also suggests that counselors become more involved with clients from the upper class than with clients from the lower class (Garfield, Weiss, & Pollack, 1973). Considering these findings, it is not surprising that clients with a lower socioeconomic status tend to drop out of counseling after one or two sessions (Berrigan & Garfield, 1981; Weighill, Hodge, & Peck, 1983). With these concerns in mind, Atkinson, Morten, and Sue (1998) noted that social class is an important variable to consider when formulating a treatment approach.

Gender

Much research has suggested that women's issues have not been adequately addressed by counseling theory, practice, and research. Gender bias in theory begins with developmental theories (a theoretical foundation for counseling). Carol Gilligan's (1982, 1991, 1993) foundational work on female moral development and identity development provides evidence of the need to create developmental theories that address men's *and* women's issues. Lucia Gilbert (1992) noted that "sexism and gender bias characterize psychological research and theory to the extent that unexamined assumptions about the sexes or untested distinctions based on gender enter into the hypotheses, rationale, norms of adjustment, or coverage of the field" (p. 387). To overcome gender bias in research, Gilbert suggested, it is essential to begin by accurately describing the experiences of men *and* women. The postmodern perspective suggests that women's experiences deserve to be valued and recognized as alternative views of knowledge and reality (Ballou, 1996) and that an understanding of relational-contextual issues that define women's existence and concept of "self" are important considerations for counseling research.

Feminists have identified systematic bias in traditional counseling theories and theories of psychopathology (Enns, 1993). From the feminist perspective, counseling theories have been written from a white male point of view that values autonomy and independence over relational considerations. In addition, theories of psychopathology tend to ascribe causality to a lack of internal conditions (such as autonomy and independence) as opposed to external forces (such as sociopolitical oppression from a male-dominated society). The practice of counseling can therefore be a process of cultural encapsulation whereby women are controlled and manipulated to conform to expectations of a white male counseling perspective. It is thus not surprising that research suggests women tend to prefer women counselors for dealing with relationship issues such as love, closeness, and sexual behavior (Snell, Hampton, & McManus, 1992).

The Intrapsychic Perspective

The intrapsychic perspective focuses on internal forces, such as the unconscious processes and endopsychic conflicts described by Freud (see Chapter 7). From the perspective of multicultural counseling, traditional schools of counseling overemphasize intrapsychic forces in conceptualizing the dynamics of behavior. The multicultural perspective suggests that external forces like oppression, racism, and discrimination can also have a direct bearing on psychological functioning (Sue & Sue, 1999).

An alternative perspective for understanding the human condition is postmodernism. From this perspective, language and narratives provide a relational-contextual perspective for defining what truth, knowledge, and reality are. This can be particularly true in terms of gender and culture, since women tend to emphasize relational issues more than do men, and minorities are directly affected by sociopolitical forces in ways that members of the dominant culture are not. A relational-contextual perspective can therefore provide an important frame of reference when counseling women and minorities.

Sexual Orientation

An important diversity issue in counseling is sexual orientation. Several key terms are associated with issues of sexual orientation (Fassinger, 1991). **Sexual orientation** refers to the complex set of behaviors, attitudes, and lifestyle factors associated with choosing a sexual partner. *Homosexuality* refers to sex with a same-sex partner; the etiology of homosexuality is to a large degree considered to be genetic or biologically based. *Gay* and *lesbian* tend to be the preferred terms (rather than *homosexual*) because they promote a more positive image that extends beyond sexual activity and includes the cultural considerations associated with gay/lesbian lifestyles. *Transgender* is a term that relates to individuals who have gender identity issues. *Lesbian, gay, bisexual, transgender* (LGBT) can be used to refer to individuals who may be lesbian, gay, bisexual, or transgender. A Q can be added to *LGBT* (**LGBTQ**) to include individuals who are questioning issues relating to their sexual identity. *Homophobia,* another commonly used term in discussions of sexual orientation, can be defined as the negative attitudes of fear and hatred that some people direct at LGBTQ people.

Heterosexism refers to the oppressive-discriminatory policies that society has imposed on LGBTQ people (Smith, Foley, & Chaney, 2008). Heterosexism is believed to maintain the privilege and power of people with heterosexual views and undermine the affectional identity of LGBTQ individuals (Smith et al.). Szymanski, Kashubeck, and Meyer (2008) noted that *internalized heterosexism* occurs when LGBTQ individuals internalize negative messages regarding homosexuality, thus undermining self-identity (e.g., self-doubt, self-hatred, and self-destructiveness). Feminist theory and multicultural/social justice counseling are examples of counseling approaches that can be used to help clients address issues associated with internalized heterosexism (Smith et al.; Szymanski et al.).

The counseling literature has to some degree been negligent in addressing issues associated with gays and lesbians, even though these individuals represent 10%–15% of the general population (Fassinger, 1991). However, models are beginning to emerge for the developmental, treatment, and spiritual issues of LGBTQ clients, and several gay-identity development models have been developed (e.g., Cass, 1979; Minton & McDonald, 1984). According to Fassinger, these models tend to acknowledge three central stages: recognition, acceptance, and affirmation.

Singh and Shelton (2011) noted very few qualitative research studies have been done regarding LGBTQ individuals, a lack they believed is unfortunate since probable small sample sizes would be ideal to provide an in-depth description of the issues of this population. Singh, Hays, and Watson (2011) conducted a qualitative research study that involved interviews with five transgender individuals regarding resiliency and coping with adversity. Results of the study indicated that all participants used the following resiliency strategies: an evolving sense of self, a belief that things will improve, a meaningful support system, feelings of self-worth, and awareness of oppressive forces. Strategies utilized by a majority of the participants included engaging in social advocacy and setting a positive example for others. The process of "coming out" (sharing one's sexual orientation with friends and family) is perceived to be an important step in promoting a positive LGBTQ identity and fostering optimal development (Fassinger, 1991). The process varies according to a number of factors, such as age, gender, and culture. For example, younger individuals may have to be especially cautious in coming out because they are still financially dependent on their parents. Black and Underwood (1998) noted that when the circumstances are right, coming out can be a very positive experience, promoting self-acceptance and psychological well-being, but that coming out prematurely can give rise to numerous problems, such as rejection by friends and family. Adolescents should wait to come out until they have worked through self-doubt and have a clear sense of identity, feel self-worth, and have an established support system, all of which may be difficult to achieve as prerequisites because some of these foundational elements are also a consequence of coming out.

Browning, Reynolds, and Dworkin (1991) addressed treatment issues pertaining to lesbian women, and Shannon and Woods (1991) provided information on counseling gay men. These scholars emphasized that it is important to look beyond sexuality when thinking about gays and lesbians and consider the special diversity and lifestyle issues that contribute to the unique features of this cultural group. For example, lifestyle considerations include career decisions, such as selecting careers where coming out could jeopardize job security and/or advancement (e.g., the military). It is also important to help gays and lesbians adjust to same-sex relationships in a homophobic world, which can involve helping gay and lesbian clients work through feelings of isolation, oppression, abandonment, and anger. In addition, counselors should strive to develop an understanding of the unique relationship issues of gays and lesbians (e.g., sexuality, communication, and parenting).

Ritter and O'Neill (1995) provided an overview of the spiritual issues involved in counseling gays and lesbians. They noted that traditional organized religion has made few positive and many negative contributions to the psychological functioning and development of gays and lesbians, suggesting that gays and lesbians experience numerous psychological and developmental problems resulting from exclusionary church doctrine and policy. Essentially, most of the organized religions (e.g., Judeo-Christian) have promoted the message that homosexuality is wrong, a sin, and a form of perversion. These religious groups tend not to recognize the evidence that homosexuality is primarily determined by biological forces (Ritter & O'Neill). The only acceptable response of a gay or lesbian person to church doctrine tends to be conversion, repentance, celibacy, or an attempt to function in spurious heterosexual relationships (Ritter & O'Neill). Gays and lesbians who fail to measure up to church policy tend to receive little support or sense of empowerment (e.g., inability to be married as gays or lesbians in the church). Without access to church functions, the church is unreachable as a source of strength and support during difficult times, such as when working through loss due to death, divorce, and other adverse life events.

On a psychological level, LGBTQ individuals can struggle with the negative feelings of guilt, shame, and isolation, which in turn can interfere with self-acceptance and identity development. Feelings of isolation are endemic to LGBTQ individuals, and it is therefore not surprising that they often feel like invisible people, living in an existential void beyond the recognized fringes of society. Counselors must take care to consider the vast array of special needs of LGBTQ clients so that they can be afforded opportunities for spiritual development and enhancement.

Stereotyping

Stereotyping can be defined as "rigid preconceptions we hold about *all* people who are members of a particular group, whether it be defined along racial, religious, sexual, or other lines" (Sue & Sue, 1999). Examples of stereotyping are beliefs that Native Americans have drinking problems and Asians are good at math. Stereotyping has negative effects on the counseling process (Sue, 1988). It can cause counselors to apply a perceived group characteristic to all members of that group without regard for individual differences, to fail to take logic or experience into consideration, and to distort all new information to fit preconceived ideas (Sue & Sue).

Communication Problems

Much of the criticism directed at multicultural counseling arises from the communication problems that interfere with the counseling process (Pedersen, 1988). Language differences can result in a variety of challenges in counseling (Sue, 1988). For example, Vontress (1973) has found that counselors who experience language difficulties with a client have trouble establishing a positive counseling relationship with the client. Sue and Sue (1977) also warned that counselors who use only standard English with a bilingual client may make an inaccurate assessment of the client's strengths and weaknesses.

The style of nonverbal communication may also vary across cultures, creating communication problems. For example, African Americans tend to use more direct eye contact when speaking than whites and as a result have been labeled more often as angry (Sue & Sue, 1999). Native Americans tend to avoid direct eye contact when listening, causing them to be incorrectly perceived as inattentive (Sue & Sue). Herring (1990) noted the particular importance of counselors being able to assess nonverbal communication accurately, because this type of communication is more ambiguous and culturally bound than verbal communication.

Westwood and Ishiyama (1990) devised the following guidelines for the communication process in multicultural counseling:

1. Counselors should check with the client on the accuracy of their interpretation of nonverbal communication.

2. Counselors can promote catharsis by encouraging clients to use their own language to express a particular feeling when another language cannot accurately describe it.

3. Counselors should try to learn culturally meaningful expressions of the client to accurately describe the client's inner process.

4. Counselors should use alternative modes of communicating, such as art, music, and photography.

Faulty Assumptions

Ten faulty assumptions can impede progress in counseling (Pedersen, 1987). Later in this chapter, these assumptions are used to evaluate the appropriateness of counseling theory in multicultural counseling.

MISCONCEPTIONS OF NORMAL BEHAVIOR People have a tendency to assume that the definition of *normal* is universal across social, cultural, economic, and political backgrounds. However, as Pedersen (1987) suggested, "what is considered normal will vary according to the situation, the cultural background of a person or persons being judged, and the time during which a behavior is being displayed or observed" (p. 17). Counselors can make an error in diagnosis if they fail to consider how the definition of normalcy can vary.

EMPHASIS ON INDIVIDUALISM Counselors with a traditional Western approach tend to emphasize the importance of the welfare of the individual. Self-awareness, self-fulfillment, and self-discovery are often used as indices of success in counseling. In addition, the task of the counselor is often perceived as "changing the individual in a positive direction even at the expense of the group in which that individual is a member" (Pedersen, 1987, p. 18). This emphasis on the interests of the individual over the group may not be consistent with the value system of some cultures. In the Chinese culture, for example, it would be inappropriate to put the welfare of an individual before the welfare of that individual's family (Pedersen). Counselors should therefore take cultural issues into consideration before promoting the virtues of individualism in counseling.

FRAGMENTATION BY ACADEMIC DISCIPLINES Counselors may have a tendency to isolate themselves from related disciplines, such as sociology, anthropology, theology, and medicine. This can result in a narrow view of people and an inability to understand individual differences. Cultural anthropology can be a particularly useful area of study in terms of addressing multicultural issues.

USE OF ABSTRACT OR OUT-OF-CONTEXT CONCEPTS Many counseling principles are based on abstract concepts, which can be easily misunderstood across cultures. In addition, the meaning of a concept will vary from one context or situation to another. It is therefore important to determine what a concept means in relation to a particular client.

OVEREMPHASIS ON INDEPENDENCE A common goal in counseling is to help clients become autonomous and independent. Pedersen (1987) warned that some cultures, such as the Japanese, believe that dependency is not only healthy but necessary. For example, the Japanese view dependency as appropriate between employer and employee, mother and son, and teacher and student. Counselors should therefore be sensitive to cultural issues in determining whether a client's dependence is excessive.

NEGLECT OF CLIENT'S SUPPORT SYSTEM A client who enters counseling may want the counseling relationship to become a substitute for existing support systems. To ensure that this does not occur, counselors should include the client's support system in treatment planning. This can be especially important for a minority client who may already feel a high degree of isolation because of cultural differences.

DEPENDENCE ON LINEAR THINKING Traditional Western counseling tends to be characterized by linear thinking or the assumption that each cause has an effect and each effect has a particular cause. However, some cultures are not tied to the linear model of analysis. For instance, the concept in Eastern culture of yin and yang does not differentiate between cause and effect but sees them as interrelated. In counseling it is therefore important to attempt to communicate in a manner that is consistent with the client's way of viewing the world.

FOCUS ON CHANGING THE INDIVIDUAL, NOT THE SYSTEM "In many minority groups counseling has a bad reputation for taking the side of the status quo in forcing individuals to adjust or adapt to the institutions of society" (Pedersen, 1987, p. 22). To overcome this obstacle, counselors should broaden their intervention strategies to include a community psychology perspective. This can include trying to change the system if it appears the system is having a detrimental effect on the client. If a client's depression appears to be related to high unemployment in the community, the counselor might become active in efforts to create employment opportunities.

NEGLECT OF HISTORY Counselors may focus only on the most recent precipitating events that led up to a crisis or mental disorder and fail to consider the client's problems from a historical perspective. For some minority clients, a historical perspective may be more appropriate because it can help the counselor understand sociocultural forces that have contributed to shaping a client's approach to problem solving and his or her outlook on life. Many African Americans, for instance, have experienced years of poverty, oppression, prejudice, racism, and exploitation. These influences can cause some to develop limited horizons and cause them to view life with, for example, a sense of despair, as well as perhaps feeling helplessness toward the self or hostility or suspicion toward others.

DANGERS OF CULTURAL ENCAPSULATION *Cultural encapsulation* blinds counselors to belief systems other than their own and causes them to fail to address cultural issues with the client. Multicultural counselors must move beyond "parochial concerns and perspectives" and develop a comprehensive perspective that integrates contrasting assumptions from other cultures (Pedersen, 1987, p. 23).

Test Bias

A variety of potential problems in multicultural testing and assessment could contribute to test bias in multicultural counseling (Lonner, 1985). These include clients' difficulties in test-taking situations and problems that relate to validity, reliability, and norms.

Test-taking situations may bring out cultural differences in terms of use of time, language, and the manner of response to test questions (Lonner, 1985). It may, for example, be culturally appropriate for some to agree with nearly every statement out of politeness. For others, it may be appropriate to give only socially desirable answers. Some individuals may view tests as unimportant and respond carelessly (Lonner).

Validity, reliability, and norms are critical in determining the use and effectiveness of tests, as discussed in Chapter 4. Validity may be the most important consideration. Construct validity is the extent to which a test measures a theoretical construct or trait, such as intelligence and verbal fluency (Anastasi & Urbina, 1997). However, the meaning and importance of these constructs may vary from one culture to another (Lonner, 1985). Tests that do not take into account differences in these constructs across cultures may therefore have invalid construct validities. Also, sociocultural factors may influence a test's reliability. Opportunities for learning may vary across cultures; for example, one culture may require formal education, whereas another may not (Lonner). It is therefore best to develop separate indices of reliability for each culture (Lonner). Another potential problem in using psychological tests multiculturally relates to norms. Most standardized tests are based on a white, middle-class norm group for setting standards or points of comparison, yet these standards often vary considerably across cultures. The norms are therefore only relevant for the particular reference group or culture in which they were developed. If the test is to be used multiculturally, new norms should be established based on the population (Lonner).

It is also important to ensure that the test results are used in an appropriate fashion. Cronbach (1984) warned that the central issue in the test bias controversy relates to how the inappropriate use of a test in decision making can create an unfair advantage for one culture over another. For example, using a culturally biased test in job selection could create an unfair advantage for some prospective employees. Culture-fair tests, several of which are described in Chapter 4, have been developed in an attempt to overcome some of the problems associated with test bias.

Prejudice

Prejudice can have adverse effects on the overall functioning of society and the peoples of the world; it plays a major role in discrimination, oppression, violence, and even war. Prejudice in the form of discrimination, cultural alienation, and restricted access to opportunities can also have detrimental effects on individuals' optimal development and self-actualization (Sandhu & Aspy, 1997). In the final analysis, prejudice is a negative force that destroys anything in its path.

Sandhu and Aspy adapted Gordon Allport's (1954) definition of prejudice: "thinking ill of others without sufficient warrant" (p. 7). Prejudice is believed to emanate from a variety of individual, social, and political forces, such as oppressive attitudes (e.g., stereotyping and racism), life-societal events (e.g., loss of job due to foreign competition), and fear (Sandhu & Aspy, 1997). An alternative explanation for the etiology of prejudice was provided by Geoseffi (1993), who suggested it can be traced to self-hatred. From this perspective, prejudice results from feelings of inadequacy that are projected onto others. Maslow's (1968) hierarchy of needs can also be used to understand prejudice. Prejudice can be seen in this context as a reflection of unmet needs (Sandhu & Aspy).

Prejudice and its reduction and prevention are important considerations in multicultural counseling (Sandhu & Aspy, 1997). The process of prevention and reduction, reduced to its most basic elements, is directed at helping clients meet their needs in a responsible manner. A comprehensive model for conceptualizing and addressing issues of prejudice in counseling is the multidimensional model of prejudice prevention and reduction (MMPPR; Sandhu & Aspy). The MMPPR regards prejudice as the result of individual, social, and political factors. Although eclectic in nature, the model draws heavily from Maslow's (1968) hierarchy of needs (people tend to meet their needs in a hierarchical manner—i.e., physiological, safety, love and belonging, and self-actualization needs). According to this theory, when people believe others are interfering with their ability to gratify needs, they attribute blame (in the form of prejudice) to the perceived source of the inhibition. Conversely, people who have healthy need systems and can satisfy their needs tend to have self-actualizing tendencies, such as harmony with self and others.

Another perspective on how Allport's theory can be used to address prejudice is provided by Utsey, Ponterotto, and Porter (2008). According to Utsey et al., Allport identified four factors associated with intergroup interactions that could contribute to prejudice reduction: equal status of individuals from different groups, common goals across groups, emphasis on cooperation across groups, and sanction and support by individuals in authority. Pettigrew and Tropp (2006) provided empirical support regarding the relationship between these four factors and prejudice reduction.

Prejudice prevention and reduction are promising topics for future discussion in the multicultural literature. They suggested that counselors become proactive in promoting multidimensional roles and interventions to fight the tide of prejudice. This can involve activities and initiatives such as addressing prejudice in all phases of the counseling process, promoting prejudice reduction in terms of need gratification and group dynamics, and becoming advocates for social reform regarding prejudice. Additional research and investigation are needed to determine how models for addressing prejudice can be effectively incorporated into multicultural counseling.

Racism

Racism is yet another potential challenge in multicultural counseling. Thompson and Neville (1999) highlighted several definitions of racism in their in-depth analysis of racism and its relationship to mental health and psychotherapy. In Cox's (1959) model, racism is "a social attitude propagated among the public by an exploiting class for the purpose of stigmatizing some group as inferior so that the exploitation of either the group itself or its resources or both may be justified" (p. 393). Cox saw racism as a way of justifying the domination and exploitation of one group of people over another. One sociological model of racism suggests that racism has a political-institutional-ideological dimension (Chesler, 1976). From this perspective, racism can often be traced to the ideology associated with political institutions whose laws maintain and propagate dominance and control of the superior group.

Thompson and Neville (1999) described a model of racism based on the earlier work of Cox and Chesler:

- Racism has evolved across geographical regions over generations.

- There are structural and ideological factors associated with racism.

- There are four forms of racism: individual, institutional, cultural, and environmental.

This model recognizes that racism in the United States has existed in different forms since the first settlers arrived. Originally, European colonizers dominated Native Americans. Later, the focus shifted to whites' domination over blacks. Over time, racism has taken different forms, as reflected in structural factors and ideology. Structural factors are those political and organizational systems that maintain and perpetuate the domination/control and oppressive forces over minority groups. The Civil War highlighted racial political views regarding the rights of blacks in America. Ideologies are the belief systems, such as prejudice, that promote racism. Racist ideologies misrepresent a cultural group in order to justify an oppressive behavior, such as slavery.

Thompson and Neville (1999) identified four forms of racism. Individual and everyday racism includes the insults and daily humiliation people experience as a result of their minority status (e.g., classmates taunt a Native American student with racially based remarks). Institutional racism is reflected in the manner in which society favors the dominant group over minority groups, an example being discriminatory hiring practices. Cultural racism is the practice of promoting the cultural beliefs and values of the dominant group and not recognizing the value of the beliefs and customs of minority groups. Cultural racism in the United States is demonstrated when individuals from the dominant culture contend their customs and beliefs are "American" and that the values and practices of minorities are not. Environmental racism is the fourth type of racism. It occurs when discriminatory laws result in minorities being exposed to unsafe environments, such as housing projects with toxic levels of lead and high rates of violence.

Racism can be a factor in mental health and psychotherapy. Thompson and Neville (1999) suggested that healthy psychological functioning promotes the necessary strength and resiliency to withstand racial oppression. Particularly important in overcoming racism are the mental health and personality factors of moral development, stable identity, self-awareness, coping skills, interpersonal skills, and the ability to accurately perceive one's environment. Although Thompson and Neville pointed out that issues relating to racism are often overlooked in psychotherapy, psychotherapy can promote mental health and healthy, functional personalities by exploring how clients' problems (such as depression) can be related to issues of racism. For example, comprehensive treatment planning may entail addressing such issues as racial discrimination and oppression in the workplace. In addition, therapists should assess how their counseling approach may foster racism. They can attempt to identify problematic ideologies (such as prejudices) and determine how they may be contributing to racial oppression within the counseling process.

Racism presents an important challenge in multicultural counseling. Thompson and Neville's (1999) model is useful for conceptualizing racism within the counseling process and, along with similar models, can play a key role in assisting counselors to overcome racial oppression. To explore and understand this complex phenomenon further will require additional research.

RACIAL MICROAGGRESSIONS Traditional "old-fashioned" forms of racism (such as blatant discrimination) are being replaced by more subtle, invisible forms of racism, referred to as **racial microaggressions** (Sue et al., 2008). Microaggressions are "brief and commonplace daily verbal, behavioral, and environmental indignities, whether intentional or unintentional that communicate hostile, derogatory, or negative racial slights and insults to the target person or group" (Sue et al., 2007, p. 273). Microaggressions occur in all types of settings and between strangers, casual acquaintances, and friends (Sue et al., 2008). They can create immediate adverse effects that undermine interpersonal relationships (e.g., generating anger, mistrust, and distortions of reality). The invisible nature of microaggressions can also make them difficult to identify and address, creating a cumulative effect over time (e.g., sapping psychic-spiritual energy, creating a general feeling of discomfort, and effectuating marginalization).

Sue et al. (2007) identified three types of microaggressions:

- *Microassault.* "Explicit racial derogation characterized primarily by a verbal or nonverbal attack meant to hurt the intended victim through name-calling, avoidant behavior, or purposeful discriminatory actions" (Sue et al., 2007, p. 274). Microassaults are similar to what has been traditionally thought of as racism—a conscious, deliberate attack (e.g., putting a person down with a racial slur).

- *Microinsult.* "Characterized by communication that conveys rudeness and insensitivity and demeans a person's racial heritage or identity. Microinsults represent subtle snubs, frequently unknown to the perpetrator, but clearly convey a hidden insulting message to the recipient of color" (Sue et al., 2007, p. 274). An example of a microinsult could be a teacher's not responding to questions from students of color during a class lesson.

- *Microinvalidation.* "Characterized by communications that exclude, negate, or nullify the psychological thoughts, feelings, or experiential reality of a person of color" (Sue et al., 2007, p. 274). An example of a microinvalidation would be a statement that negates cultural heritage: "When it comes right down to it, we are really all alike."

Sue et al. (2008) suggested that the counseling profession needs to do more to address insidious forms of racism. They contended that well-intended helping professionals must become aware of microaggressions and other forms of oppression in order to create worldviews that reflect multicultural sensitivity. Counseling psychologists could reduce disparity in health care by providing training in cultural sensitivity, empowering and advocating for clients, and engaging in culturally sensitive counseling and research (Tucker et al. 2007).

Research studies have attempted to determine how racial microaggressions impact mental health. Nadal, Griffin, Wong, Hamit, and Rasmus (2014) found that racial microaggressions had a negative effect on mental health with higher rates of depressive symptoms and negative affect. Additional research on microaggressions appears warranted.

The Efficacy of Multicultural Counseling

After reviewing the potential challenges in multicultural counseling, one may wonder whether any counselor could overcome these barriers. Research in this area has tended to focus on the effect of similarity between the counselor and client on the counseling process and counseling outcome. In an overview of the literature on racial/ethnic similarity, attitude similarity, and educational dissimilarity, Atkinson and Thompson (1992) noted that clients tend to rate counselors as more attractive when they are similar to them, except when they value dissimilarity (such as the counselor having more education than the client). Interestingly, attitudinal similarity is found to be more important in perceived counselor attractiveness than ethnic/cultural similarity. The literature on ethnic/cultural similarity reports conflicting results, with some studies favoring similarity and others suggesting clients would prefer dissimilar counselors in terms of ethnic/cultural status. There is also some evidence that similar attitudes and counselor credibility are rated as higher priorities by clients than is ethnic/cultural similarity.

Cultural mistrust, level of acculturation, and stages of identity development may be variables that should be considered in determining clients' preference for ethnic/cultural similarity. In terms of cultural mistrust, Atkinson and Thompson (1992) described several studies indicating that African American clients who rated high on cultural mistrust engaged in premature termination when paired with white counselors and rated white counselors as less credible, accepting, expert, and trustworthy. Level of acculturation also appears to play a role in preference for counselors of similar ethnic/cultural background. Studies show that clients rated low in acculturation prefer counselors who have similar ethnic/cultural status (Atkinson & Thompson). Research on stages of identity development are beginning to show that this variable can influence to some degree clients' preference for counselors with similar ethnic/cultural status (Atkinson et al., 1998).

Several other studies have investigated the relationship between personality similarity between counselor and client and the counseling process. Berry and Sipps (1991) researched the relationship between personality similarity, client's level of self-esteem, and premature termination. They found that clients who had low self-esteem tended to engage in premature termination when they also rated high on similarity with their counselor in terms of the Myers-Briggs Type Indicator. Berry and Sipps suggested that clients with low self-esteem may have a tendency to project their feelings of inadequacy onto their similar counselors, reducing these counselors' credibility and increasing tendencies toward premature termination. Towberman (1992) found that similarity between the counselor and client (as measured by the California Psychological Inventory) is related to clients' positive perception of the counseling relationship in terms of degree of involvement, support, and expressiveness.

A review of the literature regarding gender similarity and counseling outcome revealed that no clear statement has emerged regarding the efficacy of male versus female counselors or whether gender similarity between the counselor and client promotes superior efficacy over diverse gender pairings (Beutler, Machado, & Neufeldt, 1994).

Research is beginning to document different male and female styles of counseling; males use counseling approaches that tend to be more directive and controlling (Nelson & Holloway, 1990; Wogan & Norcross, 1985). Feminist counselors are investigating issues such as male dominance and control and women's oppression in the counseling process (Enns, 1993). From a feminist perspective, it is not surprising that preliminary evidence suggests women prefer women counselors for assistance with relationship issues (Snell et al., 1992). Additional research seems required to gain a clearer understanding of the role of gender in the counseling process.

Taken collectively, the literature appears to suggest that clients first and foremost want a counselor who is credible, that is, someone they believe can help them with their problems. Clients also place a high value on having a counselor who has a similar personality and attitudes, that is, someone whom they can relate to and feel comfortable with. Ethnic/racial similarity becomes important for clients who are experiencing high levels of cultural mistrust and low levels of acculturation and are processing issues of identity development. Gender also is an important variable, with women showing some tendency to prefer same-sex counselors to explore relationship issues. In addition, there appear to be some salient variables (such as self-esteem) that should be considered to gain a more in-depth understanding of the role of similarity in the counseling process.

The following *Personal Note* illustrates how a counselor can turn potential challenges in multicultural counseling to his or her advantage.

A Personal Note

I was surprised to discover in multicultural counseling that some of the barriers I envisioned turned out to be benefits. When I was a psychologist at a public health hospital on the Navajo Indian reservation, I was especially concerned about language barriers. I was told that I would need an interpreter because some Navajos could not speak English. This proved to be true in individual counseling with clients who did not speak English. In family therapy, however, I often found that some family members were bilingual. In these situations, I would have the bilingual family members act as interpreters, so an "outside" interpreter was not necessary.

Several positive outcomes resulted from having clients act as interpreters. First, they seemed to listen very carefully since they did not know when I would ask them to interpret. They seemed to take their responsibility as interpreter very seriously. Perhaps it allowed them to show respect for what other family members said. Second, clients were taking an active role in the counseling process because interpreting is basically paraphrasing.

I believe that many of the potential challenges in multicultural counseling can be overcome if the counselor develops a positive attitude and is sensitive to adjusting the approach to the unique needs of the client.

Suggestions for Incorporating a Multicultural Perspective

This section identifies suggestions for counselors to incorporate a multicultural perspective into their personal approach to counseling. It presents information on a number of emerging issues associated with multicultural counseling: multicultural counseling competencies, social justice, and worldview.

Multicultural Competency

The Society of Counseling Psychology of the American Psychological Association (APA) established a task force to identify cross-cultural competencies associated with the beliefs and attitudes, knowledge, and skills of culturally skilled counselors (see Sue et al., 1982). Sue and associates' seminal work in **multicultural competency** has played a major role in the evolution of multicultural counseling competencies during the past 20 years (Ridley & Kleiner, 2003). Sue, Arredondo, and McDavis (1992) challenged the profession to identify standards of culturally competent counselors that should be addressed in education and incorporated into counseling practice. The Association for Multicultural Counseling and Development responded by publishing the *Operationalization of the Multicultural Counseling Competencies* (see Arredondo et al., 1996). This document included 31 competencies, summarized in Table 6.1, that provide multicultural guidelines for clinical practice involving counselors' awareness of their own cultural values and biases, awareness of clients' worldviews, and multiculturally sensitive interventions.

Other professional organizations have addressed the issue of multicultural counseling competencies as a separate entity and within their ethical codes. Thomas and Weinrach (2004) noted that the American Psychological Association, in 2002, and the American Counseling Association, in 2003, endorsed their own versions of multicultural competencies. For example, in 2002, the APA issued guidelines on multicultural education, training, research, practice, and organizational change for psychologists (APA, 2002). Current revisions of the American Counseling Association (2014) and American Psychological Association (2010) codes of ethics continue to endorse the need for multicultural competencies.

Multicultural Competency and Social Justice

Multicultural competency has become one of the most widely researched areas in the helping professions. Researchers have investigated the role of multicultural competency in education (Pope-Davis & Ottavi, 1994), case conceptualization (Constantine & Ladany, 2000), clients' perspective of counseling (Pope-Davis et al., 2002), and social justice (Sandage et al., 2014; Vera & Speight, 2003). Issues of social justice have emerged as particularly well suited for integration into multicultural competency in counseling (Vera & Speight).

Social justice involves addressing social-political forces, such as cultural oppression, that undermine human rights. Martin Luther King Jr. believed that hope and faith were

Table 6.1 Multicultural Counseling Competencies

I. Counselors' Awareness of Values and Biases

   A. Attitudes and Beliefs

      1. Possess awareness of attitudes and beliefs regarding their own cultural heritage.

      2. Recognize how cultural experiences influence perceptions regarding psychological processes.

      3. Are cognizant of the limits of their multicultural expertise.

      4. Identify areas of discomfort regarding multicultural issues.

   B. Knowledge

      1. Possess awareness of how their racial/ethnic experiences can influence how counseling is conceptualized, including determining what is normal or abnormal.

      2. Determine how racism, stereotyping, and oppression impact them personally and professionally.

      3. Possess awareness of their social impact on others.

   C. Skills

      1. Acquire education and training opportunities to enhance multicultural competencies.

      2. Commit to overcoming personal issues, such as stereotyping and racism, that may undermine personal identity development.

II. Counselors' Awareness of Worldview of Clients

   A. Attitudes and Beliefs

      1. Possess awareness of how their attitudes and beliefs (both positive and negative) toward the client's cultural/ethnic heritage can influence the counseling relationship.

      2. Recognize stereotypes and preconceived notions they may have toward clients of different racial/ethnic groups.

   B. Knowledge

      1. Develop knowledge of the client's cultural heritage (e.g., where the client is functioning in terms of minority identity development models).

      2. Consider how multicultural factors such as race, ethnicity, and culture can affect a client's behavior (e.g., vocational choice and decision making) and impact the counseling process.

      3. Gain knowledge of how sociopolitical forces, such as poverty and discrimination, can undermine a client's psychological development in terms of self-esteem, self-efficacy, and other factors and how these issues can be addressed within counseling.

C. Skills

1. Utilize research and training opportunities to address mental health issues within a multicultural perspective.
2. Maintain involvement with people of different cultural/ethnic groups within and outside of the counseling setting.

III. Multiculturally Sensitive Interventions

A. Attitudes and Beliefs

1. Respect the client's spiritual and religious orientation.
2. Recognize the value of indigenous helpers utilized by clients.
3. Respect the role of bilingualism in the helping process.

B. Knowledge

1. Gain knowledge of how generic concepts from traditional counseling theories and practices may clash with ideas of different cultures.
2. Are cognizant of institutional barriers minorities face in accessing mental health services.
3. Obtain knowledge of cultural bias in assessment.
4. Gain understanding of how family life and community resources vary cross-culturally.
5. Identify how discriminatory practices may adversely affect a client's welfare.

C. Skills

1. Utilize appropriate verbal and nonverbal helping skills and modify them as necessary from a multicultural perspective, according to the unique and emerging needs of clients.
2. Implement institutional interventions to address problems such as racism and discrimination.
3. Recognize the role of traditional healers in providing culturally sensitive interventions.
4. Provide opportunities for clients to express themselves through their preferred language.
5. Utilize culturally sensitive assessment instruments and procedures.
6. Address issues of diversity, such as culture, gender, and age, that may bias evaluations and undermine interventions.
7. Empower clients so they can take an active role in formulating and implementing interventions throughout the counseling process.

Source: Adapted from Arredondo et al, (1996) Operationalization of the multicultural competencies, *Journal of Multicultural Counseling and Development*, 24, 57-74. The American Counseling Association.

necessary to maintain a commitment to human rights and social justice (Sandage et al., 2014). Counselors can advocate for social justice by expanding their role beyond counseling and psychotherapy to include engaging in work to promote social change (Hipolito-Delgado, 2014; Sandage et al.; Vera & Speight, 2003).

Feminist therapy (Brown, 1997; Enns, 1993) can be used to address issues of social justice by promoting social-political action to overcome oppression and gain equality. Crethar, Torres-Rivera, and Nash (2008) have noted that multicultural, feminist, and social justice counseling share similar paradigms, such as promoting social-environmental change to overcome marginalization and other forms of injustice. Clients are encouraged to challenge privilege inherent in the dominant society in order to promote equality, empowerment, advocacy, and inclusion.

The Multicultural Competencies Debate

There has been an ongoing debate as to the validity of multicultural competencies in advancing the practice of counseling. Weinrach and Thomas (2002) suggested there is no empirical evidence that a counselor who masters the competencies set forth by Arredondo et al. (1996) would be better off than one who has not mastered them. These authors also contended that the competencies are flawed in terms of content and assumptions. They cited a personal communication from Vontress (October 21, 1998):

> The competencies are restricted in their development to the four national minority groups: African Americans, Native Americans, Asian Americans, and Latino Americans as if culture is owned by just these groups. . . . The writers of the multicultural competencies seem to take a racio-ethnic view of culture with an emphasis on differences which bring people apart rather than on similarities which bring people together. (p. 24)

Patterson (2004) suggested that multicultural competencies are not necessary and can even be misleading and counterproductive. He cited two problems. First, positive counseling outcomes require much more than the knowledge and skills associated with multicultural competencies. Effective counseling includes a wide array of variables, such as Rogers's (1957) core conditions and rapport between the counselor and client. Second, it is a mistake to assume that client differences are more important than their similarities and to therefore classify clients into discrete groups, each requiring its own counseling approaches.

Weinrach and Thomas (2004), while stating that multicultural competencies have been a success on a symbolic level in that "they have successfully brought to professional counselors awareness of the importance of attending to the diverse counseling needs of visible minorities" (p. 91), believed that multicultural competencies have been a failure on the applied level in that they have not provided persuasive evidence that they will enhance counseling outcomes. In addition, the authors contended that the greatest flaw of the multicultural perspective is its emphasis on deficits of both clients and the counseling profession rather than on clients' strengths.

A review of 40 years of research on multicultural counseling by D'Andrea and Foster Heckman (2008b) noted that considering all the attention that had been given to multicultural counseling competencies, it was disconcerting that no studies had used the competencies as an independent variable. On the other hand, Arredondo and Toporek (2004) contended that competencies in multicultural counseling are subject to ongoing refinements, developments, and validation. They suggested there is ample empirical evidence to support the adaptation of multicultural competencies and that these competencies provide an ethically and culturally responsive standard of practice. Arredondo, Tovar-Blank, and Parham (2008) argued that those who want proof of the efficacy of multicultural counseling competencies are discounting the relevance of cultural and sociopolitical forces in counseling, suggesting that those with a "prove it" attitude represent pseudointellectual resistance to the multicultural counseling movement. More recently, Chao (2012) provided insights into the complex relationship between racial/ethnic identity and gender role attitudes, counseling training, and multicultural competencies. Results of the study showed significant interaction effects among these variables. Implications of the research suggested that multicultural competencies can be enhanced by self-exploration relating to racial/ethnic identity and gender-role attitudes.

Chao (2013) also investigated the effects of race/ethnicity, racial/ethnic identity, color-blind racial attitudes (denial of existence of racism), and multicultural training on the multicultural competency of school counselors. Results of the investigation suggested that white and racial/ethnic minority school counselors had the lowest multicultural competency when they had limited multicultural training and high levels of color-blind racial attitudes. The study also found that for white school counselors, multicultural training significantly enhanced multicultural competency; whereas the multicultural competency of racial/ethnic minority school counselors did not vary according to level of multicultural training.

Thus, the debate regarding multicultural counseling competencies is ongoing. Additional research and dialogue are essential to creating an open forum for addressing these important issues.

Worldview

It is important to have knowledge of the client's culture and to be able to understand the client as a unique individual. Worldview, a concept gaining increasing recognition in the multicultural literature, is a construct that can be used to individualize the counseling process (Ibrahim, 1991; Sue, 1978, 1981).

Worldview, which extends beyond culture or ethnic group, can be defined as assumptions and perceptions regarding the world (Sire, 1976; Sue, 1978). It is directly related to thoughts, feelings, and perceptions of social relations and the world (Ibrahim, 1991). It also has a direct effect on a client's ability to solve problems, make decisions, and resolve conflicts (Ibrahim, 1993). Knowledge of a client's worldview can promote a better understanding of the client and can lead to more sensitive and effective counseling strategies (Ibrahim, 1991).

A client's worldview should be determined during the initial client assessment (Ibrahim, 1991). One effective tool for doing so is the Scale to Assess World Views (SAWV; Ibrahim & Kahn, 1984, 1987), which assesses information regarding the client's view of human nature, social relations, relationship with nature, time orientation, and activity orientation. The SAWV can help the counselor explore the client's values, beliefs, and assumptions; gain an understanding of the client's concerns; and differentiate between the client's worldview and cultural views (Ibrahim).

Trevino (1996) proposed a multicultural perspective in a model for conceptualizing the change process that is based primarily on the concept of worldview but also incorporates concepts from anthropology and from research on the counseling process. Trevino's model of change recognizes both a general and specific worldview for both the counselor and client. According to this theory, it is advantageous for the counselor and client to have congruent general worldviews (one's basic understanding of the world in a broad, abstract sense) and discrepant specific worldviews (more definite thoughts and opinions based on life experiences). Throughout the change process in counseling, similarity in general outlook on life is believed to promote empathy and foster a positive counseling relationship; discrepant specific worldviews promote alternative perspectives for problem solving.

Identity Development

Identity development is "a process of integrating and expanding one's sense of self" (Myers et al., 1991, p. 54). Chae and Foley (2010, p. 473) found "that ethnic identity was positively related to psychological well-being." Although establishing a positive self-identity can be difficult (Myers et al.), helping clients clarify or enhance their self-identity can be a central task in counseling.

Identity development models are a means of understanding the process of identity formation and determining where clients are functioning in that process. Several of these models describe the stages of identity development for racial-ethnic groups, such as African Americans (Cross, 1995), Hispanic Americans (Casas & Pytlulk, 1995; Umana-Taylor et al., 2014), Asian Americans (Kim, 1981), white Americans (Helms, 1995; Rowe, Behrens, & Leach, 1995), and biracial Americans (Kerwin & Ponterotto, 1995).

Myers et al. (1991), however, have noted that racial-ethnic identity development models may have several limitations. For example, they may not take into account multiple oppressive factors, such as socioeconomic status and minority status (e.g., lower-class Mexican Americans) or multiracial backgrounds (e.g., Amerasians). To overcome some of these limitations, these authors developed the Optimal Theory Applied to Identity Development (OTAID) model, which allows consideration of multiple oppressive factors that can influence identity development and is based on worldview rather than restricted to racial-ethnic considerations.

Myers et al. (1991) described the OTAID model as a seven-phase process:

- *Phase 0: Absence of conscious awareness.* In this phase, individuals lack a sense of the self as a separate individual. Individuals do not develop self-awareness until 1 or 2 years of age (Dworetzky, 1996).

- *Phase 1: Individuation.* During this phase, individuals adhere to a personal identity that was generated by early familial and societal experiences. They utilize an egocentric view of themselves, which does not take into account the negative views of others.

- *Phase 2: Dissonance.* In phase 2, individuals begin to consider the opinions of others regarding who they are, even if these opinions are negative. Their perceptions of negative views from others create dissonance, and individuals begin to wonder who they really are.

- *Phase 3: Immersion.* Individuals who feel devalued by others may immerse themselves in the customs and way of life of the devalued group and react angrily toward the dominant group. For example, a 20-year-old Asian American woman who had identified with Anglo customs may reject those customs and immerse herself in Asian customs if she hears white people talking about her race in derogatory ways.

- *Phase 4: Internalization.* During this phase, individuals incorporate a number of salient aspects of the self in formulating their personal identity. This broadened self-image enables them to be more tolerant and accepting of the criticisms of others.

- *Phase 5: Integration.* As individuals gain deeper self-understanding, they begin to change their assumptions regarding the world. Their worldview is broad and accepting of individual differences. At this point, they choose friends on the basis of shared values and interest instead of ethnic-racial criteria.

- *Phase 6: Transformation.* In the transformation phase, the self is redefined according to a worldview that appreciates the interrelatedness of all aspects of life. This emerging personal identity incorporates a spiritual awareness regarding the order of life and the universe and fosters a sense of wholeness or completeness in the individual.

Recent research has investigated the relationship between ethnic identity and psychosocial functioning. For example, Umana-Taylor et al. (2014) found that for

Mexican American adolescents, high levels of ethnic identity were associated with increased academic self-efficacy and social competence and fewer depressive symptoms and externalizing problems. Umana-Taylor et al. suggested that parents can play an important role in enhancing their childrens' ethnic identity by teaching them about their ethnic background and helping them understand how their ethnicitiy contributes to their overall identity.

Methods of Evaluating Counseling Theories

To formulate a personal approach to multicultural counseling, it is necessary to determine the appropriateness of traditional counseling theory. There are several methods that can help with this process.

ACCULTURATION THEORY **Acculturation**, a complex multicultural phenomenon, is a measure of the extent of adaptation to the customs and values of the host culture. An individual's level of acculturation is associated with the degree of change (between the native and the host culture) in terms of values and behaviors, cultural awareness, and cultural loyalty (Kim & Abreu, 2001). Counselors can estimate a client's level of acculturation by examining how much the client has assimilated into mainstream society. The factors that influence acculturation include educational level, socioeconomic status, length of time lived in the United States, and extent of exposure to racism (Lee, 1991).

Acculturation theories have been developed for various ethnic/cultural groups in an attempt to understand the process of acculturation (e.g., Choney, Berryhill-Paapke, & Robbins, 1995, for American Indians). In addition, acculturation scales are available for African Americans (Helms, 1986), American Indians (Hoffman, Dana, & Bolton, 1985), Asians (Suinn, Rickard-Figueroa, Lew, & Vigil, 1987), and Hispanics (Mendoza, 1989). Acculturation theory appears to be a promising area of research and will undoubtedly stimulate additional research activity on a wide range of issues relevant to counseling within a multicultural perspective.

Researchers are beginning to explore issues that extend beyond evaluating the appropriateness of traditional counseling procedures with minority clients. "Acculturative stress," for example, is the subject of a number of studies. Smart and Smart (1995) defined *acculturative stress* as the "psychological impact of adjusting to a new culture" (p. 25). A meta-analytic analysis of 49 studies of acculturation and adjustment concluded that stress is more intense at the beginning of the acculturation process (Moyerman & Forman, 1992). Some research (Smart & Smart, 1995) has identified health factors and counseling implications associated with acculturative stress among Hispanic immigrants. Stress is related to such phenomena as impaired physical health, decision making, occupational functioning, and utility of the counseling relationship. Belizaire and Fuertes (2011) found that adaptive coping, on the other hand, is associated with enhanced quality of life and less acculturation stress. Acculturation theory will undoubtedly stimulate additional research activity on a wide range of issues relevant to counseling within a multicultural perspective.

USHER'S MODEL Using Usher's model (1989) is another way to evaluate the appropriateness of a theory. Usher suggested that the 10 faulty assumptions identified by Pedersen (1987) can be used to determine whether a traditional counseling theory can be used in multicultural counseling. A counseling theory that appears to foster one or more of these faulty assumptions can then either be modified or avoided. To illustrate her method, Usher used the 10 faulty assumptions to evaluate Rogers's (1951) person-centered therapy. Her analysis showed his theory to have some strengths and weaknesses in terms of its use in multicultural counseling. For example, two facets of Rogers's theory appear to support multicultural counseling (Usher). First, because clients define the goals and determine the evaluation process, there is less chance of their being judged in terms of the dominant culture's view of normality. Second, the elements of circularity in Rogers's approach allow clients to express themselves within a framework that is nondirective and nonjudgmental.

The method also identified some potential problems with person-centered counseling in multicultural settings. One problem relates to this therapy's emphasis on individualism and independence from others, which does not recognize the view of healthy dependencies that some cultures hold for authorities and family members. A second problem could arise from the belief that the locus of control and responsibility resides within the client, which does not take into account environmental factors, such as poverty, that can affect the client's growth process. Another potential problem relates to Rogers's emphasis on the here and now. Such a frame of reference may not be adequate for understanding problems like oppression that may affect culturally different clients.

ETIC-EMIC MODEL A third method of evaluating the efficacy of a counseling theory in multicultural counseling involves the concepts of *etic* and *emic,* terms linked to linguistics (Lee, 1984; Ridley, Mendoza, & Kanitz, 1994). The word *etic* is derived from *phonetics*, which is something common to all languages. *Etic* refers to concepts in counseling theory that are held to be universal for all cultures, for example, the contention in rational-emotive-behavioral therapy (REBT) that irrational beliefs contribute to negative emotional consequences (Ellis & Ellis, 2014). The word *emic* is derived from *phonemics*, which are things unique to a particular language. *Emic* refers to concepts that emphasize individuality, for example, neurolinguistic programming, an approach that varies with each individual (Bandler & Grinder, 1975).

There may be some advantages to using emic concepts as opposed to etic concepts in multicultural counseling. Emic concepts encourage the counselor to treat each client as an individual, thereby avoiding tendencies to engage in prejudice or stereotyping. Etic concepts, on the other hand, must be truly universal to be applied to different cultures without bias. Problems can surface with etic concepts when the theory assumes the concept is universal when in fact it is not—for example, the REBT concept that irrational thinking will generate emotional difficulties regardless of the culture (Bandler & Grinder, 1975). REBT does not appear to consider the possibility that the definition of irrational ideas may vary from one culture to another. The efficacy of REBT would therefore be significantly reduced in situations in which a counselor is using inappropriate standards to determine what thinking is rational or irrational and self-defeating.

The common-factors model of Fischer, Jome, and Atkinson (1998) can be used to address both etic (universal) and emic (culturally specific) perspectives in counseling. This model contends that all counseling is multicultural and that a framework is needed to address universal health conditions in a culturally specific context. The four common factors that research supports as having universal healing value across cultures are these:

1. *The therapeutic relationship.* Across all cultures, the word *therapy* suggests a relationship between two people. A relationship of trust and caring is considered the heart of the counseling process.

2. *Shared worldview.* A shared worldview is a common ground of understanding between counselors and clients. Although the worldviews of counselors and clients will vary, there is a communication of appreciation and mutual respect for their respective perceptions of the world.

3. *Client expectations.* For counseling to be beneficial, clients must believe that it will be of help. Faith in the benefits of counseling can be enhanced when counselors see clients in the clients' own environments, such as in their homes or churches. In these instances, clients' expectations are enhanced when counselors communicate caring and understanding of clients' worldviews.

4. *Ritual or intervention.* Ritual or intervention relates to the importance of matching counseling procedures with culturally specific issues unique to the client. Culturally sensitive interventions require a strong knowledge base in diversity issues and individual differences. For example, Lewis (1994) emphasized the importance of modifying common approaches, such as cognitive therapy, to incorporate the cultural milieu of the client. Lewis noted, for example, that African American clients place a high value on family, religion, and spirituality and suggested that in these instances, counselors might consider framing cognitive restructuring within the context of biblical passages.

Fischer et al.'s (1998) model provides a framework within which to conduct all counseling from a multicultural perspective. Reduced to its simplest elements, the model suggests counselors use the following question to frame the counseling process: "How can I continue building relationships with my clients, understanding my clients' worldviews and perceptions of distress, raising my clients' expectations, and implementing culturally relevant interventions?" (Fischer et al., p. 569). The common-factors model appears to offer much to the counseling literature in terms of bridging the gap between the etic and emic perspectives of multicultural counseling. Additional research is needed to evaluate the four common factors, specifically as they pertain to multicultural counseling.

Guidelines for Multicultural Counseling

This section provides 10 guidelines for incorporating multicultural counseling strategies into a personal approach to counseling.

ESTABLISH MUTUAL RESPECT Mutual respect forms the foundation of all relationships (Dinkmeyer & McKay, 1997). This may be especially important in multicultural counseling when a counselor from the majority culture counsels a minority client. In these situations, clients may feel they are being looked down upon and consequently resist participating in counseling.

Counselors can create opportunities to communicate respect to the client by honoring the client's unique way of perceiving and interacting with the world. Counselors can also communicate acceptance of their client whenever possible. For example, some clients may become embarrassed because they have difficulty speaking English. When this occurs, the counselor can tell these clients that it is impressive that they are becoming bilingual when most people can speak only one language.

As clients experience acceptance and respect, they may become more relaxed with and accepting of their counselor. The resulting mutual respect can contribute to a relationship of equality in the counseling process.

DON'T IMPOSE YOUR BELIEF SYSTEM When working in multicultural counseling, it is important for the counselor to be nonjudgmental. Each culture has its own norms and value system. This may influence how clients see important issues pertaining to counseling, such as their understanding of mental health. For example, the Navajos do not differentiate between physical and mental health, seeing mental problems as resulting from a person being "out of harmony" with the traditional Navajo culture (Harrar, 1984).

TREAT CLIENTS AS UNIQUE INDIVIDUALS FIRST AND AS PEOPLE FROM A PARTICULAR CULTURE SECOND It is important to consider that all people are unique, even in terms of what it means to be part of a particular culture. Focusing on the unique characteristics of a particular client will help counselors overcome stereotyping and other self-defeating processes.

DETERMINE WHETHER TRADITIONAL COUNSELING APPROACHES WOULD BE APPROPRIATE FOR A PARTICULAR CLIENT The counselor can use the three methods described in this chapter to determine the appropriateness of traditional counseling theory in multicultural settings.

PROVIDE ACCESSIBLE, DEPENDABLE SERVICES It is important for counseling services to be adequately staffed so that clients will know someone will be there if they come for help. This is especially important in rural areas, where a client may have traveled a long distance to come for counseling services. On the Navajo reservation, it was not uncommon for clients to have journeyed 100 miles and have had to get a ride from a friend or hitchhike. It would not be very welcoming for these clients to be told that they would have to come back the next day or wait a long time to receive help. It is essential for the counseling center to develop a reputation for being reliable and responsive, or clients will stop coming.

Some clients may feel that their problems are not "big enough" to warrant counseling services. These are often the clients who need help the most. They need to be reassured that the counseling service is there for them to use and that they are not "in the way," as they might feel, but are welcome.

USE A FLEXIBLE APPROACH Counselors should adjust their approach to the client's unique needs in all cases, but flexibility is especially important in multicultural counseling. In many minority cultures, such as those of Mexican Americans, African Americans, and Native Americans, a high percentage of people are struggling against the effects of poverty. These individuals may therefore need assistance with basic needs such as food, shelter, and safety. When this occurs, counselors should adjust their approach to meet these needs, becoming more action oriented and focused on the present (Sue, 1981). Counselors may even function to some degree as advocates for the client's basic rights, which may involve helping clients obtain benefits from social services or other agencies.

BE PERCEIVED AS A DOER, NOT JUST A TALKER Counselors should show they are capable of accomplishing something concrete with the client as early as possible in the counseling relationship. A counselor who is perceived as a doer and not just a talker will be valued and sought after by clients, especially those struggling to fulfill basic needs.

CONDUCT AN ENVIRONMENTAL ASSESSMENT It is important to avoid an overemphasis on intrapsychic forces in assessment and diagnosis. An environmental assessment will enable the counselor to explore sociocultural factors that could also be contributing to the client's problems. This will not only contribute to more accurate assessment and diagnosis but also help the counselor and client identify realistic treatment goals.

ALLOW YOURSELF TO BE ENRICHED BY THE CLIENT'S CULTURE Multicultural counseling can be rewarding and exciting. It can involve living and working in a different culture or simply providing a multicultural counseling service. Regardless of the degree of a counselor's multicultural experience, many opportunities exist for cultural enrichment. A counselor may soon discover some of the special facets of a culture, such as types of food, styles of dress, differences in family life, and approaches to physical and mental health. Each culture also has its special customs, beliefs, heritages, and creative arts. It may be helpful to study a culture to appreciate its special beauty. This can be done through reading, going to art exhibits and other cultural events, and, of course, learning from clients.

YOU DON'T HAVE TO BE A MINORITY TO COUNSEL A MINORITY Potential problems in multicultural counseling are language barriers, stereotyping, and a lack of awareness of the value systems of a cultural group. Counselors can overcome these problems by being sensitive to the unique needs of the client and attempting to gain the beliefs, knowledge, and skills necessary to counsel in multicultural settings.

SUMMARY

Developing a well-thought-out personal approach to counseling creates the necessary structure to work within the counseling process. An eight-stage model, including the merits of using an integrative approach, provides guidelines for formulating a personal approach that is responsive to a multicultural society.

This model suggests that counselors who utilize a central or core theory and common factors shared by different theories (e.g., establishing a positive counseling relationship is especially important) will have a solid foundation for approaching the

counseling process that will provide internal consistency.

One potential challenge associated with multicultural counseling is a tendency toward diagnostic and treatment bias. This bias can be overcome when the counselor treats the client as a person first and a member of a particular culture second; sensitively relates to the special needs and circumstances of the client; and gains the necessary awareness, knowledge, and skills to work with the populations the counselor intends to serve.

PERSONAL EXPLORATION

1. What is important to you in formulating your personal approach to counseling?

2. What intrigues you about multicultural counseling?

3. What is your position regarding diversity issues, such as sexual orientation, race, ethnicity, age, spirituality, and gender?

4. What guidelines would you follow regarding multicultural counseling?

5. What are your views regarding the place of social justice and advocacy in the practice of counseling?

6. What is the role of spirituality in counseling, and how should counselors respond to these issues?

7. What is the role of theory in developing a personal approach to counseling?

8. What are your views regarding multicultural competencies and how can they be promoted?

9. What are some guidelines for multicultural counseling that you feel are important?

10. Why is it important to have a personal approach to counseling?

LEARNING ACTIVITIES

1. Consider visiting with professional helpers or your professor to explore what their personal approach to counseling is and how they formulated their approach.

2. Consider visiting with someone who identifies as LGBTQ to explore issues associated with sexual orientation.

3. How might you advocate for social justice?

WEBSITES

Freedman, F. K. (1999). *Multicultural counseling.* Retrieved from http://www.alaska.net/~fken/html/multiculture.htm. *Presents a semi-current review of multicultural counseling, citing mostly D. W. Sue and D. Sue's 1990 text,* Counseling the Culturally Different: Theory and Practice *(2nd edition), on cross-cultural counseling.*

Green, D. (1997). *Multicultural counseling.* Retrieved from http://www.lausd.k12.ca.us/orgs/lasca/html/multicultural_counseling.html. *Provides an array of multicultural counseling resources and links.*

The Classic Theories of Freud, Adler, and Jung

The Art and Science of the Classic Theories

The art of counseling owes much to the classic theories. Freud was one of the first clinicians to really listen to clients' stories and use creative techniques such as dream analysis to explore the unconscious domain and provide insights into behavior. Adlerian psychology added another dimension to the art of counseling. Adler referred to the center or nucleus of the person as the creative self, emphasizing the individual's creative potential to interact with the world. Jung's theory, more than any other counseling theory, may capture the spirit of the art of counseling. A very sensitive individual, he would adapt his approach to meet the needs of a particular client. For example, Jung found that by mirroring the gestures of his psychotic clients, he could attempt to understand what they were trying to communicate (Douglas, 2011). In addition, Jung frequently used different modalities within the creative arts, such as having a client draw an image from a dream to provide additional means for analysis (Douglas).

The classic theories also provide a strong foundation for the science of counseling. They have played an integral role in the evolution of current psychotherapies. Some of the concepts generated by the classic theorists commonly used by clinicians include the conscious–unconscious continuum, defense mechanisms, the importance of early life experiences for personality development, the therapeutic alliance, lifestyle, and the relationship between wholeness and psychological balance to psychological growth and self-healing.

The classic theories have been the subject of much research. A review of research on Freud's theory by Henry, Strupp, Schacht, and Gaston (1994) found that current investigations are directed at gaining a better understanding of transference relationships, interpretation, and the therapeutic alliance. Adlerian theoretical constructs are of continuing interest

Chapter Overview

This chapter provides a description of the three classic theories of Freud, Adler, and Jung. Highlights of the chapter include the following:

- **The art and science of the three classic theories**

- **Background information regarding the three classic theories**

- **The theories of personality of Freud, Adler, and Jung**

- **The theories of counseling and psychotherapy of Freud, Adler, and Jung**

- **Contemporary issues regarding the three classic theories**

- **Brief-counseling approaches for the three classic theories**

- **Diversity issues with the classic theories**

(e.g., birth order [Zajonc & Mullally, 1997] and lifestyle [Stoltz & Kern, 2007]). Current research trends in Jungian psychology include the application of Jungian principles to the analysis of children and the use of bodywork and art therapy (Douglas, 2011).

As noted in Chapter 6, the trend in counseling is toward using a multicultural perspective to address diversity issues. It is especially important to think about the classic theories from a multicultural perspective because some of their concepts may appear dated and out-of-step with contemporary values and beliefs. Treating these classic theories in the context of the art and science of counseling means modifying the theories to account for findings of multicultural research and maintaining sensitivity to the evolving needs of clients.

An Overview of Freud, Adler, and Jung

The **classic psychological theories** of Sigmund Freud, Alfred Adler, and Carl Jung laid the foundation for modern clinical practice. Their influence transcended the field of psychology; their insights have a significant impact on the arts, education, child-rearing practices, and numerous other aspects of daily living.

Freud's masterpiece, *The Interpretation of Dreams,* which was originally published in 1900, caught the interest of Adler and Jung (Freud, 1900/1965). Adler and Jung were colleagues of Freud who became central figures in the psychoanalytic organization. They eventually broke ranks with Freud when they believed he overemphasized the role of sexuality in personality development. Adler and Jung then proceeded to develop their own psychological theories. The three distinct schools of psychology that evolved have a number of commonalities. Each emphasizes the importance of early life experiences on personality development and views insight as an important prerequisite to change.

The Freudian, Adlerian, and Jungian schools of psychology can be considered the "classic schools," because each developed its own comprehensive theory of personality and approach to psychotherapy. These theories can be used as the central or core theories from which one can develop an integrative counseling approach. Table 7.1 provides an overview of these three theories. The sections that follow present an overview of the three classic theories, including background information on the theorist and information on his theory of personality and theory of counseling and psychotherapy. The chapter concludes by addressing diversity issues and brief counseling from the perspective of the classic theories.

Freud's Psychoanalytic Theory

Background Information

The following overview incorporates Patterson's (1986) description of some of the significant events of Freud's life.

Table 7.1 Freud, Adler, and Jung

Theory	Key Concepts	The Counseling Process	Techniques
Freud's psychoanalytic theory	Endopsychic conflicts resulting from the id, ego, and superego; defense mechanisms; the conscious–unconscious continuum; and the effects of traumatic experiences in childhood on personality development	Has the major aim of resolving intrapsychic conflicts to restructure the personality as necessary.	Dream analysis and free association can be used to explore unconscious processes; confronting, clarification, and interpretation provide necessary insight.
Adler's individual psychology	The creative self, behavior as goal directed and purposeful, social interest, striving for significance as a motivational force, and the family constellation	Is educationally oriented, providing information to clients and guiding them and attempting to encourage discouraged clients.	The lifestyle analysis is an assessment technique, motivation modification is used to modify underlying motivational forces, and other techniques are used to reorient clients away from basic mistakes.
Jung's analytic psychology	The collective unconscious, archetypes, and personality types	Explores unconscious processes to help the self emerge so clients can be free to move toward self-realization	Analyze the interrelationship of several dreams for their symbolic content and cues to the various systems of the personality.

Sigmund Freud (1856–1939) was born in Freiberg, Moravia, a town in the Czech Republic. He was the oldest of eight children and moved with his family to Vienna when he was 4 years old. He obtained a medical degree in 1881 from the University of Vienna and, after graduation, went to Paris to study with Jean-Martin Charcot, who was known for his work with hypnosis in the treatment of hysteria. Freud then returned to Vienna and married Martha Bernays. They had six children; the youngest was Anna, who later became a distinguished child analyst.

In 1882, Freud began a private practice in medicine, initially specializing in nervous diseases. He later broadened his practice into what is known today as psychiatry. At this point in his career, Freud became interested in the "talking cure," which was being developed by the prominent Viennese physician Joseph Breuer. Breuer believed that a client could be helped by simply talking about a problem. This concept contributed to Freud's free-association technique and is an important part of the evolution of the counseling profession.

The most creative period in Freud's life was also a period during which he experienced serious emotional problems. He was tormented by psychosomatic disorders and phobias, such as an exaggerated fear of dying. At one point he was even afraid to cross the street. During this time, Freud engaged in extensive self-analysis by studying his dreams. The insights Freud gained from self-analysis became very influential in the development of his own theories, such as the Oedipus complex. He remembered that as a child he had felt hostility toward his father, whom he perceived as an overbearing authority figure. On the other hand, Freud had sexual feelings for his mother, whom he remembered as loving, attractive, and protective.

Freud's rise to prominence required perseverance and an ability to withstand severe criticism. As he developed his revolutionary theory, he was initially met with scorn and ridicule from all corners of the academic and scientific community. Alone, he forged on, typically working for 18 hours a day. Finally, with his publication of *The Interpretation of Dreams* in 1900, he became "respectable" again. Shortly thereafter, Freud was welcomed back into the intellectual community and regarded with great esteem.

In later years, Freud's struggles centered around his personal health. His fondness for cigars apparently contributed to the development of jaw cancer. During the last 20 years of his life, he was in almost constant pain and underwent 33 operations. Somehow, he still managed to maintain an active professional life. Hall and Lindzey (1978) noted that Freud was a prolific writer—his collective works fill 24 volumes. His work also stands out from a literary point of view; Freud's eloquent writing style did much to popularize his ideas.

Theory of Personality

Freud's well-developed theory of personality provided information on how behavior manifests itself in terms of the id, ego, and superego; the conscious–unconscious continuum; defense mechanisms; and other useful psychological constructs (Strachey, 1953–1974).

VIEW OF HUMAN NATURE Freud had a deterministic view of human nature. He was convinced that behavior was directed by unconscious biological urges involving sex and aggression and psychosexual experiences during the first 6 years of life.

KEY CONCEPTS The key concepts that characterize Freud's theory, as described by Freud (Strachey, 1953–1974), are incorporated into the following overview.

The Structure of the Personality In Freud's view, the personality is made up of three autonomous, yet interdependent, systems: the id, ego, and superego.

The *id* is the original system of the personality from which the ego and superego emerge (Hall & Lindzey, 1978). It is the reservoir of psychic energy, supplying energy to the other two systems. The id can be considered the "hedonistic branch" of the personality (Hall, 1954). It is driven by the pleasure principle, which attempts to reduce tension by gratification of sexual and aggressive impulses.

The *superego* is the other extreme of the personality. It can be considered the "judicial branch" and is concerned with moralistic issues, determining what is right or wrong (Hall, 1954). It represents the values and ideals of society as handed down from parent to child. The superego has three purposes: to inhibit the impulses from the id, to alter the ego's orientation from realistic to moralistic, and to encourage the personality to strive for perfection.

The *ego* can be considered the "executive branch" of the personality (Hall, 1954). It is ruled by the reality principle, which attempts to exert a realistic, reality-based influence over the id and superego.

Endopsychic Conflicts The prefix *endo-* means "within," and an **endopsychic conflict** is a conflict within the psyche. Such conflicts result from the interaction of the three parts of the personality: the id, ego, and superego. According to Freud, there is only so much "psychic energy" available to the three parts of the personality. Therefore, all three systems are in constant competition for this energy in order to take control and dominate the personality. As the three parts of the personality compete for psychic energy, they create conflicts within the psyche, which in turn create anxiety. The organism can attempt to alleviate the conflicts by creating defense mechanisms.

Endopsychic conflicts always involve the ego and either or both the id or superego. The following are possible examples of endopsychic conflicts:

- **Id versus ego.** (Id:) "I want to murder that person." (Ego:) "If you do, you will go to jail."

- **Id versus superego and ego.** (Id:) "I want to murder that person." (Superego:) "You shouldn't because it is wrong," and (Ego:) "You will go to jail."

- **Ego versus superego.** (Ego:) "I would like to go to bed with my lover." (Superego:) "Don't do it because it is a sin to have sex unless you are married."

Defense Mechanisms Freud's concept of defense mechanisms was one of his most important theoretical achievements. **Defense mechanisms** develop unconsciously when the ego feels threatened by an endopsychic conflict. When this occurs, defense mechanisms can be utilized to deny, falsify, or distort reality so the ego can cope. The role of the counselor can therefore be to help strengthen the client's ego to minimize stress from endopsychic conflicts and the resulting defense mechanisms. This process of strengthening can involve psychoeducational interventions that provide clients with information they can use to take a more realistic position regarding stresses in their environment.

Some of the more common defense mechanisms are projection, reaction formation, fixation, regression, and repression.

Projection is an attempt to attribute to another person one's own thoughts or feelings. For example, instead of saying you hate someone, you say, "That person hates me." In this example, projection occurs because the ego is threatened by aggressive id impulses. Projection can therefore be seen as an attempt to "externalize the danger."

Reaction formation is a way of coping by creating an extreme emotional response that is the opposite of how one actually feels. This results in a "falsification of reality." For example, a man may hate his wife and want a divorce. At the same time, he may have intense feelings of guilt because he believes divorce is morally wrong. If the man tells others how wonderful his wife is and how much he loves her, a reaction formation may be operating.

Fixation can occur if the demands of life become too threatening. In an attempt to avoid new responsibilities, a person can avoid growing up and fixate, or stand still, in terms of development. When this occurs during adolescence, the individual's personality remains like that of an adolescent for the remainder of life.

Regression is an attempt to cope by moving back to a point in one's development that was less threatening. For example, a person who has a major business failure may feel life is falling apart. In an attempt to cope, the person may try to escape these feelings of failure by moving back to a point in time that was not so threatening. When this occurs, the person may assume the role of a child to avoid adult responsibilities.

Repression is an attempt to cope by creating an avoidance response. In repression, the stressful situation is pushed from the conscious to the unconscious dimension of the mind.

The Conscious–Unconscious Continuum Freud was one of the first to explore the unconscious dimension of the human psyche. He believed it held the key to understanding behavior and problems within the personality. It is therefore not surprising that the majority of the techniques associated with psychoanalysis (such as free association and dream analysis) are used to explore unconscious processes.

Freud conceptualized conscious and unconscious processes along a continuum. The analogy of the iceberg can be used to understand this **conscious–unconscious continuum**, as illustrated in Figure 7.1. As shown in the figure, most of the psyche

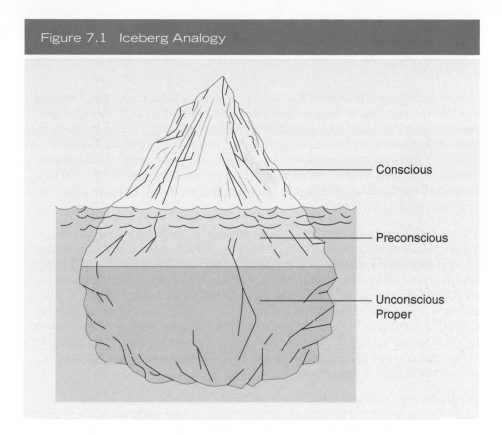

Figure 7.1　Iceberg Analogy

- Conscious
- Preconscious
- Unconscious Proper

involves unconscious processes. The *conscious* dimension contains material that the person is aware of and can readily retrieve. The *preconscious* relates to material that the person is almost consciously aware of but that is just out of mental awareness (e.g., almost being able to remember a person's name). The *unconscious proper* includes all memory traces that the person is not consciously aware of (e.g., a repressed traumatic experience such as childhood incest).

Psychosexual Stages of Development　Freud contended that personality development was determined to a large degree by early life experiences. His theory suggests that problems in the personality can result if the child has a traumatic experience or the child's basic needs are not met. When this occurs, the person could attempt to achieve indirect gratification by displacement or sublimation to restore equilibrium. Displacement is indirect gratification, such as a baby sucking his or her thumb when not allowed to eat. Sublimation is also indirect gratification, but it results in some form of social recognition. An example of sublimation is a sexually frustrated person creating a beautiful, sensuous painting.

Freud was one of the first theorists to identify stages of development through which a person progresses. He called them **psychosexual stages of development**, emphasizing the role of sexuality in the developmental process, and divided them into three periods: the pregenital period, which lasts until age 6; the latency period, which spans from age 6 to adolescence; and the genital period, which continues for the rest of a person's life.

The pregenital period is composed of the oral, anal, and phallic stages. Freud believed that the *oral stage* occurs during the first 18 months of life. It is called the oral stage because the child appears preoccupied with oral functions (e.g., sucking the mother's breast and exploring objects by putting them into the mouth). Problems that occur during the oral stage (such as extreme frustration of oral gratification) could result in the individual developing an oral personality as an adult. Adult nail-biting could be an example of displacement of latent oral needs. Becoming a teacher or orator could result from sublimation of oral needs.

The *anal stage* occurs from 18 months to 3 years of age. This stage emphasizes the impact of toilet training on personality development. Problems that can occur during the anal stage may result in an anal-explosive or anal-retentive personality. The anal-explosive personality is an aggressive type of person, a style that could result from a child using the toilet all the time as a means of keeping a parent's attention. The anal-explosive personality could develop football or boxing skills as a form of sublimation. An anal-retentive personality could result from a parent using severe punishment when the child has an "accident." Out of fear, the child could develop a pattern of not going to the toilet. An example of sublimation for the anal-retentive personality could be a person who is good at saving money.

The *phallic stage* occurs between the ages of 3 and 6. According to Freud, it is a time when male children become sexually interested in their mothers (the Oedipus complex) and female children become attracted to their fathers (the Electra complex). The boy eventually resolves his Oedipus complex out of fear of castration by his father. Problems could occur if a father had jealous tendencies and threatened to hurt his son if the boy did not stop "pestering mother," a threat that could intensify the boy's fear of castration. According to Freud, this fear could then inhibit any future thoughts of the opposite sex, promoting homosexual tendencies.

Unlike the male child, the female does not have a dramatic means of resolving her Electra complex, such as fear of castration. Instead, she may resolve her sexual feelings by reacting to the realistic barriers that are established to prohibit incestuous relationships. A problem could result during this stage if a child felt emotionally rejected by her father, possibly causing her to avoid relationships with males in the future. On the other hand, if an incestuous relationship were allowed to occur, the child could experience even more profound difficulties in her personality, such as low self-image and perhaps promiscuity.

The *latency period,* which occurs between the ages of 6 and 12, is a period of relative calm. The child has emerged from the turbulence of the pregenital period with the basic structure of the personality largely formed. During this period, the child develops new interests to replace infantile sexual impulses. Socialization takes place as the child moves from a narcissistic preoccupation to a more altruistic orientation. Problems could occur during this period if the parents do not encourage the child's interest in establishing positive social relationships. As a result, the child might not be able to develop the social skills necessary for successful interpersonal relationships.

The *genital period* begins at puberty and continues for the rest of life. The focus of this period is an opposite-sex relationship leading to the experience of intimacy. Problems during this period could occur for individuals who were discouraged from socializing or began sexual relationships before being emotionally ready to handle them.

Theory of Counseling and Psychotherapy

Freud's approach to counseling and psychotherapy is called *psychoanalysis,* emphasizing the analysis of the mind. It is a time-consuming approach that can typically involve four 1-hour sessions each week over a period of several years (Arlow, 2005).

The major aim of psychoanalysis is to restructure the personality by resolving intrapsychic conflicts. The actual process of traditional psychoanalysis involves the client lying on a couch and engaging in free association, saying whatever comes to mind. The analyst is seated out of the client's view behind the couch and listens and reacts in a noncritical manner. Arlow (2005) described four phases of psychoanalysis: the opening phase, the development of transference, working through, and the resolution of transference.

THE OPENING PHASE During this phase, the analyst obtains important history from the client. Gradually, over a period of 3 to 6 months, the analyst obtains a broad understanding of the client's unconscious conflicts.

THE DEVELOPMENT OF TRANSFERENCE During this phase, the client begins to experience a **transference** relationship with the analyst, which involves projecting thoughts and feelings onto the analyst that are associated with significant others, such as a father or mother. Transference is encouraged during psychoanalysis, for it plays a key role in bringing unresolved conflicts (which typically originated in childhood) to the surface so they can be worked through and resolved within the safety and support of the therapeutic relationship. Analysis of the transference is a cornerstone of the psychoanalytic process. It provides the client with insight into how past relationships and experiences are creating problems in present relationships. Analysis of transference also helps the client learn how to use insight to make appropriate, mature decisions regarding current relationships.

Countertransference may also occur in therapy and results when analysts unconsciously begin to see qualities in the client that remind them of someone from their past. Countertransference can interfere with the analyst's objectivity and destroy the therapeutic process. When this occurs, the analyst may need psychoanalysis to work through these tendencies.

WORKING THROUGH This phase is essentially a continuation of the previous phase. Additional analysis of transference is aimed at generating more profound insights and consolidating what can be learned from them.

THE RESOLUTION OF TRANSFERENCE During the final phase of therapy, the analyst and client work toward termination. This can involve working through resistance from the client regarding termination or preparing the client to function independently once the termination is complete.

Techniques

Freud developed many techniques for use in psychoanalysis (Strachey, 1953–1974). Their primary purpose is to make the unconscious conscious. The following list describes some of the more commonly used techniques:

- *Free association* is the primary psychoanalytic technique. As discussed earlier, it is used throughout the counseling process. Free association encourages the client to discuss whatever comes to mind, thereby overcoming his or her tendencies to suppress or censor information.

- *Dream analysis* is a technique Freud developed as a means of exploring unconscious processes. He suggested that elements of dreams contained symbolic meaning, such as a screwdriver being a phallic symbol, representing a penis.

- *Confrontation and clarification* are feedback procedures to help the client become aware of what is occurring and in need of further analysis (Prochaska, 1984).

- *Interpretation* involves providing insight to the client regarding inner conflicts reflected in resistance, transference, and other processes.

Contemporary Issues

Contemporary Freudian psychology reflects several changes and modifications from Freud's original theory. These changes evolved primarily in response to what was considered to be his overemphasis on the role of sexuality in personality development, the excessive time required to complete psychoanalysis, and the nature of the therapeutic relationship.

Strupp (1992) described several trends in psychoanalysis:

1. The role of the analyst has shifted from the detached, impersonal, classical Freudian position to the more humanistic interactive model associated with the therapeutic alliance.

2. The role of the Oedipus complex in psychopathology has been deemphasized, with earlier developmental periods playing a more central role in psychological dysfunction.

3. Treatment considerations have shifted from neurotic conditions such as obsessive-compulsive disorders and phobias to the treatment of personality disorders.

4. Transference and countertransference have been reconceptualized in terms of interpersonal theory, which emphasizes the dyadic quality of the counseling relationship. Within this context, the analyst and client continually contribute to transference and countertransference processes as a natural outcome of their ongoing relationship. Thus, negative connotations of transference and countertransference have been replaced by a more robust and positive view of how the counseling relationship can provide opportunities for insights and analysis.

Strupp (1992) identified several additional trends in psychoanalysis, including a recognition of the importance of interpersonal relations to psychological health, a reassessment of the role of the ego in psychological functioning, and the movement toward time-limited psychoanalysis. Luborsky, O'Reilly-Landra, and Arlow (2008) noted that contemporary psychoanalysts are integrating research findings from various theoretical perspectives, such as cognitive psychology, attachment theory, feminist theory, and neuroscience.

Safran and Kriss (2014) discussed the significant evolution of psychoanalysis over the past 100 years, saying that it "has become more flexible, less authoritarian, more practical, and more responsive to the needs of a wider range of clients from diverse racial, cultural, and social class backgrounds" (p. 50). In addition, a substantial amount of empirical research provides evidence of the efficacy of psychoanalytic treatment (Safran & Kriss). For example, Leichsenring and Rabung (2008) conducted a meta-analysis of 23 studies that provided evidence of the greater effectiveness of long-term psychoanalysis as compared to short-term approaches from a variety of theoretical perspectives. They found that long-term psychoanalysis was more effective than short-term approaches both in terms of overall outcome and for treatment of complex mental disorders such as personality disorders and chronic mental disorders.

THE INTERPERSONAL PERSPECTIVE The **interpersonal perspective** contends that psychoanalytic theory overemphasizes intrapsychic forces (such as inner conflicts over sexuality) and does not recognize the importance of environmental forces (such as the quality of interpersonal relationships). Interpersonal psychotherapy is an emerging form of psychotherapy based on the work of Harry Stack Sullivan (1968) and his collaborators (e.g., Adolph Meyer, 1957, and John Bowlby, 1973). It recognizes the effect of early life experiences (such as the degree of parent-child attachment) on the quality of interpersonal relationships later in life and the role that interpersonal functioning plays in depression (Prochaska & Norcross, 2010; Verdeli & Weissman, 2014).

Interpersonal theory suggests that people are motivated by interpersonal anxiety to avoid rejection and to maintain self-esteem (Schwartz & Waldo, 2003). Interpersonal psychotherapy involves identifying and working through parataxic distortions ("inappropriate ways of reacting to others . . . based on previous experiences, usually in the family of origin" (Schwartz & Waldo, p. 105.). Interpersonal psychotherapy is a time-limited approach that focuses on enhancing social skills and improving interpersonal relationships (Prochaska & Norcross, 2010; Verdeli & Weissman, 2014).

EGO-ANALYTIC THEORY The **ego-analytic position** incorporates theories associated with ego psychology and object-relations theory. Ego psychology, associated with the work of Erikson (1950) and Rapaport (1958), represents a shift in focus from the id to the ego as the primary driving force of personality (Prochaska & Norcross, 2010). In this new role, the ego is viewed as capable of functioning independently from the id in its attempt to adapt to reality and master the environment (Prochaska & Norcross).

Object-relations theory, as proposed by Kernberg (1976) and Kohut (1971), emphasizes the self and objects (people) as the primary organizing force in personality functioning (Prochaska & Norcross, 2002). Object relations are intrapsychic structures based on the mental representations of the self and others (Prochaska & Norcross).

Baker (1985) identified the following six characteristics of the ego-analytic position:

1. Noninstinctual factors are emphasized.

2. The ego is conceptualized as an autonomous structure that operates independently of the id.

3. The function of the ego has been expanded to include facilitating adaptation to the environment through the development of coping and mastery skills.

4. Psychosocial and interpersonal variables are emphasized over biological-instinctual variables.

5. Developmental stages that occur after puberty are considered as important as those occurring before puberty.

6. Psychopathology occurs when the needs associated with developmental tasks are not met and due to other forces that can cause defects in the personality structure of the individual.

Freudian Brief Approaches to Counseling

With the emergence of managed care, long-term open-ended psychoanalysis is a luxury that few individuals and insurance companies can afford (Strupp, 1992). All forms of psychotherapy (including psychoanalysis) are therefore under increasing pressure to focus on the treatment of specific mental disorders within the context of a limited number of sessions (Strupp). Brief psychodynamic psychotherapy evolved as an alternative to classic psychoanalysis. Among the brief psychodynamic approaches are Malan's (1976, 1980) focal therapy, Mann's (1973, 1981) time-limited psychotherapy, Sifneos's (1979, 1984) short-term dynamic psychotherapy, and Davanloo's (1978, 1984) short-term dynamic psychotherapy. Garske and Molteni (1985) noted that all brief psychodynamic approaches share several characteristics: They are all based on psychoanalytic theory, suggest similar efficacy, and modify psychoanalytic procedures for use in a briefer format.

The aim of brief psychodynamic psychotherapy is to go beyond symptom relief and bring out necessary changes in the client's personality (Garske & Molteni, 1985). The number of sessions required in brief psychodynamic psychotherapy tends to be limited to 12 and depends on the nature of the client's problem and the type of therapy utilized (Garske & Molteni). Mann's (1973) time-limited model involves between 1 and 12 sessions. Davanloo's (1978, 1984) short-term dynamic approach varies the number of recommended sessions from 2 to 5, 6 to 15, 16 to 25, or 26 to 40 sessions, depending on the nature of the client's problem.

Garske and Molteni (1985) identified the following six factors as promoting change in brief psychodynamic psychotherapy:

1. A contract is established with the client that includes a description of the client's problems in psychoanalytic terms.

2. A statement of goals and objectives is established, along with a time limit on the number of sessions.

3. The analyst takes an active, probing approach, clarifying and confronting the client's resistance.

4. The analyst interprets the links between the client's current problems, relationship with the analyst and significant others, and past conflicts.

5. The time-limited aspect of therapy arouses issues relating to separation and individualization within the client.

6. The termination phase of therapy is characterized by working through problems associated with separation and individualization.

Research has attempted to determine what factors contribute to the efficacy of brief psychodynamic psychotherapy. Nergaard and Silberschatz (1989) found that high measures of shame and guilt (especially guilt), as measured by the Therapy Shame and Guilt Scale, correlated with positive therapy outcomes. Mills, Bauer, and Miars (1989) noted that transference reactions should be addressed quickly and energetically by the therapist to maximize their impact.

Goldfried, Greenberg, and Marmar's (1990) review of the literature on brief psychodynamic psychotherapy found that the approach has been effective for treating stress and bereavement disorders (Marmar & Horowitz, 1988); late-life depression (Thompson, Gallagher, & Breckenridge, 1987); and adjustment, affective, and personality disorders (Marziali, 1984). In addition, in an evaluation of 34 short-term dynamic psychotherapy cases, Barth et al. (1988) found significant gains in symptom relief, adaptive functioning, and personality change at termination and over a 2-year follow-up period.

Summary and Evaluation

Sigmund Freud's place in history is secure. He is widely regarded as one of the most prominent intellectual figures of all time. His contributions to psychology and other fields are phenomenal. Freud's most remarkable achievements include the concept of defense mechanisms as a means for coping with anxiety, the mapping of the conscious–unconscious continuum, and his methods for exploring unconscious processes in psychoanalysis. The weaknesses in Freud's theory are considered to be his overemphasis of the role of sexuality in personality development and the excessive length of time required to achieve the aims of psychoanalysis. New advances in Freudian theory, as reflected in the ego-analytic position and in brief psychodynamic psychotherapy, are attempts to overcome these problems.

Adler's Individual Psychology

Background Information

Alfred Adler (1870–1937) received a medical degree from the University of Vienna in 1895. In 1902, he began what was to develop into a rather stormy relationship with Freud. Adler quickly took an active role in Freud's psychoanalytic society and was elected its president in 1910. He and Freud cofounded and became coeditors of the *Journal of Psychoanalysis*. Shortly thereafter, Adler broke with Freud over several important theoretical issues. These differences culminated in Adler's resigning from his positions as president of the society and coeditor of the journal. At this point, Adler disassociated himself from the Freudian circle and founded his own school, which he called *individual psychology*.

After serving as a medical officer during World War I, Adler returned to practice medicine in Vienna. In 1922, he turned his attention to the problems of children and established a child guidance clinic in the Vienna public schools (Dinkmeyer & Dinkmeyer, 1985). Eventually, more than 50 similar guidance clinics were opened before political turmoil restricted the growth of Adlerian psychology in Europe (Dinkmeyer & Dinkmeyer). By 1935, political unrest forced Adler to flee Europe, and he settled in the United States. Two years later, Adler died while on a lecture tour in Aberdeen, Scotland.

Adler maintained a busy schedule throughout his career. He was particularly known for his extensive lecture tours, during which he would often work with a client in front of an audience. This was revolutionary at the time because therapy was not then practiced with such openness (Dinkmeyer & Dinkmeyer, 1985). Today, Adlerians continue the tradition of demonstrating counseling strategies in front of live audiences. Adler was a prolific writer, publishing more than 100 books and articles during his lifetime. *The Practice and Theory of Individual Psychology* (Adler, 1969) is an excellent introduction to Adlerian psychology.

Theory of Personality

Adler's theory of personality is a comprehensive, in-depth analysis of how people function. It emphasizes the importance of early life experiences within the family of origin or, as Adler referred to it, the *family constellation*. From this perspective, factors such as birth order, sibling rivalry, and social interest play important roles in the formulation and functioning of the personality.

VIEW OF HUMAN NATURE Adler held an optimistic view of human nature. He believed people were basically positive and were capable of self-determination. This view of human nature stimulated the development of the humanistic movement in psychology, which focuses on the dignity and worth of the individual. Adler also emphasized that behavior is holistic, or interrelated; teleological, in that it has a purpose and is directed toward a goal; and phenomenological, because it can best be understood from the client's frame of reference.

KEY CONCEPTS Adler (1969) and Ansbacher and Ansbacher (1956, 1964) have described a number of key concepts that make up the structure of Adler's theory of personality. The following 10 principles are central to this theory.

The Creative Self This concept was Adler's "crowning achievement as a personality theorist" (Hall & Lindzey, 1978, p. 165). It lies at the heart of the Adlerian theory. The **creative self** is the center or nucleus from which all life movement generates (Ansbacher & Ansbacher, 1956). Freud called this center the ego. For Adler, the term *creative self* emphasized that each person has the potential to creatively interact with the world. Adler expressed the potential for self-determined behavior when he said:

> The important thing is not what one is born with, but what use one makes of that equipment. . . . To understand this we find it is necessary to assume the existence of still another force, the creative power of the individual. (Ansbacher & Ansbacher, 1964, pp. 86–87)

The Concept of Teleological Movement Adler saw all behavior in terms of movement: nothing is static. This movement is teleological in nature because it has a purpose and is directed toward a goal; thus, the term **teleological movement** is used. According to Adler, a person can move on the useful or useless side of life. Movement on the useful side is characterized by cooperative efforts, whereas movement on the useless side is narcissistic in nature (Ansbacher & Ansbacher, 1956).

Adler also believed that life movement was from a sensed minus to a sensed plus. According to their private logic, individuals will behave in a manner that appears to improve their position (Ansbacher & Ansbacher, 1956). This concept can be useful in understanding the motivation behind misbehavior. For example, a child may move toward a goal of power to gain recognition. In this instance, the private logic may be "I can be somebody if I fight with others."

Behavior Can Be Understood From an Interpersonal Perspective Adler emphasized that behavior can best be understood from an interpersonal perspective (Ansbacher & Ansbacher, 1956). This spirit was captured by the poet John Donne when he said, "No man is an island" (1624/1952). Adler believed that people do not behave in isolation from others but in relation to others, reasoning that can be used to identify goals of misbehavior. For example, parents can develop a tentative hypothesis by asking themselves how they feel when their child misbehaves. Feeling annoyed could indicate their child has a goal of attention, feeling angry or threatened could suggest a goal of power, feeling hurt could indicate a goal of revenge, and feeling desperate or hopeless could suggest a goal of a display of inadequacy (Dinkmeyer & McKay, 1997; Dreikurs & Soltz, 1964).

The Psychology of Use Adler stressed that all behavior has a use or payoff that is usually unconscious in nature (Ansbacher & Ansbacher, 1956). Emotions are useful in helping propel a person toward a goal. This concept of **psychology of use** can also be used to understand the symptoms associated with psychopathology, as the following *Personal Note* illustrates.

A Personal Note

Don was a 22-year-old assistant accountant. One day while he was working, his hand became numb and he was unable to move it. Don was taken to a hospital where I was the staff psychologist. The patient received a complete medical evaluation, including numerous neurological tests. After the doctors decided there was nothing physically wrong with the patient's hand, they referred him to me. When I asked Don how he liked his work, he said he hated it, largely because he wanted to go to medical school. After some additional assessment, I decided to hypnotize him. I told him he was a doctor and asked him to take my blood pressure. At this point, he was able to move his hand.

The psychology of use was quite apparent in this case since the patient's inability to move his hand could help him avoid a job he hated. It is important to point out that Don wasn't consciously aware of trying to avoid his job. He was actually relieved to discover there was nothing physically wrong with his hand.

Together, we decided that Don would try to go back to college so he could be doing something he wanted to do. With this in mind, I spent the next few sessions helping him apply for admission to college. It is interesting to note that Don could not voluntarily move his hand until he received a letter of acceptance from the college.

Don's disorder is known in the literature as a *conversion disorder.* It involves losing a bodily function, such as the use of a hand or sight, due to psychological rather than physical reasons. As illustrated in this case, the disorder can also be understood in terms of the psychology of use.

A Phenomenological Psychology The phenomenological perspective provides an understanding of clients from their internal frame of reference. Adler suggested that what individuals perceive is biased according to past experiences (Ansbacher & Ansbacher, 1964). He referred to this phenomenon as an *apperception*. A phenomenological perspective is therefore necessary to understand clients' interpretations of their experiences.

Emphasis on Social Interest Adler's term *Gemeinschaftsgefühl* has been translated into English as "social interest" (Ansbacher & Ansbacher, 1964). **Social interest** refers to an inborn tendency to cooperate and work with others for the common good (Ansbacher & Ansbacher). Social interest is considered a major motivational force in Adlerian psychology. Adler related this concept to mental health when he observed that social interest is the barometer of mental health (Ansbacher & Ansbacher). Glasser (1965) supported this position when he suggested that all people need love and affection to be fulfilled.

The Lifestyle **Lifestyle** became the recurrent theme in Adler's later writings and the most distinctive feature of his psychology (Hall & Lindzey, 1978). "The term *lifestyle* refers to the person's basic orientation to life—the set of patterns of recurrent themes that run through his or her existence" (Dinkmeyer & Dinkmeyer, 1985, p. 123). According to Adler, the lifestyle is relatively fixed by age 4 or 5. Once established, the individual's lifestyle guides the assimilation and utilization of future experiences (Hall & Lindzey).

A Holistic Psychology The individual is indivisible and undivided in Adler's individual psychology. It is therefore a holistic psychology in that it attempts to understand the overall lifestyle as a unified whole. Adlerians are interested in assessing how the person organizes the self as a whole person with interrelated and coherent beliefs, perceptions, and goals (Dinkmeyer & Dinkmeyer, 1985). This position is similar to the holistic health concept, which views the mind and body as an interactive system, not as separate entities.

Striving for Significance Adler believed that people have a basic tendency to avoid feelings of inferiority by striving for superiority (Ansbacher & Ansbacher, 1956). A person could therefore compensate for feelings of inadequacy in one area by excelling in another aspect of life. In this way, striving for superiority should not be viewed as an attempt to feel superior over others. Instead, it amounts to a striving for significance and worth as an individual and is a major motivational force (Dinkmeyer & Dinkmeyer, 1985).

The Family Constellation The **family constellation** encompasses many factors associated with a person's family of origin, such as birth order, family size, and the relationship among family members. Adler believed that each person's family constellation was unique and could therefore make a significant impact on the development of the lifestyle. Adler was particularly interested in birth order and how it affected a person's development (Ansbacher & Ansbacher, 1956). For example, first-born children tend to be bossy and talkative because they are used to telling their brothers and sisters what to do. They also tend to be conservative because they are born into a world of adults and therefore tend to affiliate with adults and adult values.

With the arrival of a second child, first-born children can feel temporarily dethroned as they have to share their parent's attention. This can cause them to be suspicious and tend to protect themselves from sudden reversals of fortune. Middle-born children attempt to compete with the oldest and so tend to be very ambitious. This can result in the "racecourse syndrome," which can foster an achievement orientation in middle-born children. It can also promote sibling rivalry or competition between siblings, which is another Adlerian principle. In addition, middle-born children can have difficulty feeling a sense of belonging because they grow up not having the special place of being the oldest or youngest. They also tend to be observers, interested in what is going on between the siblings, and mediators, willing to intervene when a conflict occurs.

The youngest child of the family is the "baby." Parents tend to be more lenient and give special favors to the baby. Youngest children usually appreciate these special considerations and learn early in life that other people will take care of them and protect them from life's difficulties.

Dinkmeyer and Dinkmeyer (1985) noted that birth-order characteristics are only tendencies that may or may not occur. Whether they manifest themselves depends on how parents relate to a child and how children interpret their ordinal position. When a person does not have the typical characteristics of a particular birth order, it can be interesting to determine what familial factors could account for the differences. For example, a middle-born female with three brothers and no sisters will usually not lack a sense of belonging because she feels special as the only girl. A middle-born male may act like a first-born child if the first-born does something extreme, such as committing murder, and is disowned from the family.

Theory of Counseling and Psychotherapy

Adlerian counseling and psychotherapy stress the role of cognition in psychological functioning. The Adlerian approach begins by using the lifestyle analysis to gain an understanding of the client. Through various techniques and procedures, such as encouragement and acting as-if, clients are helped to reorient themselves toward more positive ways of functioning.

Adlerians attempt to go beyond overt behavior and understand the motivation behind the behavior (Nystul, 1985b). This approach is therefore more concerned with modifying motivation than with modifying behavior. Sonstegard, Hagerman, and Bitter (1975) elaborated on this position:

> The Adlerian counselor is not preoccupied with changing behavior; rather he is concerned with understanding the individual's subjective frame of reference and the identification of the individual's mistaken notion or goal within that framework. Indeed, the behavior of an individual is only understood when the goals are identified. (p. 17)

Mosak and Maniacci (2011) summarized the major goals of Adlerian psychotherapy as follows:

- Increasing clients' social interest

- Helping clients overcome feelings of discouragement and reducing inferiority feelings

- Modifying clients' lifestyle in terms of views and goals

- Addressing faulty motivation

- Helping clients feel a sense of equality with others

- Assisting clients to become contributing members of society

The counseling process is educationally oriented, providing information to clients and guiding them and attempting to encourage discouraged clients. The approach attempts to reeducate clients to foster self-acceptance, acceptance of others, and a feeling of connectedness and belonging (Mosak & Maniacci, 2011). The counseling relationship is based on equality. Adlerians avoid placing the client in a subservient position, as in a doctor-patient relationship. They consider a sense of mutual respect to be vital to all relationships, including the counseling relationship.

Dinkmeyer and Dinkmeyer (1985) identified four phases of Adlerian psychotherapy: establishing the relationship, performing analysis and assessment, promoting insight, and reorientation. These authors observed that the phases are not intended to be separate or distinct processes but instead tend to overlap and blend in clinical practice. This can be especially true in the process of establishing a positive relationship. Adlerians believe it is important to maintain a positive relationship throughout the counseling process.

Techniques

Adlerian techniques can be described in terms of the four phases of Adlerian psychotherapy.

PHASE 1: ESTABLISHING THE RELATIONSHIP Adlerians utilize many techniques to establish a positive relationship. Following are three of these techniques:

1. *Use of listening skills.* Dinkmeyer and Sperry (2000) noted that effective listening skills are necessary to promote mutual trust and mutual respect—two essential elements of the Adlerian counseling relationship.

2. *Winning respect and offering hope.* Nystul (1985b) suggested that a counselor can increase the client's motivation for becoming involved in counseling by winning the client's respect and offering hope.

3. *Encouragement.* Encouragement communicates a sense of support and can help clients learn to believe in themselves. Dinkmeyer and Losoncy (1980) and Watts and Pietrzak (2000) identified important skills that are involved in the encouragement process. Some of these skills are focusing on progress, assets, and strengths; helping clients see the humor in life experiences; communicating respect and confidence; being enthusiastic; helping the client become aware of choices; combating self-defeating, discouraging processes; and promoting self-encouragement.

Watts and Pietrzak (2000) suggested that Adlerian psychotherapy is essentially a process of encouragement. In this process, clients can be assisted in restoring hope and vitality in life. For example, a client was asked what stood out for him in Adlerian psychotherapy. He responded that Adlerian psychotherapy helped him find the courage to go on living. Watts and Pietrzak noted that the Adlerian concept of encouragement is similar to the theoretical perspective underlying solution-focused brief therapy (de Shazer, 1985). Both perspectives are optimistic, focusing on strengths, solutions, and resources. They also parallel each other regarding how they conceptualize maladjustment, avoiding the medical model and focusing on overcoming discouragement (Adlerian) and identifying exceptions to the problems (solution-focused brief therapy).

PHASE 2: PERFORMING ANALYSIS AND ASSESSMENT Adlerians typically do an in-depth analysis and assessment as early as the first session. This usually involves conducting a lifestyle analysis to explore how early life experiences may have contributed to the adult personality.

Dream analysis can be a part of the lifestyle analysis (Mosak & Maniacci, 2011). Adlerians do not attempt to analyze dreams in terms of their symbolic content, as do Freudians. Instead, they see dreams as an attempt to deal with the difficulties and challenges of life. In this sense, dreams become a problem-solving activity, allowing the person a chance to rehearse for some future action (Mosak & Maniacci).

The lifestyle analysis can also be used to identify the client's strengths or assets, which in turn can be used to overcome the client's problems. In addition, it can be used to identify faulty or irrational views that may interfere with the client's growth. These are referred to as *basic mistakes,* described by the following statements (Mosak & Maniacci, 2011) with examples:

- *Overgeneralizations:* "People can't be trusted."

- *False goals of security:* "Make a mistake and you have had it."

- *Misrepresentations of life's demands:* "I never get any breaks."

- *Minimization of one's worth:* "I'm dumb."

- *Faulty value system:* "It doesn't matter how you play the game as long as you win."

PHASE 3: PROMOTING INSIGHT Adlerians believe that insight is an important prerequisite to long-term change. Insight allows clients to understand the dynamics of self defeating patterns so they can be corrected during the reorientation process. The main tool for providing insight is interpretation, which focuses on creating awareness of basic mistakes that are impeding the client's growth.

Counselors can use confrontation techniques during the insight process if they encounter resistance from clients. Shulman (1973) noted that confrontation can challenge a client to make an immediate response or change or to examine some issue. It can also foster immediacy in the relationship by enabling a client to know how the counselor is experiencing the client at the moment (Dinkmeyer & Dinkmeyer, 1985).

PHASE 4: REORIENTATION The final phase of Adlerian psychotherapy involves putting insight into action. Clients are encouraged to make necessary changes in their life as they develop more functional beliefs and behaviors. Counselors can use the following techniques during the reorientation phase:

1. *Spitting in the client's soup.* This technique can be used when clients engage in manipulative games, such as acting like a martyr. Spitting in their soup involves determining the payoff of the game and interpreting it to the client. For instance, a client may say, "My husband is such a drunk. I don't know why I put up with him." The counselor could respond by saying, "You must get a lot of sympathy from others because you have to put up with so much." As this client realizes that someone is aware of the payoffs she is receiving from her martyr syndrome, the game may seem less enjoyable.

2. ***The push-button technique.*** This technique, based on Ellis's (1962) rational-emotive therapy, involves having clients concentrate on pleasant and unpleasant experiences and the feelings they generate (Dinkmeyer & Dinkmeyer, 1985). When clients discover that their thoughts influence their emotions, they recognize that they can take control of their emotional responses. The push-button concept symbolizes the amount of control clients can exert when they "push the button" and put a stop to self-defeating processes. They can then create a constructive way of reacting to their situation, producing a more positive emotional response.

3. ***Catching oneself.*** Clients can use this technique to avoid old self-defeating patterns. Initially, clients may catch themselves in the process of self-defeating behaviors, such as playing a manipulative game. Eventually, they can catch themselves just before they start playing the game. Clients can be encouraged to use humor when they catch themselves, learning to laugh at how ridiculous their self-defeating tendencies are.

4. ***Acting as-if.*** This technique involves clients acting as if they could do whatever they would like to do, such as being more confident or being a better listener. The technique promotes a positive "can-do" spirit and a self-fulfilling prophecy, which can help clients experience success.

5. ***Task setting and commitment.*** Adlerians do not believe that change occurs by osmosis. They believe instead that it takes work and effort to change. Task setting and commitment are therefore essential aspects of Adlerian psychotherapy. Homework assignments can be useful in this regard by providing a structure through which clients can try out new modes of behaving.

Contemporary Issues

Many contemporary Adlerian concepts derive from the work of Rudolph Dreikurs (1897–1972), who was a student of Adler's. In 1939, just 2 years after Adler's death, Dreikurs moved to Chicago and established the Alfred Adler Institute of Chicago (Dinkmeyer & Dinkmeyer, 1985). In many ways, he picked up where Adler left off (Dinkmeyer & Dinkmeyer). He continued the development of Adlerian theory, especially in terms of parent education and child guidance. Dreikurs had a gift for taking Adler's writings and reworking them into concepts that are easy to understand and apply. In addition, he developed his own concepts based on Adlerian principles, such as the four goals of misbehavior (Dreikurs, 1949; Dreikurs & Soltz, 1964), encouragement (Dinkmeyer & Dreikurs, 1963), logical and natural consequences (Dreikurs & Soltz), and social equality (Dreikurs, 1971). Dreikurs maintained an active lecture tour during which he would demonstrate his approach. He is credited with having a great deal to do with the popularization and acceptance of Adlerian psychology as a major school of counseling and psychotherapy (Dinkmeyer & Dinkmeyer).

Don Dinkmeyer is another key individual in the evolution of Adlerian psychology. Dinkmeyer and his associates have incorporated a number of Adlerian and Dreikursian concepts into programs relating to children, adolescents, parents, and teachers. These programs have gained popularity among counselors and other members of the helping professions. Some of these programs are systematic training for effective parenting (STEP; Dinkmeyer & McKay, 1997) and developing understanding of self and others (DUSO-R; Dinkmeyer & Dinkmeyer, 1982).

Several other individuals have made significant contributions to contemporary Adlerian psychology. Ray Corsini (1977, 1979) developed an educational system based on Adlerian principles, which he called "individual education." Dreikurs, Corsini, Lowe, and Sonstegard (1959); Sherman and Dinkmeyer (1987); and Oscar Christenson have done much to promote the popularity of Adlerian family counseling.

A movement has begun toward integrating Adlerian psychology with other schools of thought. Shulman, in an interview with Nystul (1988), suggested that Adlerian psychology needed to develop further to incorporate new understandings in the fields of child development, neurochemistry, and cognitive psychology. Watkins (1984) pointed out the similarities between Adler's theory and vocational counseling, for example, that Adler's construct of lifestyle and Holland's personality types (such as realistic and investigative) both acknowledge the role that individual difference plays in psychological functioning.

The movement toward integration has gained momentum among the Adlerian ranks. A special issue of *Individual Psychology: The Journal of Adlerian Theory, Research, and Practice* focused on exploring the issues relating to "beyond Adler." In this special issue, Carlson (Nystul, 1991) suggested that the Adlerian movement has become isolated, focusing too much on well-developed concepts such as the four goals of misbehavior and logical consequences. Carlson contended that broader, more permeable boundaries are needed for Adlerian psychology to become part of the mainstream of contemporary psychology (Nystul). Carlson also suggested that Adlerian approaches could be developed to reach nontraditional, non-YAVIS (young, attractive, verbal, intelligent, and sensitive) clients, clients who are victims of family violence, clients with HIV/ AIDS, and clients who require sex therapy. Mosak (1991) echoed the call for change by noting that Adlerian theory focuses too much on the psychology of abnormalcy and not enough on the psychology of normalcy.

There appears to have been some progress regarding the infusing of new concepts and ideas into Adlerian psychology. Watts (2000) contended that Adlerian psychology is relevant as we enter the new millennium, suggesting that Adlerian psychology has a broad theoretical basis and is well suited for integrating. In its current form, Watts posited, Adlerian psychotherapy represents an integration of psychodynamic, cognitive, and systemic theories and can be easily adapted to emerging trends in counseling, such as approaches that are directive, time limited, present centered, and problem focused. Schwartz and Waldo (2003) noted that Adlerian psychology (Adler, 1969) and interpersonal theory (Meyer, 1957; Sullivan, 1968) share a social/interpersonal perspective that makes these two theories excellent candidates for integration. Common theoretical perspectives shared by these two theories include the following:

- Early life experiences play a role in how people develop and maintain interpersonal relationships throughout life.

- Therapy involves reorienting people from inappropriate ways of reacting to others, which are often based on early life experiences.

- People are motivated to establish and maintain meaningful interpersonal relationships.

- Mental health is associated with social interest and interpersonal functioning.

Adlerian Brief Approaches to Counseling

According to the Adlerian scholar Ansbacher (1989), Adlerian counseling and psychotherapy were the first forms of brief counseling. Adler believed that time limits in counseling could be beneficial and typically restricted his sessions to a 10-week period with two sessions per week (Ansbacher). A number of Adlerian constructs are particularly relevant to brief-counseling theory and practice. For example, the use of encouragement and focusing on clients' assets is consistent with the strengths perspective advocated in contemporary brief-counseling models. Kurt Adler (Adler's son) suggested that although Adlerian counseling is a forerunner to brief-counseling methods, it is neither a short- nor a long-term form of counseling; instead, it is a flexible approach that can be adjusted to the unique and emerging needs of clients (Adler, 1972).

Contemporary Adlerians are making innovative advances in developing brief-counseling approaches. Sperry (1987, 1989b) was one of the first Adlerians to set forth specific procedures for conducting brief counseling. He developed a simple cognitive map that clinicians can use to organize all forms of brief consultations, including "sidewalk consults" and emergency phone calls. Maniacci (1996) developed a brief-counseling model for treating personality disorders. He noted that Adlerian procedures such as the lifestyle assessment are particularly useful to understanding core personality issues. Adlerian brief therapy, a relatively new Adlerian approach developed by Bitter and Nicoll (2004), has a relational focus. These scholars contended that the therapeutic relationship and client change are interrelated.

Adlerian brief therapy represents an integration of Adlerian theory and solution-focused therapy. Factors that help keep the approach brief include time limits, therapeutic focus, counselor directiveness and optimism, symptoms as solutions, and assignments of behavioral tasks.

Postmodern Perspectives and Adlerian Psychology

The postmodern theories such as constructivism and social constructionism appear to have much in common with Adlerian psychology. Adlerian psychology has been recognized as laying the theoretical foundations for constructivism (Mahoney, 1991; Mahoney & Lyddon, 1988; Watts, 2000; Watts & Pietrzak, 2000). Constructivism and Adler's theory have several psychological constructs in common (Jones, 1995; Scott, Kelly, & Tolbert, 1995). For example, both theories emphasize the role of cognition in psychological functioning, noting the active role people play in creating their own reality. As Adler contended, the creative self allows each person an opportunity to make a unique response based on his or her past experiences and the capacity for self-determination.

Adlerian psychology also appears to have much in common with social constructionism. Social constructionism stresses the role of social forces, such as the narratives reflected in cultures, in creating personal meanings or "storied lives." Adler's construct of social interests also reflects an ecological perspective in the sense that mental health and meaning in life are to a large degree achieved through interest in, concern about, and involvement with others.

Summary and Evaluation

Adler was a man ahead of his time. His psychological insights stressed the importance of phenomenology, holism, and social interest—concepts that are incorporated into most contemporary counseling theories (Maniacci, Sackett-Maniacci, & Mosak, 2014). Adlerian psychology is perhaps best known for concepts that can be used to understand individual differences in lifestyle, family dynamics, birth order, and sibling rivalry. Another strength of Adlerian psychology is its influence on programs like systematic training for effective parenting (STEP) and other guidance programs.

A criticism of the contemporary Adlerian approach is that Adlerian counselors may be trying too hard to adhere to Adler's original concepts in terms of theory, research, and practice. As Shulman recommended in an interview with Nystul (Nystul, 1988), Adlerian psychology must be responsive to ongoing advances in counseling and psychology if it is to remain a viable theory for contemporary practitioners. Another criticism of Adlerian psychotherapy is its narrow focus on and use of the concept of basic mistakes (Nystul, 1994a). Adlerian psychology focuses on cognitions rather than behaviors, emotions, and cognitions together (Jones, 1995). It would seem that a more comprehensive treatment program would focus on all three of these domains of psychological functioning.

The manner in which cognitions are conceptualized in Adlerian psychotherapy can also be problematic. From an Adlerian perspective, cognitions are primarily thought of in terms of basic mistakes (Jones, 1995; Nystul, 1994a). Jones noted that basic mistakes are key to understanding lifestyle and emotional disorders. Nystul suggested that to a large degree, Adlerian psychotherapy involves reorienting clients from their basic mistakes. It is unfortunate that so much emphasis is placed on the concept of basic mistakes because the concept may be inconsistent with the Adlerian theory of personality (e.g., psychology of use) and discouraging to clients (see Nystul [1994a] for a detailed description of these issues).

Jung's Analytic Psychology

Background Information

Carl Gustav Jung (1875–1961) was born in Kesswil, Switzerland. His father was a pastor, which may have contributed to his fondness for religion. Jung's intellectual interests were by far the most varied of the three classic theorists. As a young man, he became intrigued by mythology, philosophy, religion, history, literature, and archaeology. While Jung was struggling to decide what to study at the university, he had an unusual dream that somehow compelled him to pursue medicine (Hall & Lindzey, 1978). Jung went on to obtain a medical degree from the University of Basel in 1900, the same year Freud published *The Interpretation of Dreams,* a work that may have influenced Jung's decision to specialize in psychiatry. Shortly thereafter, Jung obtained a position at the University of Zurich and worked under Eugene Bleuler, who was well known for his theories on schizophrenia. During this time, Jung was also fortunate to study with Pierre Janet, who was conducting research on hysteria and multiple personality disorders.

In 1907, Jung had his first meeting with Freud. They must have found many areas of common interest, as they talked continuously for 13 hours. In fact, Freud believed that Jung was his crown prince and successor (Hall & Lindzey, 1978). It was therefore not surprising that in 1910, Jung became the first president of the International Psychoanalytic Association. Their initial compatibility was short-lived, however, as Jung began to differ with Freud on important theoretical issues. Like Adler, Jung became particularly disenchanted with Freud's emphasis on the role of sexuality in personality development (Safran & Kriss, 2014). By 1914, Jung felt he could no longer participate in the Freudian movement, and he resigned from the presidency of the International Psychoanalytic Association.

At this point, Jung decided to develop his own school of psychology, which he called *analytic psychology.* It is interesting to note that as with Freud, some of Jung's most creative years occurred during a time of personal distress, between 1913 and 1916. Jung was able to make the most of these difficult times. He did extensive self-analysis through the interpretation of his dreams during this period and obtained a number of insights that had a profound effect on the development of his theory, for example, the importance of gaining an understanding of unconscious processes during psychotherapy.

Jung's analytic theory was unique in its varied theoretical foundations. He was able to integrate his early interests in religion, mythology, archaeology, literature, history, and philosophy into the study of psychology, resulting in what may be the most comprehensive understanding of the human condition (Hall & Lindzey, 1978). His collected works are extensive, filling 20 volumes (Read, Fordham, & Adler, 1953–1978). Jung's work holds particular interest for those who wish to integrate mystical ideas from the Far East with analytical concepts from the Western European and American traditions.

Theory of Personality

Jung's theory of personality is very robust, incorporating elements from disciplines including Eastern philosophy, theology and religion, medicine, and psychology. Jung's ideas are becoming increasingly popular (Harris, 1996) and can be found in such best-selling books as Estes's (1992) *Women Who Run With the Wolves*. An overview of Jung's theory of personality follows.

VIEW OF HUMAN NATURE Jung (1928) had a positive view of the human condition, believing that people have inherent tendencies toward individualization—becoming unique individuals capable of wholeness and self-realization. This process of individualization is characterized by a union or integration of conscious and unconscious processes (Jung).

KEY CONCEPTS Jung identified the following concepts associated with his theory of personality (Read et al., 1953–1978).

The Ego, the Personal Unconscious, and the Collective Unconscious According to Kaufmann (1989), Jung believed that the psyche is made up of autonomous yet interdependent subsystems of the ego, the personal unconscious, and the collective unconscious. The ego represents the conscious mind, and the personal unconscious and collective unconscious make up the unconscious domain of the psyche.

The *ego* is the center of consciousness and is made up of conscious perceptions, memories, thoughts, and feelings (Kaufmann, 1989). It provides consistency and direction in people's lives (Fadiman & Frager, 1976).

The *personal unconscious* is similar to Freud's preconscious, containing thoughts based on personal experience just beyond the reach of conscious recall (Feist, 1985). It contains forgotten or repressed material that had once been conscious and could become conscious in the future (Hall & Lindzey, 1978). The information in the personal unconscious clusters around several complexes (Kaufmann, 1989), and these revolve around themes, such as prestige or control, that can interfere with effective living (Corey, 1982). For example, a client could have a "mother complex" whereby he behaves as if he were under his mother's domination or control.

The **collective unconscious** is sometimes referred to as the transpersonal or nonpersonal unconscious since it is not associated with personal experiences. It is considered the most provocative yet controversial aspect of Jung's theory (Hall & Lindzey). The collective unconscious is made up of memory traces inherited from one's ancestral past. Jung called it *collective* because he believed that all people shared common images and thoughts regarding such things as mother, earth, birth, and death. Jung referred to these universal thoughts as **archetypes**. He believed that the collective unconscious creates the foundation for the personality. Starting from birth, the collective unconscious guides an individual's life experiences, thereby influencing perceptions, emotions, and behavior. It is therefore the most powerful and influential aspect of the personality (Hall & Lindzey).

Jung suggested that the collective unconscious was not directly amenable to the conscious but could be observed indirectly through its manifestations in eternal themes in mythology, folklore, and art (Kaufmann, 1989). Jung visited numerous indigenous cultures in Africa and the American Southwest to test his theory. He found that even though these cultures evolved independently, they shared intricate memories that could have been transmitted only by a collective unconscious.

Archetypes Jung discovered that several archetypes have evolved so completely that they can be considered separate systems within the personality (Hall & Lindzey, 1978). These are the persona, the anima and animus, the shadow, and the self.

The *persona* is the public self one projects as opposed to the private, personal view of oneself. The persona is reflected in various roles, such as work, marriage and family, and social situations. According to Jung, awareness of the persona has an inverse relation to awareness of one's personal self or individuality. For example, the more aware one is of the persona, the less aware one will be of individuality and the private, personal self.

The *anima* and *animus* refer to the suggestion that people have both masculine and feminine dimensions to their personality. The anima is the feminine archetype in men, and the animus is the masculine archetype in women. Jung believed these archetypes resulted from years of men and women living together (Hall & Lindzey, 1978). This archetype appears in dreams and fantasies as figures of the opposite sex and functions as the primary mediator between unconscious and conscious processes (Fadiman & Frager, 1976).

The *shadow* represents the negative or evil side of the personality that people do not want to recognize. The shadow is associated with thoughts that originate from animal instincts inherited through the evolutionary process.

The *self* is the center of the personality, including the conscious and unconscious parts of the mind (Feist, 1985). The self provides the personality with a sense of unity, equilibrium, and stability (Hall & Lindzey, 1978). The self cannot emerge until the other systems of the personality have fully developed, which is usually not until middle age (Corey, 1982). This is when the center of the individual shifts from the conscious ego to the midpoint between conscious and unconscious (Hall & Lindzey). This midpoint region becomes the domain of the self. It is not surprising that Jung discovered the existence of the self when he was studying Eastern meditation practices, which emphasize the interaction between conscious and unconscious processes.

Personality Types Jung noted that personality types could be differentiated in terms of attitudes and functions. He identified two types of attitudes: extroverted (or outgoing) and introverted (or introspective). According to Jung, people have both attitudes in their personality makeup. The dominant attitude is represented in the conscious mind, and the subordinate attitude exists in the unconscious psyche (Hall & Lindzey, 1978). Jung also described four functions that provide additional means of differentiating personality types. These include thinking, feeling, sensation, and intuition. Jung contended that although people rely on all these functions to react to events, the function that is the best developed will be relied on most and becomes the superior function.

Theory of Counseling and Psychotherapy

Jung's approach to counseling and psychotherapy is called *analytic psychotherapy*. It emphasizes the role of unconscious processes in psychological functioning. Through dream analysis and other procedures, the client becomes aware of unconscious processes and learns to use that understanding to maximize mental health and wellness.

The overall aim of analytic psychotherapy is to help the self emerge so that the client can be free to move toward self-realization. For this to occur, the analyst must help the client develop the other major systems of the personality. Much of psychotherapy therefore involves exploring unconscious processes in order for clients to gain insight into the structure of their personality (Kaufmann, 1989). In time, clients can learn how to make the various systems develop to their fullest and function in a complementary fashion. For example, a client describing himself as a real "macho-type" person seeks help for marital problems. The analytic psychotherapist may encourage the client to recognize the feminine (anima) dimension to his personality. According to analytic theory, this will help the client become a more fully functioning person and develop a better understanding of life.

Jung had a unique conception of psychopathology. He believed the symptoms associated with psychopathology could be instructive for both the client and analyst (Kaufmann, 1989), could serve as warning signals that something was wrong, and could provide clues into the functioning of the personality (Kaufmann). Jung was therefore reluctant to use medication to treat mental disorders because he was afraid it might mask important messages that symptoms could communicate.

The nature of the therapeutic relationship in analytic psychotherapy is also unique. Analysts are required to undertake their own analysis, which helps them gain a respect for what is involved in being a client. They do not see the counseling relationship as one in which a healthy analyst treats a sick patient. Instead, Jungian analysts view therapy as involving one person who has journeyed into the unconscious helping another person develop a meaningful dialogue with unconscious processes (Kaufmann, 1989). The Jungian analyst also believes it is critical for the client to feel a sense of acceptance during therapy (Kaufmann).

Fadiman and Frager (1976) described two major stages utilized in Jungian psychotherapy. In the *analytic stage,* clients attempt to identify unconscious material. This is followed by the *synthetic stage,* which initially involves helping clients use insight to formulate new experiences. The final phase of the synthetic stage is called *transformation,* in which clients engage in self-education and thus become more autonomous and responsible for their own development.

Techniques

Jung advocated a flexible approach to psychotherapy, believing that the method of treatment should be determined by the unique features of each client (Harris, 1996). His approach shares the characteristics of the art-of-counseling model described in Chapter 1, in that he recommended the analyst be creative and flexible in working with the client. Because Jungian psychology is based on the guiding principle that anything goes, as long as it seems to work, it is a practical approach (Kaufmann, 1989). When one client complained of difficulty falling asleep, for example, Jung simply sang the client a lullaby (Kaufmann).

Jung was skeptical of using techniques in therapy because he thought they could be unnecessarily restrictive. At the same time, he believed dream analysis could be a useful vehicle for helping clients explore unconscious processes. Unlike Freud, Jung found little value in analyzing a single dream. He believed it was essential to investigate the interrelationship of several dreams recorded over a period of time. In this process, Jung would help the client understand the symbolic meaning of dreams and how they provide clues to the various systems of the personality.

Contemporary Issues

Jungian psychology continues to be a major force in psychotherapy. As of 2009, there were more than 2,929 certified analysts in 45 countries, and there were 51 professional societies (Douglas, 2011). Douglas suggested that the Jung's analytic psychotherapy provides a meaningful theoretical perspective for understanding an increasingly complex world. He also noted that psychological constructs from Jung's theory are constantly evolving (e.g., reassessment of anima and animus in terms of changing views of masculine and feminine).

An emerging trend is the conceptualization of Jungian psychology from a paradoxical perspective (Harris, 1996). Jung's theory is founded on the concept of paradox, and *paradox* implies "ambiguity, a puzzle or dilemma, a tension between opposite poles of an issue, even incongruity between elements of a larger whole" (Harris, p. 4). Harris suggested that there are no simple answers in Jungian psychology. Instead, balance and wholeness can evolve from working with opposing paradoxical forces. In this regard, analytic psychotherapy involves helping clients seek out painful opposing forces in their lives to generate creative new solutions to old problems (Harris).

Additional trends in Jungian psychology are directed at diversification and integration. There are three schools of Jungian psychology: classical, developmental, and archetypal

(Samuels, 1985). The classical school emphasizes the role of the self as the major personality construct, the developmental school focuses on the use of transference and interpretation to work through problems associated with childhood experiences, and the archetypal school relates primarily to issues pertaining to archetypes (Spiegelman, 1989). Samuels (1989) suggested that the emerging schools of Jungian psychology need not be viewed as being in conflict. In fact, he believed differences should be encouraged to foster creative developments in Jungian psychology. Jungian psychology is also expanding its horizons in an attempt to incorporate other theories and approaches. An example is Saayman, Faber, and Saayman's (1988) exploration of how family systems theory could be integrated into Jungian marital therapy.

Jungian concepts have been incorporated into the development of a number of psychological tests, such as the Myers-Briggs, the Thematic Apperception Test, and the Rorschach (Douglas, 2011). For example, the Myers-Briggs utilizes Jung's concept of attitudes and functions in terms of introvert, extrovert, thinking, and feeling. The Myers-Briggs has become popular with individuals who want to gain self-understanding and for use in organizational and industrial psychology (McCrae & Costa, 1989).

Jungian Brief Approaches to Counseling

Analytic psychotherapy has traditionally been a long-term form of treatment directed at maximizing the functioning of the personality (Harris, 1996). Harris suggested that, owing to the restrictions on the length and nature of counseling imposed by managed care, Jungian clinicians must develop flexible practices and approaches. She contended that Jungian principles and strategies have been successfully adapted to time-limited counseling, focused on resolving specific problems with clients of various ages and socioeconomic status. Harris also believed that Jungian long-term counseling and psychotherapy can be valuable, especially in cases requiring personality restructuring. In these instances, the analyst may work with a client to provide the necessary services outside of the restrictions imposed by managed care.

Summary and Evaluation

The fundamental strength of Jung's approach lies in his comprehensive view of the human condition. Hall and Lindzey (1978) observed that "the originality and audacity of Jung's thinking have few parallels in recent scientific history, and no other person aside from Freud has opened more conceptual windows into what Jung would choose to call the 'soul of man'" (p. 149).

Jung has had a major influence on many aspects of contemporary thought, such as religion, art, music, literature, and drama (Douglas, 2011). For example, Jung's theories and interest in Eastern philosophy and spirituality appear to have played a key role in the current interest in holistic health and its use of yoga and meditation. Jung believed that wholeness and psychological balance occur when the conscious and unconscious mind learn to work in harmony. He also believed that people have the inherent capacity for psychological growth and self-healing (Douglas).

Jung's theories have also played a role in the evolution of psychological theories. For example, Jung's notion of individualization over the life span has been incorporated into life span theories such as those of Gilligan, Erikson, and Kohlberg (Douglas, 2011). Jung's deep caring for his clients and sense of hope and optimism have also laid the foundation for the humanistic theories of Maslow, Rogers, and others (Douglas). In addition, Jungian concepts have influenced counseling procedures, especially the use of the creative arts such as art therapy, dance therapy, and sand-tray therapy (Douglas). Jung used the creative arts in his own therapeutic procedures. He would, for example, encourage clients to express themselves through art or expressive movement and would also engage in these processes himself to better understand the client (Douglas). During his own self-analysis, Jung constructed a stone village as a means of working through some of his issues (Douglas), a concept later modified into what is currently known as sand-tray therapy (see Allan & Brown [1993] and Carmichael [1994] for more information on sand-tray therapy).

Jungian psychology has attracted several criticisms. The existence of a collective unconscious has been challenged more than any other of his constructs. Glover (1950) insisted that the concept is metaphysical and incapable of proof and further suggested that Jung's theory lacks developmental concepts necessary to explain the growth of the mind. Hall and Lindzey (1978) observed that many psychologists have found Jung's writing to be "baffling, obscure, confusing, and disorganized" (p. 148).

The Classic Theories and Their Use in Contemporary Practice

The classic theories of Freud, Adler, and Jung may be criticized as outdated, of little use to clinicians, and inapplicable to recent trends such as brief counseling and diversity counseling. Although these criticisms have some validity and need to be taken into consideration, the strengths of the classic theories can be of use to current practitioners. The following section is a brief overview of these theories as they relate to diversity issues and brief-counseling approaches.

Diversity Issues in the Classic Theories

Diversity issues raise some questions concerning the classic theories of Freud, Adler, and Jung. Freudian theory may be the most limited from a cross-cultural perspective. Freud tended to overemphasize intrapsychic forces, such as the endopsychic forces resulting from competition among the id, ego, and superego, at the expense of understanding sociocultural forces that can play a role in human functioning. On the positive side, Freud was a genius at describing intrapsychic forces, and a recognition of these forces is essential to the understanding of people, regardless of culture.

Adler and Jung appear to have achieved more of a balance between the intrapsychic and sociocultural perspectives. This may be especially true of Adler, who emphasized cognitive processes (intrapsychic forces) and social interest (social embeddedness), both of which play key roles in psychological functioning. Jung also sought theoretical balance in his attempt to integrate the intrapsychic working of the conscious and unconscious mind with ontological issues of spirituality, transcendence, wholeness, and healing.

Gender issues should also be considered when addressing the classic theories. Freudian psychology has come under fire from feminists and others for a number of reasons. From a feminist perspective, Freudian psychology is one of the best examples in the psychological literature of an overt display of male dominance. This anti-female spirit is perhaps captured best in his concept of penis envy, which women are supposed to have as they progress through the psychosexual stages of development. Adler (and his colleague Dreikurs) and Jung would appear to fare much better than Freud in terms of gender considerations. The theories of Adler and Dreikurs have played an important role in promoting social equality between the sexes (Dreikurs, 1971). Jung's work also appears to apply well to gender issues because of its incorporation of Eastern concepts, which have been integrated into the holistic health-and-wellness movement.

Brief Counseling and the Classic Theories

Although the classic theories (perhaps with the exception of Adlerian) were originally developed as a form of long-term therapy, they hold much promise for clinicians interested in brief counseling. First and foremost, the classic theories offer counselors a comprehensive means for understanding the personality dynamics of the client before counselors develop a treatment plan and implement interventions. Although brief-counseling approaches are not designed for personality restructuring, some comprehensive means of understanding the dynamics of behavior would seem essential in any approach to counseling.

In fact, the classic theories offer other concepts and procedures useful in brief counseling. For example, the Adlerian/Dreikursian concept of encouragement stands out as a critical counseling concept. It can foster a positive counseling relationship and help clients begin to believe in their own inherent strengths and abilities, a focal point of brief counseling. Jung's focus on psychological health and wellness is also consistent with brief counseling in its positive approach to clients. Freudian psychoanalysis has also become more appropriate to brief counseling by revising as its practitioners adapt the approach to fit within a time-limited format.

SUMMARY

The theories of Freud, Adler, and Jung are considered classic theories because of their historical significance and comprehensiveness. These theories share some elements. Freud and Adler both noted the importance of early life experiences for adult personality formation. Freud and Jung both emphasized the role of unconscious forces in personality functioning.

Each theory also has its unique psychological constructs and orientation. Freud stressed the role of sexuality and developed a psychosexual model of personality development. Adler favored the importance of social interest as a major motivating force in the dynamics of personality. Jung was known for his formulation of the collective unconscious, proposing that all people inherit a common set of memories from birth that are passed on from generation to generation.

The three classic schools of psychology continue to evolve in terms of theory, research, and practice. In addition, each has had a major impact on the evolution of current psychotherapies. Most contemporary counseling theories have incorporated psychological constructs from Freud, Adler, and Jung, most notably the wide recognition of the importance of early life experiences and the existence of unconscious processes. Some of the principles of Adlerian psychology have been particularly influential in the evolution of modern clinical practice (Corey, 2013). Adlerian concepts of holism and phenomenology are reflected in experiential theories. Adler's emphasis on cognition has also contributed to current cognitive-behavioral approaches.

The strength of the classic schools is their foundation in personality theory. They tend to be more limited in terms of their approaches to counseling and psychotherapy. In this regard, the classic schools of psychotherapy need further development and integration with modern counseling practice to enable practitioners to develop comprehensive treatment programs.

PERSONAL EXPLORATION

1. Provide an overview of Freud's concept of the id, ego, and superego. How can this theory be used to understand behavior?

2. What did Adler mean by "social interest," and how can you use this principle to enhance mental health?

3. Why do some consider dreams to be the "royal road to the unconscious"?

4. How could you use the theories of personality associated with the classic theories to understand behavior? Can you cite a couple of examples?

5. Jung's concept of the collective unconscious is controversial. What are your thoughts on this concept?

6. Provide an overview of Jung's archetypes. How might you use this concept to understand behavior?

7. Provide an overview of Freud's conscious–unconscious continuum. What do you find interesting about this concept?

8. What do you think about Adler's ideas regarding the family constellation (e.g., birth order characteristics and their impact on personality)?

9. What about Freud's theory of psycho-sexual stages of development has been controversial?

10. What is the overall aim of analytic psychotherapy, and how can it be used to promote a fully functioning person?

11. What did Adler mean when he proposed understanding behavior from a teleological perspective?

12. Why are the theories of Freud, Adler, and Jung referred to as the "classic theories"?

LEARNING ACTIVITIES

1. Consider how you would use various theoretical constructs associated with the theories of Freud, Adler, and Jung to understand behavior in yourself and others. Evaluate which constructs might be more or less useful.

2. Analyze your dreams, trying to determine what they may say about you.

WEBSITES

Boeree, C. G. (2006). *Carl Jung*. Retrieved from http://www.ship.edu/~cgboeree/jung.html. *Presents an overview of Jungian theory.*

Rose, L., et al. (n.d.). *Sigmund Freud archives*. Retrieved from http://www.freudarchives.org/.

Williams, D., Tan, E., & Clapp, M. (2005). *The Jung page: Reflections on psychology, culture, and life*. Retrieved from http://www.cgjungpage.org/. *This is the comprehensive and official Carl Jung website; updated frequently.*

The Art and Science of Experiential Counseling

The art and science of counseling and psychotherapy are reflected in experiential theories and approaches. The art of counseling plays a key role in experiential counseling, as experiential counselors, like artists, attempt to bring out the hidden beauty in their clients. They often use creative arts modalities (such as music, art, dance, drama, and bibliotherapy) to help clients discover strengths they can use to enhance their psychological functioning.

The counseling relationship is based on humanistic psychology, which recognizes the benefits of allowing one's humanness to stimulate and enhance interpersonal relationships. Open, candid interactions are common and encourage immediacy and authenticity in the counseling process. The art of experiential counseling also allows for intense therapeutic encounters. In these instances, the counselor may use self-transcendence to move beyond empathy and understanding to directly *experience* the client's joy or suffering.

The science of experiential counseling provides objectivity as a necessary balance to the art of counseling. Experiential counseling can be emotionally exhausting and taxing for both counselors and clients. The science of experiential counseling monitors the degree of psychological intensity and, like a navigator on a ship, enables the counselor and client to chart a realistic and productive course for therapy.

The science of experiential counseling is directly related to research methodology. Experiential theorists like Carl Rogers (and his person-centered approach) have played a key role in counseling research. Rogers was keenly aware of the interrelationship between theory, research, and practice (Heppner, Rogers, & Lee, 1984). He developed his

Chapter Overview

This chapter provides an overview of experiential theories and approaches to counseling. Highlights of the chapter include the following:

- **The art and science of experiential counseling**

- **Person-centered theory of personality and counseling**

- **Gestalt theory of personality and counseling**

- **Existential theory of personality and counseling**

- **Overview of the creative arts therapies (CATs) of music, art, dance, drama, and bibliotherapy and multimodality CAT**

- **Research trends**

- **Brief experiential approaches**

- **Diversity issues**

person-centered theory based on empirical research and extensive clinical practice and pioneered the research procedure of listening to counseling tapes to gain an understanding of the change process in counseling (Greenberg, Elliott, & Lietaer, 1994). Much of the recent interest in the change process can be traced to Rogers's early work (Greenberg et al.).

Other trends in experiential counseling research focus on analyzing the impact of specific experiential counseling strategies (such as the Gestalt empty-chair technique) on the change process. This line of research is qualitative in nature, whereby the counselor and client attempt to discover (as co-investigators) the subtle nuances of the change process, and much of the research in experiential counseling is directed at this type of methodology (Greenberg et al., 1994).

As noted in Chapter 6, maintaining a multicultural perspective is recommended from the perspective of both the art and the science of counseling. Experiential theories like existentialism appear to foster this perspective because they encourage an exploration of philosophical concepts—such as the meaning of life. Using experiential theories means making the necessary modifications to incorporate multicultural research findings and maintain a sensitivity to the evolving needs of clients.

Experiential Counseling

This chapter begins by providing an overview of three major theories and approaches to counseling that emphasize experiential processes: person-centered, Gestalt, and existential. The last part of the chapter describes the major creative arts therapy (CAT) modalities of music, art, drama, and dance as well as bibliotherapy and multimodality CAT. The common thread shared by these theories is their emphasis on the importance of the *experiential* aspect of counseling.

Experiential Theories

The **experiential theories** focus on what the client is experiencing during the counseling process. In person-centered counseling, the client is encouraged to experience the "self" in an open and flexible manner (Raskin & Rogers, 2005). The focus of Gestalt counseling is to help clients become aware of what they are thinking and feeling in the here and now. Existential therapy suggests that a client can obtain personal meaning by experiencing both the joys and sorrows of life. From an existential point of view, even anxiety can be instructive.

The experiential theories maintain a humanistic orientation regarding the nature of people. They tend to view people as inherently positive with self-actualizing tendencies. The experiential theories can therefore be particularly attractive to counselors who share this optimistic point of view. An overview of these three theories is provided in Table 8.1.

Table 8.1 Overview of Experiential Approaches

Theory	Founder(s)	Key Concepts	The Counseling Process	Techniques
Person-centered	Carl Rogers	Trust in the inherent self-actualizing tendencies of people; the role of the self and the client's internal frame of reference in personality dynamics	Involves an if-then process: If certain conditions are established (such as communicating empathic understanding), then the client will move toward self-actualization.	Although no techniques are identified, the approach requires the use of listening skills to communicate empathic understanding and establish other core conditions.
Gestalt	Fritz Perls	An existential-phenomenological perspective; moving from dependence to independence; being integrated and centered in the present	Involves a dialogue between the therapist and client whereby the client becomes aware of what is occurring in the here and now.	The therapist models authenticity and uses techniques to help the client become aware and centered in the present. Some techniques include the empty-chair technique and the use of personal pronouns.
Existential therapy	Victor Frankl, James Bugental, Rollo May, and Irvin Yalom	Uniqueness of the individual; search for meaning; role of anxiety; freedom of responsibility; being and nonbeing	Emphasizes the role of the counseling relationship over techniques. Counseling goals can include searching for personal meaning and becoming aware of choices.	Techniques include paradoxical reflection, dereflection, and existential encounters.

Person-Centered Therapy

Background Information

Carl Rogers (1902–1987), the fourth of six children, was raised in a close-knit family with strict religious beliefs (Rogers, 1961). In 1931, Rogers obtained a PhD degree in clinical psychology from the Teachers College of Columbia University.

Rogers then embarked on his professional career, taking a position as a psychologist with the Child Guidance Clinic of Rochester, New York. Shortly thereafter, in 1939, he wrote his first book, *The Clinical Treatment of the Problem Child*, which was based on his experience at the guidance center. This led to his appointment as a full professor in psychology at Ohio State University. It was there during the 1940s that Rogers began to formulate his own approach to counseling and psychotherapy, culminating in the publication of *Counseling and Psychotherapy* (1942).

From 1945 to 1964, Rogers held academic positions at the University of Chicago and the University of Wisconsin. During this time, he was able to continue developing his personal approach and explore its implementation in education, group process, and counseling and psychotherapy. Rogers noted that he had a somewhat negative experience with his academic peers at Ohio State University and the University of Wisconsin (Heppner et al., 1984). He felt he was not liked by his colleagues (he did not have a particularly high regard for them, either). Not surprisingly, he preferred graduate students or people outside the department as friends (Heppner et al.). In 1964, Rogers left academia permanently. During the last years of his career, he worked at the Institute for the Study of the Person in La Jolla, California. Today, the institute continues to provide training opportunities in person-centered counseling.

Theory of Personality

The theory of personality in person-centered counseling has a humanistic orientation focusing on phenomenology and the role of the self in psychological functioning. An overview of Rogers's theory of personality follows.

VIEW OF HUMAN NATURE Rogers (1951) held a positive view of human nature, noting the inherent self-actualizing tendencies of people. He believed that if the right conditions existed, people would naturally proceed toward self-actualization. His theory emphasizes the phenomenological perspective, suggesting that an individual's internal frame of reference is the best vantage point for understanding the person.

KEY CONCEPTS Raskin and Rogers (2005) noted that trust is the most fundamental concept in person-centered therapy. This theory contends that clients can be trusted to establish their own goals and monitor their progress toward these goals and that all individuals have inherent self-actualizing tendencies. Many other key concepts can be derived from Rogers's theory of personality (Rogers, 1951; Raskin, Rogers, & Witty, 2014), which is described in 19 propositions. The key concepts emphasize the role of a person's internal frame of reference and the self in understanding the dynamics of behavior. The following four propositions characterize Rogers's personality theory:

1. *People react to the phenomenal field as they experience and perceive it.* A person's phenomenal field is his or her internal frame of reference for perceiving the world. This proposition suggests that what a person perceives will be influenced by past experiences.

2. *The best point from which to understand behavior is the person's internal frame of reference.* This proposition is logically related to the first proposition. Since each person's perception

is unique, it can only be understood from the person's internal frame of reference. Rogers therefore advocated developing a phenomenological perspective, or understanding things from the client's perspective.

3. *People tend to behave in a manner consistent with their concept of self.* The self is the center of the organism and consists of how a person sees the self in relation to others. The self attempts to foster consistency within the organism by promoting behavior that is compatible to one's view of the self.

4. *The more people perceive and accept experiences, the more they will tend to be accepting and understanding of others.* Self-acceptance and understanding are viewed as contributing factors in understanding and accepting others as unique individuals.

Theory of Counseling and Psychotherapy

Rogers's **person-centered theory** can be described as an "if-then" approach. If certain conditions exist in the counseling relationship, then the client will move toward self-actualization (Rogers, 1961). Rogers identified the following three core conditions as necessary and sufficient for personal growth to occur (Rogers, 1957; Raskin et al., 2014):

1. *Counselor congruence.* Counselors are congruent in terms of what they are experiencing and what they communicate. For example, when counselors feel threatened by a client, it would be inappropriate for them to say they enjoy being with the client. This would communicate a confusing double message, and the counselor would not be genuine or authentic.

2. *Empathic understanding.* The counselor attempts to understand the client from the client's internal frame of reference. This phenomenological perspective involves understanding what the client is thinking, feeling, and experiencing and communicating this understanding to the client.

3. *Unconditional positive regard.* Rogers believed that it is essential for the counselor to communicate a sense of acceptance and respect to the client. There has been some misunderstanding of what Rogers meant by unconditional positive regard. He did not mean the counselor should tolerate and accept anything the client did (Martin, 1989). He instead believed the counselor should try to "separate the deed from the doer" (Martin). The counselor should accept the client as a person worthy of respect even though the client's behavior may be inappropriate (Rogers, Gendlin, Kiesler, & Truax, 1967).

In addition to these therapist-offered core conditions, Rogers (1957; Raskin et al., 2014) identified three other conditions that must occur for successful counseling to occur. The first two are considered preconditions for therapy: The therapist and client are in psychological contact, or aware of each other's presence, and the client is experiencing some discomfort in life to be motivated for therapy. The third condition is that the client must be able to accurately perceive and experience the core conditions set forth by the therapist.

A number of goals and therapeutic outcomes emerge from person-centered therapy. This style of counseling is unique in that it does not attempt to resolve the client's presenting problem. It instead assists the client in the growth process to become a fully functioning individual. Rogers identified the following changes that tend to occur as the client moves toward self-actualization (Rogers, 1961; Raskin et al., 2011):

- **Open to experience.** Clients are capable of seeing reality without distorting it to fit a preconceived self-structure. Instead of operating from a rigid belief system, clients are interested in exploring new horizons.

- **Self-trust.** Initially, clients tend to have self-doubts. They may believe that no matter what they decide, it will be wrong. As therapy progresses, clients can learn to trust their own judgment and become more self-confident.

- **Internal source of evaluation.** Person-centered therapy fosters the development of an internal locus of evaluation. This occurs as clients are encouraged to explore their inner choices and are discouraged from looking to others for a sense of direction or locus of evaluation.

- **Willingness to continue growing.** As a result of person-centered therapy, clients will realize that self-actualization is a process and not an end goal. In this sense, no one ever becomes self-actualized. Instead, a fully functioning person is always in the state of becoming.

Techniques

Rogers minimized the importance or use of techniques (Rogers, 1951, 1961; Raskin et al., 2014), instead emphasizing the importance of the counseling relationship. He believed that the counseling relationship could create core conditions that are the necessary and sufficient conditions for the client's self-actualization. The person-centered therapist uses listening skills to communicate empathic understanding and help the client explore inner choices. (Chapter 3 contains a counseling vignette that provides a Rogerian-oriented example of listening skills and additional information regarding Rogers's concept of core conditions in counseling.) Moon (2007) suggested that Rogers's approach can be best understood in terms of a particular attitude toward clients. Throughout Rogers's career, "he evidenced a devotion to experiencing the client's perceptions, meanings, intentions, and wishes and that he had no other agenda with clients" (Moon, p. 283).

Summary and Evaluation

Carl Rogers made a phenomenal contribution to counseling. He was the major figure behind the humanistic movement. In addition, many principles of his person-centered therapy have been incorporated into other current psychotherapies. For example, listening skills are frequently used to help establish a positive relationship, obtain a phenomenological understanding of the client, and promote the core conditions identified by Rogers.

Several studies have provided support for Rogers's theory and its application to a wide range of counseling procedures. Watkins (1993) noted that person-centered theory can be used in the contemporary practice of psychological testing, for instance when maintaining a client-centered focus to ensure that the client understands and can use test results or when using facilitating conditions (such as listening skills and core conditions) to maximize the client's readiness for positive involvement throughout the assessment process.

In a study examining the relationship between self-esteem and having a friend who communicates the core conditions of empathy, unconditional acceptance, and congruence, Cramer (1994) showed a positive relationship between self-esteem and having a friend who communicates all of these core conditions. Merrill and Andersen's (1993) qualitative study of Rogers's theory found that when the core conditions are applied to CAT, clients show gains in self-awareness, self-confidence, risk taking, and self-exploration. One limitation associated with the person-centered approach is that counseling goals are unclear, creating ambiguity in the counseling process. Usher (1989) also noted that the person-centered approach could be open to cross-cultural bias because of its emphasis on independence and individualism. In addition, research suggests that Rogers's core conditions are not necessary and sufficient but can more accurately be viewed as facilitative for personality change (Gelso & Carter, 1985; Gelso & Fretz 1992).

Gestalt Therapy
. . . .

Background Information

Frederick "Fritz" S. Perls (1893–1970), the founder of Gestalt therapy, was born in Berlin. Initially a student of psychoanalytic theory, Perls moved to the United States in 1946 and began to develop Gestalt therapy. He helped establish Gestalt Institutes in New York in 1952 and Cleveland in 1954.

Perls is best known for the work he did at the Esalen Institute of Big Sur, California, where he was a resident associate psychiatrist from 1964 to 1969. This was Perls's most productive and creative period. In 1969, he published two of his most popular books, *Gestalt Therapy Verbatim* (1969a) and *In and Out of the Garbage Pail* (1969b). Perls died a year later, after leaving the Esalen Institute to establish a Gestalt community on Vancouver Island in British Columbia.

Theory of Personality

The **Gestalt theory** of personality emphasizes the concepts of phenomenology, independence, and being integrated and centered in the now. An overview of Perls's theory of personality follows.

VIEW OF HUMAN NATURE Similar to the person-centered position, the Gestalt view of human nature is that people are self-determined, strive for self-actualization, and are best understood from a phenomenological perspective. The term *Gestalt* is taken from the principles of Gestalt psychology, which suggests that a person is a whole compiled of the interrelated parts of body, emotions, thoughts, sensations, and perceptions. Each of these aspects of a person can be understood only within the context of the whole person.

KEY CONCEPTS Perls (1969a, 1969b) and Yontef and Jacobs (2008) identified key concepts associated with Gestalt therapy, which are incorporated into the following:

1. *An existential-phenomenological perspective.* The Gestalt therapist functions from an existential-phenomenological perspective. From this perspective, the therapist attempts to understand a client from the client's perspective and helps clients gain personal meaning from their existence.

2. *Helping clients move from dependence to independence.* Perls referred to this concept when he said that Gestalt therapy helps clients make the transition from environmental support to self-support. When clients seek counseling, they tend to expect environmental support, such as reassurance, from the counselor. The Gestalt therapist avoids reinforcing clients' dependency needs and helps the client become an independent person. Clients will often resist moving toward self-support because change is threatening. When this occurs, the Gestalt therapist will usually frustrate and confront clients to help them work through the impasse.

3. *Being integrated and centered in the now.* Perls believed that nothing exists except the now, since the past is gone and the future is yet to come. From this perspective, self-actualization is centered in the present rather than oriented to the future. It requires that clients become centered in the now and aware of what they are experiencing. From a Gestalt perspective, being focused and centered in the here and now is referred to as *contact*.

Anxiety can result when clients are not centered in the now but are preoccupied with the future. When this occurs, clients may develop excessive worry about what might happen and lose touch with what is happening. Unresolved difficulties from the past can also cause problems, resulting in emotional reactions such as anger, guilt, or resentment. Being unaware of this "unfinished business" can interfere with one's functioning in the now. Resentment is seen as the most frequent and worst kind of unfinished business. Perls believed that unexpressed resentment often converts to guilt. For example, a man finds out his wife has had an affair and becomes angry and resentful. Unfortunately, he doesn't express his resentment. Instead, he wonders what he could have done to prevent the affair, resulting in feelings of guilt.

4. **Experimentation.** Gestalt therapy encourages clients to try something new to achieve genuine understanding. Experimentation goes beyond the status quo and involves thought and action versus mere behavioral change. Experimentation also generates data about the client that can be used to obtain a phenomenological understanding of the client's experience.

5. **Health.** From a Gestalt perspective, health requires

   - self-regulation (i.e., meeting one's needs via awareness, prioritizing, and organization and utilization of appropriate behavior), and

   - having contact with the person-environment field (i.e., being focused and centered in the here and now in terms of oneself in relation to the environment).

6. **Relational focus.** Gestalt therapy views personality functioning in relational-contextual terms (i.e., the self in relation to others). The interpersonal perspective emphasizes the interrelationship between the individual and the environment.

Theory of Counseling and Psychotherapy

The counseling process in Gestalt therapy is experiential. It focuses on what is occurring in the here and now of the moment (Yontef & Jacobs, 2014). "Explanations and interpretations are considered less reliable than what is directly perceived and felt" (Yontef & Simkin, 1989, p. 323). Gestalt therapy involves a dialogue between the therapist and client in which the client experiences from the inside what the therapist observes from the outside (Yontef & Simkin). Warwar and Greenberg (2000) suggested that Gestalt therapy has shifted from a focus on techniques to an emphasis on the counselor-client relationship as the key to the change process. The goals that emerge from Gestalt therapy are not specific to a client's concerns. The only goal is awareness, which includes knowledge of the environment, taking responsibility for choices, self-knowledge, and self-acceptance (Yontef & Jacobs).

Passons (1975) identified common problems that can impede a client's progress in Gestalt therapy. Difficulties can occur with clients who are overly dependent on others and lack self-responsibility, become out of touch with the world around them, allow unresolved experiences from the past to interfere with being aware of what is occurring in the now, disown their own needs, or define themselves in absolutistic, *either-or* terms.

Techniques

Authenticity symbolizes the Gestalt approach (Levitsky & Simkin, 1972). It is essential for therapists to be authentic since they cannot teach what they do not know. Training at Gestalt institutes therefore focuses on trainees playing the role of client. The Gestalt therapist also utilizes several techniques: assuming responsibility, using personal pronouns, and using the "now I'm aware" and "empty-chair" techniques.

Assuming responsibility requires the client to rephrase a statement in order to assume responsibility. For example, a client can be asked to end all statements with "and I take responsibility for it." The client may also be requested to change *can't* to *won't* or *but* to *and*. For example, instead of saying, "I want to get in shape, *but* I don't exercise," the client says, "I want to get in shape, *and* I don't exercise."

Using personal pronouns encourages clients to take responsibility by saying *I* or *me* instead of using the generalizations *we* or *us*, or *people*. Clients will tend to feel they own their thoughts and feelings more by saying, "It scares *me* to think of going to college," than by saying, "It scares *people* to go to college."

Now I'm aware is a technique that can help clients get in touch with the self. One way to use this technique is to have clients close their eyes to encourage them to get in touch with their inner world and say, "Now I'm aware," before each statement. For example, "Now I'm aware of my breathing"; "Now I'm aware of some tension in my stomach"; "Now I'm aware of feeling embarrassed and self-conscious of having my eyes closed"; "Now I'm aware of feeling afraid of something, but I don't know what." The exercise can continue after clients open their eyes to help them become aware of themselves in relation to their environment.

The *empty-chair* technique can be used to help clients work through conflicting parts of their personality, such as in an approach-avoidance conflict. For example, a client wants to ask a woman out but is afraid of rejection. The empty-chair technique involves placing an empty chair in front of the client. The client is then told that sitting in the empty chair is the part of his personality that does not want to ask the girl out. The client is encouraged to start a conversation with the empty chair by stating the reasons why he wants to ask the girl out. After the client expresses the positive side of the argument, he is asked to sit in the empty chair and respond with the reasons he does not want to ask her out. The client continues to move back and forth until he has resolved the issue. The empty-chair technique can be useful for helping clients work through unfinished business so that they can be centered in the now.

Summary and Evaluation

Gestalt therapy can be particularly appropriate for clients who lack self-awareness and feel "out of touch" with themselves. Several research studies provide some support for the efficacy of Gestalt therapy. Guinan and Foulds (1970) found clients to have increased self-actualization and self-concepts after Gestalt therapy. Clarke and Breeberg (1986) found the empty-chair technique to be more effective than problem-solving techniques in resolving decisional conflict, and Paivio and Greenberg (1992) noted that empty-chair dialogue is effective in resolving "unfinished" emotional issues clients have toward others. The main weakness of the Gestalt approach is that it lacks a strong theoretical base. It appears to emphasize techniques of therapy rather than provide an in-depth theoretical foundation for understanding human behavior or a comprehensive approach to psychotherapy. Additional research on Gestalt techniques and principles appears warranted.

Existential Therapy

Background Information

No single individual is responsible for the development of existential therapy. The theoretical origins of existential therapy can be traced to existentially oriented philosophy; Nietzsche, Heidegger, Sartre, and Buber have played influential roles. For example, Buber (1970) contended that people do not exist as isolated individuals but instead function in a state of existence that is between the I or oneself and others. Several individuals have written books on existential therapy, including Victor Frankl (1963, 1967, 1971, 1978), Rollo May (1953, 1961, 1977), Irvin Yalom (1980), and James Bugental (1976). To a large degree, the basic concepts and other tenets of existential therapy identified in this section represent an integration of the ideas of these major existential theorists.

Theory of Personality

Existential therapy sees each person as a unique individual who is struggling to derive meaning in life and focuses on attempting to understand the human condition. It rejects a fixed view of human nature and instead contends that each person must ultimately define his or her own personal existence. May and Yalom (2005) suggested that death, freedom, isolation, and meaninglessness represent four interrelated human concerns that characterize the existential theory of personality, death being the ultimate concern. Personal meaning and authenticity are associated with confronting death. Freedom to choose to confront the realities associated with death (such as a fear of isolation and extreme separateness) is necessary to overcome meaninglessness.

KEY CONCEPTS The following key concepts are associated with existential therapy (May & Yalom, 2005):

1. *Uniqueness of the individual.* The existential position suggests that no two people are alike—each one is unique. To become aware of one's uniqueness, it is necessary to encounter oneself as a separate

and distinct individual. An important part of this process is to have the experience of existential aloneness. This can be a painful experience as a person attempts to encounter the meaning of existence. Discovering the capability of becoming autonomous can facilitate this process.

2. ***The search for meaning.*** Victor Frankl's (1963, 1967, 1971, 1978) logotherapeutic approach evolved out of his experience as a prisoner of war in a Jewish concentration camp during World War II. He described these experiences as well as the basic principles of logotherapy in his book *Man's Search for Meaning* (1963). Logotherapy suggests that the most prominent psychological problem facing people is the *existential vacuum,* a lack of meaning in life. Frankl (1978) believed that a person can experience meaning by feeling valued or needed, which in turn can create a purposeful existence. Frankl (1963) cited the words of Nietzsche, who said, "He who has a *why* to live can bear almost any *how*" (p. 121).

3. ***The role of anxiety.*** Existential therapy differentiates between two types of anxiety. One is normal or healthy anxiety, called *existential anxiety,* and the other is unhealthy anxiety, referred to as *neurotic anxiety.* Neurotic anxiety is not healthy because it is an anxiety reaction that is not in proportion to the situation and can overwhelm the person. The concept of existential anxiety suggests that some degree of anxiety can be positive since it can motivate a person to make necessary changes. Another positive aspect of anxiety is that it often occurs when a person faces a difficult situation. A person who flees from this anxiety will not be able to learn from the challenges of life. In this way, existentialists believe one can draw meaning from pain and suffering. Nietzsche also related to this point when he said, "That which does not kill me, makes me stronger" (Hollingdale, 1978, p. 23).

4. ***Freedom and responsibility.*** Existential therapy contends that freedom and responsibility are interrelated. People are free to choose their own destiny, but they must also take responsibility for their actions. Existentialists help clients become aware of their choices and the control they can exert over their own destiny.

5. ***Being and nonbeing.*** Being and nonbeing are also interrelated. The reality of death brings meaning to life. Being and nonbeing are also related to freedom and responsibility. People are free to be or not to be. If individuals choose to be, they must assume responsibility for their existence. Being and nonbeing have also been related to the "I-Am" experience (e.g., "I am so therefore I exist"). "I-Am" is a proclamation of a choice of life over death, a choice of being over

nonbeing. From an existential perspective, the realization that death can occur at any time motivates people to generate meaning from their existence.

6. *Three modes of existence.* According to existential therapy, there are three modes of existence (being in the world; Nystul, 1976): the *Umwelt*, *Mitwelt*, and *Eigenwelt*. All three modes of existence are necessary to have a balanced, meaningful life. *Umwelt* is the natural world around us that helps define our existence. It includes the world of biological need gratification that is reflected in meeting basic needs such as hunger. *Mitwelt* is the social world defined by the nature of one's interpersonal relationships. *Eigenwelt* is one's "own world" and corresponds to self-understanding. *Eigenwelt* can also be associated with an ontological at-oneness with life (Kemp, 1971). For example, during meditation people can find the center of their existence and achieve an ontological at-oneness with life itself.

7. *Self-transcendence.* **Self-transcendence** involves moving beyond the subject-object dichotomy (Nystul, 1987a). For example, a student (the subject) attempts to understand the professor (the object). The subject-object dichotomy is characterized by separateness and occurs anytime a person thinks. Meditation utilizes mantras, which are non-word utterings said whenever people realize they are thinking. Self-transcendence results in an ontological at-oneness between counselors and clients. Considered the peak experience in therapy, it is characterized by a very close counseling relationship and profound levels of understanding and empathy. Self-transcendence is also associated with a distortion of time and a very close feeling of connection with whatever or whomever the person feels at one with (e.g., a client, a sunset, or a musical experience at a concert).

Theory of Counseling and Psychotherapy

The goals of existential therapy relate directly to the key concepts. They can be directed at helping clients (a) discover their own uniqueness, (b) find personal meaning in life, (c) use anxiety in a positive sense, (d) become aware of their choices and the need to take responsibility for choices, and (e) see death not as a nemesis but as an eventual reality that gives meaning and significance to life.

The actual process of existential therapy emphasizes the role of the counseling relationship over the use of specific techniques. This approach is similar to the person-centered position in that both attempt to obtain a phenomenological understanding of the client and encourage the client to become aware of inner choices. The two approaches differ in the nature of the counseling relationship. Whereas Rogers focuses on the client, existentialists focus on the therapist and the client. Counseling from an existential point of view is therefore a shared responsibility, with the counselor and client taking an active role in the counseling process.

Buber's (1970) "I-thou" concept can be used to gain insight into the nature of the counseling relationship in existential therapy. This concept suggests that counseling relationships can be experienced at different levels that reflect different degrees of humanness and authenticity. For example, the "I to it" is a depersonalized relationship in which the counselor relates to the client as an object. Buber contended that the "I-thou" relationship (which is characterized by authenticity and humanness) is necessary for a genuine encounter to occur between the counselor and client. Brace (1992) noted that Buber's "I-thou" concept can be used to enhance counseling relationships from various theoretical perspectives such as interpersonal psychotherapy.

Techniques

Some counselors working from existential theories, such as Frankl's (1963, 1967, 1971, 1978) logotherapy, utilize specific techniques. Two techniques central to Frankl's approach (Frankl, 1963, 1978) are *dereflection* and *paradoxical intention*. Dereflection, a procedure that involves helping clients focus on strengths rather than weaknesses, seems more closely aligned to the cognitive school of counseling than to existential theory. Paradoxical intention involves asking clients to do what they fear doing, such as asking them to stutter if they fear stuttering. It is not entirely clear what makes this technique existential. Paradoxical intention is simply a technique that helps a client overcome anticipatory anxiety by redefining success and failure.

Paradoxical intention appears to be particularly effective in cases that do not respond to behavior therapy (Ascher, 1979; Ascher & Efran, 1978). One particularly well-controlled study by Turner and Ascher (1979) also shows paradoxical intention to be effective in treating insomnia. Paradoxical techniques can be useful with resistant clients who are highly reactant (have high control tendencies; Dowd & Sanders, 1994). Two types of paradoxical techniques can be used with these individuals: symptom prescription and restraining. *Symptom prescription* involves requiring the client to experience the symptom he or she is trying to overcome. This technique creates a no-lose situation for control-seeking clients. Either they experience the symptom as prescribed (and feel that they now have control over their symptom), or they choose to foster resistance toward the suggestion (and do not experience their problem). *Restraining* involves asking clients to change slowly or not to change at all. In this case, a client's need for control can manifest itself in a form of resistance that results in the client changing very quickly and overcoming his or her problem.

Frankl (1963) also referred to the process of *self-transcendence,* which means moving beyond the self. This is a uniquely existential concept that can allow the therapist to transcend the limit of the self and directly experience the client's inner world of pain or joy. When this occurs, it can be referred to as an *existential encounter.* Unfortunately, Frankl did not describe a technique that could facilitate the existential encounter.

Summary and Evaluation

Existential therapy focuses on issues such as individuality and the search for meaning in life, issues that have become increasingly important in light of advances in cloning.

Existential theory will play a key role in helping people define themselves as unique individuals in an ever-changing world. The major weakness of this approach lies in its lack of a well-formulated theoretical foundation. Another weakness is that there are few, if any, unique existential techniques that can be used in the counseling process. In addition, there has been a significant decline in research on experiential therapies, and thus they are in danger of becoming extinct or being integrated into other schools of counseling (Goldfried, Greenberg, & Marmar, 1990).

Creative Arts Therapy

Creative arts therapy (CAT) can be defined as promoting psychological and physiological well-being through the use of creative modalities, such as art, music, dance, or drama. Two groups of individuals use CAT: members of the helping professions, such as counselors and psychologists, who use it as an adjunct to counseling and psychotherapy; and CAT professionals, such as music and art therapists, who are certified or registered in a particular CAT modality. CAT can be used with clients of all ages across a wide array of therapeutic modalities, including individual, group, and marriage and family counseling (Sherwood-Hawes, 1995).

CAT has been referred to by many names over the years (Fleshman & Fryrear, 1981), including *expressive therapy, expression therapy,* and *creative therapy.* CAT has been shown to (a) facilitate communication of cognitively impaired and nonverbal patients with their therapists, (b) enable therapists to readily explore patients' affect, and (c) foster therapeutic bonding (Johnson, 1984a; Robbins, 1985).

CAT is not a recognized school of counseling because it lacks a clear theoretical foundation of its own. However, creative arts therapists do make use of the major psychological theories and procedures to facilitate therapeutic outcomes. Freudian, Jungian, and existential theories are three theories with special appeal and utility in CAT. For example, art therapists often employ Freudian concepts to interpret drawings and other artwork. Jungian psychology (especially Jung's concept of the collective unconscious) can be useful in helping clients explore the symbolic nature of unconscious processes that emerge from creative expression (Sherwood-Hawes, 1995). Existential concepts of self-transcendence and the existential encounter can also provide opportunity for creative arts practitioners. CAT can foster self-transcendence, enabling the counselor to feel at one with the client (Nystul, 1987a). When this occurs, the counselor directly experiences the client's inner emotional state, resulting in an existential encounter. The case of Ron, described in a *Personal Note* later in this chapter, is an illustration of CAT and the existential encounter.

Professional Issues

Professional practitioners of CAT are individuals who have undertaken formal study in the therapeutic use of a particular creative arts modality, such as music or drama. Requirements for registration or certification vary according to the CAT specialty, from a bachelor's to a master's degree and from 6 months to 2 years of supervised clinical training. Current requirements for certification or registration can be obtained by writing to the CAT professional organizations listed in Table 8.2.

Certified and registered CAT professionals work in a variety of settings, including hospitals, nursing homes, and private practice. Their role in mental health services has been primarily as "an adjunctive, secondary form of psychotherapeutic treatment" (Johnson, 1984a, p. 212). Johnson identified several changes that need to be made for CAT to emerge as an independent profession. These include (a) using CAT to advance the knowledge of psychology; (b) identifying the unique contribution CAT can make in the helping process; (c) overcoming CAT's dependency on other disciplines, such as psychology and psychiatry, by broadening the role and function of professional creative art therapists; and (d) taking a more assertive position with other professional groups and legislative agencies.

The remaining sections of this chapter present an overview of the prominent modalities associated with CAT in terms of key concepts, procedures and outcomes, and special populations. These are summarized in Table 8.3.

Music Therapy

Music is the oldest form of art associated with curing the ill according to Fleshman and Fryrear (1981), who cited instances of primitive tribes and other people using songs and chants to obtain divine assistance.

KEY CONCEPTS The following key concepts are associated with **music therapy** (Fleshman & Fryrear, 1981):

- Music is intrinsically part of a culture.

- Music can help clients get in touch with thoughts and feelings and communicate emotions that cannot be described by words.

- Music has a basic structure characterized by rhythm, melody, pitch, and tempo that can be used to promote structure in clients whose thoughts are disorganized and chaotic (e.g., clients with schizophrenia).

PROCEDURES AND OUTCOMES Music therapy involves using musical experiences and the therapeutic relationship to enhance the client's state of well-being (Bruscia, 1987). The experiences can include a wide range of activities, including improvising, performing, composing, and listening to music (Bruscia). Bruscia contended that improvising, in which the client creates and plays simultaneously, is the fundamental approach to music therapy.

Fleshman and Fryrear (1981) suggested that music therapy involves four basic activities: (a) recreational and entertainment-oriented experiences to foster

Table 8.2 Addresses for CAT Professional Organizations

Music Therapy
American Music Therapy Association
8455 Colesville Road, Suite 1000
Silver Spring, MD 20910
http://www.musictherapy.org

National Association for Music Education
1806 Robert Fulton Drive
Reston, VA 20191
http://www.nafme.org/

Art Therapy
American Art Therapy Association
4875 Eisenhower Avenue, Suite 240
Alexandria, VA 22304
http://www.arttherapy.org

National Art Education Association
1806 Robert Fulton Drive
Reston, VA 20191
http://www.naea-reston.org

Dance Therapy
American Dance Therapy Association
10632 Little Patuxent Parkway, Suite 108
Columbia, MD 21044
http://www.adta.org

Drama Therapy
North American Drama Therapy Association
1450 Western Avenue, Suite 101
Albany, New York 12203
http://www.nadta.org

Bibliotherapy
International Federation for Biblio/Poetry Therapy
1625 Mid Valley Drive #1, Suite 126
Steamboat Springs, CO 80487
http://www.nfbpt.com/

Table 8.3 CAT Modalities

CAT Modality	Key Concepts	Procedures and Outcomes	Special Populations
Music Therapy	1. Music is intrinsically part of a culture. 2. Music can help clients get in touch with their thoughts and feelings. 3. Music has a basic structure in terms of rhythm, melody, and so forth, which helps clients overcome problems with thought disorders.	Music therapy consists of using a musical experience to enhance and facilitate counseling goals.	Music therapy can be used with all types of clients of all ages but can be particularly effective with young children and the elderly.
Art Therapy	1. Art offers a form of sublimation whereby clients can achieve indirect gratification of unconscious needs. 2. Visual symbols in art can be useful diagnostic tools. 3. Art allows for the expression of unconscious thoughts and feelings. 4. Art promotes a sense of internal equilibrium.	The process of art therapy varies according to theoretical orientation but typically includes color analysis and spontaneous drawings.	Art therapy can be used with clients of all ages but can be particularly useful with children and adolescents.
Drama Therapy	1. Drama therapy offers an opportunity to externalize and learn from experiences. 2. Drama therapy allows for the expression of strong feelings. 3. Drama therapy deals directly and openly with functions of the personality. 4. Emotional conflicts can be better understood by expressing them in action through drama.	Spontaneous role-play is the heart of drama therapy. A variety of procedures are used in drama therapy, such as movement, mime, and puppet plays.	Drama therapy can be used with clients of all ages, but its main use is with children who have physical, emotional, or mental handicaps.

(Continued)

Table 8.3 (Continued)

CAT Modality	Key Concepts	Procedures and Outcomes	Special Populations
Dance Therapy	1. Dance therapy involves the integration of mind and body. 2. Dance can reflect a client's mood and indicate flexibility or rigidity. 3. Clients can channel self-expression into dance.	Dance procedures vary according to the outcomes desired. Dance therapy can involve spontaneous or structured dance experiences and can be used to improve motor skills and interpersonal relationships; facilitate expression of moods, attitudes, and ideas; and stimulate, energize, and relax the body.	Dance therapy can be used with clients of all ages.
Bibliotherapy	Bibliotherapy can be used to foster universalizing, identification, catharsis, and insight.	Books or some form of literature are read to promote particular counseling outcomes.	Any client who can read can benefit from bibliotherapy.
Multimodality CAT	Multimodality CAT involves using the full range of CAT modalities. It can broaden the client's ability to respond to creativity.	Procedures vary according to the theoretical orientation and can include counselors setting the stage for creativity, setting an example, setting themselves at ease, and developing insights from creativity after a client has finished a creative expression.	All clients can benefit from multimodality CAT.

socialization; (b) therapeutic listening groups to promote group cohesion; (c) an adjunct to psychotherapy to stimulate emotions, encourage discussions, promote self-understanding, and facilitate socialization; and (d) individual and group music therapy to address a client's particular problem (e.g., asking clients to play a duet to foster cooperation).

Some of the research conducted on music therapy and its implications for the counseling process shows that music therapy facilitates the counseling process in terms of assessment and diagnosis (Isenberg-Grzeda, 1988; Wells & Stevens, 1984). Other studies have found music therapy exerts positive influence on perceived locus of control (James, 1988) and as a stimulus to promote group cohesion (Wells & Stevens). Moreno (1988) suggested that all procedures used in music therapy should reflect a multicultural sensitivity since musical traditions vary from culture to culture.

SPECIAL POPULATIONS Music therapy can be used with people of all ages. It can be particularly effective when working with the elderly (Gibbons, 1988). Elderly people prefer active involvement in music and can learn new musical skills, such as the guitar or piano, at a level comparable to much younger people (Gibbons, 1984). Music therapy has also been used successfully with children and adolescents. Eidson (1989) has used a behaviorally oriented music therapy program to help emotionally disturbed middle school students improve their classroom behavior. Cripe (1986) provided guidelines for how to use music therapy with children with attention deficit disorder. Wells and Stevens (1984) found that music stimulates creative fantasy in young adolescents during group psychotherapy. A meta-analysis of 11 articles on the use of music therapy with children and adolescents (Gold, Voracek, & Wigram, 2004) suggested that children and adolescents with developmental and behavioral disorders responded more positively to music therapy than did those with emotional disorders. In addition, practitioners who used music therapy as an adjunct to eclectic, humanistic, and psychodynamic approaches were more successful than practitioners who used a behavioral approach.

Other special populations, such as people with mental retardation and physical disabilities, can be served by music therapy (Fleshman & Fryrear, 1981). According to Fleshman and Fryrear, music therapy can be useful in providing stimulation and teaching social skills to individuals with mental retardation. Military marches can be used to help such individuals obtain control over their impulses. Clients with physical disabilities can also benefit from music therapy. Fleshman and Fryrear cited examples such as using wind instruments to help clients with lung disorders and using instruments that require finger dexterity to help clients overcome motor control dysfunctions.

Melodic intonation therapy is an emerging use of music therapy. According to Sparks and Deck (1994), it can be especially useful in treating aphasia (weakening or loss of language ability, which can include speech problems). Melodic intonation therapy utilizes music to stimulate portions of the brain that are associated with language functioning. The process of melodic intonation therapy involves teaching the person with aphasia to sing in a manner based on music from the early Judeo-Christian period. Family members are encouraged to participate in this process (Sparks & Deck).

Art Therapy

Art therapy is one of the oldest and most established forms of CAT. Some of the earliest examples of art therapy can be traced to the prehistoric era, when people painted pictures on the walls of their caves to express their relationship with the world (Wadeson, 1980). Art therapy encompasses many of the visual art forms, including painting, sculpture, crafts, and photography (Kenny, 1987).

KEY CONCEPTS The following are key concepts associated with art therapy:

- Art offers a form of sublimation whereby clients can achieve indirect gratification of unconscious needs (Kramer, 1987).

- Art has visual symbols that can be useful diagnostic tools (Wilson, 1987).

- Art allows for the expression of unconscious thoughts and feelings (Rubin, 1987).

- Art promotes a sense of internal equilibrium (Fleshman & Fryrear, 1981).

PROCEDURES AND OUTCOMES The origins of art therapy can be traced to psychoanalytic theory (Rubin, 1987). More recently, however, most other major schools of psychology and counseling have been incorporated, including Gestalt (Rhyne, 1987), behavioral (Roth, 1987), and cognitive (Silver, 1987). A brief review of these applications follows.

Psychoanalytic Art can be analyzed for its symbolic content (Fleshman & Fryrear, 1981; Rubin, 1987).

Gestalt Art allows the client "to experience and express immediate perceptions and awareness" (Rhyne, 1987, p. 173).

Behavioral The behavioral approach to art therapy involves applying the principles of behavior modification to traditional art therapy techniques (Roth, 1987). In this process, principles of reinforcement are used to involve the client in art therapy and other desirable behaviors (Roth).

Cognitive Cognitive art therapy involves both the assessment and development of cognitive processes (Silver, 1987). This approach is based primarily on the work of Piaget and other cognitive psychologists. Silver identified different ways art can be used to foster cognitive and creative skills. For example, the concept of sequential order can be developed through painting (Silver).

Several other authors have described procedures that are common to all approaches to art therapy. For example, color analysis can be traced to the work of Jung (1959), who noted that the use of color is related to perceptions and judgment. According to Jung, yellow is associated with intuition, red is related to feeling, green suggests sensation, and blue represents thinking. In addition, Kenny (1987) suggested that color selection is associated with emotional states, with blacks and grays indicating depression and white suggesting emotional rigidity. Additional guidelines for analyzing art include proportion, form, detail, movement, and theme to obtain an estimate of a client's psychosocial and cognitive development and level of maturity (Stabler, 1984; see Chapter 11).

Three types of drawings can be useful in art therapy: self-portraits, free drawings, and family drawings (Stabler, 1984). Bertoia and Allan (1988) emphasized the role that *spontaneous drawings,* which are essentially free drawings, can play in art therapy by providing a direct link to unconscious processes.

SPECIAL POPULATIONS Art therapy can be used with clients of all ages, and it can be particularly useful with disadvantaged youth, children with sexual identity problems, mentally retarded children, schizophrenics, and suicidal patients (Fleshman & Fryrear, 1981). For example, the "suicide slash," which is a slip of the pen or an inappropriate line in a picture, and powerful repetitious images can indicate suicidal ideations (Fleshman & Fryrear).

The following *Personal Note* provides an example of how I used art therapy as an adjunct to my counseling approach.

A Personal Note

"Sam" was a 21-year-old, self-referred client I saw at a university counseling center in Australia. He had a severe stuttering problem and complained of loneliness and boredom. During our second session, I asked Sam to draw whatever came to his mind. Sam drew the picture shown in Figure 8.1.

After Sam finished drawing, I asked him to describe himself in terms of his picture. Soon we began to acquire information regarding Sam's motivation for therapy, possible counseling goals, and barriers to the goals. The picture seemed to provide an overview of what Sam wanted from counseling. He mentioned that he had never had a girlfriend and hadn't even kissed a girl. The catapult suggested he was very motivated to have a girlfriend. Unfortunately, he didn't believe this was possible since there were several barriers standing in his way, as illustrated by the sharks swimming between him and the girl.

We went on to identify what these barriers were in terms of *basic mistakes,* as discussed in Chapter 7. For example, he thought he could not get a girlfriend if he was a stutterer. I then

(Continued)

(Continued)

Figure 8.1 Sam's Picture

Source: Adapted from Adlerian Treatment of a classical case of stuttering by Michael Nystul, 1976, *The Journal of Individual Psychology*, Vol. 32, Issue 2, pp. 194–202. Reprinted by permission.

helped Sam overcome the basic mistakes as well as other self-defeating processes during the reorientation phase of counseling. (See Nystul and Musynska, 1976, for a more detailed description of this case.)

Source: First published as the article "Adlerian Treatment of a Classical Case of Stuttering," by Michael S. Nystul and Eve Musynska, in *Individual Psychology*, Vol. 32, No. 2, pp. 194–202. Copyright © 1976 by the University of Texas Press. All rights reserved.

Drama Therapy

Psychodrama, originated by Moreno (1946), was one of the first systematic uses of drama as a form of therapy. Later, drama therapy emerged as a more flexible alternative: Drama therapy is less verbal, less structured, and less oriented toward the theater than psychodrama (Irwin, 1987). Johnson (1984b) defined **drama therapy** "as the intentional use of creative drama toward the psychotherapeutic goals of symptom relief, emotional and physical integration, and personal growth" (p. 105). Drama therapy includes any use of role-playing, but it is especially associated with the use of creative theater as a medium for self-expression (Johnson).

KEY CONCEPTS Although drama therapy is still in its formative stage of development, the following key concepts characterize its current status:

- Drama offers an opportunity to externalize and learn from experiences, both real and imagined (Irwin, 1987).

- Drama allows for the expression of strong feelings, thinking, impulses, and action (Irwin).

- Drama deals directly and openly with different functions of the personality (Fleshman & Fryrear, 1981).

- Emotional conflicts can be better understood by expressing them in action through drama (Irwin).

PROCEDURES AND OUTCOMES As in all CAT modalities, the procedures of drama therapy vary according to the theoretical orientation of the practitioner. Drama therapists draw from a variety of theoretical orientations, such as psychoanalytic, behavioral, Gestalt, Jungian, and Rogerian (Irwin, 1987).

Several authors have identified what can be considered common procedures associated with drama therapy. First, spontaneous role-playing is the heart of drama therapy and can be found in all its forms (Fleshman & Fryrear, 1981). Second, the therapist uses a variety of procedures such as movement, mime, and puppet plays to involve the client in action so inner conflicts can be expressed and better understood (Irwin, 1987). Third, drama therapy contributes to assessment and diagnosis through the analysis of roles that are enacted or rejected, themes and conflicts that emerge in fantasies and stories, and the process of the session in terms of emotional release (Irwin).

SPECIAL POPULATIONS Drama therapy can be used with people of all ages. Its main use appears to be with children, and numerous programs have been developed for children who are physically, emotionally, or mentally disabled (Fleshman & Fryrear, 1981). Drama therapy can be particularly useful in school settings to teach students how to deal with pressures relating to dating or drug and alcohol use.

Dance Therapy

The origins of **dance therapy** can be traced to modern dance, which began early in the 20th century (Fleshman & Fryrear, 1981).

KEY CONCEPTS The following key concepts are associated with dance therapy (Fleshman & Fryrear, 1981):

- The fundamental concept in dance therapy is the integration, or more specifically the reintegration, of mind and body.

- Movement can reflect a client's mood and indicate either flexibility or rigidity.

- Dance therapy provides an opportunity for clients to express themselves in movement, channeling self-expression into dance form.

PROCEDURES AND OUTCOMES In dance therapy, clients may dance by themselves or with other clients. The dance method can be spontaneous or more structured. Particular attention is paid to what the client communicates or discovers from the dance. Other factors worth noting are how the client interacts with others, the client's awareness of space, and how the dance may relate to a particular problem that the client is experiencing.

Dance therapy has the following goals (Fleshman & Fryrear, 1981; Lasseter, Privette, Brown, & Duer, 1989):

- Improving motor skills

- Enhancing the relationship between the client and therapist

- Increasing the client's movement repertoire to facilitate expression of moods, attitudes, and ideas

- Allowing for the sublimation of erotic and aggressive impulses

- Encouraging interpersonal relationships

- Stimulating, energizing, and relaxing the client's body

SPECIAL POPULATIONS Dance therapy can be used with people of all ages. It has been a primary treatment strategy for children with mental, physical, and emotional problems (Lasseter et al., 1989) and has been used successfully with children with autism (Cole, 1982), children with psychotic disorders (Gunning & Holmes, 1973), children with cerebral palsy (Clarke & Evans, 1973), children with mental retardation (Boswell, 1983), and children with emotional disturbances and learning disabilities (Polk, 1977; Wislocki, 1981).

Bibliotherapy

The earliest uses of bibliotherapy can be traced to the ancient Greeks, when a sign was hung over the entrance of a library proclaiming it to be "the healing place of the soul"

(Zaccaria & Moses, 1968). **Bibliotherapy** is "the guided reading of written materials in gaining understanding or resolving problems relevant to a person's therapeutic needs" (Riordan & Wilson, 1989, p. 506). The use of bibliotherapy as an adjunct to counseling appears to be increasing (Riordan & Wilson), with 60% of psychologists prescribing self-help books occasionally, 24% often, and 12% regularly (Starker, 1988).

KEY CONCEPTS The key concepts of bibliotherapy are derived from psychoanalytic theory and include the following (Fleshman & Fryrear, 1981):

- *Universalizing.* Clients minimize feelings of guilt, shame, and isolation when they discover that others share similar problems in life.

- *Identification.* Clients can identify with characters in books, which provide positive role models regarding attitudes and values.

- *Catharsis.* Bibliotherapy group discussions provide clients with opportunities for self-disclosure and catharsis.

- *Insight.* Clients can obtain insight by having an external frame of reference for comparison.

PROCEDURES AND OUTCOMES Bibliotherapy involves asking clients to read a book or some other form of literature to promote certain outcomes associated with the counseling process (e.g., career awareness and exploration). The nature of the reading assignment will depend on the desired outcomes. For example, *What Color Is Your Parachute?* could be used to assist a client with making a career choice. Four of the most commonly prescribed books by psychologists are *What Color Is Your Parachute?, The Relaxation Response, Your Perfect Right,* and *Feeling Good* (Starker, 1988). Once clients have read a book or other literature, they can discuss what they learned with the counselor.

SPECIAL POPULATIONS Bibliotherapy can be used with any client who knows how to read. Research on the efficacy of bibliotherapy has provided mixed results. For example, one study showed support for using bibliotherapy to effect behavioral change (Riordan & Wilson, 1989).

Multimodality CAT

A relatively recent addition to the CAT approaches involves the use of multiple CAT modalities instead of relying on a single modality such as dance or music. This broad-based approach to CAT has been called various names, including *creative-expressive arts, mixed-media arts,* and *multimedia approach to the expressive arts* (Fleshman & Fryrear, 1981; Talerico, 1986). The term **multimodality CAT** indicates using whatever CAT modality the therapist and client want to use.

KEY CONCEPTS The major premise behind multimodality CAT is that it creates limitless possibilities for creative expression, whereas using one modality can be unnecessarily restrictive, discouraging creative responses from the client (Talerico, 1986).

PROCEDURES AND OUTCOMES A four-phase model of CAT can be used with all types of creative media—for example, art, music, or dance—with clients of all ages (Nystul, 1980a, 1987a). The following are the four phases of this model:

1. *Set the stage.* The counselor sets the stage for the creative process by either having creative arts material available or encouraging the client to bring a creative outlet (e.g., a guitar) to the next counseling session.

2. *Set an example.* The counselor may wish to share a creative outlet with the client to set an example of risk taking and self-disclosure.

3. *Set yourself at ease.* The counselor should avoid analyzing a client's creative expression for psychological insights before the client is finished. Premature analysis can cause a client to become self-conscious and interfere with the counselor's direct experience of the client's creative expression.

4. *Obtain a phenomenological understanding of the client.* Once the client has completed the creative expression (e.g., a song or drawing), the counselor can attempt to gain a phenomenological understanding of the client. This can be accomplished by asking clients to describe what the creative expression said about them or describe themselves in terms of the creative expression.

The use of multiple CAT modalities in counseling and psychotherapy can promote a number of outcomes (Nystul, 1980a, 1987a). For example, it can provide assessment and diagnostic information by having clients project their thoughts and feelings into a creative expression, promoting self-disclosure in counselors and clients as they share their creative outlets. It can also increase clients' social interest as they discover the support that can result from sharing a creative expression. Counselors can also develop a phenomenological understanding of clients as they describe themselves in terms of their creative expression, and it can promote an existential encounter as counselors directly experience their clients' emotions through the release of their creative expression.

SPECIAL POPULATIONS Multimodality CAT can be used with clients of all ages. Some examples are children with autism (Nystul, 1986), children with emotional disturbance (Nystul, 1978b, 1980a), a young adult with a stutter who felt socially isolated (Nystul & Musynska, 1976), and a student in a university counseling center who had a sexual identity problem (Nystul, 1979b). In addition, the counselor is not restricted to one modality, such as art therapy, so clients have more opportunities to explore and discover creative outlets.

The following *Personal Note* provides an example of how I used multimodality CAT.

A Personal Note

One case that was very special to me involved a first-grader named Ron. I was an elementary school counselor, and Ron was referred to me for counseling services. The reason for the referral was that he spent most of his time daydreaming in class and appeared to have no friends at school.

Ron was unresponsive to my questions during our first counseling session, so I decided to see him in a play therapy setting. As described in Chapter 11, my approach to play therapy involves two parts: a self-concept program and the four-stage model associated with multimodality CAT (Nystul, 1980a).

After we finished our self-concept program, Ron was humming a song. I asked him to make up a song about how he was feeling. I attempted to accompany him on the guitar, and he responded by singing a deep, sorrowful song. These were the words to Ron's song:

> My mom comes home and daddy stays home
>
> Momma goes home, daddy stays
>
> Momma stays in the city when she wants to
>
> Momma stays in the city when she wants to
>
> Momma daddy, Momma daddy
>
> I just can't seem to go.
>
> Daddy keep care of the baby
>
> Daddy keep care of the baby
>
> Daddy keep care of the baby
>
> Please help me
>
> I want no!
>
> I need help!
>
> I can't seem to stop

> Daddy keep care of the baby
>
> Good-bye, good-bye.

As Ron sang, I did not try to identify any psychological insights from the words of the song. Instead, I went with the music and allowed myself to get caught up with his creative energy. When Ron finished singing, I felt I had gone beyond attempting to understand or empathize with Ron's pain or sorrow. Instead, I had to some degree experienced these feelings as he sang.

As a result of our existential encounter, Ron and I had established a special counseling relationship. He therefore felt free to discuss his thoughts and feelings with me. Later that day, we listened to his song again, which I had tape-recorded. This time, I was interested in exploring the song for possible psychological significance. I asked Ron what the song might say about him. He responded by telling me about different facets of his past.

As I listened, I began to identify basic mistakes—faulty views that may interfere with what a person wants out of life (described in Chapter 7). For example, he said that his father was black and his mother had said all black men are no good. This was a basic mistake since his view of being black would have a detrimental effect on feeling good about himself and others (something he wanted out of life).

To help reorient Ron from this basic mistake, I enlisted the help of Bill, a black counselor from another school, who agreed to colead some of my play therapy groups. The students loved Bill. Soon Ron began to believe that being even part black could be beautiful. (See Nystul, 1980a, for a more complete description of this case.)

Summary and Evaluation of CAT

CAT is a dynamic and powerful tool. It has many uses, such as promoting socialization, communicating thoughts and emotions, and enhancing the counseling relationship, and it can be used as a projective device in assessment and diagnosis. Although CAT can be viewed as an emerging profession or as an adjunctive strategy associated with counseling and psychotherapy, there is to date no empirical research on its precise effect on psychological functioning and the counseling process.

Research Trends in Experiential Counseling

One of the most significant advances in the 1990s was the empirical validation of experiential approaches (Warwar & Greenberg, 2000). An overview of research trends in experiential counseling approaches (Greenberg et al., 1994) includes summaries of studies directed at determining who benefits most from experiential therapies and treatment trends in experiential therapy. Studies examining the effects of client characteristics on success with experiential therapy show the following:

- Clients who rate high in social skills, affiliation, and assertiveness tend to respond well in person-centered therapy.

- Clients with high reactance (including high dominance) or resistance to influence appear to do better in person-centered therapy, whereas those low in reactance do better in Gestalt therapy.

- Internally oriented clients (open clients who are interested in inner experience) appear to do well in person-centered therapy.

Treatment trends in experiential therapies are summarized as follows (Greenberg et al., 1994):

- Experiential therapies appear to be useful across a broad range of treatment considerations, from addressing the concerns of the "worried well" to treating disorders such as anxiety and depression.

- Counselors should be aware of factors in experiential therapy (such as lack of direction and intrusiveness) that can hinder therapeutic progress.

- Counselors need to move away from uniform use of an experiential theory and adapt the theory to treat specific disorders, such as depression or panic attacks.

- Task interventions for counselors and clients can be developed, implemented, and processed to provide a focused means of treating specific problems and then analyzing their efficacy.

More recently, Elliott (2002) and Elliott and Freire (2008, 2010) conducted meta-analyses of experiential approaches, including person-centered therapy. The results of the meta-analyses provided "strong support for person-centered and experiential therapy, even when compared to cognitive-behavioral approaches" (Raskin et al., 2014, p. 133).

Rogers's emphasis on developing a positive counseling relationship has been singled out as one of the most important variables in counseling efficacy (Glauser & Bozarth, 2001). For example, Duncan and Moynihan (1994) and Hubble, Duncan, and Miller (1999) estimated that the counseling relationship is responsible for 30% of the success variance in counseling; client resources such as family support system, problem-solving skills, and level of optimism are associated with 40% of success variance; techniques represent 15% of counseling success; and the last 15% is associated with the placebo effect.

Brownell (2008) provided an overview of evidence-based practices regarding gestalt therapy and concluded that a number of challenges are associated with researching gestalt principles (e.g., awareness and being centered in the now). In 2013, Brownell helped organize an international conference to address these research issues that was cohosted by the Gestalt International Study Center and the Association for the Advancement of Gestalt Therapy (Yontef & Jacobs, 2014).

Research is also generating support for CAT, as the success of the various CATs in treating a wide array of clinical problems has been noted (Sherwood-Hawes, 1995). For example, art therapy is being used successfully to treat sexual abuse. Dance therapy has proven useful in treating eating disorders. Music therapy is used in treating a wide array of ailments, from dementia and Alzheimer's disease to chronic pain and immune system disorders. And drama and poetry therapy have been found to be effective in treating posttraumatic stress disorders and substance abuse. Gladding (2011) noted there is a need for additional research on CAT to evaluate its efficacy and identify factors that are associated with positive outcomes.

Brief Approaches to Experiential Counseling

Although experiential theories were not originally developed for brief counseling, they appear to offer much promise as a useful adjunct in a time-limited format. Person-centered therapy can be of use in establishing the counseling relationship through listening skills and facilitating the core conditions. In addition, several concepts and techniques used in Gestalt therapy could be employed in brief counseling. The key concept of awareness, for example, would seem to be a useful goal for maximizing a client's readiness for counseling, and using personal pronouns to help clients take responsibility for their behavior is among the Gestalt techniques that can be used.

The existential concepts of freedom, choice, and responsibility empower clients and enhance their motivation for involvement in the change process.

CAT is ideally suited for brief counseling. Any of the creative arts modalities can be used successfully in as little as one session (such as patients in a hospital listening to music) or can be used as an adjunct to brief-counseling models designed to treat specific disorders. CAT can make an instant impact because of the healing power of the CAT experience. Hale (1990) noted that CAT often provides a superior method of healing as compared to more traditional methods.

Diversity Issues in Experiential Counseling

Experiential theories both hold promise and raise concerns in terms of diversity issues such as age, gender, culture, sexual orientation, socioeconomic status, race, ethnicity, and spirituality. In terms of cultural issues, Rogers (in his later years) provided training all over the world in how his counseling theory could be used to foster positive interpersonal relations and overcome conflict. He hoped that his theory could provide a means of alleviating interracial tension and foster world peace (Corey, 2013). In recognition for his efforts, Rogers was nominated for the Nobel Peace Prize just before he died.

Person-centered theory provides a rich foundation for multicultural counseling (Glauser & Bozarth, 2001). Rogerian concepts that play an important role in multicultural counseling include the importance of the counseling relationship; core conditions such as empathy, respect, and genuineness; the emphasis on the "self"; and the phenomenological perspective. These concepts can be extrapolated into multicultural counseling where they are used to address issues of individual differences and diversity. Raskin et al. (2014) noted that feminist scholars have criticized experiential approaches, including person-centered counseling, for focusing on the individual and not recognizing external factors such as discrimination and racism that can undermine mental health and wellness. Raskin et al. contended, however, that although the person-centered approach does not identify specific goals, clients' feelings (e.g., oppression) often emerge within the client-centered relationship. Wolter-Gustafson (2004) and Proctor and Napier (2004) also suggested there appears to be a convergence between person-centered and feminist perspectives (Raskin et al.).

Gestalt therapy can also make positive contributions in terms of cultural issues (Corey, 2013). It can help clients integrate the opposing forces (or polarities) that they face, such as working through the conflicts between their culture and the dominant culture. In addition, Gestalt therapy emphasizes the importance of nonverbal communication as an authentic means of communication. Nonverbal communication can help overcome misunderstandings in cross-cultural counseling that result from language differences. The various creative arts modalities (such as art, music, and dance) also rely on nonverbal communication, which enhances their cross-cultural utility.

Existential therapy can play an important role in cross-cultural counseling in terms of bringing personal meaning to life and a feeling of control over one's destiny (Corey, 2013). For example, experiential counseling can help clients who feel oppressed and victimized by forces such as racism or sexism to realize that, on some level, they are making choices and decisions that are influencing the direction of their lives. Awareness of choices can foster a sense of control and responsibility, which in turn can contribute to a sense of meaning in life.

Diversity issues associated with spirituality are linked to Frankl's (1963) existential logotherapy (Ingersoll, 1995). Frankl stressed in his theory the relationship of the mind, body, and spirit, with the spirit playing the key role in one's search for meaning in the processes of self-transcendence and ontological at-oneness with others.

In the final analysis, there is promise for the utility of experiential counseling in addressing issues of diversity, yet there is more work to be done as well. It is hoped that future research will focus on how experiential theories can be broadened to create a more comprehensive, inclusive explanation of human growth and development, including psychological health and wellness.

SUMMARY

Some theories and approaches are called *experiential* because of their common view that therapeutic gains result from what the client experiences during the counseling session. The three major experiential theories—person-centered, Gestalt, and existential—reflect the spirit of humanistic psychology in their concept of human nature as inherently positive, self-determined, and self-actualizing.

The strength of experiential therapies lies in their ability to help clients become aware of their thoughts and feelings, discover their inner choices, and promote personal responsibility. The weakness of experiential therapies can lie in their overemphasis on feelings and underemphasis on cognition and behavior. Experiential therapies may therefore lack some of the counseling strategies necessary to promote a comprehensive treatment program.

Creative arts therapy is an emerging profession with opportunities for professional certification and registration in various CAT modalities, such as music, art, and drama. CAT is also an adjunctive counseling strategy that can be used to facilitate the counseling process. Multimodality CAT is a relatively new addition to the CAT field. It has the advantage of utilizing whatever CAT modality the counselor or client prefers to use.

Information on research trends, brief approaches, and diversity issues in experiential counseling shows that experiential theories and approaches can be flexible and useful in various counseling formats, from long-term to brief. Research on experiential counseling in terms of diversity issues has helped identify some of its strengths and weaknesses in this area.

PERSONAL EXPLORATION

1. Compare and contrast experiential, existential/humanistic, Gestalt therapy, and person-centered approaches. What are their strengths and weaknesses?

2. What are your favorite experiential theories, and what do you find interesting about these theories?

3. What is your opinion of creative arts therapy (CAT)? How might CAT facilitate the counseling process (e.g., assessment and diagnosis)?

4. Which CAT modalities (e.g., art, music, drama, dance, or bibliotherapy) do you find intriguing, and why?

5. How has Carl Rogers's person-centered theory influenced the field of counseling?

6. How can existential theory bring meaning to one's life?

7. What do you think the Gestalt concept "being centered in the now" means?

8. How can existential anxiety be helpful in making changes in one's life?

9. Person-centered therapy has been referred to as an "if-then" approach. What does this mean?

10. Self-transcendence has been related to a number of counseling theories. What does this concept mean?

LEARNING ACTIVITIES

1. Explore your creative outlets and identify ones that you may want to use if you were a counselor.

2. Read Victor Frankl's book *Man's Search for Meaning* (1963) and explore how the ideas expressed in it could be used to bring meaning to your life.

WEBSITES

Good-Therapy.org. (2015). *Person-centered therapy (Rogerian therapy)*. Retrieved from http://www.goodtherapy.org/person-centered.html. *Provides an overview of person-centered counseling.*

Mulhauser, G. (2014). *An introduction to person-centered counseling*. Retrieved from http://counsellingresource.com/types/person-centred/index.html. *Discusses the theory and therapeutic approach of person-centered counseling, as well as some criticisms of this approach.*

Cognitive-Behavioral Theories

The Art and Science of Cognitive-Behavioral Counseling

The goal of cognitive-behavioral counseling is to help clients identify how their thoughts and behaviors generate negative emotional consequences and to assist them with the interventions necessary to foster positive growth and development. The art of this theoretical approach is twofold. First, counselors can work *with* clients to help them discover dysfunctional thoughts from the perspective of the *client's* worldview and not from the *counselor's* view of what is rational or functional. Second, counselors can attempt to create a balance in terms of exploring the etiology of dysfunctional thoughts, addressing both intrapsychic forces and postmodern considerations that are reflected contextually between clients and sociocultural and political forces in their environments.

Behavioral counseling (which focuses on overt, observable, and measurable behavior) is founded on principles associated with the science of counseling. This position was articulated by B. F. Skinner (1990) in his ongoing goal of promoting the science of behavioral psychology. Cognitive-behavioral counseling continues the strong tradition in science. In this regard, the cognitive-behavioral school of counseling has the strongest research base of any school of counseling.

New trends in the science of counseling are reflected in mindfulness approaches to psychotherapy and postmodern theories such as constructivism and social constructionism. Mindfulness approaches include the use of meditation in psychotherapy. For example, the science of counseling is reflected in research that is exploring how meditation promotes mental and physical health and well-being (e.g., how meditation lowers blood pressure).

Postmodernism provides a perspective for understanding concepts that are fundamental to science (e.g., knowledge

Chapter Overview

This chapter provides an overview of cognitive-behavioral theories and approaches to counseling. Highlights of the chapter include the following:

- **The art and science of cognitive-behavioral counseling**
- **An overview of each cognitive-behavioral theory in terms of a theory of personality and a theory of counseling and psychotherapy (i.e., behavior therapy, rational-emotive behavioral therapy, cognitive therapy, transactional analysis, reality therapy, and feminist therapy)**
- **Trends in brief counseling**
- **Diversity issues**
- **Mindfulness approaches**
- **Postmodern perspectives**

and reality). From this perspective, *knowledge* and *reality* are relative terms that must be understood contextually. The definition of reality can vary according to culture as reflected in the culture's language and narratives. The science of cognitive-behavioral counseling can draw on qualitative research's discovery method, in which the counselor and client attempt to discover the personal meaning generated from the client's stories.

As noted in Chapter 6, using a multicultural perspective to address diversity issues throughout the counseling process is recommended on the basis of both the art and science of counseling. Cognitive-behavior theories can be associated with special concerns regarding diversity. For example, from a postmodern perspective, the nature and content of cognitive and behavioral processes vary contextually according to variables such as gender. Developmental researchers like Carol Gilligan (1982, 1990) have clearly shown that women think and behave differently than men with regard to processes such as moral decision making and identity development. Thus, it is necessary to make modifications to cognitive-behavioral theories by incorporating multicultural research findings and maintaining a sensitivity to the evolving needs of clients.

Cognitive-Behavioral Theories

Cognitive-behavioral theories emphasize the role of cognition and/or behavior in psychological functioning and well-being. The recent trend toward diversifying and integrating counseling theories has altered the focus of some cognitive-behavioral theories. Theories that originally had a cognitive focus have incorporated behavioral techniques (e.g., cognitive therapy and rational-emotive behavior therapy) and behaviorally oriented theories have incorporated cognitive techniques and concepts (e.g., behavior therapy and reality therapy).

The integration of theories represents an attempt to develop a more comprehensive approach as opposed to highlighting what is unique about a particular school of counseling. It is hoped that this trend will continue, replacing unnecessary barriers between theories with compatible concepts and procedures.

This chapter provides a description of the following theories: behavior therapy, rational-emotive behavior therapy, cognitive therapy, transactional analysis, reality therapy, and feminist therapy. Table 9.1 provides an overview of these theories, including their key concepts, counseling process, and techniques.

Behavior Therapy

Background Information

The historical roots of **behavior therapy** can be traced to three learning theories: classical conditioning, operant conditioning, and social-learning theory. Classical conditioning evolved from Ivan Pavlov's experiments with dogs. In these experiments, Pavlov (1906) demonstrated that he could condition a dog to salivate at the sound of a

Table 9.1 The Cognitive-Behavioral Theories

Theory	Founder(s)	Key Concepts	Counseling Process	Techniques
Behavior therapy	Ivan Pavlov, B. F. Skinner, Albert Bandura, Joseph Wolpe, and Donald Meichenbaum	Incorporation of principles from learning theories; grounding in the scientific method; focus on overt, observable behavior; view of psychopathology primarily in behavioral terms	Attempts to establish clear and precise counseling goals, such as modifying maladaptive behavior, strengthening desired behavior, and helping clients learn effective decision making.	Assertiveness training, systematic desensitization, token economy, cognitive behavior modification, self-control
Rational-emotive behavior therapy	Albert Ellis	Basic premise that emotional disturbance results from illogical or irrational thought processes	Helps the client learn how to dispute irrational or illogical thoughts.	Cognitive restructuring emotive techniques, shame-attacking exercises, bibliotherapy, behavioral techniques
Cognitive therapy	Aaron Beck	The role of cognition in mental health; cognitive vulnerability, cognitive distortions, systematic bias in information processing, cognitive triad of depression, the cognitive model of anxiety	Offers a short-term treatment program for depression, anxiety, and other mental disorders. Its ultimate goal is elimination of systematic bias in thinking.	Cognitive techniques such as decatastrophizing, reattribution, redefining, decentering; behavioral techniques such as skill training, progressive relaxation, behavioral rehearsal, and exposure therapy

(Continued)

Table 9.1 (Continued)

Theory	Founder(s)	Key Concepts	Counseling Process	Techniques
Transactional analysis (TA)	Eric Berne	The three ego states (parent, adult, child), transactional analysis, games people play, life scripts, the four life positions, strokes	Educative method teaches the client how to use TA concepts to make positive life decisions.	Structural analysis, transactional analysis, script analysis, analysis of games
Reality therapy	William Glasser	Success and failure identity, emphasis on responsibility, avoidance of labels associated with mental disorders, positive addiction, control theory	Primary aim is to help client develop a success identity through responsible action. Teaches clients how to use control theory to fulfill basic needs and not interfere with the rights of others.	Incorporates an eight-step approach that includes creating a relationship, focusing on current behavior, having the client evaluate behavior, making an action plan, obtaining a commitment, not accepting excuses, not using punishment, and refusing to give up.
Feminist therapy	Laura Brown, Harriet Lerner, Edna Rawlings, Carolyn Enns, and others	Marginalization, resocialization, androgyny, self-limiting horizons, social advocacy	Involves promoting equality between the sexes and overcoming oppressive forces, such as the marginalization of women, that can undermine self-actualization tendencies.	Feminist therapists use a wide range of techniques from the various schools of counseling as long as they do not reflect gender bias (e.g., feminist family therapy, cognitive-behavioral therapy, and behavioral therapy such as assertiveness training).

bell. This was the first demonstration of what Pavlov called *classical conditioning*—that dogs, or people, could be conditioned to respond to a stimulus. Pavlov's principles of classical conditioning were later applied to counseling. Joseph Wolpe (1958, 1973) played a key role in this process, integrating the principles of classical conditioning into a systematic desensitization process to treat phobias. This technique continues to be one of the most popular approaches for the treatment of phobias.

B. F. Skinner developed the second major field of learning theory, *operant conditioning*. Skinner (1938, 1953, 1961) proposed that learning cannot occur without some form of reinforcement. He contended that behaviors that are reinforced will tend to be repeated, while those that are not will tend to be extinguished. Compared to classical conditioning, operant conditioning is a more active process of learning in that the person must do something to be reinforced.

Skinner developed the principles of operant conditioning in his now-famous Skinner box experiments, in which a rat was trained to press a bar for food. More recently, the principles of operant conditioning have been utilized in programmed learning, development of self-control, behaviorally oriented discipline procedures, and management of clients in institutions by use of token economies.

The third major learning theory that helped formulate behavior therapy is *social learning theory*. Along with the various cognitive theories, social-learning theory represents a more recent dimension to the behavioral school. Among the individuals associated with these new trends are Beck (1991), Meichenbaum (1986), Mahoney (1991), and Bandura (1986). In particular, Albert Bandura was instrumental in the integration of cognition into behavior therapy.

Bandura's (1977) early work on social-learning theory focused on how learning occurs through observation, modeling, and imitation. The idea that learning could occur entirely as a function of cognitive control was a direct challenge to the traditional behavioral stimulus-response model (Mahoney & Lyddon, 1988). In addition, Bandura's (1974) "endorsement of an interactional reciprocity between person and environment marked a pivotal shift from exclusive environmental determinism" (Mahoney & Lyddon, p. 196).

Bandura (1982, 1986, 1989, 1997) developed a theory of self-efficacy, which relates to a person's belief in the ability to successfully accomplish a particular task. Perceived self-efficacy plays a central role in mediating constructive behavior change (Bandura, 1986). Bandura's theory contends that self-efficacy can directly influence what activities people will choose to engage in, how much effort they will exert, and how long they will continue when faced with adversity (Johnson, Baker, Kapola, Kiselica, & Thompson, 1989).

Theory of Personality

Behavior therapy's theory of personality is integrated into its theory of counseling and psychotherapy. In this sense, assessment and intervention are interrelated. For example, counselors and clients chart changes in behaviors to assess the relative impact of various intervention procedures.

VIEW OF HUMAN NATURE Historically, behaviorists viewed human nature as neutral. A person is not inherently good or bad but will become what the environment dictates. This position was in direct contrast to the humanistic stance, which suggested that people are capable of self-determination. More recently, the behavioral point of view recognizes the possibility of self-determined behavior, whereby individuals can take an active role in their destiny (Bandura, 1986; Meichenbaum, 1986).

KEY CONCEPTS Behavior therapy is currently in a state of rapid change and evolution (Wilson, 2011). Rimm and Cunningham (1985) and Antony (2014) identified common elements that characterize behavior therapy, as follows:

1. *Behavior therapy concentrates on overt, observable behavioral processes and cognitions.* Early behaviorists focused on overt behavior. More recently, the cognitive realm is also viewed as an important mediating factor in relation to behavior.

2. *Behavior therapy focuses on the here and now.* Information about past experience is considered important only as it relates to current treatment issues. The focus is on understanding and treating current problems relating to behavior and cognitions.

3. *Maladaptive behaviors are primarily the result of learning.* Models of learning (operant, classical, and social-learning theories) can be used to understand the etiology of maladaptive behavior. Learning principles can therefore be used to change maladaptive behavior.

4. *Well-defined, concrete goals are used.* Goals are stated in observable, measurable terms whenever possible.

5. *Behavior therapy is committed to the scientific method.* Behavior therapy utilizes the principles of the scientific method to evaluate techniques and procedures. Assessment and treatment are viewed as part of the same process, creating a built-in mechanism for research and accountability.

6. *Behavior therapy is based on empiricism.* Behavior therapy is grounded in the scientific method, utililzing evidence-based methods that are supported by research.

7. *Behavior therapy is active and transparent.* Behavior therapy is a directive process that provides clients with behavioral strategies they can use to become their own self-therapist.

Theory of Counseling and Psychotherapy

THE COUNSELING PROCESS The counselor takes an active and directive approach, which often incorporates problem-solving strategies (Wilson, 2011). The client is also expected to take an active role in the assessment aspect of the counseling process by engaging in processes such as self-monitoring and in treatment by acquiring new skills and behaviors through work and practice.

A misconception regarding behavior therapists is that they view a positive counseling relationship as unimportant to the counseling process (Wilson, 2011). Brady (1980) noted, however, that the nature of the counseling relationship can have a direct bearing on the outcome of behavior therapy. In addition, Swan and MacDonald (1978) have found that behavior therapists report that relationship-building procedures are among the most frequently used.

Behavior therapy has concrete, specific goals that include acquiring necessary behaviors and coping skills and overcoming self-defeating cognitive processes. When possible, clients assume primary responsibility for determining treatment goals. The therapist's role and function are therefore directed at how to accomplish goals in therapy rather than focusing on which goals to work on (Wilson, 2011).

TECHNIQUES Most behavior therapy procedures are short-term, although some may extend for as long as 25 to 50 sessions (Wilson, 2011). Behavior therapists use a wide variety of techniques and procedures: cognitive behavior modification, self-management and self-control, self-efficacy, participant modeling, assertiveness training, systematic desensitization, and token economy.

Cognitive Behavior Modification Donald Meichenbaum's (1986) cognitive behavior modification employs several useful strategies, such as self-instructional therapy and stress-inoculation training. Self-instructional therapy is a form of self-control therapy in which clients learn to use tools to take control of their lives. Behavior change occurs "through a sequence of mediating processes involving the interaction of inner speech, cognitive structures, and behaviors, and their resultant outcomes" (Meichenbaum, 1977, p. 218).

This theory suggests that people have a set of beliefs or cognitive structures that influence how they react to events in terms of an inner speech or self-talk. To a large degree, cognitive structures and inner speech determine how people behave. The focus of therapy is on restructuring faulty cognitive structures, altering inner speech so that it triggers coping behaviors, and, if necessary, using behavior therapy to teach coping responses.

Stress-inoculation training is another useful approach that employs a number of cognitive-behavioral techniques, such as "cognitive restructuring, problem-solving, relaxation training, behavioral and imaginal rehearsal, self-monitoring, self-reinforcement, and efforts at environmental change" (Meichenbaum, 1985, p. 21). It can be used to treat different disorders but is especially useful in treating anxiety. The procedure focuses on helping clients learn coping mechanisms that they can use to "inoculate" or protect themselves against stress-related reactions. A major premise of this approach is that clients can be taught to cope with stressful situations and enhance their performance by modifying their self-statements. Stress-inoculation training is comprehensive, attempting to go beyond symptom relief and teach skills that can be useful to prevent problems in the future, including relapse. The process of implementing stress inoculation typically involves three stages: conceptualization, skill acquisition and rehearsal, and application and follow-through.

Self-Management and Self-Control Kanfer and Goldstein (1986), Bandura (1986), and Meichenbaum (1986) are associated with self-management and self-control procedures, which are directed at helping clients become their own agents for behavior change (Gintner & Poret, 1987). In this process, the counselor provides support and expertise in terms of behavioral management. The client assumes responsibility for implementing and carrying out the program (Kanfer & Goldstein).

A wide range of skills can be used to promote self-management and self-control. For example, Kanfer and Goldstein (1986) identified skills in (a) self-monitoring, (b) establishing rules of conduct by contracting, (c) obtaining environmental support, (d) self-evaluating, and (e) generating reinforcing consequences for behaviors that promote the goals of self-control. Other self-control skills are progressive relaxation to reduce stress; biofeedback to treat psychophysiological disorders; and self-instructional training for control of anger, impulsivity, and other coping problems (Wilson, 2011).

Self-Efficacy As noted earlier, self-efficacy is a theory developed primarily by Bandura (1982, 1986, 1989) that relates to a person's belief in his or her ability to accomplish a particular task. Self-efficacy is not a behavioral technique. It can be better viewed as a concept that should be considered when implementing a technique. Rimm and Cunningham (1985) noted that treatments that foster the greatest change in self-efficacy should be the most effective. They suggested that treatment efficacy can be increased by promoting methods that foster the communication of efficacy information to clients. Efficacy information can be transferred to clients by (a) actual performance, which is the most powerful information source; (b) vicarious learning or modeling; (c) verbal persuasion; and (d) psychological arousal (Bandura, Reese, & Adams, 1982).

Self-efficacy theory has stimulated a proliferation of research activity, which has shown it to predict many behaviors, such as depression (Davis-Berman, 1988), cessation after treatment (Gooding & Glasgow, 1985; Nicki, Remington, & MacDonald, 1984), recovery from heart attacks (Bandura, 1982), sports performance (Lee, 1982; McAuley, 1985), and success in weight reduction programs (Weinberg, Hughes, Critelli, England, & Jackson, 1984). Based on a review of the literature on self-efficacy, Johnson et al. (1989) concluded that "across varied behavioral domains, self-efficacy has predicted differences in the degree to which people choose, present, and succeed in performing targeted behaviors" (p. 206).

Participant Modeling Participant modeling is based on Bandura's (1977, 1986, 1989) social learning theory, which emphasizes the role of observation and imitation in learning. It is used primarily to treat phobias and fears (Rimm & Cunningham, 1985). Participant modeling involves two stages: observation and participation. During the observation stage, the client observes a model engaged in the feared behavior (e.g., petting a dog). Research suggests that efficacy increases when the model is similar to the client in terms of age and gender (Raskin & Israel, 1981) and the manner in which the model approaches the feared task (Meichenbaum, 1972). The second stage involves the client participating or engaging in the feared behavior. During this process, the counselor guides the client through a series of exercises relating to the feared task (Rimm & Cunningham, 1985).

Assertiveness Training Assertiveness training can be used for clients who find it difficult to stand up for their rights or who are unable to express their feelings in a constructive manner (Wilson, 2011). Rimm and Cunningham (1985) described the following steps involved in assertiveness training. First, the therapist and client determine whether there is a need for assertiveness training. Second, the therapist describes how increased assertiveness can be beneficial. The third and most important step involves a process of behavioral rehearsal, during which the therapist models an assertive behavior, then asks the client to "rehearse" the assertive behavior, and finally provides feedback and appropriate reinforcement.

Systematic Desensitization Systematic desensitization is a technique developed by Wolpe (1958, 1973) to treat problems resulting from classical conditioning, such as phobias. It has also been used to treat a variety of other maladaptive behaviors, including excessive fears about issues such as death, injury, and sex (Kazdin, 1978).

The following steps can be used to implement this technique:

1. **Teach deep relaxation.** Systematic desensitization utilizes the principle of counterconditioning by introducing a relaxation response to replace the previously conditioned adverse response. It is based on the assumption that a person cannot be anxious and relaxed at the same time. The client is therefore taught to experience a state of deep relaxation as the therapist describes a relaxing scene.

2. **Develop a hierarchy.** The therapist and client develop a hierarchy of situations that elicit a fear response. The situation that elicits the lowest level of anxiety is the first item in the hierarchy, and the one that elicits the highest level of anxiety is last. It is important that the statements are specific enough so the client can visualize the situation. For example, if a client has a fear of heights, the first situation visualized might be "I walked up a flight of stairs to the fourth floor and looked out the window."

3. **Proceed through the hierarchy.** The therapist helps the client enter into a state of deep relaxation. The therapist then asks the client to imagine the first item in the hierarchy. By introducing a relaxation response to a situation that previously elicited a fear response, the therapist helps the client become desensitized by the counterconditioning process.

4. ***Address the fear in vivo.*** This step involves desensitizing the client to in vivo or real-life situations associated with the fear. For example, if the client has a snake phobia, an item on the hierarchy may be to imagine looking at a snake. During the in vivo experience, the client will be asked to look at a real snake.

5. ***Follow up and evaluate.*** The final step is to evaluate how successful the client is in dealing with the fear response in a variety of situations over an extended period of time.

Token Economy Ayllon and Azrin (1968) developed the technique of *token economy* to teach psychiatric patients to become more responsible. The technique, used primarily in hospitals, residential settings, and schools, is based on the principles of operant conditioning and involves giving tokens to reinforce a desired behavior, such as cleaning one's room. After collecting enough tokens, clients can exchange them for goods or privileges, such as being able to watch TV. To increase intrinsic motivation, the tokens must be gradually eliminated and replaced by social reinforcers, such as encouragement, to enable clients to maintain newly acquired behaviors after they leave the treatment setting.

Summary and Evaluation

Behavior therapy focuses on overt behavior. The counseling process emphasizes the importance of establishing clear goals stated in behavioral terms. Progress in therapy is indicated when there is a change or modification in behavior. Treatment and assessment are seen as part of the same process, creating a built-in mechanism for research and accountability.

Emmelkamp (1994), in summarizing the research on behavior therapy, concluded that it has been effective in treating a number of mental disorders and client concerns. Examples include the following:

- Anxiety disorders such as phobias, posttraumatic stress disorder, generalized anxiety, and aggressive-compulsive disorder

- Depression (Behavioral counseling is especially effective when used in conjunction with cognitive approaches such as cognitive therapy.)

- Alcoholism, including treatment of controlled drinking

- Sexual disorders (Behavioral counseling is quite useful in treating sexual dysfunctions such as premature ejaculation and missed orgasm but not so effective in treating paraphilias such as exhibitionism and pedophilia.)

The behavioral approach has some weaknesses, such as disregarding the importance of feelings and emotions in the counseling process. It also tends to ignore historical factors that can contribute to a client's problem and to minimize the use of insight in the counseling process.

Rational-Emotive Behavior Therapy (REBT)

Background Information

Albert Ellis (1913–2008) received MA and PhD degrees in clinical psychology from Columbia University and went on to practice in the areas of marriage, family, and sex therapy. In the 1950s, Ellis initially developed his theory of counseling, which he called *rational therapy*. In 1962, Ellis published *Reason and Emotion in Psychotherapy*, laying down the foundation for his revised theory, which he called *rational emotive therapy (RET)*. Ellis changed the name of his theory again in 1993 to **rational-emotive behavior therapy** (REBT) to acknowledge the interrelationship among thoughts, feelings, and behaviors in human functioning (Ellis, 1993; Ellis & Ellis, 2014).

Ellis, who served as the executive director of his REBT institute starting in 1960, was a prolific writer and an active clinician. The following *Personal Note* provides additional information about his interests and professional activities.

A Personal Note

I had the privilege of interviewing Albert Ellis when he was 71 years old, and I found him to be very energetic (Nystul, 1985a). He noted that his typical daily schedule involved providing individual and group counseling and psychotherapy from 9:30 a.m. until 11:30 p.m. Ellis's other activities included directing his institute, supervising numerous therapists, making many presentations, conducting workshops, and writing approximately 20 articles and 1 or 2 books each year.

Although Ellis had already written more than 45 books and 500 articles, he had no intention of retiring. At the end of our interview, he said:

> All this activity is infinitely more enjoyable to me than would be lying on a beach, sightseeing, or reading romantic novels. I hope that my good health continues, in spite of the diabetes that I have had for the last 30 years, and that I shall die in the saddle a few decades from now.
>
> Many years ago, I reluctantly came to the conclusion that when I die, I shall still have at least 100 books unwritten, and that is a frustration I had better realistically accept. I would prefer to live forever and to keep exploring the realm of human disturbance and potential realms to happiness and self-fulfillment for eons to come, but no such luck! One of these days in the not-too-distant future, I shall run down. Too damned bad! But hardly awful and terrible. (Nystul, 1985a, p. 254)

Theory of Personality

The REBT theory of personality emphasizes the role of cognitions (and to some degree behaviors) on emotions. REBT contends that people can be best understood in terms of the nature of their *self-talk* (internal cognitive dialogue).

VIEW OF HUMAN NATURE Ellis believed that humans have a potential to be rational or irrational—to be self-preserving or self-destructive. He contended that people perceive, think, emote, and behave simultaneously. Thus, to understand self-defeating conduct, it is necessary to understand the interrelationship among thinking, feeling, and behavior (Ellis, 1996; Ellis & Ellis, 2014).

KEY CONCEPTS The major concepts in REBT relate to the role of cognition and how irrational thoughts can create self-defeating, emotionally disturbing outcomes (Ellis, 1962, 1996; Ellis & Ellis, 2014).

The Role of Cognition The basic premise is that emotional disturbance results primarily from cognitive processes that are fundamentally irrational or illogical in nature (Ellis & Ellis, 2014). Ellis and Harper (1975) defined as *rational* anything that promotes happiness and survival for the individual and as *irrational* anything that inhibits personal happiness and survival. One way to identify illogical or irrational thought processes is to look for statements that contain the unconditional *should* or the absolutistic *must* or *ought* (Ellis & Ellis; Ellis & Harper). Here are some examples of such self-defeating statements:

- "I should get all As, and if I don't, I'm stupid."

- "I ought to know better when it comes to choosing a boyfriend. The ones I pick are all duds."

- "I must do well at my job, and if I don't, I'm no good."

Ellis suggested that not all statements of irrational beliefs contain shoulds, oughts, and musts (Ellis, 1977; Ellis & Ellis, 2014). According to Ellis, irrational thoughts can also be in the form of other self-defeating self-statements, such as these:

- *Self-damnation:* "I am a worthless good-for-nothing."

- *I-can't-stand-it-itis:* "I can't stand the thought of losing my girlfriend."

- *Awfulizing:* "I would never want to bring a child into this insane and awful world."

The A-B-C-D-E Acronym In part, REBT's popularity is due to its simplicity. The basic procedures associated with REBT can be taught to the client by using the A-B-C-D-E acronym. The letter *A* in the acronym stands for the activating event. This can be whatever the client may be reacting to, such as a recent phone conversation or a report that was received by a supervisor. *B* represents the client's belief system or cognitive reaction to the activating event. *C* is the emotional consequence that the client is experiencing, such as feeling anxious or depressed. *D* suggests that the client learn to dispute self-defeating thought processes, and *E* is the effect of the disputing process. Ellis (1962, 2008) contended that it is not *A* that causes a serious emotional reaction (*C*). For *C* to occur, a self-defeating thought process must occur at *B*. The client is therefore taught how to dispute self-defeating processes (*D*) to generate a positive effect (*E*).

Ellis also suggested that self-defeating cognitive reactions follow a predictable pattern. People usually start with a sane or rational reaction to the activating event. Next, they tend to engage in self-talk that is illogical or irrational. Finally, they grossly overreact to the situation, making it seem like a catastrophe (Ellis, 1962, 1996; Ellis & Ellis, 2014).

It is important to note that for REBT to be effective, counselors must be careful not to focus just on the client's sentences and self-statements. They should also help clients explore and dispute self-defeating "meanings, evaluations, images, and other forms of cognitions" (Ellis, 1986, p. 648). From this perspective, Ellis contended that REBT has always been consistent with postmodern trends, which recognize the multiple voices reflected in social forces such as culture, language, and narratives (Ivey, 1996). The following *Personal Note* provides an illustration of REBT.

A Personal Note

Tim was a 30-year-old, self-referred male who came to a mental health clinic complaining of anxiety and depression and threatening suicide. Tim told me he had recently started a new job as an accountant for a firm. Two days earlier, his boss had returned a report he had written with several suggestions and one or two indications of possible errors in his statistics. His boss had asked him to look over the suggestions and revise the report accordingly. Tim told me all he could think about since then was the report and how his boss "*must* be out to get me."

I decided to use REBT, so I provided Tim with an overview of the A-B-C-D-E acronym. Together, we decided that the activating event *A* was the boss returning the report; *B* was his cognitive reaction to *A* (i.e., "My boss must be out to get me"); and *C* represented his feelings of being anxious, depressed, and suicidal. Since REBT focuses on cognition, we then explored his cognitive reactions to *A*. Tim's thought process followed the predictable pattern described earlier. He started with a sane reaction, "It looks like there are some mistakes here." He then began to think irrationally and said things like, "He *must* be out to get me. I know he has decided he made a mistake in hiring me and is looking for a way to let me go." Finally, his thoughts became catastrophic as he concluded, "It's just a matter of time until he fires me, and I'll never get another job. I guess there is just no hope for me."

(Continued)

(Continued)

We also explored how sociocultural forces could influence the personal meanings, evaluation, and images associated with his story. In this regard, he mentioned that he could be overreacting to this situation, owing to repeated parental messages of "No matter what, you have to do well at work."

When I asked Tim how he felt when he said these things to himself, he replied, "Terrible." He began to realize that his thoughts could cause an intense emotional reaction at C. Tim and I then attempted to restructure his cognitive reactions. We disrupted, D, his irrational reactions with rational reactions. For example, he changed "My boss *must* be out to get me," to "My boss seems to have some concerns about my report." We also co-constructed new narratives that more realistically conceptualized work in terms of success and failure.

By the end of our first counseling session, Tim no longer had intense feelings of being anxious, depressed, or suicidal. He said he had no idea how much power thoughts could have on emotions, and he was glad he had a tool he could use to help control his emotional reactions. Tim also commented that he still felt somewhat uncomfortable about his relationship with his boss. He wanted to know how his boss thought he was doing in his job. Tim agreed to ask his boss this question as a homework assignment. At the start of our next session, Tim smiled and said, "I guess I caused myself a lot of needless worry. My boss said he thought I was doing just fine, and he really appreciated me revising my report." Counseling was terminated shortly thereafter.

Theory of Counseling and Psychotherapy

THE COUNSELING PROCESS The primary goal of REBT is to restructure the client's self-defeating cognitions and help the client acquire a more realistic philosophy of life (Ellis & Ellis, 2014). The process of therapy is educational and confrontational in nature. The therapist teaches the client how to dispute irrational thoughts and confronts and even attacks, if necessary, the client's self-defeating belief system. Once clients become aware of their negative self-talk, they can create a cognitive reaction that generates a more positive emotional consequence.

In terms of the counseling relationship, Ellis and Ellis (2014) did not believe that a warm relationship is either a necessary or sufficient condition for personality change. They believed the therapist must fully accept clients but must also point out discrepancies in clients' behavior when necessary (Ellis, 1996; Ellis & Ellis).

TECHNIQUES The therapeutic REBT techniques that Ellis identified include cognitive, emotive, and behavioral techniques (Ellis, 1962, 1996; Ellis & Ellis 2014).

Cognitive Techniques To a large degree, REBT focuses on helping clients overcome self-defeating cognitions. Cognitive restructuring is the main technique used. It involves restructuring irrational and illogical cognitions through the steps represented by the A-B-C-D-E acronym. Other cognitive methods include techniques such as *reframing,* or redefining a negative situation from a more positive perspective, and *referenting,* or helping clients conceptualize problems from a holistic rather than a fragmented perspective (Livneh & Wright, 1999). Bibliotherapy is also used in REBT to help clients learn how to apply REBT in everyday life.

Emotive Techniques Emotive (or emotive-evocative) techniques focus on the client's affect or emotional domain. These techniques can play a major role in helping clients learn how to accept themselves (Corey, 2013). For example, humor can be used to help clients put their situation in perspective and stop putting themselves down. Other emotive techniques include the use of imagery to create more positive emotional patterns (e.g., imagining what it would feel like to overcome fear) and shame-attacking exercises, in which clients learn to overcome shame by becoming less concerned about how they are perceived by others.

Behavioral Techniques REBT utilizes the full range of behavioral techniques to help clients achieve their goals. Examples of behavioral techniques include the use of operant conditioning (e.g., behavior modification), assertiveness training, systematic desensitization, relaxation therapy, and self-management (including self-monitoring). Homework assignments play an integral role in the application of behavioral techniques, whereby clients try out and practice what they learn in counseling in their day-to-day activities.

Summary and Evaluation

A literature review of REBT concludes that there is some encouraging support for its efficacy (Weinrach, 1995). For example, a meta-analysis of 70 REBT studies showed REBT to be significantly superior to no other treatment and having similar efficacy as other approaches such as cognitive behavior modification and cognitive therapy (Lyons & Woods, 1991).

REBT is an educationally oriented approach that attempts to teach a client how to overcome self-defeating cognitive reactions. One of its strengths is its simplicity. It can be taught to the client in terms as simple as the A-B-C-D-E acronym. In time, clients can learn to use the tools necessary to become their own self-therapists and gain control over their mental health.

The major weakness of REBT may be its overemphasis on the role of cognition in the etiology of mental disorders and emotional disturbances. In addition, it may oversimplify what is required to effectively restructure cognition. For many clients, much more may be required than simply changing irrational statements to rational statements. REBT also avoids exploring other factors, such as traumatic early-life experiences, which could represent important treatment considerations.

Cognitive Therapy

Background Information

During the mid-1950s, Aaron Beck (b. 1921) developed a cognitively oriented approach to treat mental disorders, rejecting his early training in psychoanalysis. Beck is best known for his work on depression (Beck, 1987, 1991; Beck, Rush, Shaw, & Emery, 1979) and anxiety (Beck & Emery, 1985). His early work on depression resulted in the development of the Beck Depression Inventory, which is widely used as a clinical and research instrument.

Theory of Personality

"Cognitive therapy is based on a theory of personality that maintains that people respond to life events through a combination of cognitive, affective, motivational, and behavioral responses (Beck & Weishaar, 2014, p. 231). The theory of personality for cognitive therapy emphasizes the role of cognitive processes on the development of mental disorders such as depression and anxiety. Cognitive therapy contends that the etiology of many mental disorders can be directly traced to cognitive dysfunctions involving misinterpreting environmental cues (e.g., "My friend did not show up, so he must not like me").

VIEW OF HUMAN NATURE Beck contended that people are a product of the interaction of innate, biological, developmental, and environmental factors (Beck & Weishaar, 2014). Also, by emphasizing the role of cognition in mental health, he suggested that people have the capacity for self-determination.

KEY CONCEPTS Beck and Weishaar (2011, 2014) described the following key concepts associated with cognitive therapy.

The Role of Cognition in Mental Health Emotions and behaviors are determined primarily by how a person perceives, interprets, and assigns meanings to events.

Cognitive Vulnerability Personality structures have vulnerabilities that predispose them to psychological distress. These vulnerabilities are characterized by *schemata,* which are fundamental beliefs and assumptions that develop early in life and are reinforced by learning situations throughout life. They create beliefs, values, and attitudes about oneself, others, and the world. A schema can be functional or dysfunctional. Examples of statements indicating dysfunctional schemes of a borderline personality are "There is something fundamentally wrong with me," and "People should support me and should not criticize, abandon, disagree with, or misunderstand me and my feelings" (Beck & Weishaar, 1989, p. 294). A dysfunctional schema can contribute to cognitive distortions, systematic bias in information processing, and other problems associated with emotional distress.

Cognitive Distortions A cognitive distortion is a systematic distortion in reasoning that results in psychological distress. Cognitive distortions identified by Beck and Weishaar (2014) include the following:

- *Arbitrary inference,* drawing a conclusion that has no supportive evidence or contradicts existing evidence

- *Selective abstraction,* taking information out of context or ignoring other information

- *Overgeneralization,* constructing a general rule on the basis of one or more isolated incidents and then applying it to unrelated situations

- *Magnification and minimization,* viewing something out of proportion, as either less or more significant than it actually is

- *Personalization,* attributing external events to oneself without evidence of a causal connection

- *Dichotomous thinking,* conceptualizing an experience in either-or terms, such as seeing it as good or bad

Systematic Bias in Information Processing Mental disorders are characterized by a bias in information processing. Typically, the bias begins when a person "misreads" external events, thereby creating dysfunctional responses. For instance, someone who suffers from claustrophobia may "misread" taking an elevator as a very dangerous situation. The systematic bias then tends to shift to internal messages, such as physiological responses. In this example, the person may "misread" feelings of tension and apprehension as an impending anxiety attack.

Cognitive Triad of Depression The cognitive triad is characterized by a negative view of the self, the world, and the future. Psychological and physical symptoms of depression can evolve from the cognitive triad. Beck and Weishaar (2014) cited several examples of this phenomenon. A feeling of being unable to cope or control events can lead to a paralysis of will. Negative expectations about life can contribute to physical symptoms of depression, such as low energy, fatigue, and inertia.

Cognitive Model of Anxiety Anxiety results when a person's information processing is faulty, resulting in perceptions of danger when no danger exists. People with this anxiety have difficulty correcting their misconception by recognizing safety cues or other evidence. The cognition of anxious individuals is characterized by themes of danger and the likelihood of harm.

Theory of Counseling and Psychotherapy

THE COUNSELING PROCESS Beck summed up the major thrust of cognitive therapy in an interview with Weinrach (1988):

> Cognitive therapy is a short-term treatment that was developed primarily for the treatment of depression and anxiety. It is now being used for personality disorders, eating disorders, and some of the other types of problems that have been more

refractory to psychotherapy in the past. It is based on a view of psychopathology that stipulates that people's excessive affect and dysfunctional behavior is due to excessive or inappropriate ways of interpreting their experiences. It is also based on the notion that people who are depressed or anxious have in some way a distorted image of themselves and their external situation. (p. 160)

Beck and Weishaar's (2014) insights into the counseling process are incorporated into the following overview. The counselor initially attempts to promote a positive relationship by establishing the core conditions identified by Rogers: warmth, accurate empathy, and genuineness. The client is then encouraged to take an active role in the process by setting goals, recounting cognitive and behavioral reactions to problem situations, and doing homework assignments.

The counselor functions as a guide by helping the client understand the role of cognition in emotions and behaviors. The counselor also acts as a catalyst by promoting corrective experiences that result in necessary cognitive restructuring and skill acquisition. Counselors avoid the role of passive expert. They instead engage in a process of collaboration with the client with the ultimate goal of eliminating systematic biases in thinking. Counselors do not tell the client that a particular belief is irrational or wrong. Instead, they explore with the client the meaning, function, usefulness, and consequences associated with the belief. The client then decides whether to retain, modify, or reject a belief.

TECHNIQUES Beck and Weishaar (2014) described the following techniques associated with cognitive therapy.

Decatastrophizing This process, also known as the *what-if* technique, involves preparing clients for feared consequences by identifying problem-solving strategies.

Reattribution Technique This technique encourages challenging thoughts and assumptions by exploring other possible causes of events.

Redefining Redefining helps mobilize clients who feel they have no control over a problem by rephrasing the problem in a manner that promotes action. For instance, a student could change "I'm not a good student," to "I'm going to study more."

Decentering This technique involves having the client make observations to obtain a more realistic understanding of other people's reactions. It can alleviate anxiety by helping clients realize that they are not the center of attention.

Behavioral Techniques Cognitive therapy utilizes a wide range of behavioral techniques to help clients: modifying automatic thoughts and assumptions (e.g., hypotheses testing to challenge thoughts and assumptions), reducing negative thinking (e.g., diversion techniques such as physical activity), preparing for difficult situations (e.g., behavioral rehearsal to prepare for a future event), and exposing themselves to feared situations (e.g., exposure therapy).

Summary and Evaluation

Cognitive therapy has become an increasingly popular form of counseling. It has primarily been a short-term treatment for depression. More recently, cognitive therapy has been used to effectively treat a variety of disorders, such as anxiety (Chambless & Gillis, 1993), eating disorders (Wilson & Fairburn, 1993), and substance abuse (Beck, Wright, Newman, & Liese, 1993).

Its popularity is due in part to the massive research efforts that have evaluated the efficacy of cognitive therapy in the treatment of depression. Beck and Weishaar's (2011, 2014) review of the literature showed that cognitive therapy is superior to drug therapy (Blackburn, Bishop, Glen, Whalley, & Christie, 1981; Hollon et al., 1992; Maldonado, 1982) or equal to drug therapy (Blackburn, Eunson, & Bishop, 1986; Hollon, Evans, & DeRubeis, 1983; Murphy, Simons, Wetzel, & Lustman, 1983; Simons, Murphy, Levine, & Wetzel, 1986). Studies indicate that a combination of cognitive therapy and antidepressant medication is the most effective treatment for depression (Blackburn et al., 1981, 1986; Maldonado; Teasdale, Fennell, Hibbert, & Amies, 1984). Cognitive therapy also appears to have stronger long-term effects than drug therapy (Blackburn et al., 1986; Hollon et al., 1983; Kovacs, Rush, Beck, & Hollon, 1981; Maldonado).

Dobson's (1989) meta-analysis of the efficacy of cognitive therapy for the treatment of depression analyzed 28 studies that used the Beck Depression Inventory as the outcome measure. Results of the study indicate that cognitive therapy clients do better than 98% of control subjects, 70% of drug-therapy clients, and 70% of other psychotherapy clients. These results were consistent with the results of an earlier meta-analysis study by Nietzel, Russell, Hemmings, and Gretter (1987).

More recently, Butler, Chapman, Forman, and Beck (2006) conducted a review of 16 meta-analyses that provided evidence of the efficacy of cognitive therapy and cognitive behavioral therapy. Large size effects were noted for a variety of conditions associated with anxiety and depression. Moderate size effects were found for marital problems, somatic complaints, and chronic pain. Small size effects were related to treatment of schizophrenia and bulimia nervosa. In addition, a study by Hollon et al. (2005) found that clients treated with cognitive therapy had lower rates of relapse than did those treated with antidepressant medication. Hollon and Beck (1994) cautioned that the literature suggesting cognitive therapy is superior to drug therapy may be oversimplified and prone to methodological problems. Their extensive review of the literature cast doubts on the claims that cognitive therapy is superior to drug therapy in the treatment of depression. Methodological problems include a lack of placebo controls to allow for adequate comparisons between treatment groups. In addition, severity of symptomology may play an important role in the efficacy of cognitive therapy as a treatment for depression. In this regard, there is some indication that cognitive therapy may be less effective than drug therapy for individuals who have severe depression and more effective than drug therapy for individuals with mild or moderate depression (see the National Institute of Mental Health's Treatment of Depression Collaborative Research Program, Elkin et al., 1989).

There is some indication in the research that the effectiveness of cognitive therapy depends to some degree on the personal characteristics of the client. A review of this literature concluded that clients who were depressed and tended to externalize did better in cognitive therapy, whereas clients who were depressed and internalized tended to do better in supportive/self-directed counseling (Prochaska & Norcross, 2010). In addition, clients who rated low on defensiveness seemed to do better in cognitive therapy than did those who rated high in defensiveness.

Transactional Analysis (TA)

Background Information

Eric Berne (1910–1970) is the originator of **transactional analysis (TA)**. He received an MD degree from McGill University in Montreal in 1935 and then completed psychiatric training at Yale University.

TA is unique in its effort to avoid psychological jargon. Instead, the language of TA is easy to understand, using such terms as *parent, adult, child, strokes, games, rackets, decisions,* and *redecisions.* Its use of clear, simple language helped TA become attractive not only as a form of therapy but also as a self-help approach. As evidence of its popularity, two major books on the topic were international best sellers at various times: *Games People Play* (Berne, 1964) and *I'm OK—You're OK* (Harris, 1967).

More recently, TA has become an example of an emerging school of counseling that emphasizes the role of interpersonal relationships in psychological functioning (Prochaska & Norcross, 2002). In this regard, TA can be considered one of the first major theories of counseling to focus on interpersonal relations (Adlerian psychology also stresses the importance of the interpersonal perspective). The interpersonal orientation is reflected in the name of the theory (i.e., *transactional analysis* suggests that people can learn to understand and enhance the transactions and communication patterns between people).

TA's interpersonal focus shares commonalties with another interpersonally oriented theory of counseling, interpersonal psychotherapy, which is gaining recognition as an important new counseling approach (Prochaska & Norcross, 2002). Interpersonal psychotherapy is based primarily on the work of Harry Stack Sullivan (1968) and his school of interpersonal psychoanalysis. Sullivan proposed a modified version of Freud's theory that emphasizes social relations over the drives of sex and aggression as being primarily responsible for mental health and well-being. Adolph Meyer (1957) and individuals associated with the family therapy movement, such as John Bowlby (1973, 1988a) who did work on attachment, also contributed to the early development of interpersonal psychotherapy. Together they provide additional information on how environmental factors (such as psychosocial stressors) and family interaction patterns can influence psychological functioning.

Several other individuals have gone on to develop interpersonal psychotherapy as a short-term, present-centered approach to treat depression (e.g., Klerman & Weissman, 1993). Teyber (2000) summarized the basic premises in interpersonal psychotherapy as follows:

- Problems are conceptualized from an interpersonal perspective.

- Familial interaction patterns are the best means of understanding oneself and others.

- The counselor-client relationship can be used to work through relationship issues.

Interpersonal psychotherapy appears to be an important emerging theory of counseling. Verdeli and Weissman (2014) conducted an overview of research studies that provides evidence of the effectiveness of interpersonal psychotherapy to treat mood disorders, eating disorders, posttraumatic stress disorder, and substance abuse disorders. A more detailed description of this approach is beyond the scope of this text; for additional information and an excellent overview of interpersonal psychotherapy, see Teyber (2000) and Verdeli and Weissman.

Theory of Personality

TA possesses a rich tapestry of concepts with which to generate a theory of personality. The concepts that can be used to provide an in-depth understanding of personality dynamics include *stroking, the games people play,* and *the four life positions.*

VIEW OF HUMAN NATURE Berne (1961, 1964) believed that people have the capacity to determine their own destiny but that few people acquire the necessary self-awareness to become autonomous. Berne (1961) also stressed the importance of early life experiences in personality development, suggesting that people develop scripts at that time that they follow throughout life. These scripts are derived from parental messages and other sources, such as fairy tales and literature.

KEY CONCEPTS Berne (1961, 1964), Dusay and Dusay (1989), and Prochaska and Norcross (2002) provided an overview of the key concepts associated with TA.

The Interpersonal Perspective As noted earlier, TA is considered one the first major theories of counseling to emphasize the role of interpersonal functioning in mental health. Many of the key concepts in TA (such as transactional analysis and analysis of games) are directed at understanding and enhancing interpersonal relations.

Prochaska and Norcross (2002) noted that in TA, psychopathology is understood as a manifestation of intrapersonal (within the individual) and interpersonal (between people) forces. Regardless of the origins of a psychological disorder, it is always interpersonal in terms of its expression (Prochaska & Norcross). TA is therefore usually conducted in group counseling to encourage interpersonal expression. In this format, clients can gain valuable insights into their problems and learn how to use TA techniques and other counseling strategies to overcome their difficulties (Prochaska & Norcross).

Ego States Berne identified the three ego states of parent, adult, and child. The *parent ego state* represents the person's morals and values and can be either critical or nurturing. The critical parent attempts to find fault, whereas the nurturing parent is supportive and promotes growth. The *adult ego state* is the rational-thinking dimension. It is devoid of feelings and acts as a mediator between the child and parent ego states. The *child ego state* is the uninhibited side of the personality, characterized by a variety of emotions such as fear, happiness, and excitement. The child ego state has two dimensions: the free child and the adapted child. The *free child* is uninhibited and playful, whereas the *adapted child* is rebellious and conforming.

An egogram can be used to assess the relative strengths and weaknesses of the various ego states. The egogram "reflects the type of person one is, one's probable types of problems, and the strengths and weaknesses of the personality" (Dusay & Dusay, 1989, p. 420). Interpreting an egogram is a complex process that requires specialized training. Clinicians are especially interested in ego states that are high or low relative to the client's other ego states. For example, low critical parent (CP) suggests problems with exploitation, low nurturing parent (NP) implies loneliness, low adult (A) indicates difficulty concentrating, low free child (FC) suggests a lack of zest for life, and low adapted child (AC) indicates a person who is rigid and difficult to get along with (Dusay & Dusay). A healthy egogram is indicated when there is relative balance among the strength of the ego states, as illustrated in Figure 9.1.

Transactional Analysis The concept of transactional analysis involves analyzing transactions between people. It entails assessing the three ego states of parent, adult, and child of each person to determine whether the transactions between people are complementary, crossed, or ulterior.

Complementary transactions occur when each person receives a message from the other person's ego state that seems appropriate and expected. Figure 9.2 provides three examples of complementary transactions. In each example, both people are sending and receiving messages as expected.

Crossed transactions occur when one or more of the individuals receives a message from the other person's ego state that does not seem appropriate or expected. Figure 9.3 illustrates two examples of crossed transactions.

Ulterior transactions occur when a person's communication is complex and confusing. In these transactions, a person sends an overt message from one ego state and a covert ulterior message from another ego state. The ulterior message can be communicated verbally, nonverbally via body language, or by tone of voice. Figure 9.4 gives examples of each possibility.

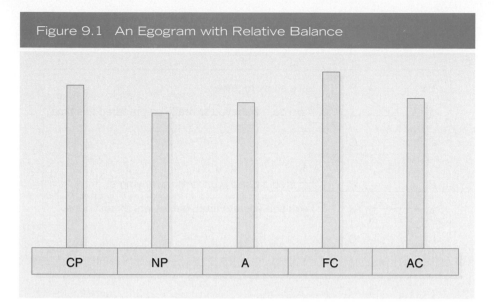

Figure 9.1   An Egogram with Relative Balance

| CP | NP | A | FC | AC |

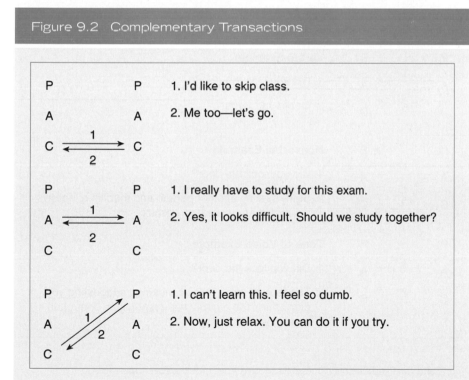

Figure 9.2   Complementary Transactions

P   P   1. I'd like to skip class.

A   A   2. Me too—let's go.

C   C

P   P   1. I really have to study for this exam.

A   A   2. Yes, it looks difficult. Should we study together?

C   C

P   P   1. I can't learn this. I feel so dumb.

A   A   2. Now, just relax. You can do it if you try.

C   C

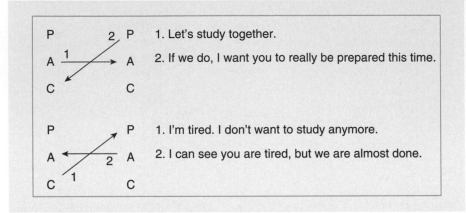

Figure 9.3 Crossed Transactions

P 2 P   1. Let's study together.
A 1 A   2. If we do, I want you to really be prepared this time.
C   C

P P   1. I'm tired. I don't want to study anymore.
A 2 A   2. I can see you are tired, but we are almost done.
C 1 C

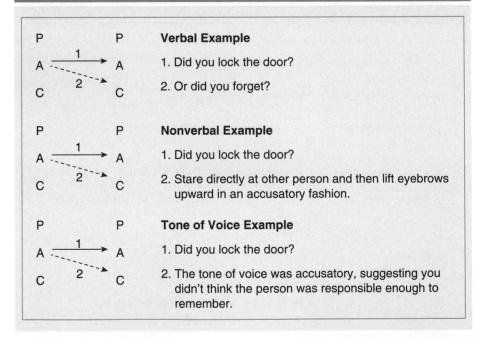

Figure 9.4 Ulterior Transactions

P P   **Verbal Example**
A 1 A   1. Did you lock the door?
C 2 C   2. Or did you forget?

P P   **Nonverbal Example**
A 1 A   1. Did you lock the door?
C 2 C   2. Stare directly at other person and then lift eyebrows upward in an accusatory fashion.

P P   **Tone of Voice Example**
A 1 A   1. Did you lock the door?
C 2 C   2. The tone of voice was accusatory, suggesting you didn't think the person was responsible enough to remember.

Note: Solid lines indicate overt messages; dotted lines indicate covert messages.

Games People Play Berne (1964) defined *games* as "an ongoing series of complementary ulterior transactions progressing to a well-defined, predictable outcome" (p. 48). These games are usually played at an unconscious level, with the people involved unaware they are playing a particular game. Some of the games people can play are "Now I've got you, you SOB," and "Kick me." Although game playing results in bad feelings for both players, it also offers payoffs for the participants (Dusay & Dusay, 1989). The following example illustrates what might occur during the game of "Kick me."

Mary fears dating because she believes things will never work out. She reluctantly accepts a date with John, whom she finds attractive. Within the first 10 minutes of the date, she criticizes John's hairstyle and then complains about the movie they are going to see. After the movie, John gets tired of Mary's insults and takes her home. As he pulls up to her house, he proceeds to tell her off ("kicks her"), saying what an ungrateful person she is.

Although Mary initially feels hurt by John's comments, she will receive a payoff from her game. As she goes into the house, she can ask herself, "Why do I always get rejected? Things never work out. I guess dating isn't for me." The game therefore provides Mary with the payoff of having an excuse to avoid dating in the future. John also receives a payoff in that her rudeness made him feel free to "kick her."

The Four Life Positions Berne (1961) suggested that in developing life scripts, people put themselves in the role of being "OK" or "not OK." They also tend to see others as basically friendly (OK) or hostile (not OK). The following four possible life positions represent combinations of how people define themselves and others:

1. "I'm OK, you're OK" represents people who are happy with themselves and others.

2. "I'm OK, you're not OK" suggests people who are suspicious of others, could have a false sense of superiority, or may be suffering from a mental disorder such as paranoia.

3. "I'm not OK, you're OK" indicates people who have a low self-concept and feel inadequate in relation to others.

4. "I'm not OK, you're not OK" implies people who have given up on themselves and life and may even be suicidal.

Life Scripts A major part of personality structure relates to the life scripts that are created beginning in childhood. A life script is composed of parental messages—for example, a parent saying, "You're my darling angel"—and complementary messages from other sources that may include fairy tales, movies, and literature. These messages create a role that a person identifies with and acts out throughout life. For instance, a person could identify with the Superman character and play the role of the "good person who comes to the rescue" in interpersonal relations. Another possible life script is identifying with the Cinderella character, which might lead to feelings of self-pity, being taken advantage of, and never having a chance to get out and have fun.

Strokes TA suggests that the basic motivation for social interaction is related to the need for human recognition, or *strokes* (Dusay & Dusay, 1989). Strokes can be physical, verbal, or psychological and can be positive, negative, conditional, or unconditional. Positive strokes tend to communicate affection and appreciation and are essential to psychological development. TA attempts to identify what types of strokes are important to clients and encourages them to take an active role in getting these strokes. For instance, after having a rough day, people could tell their partner that they need some extra strokes that evening.

Theory of Counseling and Psychotherapy

THE COUNSELING PROCESS The ultimate goals of TA are to help clients become autonomous, self-aware, and spontaneous and have the capacity for intimacy (Berne, 1961). Following are some of the short-term goals TA uses to help clients achieve these ultimate goals:

- Making new decisions, called *redecisions,* regarding their behavior and approach to life

- Rewriting their life script so they feel OK about themselves and can relate effectively to others

- Ceasing to play games that confuse communication and interfere with authentic interpersonal functioning

- Understanding their three ego states of parent, adult, and child and how they can function in an effective and complementary fashion

- Avoiding communicating in a manner that promotes crossed or ulterior transactions

- Learning how to obtain and give positive strokes

The counseling process in TA is educative in nature. The therapist takes on the role of teacher, providing clients information on how to use the TA concepts. TA emphasizes cognition in its approach by showing clients how they can use their intellect to apply TA principles to overcome mental disorders.

The counseling process in TA is also active, in that it emphasizes the importance of clients doing something outside of counseling via homework assignments. In addition, TA relies on the use of a counseling contract, which the therapist and the client develop together. The contract is very specific in identifying the counseling goals, treatment plan, and roles and responsibilities for achieving these goals.

TECHNIQUES The following TA techniques relate to the key concepts described earlier:

- *Structural analysis* is a technique that helps clients become aware of their three ego states and learn to use them effectively.

- *Transactional analysis* helps clients learn to communicate with complementary transactions (e.g., adult to adult).

- *Script analysis* is a process that explores the type of life script the client has developed and how it can be rewritten in a more effective manner.

- *Analysis of games* involves clients identifying what games they play and how the games interfere with interpersonal functioning.

Summary and Evaluation

TA is an educative, cognitively oriented process in which clients learn to apply TA principles so that they can become self-therapists and lead autonomous, fully functioning lives. It was one of the first theories of counseling whose goal was to focus on the role that interpersonal relations play in mental health and well-being. Its valuable tools include analysis of games, which can help clients understand and enhance their interpersonal functioning as an important step in overcoming their psychological problems. The strength of TA is that the concepts are written in easily understandable words—such as *parent, adult, child, strokes,* and *games*—instead of psychological jargon. One weakness of TA is the possibility of focusing too much attention on self-analysis and intellectualization. When this occurs, clients may become self-absorbed and calculating in their relationships with others.

There is evidence to suggest that TA is becoming more popular with practitioners as they begin to integrate it with other schools of counseling, such as Gestalt and psychodrama (Poidevant & Lewis, 1995). This wider base of application has allowed TA to be used in industry, for example, by airlines and utility companies (Poidevant & Lewis). TA has also been shown to promote a variety of positive outcomes such as wellness, communication skills, parent education, family counseling, and school functioning (Poidevant & Lewis). For example, there appears to be a positive relationship between getting strokes and overall physical and psychological wellness (Allen & Allen, 1989). In addition, TA has been used to enhance communication skills and productivity (Nykodym, Rund, & Liverpool, 1986; Spencer, 1977). In terms of parent education, TA has been shown to foster the self-esteem of parents in parent education programs (Bredehoft, 1990). In addition, TA's concepts and procedures (such as ego states and transactional analysis) have been useful in family counseling (Zerin, 1988). In terms of school functioning, Miller and Capuzzi (1984) found that TA can be used to enhance the self-esteem of elementary school students, increase rates of attendance of high school students, and promote positive academic performance in higher education students. Poidevant and Lewis went on to note that TA does not seem to be appropriate for some populations, such as people who suffer from schizophrenia and severe anxiety disorders such as phobias.

An extensive review of the TA research literature by Prochaska and Norcross (2002), including the meta-analysis by Smith, Glass, and Miller (1980), showed overall support for TA, suggesting "it was consistently more effective than no treatment and usually more effective than placebo treatments in adult samples" (p. 217). The review also identified limitations with TA. A major problem with TA is that many of the concepts (such as parent, adult, and child) are difficult to evaluate empirically. In addition, these concepts (while easy to understand) may be an oversimplification of Freud's theory in that they appear to have left major theoretical constructs "lost in the translation" (such as the id as the major driving force in the personality). From a postmodern perspective, TA may be lacking in terms of not going far enough with its interpersonal perspective. For example, additional emphasis could be placed on sociocultural forces that can have an impact on psychological functioning.

Reality Therapy

Background Information

William Glasser (1925–2013) was the founder of **reality therapy**. He was a consulting psychiatrist for the Ventura School for Girls in California when he attempted his first large-scale implementation of reality therapy. The program was well received, prompting an interest in the merits of reality therapy. This approach appeared to be a realistic one, especially for clients like delinquent children and substance abusers who had a pattern of being irresponsible.

In 1961, Glasser published his first book, *Mental Health or Mental Illness?* in which he took an antipsychiatry position, exploring how labels such as *mental disorder* and *schizophrenia* can be harmful to a client. Glasser persisted with this position by not recognizing the various mental disorders described in the *DSM-IV-TR* (2000).

Glasser wrote several other books that contributed to the evolution of reality therapy. He published *Reality Therapy* in 1965, which established his approach as a major force in counseling and psychotherapy. In *Schools Without Failure,* Glasser (1969) attempted to apply the principles of reality therapy to education. His later publications broadened the theoretical base of his approach. In *Positive Addiction* (1976), he described how positive addictions can be substituted for negative addictions. In *Stations of the Mind* (1981), he described the neurological and psychological basis of reality therapy.

In the mid-1980s, Glasser began to focus on the role of control in mental health. Reality therapy was therefore expanded to include control theory (Glasser, 1984, 1985).

Glasser also applied the concepts of control theory to education (1986, 1990). Later, Glasser replaced control theory with choice theory (Glasser, 1998; Glasser & Glasser, 1999). Choice theory recognizes the importance of helping clients learn how to make effective choices to meet their needs in a responsible manner.

Glasser then published *Counseling With Choice Theory: The New Reality Therapy* (2000). This volume represents a direct integration of choice theory into reality therapy, suggesting that 99% of the problems in relationships stem from external control psychology characterized by thinking, "I know what is right for you." Glasser contended that choice theory can be used to overcome the adverse forces of external control psychology, noting that choice determines one's happiness and fulfillment and that controlling others will not bring happiness. He summed up the essence of reality therapy saying, "It is what you choose to do in a relationship, not what others choose to do, that is the heart of reality therapy" (p. 1). Corey (2013) noted that "a primary goal of contemporary reality therapy is to help clients get connected or reconnected with the people they have chosen to put in their quality world" (p. 340).

Wubbolding (2000, 2003, 2010) has also played a key role in the evolution of reality therapy. He has been influential in expanding on Glasser's theory in terms of counseling procedures. His work on the four stages of reality therapy and the questions associated with these stages (e.g., "What are you doing?" and "Is what you're doing working for you?") are very useful in terms of providing a structure to the process of reality therapy.

Theory of Personality

Reality therapy emphasizes the role of choice and responsibility in human functioning. Its theory of personality proposes that enhanced awareness of choices helps clients assume responsibility for their behavior. As clients learn to make appropriate choices, they can create "quality worlds" characterized by success identities and appropriate need gratification.

VIEW OF HUMAN NATURE Glasser believed that the primary motivational force of people is directed at fulfilling basic physiological and psychological needs of survival, love, belonging, power, freedom, and fun. He emphasized the choice people have over fulfilling their needs and creating their own destiny.

KEY CONCEPTS Several key concepts characterize reality therapy (Glasser, 1965, 1985, 1998; Glasser & Wubbolding, 1995; Wubbolding, 2000, 2003, 2010).

Success and Failure Identity A *success identity* results when a person is able to fulfill the psychological needs of loving and of feeling worthwhile to the self and others in a manner that does not interfere with the rights of others. When a person is unable to meet these basic psychological needs, a *failure identity* results. Failure identities are associated with problematic approaches to life, such as delinquency and mental disorders.

Emphasis on Responsibility Reality therapy encourages clients to evaluate their behavior in terms of whether it is helping or hurting themselves and others. When people make an honest evaluation of their behavior, they can assume responsibility for it. Glasser believed that responsibility is critical to mental health and therefore a primary goal of reality therapy.

View of Psychopathology As mentioned earlier, Glasser (1961) first published his antipsychiatry stance with his first book, *Mental Health or Mental Illness?* Thereafter, he consistently maintained that there are no mental disorders and that the labeling process can do more harm than good. In addition, Glasser believed that people are in control of their mental health. According to this theory, a person must behave in a manner associated with depression in order to be depressed. When clients say they are depressed, Glasser would suggest that they say instead, "I'm depressing." As a result, clients will realize the control they have over their mental health.

Positive Addiction Glasser's (1976) *Positive Addiction* was an innovative attempt to redefine the concept of addiction. Up to that time, the tendency was to understand addiction as something negative and to be avoided. Glasser observed that some positive behaviors, such as jogging and meditation, appear addictive in that the person becomes uncomfortable if these behaviors are not allowed to occur. Glasser suggested that people with a negative addiction such as alcoholism can try to discover a positive addiction that becomes a substitute for it.

Control Theory Control theory, once a central concept in reality therapy, suggests that each person has a control system that serves to exert control over the environment. This theory represents a direct challenge to the traditional stimulus-response notion, which suggests that people's responses are conditioned by the environment. Glasser (1986) insisted that "what goes on in the outside would never 'stimulate' us to do anything. All of our behavior, simple to complex, is our best attempt to control ourselves to satisfy our needs" (p. 17). Simply stated, people feel good when they believe they have control over their lives and feel bad when they feel their lives are out of control. As noted, the basic tenet of control theory is that all behavior results from people attempting to satisfy basic needs, which include the psychological needs of belonging, freedom, power, and fun and the physiological need for survival.

Choice Theory Glasser (1998) made a major revision to reality therapy by replacing the concept of control theory with choice theory. The overall aim of choice theory is to help clients learn to make choices that can help them meet their needs in a responsible manner and get what they want in terms of creating a "quality world." Glasser emphasized the role of behavior in learning how to make appropriate choices and contended for the most part that behavior is intrinsically motivated.

Glasser (1998) identified the following 10 axioms of choice theory:

1. People can control only *their own* behavior.

2. Information is essentially all that people exchange, and people must choose how they deal with the information they get from others.

3. Long-lasting problems tend to be relationship problems.

4. Problem relationships affect our *present* lives.

5. Focusing on the *past* can do little to improve current significant relationships.

6. People are motivated to fulfill needs of survival, love and belonging, power, freedom, and fun.

7. Need satisfaction is dependent on satisfying pictures in a person's "quality world."

8. People engage in behaviors relating to acting, thinking, feeling, and physiology throughout life.

9. Awareness of choice associated with behavior is enhanced by the use of language such as "I am choosing to feel anxiety" (or "I'm anxieting") as opposed to "I am suffering from anxiety."

10. People have direct control over their acting and thinking and indirect control over feelings and physiology.

Theory of Counseling and Psychotherapy

THE COUNSELING PROCESS The primary goal of reality therapy is to help clients choose to live their lives in a manner that is responsible and does not interfere with the rights of others. The counseling process is educational in nature, and clients learn how to apply choice theory to effective living. Reality therapy contends that a positive counseling relationship promotes efficacy in the counseling process. It focuses on present behavior and makes no attempt to explore past events such as childhood trauma. It also does not recognize mental disorders, because they represent harmful labels.

TECHNIQUES The main technique in contemporary reality therapy is teaching clients how to use choice theory to meet their basic needs in a responsible manner (Glasser, 1998). Glasser (1980, 1984) set forth an eight-step approach for implementing reality therapy: create a relationship, focus on current behavior, invite clients to evaluate their behavior, make a plan of action, get a commitment, refuse to accept excuses, refuse to use punishment, and refuse to give up. Glasser (1984) suggested using a flexible approach when applying these steps and proposed that the steps are interrelated and overlapping processes rather than discrete steps.

A more recent version of reality therapy emphasizes a four-stage approach that is expressed in the acronym WDEP (Glasser & Wubbolding, 1995; Wubbolding, 2000, 2003, 2010). The following is a brief overview of these four steps:

1. *W* stands for the client's wants, needs, and perceptions. In this first stage of counseling, the counselor explores what the client wants out of life by asking questions such as "What do you want?" (from your job, spouse, and so forth). Various techniques and procedures can be used in this process, such as exploring the client's inner "picture album," which reflects perceptions of his or her wants and needs.

2. *D* stands for what the client is doing and the direction he or she is taking in life. In this stage, the counselor can ask, "What are you doing?" or "Where will you go with your life if you continue doing what you are doing now?" This step focuses on evaluating the client's current behaviors as expressed in the here and now (rather than delving into the past).

3. *E* stands for self-evaluation, which Glasser believed is the central concept in reality therapy. Self-evaluation involves helping clients engage in a process of self-analysis to determine whether "what they are doing is working for them." Self-evaluation is a critical stage in counseling in terms of helping clients get motivated to engage in the change process.

4. *P* involves helping clients plan to make the necessary changes to meet their needs more effectively. Plans are directed according to the insights gained from self-evaluation. Wubbolding (1986) identified the characteristics of effective planning as simple, attainable, measurable, immediate, involved, controlled by the client, committed to, and consistent.

Summary and Evaluation

Reality therapy is a popular short-term form of intervention that focuses on behavior that is occurring in the present. It is a particularly attractive type of treatment for people who have a pattern of acting irresponsibly, such as delinquent children, students with school-related behavioral problems, and people with substance abuse problems.

A limited number of studies have evaluated the efficacy of reality therapy. Most of the studies cited in Glasser and Wubbolding (1995) and Wubbolding (2000, 2003, 2010) as evidence of the effectiveness of reality therapy were published before 1990. One study by Honeyman (1990) cited as providing support for reality therapy suggested that this approach could be used in group counseling with addicts to enhance their self-esteem, help them take more responsibility for their behavior, and improve their relations with others. Graham, Sauerheber, and Britzman (2013) suggested that choice theory and reality therapy can be integrated into family therapy, providing an understandable-practical approach to address the complex issues associated with family dynamics. Additional research seems warranted to evaluate the key concepts (e.g., choice theory) and procedures (e.g., their application to different theoretical perspectives) of reality therapy.

Feminist Therapy

Background Information

A number of creative individuals in the counseling profession have contributed to the evolution of feminist therapy. Some of the early pioneers were Laura Brown (1988), Harriet Lerner (1988), Edna Rawlings (1993), and Carolyn Enns (1993). Feminist therapy continues to evolve into the 21st century as a highly provocative, stimulating school of counseling. The following overview incorporates the feminist perspectives as set forth by Elliott (1999); Enns; Evans, Seem, and Kincade (2005); Forisha (2001); Gilbert and Scher (1999); and Kottler and Montgomery (2011).

Feminist therapy has evolved as an alternative to traditional schools of counseling, which, in large part, have been developed by men. A few exceptions are the theorists Anna Freud, Karen Horney, Melanie Klein, and Virginia Satir. The roots of feminist therapy can be traced to the early 1960s and the work of Betty Friedan (1963) and others associated with feminism and the Women's Liberation Movement. Feminism became a force for promoting equality between the sexes and for addressing oppression directed toward women.

Different forms of feminism have contributed to this movement. Evans et al. (2005) suggested that feminist perspectives (such as liberal, cultural, socialist, and radical feminism) can be differentiated in terms of how they define underlying causes of oppression. For example, socialist feminism contends that women are oppressed as a result of economic policies that exploit women as a source of cheap labor. Radical feminism suggests that oppression results from a male-dominated and male-controlled society and that a restructuring of society is necessary for meaningful change.

Feminist therapy reflects an integration of feminist principles into the counseling process. Numerous theoretical perspectives have emerged from this process (e.g., liberal, cultural, socialist, and radical feminist therapies; empowerment feminist therapy; feminist standpoint theory; feminist postmodernism; gender-awareness therapy; and feminist family therapy). Feminist therapy may be the most misunderstood major school of counseling, resulting in the underutilization of this promising theoretical perspective. Misconceptions include the following:

- Feminist therapy evolved from the Women's Liberation Movement and is therefore anti-male.

- Feminist therapy has been used to address lesbian issues and is therefore a school of counseling restricted to lesbian issues.

- Feminist therapy was developed to create a voice for women and not men. hooks (1995) addressed the relevance of feminist therapy for men and women, saying:

  I believe that we have to start seeing sexism and racism as practices that are profoundly antispirit and antilove. For me feminism is not a movement of women against men. It's a way of thinking that allows *all* of us to examine the harmful role sexism plays in our personal lives and public world and to figure out what we can do to change this. It's a movement that creates space for the spirit and for being a whole person. (p. 188)

As hooks (1995) noted, feminist therapy can have important implications for men. For example, men can benefit from androgynous socialization processes that foster the feminine side of development. In addition, male socialization can include an emphasis on emotional understanding and communication. Men can also benefit from sociopolitical action that promotes attachment and bonding with their children (e.g., paid time off from work after the birth of a child).

Theory of Personality

VIEW OF HUMAN NATURE Feminist therapy appears to have a postmodern-contextual perspective in terms of its view of human nature. The postmodern position conveys a healthy skepticism toward universal truths, such as a unified view of human nature (Enns, 1993). The feminist perspective recognizes the inner strength and resiliency of the human spirit and the inherent drive for freedom and equality. Feminist therapy also contends that contextual factors like sociopolitical forces can create oppression and undermine self-actualizing tendencies.

KEY CONCEPTS

RELATIONAL FOCUS The relational focus in feminist therapy is, to a large degree, associated with relational-cultural theory (Miller, 1976, 1987; Miller & Stiver, 1995), which was developed by Jean Baker Miller and others associated with the Stone Center for Developmental Services and Studies at Wellesley College. The Stone Center model represents an integration of principles from human development, psychodynamic theory, and feminist therapy. It also defines the "self" in relational terms (e.g., "the self in relation" or "the relational self").

Duffey and Somody (2011) noted there has been a resurgence of interest regarding Relational Cultural Theory (RCT) with RCT incorporating characteristics that are hallmarks of the counseling profession (e.g., strengths perspective, contextual focus, and emphasis on wellness). The authors suggested that RCT's relational focus is relevant to both males and females in terms of addressing issues that promote positive interpersonal relationships (e.g., mutual empathy, authenticity, relational resilience, and relational competency). Additional research on this theory appears warranted.

Carol Gilligan's (1991, 1993) highly influential work on identity development and moral decisions also plays a central role in the relational focus utilized in feminist therapy. Gilligan contended that male development emphasizes autonomy and independence, whereas female development tends to revolve around relational issues such as nurturing, empathy, and connecting. Failure to recognize and value the relational qualities of women results in marginalizing (undervaluing) the role and function of women in society.

Social Constructionist Perspective The postmodern perspectives, such as social constructionism, attempt to address the interrelationship between internal and external forces (e.g., people construct their view of reality based on internalized narratives from society). Feminist therapy attempts to deconstruct problematic narratives such as socialization processes that oppress, devalue, or control women.

Diversity and Complexity of Women's Lives Feminist therapy recognizes the diversity and complexity of women's lives (Enns, 1993), aspects that are reflected in the multiple roles and functions associated with being a woman (e.g., individual, friend, wife, and mother).

Theory of Counseling and Psychotherapy

THE COUNSELING PROCESS Feminist therapy is both a form of humanistic psychotherapy and a means of engaging in needed social reform (Forisha, 2001). In this regard, feminist therapy promotes personal power and self-efficacy that transcends the individual (e.g., "the personal is political"). Feminist therapy can be used with a wide range of clients who reflect various forms of diversity, such as age, gender, and sexual orientation. For example, gender-aware therapy (Good, Gilbert, & Scher, 1990) provides a conceptual framework for addressing gender issues throughout the counseling process. In addition, feminist therapy is not anti-male but is instead a positive perspective for both sexes. In this regard, feminist therapy provides a forum for freeing men and women from oppressive forces, such as gender-role stereotyping. It also promotes egalitarian relationships and mutual respect between the sexes. Enns (1993) suggested that men could play a role as pro-feminist therapists by promoting justice and equality between the sexes. For example, men can take an active role as feminist therapists by confronting clients who undermine, control, and devalue women.

Feminist therapy can be conceptualized within several stages of the counseling process as follows.

The Counseling Relationship Feminist therapists promote egalitarian relationships between counselors and clients by removing power and control boundaries. In this process, counselors use self-disclosure (including sharing values and beliefs) to "bring to life" and personalize feminist ideologies and concepts. Therapists demystify the therapy process by educating clients on the theory and practice of feminist therapy. Clients are encouraged to take an active role in therapy, including having candid discussions about feminist principles.

Goals The goals of feminist therapy are directed at relieving client distress; promoting social, economic, and political equality between the sexes; and overcoming oppressive forces such as the marginalization of women. In addition, Forisha (2001) suggested that feminist therapy fosters a number of self-actualizing tendencies such as self-awareness, self-acceptance, self-integration, self-affirmation, self-nurturance, and independence. For example, self-integration can involve integrating opposing sides of one's personality by promoting an androgynous view of the self.

Assessment and Diagnosis Feminist therapy considers internal and external forces in assessment and diagnosis. In this process, emotions may serve adaptive functions (e.g., anger and rage can be coping responses to oppression). Anxiety may also serve a purpose as it can motivate necessary change, such as a reassessment of sex-role expectations. In addition, Forisha (2001) proposed that the marginalization of women has resulted in women being overdiagnosed for mental disorders. For example, women are two times as likely as men to be perceived as having psychiatric and emotional problems. Kottler and Montgomery (2011) noted that diagnostic manuals contribute to overdiagnosis by portraying normative female traits as criteria for psychopathology (e.g., passive, dependent, and seductive).

TECHNIQUES According to Enns (1993), feminist therapists utilize an integrative approach to counseling. They incorporate techniques and models from the various schools of counseling as long as they do not reflect gender bias. Some of these techniques are as follows.

Feminist Family Therapy Feminist family therapy provides an excellent forum for exploring feminist issues such as equality between the sexes and oppression. Feminist family therapy goes beyond traditional family therapy by addressing the role of gender and sociopolitical forces in family dynamics. It also promotes gender-sensitive models for socialization and identity development.

Career Counseling The field of career counseling has made great strides in identifying the personal, family, and cultural factors that affect career choice and decision making. Feminist therapists utilize these models to help clients overcome self-limiting horizons associated with gender-role expectations.

Existential Therapy Feminist therapists use existential therapy as a forum for exploring the meaning of life. They engage in philosophical discussions with clients on a variety of topics, such as the importance of personal autonomy and what it means to live life to the fullest. Existential discussions can be useful in promoting self-realization in terms of resocialization, personal identity formation, and enhancement of self-concept.

Cognitive-Behavioral Therapy To promote symptom relief (e.g., overcoming anxiety and depression), feminist therapists use cognitive-behavioral techniques such as cognitive restructuring, a technique that can also be used to deconstruct self-defeating narratives associated with issues such as weight and body image.

Behavioral Techniques To promote personal autonomy and to empower clients to stand up against the tide of oppression, feminist therapists use behavioral techniques such as assertiveness training. Assertiveness training can also be used to promote androgyny (Gilbert & Scher, 1999).

Person-Centered Therapy Feminist therapists use person-centered therapy to empower clients and to help them become aware of their inner choices and strengths. Person-centered techniques such as listening skills are used for a variety of counseling outcomes, including fostering self-awareness and validating emotions.

Adlerian Counseling Adlerian counseling techniques, such as encouragement, are used in feminist therapy to promote self-efficacy and self-esteem. The lifestyle analysis is an Adlerian technique that can be used to enhance self-understanding and social interest.

Bibliotherapy Bibliotherapy is used to encourage clients to read books that provide information on feminist issues. Bibliotherapy also offers clients opportunities for normalizing and universalizing the experiences of women.

Gay and Lesbian Therapy Feminist therapists were among the first counseling professionals to normalize homosexuality (Elliott, 1999). Feminist therapy has developed models and techniques for addressing gay and lesbian issues within the counseling process (e.g., gay and lesbian identity development models). Feminist therapists also assist gay, lesbian, bisexual, and trangendered individuals with issues associated with "coming out."

Political Advocacy Feminist therapists contend that the "personal is political." From this perspective, problems such as oppression can only be overcome by involvement in social advocacy, such as by taking social and political action.

Summary and Evaluation

Feminist therapy is an emerging theoretical perspective in the counseling literature. The overall aim of feminist therapy is to promote equality between the sexes and to overcome tendencies toward oppression. Feminist therapy has also provided a forum for addressing diversity issues, such as gender and sexual orientation, within the counseling process.

Elliott (1999) noted that it is difficult to find universities that offer training and supervision in feminist therapy. The lack of training opportunities is compounded by the fact that some programs appear to exclude feminist therapy from the curriculum on ideological grounds. This form of discrimination is unfortunate, to say the least. Future research efforts may provide the support necessary for feminist therapy to be fully integrated into the mainstream of counseling.

Special Issues in Cognitive-Behavioral Counseling

Cognitive-Behavioral Theories From a Brief-Counseling Perspective

Cognitive-behavioral theories have particular utility in brief counseling because their techniques and procedures can easily be integrated into a brief-counseling format (e.g., they are solution focused). The following highlights some of the characteristics cognitive-behavioral theories share with the brief-counseling perspective.

BEHAVIOR THERAPY Behavior therapy is well suited for brief counseling. It tends to be time limited, with the counselor contracting with the client to resolve concerns within a 2- to 3-month period (or 8 to 12 sessions; Wilson, 2011). Many of the techniques and procedures used in behavior therapy fit well with the brief-counseling model in that they are solution focused (e.g., systematic desensitization and stress inoculation to treat anxiety).

RATIONAL-EMOTIVE BEHAVIOR THERAPY REBT is an ideal form of brief counseling (Ellis & Ellis, 2014). Although REBT can be used as a form of brief therapy for all clients, it is especially productive for clients who have a specific problem, such as sexual inadequacy or hostility toward a boss, but do not have a serious disturbance (Ellis & Ellis). Ellis and Ellis contended that REBT can help clients in just 1 session but typically lasts for 1 to 10 sessions. Ellis and Ellis believed that the efficacy of REBT as a form of brief counseling can be enhanced when counselors have clients listen to tape-recorded sessions to process how they can apply therapy and when counselors use the REBT Self-Help Form to help clients learn how to apply REBT to a variety of problems they encounter between sessions.

COGNITIVE THERAPY Beck and Weishaar (2011, 2014) described cognitive therapy as a highly structured form of short-term counseling that usually lasts from 12 to 16 sessions. This solution-focused approach attempts to address problems with depression and anxiety and, to some degree, other disorders, such as eating disorders and substance abuse. Cognitive therapy has received substantial research support as an effective short-term treatment approach for treating specific disorders. Managed-care organizations have therefore recognized the utility of cognitive therapy (Beck & Weishaar, 2011).

TRANSACTIONAL ANALYSIS Although TA was not initially designed as a brief-counseling approach, many of its concepts and procedures can be incorporated into a brief-counseling model. The techniques and concepts in TA can be particularly useful for generating a solution-focused approach to counseling. For example, the concepts and strategies of stroking, game playing, ego states, and transactional analysis (analyzing the transactions between people in terms of parent, adult, and child) can play a useful role in helping clients enhance their interpersonal functioning and foster mental health and well-being.

REALITY THERAPY Reality therapy has not traditionally been considered a form of brief counseling, but recent revisions of the theory appear to have made it more attractive. Some of these revisions include emphasizing choice theory and how clients can learn to meet their needs in a manner that does not interfere with the rights of others, the concepts of success identity and failure identity and positive addictions, and Glasser's new way of conceptualizing the counseling process in terms of questions like "What are you doing?" and "Is it working for you?" Each of these concepts and processes can be used to create a brief-time, limited-solution-focused approach to counseling. In addition, reality therapy shares common characteristics with the brief-counseling perspective. For example, current behavior is the focus for change (the past is avoided), psychological jargon is minimized, clients are encouraged to take an active role in their therapy, and the counseling process is solution focused (Palmatier, 1990).

FEMINIST THERAPY Feminist therapy is a flexible form of therapy that can be adapted to a brief-counseling format. A number of feminist therapy interventions can promote brief counseling because they can be conducted outside of formal counseling. For example, clients can be encouraged to engage in bibliotherapy by reading books about feminism and how to become an effective change agent for social reform.

Diversity Issues

Having an awareness of diversity concerns in counseling implies addressing issues such as the client's degree of acculturation, identity development, cultural background (including values and beliefs), and worldview before implementing counseling theories. For example, degree of acculturation can suggest how appropriate traditional theories may be (the higher the acculturation, the higher the probability of appropriateness).

BEHAVIOR THERAPY The essence of behavior therapy is to assess the relationship between the environment and the client's behavior and to adjust counseling to address environmental conditions, such as culture, as necessary (Tanaka-Matsumi & Higginbotham, 1994). Although behavior therapy attempts to include environmental assessment, it often falls short of this goal, especially in terms of expressing sensitivity to cultural or family systems perspectives (Prochaska & Norcross, 2010).

RATIONAL-EMOTIVE BEHAVIOR THERAPY AND COGNITIVE THERAPY REBT and cognitive therapy focus on the role of cognition in mental health and well-being. It is important to consider diversity issues, such as gender, culture, and worldview, in applying these theories. Cognitive therapies may reflect a male bias, valuing "rational thinking" over what could be considered female characteristics, such as intuition and connection, and therefore may be inappropriate and offensive to women (Prochaska & Norcross, 2010). Cultural problems could emanate from REBT's notion that absolutistic thinking (characterized by *shoulds*, *oughts*, or *musts*) creates emotional distress. It is critical to ensure that a client's culture does not value absolutistic thinking as a sign of mental health before trying to dispute this type of thinking. In addition, the concept of worldview recognizes that each person has a unique way of understanding and viewing the world. It is therefore important to gain a phenomenological perspective when conceptualizing a client's cognitions.

TRANSACTIONAL ANALYSIS On the positive side, TA has done a good job in moving beyond an emphasis on intrapsychic forces to recognizing the role of relational issues in psychological functioning. TA could go further in this regard by incorporating a systemic perspective and being more sensitive to cultural issues (Prochaska & Norcross, 2002). Although TA includes a number of concepts that could have wide cross-cultural appeal (e.g., the need for strokes), some of its terminology may be difficult to understand from a cross-cultural perspective.

REALITY THERAPY Several concepts in reality therapy—among them control, choice, and responsibility—may pose problems in terms of cultural issues. Although these concepts may be valued in Western cultures (since they promote individualism), they may not fit well with Eastern cultures (which value the group over the individual). In this sense, Eastern cultures are not as concerned with who broke something (identifying who must take responsibility) but how to fix or correct what is wrong.

Wubbolding (1990), in recognizing the differences among cultures, recommended that reality therapy be adjusted to fit the needs of the client's milieu, including being sensitive to language differences (e.g., "I'll try," in Japan may be equivalent to "I'll do it," in the United States). However, some of the newer trends in reality therapy may be well suited to cross-cultural counseling. One example is structuring counseling along themes such as "What are you doing?" and "Is it working for you?" This enables clients to take an active role in personalizing counseling from the standpoint of their worldview.

FEMINIST THERAPY Feminist therapy has emerged as a major school of counseling and psychotherapy because it addresses diversity issues, such as gender and sexual orientation. Recent research initiatives in feminist therapy have also addressed cultural issues. For example, McNair (1992) suggested that non–African American counselors should not impose their value system when counseling African American women. African American women's values—family, community, and church—should be recognized and not marginalized in favor of values relating to autonomy.

Mindfulness-Based Approaches

An interest in integrating Eastern philosophies, such as Zen Buddhism, into psychotherapy can be traced to the pioneering work of Fromm, Suzuki, and DeMartino (1960). The increasing application of Eastern principles to psychotherapy over the past half century reflects a cultural shift that may be in its infancy (Kabat-Zinn, 2003).

Kabat-Zinn (2003) noted that although mindfulness is the "heart" of Buddhist meditation, it is a universal concept that extends beyond Buddhism. He defined **mindfulness** as "the awareness that emerges through paying attention on purpose, in the present moment, and nonjudgmentally to the unfolding of experience moment by moment" (p. 145). Most people are rarely mindful (Germer, 2013). Instead, they tend to function in a state of mindlessness, robotically going through life on "automatic pilot"; they pay little attention to what they are experiencing and are distracted by thoughts of the past and future. Kabat-Zinn considered mindfulness a form of deep inquiry that cultivates insights into the nature of the human experience. Mindfulness is also referred to as insight meditation: "a deep, penetrative non-conceptual seeing into the nature of mind and world" (Kabat-Zinn, p. 146).

A second revolution going on in cognitive psychology recognizes that much of what is experienced is influenced by unconscious processes (Germer, 2013). The task of therapy is therefore "to *access* implicit, automatic, dysfunctional thought patterns" (Germer, p. 21). Johanson (2006) suggested that mindfulness is a distinct state of consciousness that has vast implications for exploring unconscious processes and reorganizing deep cognitive structures. Mindfulness has been incorporated into a wide range of psychotherapeutic approaches, such as the humanistic, psychodynamic, and cognitive-behavioral (Germer). Mindfulness-based interventions, such as meditation, have come of age, empowering clients to take an active role in treating a wide range of medical conditions like cancer, chronic pain, sleep disturbances, and depression (Krasner, 2004).

Within the perspective of psychotherapy, Germer (2013) described mindfulness as being composed of three interrelated processes—awareness, present experience, and acceptance. Awareness and being centered in the "now" are therapeutic concepts that can be traced to Perl's (1969a, 1969b) Gestalt therapy. The therapeutic concept of acceptance has been more recently emphasized in cognitive therapies.

Krasner (2004), Johanson (2006), and Segal, Williams, and Teasdale (2013) provided an overview of four cognitive-behavioral approaches that incorporate mindfulness interventions.

- *Dialectical behavioral therapy (DBT; Linehan, 1993; Linehan et al., 2006).* DBT "integrates mindfulness and acceptance strategies associated with Zen traditions with traditional cognitive behavior therapy" (Lenz, Taylor, Fleming, & Serman, 2014, p. 27).

- *Mindfulness-based cognitive therapy (MBCT; Segal et al., 2013).* This form of group therapy utilizes mindfulness interventions to promote relapse prevention in individuals who have a history of depression.

- *Mindfulness-based stress reduction (MBSR; Kabat-Zinn, 2003).* MBSR was initially developed as a psychoeducational group process in which clients were taught mindfulness interventions to promote stress reduction, health, and wellness.

- *Acceptance and commitment therapy (ACT; Hayes, Follette, & Linehan, 2004; Hayes, Strosahl, & Wilson, 2012).* Practitioners of ACT contend that mindfulness interventions can help clients accept (not evaluate) experiences and be committed to clarifying values, taking action, and promoting personal meaning in life.

ACT (Hayes et al., 2012) employs the concept of cognitive diffusion—accepting a thought as just a thought without interpretation or evaluation. "Acceptance" is essentially the opposite of what traditional cognitive behavioral approaches recommend, such as disputing irrational or self-defeating thoughts (e.g., Ellis's REBT; see Ellis & Ellis, 2014). ACT suggests that clients react to particular thoughts in the context of a stream of consciousness—each thought is one of many thoughts one is aware of and accepts, regardless of whether it is painful or joyous.

The following *Personal Note* provides an example of how I have been able to incorporate my experiences with meditation into emerging trends in mindfulness-based approaches.

A Personal Note

I have been doing Transcendental Meditation (TM) for 47 years—20 minutes in the morning and evening. When I first started meditating, I did not think I had time to meditate. Almost immediately after starting, however, I began to look forward to having the 20 minutes to myself, as it was very relaxing and a good way to obtain important insights and release stress. It is therefore not surprising that I have only missed approximately 20 meditations in 40 years. I meditate because I enjoy it, not because I think it is good for me—as I sometimes do when I exercise.

Over the years, I have been very interested in how Eastern concepts like meditation and mindfulness could be integrated into psychotherapy, such as self-transcendence and the existential encounter discussed in Chapter 8. My experiences with meditation have helped me understand concepts associated with mindfulness in psychotherapy.

I have marveled at the exquisite simplicity and power of the ACT concept of cognitive diffusion. It makes sense to be aware of and accept thoughts for what they are—one thought at a time in the moment. For example, when I feel anxiety, I accept my anxiety as unpleasant and discomforting but do not get "bogged down" with this thought. Instead, I become aware and accept this thought and then experience the next thought (such as "There goes a beautiful butterfly") in my ongoing stream of consciousness.

The concept of stream of consciousness comes easily for me, as it reflects what I experience when I meditate (thoughts and feelings bubble up into my awareness as I transcend deep into my inner psyche). I am also aware of how meditation can be an extremely effective/efficient way to explore and become mindful of thoughts and feelings in my unconscious mind. The resultant insight, stress release, catharsis, and inner peace have done much for my physical and mental health.

My research and clinical experience have also taught me that meditation is not easy or enjoyable for some people. One study investigated whether there is a difference in the psychological profiles of nonmeditators, meditators, and dropout meditators (Nystul & Garde, 1979). Results showed that regular meditators had the most positive mental health, followed by nonmeditators, with dropout meditators being the most prone to personality disorders. Perhaps people with in-depth psychological problems may find the release of repressed thoughts during meditation overwhelming and stressful. For others, meditation may simply not be something that is compatible with their way of being in the world.

RESEARCH ON MINDFULNESS-BASED APPROACHES Research studies have provided evidence of the efficacy of mindfulness-based approaches to enhance health, wellness, and other psychological factors.

In an overview of research investigations on mindfulness and meditation, Lazar (2005) noted that preliminary results support the use of mindfulness and meditation in psychotherapy in conjunction with other approaches for managing pain and treating anxiety, depression, eating disorders, cancer, and psoriasis. She also noted that meditation appears to promote neurophysiological changes that enhance mental and physical health.

Wisner and Norton (2013) conducted a study that assessed the effects of mindfulness-based group counseling on students attending an alternative high school. Results of the study showed that mindfulness skills increased the behavioral and emotional strengths of students who were at risk of dropping out of high school.

Ricard, Lerma, and Heard (2013) investigated the effects of dialectical behavioral therapy (DBT) skills group counseling on students attending a disciplinary alternative educational program. DBT skills addressed included mindfulness, emotional regulation, interpersonal effectiveness, and distress tolerance. Results of the study showed a reduction in student- and parent-reported measures of behavioral distress.

Lenz et al. (2014) conducted a meta-analytic study to investigate the use of dialectical behavior therapy (DBT) to treat individuals who had been diagnosed with eating disorders and had co-occuring depressive symptoms. Results of the study provided "preliminary support for DBT as a potentially effective strategy for treating eating disorder episodes and comorbid depression concurrently" (p. 33).

A literature review by Nystul (2010) also provided research evidence for the psychological and physiological effects of meditation. He found that Transcendental Meditation can be a useful adjunct to psychotherapy in addressing unhealthy lifestyle factors such as chronic stress, alcohol abuse, and smoking. TM has also been associated with reducing the risks of coronary heart disease and high blood pressure. In addition, TM promotes positive psychological well-being in terms of personality functioning, self-concept, ego development, and mental functioning across the life span.

Mindfulness appears to be an effective way to access unconscious processes, provide new perspectives for reacting to thoughts and overcoming disorders such as anxiety, reduce the risk of disease, and promote a mindful/meaningful quality to life. Additional research on this exciting new dimension in psychotherapy is warranted.

Postmodern Theories

The postmodern theories such as narrative psychology, constructivism, and social constructionism have played an important role in the evolution of cognitive-behavioral counseling (Mahoney, 1995b). Their reevaluation of such basic concepts as knowledge and reality is central to this evolution. From a postmodern perspective, knowledge and reality are relative concepts that vary according to sociopolitical forces reflected in the narrative of cultures. Gergen (1982) emphasized the social dimension of cognition when he said that "knowledge is not something that people possess in their heads, but rather something that people do together" (p. 270).

Postmodernism has created a paradigm shift within cognitive-behavioral counseling, changing its focus from intrapsychic causality to a recognition of contextual forces that impact human functioning. The process of counseling is therefore becoming more of a creative than a corrective endeavor (Lyddon, 1995). It is less concerned with overcoming internal cognitive deficits and more concerned with the counselor and client creating new narratives that are not associated with problems or concerns of the client (Lyddon).

Ellis and Ellis (2014) contended that REBT embraces the major tenets of postmodernism, such as considering the role of contextual (relational) issues in creating personal meaning and defining reality. In this regard, Ellis and Ellis suggested that cognition, emotions, and behavior are best understood and addressed within a sociocultural and sociopolitical context. D'Andrea (2000), however, questioned whether Ellis's REBT qualifies as a postmodern approach, contending that REBT does not assess clients' beliefs contextually from a multicultural perspective. On the contrary, REBT classifies beliefs as "impractical" or "irrational" if they conflict with the value system of mainstream society (D'Andrea, p. 8). Additional research appears necessary to assess the nature of postmodernism within REBT.

SUMMARY

Theories included in this chapter emphasize the role of cognition and/or behavior in the counseling process. Cognitive-behavioral approaches integrate concepts and counseling strategies. This is especially true for behavior therapy, rational-emotive behavior therapy, and cognitive therapy. These three theories share a common focus on the integral role that cognition plays in the development of mental disorders. They also incorporate behavioral techniques to teach clients the skills and behaviors necessary to overcome their problems. But there are also subtle differences among these three theories. Ellis's REBT focuses on confronting and disputing the client's irrational and illogical thoughts. Beck's cognitive therapy is concerned with whether a client is interpreting an event in a functional or dysfunctional manner. For Meichenbaum, the central issue in behavior therapy is the nature of the client's inner speech, or self-talk; he contended that a client must learn self-talk that triggers effective coping mechanisms.

Transactional analysis emphasizes the relational aspect of human behavior and how clients can use certain concepts to enhance their interpersonal functioning. Reality therapy stresses the role of choice in mental health and how clients can be helped to make appropriate choices to meet their needs in a manner that does not interfere with the rights of others. Cognitive-behavioral strategies are also utilized by these two theories. For example, transactional analysis helps clients understand how to rewrite life scripts to overcome self-defeating tendencies. And reality therapy promotes cognitions and behaviors that will "work" for a client" (i.e., get the client's needs met in a manner that does not interfere with the rights of others).

Feminist therapy employs interventions that are both cognitive and behavioral in nature. Cognitive-behavioral interventions are directed at a number of concerns in feminist therapy, such as resocialization, gender expectancies, and self-concept. Cognitive restructuring can be used to promote symptom relief and to overcome cognitive distortions associated with weight and body image. Behavioral interventions can include homework assignments associated with political advocacy.

Cognitive-behavioral counseling is particularly well suited for use in a brief-counseling format, for it provides a time-limited approach to the treatment of specific disorders such as depression and anxiety. However, cognitive-behavioral theories have both strengths and weaknesses in terms of their effectiveness in addressing issues of diversity.

Eastern concepts such as mindfulness and meditation are being integrated into psychotherapy to promote psychological and physiological well-being. Postmodern perspectives in cognitive-behavioral counseling have provided an important paradigm shift that will accommodate emerging diversity issues such as gender and culture.

PERSONAL EXPLORATION

1. What cognitive-behavioral theories do you like best, and why?

2. What is your opinion of feminist theory? Can it also be used with men and, if so, how?

3. How can transactional analysis be used to improve interpersonal relationships?

4. What is your opinion of mindfulness-based approaches? Would you consider using them and, if so, why?

5. How might you use behavior theories such as Pavlov's classical conditioning, Skinner's operant conditioning, and Bandura's social learning theory?

6. What do you think about reality therapy and choice theory, and how might you use concepts associated with these theories?

7. What do you think about the relational focus in feminist theory, and how might this concept impact you?

8. How might you use the A-B-C-D-E acronym from Ellis's rational-emotive behavior therapy to overcome self-defeating thought processes?

9. How can Beck's cognitive therapy be used to address issues of depression and anxiety?

10. Which one of the four life positions described in transactional analysis do you identify with, and why?

LEARNING ACTIVITIES

1. Consider applying concepts associated with cognitive behavioral theories to enhance your life (e.g., mindfulness-based techniques such as meditation).

2. Consider reading one or more of the best-selling books relating to transactional analysis (e.g., Berne's *The Games People Play* and Harris's *I'm OK—You're OK*).

WEBSITES

Edelstein, M. R. (n.d.). *REBT therapy.* Retrieved from http://www.threeminutetherapy.com/rebt.html. *Provides a brief description of rational-emotive behavior therapy.*

Psychnet-UK. (n.d.). *Feminist psychotherapy.* Retrieved from http://www.psychnet-uk.com/x_new_site/psychotherapy/psychotherapy_feminist_therapy.html. *Provides links to several articles describing feminist therapy.*

Cherry, K. (n.d.). *What is cognitive behavior therapy? Process, types, components, uses, and effectiveness.* Retrieved from http://psychology.about.com/od/psychotherapy/a/cbt.htm. *Provides an overview of behavior therapy.*

Special Approaches
and Settings

Part Three provides an overview of the special approaches and settings associated with the counseling profession. The following six chapters are covered in Part Three:

CHAPTER 10

Marriage and Family Counseling

The Art and Science of Marriage and Family Counseling

Marriage and family counseling is both an art and a science. It is an art to attempt to formulate and maintain a positive counseling relationship with a couple or family and understand and work with the complex issues that emerge within the family system. This process requires patience, flexibility, creativity, and all the other dimensions associated with the art of counseling.

The spirit of the art of counseling appears to be incorporated into the recent trend toward a postmodern/social constructionist approach to marriage and family counseling. This approach recommends that marriage and family counselors enter family systems not as experts but as inquisitive learners who want to discover how family members define their strengths and weaknesses individually and collectively. The process is similar to the discovery-oriented methods used in qualitative research, whereby the investigator and participant function as co-investigators. The focus of marriage and family counseling from this perspective is on helping couples and families discover new options and opportunities for effective family living through analysis of family stories and narratives. The postmodern/social constructionist approach to marriage and family counseling may represent a bridge between art and science (i.e., between counseling and qualitative research).

The science of marriage and family counseling can be found in the use of assessment and research procedures. Assessment instruments like marital satisfaction inventories provide objective information on areas in which the couple is satisfied or dissatisfied. Both qualitative and quantitative research strategies provide information on the effectiveness of marriage and family counseling. Recent advances in quantitative research have done much to overcome methodological

Chapter Overview

This chapter provides an overview of the field of marriage and family counseling. Highlights of the chapter include the following:

- **The art and science of marriage and family counseling**

- **The evolution of marriage and family counseling**

- **Theoretical foundations, including systems theory and the family life cycle**

- **Postmodern perspectives on marriage and family counseling**

- **Diversity issues in marriage and family counseling**

- **Evaluation of marriage and family counseling**

weaknesses and clearly demonstrate the efficacy of marriage and family counseling (Shadish, Ragsdale, Glaser, & Montgomery, 1995). Qualitative research also seems to offer promise in that it is congruent with systems theory (Moon, Dillon, & Sprenkle, 1990). Qualitative research and systems theory emphasize "social context, multiple perspectives, complexity, individual differences, circular causality, recursion, and holism" (Moon et al., p. 364).

Evolution of Marriage and Family Counseling

The field of marriage and family counseling has evolved over the last 60 years (Everett, 1990). The key events associated with this evolution are incorporated into the following overview (Goldenberg & Goldenberg, 2013).

Psychoanalysis

Nathan Ackerman's (1937) work on the family as an important psychosocial unit set the stage for the adaptation of Freudian concepts to family counseling. Prior to Ackerman's work, psychoanalysis was strictly a process for individual psychotherapy.

General Systems Theory

Ludwig von Bertalanffy introduced general systems theory in the 1920s. This theory contends that seemingly unrelated phenomena represent interrelated facets of a larger system (von Bertalanffy, 1968). General systems theory was later applied to marriage and family counseling, providing an important theoretical foundation.

Research on Schizophrenia

Numerous studies since the late 1940s have investigated the relationship between family dynamics and schizophrenia. Although this massive research effort has as yet determined nothing conclusive, it has raised the profile of family therapy as a potentially useful treatment modality.

Marriage Counseling and Child Guidance

Marriage counseling and child guidance were the first counseling approaches to recognize that problems relate to both intrapersonal (within the person) and interpersonal (between people) forces. The inclusion of the interpersonal perspective prompted counselors to work with the parent and child or husband and wife together in a counseling session.

Group Therapy

Around 1910, Morino developed what can be considered the earliest uses of group processes in counseling. Since then, many other forms of group counseling have evolved. Group counseling influenced marriage and family counseling in terms of how marriage and family counselors could use effective group leadership skills, how the knowledge of group processes could contribute to the understanding of interactions among family members, and how the concept of "the group" as a change agent could be applied to "the family" as a change agent.

Changing Family Structure

The traditional intact family characterized by a wage-earning father, a homemaker mother, and biological children is now in the minority. Current family structures in the United States represent a wide range of family systems that include single parents rearing children; blended families, in which the husband and wife live with children from a previous marriage; cohabiting couples, or unmarried individuals living together for an extended period of time; and same-sex couples living together rearing children.

Numerous problems emerge as family members attempt to adjust to changing family structures. For example, family members often experience financial problems following a divorce (especially women with children). Marriage and family counseling has to some degree evolved as a means of assisting with these common problems of modern family life.

Marriage Counseling Versus Couples Counseling

The continuing evolution of marriage and the family within the changing fabric of contemporary society requires a reconsideration of the terminology used in the helping process. Generally speaking, marriage counselors loosely define their services as appropriate for any couple, married or not married, who is in need of assistance. Using this definition, marriage counseling can also be referred to as *couples counseling*. Family therapists also tend to define *family* broadly to include two or more people cohabiting in the same household. Olson and DeFrain (1997) supported this inclusive definition: a "family is two or more people who are committed to each other and who share intimacy, resources, decisions, and values" (p. 9).

Although this chapter adheres to the traditional terminology of *marriage and family counseling* (versus *couples counseling*), many of the concepts described in the sections on marriage counseling may also have relevance for nonmarried couples. For example, Gottman's factors that predict divorce may also be warning signs of the impending breakup of a serious nonmarried relationship.

Professional Issues and Organizations

The field of marriage and family counseling is both a professional discipline and a specialized counseling strategy practiced by various members of the helping profession. R. L. Smith (1994) recommended that the appropriate sequence for becoming a marriage and family counselor is first to master personal and human relations skills, then to develop general counseling skills and theory, and finally to specialize in marriage and family skills and theory.

The two main professional organizations for marriage and family counselors are the American Association for Marriage and Family Therapy (AAMFT) and the American Counseling Association (ACA)—formerly known as the American Association for Counseling and Development (AACD). The AAMFT has a much longer history; it was originally called the American Association of Marriage Counselors in 1942. As of 2015, there were over 25,000 members. The current address of AAMFT is as follows:

American Association for Marriage and Family Therapy

112 South Alfred Street

Alexandria, VA 22314

http://www.aamft.org

In 1989, the ACA established the International Association of Marriage and Family Counselors (IAMFC) as a division. As of 2010, there were over 2,800 IAMFC members (Wilcoxon, Remley, & Gladding 2012). The current address of the ACA is as follows:

American Counseling Association

6101 Stevenson Avenue, Suite 600

Alexandria, VA 22304

http://www.counseling.org

The AAMFT and ACA have done much to promote the professional standards of marriage and family counseling, including establishing ethical codes and promoting state licensure. By 2009, all 50 states (as well as the District of Columbia) had licensure laws regarding marriage and family counseling.

Theoretical Foundations

Several important theoretical foundations have contributed to marriage and family counseling. Theories described in this section include systems theory and the family life cycle.

Systems Theory

Systems theory is the foundation of and integrating force in marriage and family counseling (Smith, Carlson, Stevens-Smith, & Dennison, 1995). The systems perspective is based on the principle of circular causality (Everett, 1990). According to this principle, actions caused by one family member influence the actions of all other family members, affecting the functioning of the family system, including the person who was responsible for the initial action (Goldenberg & Goldenberg, 2013).

In addition, systems theory focuses on the family system rather than the individual. From this perspective, problematic individuals are viewed in terms of family interaction patterns and are therefore considered within the social context in which their problems occur (Hazelrigg, Cooper, & Borduin, 1987).

KEY CONCEPTS   An overview of key concepts associated with systems theory (based on Goldenberg & Goldenberg [2013] and Sperry & Carlson [1991]) follows.

Organization   The organizational structure of the family system can be understood in terms of wholeness, hierarchies, and boundaries (Gurman & Kniskern, 1981). *Wholeness* relates to the recurrent patterns reflected in the family system as opposed to individual elements of the family (Sperry & Carlson, 1991). Wholeness suggests that the family is more than the sum of its parts, with the family system having a life of its own (Everett, 1990). *Hierarchies* involve the different levels of subsystems that make up the family system, for example, parents, siblings, and relatives. *Boundaries* represent the degree of relatedness between family members (Goldenberg & Goldenberg, 2013). Extreme separateness between family members can occur when boundaries are rigid, and extreme togetherness is associated with diffuse boundaries (Sperry & Carlson).

Communication   All behaviors, verbal and nonverbal, are considered important aspects of communication. Systems theory also attempts to identify and assess familial communication patterns.

Family Rules   Families are governed by rules that influence how family members interact and how well the family functions. For example, an alcoholic's family might have an unwritten rule that no one may talk about that family member's drinking problem.

Family Homeostasis   Family homeostasis is the tendency of family systems to maintain equilibrium or restore balance if the system becomes disrupted. Family systems can resist change in an attempt to maintain homeostasis.

Information Processing   Information processing involves the exchange of information between the family and the outside world. It provides essential feedback for families to make necessary alterations in functioning. A family system is considered open if there is sufficient opportunity for information processing and closed if there is insufficient opportunity. Healthy family systems are neither too open nor too closed (Sperry & Carlson, 1991).

Change   Watzlawick, Weakland, and Fisch (1974) noted that there can be first-order or second-order change. First-order changes are alterations that leave the organizational structure unchanged, whereas second-order changes result in fundamental change to the system's organization (Sperry & Carlson, 1991).

The Functional Family System   It would be presumptuous to set forth a definitive description of what constitutes a **functional family system**, since any definition would vary from culture to culture and family to family. Therefore, findings from the following studies on this topic are presented with that caution.

From a survey of 310 members of AAMFT about what they believe constitutes a healthy family, Fisher and Sprenkle (1978) suggested that the fully functioning family is one in which the family members feel valued, supported, and safe. In addition, the researchers noted, "They can express themselves without fear of judgment, knowing that opinions will be attended to carefully and emphatically. Family members are also able to negotiate when necessary" (p. 9).

Many additional characteristics of healthy family functioning can be summarized as follows (Ebert, 1978; Stinnet & DeFrain, 1985; Watts, Trusty, & Lim, 1996):

- *Sharing of feelings.* Family members feel free to openly share positive and negative feelings with each other.

- *Social interest.* Healthy families tend to have many of the characteristics associated with the Adlerian concept of social interest (e.g., social relatedness and sense of connectedness to others, community feeling, and empathy).

- *Adaptability.* These families take a flexible-adaptive approach to problem solving and problem prevention as opposed to a rigid-restrictive approach to the challenges of life.

- *Boundary clarity.* These families allow for a balance between promoting a sense of community, cohesion, and belonging and encouraging family members to grow as autonomous individuals.

- *Understanding of feelings.* All members of the family sense that they are being understood by the other family members.

- *Acceptance of individual differences.* Individual differences among family members are permitted and even encouraged so all family members can develop their unique potential.

- *Highly developed sense of caring.* Family members communicate a sense of love and caring toward each other. This contributes to family members feeling valued and having a sense of belonging within the family.

- *Cooperation.* Each family member is willing to work in a cooperative manner to help the family function effectively.

- *Sense of humor.* Family members are capable of laughing at themselves and joking about family events.

- *Provision for survival and safety needs.* The basic needs of food, shelter, and clothing are provided.

- *Nonadversarial problem solving.* Problems are usually solved in a democratic fashion.

- *Overall philosophy.* The family has a set of values that provides a structure for family living.

- *Commitment.* Family members are committed to each other's well-being.

- *Expression of appreciation.* Family members regularly express appreciation to each other.

- *Communication.* Good communication patterns are established between family members.

- *Time spent together.* Family members spend time together to foster positive relationships and a sense of family unity.

- *Spirituality.* Family members can draw strength from their spirituality.

- *Coping skills.* The family has the coping skills necessary to meet the challenges of family life.

These characteristics collectively suggest that a functional family system creates a positive environment for individuals to grow and develop. It is characterized by love, caring, and mutual respect. Family members can communicate with each other effectively and be responsive to forces outside the family. The family has the necessary coping mechanisms to be successful in meeting the developmental tasks of family life.

PROMOTING HEALTHY FAMILY FUNCTIONING Family systems theories can be used to understand healthy and problematic patterns of family functioning (Waldo, Horne, & Kenny, 2009). Figure 10.1 incorporates the following family systems concepts:

- positive/problematic communications (Satir, 1988);

- secure/insecure attachments (Ainsworth & Bowlby, 1991);

- clear/diffuse boundaries and differentiation between family members (Bowen, 1978; Minuchin, 1974); and

- conflict resolution skills (Rahim, 1983).

According to Waldo et al. (2009), Figure 10.1

depicts the potential relation among family systems concepts. Bowen's concept of differentiation forms the vertical "Y" axis of the figure, and Minuchin's concept of structural boundaries forms the horizontal "X" axis of the figure. Healthy family systems employ assertive and empathic communication, engage in integrative conflict resolution, and promote secure attachment. Family systems with lower levels of differentiation are likely to have either an enmeshed structure with diffuse boundaries or a disengaged structure with rigid boundaries. Enmeshed family structures promote passive communication, obliging conflict resolution behaviors and preoccupied attachment. Disengaged family structures promote aggressive communication, dominating conflict resolution behaviors, and dismissive attachment. Family systems that have very low levels of differentiation may fluctuate between highly disengaged and enmeshed structures. These fluctuations promote withdrawal or confused communication, avoidance of conflict resolution, and fearful attachment. (pp. 215–216)

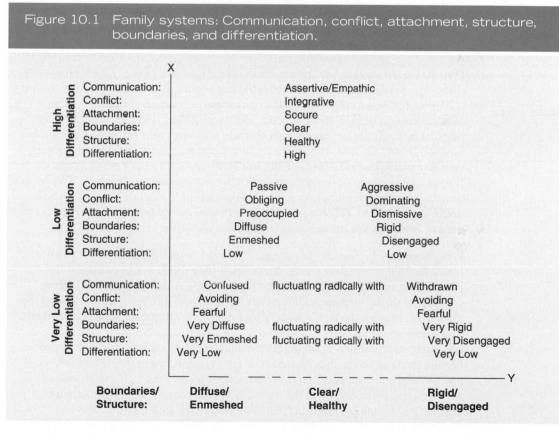

Figure 10.1 Family systems: Communication, conflict, attachment, structure, boundaries, and differentiation.

Source: Adapted from Waldo, M., Horne, A.M., & Kenny, M.E. (2009), Developing healthy family relationships. In M.E. Kenny, A. M. Horne, P. Orpinas, & L.E. Reece (Eds.), *Realizing Social Justice: The Challenge of Preventive Interventions* (pp. 207–227). Washington, D.C. American Psychological Association.

Waldo and associates (2009) suggested that preventative programs, such as parent education, can play an important role in strengthening families by addressing risk factors (e.g., lack of parental involvement) and promoting protective factors (e.g., resiliency) associated with healthy family functioning. Protective factors can vary according to culture (Waldo et al.). For example, racial pride, community resources, and economic opportunity have been associated with resiliency in African American families. Protective factors can be useful in overcoming stressors within and outside of the family (such as racism and other sources of conflict) and can therefore promote advocacy and social justice.

EVALUATION OF SYSTEMS THEORY Systems theory has added an important dimension to the counseling literature. It has contributed to the understanding of how systems work and their influence on psychological functioning. The systems perspective has been particularly useful in describing the structure and process of family life and how the family system creates an entity that is greater than the sum of its individual parts (Goldenberg & Goldenberg, 2013). According to Goldenberg and Goldenberg, systems thinking provides a mechanism for seeing wholes: relationships rather than isolated units and patterns of change rather than static snapshots (Senge, 1990).

Systems theory also has weaknesses (Enns, 1988; Epstein & Loos, 1989). First, systems theory has been accused of overlooking the importance of intrapsychic issues, ignoring clients' emotions and affect, and failing to address issues of responsibility (Golann, 1987; Nichols, 1987a, 1987b). Second, feminists contend that systems theory does not take into account important familial issues such as power, equality, and sex-role function (Enns; Goldner, 1985). Third, the systems perspective does not adequately consider factors that occur outside the family system, such as at a job or in school (Elkaim, 1982). Fourth, the systems approach is not realistic in that it attempts to "heal the cracked bones of a whole number of people rather than stop the hand of those delivering the blows" (Elkaim, p. 345). Finally, systems concepts and practices are in need of empirical validation (Liddle, 1982; Shields, 1986).

Ecosystems theory (Sherrard & Amatea, 2003) and postmodern/social constructionist trends in family counseling (Anderson & Goolishian, 1992; White & Epston, 1990) provide new opportunities to overcome some of these criticisms of systems theory. Ecosystems theory emphasizes holism and is concerned with relationships among the individual, couples, the family, and the sociocultural environment (Sherrard & Amatea). The theory appears inclusive, attempting to create a balance between intrapsychic and interpersonal forces. It recognizes the individual and expands systemic horizons beyond the family to include sociocultural forces that represent the individual's social and physical environment. Trends in postmodern/social constructionist theories are consistent with ecosystems theory. From a postmodern/social constructionist perspective, individuals construct their own reality based on the languages and narratives passed on from culture to culture. The trend toward using ecosystems and postmodern/social constructivist theories is important in counseling, especially in terms of creating a more inclusive, comprehensive model for marriage and family counseling.

The Family Life Cycle

Duvall's (1977) eight-stage model for understanding family life (summarized in Table 10.1) provides another important theoretical foundation for marriage and family counselors.

Table 10.1   Duvall's Family Life Cycle Model

Stage of the Family Life Cycle	Positions in the Family	Stage-Critical Family Developmental Tasks	Approximate Number of Years in Stage
1. Married couples (without children)	Wife Husband	Establishing a mutually satisfying marriage Adjusting to pregnancy and the promise of parenthood	2 years
2. Childbearing families (oldest child birth–30 months old)	Wife-mother Husband-father Infant daughter or son or both	Giving birth to, adjusting to, and encouraging the development of infants	2–5 years
3. Families with preschool children (oldest child 30 months–6 years old)	Wife-mother Husband-father Daughter-sister Son-brother	Adapting to the critical needs and interests of preschool children Coping with energy depletion and lack of privacy as parents	3–5 years
4. Families with school children (oldest child 6–13 years old)	Wife-mother Husband-father Daughter-sister Son-brother	Fitting into the community of school-age families Encouraging children's educational achievements	7 years
5. Families with teenagers (oldest child 13–20 years old)	Wife-mother Husband-father Daughter-sister Son-brother	Balancing freedom with responsibility as teenagers mature Establishing postparental interests and careers as parents of growing children	7 years

(Continued)

Table 10.1 (Continued)

Stage of the Family Life Cycle	Positions in the Family	Stage-Critical Family Developmental Tasks	Approximate Number of Years in Stage
6. Families as launching centers (first child gone to last child leaving home)	Wife-mother-grandmother Husband-father-grandfather Daughter-sister-aunt Son-brother-uncle	Releasing young adults into work, military service, college, and marriage with appropriate rituals and assistance Maintaining a supportive home base	8 years
7. Middle-aged parents (empty nest to retirement)	Wife-mother-grandmother Husband-father-grandfather	Rebuilding the marriage relationship Maintaining kin ties with older and younger generations	15± years
8. Aging family members (retirement to death of both spouses)	Widow/widower Wife-mother-grandmother Husband-father-grandfather	Coping with bereavement and living alone Closing the family home or adapting it to aging needs Adjusting to retirement	10–15± years

Source: Duvall, E.M. (1977). *Marriage and family development* (5th ed.). Philadelphia: Lippincott.

The eight stages begin with marriage and end with the death of both spouses. The model identifies developmental tasks associated with each stage as well as the approximate number of years that each stage will last.

Duvall's **family life cycle** model has been integrated into theories of marriage and family counseling (Carter & McGoldrick, 1988; Haley, 1971, 1973; Kovacs, 1988; Solomon, 1973) and can be useful in identifying past, present, and future developmental tasks associated with family life (Carter & McGoldrick). Failure to master the developmental tasks associated with a particular stage could have adverse effects on a family's functioning (Solomon). Marriage and family counselors could play an important role in assisting families to develop the necessary coping skills associated with particular developmental tasks (Wilcoxon, 1985).

Therapeutic implications of the family life cycle involve the transition points between stages, which are the most stressful times for families and when familial problems typically occur (Haley, 1973). A central therapeutic task is to help families resolve developmental issues so that they can move forward in the family life cycle (Haley).

EVALUATION OF THE FAMILY LIFE CYCLE The family life cycle is a valuable model for understanding how family life proceeds through time. It has also been studied extensively in research on families, including how it can be integrated with systems concepts (Kovacs, 1988). In addition, the model provides a focus for counseling by identifying developmental tasks that require assistance from the counselor.

The model does have weaknesses, however (Goldenberg & Goldenberg, 2013). For one, it does not take into account the wide array of contemporary family structures that result from divorce and remarriage. In addition, Duvall's model does not provide enough information on the transition points between stages, which can be especially problematic for families.

Marriage Counseling

Marital problems rank highest among reasons for referral to mental health services (Sperry & Carlson, 1991). Sholevar (1985) estimated that 75% of all clients entering counseling are seeking assistance with marital difficulties, as well as help with other problems. People tend to seek marriage counseling when a family system is experiencing a state of disequilibrium owing to problems such as infidelity, sexual incompatibility, disagreements over child-rearing practices, divorce, ineffective communication, and issues relating to power and control (Goldenberg & Goldenberg, 2013).

Marriage counseling can also be useful to treat individual problems, such as depression and alcoholism (Friedlander & Tuason, 2000). For example, depression linked to a distressed marriage is better treated in marriage counseling, whereas depression not related to marital problems responds better to individual counseling. In the treatment of alcoholism, marriage counseling is viewed as superior over individual counseling in overcoming violent tendencies, maintaining abstinence, and enhancing marital satisfaction. Marriage counseling is considered particularly useful in treating alcoholism by way of promoting alcohol education and emphasizing the motivational influences of a caring partner.

Marriage counseling can be a very challenging and rewarding experience for marriage counselors and clients. Individuals requesting marriage counseling often wait "until the last minute" to seek help (Friedlander & Tuason, 2000). By the time they enter counseling, their problems are usually well entrenched. It is therefore not so surprising that 50% of clients continue to be dissatisfied with their partner after completing marriage counseling. Counselors can also derive rewards from marriage counseling. It can be very gratifying to help clients overcome problems successfully and build the foundations for lasting, meaningful relationships.

The Counseling Process

Marriage counseling tends to be brief, problem centered, and pragmatic (Goldenberg & Goldenberg, 2013). The most popular form of marriage counseling is *conjoint marriage counseling* (Nichols & Everett, 1986), which involves the counselor working with the couple together. Humphrey (1983) described a slight modification of the conjoint session, suggesting that the counselor see each individual separately before the conjoint session. He contended that when individuals are seen separately, they will more openly discuss sensitive issues such as an extramarital affair. When this approach is used, the counselor must establish a clear policy regarding confidentiality: The counselor must clarify with the client what information from individual sessions can be introduced during conjoint sessions and how it will be conveyed.

The process of marriage counseling varies according to the theoretical orientation of the counselor. Marriage counselors make use of a wide variety of counseling theories, such as psychoanalytic, cognitive-behavioral, strategic, and structural (Sperry & Carlson, 1991). To a large degree, these theories can be considered adaptations of those used in individual counseling (discussed in Chapters 7, 8, and 9) and those associated with family counseling (presented later in this chapter). There also appear to be some commonalities across marriage counseling approaches. Sperry and Carlson noted that all approaches use a systems perspective. Goldenberg and Goldenberg (2013) suggested that marriage counselors address thoughts, feelings, and behaviors within the context of marital and family systems.

Several integrative models of marriage counseling have been developed that provide a broad, flexible approach. For example, Glick, Clarkin, and Kessler (1987) and Nichols (1988) contended that marriage counseling has three stages: early, middle, and termination. Nichols's model has three tasks associated with the early stage: establishing a positive relationship, assessment and goal setting, and providing immediate assistance to the couple. The middle stage is primarily concerned with using intervention strategies to resolve counseling goals. The termination stage allows for the transition toward termination once the counseling goals have been achieved.

Skills-Based Marriage Counseling

A practical approach to marriage counseling that can be utilized by counselors of different theoretical orientations is the skills-based approach (Sperry & Carlson, 1991), which has been adapted from Dinkmeyer and Carlson's (1984) earlier work on marital enrichment. **Skills-based marriage counseling** evolved from the following principles: (a) Healthy, productive marriages require time and commitment; (b) the skills necessary for a satisfying marriage can be learned; (c) change requires each partner to assume responsibility; (d) positive feelings such as love and caring can return with behavior change; and (e) small changes can help bring about big changes.

According to Sperry and Carlson (1991, p. 45), the 10 skills that are believed to contribute to effective marriages involve both partners doing the following:

1. Individually accept responsibility for their behavior and self-esteem

2. Identify and align their personal and marital goals

3. Choose to encourage each other

4. Communicate their feelings with honesty and openness

5. Listen emphatically when feelings are expressed

6. Seek to understand the factors that influence their relationship

7. Demonstrate that they accept and value each other

8. Choose thoughts, words, and actions that support the positive goals of their marriage

9. Solve marital conflicts together

10. Commit themselves to the ongoing process of maintaining an equal marriage

The skills-based approach to marriage counseling is educative in that it provides the couple with opportunities to learn how to use the 10 skills. For example, the couple can learn how to use some of these skills in a four-step approach to conflict resolution: (1) show mutual respect, (2) pinpoint the real issue, (3) seek areas of agreement, and (4) mutually participate in decisions. Additional guidelines for conflict resolution include being specific and oriented in the present and future; using good communication skills, such as "I" messages and active listening; avoiding absolutes; and avoiding attempting to determine who was right or wrong (Sperry & Carlson, 1991).

Marital Assessment

Marital assessment is an aspect of the counseling process that deserves special attention. Comprehensive assessment is essential in marriage and family counseling (Sperry & Carlson, 1991) since 83% of treatment failures are associated with inadequate assessment (Coleman, 1985). Comprehensive assessment in marriage counseling involves assessing the situation, the system, each spouse, and the suitability of the couple for marriage counseling (Sperry, 1989a). The following is a description of these four factors:

1. *The situation.* Assessing the situation means identifying stressors, precipitating factors to marital discord, and other factors that affect the situation.

2. **The system.** Systems theory can be used to assess the marital system to gain an understanding of its functional and dysfunctional characteristics.

3. **Each spouse.** Each spouse is evaluated to determine his or her level of physical and psychological health as well as personality style.

4. **Suitability for treatment.** It is also important to determine whether marriage counseling is appropriate for a couple. Beutler (1983) suggested that clients need to be motivated to change and have reasonable expectations regarding outcomes to be suitable for marriage counseling.

The assessment procedures commonly used in marriage counseling include the clinical interview (Framo, 1981); enactment, in which clients act out conflicts or problems during a counseling session (Nichols, 1988); and standardized tests designed for marriage counseling (Boen, 1988).

Marital assessment instruments have become popular in marriage counseling. These instruments are especially useful during initial counseling sessions, but they can be used throughout the counseling process as the need arises (Boen, 1988). An overview of the most widely used marital assessment instruments follows (Boen):

- **Stuart's Couples Precounseling Inventory (SCPI).** The SCPI was developed by Stuart (1983). It identifies 15 areas in which the couple is satisfied or dissatisfied, such as child-rearing practices or sexual practices. The SCPI also identifies the amount of commitment each member has to the relationship as well as which individual has more to gain or lose by maintaining the relationship.

- **Russell and Madsen's Marriage Counseling Report (MCR).** The MCR, developed by Russell and Madsen (1985), is based on the 16 Personality Factors Questionnaire (16PF), which was developed by Raymond Cattell, as discussed in Chapter 4. The MCR provides information on the personality of each spouse, how these personalities may be contributing to marital difficulties, and how the marriage may be exacerbating psychological problems of the spouses.

- **Taylor-Johnson Temperament Analysis (TJTA).** The TJTA (Taylor & Morrison, 1984) is a revision of the Johnson Temperament Analysis developed by R. H. Johnson in 1941. It "can be used to show where a couple are similar or different to the normal population as well as where they are similar or different to each other and the degree of understanding they have for each other's personality characteristics" (Boen, 1988, p. 485).

- *Snyder's Marital Satisfaction Inventory* (MSI). The MSI, developed by Snyder (1981), identifies basic areas in which the couple is satisfied or dissatisfied, such as communication or problem solving. The MSI is particularly useful for couples who do not know where to begin in terms of dealing with their concerns.

- *Assessment of Divorce.* One intriguing method of assessing marriages is to identify **factors that predict divorce**. A series of studies by Gottman (1994) and Gottman, Coan, Carrere, and Swanson (1998) have identified the following variables for predicting divorce:

  o Criticism, contempt, defensiveness, and emotional withdrawal occur during conflict resolution (Gottman, 1994).

  o Lack of positive affect, such as humor, interest, and affection. Successful marriages have higher rates of positive affect interactions, and their ratios of positive to negative affect during conflict resolution is 5:1 while in unstable marriages the ratio is 0.8:1 (Gottman, 1994).

  o Husband rejects the wife's influence during a conflict (Gottman et al., 1998).

Gottman et al. (1998) have identified the following variables for predicting marital satisfaction:

- Wives soften the start-up of addressing the potential conflict (e.g., they take a more tentative rather than confrontational approach).

- Husbands deescalate low-intensity negative affect of wives (e.g., anger, sadness, and tension).

- Wives deescalate high-intensity negative affect of husbands (e.g., contempt, defensiveness, and belligerence).

- Physiological soothing of self or partner occurs for stress management (especially important for men, who are considered to have higher levels of autonomic arousal during conflict than women).

In addition, Gottman et al. (1998) have found that listening skills may not be very useful during a conflict. Communication using listening skills may be too direct and confrontational and require spouses to empathize with a partner when they are emotionally unable to do so (e.g., after a spouse has just gotten angry at them).

Gottman et al. (1998) noted that negative emotions such as anger are not predictors of divorce. In fact, successful marriages need to include expression of both positive and negative emotions. What appears to be important is "gentleness, soothing, and deescalation of negativity (negativity of one spouse followed by the partner's neutral affect)" (Gottman et al., p. 16). Gottman and Notarius (2000) provided a review of a decade's research on marital interactions. The research did not focus on predicting divorce but on factors that tend to enhance or undermine marital (or couples') satisfaction. Some of these findings are as follows:

- Within 1 year of the birth of the first child, couples tend to revert to stereotypical gender roles, males withdraw into work, and the quality of communication and sexual relations reduces dramatically (pleasure is derived from interacting with the baby).

- Distressed couples emotionally invalidate and inhibit problem solving, whereas nondistressed couples emotionally validate, self-disclose, and facilitate problem solving.

- Engaging in a demand/withdrawal pattern (wife demands a change and husband withdraws through inaction or defensiveness) is associated with a decline in wives' marital satisfaction within 2.5 years.

- The effects of humor on problem solving appear to change over the life span from negative during the middle adult years to positive during the late adult years. (Middle adults tend to use humor as an avoidance mechanism, and late adults use humor as a way to express genuine positive affect.)

- Couples who maintain change after termination of couples counseling are able to do a better job of keeping work stress out of the marriage than are couples who experience relapse.

Family Counseling

No clear definition of family counseling has emerged. Its hallmark, however, is that it involves problems experienced by an individual that seem to indicate more fundamental problems within the family system (Horne & Ohlsen, 1982). Family counseling is superior to individual counseling in the treatment of some disorders. For example, Campbell and Patterson (1995) have found that adolescents who had anorexia for 3 years or fewer had more positive treatment outcomes with family counseling than when they were treated with individual counseling. The systems perspective continues to characterize family counseling, in which family counselors treat problems within a relationship context rather than working separately with individuals (Goldenberg & Goldenberg, 2013).

This section first provides an overview of six major family counseling theories (summarized in Table 10.2) and then discusses the family counseling process.

Table 10.2 Theories of Family Counseling

Theory	Founder(s)	Key Concepts	Process	Goals
Psychodynamic family counseling	Nathan Ackerman, James Framo	Intrapsychic forces play a key role in family dysfunction; object relations such as meaningful relationships are the primary motivational force in life.	Focuses on intrapersonal and interpersonal forces (e.g., strengthening the ego, clarifying roles, helping clients obtain more satisfying relationships).	To promote change and growth by altering patterns of communication, resolving pathological inner conflicts, and defining roles of family members in complementary fashion
Experiential family counseling	Virginia Satir, Carol Whitaker, William Bumberry	Self-actualization, awareness, choice, and responsibility	Frees family members to move toward self-actualization; has an experiential focus; relates to the here and now rather than past issues.	To promote clear communication, help family members become authentic, autonomous individuals, and promote a positive family climate
Structural family counseling	Salvador Minuchin	Systemic concepts such as boundaries and reframing	Counselor joins the family to alter the structure of interaction among family members.	To clarify boundaries, increase flexibility of family interactions, and modify dysfunctional family structure

(Continued)

Table 10.2 (Continued)

Theory	Founder(s)	Key Concepts	Process	Goals
Strategic family counseling	Jay Haley, Cloe Madanes	Communication patterns and power struggles determine the nature of relationships between family members.	Attempts to directly resolve presenting problems with little attempt to gain insight from past events.	To resolve symptomology of family members by redefining relationships between family members
Adlerian/Dreikursian family counseling	Alfred Adler, Rudolph Dreikurs	Family constellation, mutual respect, goals of misbehavior, use of consequences, encouragement, communication	Has an educational focus to help parents learn skills to foster positive parent-child relationships.	To understand the dynamics of problems occurring within the family and promote positive parent-child relationships
Postmodern/social constructionism	Tom Andersen, Michael White, and others	Problems are conceptualized in terms of language and narratives.	Uses stories reflecting family life that are developed and rewritten, creating opportunities for a more meaningful family life.	To help families create new stories, fostering improved family functioning

Psychodynamic Family Counseling

Nathan Ackerman (1937, 1956, 1966, 1970) is credited with integrating Freud's psychoanalytic theory into family counseling. His model emphasizes the importance of both intrapersonal and interpersonal forces. Ackerman (1970) viewed the family as a system of interacting personalities, with each family member representing a subsystem. The primary aim of Ackerman's approach is to promote change and growth by altering patterns of communication, resolving pathological inner conflicts, and helping family members define their roles in a complementary manner (Goldenberg & Goldenberg, 2013).

Framo (1992) later integrated object-relations theory (see Chapter 7) into **psychodynamic family counseling**. The basic premise of object-relations theory is that the fundamental motivation in life is the drive to satisfy object relations (e.g., satisfying relationships; Goldenberg & Goldenberg, 2013). In addition, object-relations theory contends that intrapsychic conflicts that evolved from the family of origin play a key role in relationship difficulties. As part of the overall treatment program, psychodynamic family counselors may conduct individual counseling, couples counseling, and family counseling that includes members of the client's family of origin (Goldenberg & Goldenberg).

Experiential Family Counseling

The theoretical origins of **experiential family counseling** can be traced to the humanistic-existential schools of counseling, as discussed in Chapter 7. Virginia Satir (1983, 1988), Carol Whitaker (1976, 1977), and William Bumberry (Whitaker & Bumberry, 1988) are credited with incorporating the major concepts of the humanistic-existential schools into family counseling. The basic premise of this approach is that if individual family members can be freed to move toward self-actualization, the family will function effectively. The goals of experiential family counseling include promoting clear communication among family members; helping family members become authentic, autonomous individuals; assisting the family in developing a positive family climate characterized by encouragement, caring, and intimacy; and promoting awareness of choice and responsibility in family members.

The counseling process in experiential family counseling focuses on the here and now instead of dealing with problems from the past. The emphasis within counseling is on experiencing rather than intellectualizing. The counselor uses a variety of techniques—such as sculpting, confrontation, communication skills training, and Gestalt exercises—to help family members become aware of their feelings. The technique of *sculpting,* for example, involves having one person physically arrange the other family members to create a "sculpture." The person creates the sculpture by using space and form to represent perceptions of family relationships, for instance, placing a child between the mother and father, to symbolize interference between the marital dyad. All family members are then invited to discuss the creation. Typical themes that result from such discussions are closeness, isolation, alignment, intimacy, and power.

Structural Family Counseling

Salvador Minuchin (1974, 1984) is credited with developing **structural family counseling**. The role of the counselor in this approach is to join the family in a position of leadership. The goals are to clarify boundaries between family members, increase flexibility of family interactions, and modify dysfunctional family structure (Goldenberg & Goldenberg, 2013).

Minuchin (1974, 1984) developed several innovative concepts that have played a key role in the evolution of systems theory (Goldenberg & Goldenberg, 2013). One example is the concept of *boundaries,* which are the unwritten rules that help define roles and functions of family members. Boundaries determine what will be allowed to occur between family members and can ensure privacy or allow for intimacy. Family dysfunctioning can result when boundaries become rigid, confused, or conflicting.

Another concept that Minuchin (1974, 1984) developed is *reframing,* a family counseling technique used to help the family see things from a more positive perspective. For example, an adolescent might complain that his mother spends too much time working. Using the technique of reframing, the counselor might help the adolescent focus on the fact that his mother enjoys her job and that it makes her a pleasant person to be with.

Strategic Family Counseling

Jay Haley (1963, 1971, 1973, 1976, 1980) and individuals such as Cloé Madanes (1981, 1984) have played key roles in the development of **strategic family counseling**. This approach focuses on communication patterns between family members and views intrapsychic forces as unimportant. Haley (1976, 1980) contended that the relationships between family members can be determined by the manner in which the family members communicate and how they position themselves in terms of power issues.

This approach is considered strategic because it focuses on resolving the presenting problem directly, with little attempt to elicit insight into past events. To resolve the presenting problem, counselors use procedures oriented to concrete actions, including assigning homework, teaching new skills, and giving advice. They also use paradoxical techniques, which involve prescribing the symptom. For example, if a husband and wife have a habit of yelling at each other, the counselor might ask them to spend 10 minutes yelling at one another every day.

Strategic family counseling can be a powerful and effective form of counseling. Strategies such as advice giving and paradoxical techniques must be used carefully, however, or they may do more harm than good to the family (Nichols, 1984).

Adlerian Family Counseling

Alfred Adler's school of individual psychology and the later writings of Rudolph Dreikurs (see Chapter 7) have been applied to a variety of helping processes, including family counseling and parent education. **Adlerian family counseling** focuses on individual family members as well as the overall functioning of the family. The main goal of this approach is to improve parent-child relationships (Lowe, 1982). Carlson and Robey (2011) noted that Adlerian family counseling can be enhanced by integrating concepts from other theoretical perspectives and methodologies (e.g., attachment theory, multiculturalism, and research regarding blended families). In addition, Sutherland (2011) described how art therapy can be incorporated into Adlerian family counseling to explore family dynamics, promote social interest and encouragement, and move the focus of therapy from problem behaviors to healthy family functioning.

Adlerian family counseling is psychoeducational—helping parents learn principles and understand the dynamics of problems occurring within the family (Lowe, 1982). In this process, the counselor identifies basic mistakes, teaches the parents concepts that will help them understand misbehavior, helps parents deal effectively with discipline problems, and assists in establishing positive parent-child relations. The key concepts of this approach are family constellation, goals of misbehavior, use of natural and logical consequences, encouragement, and communication. Although these Adlerian concepts are discussed in Chapter 7, they are presented here in terms of the family counseling approach.

- *Family constellation.* The family constellation relates to the overall structure of the family. Particular attention is paid to how birth-order characteristics can be used to understand the personality of the children (e.g., first-born children tend to be bossy).

- *Goals of misbehavior.* Children's misbehavior is seen as movement toward one of four goals of misbehavior: attention, power, revenge, and display of inadequacy. Additional goals of misbehavior for teenagers include excitement, peer acceptance, and superiority (Dinkmeyer, McKay, & Dinkmeyer, 1997).

- *Use of natural and logical consequences.* Parents are taught to use natural and logical consequences as opposed to punishment to discipline children. Among the advantages of this approach over punishment are that consequences are more logically tied to misbehavior, promote choice and responsibility in the child, and minimize animosity between the parent and child.

- *Encouragement.* Parents are taught to use encouragement with their child. Offering encouragement focuses on effort and helps build self-esteem, confidence, and self-efficacy.

- *Communication skills.* Parents learn how to use effective communication skills with their child. A philosophy of mutual respect is essential for effective communication. When parents respect the child, they will tend to communicate empathic understanding of the child's point of view. Parents may also be taught listening skills and problem-solving skills, which can be used to help their child deal with personal problems.

The concepts utilized in Adlerian family counseling have also been incorporated into parent education programs such as Dinkmeyer, McKay, and Dinkmeyer's (1997) systematic training for effective parenting (STEP) and Popkin's (2014) active parenting programs (Lowe, 1982; Lindquist & Watkins, 2014). Parent education programs typically involve small groups of individuals meeting to discuss parenting concepts and concerns, usually for approximately 1.5 hours each week over a 10-week period. Research efforts show that the effectiveness of parent educators is not related to whether the educators have been parents themselves (Schultz, Nystul, & Law, 1980). Research also suggests that it is important to include role-play activities to allow for the internalization and transfer from attitudes to behaviors (Schultz & Nystul, 1980). More recently, Pan and Wu (2008) reported that STEP was effective in improving parent-child relationship, and Spence (2009) found that STEP increased parenting skills and provided insights into family dynamics.

I developed an approach to family counseling called *marathon family counseling* while working on the Navajo Indian reservation. The approach evolved out of my work with Katherine Hillis, a Navajo mental health counselor. Marathon family counseling shares the following characteristics with Mara Selvini-Palazzoli's (1980) approach. Both utilize extended family sessions lasting up to 8 hours approximately once a month, and both serve clients who live in rural areas and have had to travel hundreds of miles for the session. Marathon family counseling is based on the principles of Adlerian family counseling, which include using encouragement, establishing mutual respect, identifying basic mistakes, and providing reorientation from basic mistakes. The following *Personal Note* illustrates this approach.

A Personal Note

A 74-year-old grandmother arrived at the mental health center at the Navajo Indian reservation where I was working. Accompanied by her daughter, the woman appeared depressed and tearful during the initial interview. She lived with her husband 100 miles from the center and had 3 daughters, 2 sons, and 12 grandchildren.

The grandmother complained that two of her grandchildren had wrecked four of her automobiles over the years. She thought that the situation was hopeless and that it would probably happen again because "kids will be kids." While she talked, my Navajo mental health aide and I identified

some basic mistakes. As discussed in Chapter 7, the Adlerian concept of a basic mistake is a self-defeating idea, such as an overgeneralization, false goal of security, misconception of life's demands, or minimization of one's worth. The client's basic mistakes were as follows.

1. Others can't survive without me.

2. The children of my family aren't responsible, so I'll have to take care of everything.

3. I'm not important. Other people are more important than I am.

At this point, my aide and I decided that the client could benefit from marathon family counseling because of the great distance she and her daughter had traveled and the depth of her distress. We then discovered that the grandchild who had most recently wrecked her car was in jail for a DWI citation. Since we wanted to include that family member in the session, we decided to have the family counseling session at the local jail. We phoned several other family members, and they agreed to meet us there.

We began the session by asking the grandmother to share how she was feeling. She started to cry and said she was very sad. She didn't feel her grandchildren cared about her but instead just wanted to use her and her cars. She said she felt that they had no respect for her or her feelings. I asked how the family members felt about what the grandmother was saying. The two grandchildren who had wrecked her cars seemed uneasy and defensive. After these feelings were explored, they were able to make some statements that seemed to express genuine concern.

I mentioned that all people make mistakes and have room for improvement. The family members agreed. My aide and I then explored ways each family member had contributed to the current problem and what they could do to help. With much encouragement, each person was able to make a specific plan for improvement.

At the end of the session, I asked the family members to express how the session had affected them and what they wanted to do differently to help their family. I arranged to see them all in 2 weeks at the grandmother's house. We finished the session by thanking the family members and shaking their hands. Several family members also shook hands with one another and gave each other warm embraces.

We then talked with the grandmother privately and explored how she was feeling. She said she was relieved but still felt somehow responsible for her family's behavior. At this point, we discussed the basic mistakes we had identified earlier. We then used a variety of procedures to reorient the grandmother from her basic mistakes. For example, we read the section on children from *The Prophet* (Gibran, 1965). This helped her realize that she was not responsible for her grandchildren. Her job was to provide guidance and love and let them—like arrows— fly freely into the challenges of life. She began to realize that if she didn't let go, they wouldn't have the opportunity to become responsible people. She had a very positive response to the reading from *The Prophet* and wanted a copy of the book. I let her borrow mine until she could get a copy. She then left for home with her daughter.

After the initial marathon counseling session, my mental health aide and I provided counseling services for the family over an 18-month period. The grandmother was eventually able to let go of her tendency to feel responsible for her grandchildren's behavior. Her signs of depression were gone after 1 month. The two grandchildren who had wrecked her cars both had minor problems with the law (e.g., public intoxication) during the counseling period. On the positive side, however, they didn't wreck any more cars during that time.

Source: From "Marathon Family Counseling" by M. Nystul, 1988, *Individual Psychology: The Journal of Adlerian Theory, Research, & Practice, 32*(2), pp. 194–202, by permission of the University of Texas Press. Reprinted by permission.

Postmodern/Social Constructionist Perspectives in Family Counseling

The postmodern/social constructionist perspective plays a vital role in family therapy (Bitter & Corey, 1996). As noted earlier, social constructivism recognizes the multiple realities reflected in the languages of different cultures and the stories internalized by individuals in those cultures. Social constructionism, therefore, parallels the postmodern position, which recognizes a subjective reality based on the context of the observational process used. The social-constructionist perspective is thus particularly useful in infusing issues of diversity (such as gender, feminism, and culture) into family counseling.

The process of counseling (from a postmodern/social constructionist perspective) is similar to the qualitative research method of discovery. The counselor enters the relationship without preconceived ideas of what should or should not happen in therapy but instead attempts to discover with clients what is important from their phenomenological perspective. In this process, families are encouraged to engage in conversations that explore the meanings family members have given to their problems (Goldenberg & Goldenberg, 2013). In this process, "past experience is viewed as helpful not as a source of objective fact but as a source for determining and understanding the language, assumptions, and views of clients" (Giblin & Chan, 1995, p. 326). The counseling relationship is a collaborative relationship that fosters empowerment in clients. Goals and procedures vary according to clients' needs and the theoretical perspective of counselors but typically focus on helping families create new stories that enlarge their perspective and options and can bring new meaning to family life (Bitter & Corey, 1996). "Clients are invited into a reflective process, and the goal is to open up new meanings and possibilities for alternative behaviors" (Giblin & Chan, p. 326).

Bitter and Corey (1996) identified the following postmodern/social constructionist approaches to family counseling.

THE REFLECTING TEAM Family therapy can be enriched by the dialogues that are generated between families and professionals who are observing and processing the family counseling session (Tom Andersen, 1991, 1992). The overall process and goal of the reflecting team approach is to help families create new life stories through dialogue and reflection. For example, a reflecting team that has observed a family session through a one-way mirror can then join the family and process the central story that characterized the session. For example, the story might be one of concern that family members don't seem to care about each other. Together, counselors and family members can reflect on various aspects of the dynamic, such as when the family does get along. The resulting dialogue can create new stories that promote hope and encouragement for the family.

THE LINGUISTIC APPROACH The key individuals associated with the linguistic approach to family counseling are Harlene Anderson and Harold Goolishian (1992). They contended that narratives emerge from social interactions over time and the nature of the narratives is associated with the meaning experienced in life. In this approach, the counselor enters into the session with compassion and caring and a keen interest in discovering meaning from the families' stories. The goal of counseling is to help the family create alternative stories that can enhance meaning for the family.

The linguistic approach involves helping families explore the evolution of stories that characterize family life. For example, dysfunctional stories can emerge from the narratives shared between family members, which are then passed on from generation to generation (e.g., "blacks don't trust whites" or vice versa). Families can use these insights to help overcome dysfunctional elements in their stories (such as stereotyping and prejudice) and then create more meaningful and functional stories.

THE NARRATIVE APPROACH The narrative approach is associated with Michael White and David Epston (1990) and the earlier work of Michel Foucault (1980). This approach contends that narratives are a reflection of the dominant culture and therefore must be challenged to ensure that they are sensitive to diversity issues, such as gender, sexual orientation, and culture. The process and goal of the narrative approach is to help families deconstruct dysfunctional narratives (from the dominant culture) and reauthor new, more functional narratives.

The narrative approach encourages families to question the assumptions on which their stories are based in terms of potential influence from the dominant society. For example, a family member who is "coming out" with his or her family in terms of sexual orientation may encounter excessive resistance from the family. In some instances, this may result in the family being torn apart and the gay or lesbian individual being psychologically abandoned. Counselors can help these families separate their values, wants, and needs from external forces that may perceive things in rigid, either-or terms. This process may contribute to more functional family narratives that are based on their cultural identities and worldviews and not the worldviews projected by the dominant society.

SOLUTION-ORIENTED THERAPY Among the individuals who have promoted a solution-oriented approach to counseling are Steve de Shazer (1991) and William O'Hanlon and Michele Weiner-Davis (1989). The solution-oriented approach can be used across all domains of counseling, from individual to group to marriage and family. This approach suggests that it is more productive to focus on solutions and strengths than on problems and weakness and that families can be assisted in creating narratives that reflect positive change. The solution-oriented approach focuses on family strengths and problem resolution. An example would be Adlerian/Dreikursian family counseling, in which parents are taught to use encouragement to foster their children's self-efficacy and to use consequences to overcome discipline problems by promoting choice and responsibility.

FEMINIST PSYCHOTHERAPY Carolyn Enns (1993), Edna Rawlings (1993), Judith Avis (1986), and others have set forth the major issues associated with feminist psychotherapy. As applied to family counseling, feminist psychotherapy contends that the family system is a male-dominated, patriarchal system. Male domination exists even when the father is absent from the family. From a feminist perspective, male domination and control are maintained by public patriarchy, as represented by government structures such as welfare and other family assistance programs. Male-dominated narratives are perpetuated in many ways—through the media, research, and even the theories that describe normal family life and human development. Carol Gilligan's (1982) important work on the moral development of women provides an example of how male-dominated research can ignore gender difference in human growth and development.

The overall aim of feminist family therapy is to help family systems overcome oppressive forces and foster mutual respect, equality, and gender sensitivity between the sexes. Some of the goals of therapy include deconstructing patriarchal narratives and reconstructing narratives that recognize gender differences and the special needs of women in all aspects of living, empowering women within the context of egalitarian families, valuing what is considered feminine or nurturing, and promoting a positive attitude toward women.

The Counseling Process

The process in family counseling varies according to the theoretical orientation of the practitioner. Family counseling approaches share many commonalities, however, regardless of the theoretical perspective. For example, family counselors do the following (Friedlander & Highlen, 1984; Friedlander, Highlen, & Lassiter, 1985; Friedlander & Tuason, 2000):

- View the marital subsystem as the most stressed

- Align themselves with the family's established hierarchy, interacting more with parents than children

- Focus on the nuclear family, especially the parental subsystem

- Avoid direct confrontation with family members, preferring to direct messages to other family members (such as asking the wife why she thinks her husband is afraid of her)

- Actively engage in interpretation and educational processes

- Attempt to establish a therapeutic alliance with the family by being perceived as warm, trustworthy, and having clear goals

In addition, these authors found that family counselors make few references to the future, parents emphasize current issues, and children tend to relate to here-and-now issues regarding sibling relationships.

There is interest in developing integrative models for family counseling that can be responsive to different populations (Goldenberg & Goldenberg, 2013). L'Abate (1986) proposed the following four-stage integrative model for family counseling:

1. **Stress reduction.** The tasks associated with this stage are establishing a positive relationship, reducing stress and conflict, resolving an existing crisis if necessary, and reducing symptomatic behavior to a tolerable level.

2. **Training and education.** This stage involves helping the family learn the skills necessary to function effectively. Counselors frequently assign homework so that family members can practice the skills they are learning.

3. **Issue of termination.** During this stage, the family is given an opportunity to deal with issues that have not been resolved, such as dealing effectively with intimacy. When all issues have been resolved, the counselor helps the family move toward termination of the counseling process.

4. **Follow-up.** Follow-up involves determining the efficacy of counseling and allows for additional counseling as needed.

ETHICAL AND LEGAL ISSUES RELATING TO MARRIAGE AND FAMILY THERAPY Wilcoxon et al. (2012) described ethical and legal issues in marriage and family therapy in terms of client welfare, confidentiality, informed consent, and dual relations.

Client Welfare The following is AAMFT's (2015) ethical position relating to client welfare:

> Marriage and family therapists advance the welfare of families and individuals and make reasonable efforts to find the appropriate balance between conflicting goals within the family system. (Standard 1)

The issue of client welfare can become complex in marriage and family therapy because the counselor is working with more than one client. Margolin (1982) noted that the goals of individuals seeking marriage and family therapy can conflict. This can occur in marriage therapy, for example, when one person wants a divorce and the other does not. Wilcoxon et al. (2012) suggested that a counselor can avoid these problems by utilizing a systems perspective rather than focusing on the problems of individual clients.

Confidentiality The following is AAMFT's (2015) ethical position on confidentiality:

> Marriage and family therapists have unique confidentiality concerns because the client in a therapeutic relationship may be more than one person. Therapists respect and guard the confidences of each individual client. (Standard 2)

Respecting the confidence of clients in marriage and family therapy can often create an ethical dilemma; for example, the counselor might be asked to keep information about a client's affair from the client's spouse.

Margolin (1982) noted that counselors tend to take one of two positions regarding confidentiality when working with couples and families. In one position, the counselor views each marital partner or family member as an individual client. The counselor may routinely see the clients individually before seeing them together in couples or as families. A counselor who utilizes this approach needs to develop a clear position on confidentiality and communicate it to the clients. Typically, the counselor will either reserve the right to use professional judgment to maintain individual confidence or avoid disclosing sensitive information unless the client gives permission. A second approach to confidentiality is based on nonsecrecy (Margolin). From this perspective, the counselor does not feel any obligation to withhold information from the other marital partner or family member. A counselor who takes this approach usually avoids seeing the clients individually. In addition, the counselor should inform clients of the policy on confidentiality before they commence counseling.

In view of the varying litigation regarding privileged communication, it is important for counselors to determine the laws in their state concerning multiperson therapies (Gumper & Sprenkle, 1981). The concept of privileged communication originally developed within the context of one-to-one relationships, for example, doctor-patient and attorney-client (Wilcoxon et al., 2012). It is therefore not surprising that conflicting legal precedents have arisen when this concept has been applied to situations involving more than one client. Several legal cases have tested the validity of privileged communication for clients involved in marriage counseling. Herrington (1979) noted that a Virginia judge ruled that there was no confidentiality because statements were not made in private to a doctor but were made in the presence of a spouse. Another case, reported by Margolin (1982), supported privileged communication in marriage counseling. This case involved a man who had decided to divorce his wife. He had his counselor subpoenaed to testify in court about statements his wife had made during their conjoint sessions. In this case, the husband was waiving his right of privileged communication, but the wife was not waiving hers. The judge ruled in favor of protecting the wife's right to confidentiality.

Informed Consent The AAMFT (2015) has stated the following ethical position relating to informed consent:

> Marriage and family therapists obtain appropriate informed consent to therapy or related procedures and use language that is reasonably understandable to clients. When persons, due to age or mental status, are legally incapable of giving informed consent, marriage and family therapists obtain informed permission from a legally authorized person, if such substitute consent is legally permissible. The content of informed consent may vary depending upon the client and treatment plan; however, informed consent generally

necessitates that the client: (a) has the capacity to consent; (b) has been adequately informed of significant information concerning treatment processes and procedures; (c) has been adequately informed of potential risks and benefits of treatment for which generally recognized standards do not yet exist; (d) has freely and without undue influence expressed consent; and (e) has provided consent that is appropriately documented. (Standard 1.2)

Applying the concept of informed consent can be more difficult in marriage and family therapy than in individual counseling. Margolin (1982) noted that the individuals who undergo marriage and family therapy together do not always begin therapy at the same time. It may therefore be necessary to repeat the procedures associated with informed consent as new clients begin the counseling process.

Dual Relationships The AAMFT (2015) takes the following ethical position on dual relationships:

> Marriage and family therapists are aware of their influential positions with respect to clients, and they avoid exploiting the trust and dependency of such persons. Therapists, therefore, make every effort to avoid conditions and multiple relationships with clients that could impair professional judgment or increase the risk of exploitation. Such relationships include, but are not limited to, business or close personal relationships with a client or the client's immediate family. When the risk of impairment or exploitation exists due to conditons or multiple roles, therapists document the appropriate precautions taken. (Standard 1.3)
>
> Sexual intimacy with current clients or with known members of the client's family system is prohibited. (Standard 1.4)
>
> Sexual intimacy with former clients or with known members of the client's family system is prohibited. (Standard 1.5)

Dual relationships can pose problems in all types of counseling, including marriage and family counseling. One potential problem in marriage and family counseling is providing individual counseling and marriage counseling to the same individual and attempting to ensure that confidentiality is maintained.

Hertlein, Blumer, and Mihaloliakos (2015) identified ethical concerns regarding online marriage and family therapy based on a survey of 226 licensed marriage and family counselors. Results of the study suggest that marriage and family counselors report concerns relating to the following five themes: confidentiality, potential problems maintaining a therapeutic relationship, responding appropriately to crisis and other serious clinical issues, licensure and liability concerns, and education and training. The authors noted that the ACA (2014) and AAMFT (2015) codes of ethics regarding online counseling could be used to address these issues.

Diversity Issues in
Marriage and Family Counseling

Diversity issues such as age, gender, culture, sexual orientation, socioeconomic status, race, ethnicity, and spirituality are important in all aspects of counseling, including marriage and family counseling (Hayes, 1995; Paniagua, 1996). Marriage and family counselors must be sensitive to a wide array of diversity issues—gender, culture, age, sexual orientation, and socioeconomic status—to be effective in their practice. Hayes noted that Rothenberg's (1995) book on race, class, and gender may be particularly useful to marriage and family counselors. It contains numerous personal narratives that depict the struggles of families with issues such as racism, oppression, and sexism. Hayes also suggested that Linda James Myers's (1988) optimal theory may help family therapists overcome oppression through self-knowledge and positive identity development.

As noted earlier, feminist therapy also has much to offer in marriage and family counseling. Giblin and Chan (1995) described several common themes in the feminist literature that may have relevance for marriage and family counselors. Some of these themes are communicating respect; validating feelings; supporting social and political change to overcome oppression; promoting social equality over power, control, and dominance; understanding behavior contextually; becoming aware of the relational connectedness associated with being human; and promoting mutual empathy, mutual engagement, and mutual empowerment.

Johnson (1995) identified 10 resiliency mechanisms in culturally diverse families. Johnson defined *family resiliency* as the manner in which the family renews itself each day and maintains homeostasis and a sense of collective identity as a unique living system. Resiliency also relates to the ability of family members to cope with everyday problems without compromising their moral or cultural values. These resiliency mechanisms are summarized as follows. The family serves as a "sacred ark," protecting its members from the storms of adversity and providing safety and refuge for them. These families utilize multiple support systems that include spirituality, the recognition of what the elders of the family or society can offer, and the role of the extended family in daily family life. Other resiliency characteristics include use of the native language, a high value on family socialization and communication, insulation from racism and the adverse effects of migration, and support of the individual resiliency of each family member.

Paniagua (1996) provided suggestions for incorporating a cross-cultural perspective into family counseling. First, how the extended family is defined varies considerably from culture to culture. For example, in Hispanic cultures, the extended family can include the *comadre* (co-mother) and the *compadre* (co-father) as well as folk healers. Family counselors should therefore have families define their concept of the extended family and explain how their extended family affects the overall role and function of the family.

Second, family counselors should assess the levels of acculturation in the family (Paniagua, 1996). Significant discrepancies in acculturation between family members (e.g., between children and parents or between husband and wife) can create family dysfunction and should be identified and addressed as necessary. It is also important to recognize that although a family is from a particular ethnic minority, its members may not feel that way (they may identify with the majority culture; Dana, 1993). Acculturation scales have been developed for different cultures (see Chapter 6) that can be used to determine the degree of a family member's acculturation.

Third, Paniagua (1996) noted that it is not critical for a family and a counselor to be of the same race. It is more important for the counselor to have some compatibility in terms of lifestyle and values and to be sensitive to cultural variables in the assessment and treatment of family dysfunction. It is also important that the counselor has the necessary skills to be successful in cross-cultural counseling. Paniagua provided some suggestions in terms of what counselors should communicate cross-culturally during the first and subsequent family sessions. For example, during the first session, it is important for counselors to demonstrate expertise and authority with Asian families, avoid discussing the behavior of African American parents in the presence of their children, and explore levels of acculturation and provide concrete and tangible advice to all groups. In subsequent sessions, family counselors can focus on other issues associated with a cultural group or all groups, such as being sensitive to the family's sense of powerlessness (for all families but especially African American families) and personalizing the session through the use of first names and handshaking (Hispanic families).

Brown (1997) advocated using a cross-cultural perspective in consulting with parents. Consultation with parents frequently involves using parenting programs to help parents improve parent-child relationships and foster optimal development in children. Brown suggested that cross-cultural parenting consultants "be aware of their personal values and biases, be culturally empathic, be aware of their consulting paradigm, and be able to make culturally sensitive adaptations to their approach to consultation" (p. 29). In their study of possible bias relating to cross-cultural perceptions of family functioning, Gushue, Constantine, and Sciarra (2008) found that white family counselors perceived Latino families as healthier than white families (perhaps due to a belief that Latinos emphasize family life more than white families). The study also found that stereotypes regarding family functioning were moderated by multicultural counseling knowledge and awareness.

Evaluation of Marriage and Family Counseling

Between 1970 and 1990, at least 20 literature reviews, involving the analysis of approximately 300 studies of marriage and family counseling, were conducted (Raffa, Sypek, & Vogel, 1990). Unfortunately, methodological flaws in many of the studies reviewed called into question the efficacy of marriage and family counseling. Some of the methodological problems included inadequate information regarding intervention strategies (Bednar, Burlingame, & Masters, 1988), a lack of controlled studies, inadequate research design, the use of assessment instruments with questionable reliability and validity, and the need for replication of results (Raffa et al.).

However, more recent research and the use of meta-analysis to analyze multiple studies simultaneously have been able to adequately address these methodological problems and provide clear evidence of the efficacy of marriage and family counseling (Dunn & Schwebel, 1995; Lebow & Gurman, 1995; Shadish et al., 1995). Results of a meta-analysis of 163 marriage and family counseling studies (62 marital and 101 family) provide clear support for the efficacy of marriage and family counseling, no evidence of one theoretical approach being superior to others, and no evidence that marriage and family counseling is superior to individual counseling (Shadish et al.).

Dunn and Schwebel's (1995) evaluation of marriage counseling suggested that conducting meta-analyses of marriage and family counseling could obscure the results. These researchers evaluated 15 methodologically rigorous marital outcome studies. They found that behavioral marital therapy, cognitive-behavioral marital therapy, and insight-oriented marital therapy are all successful in bringing about positive change in spouses' relationship-related behavior; insight-oriented marital therapy was the most successful in enhancing the spouses' assessment of the quality of their relationship; and cognitive-behavioral marital therapy was the best at contributing to the spouses' posttherapy relationship-related cognitions.

An extensive review of research (including meta-analytic reviews) concluded that there was an enormous enhancement in the quality of the research on marriage and family counseling between 1985 and 1995 (Lebow & Gurman, 1995). Much of the research has focused on behavioral approaches, but nonbehavioral methods are beginning to receive more attention in the literature. In addition, both marriage counseling and family counseling are becoming more integrative of various theoretical approaches and recognizing the merits of designing treatment approaches that are directed at the individual, family, and larger systems, such as cultural, societal, and economic systems (Lebow & Gurman).

SUMMARY

The field of marriage and family counseling is both an emerging profession and a counseling specialty practiced by various members of the helping profession. Systems theory and the family life cycle model are important theoretical foundations for this specialty.

Although there are theoretical differences with regard to key concepts, goals, and counseling approaches, the field shares a common focus on the relationship between family members and the overall family system rather than on individual family members. The field also appears to share a trend toward integration of theories in an attempt to meet the needs of different populations.

Major reviews of the research that has been conducted on marriage and family counseling note that recent studies provide strong support for the efficacy of marriage and family counseling.

PERSONAL EXPLORATION

1. How might Gottman's work on predicting divorce be useful in preventing interpersonal problems in your life?

2. What do you think is important in making a marriage or life partnership work, and how can you take an active role in this process in your current relationship or a future one?

3. What are characteristics of healthy family functioning, and how can you foster this in your family life?

4. What type of counselor would you want to see if you were having marriage or family problems?

5. What are your thoughts regarding Adlerian parenting concepts such as the family constellation, goals of misbehavior, the use

of natural and logical consequences, and communication skills?

6. How can general systems theory be used to conceptualize family functioning?

7. How can you use the family life cycle to understand family life?

8. Do you think marital assessment instruments, such as Stuart's Couples Precounseling Inventory, can be useful in marriage counseling?

9. What are your views regarding marathon family counseling?

10. Which of the postmodern trends in family counseling do you find interesting, and what do you like about them?

LEARNING ACTIVITIES

1. Consider using parenting concepts of encouragement to promote self-efficacy and the "can-do" spirit in children and adolescents.

2. Consider applying Gottman's research regarding factors associated with divorce (e.g., criticism, contempt, defensiveness, and emotional withdrawal) to assess your own relationships.

WEBSITES

Franklin, D. J. (2010). *Couples therapy*. Retrieved from http://psychologyinfo.com/treatment/couples_therapy.html. *Provides a description of couples therapy.*

Franklin, D. J. (2010). *Family counseling*. Retrieved from http://psychologyinfo.com/treatment/family_therapy.html. *Provides a description of family therapy.*

Niolon, R. (1999). *Bowenian family therapy*. Retrieved from http://www.psychpage.com/learning/library/counseling/bowen.html. *Includes information on Bowen's theory of family therapy.*

CHAPTER 11

Child and Adolescent Counseling

The young . . . are full of passion, which excludes fear; and of hope, which inspires confidence.

—Aristotle, *Rhetoric Book II*

Child and adolescent counseling is an emerging specialty within the counseling profession. Some of the most promising advances in counseling and psychology are occurring in this field. These are reflected in our understanding and treatment of common problems that children and adolescents experience, including child abuse and neglect, child/adolescent depression, and antisocial behavior. In this chapter, information is presented on these types of problems as well as other conceptual and treatment issues.

The Art and Science of Child and Adolescent Counseling

Child and adolescent counseling, like all aspects of counseling, is an art and a science. Discovering the private world of children and adolescents is an art. The challenge when working with children is finding ways to communicate that are not restricted by language and cognitive development.

When working with adolescents, the challenges include keeping lines of communication open and maintaining trust. Possible strategies that can be used to transcend these potential barriers include play therapy, conflict resolution, parent education, family therapy, consultation with teachers and parents, and ecological-environmental approaches directed at enhancing the world of children and adolescents.

One way to conceptualize the art of child and adolescent counseling is as "reaching in–reaching out" (Nystul, 1986); that is, the counselor attempts to enter the child's or adolescent's internal frame of reference—the world that

Chapter Overview

This chapter provides an overview of child and adolescent counseling. Highlights of the chapter include the following:

- **The art and science of child and adolescent counseling**

- **Children and adolescents from a historical perspective**

- **Developmental theories**

- **Emerging developmental theories (optimal development, attachment theory, resiliency, and emotional intelligence)**

- **Special approaches to child and adolescent counseling (play therapy, conflict resolution, and guidelines for child and adolescent counseling)**

- **Special problems of children and adolescents (child abuse and neglect, depression, and antisocial behavior)**

- **Diversity and postmodern issues in child and adolescent counseling** makes sense to the young person and in which they feel safe. As trust and respect are established, the child or adolescent may then feel encouraged to reach out into the world of others, for example, by moving toward success-oriented rather than failure-oriented activities in school. Throughout this process, the counselor communicates a wide range of emotions, such as caring, compassion, and perhaps even anger, to provide the structure and emotional support necessary for optimal development.

The science of child and adolescent counseling is grounded in developmental theory, research, and practice, which recognize that counseling across the life span must be cognizant of the physical, cognitive, and psychosocial aspects of development and their impact on the counseling process. From a developmental perspective, children and adolescents need assistance in acquiring the coping skills necessary to master the various tasks that are part of moving forward in their development. Counseling strategies can be directed at helping children and adolescents acquire these coping skills by fostering resiliency, positive attachment relationships, emotional and intellectual intelligence, and other qualities that promote optimal development. Recent research on diversity issues and postmodernism must also be addressed when formulating counseling strategies with children and adolescents.

Children and Adolescents from a Historical Perspective

Children

The concept of childhood as a distinct developmental stage is relatively new (LeVine & Sallee, 1992). In the past, children were viewed as miniature adults and worked alongside adults in fields and factories and fought in wars. Children had no special privileges and lacked the protection of child labor laws and the advantages of formal education. They were to be "seen and not heard" and used in whatever way their parents dictated (LeVine & Sallee).

Children were often lucky to survive long enough to become adults. Until the 19th century, parents had the right to kill a newborn child who was deformed, sickly, retarded, or even the "wrong" sex (Radbill, 1980). If children survived that possibility, there was still a very good chance they would die of illness or accident. In the 1600s, 59% of children in London died before they were 5 years old, and 64% died before they turned 10 (LeVine & Sallee, 1992). The following story illustrates how a 7-year-old girl was viewed and treated in 1713 (Kanner, 1962).

> This 7-year-old girl, the offspring of an aristocratic family, whose father remarried after an unhappy first matrimony, offended her "noble and god-fearing" stepmother by her peculiar behavior. Worst of all, she would not join in the prayers and was panic-stricken when taken to the black-robed preacher in the dark and gloomy chapel. She avoided contact with people by hiding in closets or

running away from home. The local physician had nothing to offer beyond declaring that she might be insane. She was placed in the custody of a minister known for his rigid orthodoxy. The minister, who saw in her ways the machinations of a "baneful and infernal" power, used a number of would-be therapeutic devices. He laid her on a bench and beat her with cat-o'-nine-tails. He locked her in a dark pantry. He subjected her to a period of starvation. He clothed her with a frock of burlap. Under these circumstances, the child did not last long. She died after a few months, and everybody felt relieved. The minister was amply rewarded for his efforts by Emerentia's parents. (p. 97)

LeVine and Sallee (1992) cited the following events as contributing to the recognition of childhood as a distinct stage of development. In 1744, Pestalozzi published what was the first scientific record of the development of a young child. In the late 19th century, two books were published that served as models for observational and experimental approaches to analyzing child development: Charles Darwin's *Biographical Sketch of an Infant* in 1877 and Wilhelm Preyer's *The Mind of a Child* in late 1892. It was also during the latter part of the 19th century that G. Stanley Hall at Clark University studied the physical and mental capabilities of children. Then, in the early 1900s, child guidance clinics were founded to provide counseling and guidance services to children. In 1910, the Stanford-Binet IQ tests were published, and in 1917, John B. Watson conducted his now-famous "Little Albert" experiments, which demonstrated that a child could be conditioned to cry at the sight of a furry object.

Although Western society's understanding of childhood has come a long way from the dark ages of the past, there are still signs that being a child is not easy. Children are faced with a wide array of sociocultural conditions that often have an adverse effect on their development (Wagner, 1994). For example, 25% of children under 5 years of age in the United States live in poverty, and the number of children born into a single-parent home increased from 4% to 25% between 1950 and 1988 (Wagner). Parents are spending an increasing amount of time at work, significantly reducing their involvement in child rearing (Committee for Economic Development, 1991). The void left by a lack of parental involvement is being filled by several negative activities, including viewing television programs that are often laden with sex and violence (3- to 4-year-olds watch an average of 2 or more hours a day; DeHart, Sroufe & Cooper, 2004); escaping into substance abuse; and attempting to meet the basic needs of love, belonging, and self-esteem through gang involvement.

Adolescents

It was not until the 20th century that **adolescence** was considered a separate stage of development (DeHart et al., 2004). Before that time (and in some underdeveloped countries today), puberty marked the transition from childhood to adulthood. G. Stanley Hall (1904) was one of the first to recognize adolescence as a distinct stage of development, which he characterized as a conflict-ridden period resulting from rapid and profound physical changes set off by the onset of puberty.

Hall's characterization has been modified by the contemporary views of adolescence as not normally a period of "storm and stress" but a time of relatively healthy development (DeHart et al., 2004; Wagner, 1996). Current estimates suggest that 80% of adolescents manage very well in terms of their overall psychological functioning, with the remaining 20% having significant behavioral difficulties requiring some form of clinical intervention (Weiner, 1992). More specifically, 20% pass through adolescence with virtually no recognized mental disorders, 20% have mental disorders, and the remaining 60% have mild psychological problems that do not significantly interfere with daily functioning (Weiner).

Although adolescence is not typically the stormy period claimed by Hall, evidence suggests it is a time of increasingly high risk for problems that adversely affect healthy development, such as substance abuse, teenage pregnancy, depression, and violence (Takanishi, 1993; Wagner, 1996). Approximately 25% of US adolescents face serious risk and 25% face moderate risk for health- and safety-related problems—problems that appear to be growing at an alarming rate (Takanishi). For example, more US children and adolescents are experimenting with alcohol and illegal drugs than ever before, and at a younger age (15 and younger); depression affects between 7% and 33% of adolescents; suicide rates tripled between 1968 and 1985 for 10- to 14-year-olds and doubled during that time period for 15- to 19-year-olds; homicide rates have escalated, especially for African-American males between 15 and 19 years of age, increasing by 111% between 1985 and 1990; and pregnancy rates have increased 23% between 1973 and 1987 for 10- to 14-year-olds (Takanishi). With all the challenges facing adolescents, the resurgence of interest in the counseling profession in the field of adolescent counseling is not surprising (see, for example, the special issues on adolescence in *The American Psychologist, 48*(2), 1993, and *The Counseling Psychologist, 24*(3), 1996).

With approximately 12% of individuals under the age of 18 having a serious emotional or behavioral disorder and only a minority receiving adequate mental health services, Collins and Collins (1994) have suggested that the current mental health delivery system for children and adolescents is inadequate and that it is necessary to develop a community-based system of care. This community system should be an ecological one, that is, a unified attempt of all community organizations and agencies to promote family strength and optimal development.

Developmental Theories

Counseling children and adolescents is significantly different from working with adults. Unlike adults, children and adolescents are undergoing constant changes in their physical, cognitive, and psychosocial abilities. A child or adolescent may therefore express certain symptoms at one stage of development and entirely different symptoms at another stage (LeVine & Sallee, 1992). For example, a child at age 3 may resort to temper tantrums when under stress. The same child at age 13 may turn to drugs as a means of dealing with stress (LeVine & Sallee).

It is therefore important to work with children from a developmental perspective. This section provides an overview of developmental theories relating to cognitive, moral, and psychosocial development as well as issues that relate to psychopathology; and the classic theories of personality (summarized in Table 11.1). A more detailed description of developmental characteristics (physical, cognitive, and social-emotional) and associated counseling and consultation strategies in early childhood through adolescence can be found in Stern and Newland (1994) and Vernon (1995).

Cognitive Theories

Many theories have attempted to explain how cognitive development occurs throughout the life span (Brunner, 1973; Piaget, 1952). Among these, Jean Piaget's theory has received significant attention in literature. Piaget divided cognitive development into four distinct stages: sensorimotor (birth to 2 years of age); preoperational (2 to 6 years of age); concrete operational (ages 7 to 11); and formal operational (age 12 through adulthood). According to Piaget, the cognitive development of children and adolescents becomes more sophisticated as they progress from one stage to the next. For example, children are usually unable to understand cause and effect during the preoperational stage (2 to 6 years old), and therefore concepts such as divorce or death may be difficult for them to understand. They may become confused and even blame themselves. It is therefore important for counselors to be aware of a child's or adolescent's level of cognitive development during the counseling process.

Cognitive development can also play an important role in how children respond to questions. The cognitive style of children aged 7 to 11 tends to be concrete in nature (concrete operational stage). Children therefore tend to respond well to questions that ask for specific information (probing questions), such as "Do you like school?" Open-ended statements such as "How are you doing?" can be difficult for children and often result in limited responses, such as "Fine." Adolescents typically function at the formal operational stage and have the ability to think abstractly, which enables them to generate more robust responses to open-ended questions. Most of the other listening skills discussed in Chapter 3 can be used with children and adolescents (e.g., reflection of feeling, paraphrasing, clarifying, minimal encouragers, summarizing, and so forth).

David Elkind (1984) extended Piaget's theory of cognitive development to include information on adolescent egocentrism. According to Elkind, adolescent thinking tends to be self-centered or egocentric, and this tendency can impede communication and psychological functioning. For example, since adolescents tend to see things from their point of view, they are inclined to argue with opposing positions (especially those of adults). Two other characteristics associated with adolescent egocentricism are the imaginary audience and personal fable. *Imaginary audience* relates to the adolescent tendency to be self-conscious. For example, when adolescents play tennis, they may think everyone's eyes are on them, leading to frequent bouts of giggles and other

Table 11.1 Developmental Theories

Developmental Theories	Founder	Key Concepts	Implications for Counseling
Cognitive theory	Jean Piaget, David Elkind	Divided cognitive development into four distinct stages: sensorimotor (birth to age 2), preoperational (age 2–7), concrete operations (age 7–11), and formal operations (after age 11).	Counselors should adjust the counseling approach to the child's or adolescent's level of cognitive functioning.
Theory of moral development	Lawrence Kohlberg, Carol Gilligan	Identified three levels of moral development, beginning with an egocentric view regarding morality (i.e., a child controls behavior out of a fear of punishment).	An understanding of moral reasoning can be useful to promote self-control.
Psychosocial development theory	Erik Erikson	Identified seven psychosocial stages and their associated developmental tasks (e.g., from birth to 1 year of age, the central task is trust).	Counselors can help clients obtain the coping skills necessary to master developmental tasks so they can move forward in their development.
Developmental psychopathology	Alan Kazdin, Maria Kovacs, and others	Study of child and adolescent psychopathology in the context of maturational and developmental processes.	Provides a framework for understanding child and adolescent psychopathology as distinct from adult psychopathology and aids in accurate assessment, diagnosis, and treatment.
The classic theories	Sigmund Freud, Alfred Adler, and Carl Jung	The theories of personality posited by the classic theorists emphasize the role of early life experiences on child and adolescent development.	Provide useful information for counselors to understand the dynamics of behavior *before* they begin to use counseling techniques to promote behavior change.

expressions of embarrassment. *Personal fable* involves adolescents feeling invulnerable because they believe that what they do is so special and no harm will come to them. For example, adolescents may feel that pregnancy is impossible because they are so in love and their love is so perfect that nothing bad can happen.

Counseling implications of adolescent egocentricism include being aware of this tendency and guarding against it by not overreacting (e.g., getting angry at an adolescent's self-centered point of view). Counselors can also exercise patience when helping adolescents to discover the value of appreciating different points of view as a means of enhancing communication. Group counseling with adolescents may be particularly useful in this process. Counselors may also wish to use reality testing to help adolescents overcome the tendency to be self-conscious and feel invulnerable. This can involve objectively examining various activities (such as engaging in sex) to help them develop a realistic understanding of the consequences of their behavior.

Theories of Moral Development

Counselors are facing an increasing number of children and adolescents who are out of control and engaging in various acts of misbehavior (McMahon & Forehand, 1988). Theories of moral development can provide a better understanding of children and adolescents who misbehave by explaining their moral reasoning.

Piaget (1965) and later Lawrence Kohlberg (1963, 1973, 1981) both developed theories of moral development, with Kohlberg's theory, which is based on Piaget's work, being widely accepted in the literature. In Kohlberg's theory, moral development is divided into three levels, with each level containing two stages. These levels and stages are hierarchical, meaning that a person moves through them one at a time without skipping any.

According to Kohlberg, children functioning at Level 1 have an egocentric point of view regarding morality. They control their behavior out of fear of punishment. Individuals at Level 2 of moral development control their behavior and abide by laws out of concern over how others will view them as a person and also how they will view themselves. At Level 3, people control their behavior and abide by laws on the basis of a rational decision to contribute to the good of society. Individuals who have reached the age of 11 or 12 are often capable of functioning at Level 3.

Carol Gilligan (1982, 1987, 1990) contended that Kohlberg's theory does not take into account gender issues associated with moral development. According to Gilligan (1982, 1987), Kohlberg's theory is based primarily on the way men perceive morality, as a set of values and moral principles that can be applied to all situations regardless of the social context and that are concerned with what is fair and equitable. Gilligan argued that female moral reasoning is more concerned with caring for the needs of others than with equity and is also directly related to the social context, in that one's moral reasoning is influenced by how one will be viewed by significant others.

Parr and Ostrovsky (1991) have described how theories of moral development can be used as guides to counseling children and adolescents. For example, a behavior modification technique such as a token economy may be useful with first graders, since their moral decision making is strongly influenced by obeying rules and the fear of being punished. The same approach may not be as effective with adolescents since they may be more concerned with social issues, such as how their behavior conforms to shared norms and how their decisions will be perceived by their peer group. Group counseling can provide teens with a social milieu to work through their concerns and facilitate moral decision making.

Psychosocial Theories

Psychosocial development are another important issue in counseling children and adolescents. Erik Erikson's (1963, 1968) theory identified seven psychosocial stages, from birth to death. Each stage involves a particular task that must be accomplished before the individual can proceed effectively to the next developmental task. From birth to age 1, for example, the central task is to experience a sense of trust from the environment. Without that experience, an infant will develop a mistrustful attitude. The developmental task of adolescence is identity versus identity confusion (the ability to establish a clear sense of personal identity). To accomplish each task, the individual must master its various associated coping skills. To promote positive psychosocial development, counselors can help children and adolescents acquire these coping skills (Blocher, 1987; Stern & Newland, 1994). Chapter 14 provides a more detailed description of the role of developmental tasks in the counseling process.

Developmental Psychopathology

Recently, the counseling field has attempted to view psychopathology from a developmental perspective (Bergman & Magnusson, 1997; Kazdin, 1993; Sroufe, 1997; Wakefield, 1997). **Developmental psychopathology** is "the study of clinical dysfunction in the context of maturational and developmental processes" (Kazdin, 1989, p. 180). Developmental psychopathology attempts to address three issues: (a) how the developing organism mediates the development of mental disorders; (b) the impact of mental disorders on age-appropriate abilities; and (c) whether mental disorders develop continually or in stages (Kovacs, 1989).

According to Alan Kazdin (1989), the greatest advance in developmental psychopathology occurred with the publication of the *Diagnostic and Statistical Manual for Mental Disorders* (*DSM-III* and later *DSM-III-R*; American Psychiatric Association, 1980, 1987). Kazdin noted, "It represented a quantum leap in the attention accorded disorders of infancy, childhood, and adolescence" (p. 183). The *DSM* recognized the variations from childhood to adulthood in the nature and course of psychopathology. For example, the *DSM-IV* notes that it is common for a depressed child to experience problems that are usually not found with adult depression. Some of these are somatic, or bodily, complaints; psychomotor agitation; and mood-congruent hallucinations. The *DSM-5* notes that disruptive mood dysregulation disorder (characterized by severe irritability) is common among children, with the symptoms of the disorder changing as children get older. Comorbidity (two or more diagnoses) is also common in children and adolescents (Sroufe, 1997). Such multiple diagnoses can obscure or mask a psychological problem, making an accurate assessment difficult. For example, if a child has a substance abuse problem, an oppositional-defiant disorder, and an anxiety disorder, the clinician may focus on the drug and oppositional problems and miss the anxiety problem.

A great deal of research and theoretical development is occurring in the field of developmental psychopathology. A wide range of topics have been explored, among them the role of nature and nurture (Rutter et al., 1997), transition and turning points (Rutter, 1996), and emotions (Cicchetti, Ackerman, & Izard, 1995). From their investigation of the role of emotional regulation in developmental psychopathology, Cicchetti et al. contended that the primary function of emotional regulation is to initiate, organize, and motivate adaptive behavior, thereby preventing abnormal conditions and responses.

However, research specifically directed at the developmental psychopathology of adolescence has not received much emphasis. Developmental psychopathology has tended to focus on children and overlook adolescence (Kazdin, 1993) because adolescence had been viewed as a transitional period between childhood and adulthood that was in constant change due to biological flux, making it difficult to identify clear mental health patterns. This point of view is changing as the unique developmental characteristics of adolescence have become recognized and accepted as an important domain for scientific investigation (Kazdin).

In terms of refining the process of assessment and diagnosis in child and adolescent counseling, advances in the study of developmental psychopathology hold promise. Additional research is required to determine how different developmental levels may influence symptom expression and treatment (Kazdin, 1989).

The Classic Theories

The classic personality theories of Sigmund Freud, Alfred Adler, and Carl Jung (see Chapter 7) can also provide useful information for understanding children and adolescents. These theories all emphasize the role of early life experiences in child and adolescent development. Freud, one of the first to look at stages of development in children and adolescents, viewed them from a psychosexual perspective: the oral, anal, phallic, latency, and genital stages. According to Freud's theory, traumatic experiences during any of these stages can fixate development at that level, and adults can spend the rest of their lives attempting to resolve the needs unmet in childhood or adolescence. For example, if children do not have opportunities to fulfill their oral needs, they may continually attempt to meet those needs in later life and in the process develop an orally fixated personality. Such tendencies can be positive, such as becoming an orator, or negative, such as nail biting.

Adler, his colleague Rudolf Dreikurs, and others of the Adlerian school offered much insight into child and adolescent development. They developed numerous psychological constructs that can be used to understand and counsel children and adolescents, including birth order, the family constellation, lifestyle, goals of misbehavior, encouragement, and the use of consequences as a disciplinary technique.

Jungian psychology adds another valuable dimension to the conceptualization of child and adolescent development. Jung's concepts of holism and balance, for example, have been integrated into Jungian forms of play therapy, which is described later in this chapter.

Emerging Developmental Trends

There has been a major shift in orientation in the field of counseling from pathology to wellness. The recognition that strength is required to overcome adversity has come to play a central role in virtually all aspects of counseling, from holistic health, which suggests that clients develop a wellness orientation, to brief-solution-focused counseling, which encourages clients to use what has worked before (exceptions to the problem) to overcome current difficulties. Given this ongoing emphasis on strengths, it is not surprising that developmental theories and concepts are beginning to take on a strengths perspective. This section reviews four emerging trends in the developmental orientation that have a strengths perspective (optimal development, resiliency, attachment theory, and emotional intelligence; see Table 11.2). Because resiliency, secure attachment, and emotional intelligence facilitate optimal development, these concepts appear to be interrelated.

OPTIMAL DEVELOPMENT The roots of **optimal development** lie in the work of humanistic psychologists like Carl Rogers (1951) and Abraham Maslow (1960), who proposed a model of human growth and development based on inherent self-actualizing tendencies. Rogers believed that a person will move toward self-actualization (optimal development) if the right conditions are established. More recently, Wagner (1996) has presented optimal development as a developmental perspective that emphasizes health and wellness over pathology. Wagner noted that what constitutes optimal development varies to some degree contextually in terms of culture and so forth. Wagner went on to review the literature to identify biophysical, cognitive, and psychosocial competencies that appear to characterize optimal development in adolescence. These research findings are summarized as follows:

- *Biophysical.* "Upon reaching the age of 18, an adolescent will be alive and healthy, physically mature, and engaged in health-enhancing behaviors, including proper diet and regular exercise" (Wagner, p. 364).

- *Cognitive.* "Upon reaching the age of 18, adolescents will engage in efficient and purposively idiosyncratic thinking of a more hypothetical, multidimensional, future-oriented and relative nature that is based on prior life experiences, including the completion or near completion of at least 12 years of formal education" (Wagner, p. 368).

- *Psychosocial functioning.* "Upon reaching the age of 18, adolescents will be emotionally aware, feel secure and self-confident, be determined and optimistic about the future, and possess the resilience needed to overcome adversity" (Wagner, p. 371).

Table 11.2 Emerging Developmental Trends

Developmental Theories and Concepts	Founder	Key Concepts	Implications for Counselors
Optimal development	No one individual; contributors include Carl Rogers, Abraham Maslow, and William Wagner	A view of human development that focuses on positive, healthy development as opposed to a pathological view of development	Optimal development can help counselors take a strengths perspective by focusing on what people can do rather than what they cannot do. This perspective promotes a positive, self-fulfilling prophecy.
Resiliency	No one individual; Emmy Werner's research stands out	Coping mechanisms that provide a buffer to harmful stress and obstacles to development	Resiliency characteristics can provide useful survival responses to stress, which in turn can promote optimal development. Counselors can promote resiliency characteristics in their approach with clients.
Attachment theory	Mary Ainsworth, John Bowlby, and others	A study of the relationship between the emotional bond between a parent and child and that child's psychosocial development over the life span	An understanding of a client's present and past attachment relationships can provide useful insights into how to move toward optimal psychosocial development.
Emotional intelligence	John Mayer and Peter Salovey	A study of the role that social emotions play in psychological functioning (e.g., the ability to accurately perceive emotions and respond to them appropriately)	Counselors can promote emotional intelligence in clients by helping them gain a better understanding of how emotions foster optimal development. Counselors can also help clients enhance their emotional intelligence through such activities as social-skills training in groups.

Several authors have proposed a person-environmental fit model of development that can be used to understand how optimal development occurs (Chu & Powers, 1995; Eccles et al., 1993). According to this model, a person moves forward toward optimal development when there is a good fit between his or her needs and the social environment. Synchrony occurs when the social environment is responsive to the individual in terms of promoting personal independence, self-determination, and decision making. In addition, synchrony plays a key role in promoting important competencies in children and adolescents, such as attachment, autonomy, and social competency (Chu & Powers).

When the fit between the social environment and the individual is strained, the person can become discouraged and lack motivation for positive involvement (Eccles et al., 1993). This can lead to disruptions in the developmental process, such as excessive rebelliousness during adolescence, dropping out of school, and drug abuse. The person-environmental fit model may provide an explanation for why early and middle adolescence is particularly problematic for some adolescents. Once an adolescent goes to middle school, parents tend to renegotiate rules relating to autonomy and control (e.g., how late the teen can stay out; Chu & Powers, 1995). At the same time, it is not uncommon for middle school teachers to also place a high premium on discipline and control. When the adolescent no longer feels a sense of empowerment, he or she can feel discouraged and lack motivation for involvement in family life or school, resulting in a variety of serious problems.

Optimal development can be facilitated in children and adolescents by building strengths in resiliency, coping, and problem solving (Van Slyck, Stern, & Zak-Place, 1996). Preventative programs that focus on conflict resolution are effective interventions for fostering these strengths, especially for adolescents since they are prone to problems that stem from interpersonal conflicts. Guidelines for promoting synchrony in child- or adolescent-adult relationships include maintaining flexibility and openness to change and exercising sensitivity and activeness in terms of encouraging problem solving and decision making (Chu & Powers, 1995). These characteristics also seem to be valuable in promoting strengths associated with optimal development in children.

RESILIENCY **Resiliency** is a term that has been used to describe why some at-risk children and adolescents thrive, whereas others experience disruptions in their development. It can be defined as a tendency to overcome adverse conditions as a result of having growth-facilitating characteristics that promote optimal development. Research investigations have attempted to understand the dynamics of resilience. Perhaps the most significant study on resiliency was one conducted by Werner and her colleagues (Werner, 1992; Werner & Smith, 1982, 1992) that attempted to identify resiliency characteristics for 200 at-risk children in Hawaii over a 32-year period. These children had experienced at least four risk factors, such as family dysfunction, parental alcoholism, and poverty. Surprisingly, 1 out of 3 of these at-risk children grew into competent, happy, productive young adults.

In an overview of the literature on resilience in terms of its characteristics and implications for counseling and development, Rak and Patterson (1996) identified some of these resiliency characteristics: a positive self-concept, an optimistic outlook, good interpersonal skills resulting in positive social experiences, good problem-solving and decision-making skills, a well-developed sense of personal autonomy, an environmental support system (within or outside of the family), and a significant other who can provide adequate mentoring. Adams's (1997) qualitative study involving interviews with 10 individuals 85 years or older suggested that resiliency is related to a wide array of health factors (e.g., emotional, physical, spiritual, social, and internal). Lee et al. (2013) conducted a meta-analysis of 33 studies that addressed factors associated with promoting resiliency. Results of the study showed that protective factors (e.g., self-efficacy and positive affect) had the largest effect in terms of promoting resiliency, risk factors (depression and anxiety) had a medium effect, and demographic factors (e.g., gender and age) had the smallest effect.

Resiliency research poses a new way of conceptualizing counseling and development. It has revealed that resiliency characteristics act as a buffer to help children and adolescents cope with stress so they can move toward optimal development (Rak & Patterson, 1996). From a strengths perspective, counselors can foster resiliency characteristics in their clients, thereby promoting survival responses and maximizing developmental opportunities. The field of resiliency research appears to offer opportunities for counselors to utilize a strengths perspective in counseling.

ATTACHMENT THEORY **Attachment theory** was originally developed by Mary Ainsworth and associates (Ainsworth, Blehar, Waters, & Wall, 1978), John Bowlby (1969/1982), and others as an investigation into the emotional bond between parents and child and the implications that bond has for psychosocial development throughout the life span. Ainsworth et al. devised an experiment, called the Strange Situation, that investigated attachment patterns of 1-year-olds. An overview of the experiment (Feldman, 2008) follows:

A mother enters a room with an infant. She sits down and lets her child freely explore the room. A stranger enters the room and converses with the mother and infant. The mother then leaves the infant alone in the room with the stranger. The mother returns and greets and comforts the infant, and the stranger departs. The mother then leaves the infant alone in the room. The stranger goes back into the room. The experiment concludes with the mother returning and the stranger exiting the room.

Based on the Strange Situation experiment, Ainsworth suggested there are three patterns of attachment: secure, avoidant, and ambivalent. Feldman's (2008) description of these three attachment patterns follows:

- *Secure attachment* occurs with the majority of children in North America. Securely attached infants have a special-nurturing relationship with their caregivers. The caregiver is sensitive to the infant's needs, promoting feelings of safety and security. These infants are able to explore their environment independently. They become upset when their caregiver leaves and seek contact when the caregiver returns.

- *Avoidant attachment* occurs with approximately 20% of infants. Avoidant attachment is characterized by infants who appear to avoid contact with their caregiver and seem indifferent to their caregiver. They do not get upset when separated from the caregiver or seek out the caregiver when the caregiver returns.

- *Ambivalent attachment* occurs with about 10% to 15% of infants. Ambivalent attachment is associated with infants who display both positive and negative feelings toward their caregiver. They tend to stay close to their caregiver, undermining their ability to engage in independent exploratory behavior. When separated from the caregiver, these infants become very upset. When reunited, they display mixed emotional responses towards the caregiver (e.g., fluctuating between affection and anger).

A fourth attachment pattern relating to Ainsworth's work has been identified (Feldman, 2008). *Disorganized/disoriented attachment* occurs with 5% to 10% of infants. These infants appear to have the most insecure attachment patterns. Disorganized/disoriented attachment is characterized by inconsistent, confused, and contradictory emotional and behavioral responses to the caregiver. For example, after a period of separation, an infant may seek out the caregiver but avoid eye contact. Emotional expressions with the caregiver can fluctuate dramatically for no apparent reason (e.g., one moment appearing calm and then engaging in a crying tantrum).

The first 3 to 4 years of life can be considered the sensitive period for establishing a secure attachment. A sensitive period is "a point in development when organisms are particularly susceptible to certain kinds of stimuli in their environments, but the absence of those stimuli does not always produce irreversible consequences" (Feldman, 2008, p. 12). When a child has significant problems formulating a secure attachment, serious psychological impairment can result. In extreme cases (often involving child abuse or neglect), a reactive attachment disorder may occur, undermining a child's ability to formulate meaningful relationships with others (Feldman).

Ainsworth (1989, 1991) and Bowlby (1988a, 1988b) advocated for what is known as a *continuity theory* regarding attachment. According to this theory, the nature of the attachment in early life influences development throughout the life span. Much research has tested this hypothesis and has investigated the relationship among attachment styles and affect regulation and social competence in adults (Lopez, 1995), producing some evidence in support of the continuity hypothesis (Lopez). For example, securely attached infants and children tend to become adults who have secure attachment styles (Brennan, Shaver, & Tobey, 1991; Carnelley, Pietromonaco, & Jaffe, 1994) and become parents who are able to establish secure attachments with their family members (Ricks, 1985). The true test of the continuity hypothesis will require longitudinal studies that investigate the relationship between early attachment and development throughout the life span (Lopez).

A compelling body of research suggests a relationship between adult attachment styles and adult affect regulation and social competence (Lopez, 1995). For example, securely attached adults tend to have superior communication and problem-solving skills (Pistole, 1993; Shaver & Brennan, 1992), higher levels of marital adjustment (Kobak & Hazan, 1991), and the ability to provide more emotional support to distressed partners and solicit emotional support when they need it (Lynch, 2013; Simpson, Rholes, & Nelligan, 1992).

There are several commonalities between attachment theory and Adler's individual psychology (Peluso, Peluso, White, & Kern, 2004). Two key theoretical constructs in Adlerian psychology are lifestyle analysis and social interest. *Lifestyle* refers to a person's basic orientation to life. *Social interest* relates to inborn tendencies to cooperate and work with others (which is believed to increase with mental health and wellness). Attachment and lifestyle are similar in terms of their emphasis on early family relationships. Being securely attached can contribute to a person's being self-confident and having an active lifestyle. Attachment and social interest are also similar constructs, for both suggest that the ability to establish meaningful social relationships is influenced by the nature of early parent-child relationships. Securely attached individuals are better able to establish and maintain meaningful social relationships.

One intriguing area for the application of attachment theory is in career development. Securely attached individuals tend to have adaptive characteristics that promote success in career exploration and decision making (Blustein, Prezioso, & Schultheiss, 1995). Some of these characteristics are enhanced ego identity development (Rice, 1990), enhanced adult work behavior (Hazan & Shaver, 1990), and enhanced exploratory behavior (Hazan & Shaver).

Attachment theory is a view of a healthy personality in terms of relational issues in development (Lopez, 1995) and therefore provides a strengths perspective for counseling. Concrete strategies for applying attachment theory in counseling practice are beginning to emerge, and several instruments have been developed to assess the nature and scope of a person's attachment style (for adolescent and adult attachment instruments, see Lyddon, Bradford, and Nelson [1993] and Bradford and Lyddon [1994]). Krause and Haverkamp (1996) have suggested that it may be productive to assess adults' current attachment relationships with their parents to gain insights into adult or child–older parent relationships. Clients who appear to have problematic histories or current problems with attachments may wish to address attachment issues in counseling to free the way for optimal development (Blustein et al., 1995).

EMOTIONAL INTELLIGENCE Mayer and Salovey are credited with developing the concept of **emotional intelligence** (Mayer, Dipaolo, & Salovey, 1990; Mayer & Salovey, 1997; Salovey & Mayer, 1990). Based on their scientific description of emotional intelligence (or EI), Mayer (1999, 2001) contended that it is a unitary ability that can be measured reliably and is related to but independent of standard intelligence. Emotional intelligence is a form of alternative intelligence that can be traced to Thorndike's (1920) work on social intelligence (Mayer, Salovey, & Caruso, 2000), which essentially explores how people make judgments regarding others and examines the accuracy of those judgments (Mayer & Geher, 1996). Emotional intelligence has evolved into a more complex construct, defined as

> an ability to recognize the meanings of emotions and their relationships, and to reason and problem-solve on the basis of them. Emotional intelligence is involved with the capacity to perceive emotions, assimilate emotion-related feelings, understand the information of those emotions, and manage them. (Mayer, Caruso, & Salovey, 1999, p. 267)

Goleman's (1997) best-selling book *Emotional Intelligence* presented a popularized version of emotional intelligence theory. The book refers to emotional intelligence as *EQ,* as opposed to the intellectual quotient (IQ), and provides information on the practical applications of emotional intelligence to everyday life, suggesting that emotional intelligence may be more important to determining personal success than is intellectual intelligence. According to Goleman, IQ may get you hired, but it is EQ skills that are primarily responsible for promotions and other job-related successes. Goleman noted that self-awareness may be the cornerstone of emotional intelligence since it is necessary for a wide range of pro-social behaviors, such as self-control. Other key characteristics that have been linked to success are empathy and interpersonal skills (Goleman), optimism (Seligman, 1991), practical intelligence or common sense (Sternberg, Wagner, Williams, & Horvath, 1995), and delay of gratification (Mischel, Shoda, & Rodriguez, 1989; Shoda, Mischel, & Peake, 1990). Optimistic responses to setbacks have been associated with job-related success, such as increased sales in the life insurance profession (Seligman), and practical intelligence or common sense is a better predictor of success in employment than is intellectual intelligence (Sternberg et al., 1995).

Mischel et al.'s (1989) "marshmallow" study on delay of gratification is another example of the effects of emotional intelligence on psychological functioning. In this study, 4-year-olds were told they could have one marshmallow now or two when the researcher returned from an errand. Those who waited for two marshmallows utilized a variety of delay-of-gratification coping skills, such as singing, playing games, and so forth. The researchers then conducted a longitudinal study that extended from childhood into adolescence (Mischel et al.; Shoda et al., 1990). They found that the 4-year-olds who waited for two marshmallows were rated as more intelligent, better able to concentrate, and more goal oriented than those who preferred instant gratification. In addition, children who could delay gratification went on to become adolescents who tended to have significantly higher SAT scores (Shoda et al.).

Many of the ideas and behavior being studied in the field of emotional intelligence is also being explored in the emerging field of evolutionary psychology (Gibbs, 1995). Evolutionary psychology, which is based on the work of Charles Darwin, explores all aspects of development in terms of survival of the human species (Daly & Wilson, 1983; Wright, 1994). From an evolutionary perspective, human emotions like anger may trigger a fight-or-flight response (Goleman, 1997), empathy can act as a buffer to cruelty (Goleman), and facial beauty and attractiveness can be related to reproductive capacity (Johnston & Oliver-Rodriguez, 1997). The research in evolutionary psychology appears promising in terms of understanding human development, including the realm of emotional intelligence.

Emotional intelligence provides a strengths perspective for counselors by recognizing the vital role that social emotions play in human functioning. For example, counselors can help clients use the power of encouragement to foster self-efficacy. In addition, preventative programs in schools can promote strengths in emotional literacy to overcome the negative tendencies of violence, loneliness, and despair (Goleman, 1997). School counselors have an ideal setting in which to promote emotional intelligence through classroom presentations, counseling (especially group), and consultation with parents and teachers.

Treatment Issues

This section addresses treatment issues in child and adolescent counseling. It begins by describing some of the commonly used assessment procedures. The chapter then provides information on treatment in terms of research findings, a description of special counseling approaches with children and adolescents, and an overview of ethical issues relating to children and adolescents.

Assessment Procedures

Child and adolescent counseling encompasses the full range of standardized and nonstandardized assessment procedures described in Chapter 4. Two additional child and adolescent assessment procedures are the use of drawings as an assessment tool, a procedure clinicians have used for some time, and the use of clinical interviews with children, adolescents, and parents. Although clinical interviews have been used with adults for many years, their use with children and adolescents is more recent (Edelbrock & Costello, 1988) and represents a major advance in the assessment of childhood and adolescent disorders (Kazdin, 1989).

DRAWINGS Drawings can be used in both standardized and nonstandardized assessment procedures. One standardized test is the Goodenough-Harris Drawing Test (Harris, 1963). This test requires children and adolescents to make a picture of a man or woman (depending on the sex of the child) and a picture of themselves. Another commonly used standardized test is the House-Tree-Person Test (Buck, 1949), in which children and adolescents first draw a house, then a tree, and last a person. More recent is the Kinetic Drawing System for Family and School (Knoff & Prout, 1985), in which children and adolescents draw one picture of their family and another that relates to school. This test assesses important relationships at home and school.

Drawings by children and adolescents can also be used in a nonstandardized way to obtain an estimate of a child or adolescent's cognitive and psychosocial development and level of maturity (Stabler, 1984). The following five factors are important in assessing drawings (Stabler):

1. *Proportion or form.* Do figures in the drawings have appropriate proportion or form?

2. *Detail.* What is the degree of detail in the drawing (are there ears, eyes, a mouth, and a nose on the face)?

3. *Movement or action.* Is there movement or action depicted in the drawing, and do human figures have the appearance of three dimensions?

4. *Theme.* Is a theme or story conveyed in the picture, such as two people in love or Superman stopping a villain?

5. *Gender identity.* Is there evidence that the child or adolescent has a clear concept of gender identity?

There are also guidelines for assessing drawings in terms of cognitive functioning and overall maturity for children and adolescents in three age groups: aged 5 to 7, 8 to 9, and 10 to 12 (Stabler, 1984). For example, children from age 5 to 7 tend to be able to draw pictures that are more or less proportional, have limited detail, show some evidence of gender identity emerging, depict rather poor movement or action, and typically have no theme. Figure 11.1 illustrates a typical drawing by a 6-year-old and a 12-year-old.

Three types of drawings are particularly useful in the assessment process: free drawings, where children are encouraged to draw whatever they like; self-portraits; and family drawings, in which children draw themselves with their family (Stabler, 1984). These drawings enable the counselor to make hypotheses about what to explore with a child. For example, a free drawing may have themes that represent children's concerns, so a child who repeatedly draws a house with a child by a mother and father in the home could suggest the child is concerned with issues relating to home and family life. A self-portrait with no arms or legs could indicate a sense of lack of control over the environment. Children who draw a self-portrait without a mouth may think that others do not value their views. A family drawing with a significant distance between the child and other family members could suggest a feeling of isolation or alienation.

CLINICAL INTERVIEWS The clinical interview has become an increasingly popular tool for assisting with assessment and diagnosis (see Chapter 4 for a description of the clinical interview). The clinical interview does not replace other forms of assessment, but it can be viewed as an adjunct to the process of assessment and diagnosis. In this role, the clinical interview has been shown to increase diagnostic reliability (Robins, Helzer, Croughan, & Ratcliff, 1981). Although clinical interviews have been used with adults for some time, their development and use with children and adolescents have occurred primarily during the last 20 years, corresponding to the increased differentiation of mental disorders in children and adolescents.

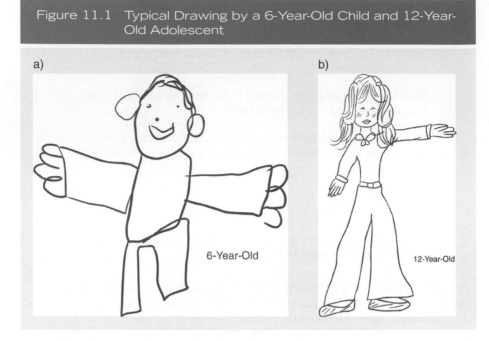

Source: Typical drawing by a 6-year old child and 12-year-old adolescent. From *Children's drawings* (pp. 5, 8) by B. Stabler, 1984, Chapel Hill, NC: Health Science, Consortium. Copyright 1984 by Health Sciences Consortium. Reprinted by permission.

There are several advantages and disadvantages of clinical interviews compared to other child and adolescent assessment procedures, such as observation and psychological tests (Edelbrock & Costello, 1988). Advantages include enabling the counselor to establish rapport; clarify misunderstandings; and obtain self-report data from parents, children, and adolescents. The primary disadvantages relate to questionable levels of validity and reliability owing to the newness of these instruments and the consequent lack of empirical evaluation.

Many clinical interview instruments for children and adolescents are currently available. The commonly used clinical interviews vary in terms of structure, and the more structured interviews require less training to administer (Edelbrock & Costello, 1988). The following are three examples:

1. *The Diagnostic Interview for Children and Adolescents* (Herjanic & Reich, 1982). This highly structured diagnostic interview can be used with children 6 years of age or older. It covers a broad range of childhood symptoms in terms of frequency and duration. There is also a version for parents, which solicits pertinent developmental and family history.

2. ***The Interview Schedule for Children*** (Kovacs, 1982). This is a semistructured interview for children ages 8 to 17. It is symptom oriented and focuses primarily on depression, although it also assesses other diagnostic criteria. A separate interview can be conducted with parents, children, and adolescents.

3. ***The Diagnostic Interview Schedule for Children*** (Costello, Edelbrock, Kalas, Kessler, & Klaric, 1982). This highly structured interview for children and adolescents ages 6 to 18 provides information on a wide range of symptoms and behaviors in terms of onset, duration, and severity. A parallel version can be used with parents and children or adolescents.

Child and Adolescent Counseling Goals

One way to conceptualize counseling goals in child and adolescent counseling is from a developmental perspective. The developmental perspective can be applied to clients of all ages. It can be especially useful in child and adolescent counseling (such as in school counseling) where developmental issues are continuously addressed. The developmental perspective differentiates between two types of counseling goals: universal-primary goals and secondary goals. Universal primary goals address developmental issues; secondary counseling goals relate to specific problems, such as procrastinating and not turning in schoolwork on time.

Universal-primary goals promote optimal development through the enhancement of developmental competencies such as self-esteem, attachment, resiliency, emotional intelligence, self-awareness, self-control, self-efficacy, intrinsic motivation, and internal locus of control. They are considered primary counseling goals because they relate to the child's or adolescent's overall growth and development. In addition, universal-primary goals may promote developmental competencies necessary to successfully address secondary counseling goals to which they may be directly or indirectly related. For example, greater intrinsic motivation and self-control are universal-primary goals that may be directly related to overcoming procrastination. Increased self-awareness may be a developmental goal that is indirectly related to the procrastination problem but could be important to the child's or adolescent's overall growth and development.

It is important to consider both universal-primary and secondary counseling goals when assessing progress in counseling. From a developmental perspective, success should be measured both in terms of whether problems have been resolved (secondary goals) and how clients are progressing relative to their overall growth and development (universal-primary goals). Counselors and clients should be encouraged if progress is being made with either universal-primary or secondary counseling goals.

Child and Adolescent Counseling Research

Overviews (Kazdin, 1993; Weisz, Weiss, & Donenberg, 1992) of a number of meta-analyses on child and adolescent counseling (e.g., Hazelrigg, Cooper, & Borduin, 1987;

Kazdin, Bass, Ayers, & Rodgers, 1990) report strong support for the efficacy of child and adolescent counseling. For example, the effects of child and adolescent counseling are superior to no treatment, the degree of positive change is comparable to that in adult counseling, there is little variation in efficacy of treatment modalities such as behavioral versus nonbehavioral, and treatment outcomes are similar for internalized problems such as depression and externalized problems such as aggression (Kazdin, 1993). Research also suggests that a developmental perspective is critical in identifying appropriate counseling interventions for children and adolescents. For example, behavioral approaches such as behavior modification have been useful in treating children (Kazdin), and adolescents (owing to their ability to think abstractly) are able to utilize cognitive-behavioral approaches better than are children (Durlak, Fuhrman, & Lampman, 1991).

Kazdin (1993) also noted that there is strong support for preventative programs with children and adolescents (Goldston, Yager, Heinicke, & Pynoos, 1990; Weissberg, Caplan, & Harwood, 1991). Programs that provide support to a family during a child's formative years appear to prevent problems, such as a child engaging in antisocial behavior later in childhood and adolescence. Research also suggests that school-based programs appear to be effective in preventing a wide array of problems, such as substance use and abuse and school dropout. Kazdin proposed that the success of preventative programs depends to some degree on the ability to not only change attitudes but also change behavior. Schultz and Nystul (1980) found in an earlier study on parent education that the internalization and transfer from an attitude to a behavior requires some form of action, such as role-playing.

Special Counseling Approaches for Children and Adolescents

Most counseling approaches used with children and adolescents (such as behavioral and cognitive-behavioral) are adaptations of strategies used with adults (Tuma, 1989). Play therapy and conflict resolution are two counseling approaches that have been specifically designed for working with children and adolescents. This section is an overview of these unique methods and provides guidelines for child and adolescent counseling.

PLAY THERAPY Play represents an important developmental tool for children and adolescents. It is a natural form of communication (Campbell, 1993) and an expression of creativity linked to learning, coping, and self-realization (Rogers & Sharapan, 1993). Through play, children and adolescents are able to enhance cognitive, physical, and psychosocial development (Papalia, Olds, & Feldman, 2007). For example, playing hide-and-seek involves deciding where and how to hide (cognitive); mobility, such as running and squatting (physical); and cooperating with others (psychosocial). Sports like basketball and baseball become favored forms of play for adolescents and adults and continue to provide opportunities to enhance development.

Play therapy is a counseling strategy that has been used primarily with children for a variety of purposes: to build relationships, conduct assessment, promote communication, provide psychological healing, and foster growth (Orton, 1997). Play therapy uses play media—such as sand play, art, and music—to help children learn skills and work through problems so they can progress in their development. Sand play, an emerging form of play therapy (Carmichael, 1994), involves the use of two 20″ × 30″ × 4″ trays (one with wet sand and one with dry sand) and numerous objects that represent everyday life (people, fences, animals, and so forth). Children are encouraged to use the objects to express themselves in fantasy play. The three stages of play therapy (including what one would expect in sand play) are chaos, struggle, and resolution (Allan & Brown, 1993). During the initial stage (chaos), children tend to express negative feelings, such as anger and confusion, and project those feelings onto their play activities. As play therapy progresses, the therapist encourages children to utilize play as a means of working through their struggles. The last phase of play therapy is characterized by creative expressions that are more positive in nature (such as cooperation), reflecting resolution of conflicts.

The historical roots of play therapy can be traced to two major schools of counseling, Freudian and Rogerian. Anna Freud (1928), the daughter of Sigmund Freud, was perhaps the first to use play therapy with children, and Melanie Klein (1960) further developed the psychoanalytic school of play therapy. These clinicians incorporated the major principles of psychoanalysis into their approach, for example, strengthening the ego to minimize endopsychic conflicts and utilizing the transference relationship to help children overcome traumatic experiences. The psychoanalytic counselor conceptualizes play in a manner similar to free association. From this perspective, play allows children to express themselves freely and spontaneously. The counselor's role in this process is passive and interpretive. For example, if a child painted a picture with dark objects, the counselor might ask, "Are you feeling sad or gloomy today?"

The theoretical foundation of Virginia Axline's (1964, 1974) school of play therapy can be traced to Carl Rogers's person-centered school of counseling; it is therefore a humanistic-phenomenological approach. The counselor conveys a warm and accepting attitude toward the child and encourages the child to freely explore the different play materials (Axline, 1964, 1974). The role of the counselor is similar to that in person-centered counseling. As the child plays, the counselor attempts to convey empathic understanding by reflecting what he or she senses the child is experiencing. A more detailed description of Axline's approach can be found in *Dibs: In Search of Self* (Axline, 1964).

Contemporary forms of play therapy are based on a number of theoretical orientations, such as Rogerian (Landreth's child-centered therapy, 1993, 2012); Jungian (Allan & Brown, 1993); and Adlerian (Kottman & Johnson, 1993; Kottman, 2003; & Nystul, 1980a). Taylor and Bratton (2014) noted that child-centered play therapy was the main theoretical orientation used in play therapy followed by Adlerian play therapy. Jungian play therapy therapy is also popular, especially when used with sand play therapy (Carmichael, 1994).

Current trends in Rogerian child-centered play therapy reflect the earlier model developed by Axline and are being used to treat a wide range of problems—regressive behavior, depression, abuse, and socially inappropriate behavior (Landreth, 1993, 2012). Blanco and Ray (2011) reported that child-centered play therapy significantly increased achievement in academically high-risk first-grade students.

Child relationship therapy (Landreth & Bratton, 2006) is an emerging form of play therapy that involves helping parents learn the skills associated with child-centered therapy so they can play an active role in addressing their children's needs. Post, Ceballos, and Penn (2012) provided guidelines that therapists could use to establish behavioral goals with parents during child relationship therapy. They noted that behavioral goals should be consistent with the Rogerian child-centered perspective (e.g., self-acceptance, self-reliance, better problem solver, and able to assume responsibility for behavior). Carnes-Holt and Bratton (2014) conducted research on the use of child relationship therapy to address attachment issues with adopted children. Results of the study showed that child relationship therapy reduced child behavioral problems and increased parental empathy. Jungian play therapy involves an application of the major Jungian principles (see Chapter 7). Jungian play therapy uses the therapeutic alliance to help the child work through unconscious struggles and conflicts reflected in play (Allan & Brown, 1993). A central goal is to help the child create a balance between the inner world of feelings, drives, and impulses and the demands of the outer world as reflected in school, peers, and family. Another major goal in Jungian play therapy is to strengthen the child's ego so it can become an effective mediator between the child's inner and outer world. In fact, Jungians have found sand play therapy to be particularly useful as a means of strengthening the child's ego to create a balance between the child's inner and outer world (Carmichael, 1994).

Adlerian play therapy is based on the work of Adler (1930) and of Dreikurs and associates (Dreikurs & Soltz, 1964). It is used to foster a positive counseling relationship, help parents and teachers gain a better understanding of children, enable children to gain insight and self-awareness, and provide skills and experiences necessary for children to work through conflict and enhance their development (Kottman, 2003; Kottman & Johnson, 1993; Nystul, 1980a).

Consultation with parents and teachers can be an important adjunct to Adlerian play therapy (Kottman & Johnson, 1993; Nystul, 1987b). Meany-Walen, Bratton, and Kottman (2014) reported that Adlerian play therapy can be used to reduce behavioral problems of students and also lower the stress level of teachers working with these students. Counselors can use Adlerian/Dreikursian concepts to help parents and teachers develop tools to better understand and work with children. Some of the more widely used concepts are the goals of misbehavior, the birth-order factor in personality development, encouragement versus praise, and consequences versus punishment. Programs such as Systematic Training for Effective Parenting (STEP) by Dinkmeyer and McKay (1997) provide an excellent summary of these ideas as well as structured activities for applying them.

The following *Personal Note* provides an example of how I developed my own approach to play therapy.

A Personal Note

I have developed my own approach to play therapy (Nystul, 1980a). Grounded in Adlerian/Dreikursian psychology, it also integrates the four phases of multimodality creative arts therapy described in Chapter 8: set the stage, set an example, set yourself at ease, and obtain a phenomenological understanding of the child. My approach to play therapy is based on the following seven assumptions:

1. The counselor attempts to establish a feeling of mutual respect with the child.

2. The counselor uses encouragement whenever possible.

3. The counselor attempts to understand the child by exploring the child's private logic.

4. The counselor tries to redirect the child's teleological movement to increase the child's motivation for change.

5. The session starts with 15 to 30 minutes of self-concept development and ends with 15 to 30 minutes of multimodality creative arts therapy.

6. The counselor uses logical and natural consequences to establish realistic limits.

7. The counselor recognizes the importance of parent and teacher involvement as an adjunct to play therapy.

Over the years, I have found play therapy to be a very effective way to work with children. I believe play is a natural medium for communicating with them. Play allows children an opportunity to relax and be themselves as they work through issues that concern them.

Guidelines for Play Therapy The following guidelines may be useful when implementing a play-therapy program.

Play therapy can be conducted individually or in small groups of two or three children. The play therapy room should be approximately 15′ × 15′. It should be big enough for two adults and four children but small enough to promote a sense of closeness between the counselor and the child. If the room is too large, for example, the child may wander off. The counselor should ensure privacy. No one should be permitted to come into the play therapy room while a session is in progress. Interruptions can be a major distraction from the counseling process.

Different play materials, such as playhouses, puppets, babies, and other family members, should be on hand. Art supplies, like molding clay and watercolors, and musical instruments, like bongo drums and a tambourine, are also useful.

The counselor should establish limits with the child during the first session regarding time and behavior. In terms of time, the session length can vary according to the time available but should not exceed 1 hour. The length of time should be determined before the first session and adhered to as much as possible. Regarding behavior, the counselor should restrain a child who acts in an aggressive, hostile manner. It may even be necessary to discontinue the play therapy session if the child persists in being hostile. When a child abuses a toy, the counselor can use a logical consequence. For example, a counselor might say, "It looks like you're not ready to use the drum today. I'll put it up for now. Some other time, you can try to use it the way it is supposed to be used."

In communicating, counselors should use a friendly, kind voice, especially if they sense a child feels insecure and use an appropriate vocabulary level so that the child will understand their words. They should avoid using a tone of voice that seems to talk down to a child. Although it may be necessary to be firm with a child, it is probably counterproductive to be stern. Counselors should let themselves laugh and have fun with the child, and they should talk from a positive perspective, using encouragement whenever possible.

Play therapy offers a means to reach into the world of the child and help the child reach out to the world of others. It can be used to treat a wide range of problems and concerns. For example, play therapy can be used to help children with autism learn language and other skills necessary to overcome some autistic tendencies (Nystul, 1986).

Play therapy can provide an important dimension to comprehensive developmental counseling programs by helping children overcome tendencies toward reluctance and resistance, fostering problem solving, and so forth (Campbell, 1993). Play therapy has cross-cultural potential by creating a universal language through play and involvement in the creative arts (Cochran, 1996). It can help overcome language barriers and other sources of resistance in order to foster school success in children and adolescents (Cochran).

Several research studies have provided evidence of the efficacy of play therapy. A meta-analysis of 15 research reports on play therapy shows that this approach is superior to nontreatment and promotes general adaptation and intellectual skills (Reams & Friedrich, 1983). Erford et al. (2011) provided additional evidence of the efficacy of play therapy. They conducted a meta-analysis of 42 studies that investigated the effects of counseling and psychotherapy on depression for children and adolescents age 6 to 17. Results of the study provided evidence of the efficacy of counseling and psychotherapy as a treatment for depression in both school and outpatient settings. The effects were maintained at 2 years following termination, and results did not vary according to theoretical orientation (cognitive-behavioral, interpersonal, or family based) or individual versus group format. Additional research seems warranted to gain a clearer understanding of how play therapy can be used with children.

CONFLICT RESOLUTION Specially designed youth-oriented conflict resolution procedures can be used with children (Stern & Newland, 1994) and adolescents (Van Slyck et al., 1996). As noted in Chapter 14, **conflict resolution** is particularly useful in middle school counseling, where problems tend to be related to interpersonal conflict. Youth-oriented conflict resolution, which is used in both school and mental health counseling, has its own unique theories, techniques, and training requirements (Van Slyck et al.).

An overview of the field is as follows (Van Slyck et al., 1996). Youth-oriented conflict resolution is considered distinct from adult conflict resolution in that the youth takes an active role in the process by learning how to manage his or her own conflicts; adults tend to take a more passive role by bringing in a mediator to resolve the conflict (such as in divorce mediation). The overall goal of youth-oriented conflict resolution is to foster problem-solving skills, coping skills, and resiliency characteristics that can be used to overcome conflict and foster optimal development.

Youth-oriented conflict-resolution programs can be both preventative and remedial in nature. Preventative programs are directed at helping young people learn how to apply conflict resolution theory and skills to foster a life with minimal adverse conflicts and stress. Large- and small-group guidance activities to promote conflict resolution as well as adaptations to the school curriculum can play a major role in implementing preventative programs. In contrast, remedial conflict resolution relates to overcoming currently existing conflicts. This can involve the use of peer counseling (e.g., peer mediation) or direct intervention by teachers, staff, and counselors. Regardless of the level of intervention (prevention or remedial), the focus is on helping young people use problem-solving skills to successfully mediate and negotiate problems of living.

Several steps of Dysinger's (1993) youth conflict resolution model have been incorporated into the following framework for conflict resolution problem solving:

1. *Take a positive approach.* Begin by encouraging young people to approach conflict resolution from a win-win perspective. Ground rules are established that promote a positive, strengths perspective rather than an adversarial approach (e.g., no name-calling or threatening).

2. *Listen and respond appropriately.* Help the conflicting parties learn to use listening skills to understand opposing points of view and to respond constructively. Ground rules include no interrupting while others are talking (so that the parties can be in the role of listener and learner) and responding from a position of caring.

3. *Become aware of choices and responsibility.* Youths are encouraged to become aware of the choices they have made and the responsibility they must assume in relation to the conflict. Ground rules include no blaming or whining. Use of personal pronouns can be encouraged to help young people take responsibility for their behavior.

4. *Create solutions that promote friendship.* Identify a new approach that can be used to overcome the conflict. The nature of the new approach will vary with the situation and people involved. For some,

assurance that the other person will not engage in a certain behavior will be enough; for others, simply understanding the other person's point of view can resolve the conflict.

5. ***Follow up.*** Check to see whether the conflict has been resolved and encourage the youths to engage in conflict resolution problem solving if the problem continues. Through cooperation and caring, friendships can be enhanced, and conflicts and stress can be minimized. Lancaster, Lenz, Meadows, and Brown (2013) provided evidence of the efficacy of conflict resolution group counseling for urban African American adolescent girls. The study assessed the effects of six 1.5-hour group conflict resolution counseling sessions that addressed topics such as understanding anger styles and assertive-based conflict resolution. Results of the study provided evidence that conflict resolution group counseling promotes more positive assertive attitudes regarding how to handle conflict, but unfortunately the study did not show evidence of a decrease in tendencies to engage in violence. Additional research relating to these issues appears warranted.

Guidelines for Child and Adolescent Counseling

The following guidelines can be integrated into one's personal approach to counseling children and adolescents.

MAINTAIN A LINE OF COMMUNICATION Parents, teachers, and counselors can get discouraged when counseling children and adolescents. Parents can contribute to communication problems by utilizing a rigid parenting style, for example, using ultimatums like "While under my roof, you'll do as I say—or else." Children and adolescents may create special challenges for adults as they act out rebellious stages, say and do hurtful things, and find ways to annoy others. When this occurs, it is important for concerned adults to maintain a line of communication with the child or adolescent.

The following *Personal Note* provides examples of clinical issues associated with maintaining a line of communication.

A Personal Note

I will always remember what a woman who specialized in working with adolescents told me. She said the most important thing in counseling adolescents is to always maintain a line of communication. It is very easy to lose that connection with adolescents due to a variety of factors, such as the rebelliousness of adolescents and parents who have autocratic parenting styles (e.g., insist on having things their way). Without communication, problems cannot be resolved, and bad situations only get worse.

I have found that several theoretical perspectives can be used to maintain a line of communication with children and adolescents. For example, Glasser (1980) suggested that counselors convey to their clients that they will never give up on them regardless of what they do. Children and adolescents often test their counselors by escalating misbehavior to see if their counselors really mean it. My theory of emotional balancing (described in Chapter 3; see also Nystul, 2002a, 2002b) provides another tool for maintaining a line of communication. According to this theory, a person can maintain meaningful communication and emotional balance by avoiding both emotional disengagement and emotional enmeshment.

USE INTERVENTIONS GROUNDED IN THEORY Theory provides a conceptual framework for understanding and addressing clinical issues. The following *Personal Note* describes why I have found theory to play a key role in child and adolescent counseling.

A Personal Note

Once when I went to an Adlerian conference, I attended a presentation by Professor James Croake. During the presentation, he said that having a solid grounding in theory could be very beneficial for helping relationships and it should be emphasized over technique. I could not agree with him more. I have found that theories (such as theories of personality and theories of child development) promote understanding of *why* the child is misbehaving and so on, and understanding tends to promote interest and compassion, which in turn can foster positive outcomes such as problem resolution.

Interventions grounded in theory are also useful to those in the role of consultant. As a school psychologist, I am often asked by teachers what they should do about a student's misbehavior. My consultation usually focuses on helping them understand the dynamics of the child's or adolescent's misbehavior. In this process, we explore the application of simple, practical theories such as Glasser's (1969) concept of success versus failure identity and Dreikurs's concepts of goals of misbehavior and encouragement versus praise (Dreikurs & Soltz, 1964). These theories are great because they have stood the test of time.

INCORPORATE PARENTING CONCEPTS IN ONE'S APPROACH Parenting programs like Dinkmeyer and McKay's (1997) Systematic Training for Effective Parenting (STEP) can be important adjuncts to child and adolescent counseling. Parenting concepts and ideas can be used to address child/adolescent problems and enhance family relationships (Nystul, 1980b, 1982, 1984, 1987b). Parenting programs such as STEP do not require licensed professionals and are often led by interested parents.

In some instances, more in-depth parenting interventions are required. In these cases, counselors can utilize parenting programs as an adjunct to child and adolescent counseling. Parent management training (PMT) is the most popular parenting program used by counselors to assist parents (Friedlander & Tuason, 2000). PMT is a psychoeducational intervention that helps parents learn procedures to address a number of child and adolescent problems, such as oppositional and conduct disorders, attention-deficit hyperactivity disorder, and delinquency (Estrada & Pinsoff, 1995). PMT has also been used to enhance overall family functioning by reducing family conflict and increasing family cohesion and expression (Sayger, Horne, & Glaser, 1993). Positive gains associated with PMT can be significantly reduced, however, when parents are depressed or experiencing high levels of stress (Webster-Stratton, 1990) or families are disadvantaged or isolated (Estrada & Pinsof).

EMPHASIZE CHOICE AND RESPONSIBILITY Glasser (1998) emphasized the role of choice and responsibility in promoting mental health. Choice and responsibility can be especially useful in child and adolescent counseling strategies to promote optimal development. Parents, teachers, and others can help children and adolescents become aware of their choices and assume responsibility for those choices, resulting in personal and relational benefits. Personal growth resulting from choice and responsibility can include increases in self-efficacy, self-control, self-esteem, and internal locus of control. Relational benefits can include minimizing conflict between the adult and child or adolescent (because the parent is focusing on the child's or adolescent's choices rather than getting sidetracked into issues such as power and control).

UTILIZE THE REACHING IN–REACHING OUT MODEL The **reaching in–reaching out model** can be useful in child and adolescent counseling (Nystul, 1986). Using this approach, counselors find a way into the world of the client and then help the client reach out to the world of others. The more rigid and ritualistic clients are, the more resistant they can be, and therefore the more important it is to meet them on their terms. When clients are met on their terms, they tend to feel safe, thereby lowering their resistance to being with their counselor. As clients let counselors into their world, the resultant existential encounter can be enhanced by enjoyable experiences such as "having fun" with puppets, music, or other creative play modalities.

"Having fun" can set the stage for the reaching-out phase of counseling by increasing the client's motivation for working with the counselor. The reaching-out phase involves a transformation of the self, reflected in a shift in the client's private logic toward increased social interest and willingness to cooperate with the counselor (e.g., "I want to listen and cooperate with my counselor because he can be fun"). Once the transformation of the self has occurred, counselors can help clients reach out to the world of others by directly addressing their problems (such as helping a child with autism learn language skills). Counselors can then work with other concerned adults, like parents and teachers, to help them effectively relate to children and adolescents by applying the reaching in–reaching out approach.

The following *Personal Note* (first described in Chapter 1 in a *Personal Note* relating to the art of counseling) illustrates how to reach into a child's world. The case involved a first-grade girl who had been placed in a class for the mentally retarded. As it turned out, she had been misdiagnosed and was not retarded but autistic.

A Personal Note

When I first saw her, I was not aware that she was autistic. I had brought puppets that I was going to use to present self-concept material and other activities. Her idea of using the puppets was to throw them all in a pile and redo a throw if it didn't land right on the other puppets (that type of ritualistic behavior is common with autistic children). As I attempted to reach into her world (a world in which she felt safe and understood), I became a "puppet basketball net." I circled my arms around her pile of puppets and yelled, "Two points!" when she threw one into my circle. Over time, she felt safe with me and began to welcome my company. I used this interest to encourage her to reach out to the world of others by fostering her language development and eventually finding ways to help her break out of some of the rigidity of her autistic world.

Over the years, I have reflected on this case and have come to believe that, to some degree, all counseling is a reaching in–reaching out process. Initially in counseling, I find ways to reach into my client's world. With children, this can be through play therapy; with adults, perhaps I discover the personal meaning of their stories through creative arts therapy or listening skills. After a while, we establish a positive counseling relationship that provides the basis for encouraging my clients to reach out in new directions, expand their horizons, and foster their optimal development.

ETHICAL ISSUES RELATING TO CHILD AND ADOLESCENT COUNSELING Lawrence and Kurpius (2000) noted that ethical-legal issues regarding counseling minors are an emerging area of concern. Counseling children and adolescents is a specialty that requires unique competencies—such as ethical-legal decision making—in clinical practice. Ethical-legal issues relating to informed consent, confidentiality, and reporting child abuse and neglect raise particular challenges for counselors. It is important for counselors to be aware of this information to determine the rights parents and minors have to confidential information and how these issues impact the counseling process.

Informed Consent Corey, Corey, Corey, and Callanon (2015) noted that most states require parental consent for minors to receive counseling services. Some states permit minors in crisis situations, such as those involving substance abuse, to enter into a counseling relationship without parental permission (Corey et al.). Counselors should therefore be aware of the laws relating to informed consent in their state.

Confidentiality Confidentiality is handled in a distinct way when counseling minors, and the rules vary according to federal and state laws, settings, and ethical codes. Ansell (1987) described confidentiality as a gray area that requires the counselor to proceed with caution when dealing with minors. Conflicts can result from the counselor's legal responsibility to respect a parent's right to be informed of counseling services and the ethical responsibility to maintain the confidentiality of the minor (Huey, 1986).

Ansell (1987) suggested that counselors establish guidelines with the parents and the minor regarding the nature of information that can be released to parents. The ACA's (2014) ethical code can be used to structure these guidelines:

> When counseling minor clients or adult clients who lack the capacity to give voluntary, informed consent, counselors protect the confidentiality of information received—in any medium—in the counseling relationship as specified by federal and state laws, written policies, and applicable ethical standards." (B.5.a)

The counselor can therefore suggest that confidential information will be released to parents when the counselor believes it is in the child's best interest.

Parents are also legally entitled to have access to their child's or adolescent's confidential records (Thompson & Rudolph, 2007). Personal notes are exempt from this requirement when they are kept separate from institutional files; when they are not seen by anyone, including clerical staff; and when they were not discussed with anyone in the process of decision making (Thompson & Henderson, 2007).

Child Abuse All states have laws relating to child abuse (Thompson & Henderson, 2007), and most require counselors to report suspected abuse (Congdon, 1987). These laws usually "include penalties for failure to report and provide immunity for the reporter from criminal and civil liability" (Congdon). Counselors should limit their reporting of information to that required by law. Reporting additional information can make the counselor guilty of releasing privileged information (Congdon).

Special Problems of Children and Adolescents

This section is an overview of some of the special problems experienced by children and adolescents: child abuse and neglect, depression, and antisocial behavior. For each type of problem, information is presented on incidence, assessment, causes, effects, and treatment.

Child Abuse and Neglect

Children have been abused and neglected throughout history, but it was not until the early 1960s that child abuse and neglect became recognized as social problems that require comprehensive treatment (Wolfe, 1988). This section reviews some of the issues associated with child abuse and neglect.

INCIDENCE Papalia et al. (2007) noted that the incidence of child abuse and neglect in the United States had decreased by 20% since 1993, when it was at its highest level. In 2002, state child protective service agencies in the United States investigated and confirmed 896,000 cases of child abuse and neglect, although the actual number was estimated to be much higher. In addition, approximately 1,400 children died of abuse and neglect in the United States in 2002, with 76% being 3 years old or younger. Papalia et al. also noted that of the children who experience abuse or neglect, approximately 60% were neglected, 20% were physically abused, 10% were sexually abused, and 7% experienced emotional (psychological) abuse.

ASSESSMENT Early identification and treatment of child abuse and neglect are critical to minimizing negative effects on the child. The following are warning signs of the various forms of child abuse and neglect (Salkind, 1994):

- *Physical abuse.* Signs of bruises, burns, and broken bones

- *Child neglect.* Poor health and hygiene and excessive school absenteeism

- *Sexual abuse.* Use of sexually explicit terminology, nightmares, genital injury, and sexually transmitted disease

- *Psychological (emotional) abuse.* Depression, self-deprecation, somatic (bodily) complaints such as headaches or stomachaches, and fear of adults

The assessment of child abuse and neglect is a multistage process (Wolfe, 1988). It usually begins with impressionistic data from the reporting and referral source. That stage is followed by a refinement of information during interviews with parents and the child (Wolfe). Much of the initial information regarding the functioning of the parent and child can be obtained in a semistructured interview with the parent (Wolfe). The Parent Interview and Assessment Guide can be used to structure the interview and provide information on family background, marital relationship, areas of stress and support, and symptomatology (Wolfe). Several instruments can be used to survey the attitudes of parents on topics relating to marriage and the family. The Child Abuse Potential Inventory (Milner, 1986) identifies familial patterns associated with child abuse. The Childhood Level of Living Scale (Polansky, Chalmers, Buttenwieser, & Williams, 1981) measures the degree of positive and negative influences in the home and is particularly useful for assessing neglect (Wolfe).

CAUSES Research shows that child abuse results from a complex interaction of events. Wolfe (1988) summarized the research by noting that child abuse is a special type of aggression resulting from proximal and distal events.

Proximal events are those that precipitate abuse. A proximal event can involve a child's behavior or an adult conflict that triggers the abuse. Common child behaviors that can trigger child abuse are aggression, unspecified misbehavior, lying, and stealing (Kadushin & Martin, 1981). Marital problems and violence are also associated with child abuse (Straus, Gelles, & Steinmetz, 1980). *Distal events* are those that are indirectly associated with child abuse. These factors include low socioeconomic status and poverty, restricted educational and occupational opportunities, unstable family environment, excessive heat, overcrowding, ambient noise level, and unemployment (Wolfe, 1988).

Other research has attempted to identify characteristics of abusive parents as a means of understanding the causes of child abuse. Abusive parents tend to have been abused as children, have difficulty coping with stress, suffer from substance abuse problems, be immature and hold unrealistic expectations of children, and have children with special needs that require extra time and energy (Talbutt, 1986). A typical profile of parents at high risk for child abuse describes them as tending to be young, poorly educated, single, living in poverty, socially isolated, and feeling little support from a significant other (DeHart et al., 2004). Abusive mothers tend to have a negative attitude toward their pregnancy (DeHart et al.). Compared to nonabusive parents, they tend to have less understanding of what is involved in caring for an infant, are less prone to plan for pregnancy, do not attend childbirth classes, do not have special living quarters for the baby to sleep, and have unrealistic expectations about raising an infant.

EFFECTS Physical neglect that results from not meeting a child's basic needs, like food and shelter, tends to produce a lack of competency in dealing with the tasks of daily living, such as personal hygiene. Physical abuse and emotional unavailability often result in behavioral and emotional problems, such as avoidance of intimacy in relationships, aggressiveness with peers, and blunted emotions (DeHart et al., 2004). Psychologically abused children can develop neurotic traits, conduct disorders, negative self-image, and distorted relations with others (Craig, 2002; Hart & Brassard, 1987).

Sexual abuse can have traumatic and enduring effects. Children who have been victimized by sexual abuse often suffer significant psychological distress, with approximately half meeting the criteria for posttraumatic stress disorder (PTSD; Putman, 2009). A number of symptoms are associated with child sexual abuse and PTSD (Putman):

- Fear reactions and phobic avoidance of males

- Reenactment of the traumatic event via nightmares, traumatic play, flashbacks, and intrusive thoughts

- Dissociation or altered state of consciousness (can include amnesia, sleepwalking, and trancelike states) contributing to loss of memory and loss of personal identity

- Avoidance of stimuli associated with trauma via cognitive suppression and behavioral avoidance, undermining overall functioning

- Emotional detachment characterized by blunted affect

- Negative sense of self (self-blame and reduction in self-efficacy) and the future

- Heightened state of arousal, including sleep problems, exaggerated startle response, trouble concentrating, and aggression

Putman (2009) noted it is common for children who have been victimized by sexual abuse to have suicidal ideations and multiple *DSM* disorders. *DSM* disorders that commonly occur with PTSD include attention deficit hyperactivity disorder (ADHD), mood disorders (e.g., major depression), and anxiety disorders (e.g., social phobias). Putman suggested that it is important to obtain an accurate diagnosis, screen for possible risks for suicide, and address these clinical issues as necessary.

Sexual abuse can damage a child in several ways (O'Brien, 1983):

- *Psychological effects.* Sexual experiences can be confusing for children because they are unable to understand the strong emotional feelings associated with sex.

- *Low self-esteem.* Children may blame themselves for permitting the sexual contact or may feel dirty or ashamed as a result of the experience.

- *Exploitation.* Sexually abused children may feel used and develop a hostile, suspicious attitude toward others.

- *Vulnerability.* Because children are dependent on adults, they are vulnerable to and trusting of adults. When that trust is broken, children may develop a negative attitude toward vulnerability, making it difficult for them to develop trust and intimacy in their relationships.

- *Distorted view of sexuality.* It is common for sexually abused children to develop a very negative or perverted attitude toward sex. As they grow up, they may avoid sex or become sexually promiscuous.

- *Violation of the child's privacy.* After an incestuous relationship is discovered, the abused child must cooperate with the authorities. This violation of the child's privacy can be traumatic and anxiety provoking.

- *Distorted moral development.* Sexual abuse often occurs between the ages of 9 and 11, when a child's moral development is being formulated. Children can become confused about what is right and wrong when an adult is allowed to violate them sexually.

The following *Personal Note* illustrates how difficult it can be for a child to deal consciously with the trauma of sexual abuse.

A Personal Note

When I was a psychologist at a hospital, I worked with several girls who had babies as a result of sexual trauma (e.g., being raped by their fathers). These girls tended to use denial as a means of coping with what had happened.

For example, I met a 14-year-old girl the day before she had her baby. She insisted that she was not even pregnant. After she had the baby, she said that the baby was not hers. This patient required extensive counseling and psychotherapy to develop a realistic approach to her situation.

TREATMENT The most hopeful treatment for abusive parents involves "resocialization" tasks, which help parents overcome isolation and foster interpersonal relations and support (Brockman, 1987). These efforts can include encouraging parents to join Parents Anonymous or other self-help groups. Several preventative programs can also be promoted in schools (Brockman), including adult education, interpersonal training for students, courses on sexuality and parenting in high school, and guest speakers from organizations like Parents Anonymous.

Thompson and Wilcox (1995), on the other hand, noted that little empirical evidence supports the social-isolation theory of child abuse, citing numerous examples of parents who are provided social support and who continue to engage in child abuse because of many other stressors (such as substance abuse problems). They contended that child abuse and neglect are a cross-disciplinary problem that should be addressed by research and intervention teams composed of people from disciplines like psychology, social work, and sociology, because such teams can gain a more comprehensive understanding of the causes and treatment strategies associated with child mistreatment.

Treatment efforts can also be directed at the abused child. Group counseling can be especially effective in working with abused and neglected children (Damon & Waterman, 1986) and adolescents (Hazzard, King, & Webb, 1986) to foster self-esteem, overcome problems with trust, correct distorted cognitions, and enhance self-control skills (Kitchur & Bell, 1989). Play therapy has also been used extensively with abused children (White & Allers, 1994). A review of this literature shows a pattern of unique behaviors that emerged in conducting play therapy with abused children. Some of these behaviors include developmental immaturity, repetitive and compulsive behavior, opposition and aggression, withdrawal and passivity, self-depreciation and self-destructive behavior, hypervigilance, sexual behavior, and dissociation (an unconscious denial of abuse). The nature of play among these children is also distinctive; abused children are not very imaginative in their play, and their play does not seem to alleviate their anxiety.

Special treatment considerations relating to sexual abuse can be represented using a three-stage model called the *resolution model* (Orenchuk-Tomiuk, Matthey, & Christensen, 1990). The three stages are (a) the noncommittal or oppositional stage, (b) the middle stage, and (c) the resolution stage. The model differentiates among treatment issues for the child, the nonoffending parent, and the offending parent at each stage, as follows:

- The child feels responsible for the abuse during the noncommittal or oppositional stage, feels angry and experiences symptoms associated with posttraumatic stress disorder during the middle stage, and no longer feels responsible for the sexual abuse or experiences problematic symptoms during the resolution stage.

- The nonoffending parent denies the occurrence of sexual abuse, blames the child for disclosure, and defends the offender during the noncommittal or oppositional stage; believes the abuse has taken place and begins to become an ally for the child during the middle stage; and becomes a positive ally for the child and works through guilt associated with not protecting the child during the resolution stage.

- The offender refuses to accept responsibility for abuse and/or denies its occurrence during the noncommittal or oppositional stage, is able to admit to the abuse but may blame the child during the middle stage, and assumes responsibility for the abuse and establishes a more positive parental role during the resolution stage.

The resolution model recommends that individual and group counseling can be useful during the noncommittal or oppositional stage. Couples and family counseling should not be used until the middle or resolution stages and should involve the child only if the child is ready.

Some guidelines that counselors can use with children who have been sexually abused are that counselors should take on the role of advocate for sexually abused children; help them overcome feelings of guilt and shame, emphasizing that the abuse was not their fault and that it will stop; use open-ended questions when assessing for sexual abuse and thus avoid leading questions; and take accusations seriously, since children tend not to lie about sexual abuse and psychological harm can occur if they are not taken seriously (England & Thompson, 1988).

Additional counseling strategies that can be used to treat PTSD associated with sexual abuse are art and play therapy, which can facilitate expressions of trauma associated with sexual abuse. Cognitive-behavioral therapy is believed to be the most effective approach for treating PTSD symptoms. For example, cognitive-behavioral strategies can be directed at overcoming cognitive confusion and intrusive memories of the abuse; group counseling can also be included in the treatment plan to promote coping skills, problem-solving strategies, and peer support and encouragement (Putman, 2009).

Depression

The recognition of childhood and adolescent depression is a relatively recent occurrence (Petersen et al., 1993; Wagner, 1994, 1996). This section reviews some of the major issues associated with depression in children and adolescents.

INCIDENCE Research suggests that children are as capable of experiencing clinical depression as adults (Alper, 1986; Kovacs, 1989). Serious depression has been found in infants (Field et al., 1988; Spitz, 1946), preschool and school-age children (Digdon & Gotlib, 1985; Kazdin, 1988; Kovacs), and adolescents (Petersen et al., 1993; Rice & Meyer, 1994; Wagner, 1996). One in 8 adolescents (ages 10–19) experience depression (Dixon, Scheidegger, & McWhirter, 2009), with 30% of adolescents exhibiting some symptoms of depression (Erford et al. 2011). The average duration of a major depression in children and adolescents is 7 to 9 months, and a dysthymic depression lasts an average of 3 or more years (Kovacs).

Manic disorders in their classic form are rare and hard to diagnose accurately in children and adolescents (Strober, Hanna, & McCracken, 1989). An overview of bipolar disorder in children reveals that children experience much higher rates of this disorder than previously believed (Hammen & Rudolph, 2003). The disorder was apparently underdiagnosed because children do not present with the symptoms of bipolar disorder typically experienced by adults. For example, children can cycle through their manic-depressive states in one day (versus adults, who spend days in each state). In addition, children do not experience the euphoria and grandiosity states common in adults with bipolar disorder. Diagnosing bipolar disorder in children is also difficult due to the wide array of psychological symptoms that may present, including rapid mood shifts often characterized by intense irritability, aggression, and rage; destructive, social, and academic problems; and psychosis, delusions, and suicidal thoughts and behaviors (Hammen & Rudolph). Bipolar disorder in children typically is comorbid with other mental disorders, such as ADHD, anxiety disorders, oppositional-defiant disorder, and substance abuse.

ASSESSMENT As noted earlier in this chapter, developmental psychopathology provides a framework for understanding how mental disorders such as depression vary over the life span (including during childhood and adolescence). Some major symptoms associated with childhood depression include the following (Sakolske & Janzen, 1987). Changes in mood and affect are the most obvious indications. Examples include children who were relatively happy and had positive self-images suddenly saying they are sad, miserable, and no good. Another indication is that depressed children tend to show a lack of interest in activities that were previously enjoyable, such as hobbies and sports. They may also lose interest in friends and family members. Other symptoms include physical complaints such as headaches and abdominal discomfort; sleep disturbances including nightmares; changes in appetite; impaired cognitive processes such as difficulty concentrating; and problems in school, work, and interpersonal relationships. Depressed adolescents typically show signs of unhappiness and have a number of fears and worries, such as a fear of not being loved or not having friends, and they may worry about their appearance and relationships (Petersen et al., 1993). In addition, it is estimated that adolescents experience major depression at a much higher rate than do children (Petersen et al.).

To be diagnosed with major depression, a person (regardless of age) must meet the established criteria. For example, the *DSM-5* (American Psychiatric Association, 2013) includes such factors as depressed mood, decreased ability to experience pleasure, weight loss (or failure to thrive in children), loss of energy, thoughts of death, and so forth. The *DSM-5* also notes that certain symptoms such as hypersomnia (excessive sleepiness) and hyperphagia (obsessive-compulsive behavior toward food, such as continuing to eat when full) are more common in younger individuals. Onset of depression at earlier ages is associated with familial issues and personality disturbances (American Psychiatric Association).

Multiple diagnoses (comorbidity) are common with depressed children and adolescents. Depression under these circumstances is sometimes referred to by clinicians as a "masked depression," since the symptoms of depression are obscured by the additional diagnosis (Kovacs, 1989). Bipolar disorder is particularly difficult to diagnose in children, because it typically occurs in conjunction with severe symptoms such as psychosis and mental disorders such as ADHD and anxiety disorders (Hammen & Rudolph, 2003). Because it potentially masks bipolar disorder, ADHD poses a significant challenge to the diagnostic process.

Several instruments have been designed specifically to assess childhood and adolescent depression. For example, diagnostic interviews have been developed to assess child and adolescent mental disorders (Edelbrock & Costello, 1988). Most other instruments are directed at children, one of the most widely used being the Children's Depression Inventory (Kovacs, 2003), which was developed from the Beck Depression Inventory. It assesses the cognitive, affective, and behavioral signs of depression. The Hamilton Rating Scale for Depression (Hamilton, 1960) has been updated over the years and is considered one the best clinician-administered interviews for screening depression in children (Muller & Erford, 2012). Muller and Erford also noted that the Beck Depression Inventory II (Beck, Steer, & Brown 1996) and the Reynolds Adolescent Depression Scale (Reynolds, 2002) are two excellent screening instruments for adolescent depression. Other instruments include the Short Children's Depression Inventory (Carlson & Cantwell, 1979), the Children's Depression Scale (Lang &

Tisher, 1978), and the Schedule for Affective Disorders and Schizophrenia for School-Age Children (Chambers, Puig-Antich, & Tabrizi, 1978). All of these instruments are described in Kazdin (1988).

CAUSES Several factors have been associated with childhood depression, including parents who have high standards and do not express positive affect to their child (Cole & Rehm, 1986); children who have negative cognitive schemata characterized by self-deprecation, hopelessness, and despair (Hammer & Zupan, 1984); and social-skill and problem-solving deficits (Altmann & Gotlib, 1988). The underlying etiology of bipolar disorder in children is primarily associated with genetics (Hammen & Rudolph, 2003). The ecological perspective for conceptualizing mental health problems of children recognizes the effects of the "povertization of childhood" (Wagner, 1994). Wagner noted that 25% of children aged 5 or younger are living in poverty, and a great number of these children are born to single mothers. This "povertization" has been associated with impeding the development of children and having a devastating effect on their well-being (Wagner).

Major causes of adolescent depression (many of which also seem relevant to childhood depression) include pessimistic-negative cognitions; genetic predisposition (a parent with a history of depression); and social-systemic factors such as excessive environmental stress, problems with home (including family and marital discord), school, and peer group (Petersen et al., 1993). Ashby, Dickinson, Gnilka, and Noble (2011) found that adolescents who are adaptive perfectionists (who believe that setbacks are necessary for success) tend to have more hope and less depression than maladaptive perfectionists (who contend that setbacks are a sign of failure) and nonperfectionists. It is interesting to note that one of the best predictors of adult depression is impaired peer group relations during adolescence. The importance of social networking and mental health was revealed in research that found adolescents who perceived they mattered to others were less prone to develop anxiety or depression (with mattering to others and anxiety and depression having an inverse correlation; Dixon et al., 2009).

From an existential perspective, Frankl's (1963) logotherapy seems ideally suited to addressing adolescent depression, because adolescence can be a challenging period of development as youths struggle with issues of self-awareness; personal identity; peer pressure; and experimentation with alcohol, drugs, and sexuality (Blair, 2004). As adolescents attempt to define their existence, they can experience an existential vacuum or a lack of meaning in life associated with not living up to one's potential. Adolescents who struggle with identity issues, as they attempt to define themselves and give their life meaning, can experience symptoms of depression such as sadness and despair (Blair). Problems regarding the emergence of the "self" can result from the conflicting demands from the adolescents' peer group and the expectations of their parents.

EFFECTS Depression in childhood and adolescence can have serious consequences: impaired cognition (Kovacs, Palauskas, Gatsonis, & Richards, 1988; Petersen et al., 1993); problems with social and educational progress (Kovacs et al.; Petersen et al.);

and suicidal tendencies (Garland & Zigler, 1993; Kovacs, 1989). Bipolar disorder in children is associated with suicidal tendencies and impairment in social relationships, academic achievement, self-control, and ability to maintain contact with reality (Hammen & Rudolph, 2003). Even if a person does not become depressed as a child, childhood experiences can make an individual prone to depression as an adult. For example, children who experience the death of their mother before they are 11 years of age are more prone than other children to develop depression as adults (Brown & Harris, 1978).

TREATMENT Treatment considerations for depression and bipolar disorders vary when working with children and adolescents. Antidepressant medication can be considered in the treatment of depression, although there are mixed reports regarding its efficacy for children (Puig-Antich et al., 1987) and some concern that antidepressants can cause an increased risk for suicide in children and adolescents (Erford et al., 2011). Several counseling approaches are available for treating childhood depression. Among them, cognitive approaches have been particularly effective (Reynolds & Coats, 1986). Rasmussen (2014) noted that inherent in virtually all *DSM-5* disorders (including depression) is a sense of discouragement and despair. Parent education can be used to encourage children and adolescents and increase their social interest (Rasmussen). Play therapy can also be used to treat depression in children by creating a supportive environment for children to work through their social-emotional issues (Landreth, 1993, 2012).

An overview of existential strategies, based on Frankl's (1963) logotherapy, that can be used to treat adolescent depression can be summarized as follows (Blair, 2004):

- Counselors should build a relationship of respect and trust by emotionally connecting with clients and maintaining a nonjudgmental position.

- Counselors should help clients understand the purpose behind the depression (e.g., it can create motivation for self-exploration and change).

- Counselors should assist clients in identifying what is missing in their lives (i.e., what is necessary to reach their full potential).

- Counselors should address the clients' strengths, talents, and interests that they can use to achieve necessary change.

- Counselors should facilitate clients' search for meaning by emphasizing that they have choices, are free to make choices, and must ultimately take responsibility for their choices.

Dixon et al. (2009) suggested that since adolescent anxiety and depression have been related to perceived mattering to others, counselors can explore how adolescents perceive their relationships with others. In this process, counselors can explore perceptions regarding peer group, friends, and family to enhance social support systems, personal meaning, and mental health. McCarthy, Downes, and Sherman (2008) conducted qualitative research that involved interviewing young adults who had been diagnosed and treated for major depression when they were adolescents. Themes that emerged from the study included the following:

- Simply talking about depression helped.

- Counseling brought relief from the depression and was viewed as more helpful than medication.

- Friends often provided important support.

- Parents played critical roles (e.g., were copartners in the recovery process).

Bipolar disorders in children and adolescents require special treatment considerations. The most important treatment issue is an accurate diagnosis. In fact, some clinicians contend that early detection and treatment of bipolar disorder in children can lessen the effects of the disorder and that misdiagnosis can make the course of the disorder worse (Hammen & Rudolph, 2003). However, accurate diagnosis of bipolar disorder in children can be a daunting task since, as noted earlier, it is often comorbid with other disorders such as ADHD and a wide range of psychological features like extreme mood changes and rage.

Medication can play a major role in the treatment of bipolar disorder. Establishing an effective treatment regime can be challenging, however, since medications used to treat one disorder can undermine the treatment of a coexisting disorder. For example, antidepressant medications may trigger hypomania and the rapid cycling associated with bipolar disorder, and psychostimulants used to treat ADHD can have an adverse effect on both depression and mania (Hammen & Rudolph, 2003).

Suicide

Child and adolescent suicide is a special problem that has far-reaching consequences extending beyond the victim to the family, community, and society. It is a complex phenomenon that has been linked to factors such as depression. This section reviews some of the trends in research on suicide among children and adolescents in the United States based on Capuzzi and Nystul (1986), Goldman and Beardslee (1999), and Feldman (2008).

INCIDENCE Suicide rates for children and adolescents have increased dramatically since 1950. For example, adolescents committed 2.7 suicides per 100,000 in 1950, 5.2 per 100,000 in 1960, and 13.8 per 100,000 in 1994. In addition, it is estimated that every 90 minutes an adolescent commits suicide and, for every successful suicide, there are approximately 200 suicide attempts (Feldman, 2008). The suicide rate for children is approximately one tenth of that for adolescents. Among children, suicide is the fifth leading cause of death; it is the third leading cause of death among adolescents. Of particular concern is the fact that children's suicide rates appear to be increasing.

The disparity of suicide rates between children and adolescents has been attributed to a number of factors. Children have less ability to plan and carry out a successful suicide than adolescents, in part due to their lower level of cognitive functioning and the fact that they have less access to lethal weapons. Children also have fewer problems with feelings of hopelessness and helplessness that are often associated with suicide. They tend to live in the present and therefore do not believe that feelings of hopelessness and helplessness will be ongoing. In addition, children tend to be more comfortable with feelings of helplessness because childhood is characterized by high levels of dependence for survival. Lower suicide rates among children can also be attributed to parents monitoring them more closely than adolescents.

The incidence of suicide varies according to gender, sexual orientation, and culture. Females think about and attempt suicide at significantly higher rates than do males (4:1 and 3:1, respectively), yet males commit 5 times as many successful suicides as females. In part this may be due to males using more violent suicidal methods, such as lethal weapons, and females tending to use pills, which may allow for successful medical interventions. Sexual orientation has also been associated with increased risk of suicide. The rate of successful suicide is much higher for LGBTQ adolescents than for the general population. In these instances, a lack of acceptance of sexual orientation by friends, family, and society may have undermined identity formation during adolescence. Culture has also been associated with different rates of childhood and adolescent suicide. Native Americans have the highest rates of adolescent suicide, followed by Anglos and then African Americans. Native American youth suicide rates appear to be higher in tribes that place a lower emphasis on traditional values.

ASSESSMENT The pathway to child and adolescent suicide involves a complex set of factors. Increased vulnerability is associated with psychopathology, such as depression and substance abuse; stress from problems of living (e.g., teen pregnancy); family factors, such as family dysfunction, violence, and abuse; a lack of coping and problem-solving skills; and an insufficient social-emotional support system. The MMPI (means, motive, plan, and intent) acronym can be used to assess for suicide. For example, an adolescent who insists he wants to kill himself because of a recent breakup would have high intent and motive. If he had a loaded gun in his car, he would also have the means and a plan and would be considered a high risk for suicide.

CAUSES Suicide can be understood from a number of perspectives. The biochemical model is based on the chemical imbalance associated with depression and resultant increased risk for suicide. The psychological perspective focuses on feelings such as hopelessness and despair and how a child or adolescent can view suicide as a way out of his or her problems. Developmental theory suggests that a child or adolescent may commit suicide as a response to conflict over identity formation.

EFFECTS The effects of suicide transcend the victim, affecting the victim's family, school, community, and society. Loved ones are left to contend with a wide array of feelings, such as anger and guilt. It is also common for friends and family members to spend considerable time and energy wondering why the act was committed and whether there was anything they could have done to prevent the suicide.

TREATMENT Suicide prevention plays a central role in treatment. Children and adolescents must be assessed and monitored for suicidal ideations and actions, and parents and school officials are an important part of this process. Any child who appears sad or depressed should be referred to the school counselor for assessment of possible suicide. Schools can take other preventive actions, such as promoting resiliency characteristics to enhance coping mechanisms for stress. Once a child or adolescent is identified as suicidal, suicide contracts can be used that require a parent and/or child/adolescent to notify a mental health worker if the child/adolescent becomes actively suicidal. Hospitalization and treatment should be considered when a child/adolescent is at high risk for suicide. Once children/adolescents are stabilized in terms of their suicidal ideations, counseling can focus on identifying underlying causal factors associated with their suicidal tendencies. Treatment can then be directed at resolving these issues to enhance overall psychological functioning.

Antisocial Behavior

Antisocial behavior in children and adolescents includes acts that violate major social rules—among them violence and aggression, bullying, lying, stealing, and truancy (Kazdin, Bass, Siegel, & Thomas, 1989). This section reviews some of the issues associated with antisocial behavior.

INCIDENCE Some researchers suggest that children and adolescents are being raised in a "culture of violence" as reflected in increasingly high rates of domestic violence, hate crimes, and other antisocial activities (Weinhold, 2007, p. 186). The incidence of children engaging in antisocial behavior is high, and one third to one half of all mental health clinical referrals involve such behavior (Kazdin et al., 1989). Rates of antisocial behavior in the form of delinquency are also high, with 6% of violent crimes in the United States—such as rape, murder, assault, and robbery—being committed by youths under 15 and 16% committed by adolescents 15 to 18 years of age (Berger & Thompson, 2000). Worldwide, a person is more likely to be arrested during adolescence and young adulthood than at any other time.

Incidents of school shootings are increasing. Although multiple factors can be associated with violence, bullying is receiving attention as a contributing factor to school violence. Bullying is unprovoked and repeated aggressive behavior that causes distress to its victim and verbal or physical behavior that disturbs someone who is less powerful (Goldstein, 1999; Nansel et al., 2001). The incidence of bullying varies with age and setting and appears to peak in middle school (Goldstein, 1999). Bullying appears to be widespread, affecting 1 in 3 students between 6th and 10th grade (Nansel et al., 2001). Children and adolescents who were bullied may later retaliate with violence (Wartik, 2001). The two Columbine High School shooters and the Santee, California, shooter are believed to have been victims of bullying.

ASSESSMENT Children or adolescents who engage in a well-established pattern of antisocial behavior may receive a *DSM-5* diagnosis of either conduct disorder or oppositional-defiant disorder (ODD). Conduct disorder is the more serious mental disorder and "is a repetitive and persistent pattern of behavior in which the basic rights of others or major age-appropriate societal norms or rules are violated" (American Psychiatric Association, 2013, p. 472). The main feature of ODD "is a frequent and persistent pattern of angry/irritable mood, argumentative/defiant behavior, or vindictiveness" (American Psychiatric Association, p. 463). ODD is one of the most common and challenging mental health disorders of children and adolescents, affecting 5% to 10% of children ages 8 to 16 (Erford, Paul, Oncken, Kress, & Erford, 2014). Erford et al. also noted that ODD is more common in males than females and often occurs with other disorders such as anxiety, depression, and ADHD (e.g., 30% to 60% of individuals diagnosed with ADHD are also diagnosed with ODD).

A number of instruments can be used to assess antisocial behavior (McMahon & Forehand, 1988), including several structured interviews developed especially for children. One of these is the Diagnostic Interview Schedule for Children, a highly structured interview that can be used with children aged 6 to 18 and their parents (Costello, Edelbrock, Dulcan, & Kalas, 1984). The Child Behavior Checklist (Achenback & Edelbrock, 1983), one of the most popular instruments, can be used with children aged 2 to 16 and provides a comprehensive assessment of behaviorally disordered children (McMahon & Forehand). An advantage of this scale is that it has parallel forms for the child, parent, teacher, and observer. The Revised Behavior Problem Checklist (Quay & Petersen, 1983) can be used to detect tendencies toward conduct problems, personality problems, inadequacy and immaturity, and socialized delinquency. This scale is completed by parents or teachers.

Assessment of aggression can involve identifying types of aggression. Strassberg, Dodge, Pettit, and Bates (1994) suggested that there are three types of aggression: instrumental, reactive, and bullying. *Instrumental aggression* involves the use of aggression to retaliate against someone who is caught doing something wrong (e.g., someone who has stolen or is trying to steal something). *Reactive aggression* is impulsive violence in response to a perceived wrongdoing and involves attributing blame without understanding whether the act was intentional or accidental. *Bullying aggression* is a hostile response to others for no apparent reason. A different perspective on bullying aggression is to view it as as *proactive aggression* (Brown & Parsons, 1998). Proactive aggression is a socially learned response; the aggressive individual may believe that problems can be solved by aggression. Proactive aggression tends to be well planned and goal directed and includes bullying or other acts of aggression to achieve a desired goal.

CAUSES Patterson, DeBaryshe, and Ramsey (1989) suggested that antisocial behavior is a developmental trait that begins in childhood and often continues into adolescence and adulthood. These authors utilized a social-interactional perspective, which suggests that family members train children to engage in antisocial behaviors

(Snyder, 1977; Wahler & Dumas, 1987). According to this theory, when parents do not adequately reinforce pro-social behavior or effectively punish deviant behavior, children learn to use antisocial behaviors to stop aversive intrusions from other family members. From this perspective, antisocial behavior can be viewed as the manifestation of survival skills necessary to cope with a dysfunctional family.

Aggression has been linked to the parents' use of spanking as a disciplinary measure (Strassberg et al., 1994). Spanking does not appear to be related to instrumental aggression (i.e., children retaliating for a known wrong regardless of whether they were spanked). Instead, spanking is related to reactive aggression. Children who were spanked are twice as likely as children who were not spanked to use an aggressive response to an accidental or intentional provocation. Bullying aggression is related to children who have been severely punished.

McMahon and Forehand's (1988) overview of studies that identify factors associated with conduct disorders and antisocial behaviors indicates that children with conduct disorders also tend to exhibit impaired peer relationships (Achenback & Edelbrock, 1983), misattribute hostile intentions to others (Milich & Dodge, 1984), have deficits in social problem-solving skills (Asarnow & Calan, 1985), lack empathy (Ellis, 1982), are prone to hyperactivity (Loeber & Schmaling, 1985) and depression (Chiles, Miller, & Cox, 1980), have low levels of academic achievement, and have a genetic predisposition to develop antisocial tendencies (Kazdin, 1985). Antisocial children also have deficits in interpersonal cognitive problem-solving skills (such as formulating solutions to problems), impaired cognitive development (such as moral reasoning), and maladaptive cognitive strategies (such as impulsiveness; Kazdin et al., 1989). Another series of studies has found a link between the influence of the peer group and acts of delinquency and substance abuse (Elliott, Huizinga, & Ageton, 1985; Huba & Bentler, 1983; Kandel, 1973).

EFFECTS Many factors that are typically seen as causes of antisocial behavior, such as academic failure and peer rejection, can more accurately be understood as effects (Patterson et al., 1989). For example, research has shown that childhood aggression leads to rejection by the peer group, not the reverse (Cole & Kupersmidt, 1983; Dodge, 1983). The effects of antisocial behavior tend to last from childhood into adulthood (Kazdin et al., 1989). Individuals diagnosed with antisocial behavior disorders tend to disproportionately experience problems as adults, including criminal behavior, alcoholism, and antisocial personality disorders. Children who engage in antisocial behavior are also prone to become delinquents (Patterson et al.). Approximately one half of antisocial children become delinquent adolescents, and one half to three fourths of delinquent adolescents become adult offenders. The impact of delinquency on society is great, with 16% of arrests for serious crimes being committed by individuals under 18 years of age (Feldman, 2008).

Another effect of childhood/adolescent aggression is that it can evolve into bullying if the bullying is rewarded (i.e., if the child/adolescent gets away with being a bully). Victims of bullying are believed to have an increased risk of suicide and be more likely to engage in retaliatory violence against others (Wartik, 2001).

TREATMENT Counseling antisocial individuals can be a very difficult endeavor, as it involves trying to stop a pattern of behavior that began during childhood and has evolved into a lifestyle. By the time these individuals are adolescents, many are active in gangs and find the possibility of getting out of a gang either undesirable or impossible. It is therefore not surprising that there has been limited success in overcoming antisocial behavior (Kazdin, 1987; Wilson & Herrnstein, 1985).

Erford, House, and Martin (2013) conducted a meta-analysis of 31 studies regarding youths aged 6 to 17 years with oppositional behavior. Results of the study showed counseling and psychotherapy approaches (including individual, group, family, and parent training) generate positive outcomes regarding the reduction oppositional behavior following termination. Long-term gains were less consistent, suggesting problems with relapse that could be addressed by incorporating follow-up sessions following termination.

Special education programs are another form of intervention that has shown some success in treating antisocial youth. In the United States, public schools provide closely supervised educational experiences for students with serious emotional disturbance and behavioral disorders, many with a history of antisocial behavior (Thompson & Henderson, 2007). These classes utilize a number of strategies to help students overcome emotional and behavioral barriers to learning. Several studies have provided evidence that teachers can make a difference in overcoming antisocial tendencies (Kupersmidt & Patterson, 1991; Tremblay, LeBlanc, & Schwartzman, 1988). The following *Personal Note* provides an example of my involvement in these programs.

A Personal Note

Over the past 20 years, I have been involved in working with special education students in elementary schools who have been placed in a classroom for students with serious emotional disturbance and behavioral disorders. During this time, I have been amazed by the "miracle" that special education programs can achieve with students. The miracle is that the students go from what Glasser (1969) would refer to as a *failure identity* to a *success identity*. When they come into the program, they have a failure identity. They hate school because they have never been successful at it. Many are a step away from dropping out. They are some of the best blamers and whiners I have ever encountered. Their problems are always someone else's fault. In addition, they are usually so busy trying to avoid doing schoolwork and have fun that they are constantly running into problems with their teachers and experiencing adverse consequences, such as not having the privileges that others are getting.

With these programs, these students begin to gain a success identity. They learn to follow the rules and get their work done. Gradually, they begin to feel pride in accomplishment, which plants the seed for intrinsic motivation. In addition, they become aware of choices regarding their behavior and learn to assume responsibility for what they have done. An example of this

(Continued)

(Continued)

occurred when I walked into a class and asked a student how he was. He told me, "I got caught hitting some guy on the bus and got a level drop." That was it—no whining or blaming. Becoming responsible leads to self-respect, which in turn earns the respect of others.

Perhaps the best example that illustrates the success of these programs was what I experienced at a Christmas party. I was observing a new boy who had only been in the program for about 10 weeks. When he came into the program, he hated everything, and his parents had to "drag him to school." Now he was doing really well in the program and felt pride in his achievements (instead of frowning, he was usually beaming). When the Christmas show finished, it was about 2:00 p.m. and school got out at 3:00 p.m. As his mom was about to leave, the teacher asked the boy if he wanted to go home with his mom. To my surprise, he said, "No, I want to stay until school gets out." Now that indeed is a miracle, to see a boy go from hating school and wanting no part of it to taking pride in school and enjoying it!

The research of Cashwell and Vacc (1996) provided some guidance for preventing and overcoming delinquency in adolescents. They found that two of the strongest predictors of adolescent delinquency are being involved with delinquent peers and a lack of family cohesion. They suggested that preventative programs should be started in elementary school to promote social-skills training and an awareness of the dangers of involvement in antisocial groups such as gangs. In addition, counseling could be directed at enhancing family cohesion through such efforts as parenting training and family counseling.

Treatment of aggression can involve various interventions. Brown and Parsons (1998) emphasized the importance of developing different strategies for different types of aggression. The concept of proactive aggression (including bullying aggression) views aggression as a learned response. Treatment approaches should, therefore, be directed at helping children/adolescents learn alternative responses to problem solving that do not entail aggression. As part of this approach, parents can be urged to avoid using severe punishment to prevent bullying aggression in their children/adolescents. Therapists can also use behavioral approaches, such as shaping and reinforcement, to promote pro-social and appropriate goal attainment behaviors.

Reactive aggression involves impulsive, nonmediated aggression. Children/adolescents engaging in reactive aggression can benefit from interventions that help with impulse control. Behavioral interventions can be used to target the antecedents to aggressive responses (e.g., moving a student away from other students to prevent potential conflict situations). Cognitive approaches can also be used to help children/adolescents reframe an intrusion as a potentially nonthreatening accident.

Counseling and mental health services for children and adolescents with antisocial behavior problems call for additional research and development. The casualties of this problem extend beyond the victim, infusing fear and negativity into society itself. There is a great need for realistic and effective means of defeating needless violence, aggression, and hostility.

Diversity and Postmodern
Issues in Child and Adolescent Counseling

Diversity and postmodernism are redefining the foundation and evolution of child and adolescent counseling in terms of theory, research, and practice. From a theoretical perspective, child and adolescent counseling is grounded in developmental theory. Carol Gilligan's (1982) seminal work on female moral development is credited with generating an awareness of male bias in developmental theory.

Gilligan's research (1982, 1991) has contributed to a wave of interest in reassessing gender issues in developmental theory. Gilligan and, more recently, Allen and Stoltenberg (1995), Horst (1995), and Wastell (1996) have reassessed other developmental theories. For example, they contended that Erikson's (1968) theory of psychosocial development needs to be modified to overcome gender bias in favor of males. From a feminist perspective, two of Erikson's stages are in particular need of revision (identity formation during adolescence and intimacy during young adulthood). With respect to identity formation, Erikson appeared to acknowledge the male values of autonomy and individualism over the relational values favored by females. A more accurate conceptualization of female identity development would describe the self as being organized around the goal of establishing and maintaining meaningful relationships.

Sexual orientation can be an important diversity issue in counseling adolescents and young adults, who are striving for identity formation and intimacy. LGBT adolescents face a wide array of obstacles to development, such as homophobia, discrimination, negative stereotyping, and even violence (Kottman, Lingg, & Tisdell, 1995). The grip of homophobia often extends into the adolescent's support system, with friends and family often unable to recognize and accept an LGBT orientation. This often leaves the LGBT adolescent feeling alienated and isolated, with self-esteem and self-acceptance problems (fundamental building blocks for identity development and intimacy). In the face of so much negativity, it is not surprising that LGBT adolescents are at risk for mental health problems (Kottman et al.). Approximately one third of gay teens in a study had attempted suicide and/or been hospitalized for mental health problems, 48% had run away from home, and 58% regularly abused substances (Remafedi, 1987). Approximately one third of all successful adolescent suicides are individuals with LGBT orientations (O'Connor, 1992).

Hammond and Yung (1993) have addressed issues concerning violence and death among ethnic minority adolescents. They reported that African American male adolescents experience a disproportionate risk of death or injury due to violence. Perhaps the most telling statistic regarding this problem is that the number one reason for African American male adolescent death in the United States is assaultive gunshot by a friend or acquaintance. According to Hammond and Yung, causes of violence among African American adolescent males can be attributed to psychosocial, cognitive-behavioral, and environmental factors, with environmental-ecological factors appearing to be major forces in promoting violence. For example, many of these individuals live in the inner city, where violence and crime are a part of everyday life. Hammond and Yung suggested that preventative programs need to be directed at overcoming the legacy of violence. They described a multifaceted program directed at challenging beliefs and assumptions regarding violence, overcoming sociopolitical and ecological barriers to optimal development (e.g., family and community instability), and fostering cultural awareness and sensitivity.

Mental health issues like depression in children and adolescents could also be approached from the perspective of gender. For example, female adolescents are more prone to depression than male adolescents (Petersen et al., 1993). Female adolescents also respond differently to depression because they tend to internalize (ruminate), whereas males tend to externalize (distract themselves with activities). Comorbitity in depression also tends to vary between male and female adolescents, with female depression often occurring along with eating disorders and male depression co-occurring with disruptive disorders (Petersen et al.).

The postmodern considerations of cultural and environmental-ecological factors also affect the assessment and treatment of mental disorders of children and adolescents. The prevalence of mental disorders varies from culture to culture. Some cultures (such as Native American) have significantly high rates of depression and suicide, owing in part to environmental forces like high levels of unemployment (Harrar, 1984). Community psychology that utilizes an ecological perspective can provide a useful dimension to mental health services for Native Americans (Harrar). The experience of mental disorders may also vary widely from culture to culture in terms of the language and knowledge bases associated with mental health and mental illness. Members of some cultures (such as Latino) experience depression in mainly somatic terms, such as complaints of nerves or headaches, whereas individuals from other cultures (such as Asian) may experience depression as feelings of being tired or off-balance (American Psychiatric Association, 2000). It is therefore important to consider cultural forces reflected in the language and narratives of children and adolescents when assessing and treating problems like depression.

SUMMARY

Child and adolescent counseling is an emerging specialty in counseling. The concept of childhood and adolescence as distinct developmental stages is relatively new; previously, the special needs of children and adolescents were generally ignored. However, theories of child and adolescent development have provided information on child and adolescent cognitive, moral, psychosocial, and mental health development. The theories are an important conceptual framework for understanding and treating children and adolescents.

Assessment procedures unique to the field of child and adolescent counseling include the use of drawings and clinical interviews. Treatment includes play therapy, conflict resolution skill building, cognitive-behavioral therapy, and psychotropic medications.

Some of the current trends in child and adolescent counseling focus on the incidence, assessment, causes, effects, and treatment issues surrounding child abuse and neglect, childhood and adolescent depression, suicide, and antisocial behavior.

PERSONAL EXPLORATION

1. How can parental education be useful in enhancing parenting skills?

2. What are the strengths and limitations of play therapy, including the use of art and puppets in counseling?

3. How can narrative therapy be used in child counseling?

4. What are the theoretical constructs associated with Adlerian play therapy?

5. Describe projective techniques in child counseling.

6. What do you think is behind the increase in school shootings, and what should be done about it?

7. What role does attachment theory play in promoting social-emotional development?

8. What do you think are the main causes of child abuse and neglect, and what should be done about this problem?

9. What are your thoughts regarding cyberbullying?

10. What factors are associated with child and adolescent depression, and what do you think can be done to help young people with depression?

11. How can family therapy be used to address common issues of adolescents?

12. What characteristics of resiliency do you have, and how have they helped you cope with adversity?

13. How would you assess yourself in terms of emotional intelligence?

14. What are your views regarding optimal development?

LEARNING ACTIVITIES

1. Read a book on emotional intelligence, such as Goleman's (1997) best-selling book *Emotional Intelligence*, and apply some of these principles in your life.

2. Take a parent education course to enhance your parenting skills.

WEBSITES

Association for Play Therapy. (2009). Retrieved from http://www.a4pt.org.

Henderson, N. (2014). *The resiliency quiz*. Retrieved from http://www.resiliency.com/htm/resiliencyquiz .htm. *Provides a resiliency quiz to help make the concept of resiliency more concrete.*

Group Counseling

The Art and Science of Group Counseling

Group counseling is an art in the sense that the group facilitator must be flexible and creative in adapting to ongoing movement within the group process. Groups are dynamic entities and in that regard have a life and purpose of their own. Facilitators need to let go of preconceived ideas of what will occur within a group and allow the group to move toward the realization of its own unique potential. Facilitators must also be sensitive to diversity issues within the group. In doing so, facilitators, like artists, can help members create opportunities for sharing and learning.

The science of group counseling is directed at a number of important issues relating to group work. Contemporary group work emphasizes the capacity of the group to give individuals and the group as a whole a focus in order to enhance motivation and productivity. Structure can include ensuring that prospective members are appropriate for the group, establishing rules or guidelines for the functioning of the group, encouraging members to formulate personal counseling goals, and using a conceptual frame of reference for facilitating the group (such as a solution-focused brief-counseling perspective). The science of group counseling can also involve research and evaluation to determine the efficacy of group theory and practice. In 1997, a special issue of the *Journal for Specialists in Group Work* (November 1997) was published in an effort to create a balance between the art and science of group counseling. Numerous articles in this issue encourage collaboration between science and practice in group work.

Group Counseling

Group counseling is an important specialty within the counseling profession. This practice is part of most counseling programs and is therefore an integral part of the counselor's

Chapter Overview

This chapter provides an overview of group counseling. Highlights of the chapter include the following:

- **The art and science of group counseling**
- **Group counseling from a historical perspective**
- **Comparison of group counseling to individual and family counseling**
- **Types of groups; group size, composition, and duration; and group goals**
- **Problem solving and group process**
- **Pregroup screening and orientation and stages in group counseling**
- **Brief-solution-focused group counseling**
- **Dealing with disruptive group members**
- **Qualities of effective group leaders, use of coleaders, and common group leadership mistakes**
- **Diversity issues in group counseling**

identity (Fuhriman & Burlingame, 1990). Several organizations have done much to advance the professionalization of group counseling. The American Counseling Association (ACA) chartered a special division for group counseling in 1973 called the Association for Specialists in Group Work (ASGW). Ethical guidelines were established in 1980 and revised in 1989 and 2007 (Thomas & Pender, 2008).

The ASGW also established professional standards for the training of group workers (Wilson, Rapin, & Haley-Banez, 2000) and standards for multicultural counseling (Haley-Banez, Brown, & Molina, 1998). Several other professional organizations have furthered the cause of group counseling, including the Association for Multicultural Counseling and Development; the American Group Psychotherapy Association; the International Association for Group Psychotherapy; and the American Society of Group Psychotherapy and Psychodrama.

This chapter provides an overview of group counseling. It begins by describing group counseling from a historical perspective and then differentiates group from individual and family counseling. The chapter also includes information on the practice of group counseling, a description of the stages of group counseling, ethical-legal issues in group counseling, and diversity issues in group counseling.

Group Counseling From a Historical Perspective

The rich and fascinating history of the group movement can be traced to the pioneering work of J. L. Morreno and Kurt Lewin in the 1920s and 1930s (Bonner, 1959). Lewin's field theory provided an important theoretical foundation for group work, and Morreno developed a unique approach to group counseling called *psychodrama*.

Initially, the professional community was skeptical of group counseling. Some perceived the new technique as a radical, unorthodox procedure that would undermine confidentiality. It also conflicted with the basic model of counseling—counselors working with individual clients. Gradually, however, group counseling gained respectability. In 1946, the National Training Laboratory (NTL) was founded in Bethel, Maine (Baruth & Robinson, 1987), and it soon became a major training institute for group work. The institute focused on how to use group dynamics to promote personal growth and interpersonal functioning.

During the 1960s, encounter and sensitivity groups became popular in general and the "in" thing on many college campuses. The spirit of the group movement seemed to blend with the cultural revolution also taking place in the 1960s. Both encouraged self-exploration, mind expansion, spontaneity, openness, honesty, and confrontation when necessary. Perhaps in part due to its association with the hippies of the 1960s, the group movement became a target of criticism. Because of a few unusual encounter groups that were conducted in Northern California with nude participants, inferences were drawn that all group counseling devolved into sex orgies. The group movement was also charged with contributing to social unrest among youth. As a result, an antigroup movement began in California in the late 1960s. Some of its leaders even suggested that group counseling was part of a communist conspiracy to undermine young people. Patterson contended that there were legitimate criticisms of many of the groups run in the 1960s (Vacc, 1989). He believed that problems resulted from inadequate training of group leaders; too much emphasis on uncovering people's problems and doing whatever "feels right" without concern for the effect on other group members; and the use of gimmicky, manipulative techniques and games.

During the 1970s and 1980s, several factors contributed to group counseling's return to respectability. The most significant was a shift away from the lack of structure associated with sensitivity and encounter groups, which was seen as a contributing factor not only to negative perceptions about the specialty but also to "casualties" in counseling. Professionals believed that groups based on clear goals and objectives could generate more productive outcomes.

Gazda (Elliot, 1989) suggested that group counseling in the 1990s would be associated with family group work, social-skills training, and life skills training groups. He also believed that the popularity of self-help groups would grow faster than that of any other type. Horne (1996) provided additional information on group counseling in the 1990s noting that group counseling was accommodating increasingly diverse populations in various types of settings and was incorporating strategies utilized in individual counseling such as the solution-focused brief-counseling perspective.

More recently Corey (2016) reported there has been an increased use of group counseling within the helping professions to assist a wide range of clients in a variety of settings such as school and community agencies. Corey also cited research evidence of the efficacy of group counseling noting that in some instances it can be more effective than individual counseling.

Comparison to Individual and Family Counseling

Although the specialty of group counseling has unique features in terms of theory and practice, it has elements in common with other forms of counseling, such as individual and family counseling. This section describes the similarities and differences between group counseling and individual and family counseling and identifies advantages and disadvantages of group counseling.

Group Counseling Versus Individual Counseling

There are actually few differences between group counseling and individual counseling (Fuhriman & Burlingame, 1990). This is not surprising because theories and techniques tend to transfer from individual counseling to group counseling. But even though the techniques used in group counseling and individual counseling are similar, the counseling process varies in group counseling to accommodate the increased complexities that result from multiple clients. Drawing primarily from Yalom's (1995) 11 therapeutic factors for group work, Fuhriman and Burlingame (1990) identified the following 6 factors that differentiate group counseling from individual counseling:

1. *Vicarious learning.* Group counseling offers opportunities for members to learn from observing other group members, or via **vicarious learning**, as they explore their concerns.

2. *Role flexibility.* Clients in group counseling can function both as helpers and helpees, thus having the benefits of **role flexibility**. Clients in individual counseling can only maintain the role of helpee.

3. *Universality.* Group counseling creates opportunities for clients to discover that other group members have similar concerns, fears, and problems. This experience of **universality** can help clients put their problems in perspective and not overreact to them.

4. *Altruism.* During group counseling, members are encouraged to offer help to other group members. Clients who engage in altruistic behavior can provide support for other group members and enhance their self-image.

5. *Interpersonal learning.* Interaction between group members creates opportunities to enhance interpersonal skills.

6. *Family reenactment.* The therapeutic climate created in a group can be similar to what was experienced in a client's family of origin. Group counseling can therefore be particularly useful in working through early familial conflicts.

The following *Personal Note* is an illustration of how I helped a client work through an early familial conflict in group counseling.

A Personal Note

When I was a counseling psychologist at a university counseling center, a client in the group, "Tom," a man in his early 20s, was having problems. Specifically, he was feeling a lack of confidence and courage.

During one session, Tom told the group about an experience he'd had as a teenager. He said his father was an alcoholic who verbally and physically abused Tom's mother. Tom described one instance that he often thought about. He and his mother were sitting in the living room when his father started yelling terrible things at his mother, then went over and slapped her across the face. Tom just sat and watched. He felt angry at his father but also at himself because he couldn't help his mother. As he reflected on the incident, he said he just wished he'd had the courage to "stand up like a man" and come to the aid of his mother.

I suggested that we reenact the situation. I arranged to have a group member play the role of mother, Tom would be himself, I would play the

(Continued)

(Continued)

role of father, and the rest of the group members would be the audience and provide feedback.

When we started the scene, Tom initially had a difficult time taking his role seriously. He started to laugh and said, "You don't look like my father." I intensified my yelling and abusive language toward his "mother." I then went over and started to shake her. The next thing I realized was that Tom was standing in front of me. He grabbed my shoulders and told me to leave his mother alone. His face was bright red with anger. He was breathing hard and then started to cry.

At this point, I stopped the reenactment and held the client for a few moments and encouraged him to cry and get his feelings out. We then discussed the experience with the group members. Tom said something seemed to snap in him when I began to yell at his "mother." He really felt he was there with his mother and father. Tom said it made him feel better to be able to tell his father how he felt and to stand up for his mother. He went on to say that his tears were tears of relief that he was finally able to let go of his feelings of helplessness and shame.

This case illustrates the intense emotions that can result from group counseling procedures. The procedures should therefore be used carefully. It is especially important not to push clients to the point where they are forced to deal with emotions they are not ready to handle.

A number of research studies have been undertaken to compare the efficacy of individual counseling versus group counseling. A meta-analysis of 23 outcome studies that compared individual counseling to group counseling showed no difference in overall efficacy and that both forms of counseling were more effective than no counseling (McRoberts, Burlingame, & Hoag, 1998). The study noted that efficacy rates vary to some degree according to clients' problems. Group counseling appears superior to individual counseling for treatment of chemical dependencies, vocational choice, stress syndromes, and V-codes (problems of living, such as parent-child relational difficulties). Individual counseling appears particularly well suited to the treatment of depression, especially when the treatment program utilizes a cognitive-behavioral theoretical orientation. The researchers concluded that under most conditions, group counseling is an effective, cost-efficient alternative to individual counseling. One of the most robust findings of a review of therapeutic applications of groups over the past four decades is that clients are better off utilizing both individual and group counseling versus only individual counseling or group counseling alone (Barlow, Burlingame, & Fuhriman, 2000).

Group Counseling Versus Family Counseling

Group counseling and family counseling also have similarities and differences. Both "bring people together to resolve problems by emphasizing interpersonal relationships" (Hines, 1988, p. 174). Their processes are also similar. The focus of the initial sessions in both is on the counselor defining the presenting problem from an interpersonal perspective (Hines; Whitaker & Keith, 1981; Yalom & Leszcz, 2005). The working stage in both is an interactive process in which the client and counselor are actively engaged (Hines; Whitaker & Keith; Yalom & Leszcz).

Differences between group counseling and family counseling concern inclusion, structure, and interrelatedness (Hines, 1988). Inclusion must be gained by participation in a group, whereas it is a biological given in a family (Hines). Structurally, group members have equal power, whereas family members have hierarchical power (Couch & Childers, 1989; Hines). Group members have a lower degree of interrelatedness than family members, who have spent years living together (Hines). As a result, family members have well-established interpersonal processes, whereas group members are strangers to one another when they form the group (Couch & Childers).

The role of the counselor is also different in group counseling and family counseling. During the initial stage of group counseling, the leader attempts to assist group members with the process of inclusion (Hines, 1988; Schultz, 1977). The reverse is true in family counseling, since the counselor initially feels like an outsider and attempts to be included in the family (Hines). The counselor's role is also different in terms of establishing norms (Couch & Childers, 1989; Hines). During the initial phase of group counseling, the leader plays an active role in establishing group norms, which is not the case in family counseling, because the family already has a well-established norm system (Couch & Childers; Hines).

Perhaps the biggest difference between group counseling and family counseling is the goals of each process. Group counseling has goals for the group, such as creating a climate of trust and acceptance, as well as specific goals for each individual member (Couch & Childers, 1989). In contrast, the goal of family counseling is to improve the overall functioning of the family unit.

Despite the differences between group and family counseling, opportunities exist for integration (Vinson, 1995). A systemic perspective can be used in both forms of counseling to enhance awareness of the interactional processes between clients and the system as a whole (Horne, 1993). Vinson has described numerous instances of how family therapy can be integrated into group counseling (e.g., psychoeducational support groups [Gregg, 1994] and separation divorce/adjustment groups [Addington, 1992]). Vinson also suggested that many family counseling techniques can be used in group counseling, such as the genogram to explore family-of-origin issues.

Advantages and Disadvantages of Group Counseling

Like other counseling strategies, group counseling has potential advantages and disadvantages. The main advantage is that group counseling provides a safe environment for clients to try out and experience new behaviors with other group members. Other advantages include the following:

- Clients can learn from other group members as they explore their personal concerns.

- The process is more economical in terms of time, since several clients can be seen during a session.

- Clients can have an opportunity to help others during the session, thereby minimizing tendencies to be overly concerned with their own problems.

- Problem solving can be enhanced by the ideas generated by other group members.

- The group can foster energy and enthusiasm, which can help motivate a client to pursue personal goals.

The main disadvantage of group counseling is that it may be inappropriate for some clients, especially for clients with serious mental disorders or a low self-concept. It may even be dangerous for these clients to participate in a group because they may feel threatened or personally attacked by the feedback they receive from other members. In these cases, the client may first need to participate in individual counseling to be able to make use of group counseling successfully. Other risks associated with group counseling include problems with confidentiality that can arise in groups, inappropriate self-disclosure owing to group pressure, participants feeling attacked as a result of confrontation, and negative emotional consequences that result from scapegoating (Corey, Corey, & Corey, 2014).

Group Goals and Processes

The science of counseling is reflected in the structure that goals can bring to the counseling process. Goals create a focus for individuals and the group itself, enhancing motivation and constructive action. Both **group goals and individual goals** are part of group counseling. To a large extent, group goals vary according to the type of group. Some groups focus on providing guidance on topics such as parent education; others have the goal of overcoming mental problems such as depression.

Group goals can also relate to the counseling process, including fostering trust and acceptance and promoting self-disclosure, feedback, and risk taking (Corey et al., 2014). Most approaches to group counseling also encourage group members to formulate individualized goals (Couch & Childers, 1989). Members are then assisted in learning problem-solving strategies they can utilize outside the group setting (Couch & Childers).

In the view of Waldo and Bauman (1998), it is critical to describe groups in terms of the interrelationship of group goals and processes. These authors suggested that a new method of categorizing groups, the Goals and Process Matrix (GAP), be used as a classification system for group work. This model attempts to define (or classify) groups by answering the question "Which group process is best for pursuing which group goal?" (Waldo & Bauman). The GAP appears to promote individualized description of groups, which allows for integration of group formats (e.g., task groups and guidance groups) in terms of their goals and processes. At the very least, the GAP model seems to offer opportunities for enhancing existing models for categorizing group counseling by recognizing the overlapping function of groups in terms of goals and processes. Additional research on the GAP seems warranted to obtain a clearer understanding of how it can be used to describe the types of groups used in group counseling.

Types of Groups

The ASGW revised its *Professional Standards for Training of Group Workers* in 2000. This publication presents a broad definition of group counseling within the context of group work, which is defined as processes that involve giving help and accomplishing tasks in a group setting. The major types of group work used by people in the helping profession are summarized as follows:

- *Task/work groups* encompass all the different types of groups used in contemporary society to accomplish various tasks. Examples of task/work groups include committees, study groups, and discussion groups.

- **Guidance/psychoeducational groups** focus on providing information that can be used to facilitate human growth and development and prevent problems from occurring. These groups are widely used in schools and other settings. They provide an opportunity to explore a variety of topics, such as how to avoid involvement in gangs and how to be an effective parent.

- *Counseling/interpersonal problem-solving groups* use interpersonal support and problem-solving methods to help individuals with problems of living. These groups also attempt to help group members learn how to use various counseling strategies so that they can work through or prevent future problems.

- *Psychotherapy/personality reconstruction groups* are designed to help individuals overcome in-depth personal or mental health problems such as anxiety or depression. These groups attempt to remediate or overcome significant psychological difficulties by a variety of processes, which can include personality restructuring.

Additional types of groups are as follows (Jacobs, Masson, Harvill, & Schimmel, 2012; Nelson-Jones, 1992):

- *Life-skills training groups,* also called *education groups,* are defined as "time-limited, structured groups in which one or more leaders use a repertoire of didactic and facilitative skills to help participants develop and maintain one or more specific life skills" (Nelson-Jones, 1992, p. 6). These groups are characterized by an emphasis on wellness versus sickness, systematic instruction, an experiential focus, and participant involvement. Life skills training groups promote skills relating to all aspects of life, such as parenting, intellectual development, self-management, and physical development.

- *Mutual-sharing groups,* also called *support* or *self-help groups,* are composed of people with similar concerns who provide support to one another. The fundamental goal of mutual-sharing groups is to provide support to members. Examples of these groups are children of divorced parents, adult children of alcoholics, and adults who are prone to engage in child abuse.

- *Growth groups* are designed to help group members increase their self-awareness. Their goal is to assist members in improving their lives by clarifying their values, personal concerns, and interpersonal relationships.

- *Family groups* involve inviting different families to a group setting to discuss issues of concern. The primary goal is to enhance the functioning of the family system. Multiple-family group work can be used when a counselor wants to work with several families at a time. Family network groups can be established with the goal of providing information and support to families.

- *Discussion groups* provide an opportunity to discuss a topic of interest rather than the personal concerns of group members. Examples of discussion group topics are the pros and cons of having children, the effects of drug abuse, and attitudes toward marriage. The goal of discussion groups is to have members share ideas and knowledge regarding a particular topic.

- *Online group counseling* represents an emerging trend in group work. The Internet offers a unique opportunity for computer-based group counseling. Mutual sharing (as in a support group) is particularly well suited to online group work; as of 1999, there were approximately 900,000 listings for support groups such as recovery from addictions. Guidelines for setting up online support groups have been established (Page et al., 2000).

The future of technology in group counseling appears promising. McGlothlin (2003) has reviewed innovative technology applications in group work. For example, PalTalk, software for online audio group conferencing, can be used in nonconfidential discussions relating to counseling supervision (Page et al., 2003). Students had an overall positive response to PalTalk, noting that the audio dimension in online discussions provided group members with a chance to participate, facilitated meaningful connections between students, and promoted learning. Problems with PalTalk were associated with difficulty obtaining clear audio signals in rural areas, which created frustration for group members and delayed the start of some groups.

The advantages and disadvantages of online support groups and online counseling have been discussed by Page et al. (2000) and McGlothin (2003). Advantages include the enhanced opportunity to reach large numbers of interested persons and the fact that online group counseling is not restricted by time or facilities. Thus, individuals who do not ordinarily have access to groups due to geographic isolation or personal disabilities can be served through online group work. In addition, some group members find it easier to participate online than face-to-face. Supplemental materials can also be easily accessed and downloaded from Internet sites. The potential disadvantages include impersonalization due to a lack of human contact and communication problems resulting from a lack of visual or auditory cues. In addition, problems can arise from inadequate training in technology, technological breakdown, and lack of access to technology. There are also a number of hard-to-deal-with group process issues, such as screening members to ensure suitability for the group, and ethical issues, such as informed consent and confidentiality.

Problem Solving and Group Process

Two dimensions of group counseling are critical to the success of the group: problem solving and group process. These dimensions are interrelated, and success in one dimension fosters success in the other.

The problem-solving strategies of individual counseling discussed in Chapter 3 can also be used in group counseling. These strategies typically involve the group leader and members first listening to a particular concern of a member and then helping that member resolve the concern. An important part of the problem-solving process is members taking action and assuming responsibility (Burlingame & Fuhriman, 1990).

Burlingame and Fuhriman (1990) identified the following factors associated with group process:

- *Engagement.* Engagement entails members sharing their feelings with one another. This practice is believed to foster cohesion (Aiello, 1979) and universality (Brabender, 1985).

- *Group versus individual focus.* Opinions vary as to whether the process in group counseling should focus on the group, on the individual, or alternately on the group and the individual (Burlingame & Fuhriman, 1990). A more equitable position might be to focus simultaneously on the individual and the group. Having coleaders is a useful format, with one leader focusing on the concerns of an individual client and the other on issues that relate to the group process.

- *Here-and-now focus.* Most approaches to group counseling emphasize the importance of maintaining a focus on the here and now in terms of group process (Burlingame & Fuhriman, 1990).

Yalom (1995) suggested that a primary task of the group leader is to encourage group members to relate in the here and now and then to have the group reflect on the here-and-now behavior that has just transpired. The here-and-now focus is believed to help group members learn about themselves through self-disclosure and feedback as they interact with each other (Sklare, Keener, & Mas, 1990).

- *Goals of the group.* To some degree, a group's goals determine the nature of the group. For example, a group designed to discuss parenting may have a didactic emphasis, whereas groups designed to improve interpersonal relationships tend to be experiential in nature.

Group Size, Composition, and Duration

Appropriate group size varies according to the type of group and the ages of its members. For example, a play therapy group should not exceed four children for the counselor to be effective. In contrast, a school counselor may effectively work with a classroom full of students. For group counseling and psychotherapy, the average group size ranges from 4 to 10 members (Burlingame & Fuhriman, 1990), a size large enough to include a diversity of ideas yet small enough to provide an opportunity for each member to participate.

Group composition is another important issue to consider in forming a group. Groups can be either heterogeneous or homogeneous. Heterogeneous groups are composed of individuals of different ages, genders, cultures, socioeconomic statuses, and so forth. These groups can help promote a diversity of ideas for group members to consider. Heterogeneous groups are also believed to foster greater individualization because of the wide range of issues they can address (Unger, 1989). Heterogeneous groups are commonly used in schools, where a counselor might conduct a session on alcohol and drug use with an entire classroom, or in community mental health centers, where a counselor might have several clients participate in group counseling to resolve personal problems.

Homogeneous groups, on the other hand, are composed of individuals who have something in common, such as parents who want to learn about parenting or clients who suffer from eating disorders. An advantage of homogeneous groups is that they enhance universality by bringing together individuals with similar problems or concerns. Homogeneous groups are also believed to promote more cohesion and identification than heterogeneous groups (Unger, 1989).

Duration relates to three issues: whether the group is open or closed, the length of each session, and the number of sessions. *Open groups* are ongoing, with no termination date, and they allow new members to join at any time. Alcoholics Anonymous uses an open-group format, encouraging new members to start attending sessions whenever they can. *Closed groups* have a specific starting date, and they do not allow new members to join after the first session. Closed groups are often used when the members want to learn certain principles and do not want to have to keep reviewing what was covered in an earlier session. A parent education group designed to help members learn about parenting might be an example of a closed group. About half of hospital outpatient groups are open while half are closed, whereas inpatient groups tend to be open to accommodate new patients as they are admitted to the hospital (Burlingame & Fuhriman, 1990).

In most groups, each session lasts approximately 90 minutes (Burlingame & Fuhriman, 1990). The group leader and members should determine the length of the session in advance and adhere to it as much as possible so that group members can plan accordingly. The number of sessions associated with group work varies according to the type of group, the needs of the group members, and the theoretical orientation of the group leader. Educational groups might require from 6 to 10 sessions or extend over an entire school year. For counseling and psychotherapy groups, the number of sessions varies according to the setting. Groups for inpatient psychiatric patients usually meet at least once each day while the patients are in the hospital. Ideally, group counseling and psychotherapy in outpatient mental health settings, such as private practice, occur once a week for several months. Managed care's emphasis on short-term, symptom-focused treatment is making it increasingly difficult to obtain approval for these types of treatment programs.

Use of Coleaders

Several advantages are associated with having a leader and **coleader** in group counseling. First, group members can benefit from the expertise of two counselors. Second, there may be an advantage in having male and female counselors to create a more balanced perspective. Third, at the end of a session, the leader and coleader can spend time debriefing, or sharing ideas about the session. As a result, they can gain a more comprehensive understanding of what occurred. A fourth advantage is that the leader can focus on helping a client work through a personal problem while the coleader focuses on the group process. Facilitating the group process can involve creating a positive, trusting climate; keeping the group on task; helping each member feel valued; assisting reluctant clients in becoming involved in the group; and dealing with difficult members who may want to monopolize or sabotage the group.

There are additional advantages of using coleaders in groups (Corey et al. 2014). These include avoiding burnout, allowing for coverage if a group leader is ill, processing strong emotional reactions of group leaders, and working through countertransference if it occurs. There can be potential disadvantages to using coleaders as well (Corey et al.). For example, problems can arise from a lack of trust and cooperation between the leaders. When this occurs, one leader may compete with the other for the support and admiration of the group members. Problems between group leaders can take up group time as the leaders deal with their unresolved issues.

Pregroup Screening and Orientation

There appears to be a positive correlation between the amount of time spent in preparation for a group and positive outcomes for the group (Lynn & Frauman, 1985). A pregroup interview is typically used to help screen and orient prospective group members. The four steps in a pregroup screening interview are identifying needs, expectations, and commitment; challenging myths and misconceptions; conveying information; and screening (Couch, 1995). In this process, the counselor attempts to ensure that client expectations are consistent with group goals. The counselor can also screen out potential members who may lack the necessary ego strength for handling the open feedback that commonly occurs within group counseling.

Pregroup orientation is designed to help members prepare for entry into the group. The following list of issues should be discussed with prospective group members before they join the group (Corey et al. 2014):

- The purpose of the group

- The group format, procedures, and ground rules

- The appropriateness of the group for the client

- Client concerns

- The leader's education, training, and qualifications

- Possible psychological risks that could result from the group

- Fees and expenses

- Limits of confidentiality

- What services can be provided by the group

Pregroup screening issues can vary according to setting. For example, in school counseling, pregroup screening can be used to promote appropriate group composition (Hines & Fields, 2002). School counselors should consider diversity issues such as age, level of maturity, gender, and culture to create a balance in terms of group composition. Other factors deemed important in forming a group include ensuring a good fit between the type of group and the needs of the student and ensuring that the students will work well together.

Stages in Group Counseling

Several attempts have been made to delineate the **stages in group counseling** (Corey, 2016; Gazda, 1989) under the assumption that a model of the stages provides a structure for the process that helps us better understand it. Corey et al.

(2014) have developed the following model consisting of four stages: the initial, transition, working, and final stages.

Stage 1: The Initial Stage

The initial stage of group counseling involves screening, orientation, and determining the structure of the group. The major functions of the group leader during this stage are establishing ground rules and norms for the group, helping members express their fears and expectations, being open and psychologically present, assisting group members in identifying concrete personal goals, and sharing expectations and hopes for the group. During the initial stage, members attempt to create trust; learn to express their feelings and thoughts, including fears or reservations about the group; become involved in establishing group norms; establish personal goals; and learn about the dynamics of the group process.

Stage 2: The Transition Stage

The transition stage is characterized as a time when group members experience anxiety and defensiveness as they begin to question the value of the group. The major functions of the group leader during this stage are encouraging members to express their anxiety, dealing openly with conflicts that occur in the group, and helping group members become autonomous and independent. During this stage, it is common for group members to become concerned about being accepted by the group. A central task for members is to recognize and express feelings of resistance toward the group process.

Stage 3: The Working Stage

The working stage occurs when group members feel free to explore their thoughts and feelings and work on their concerns. The major functions of the group leader during this stage are encouraging members to translate insight into action and helping them make the necessary changes to achieve their goals. The working stage is characterized by group members introducing personal issues that they are willing to work on, providing and receiving feedback, applying what they learn in the group to their daily lives, and offering support and encouragement to other group members.

Stage 4: The Final Stage

The final stage should offer group members a smooth transition toward termination of the group. The major functions of the group leader during the final stage are assisting clients in working toward termination, providing opportunities for them to receive additional counseling if necessary, and helping them gain a useful understanding of what they have learned. This stage is often characterized by sadness and anxiety regarding the termination of the group. Members may begin to decrease the intensity of their participation to prepare for termination, and they may also evaluate how they experienced the group.

RESEARCH REGARDING STAGES IN A GROUP Young (2013) noted that motivational interviewing (MI) can be used during the early stages of group counseling to promote trust and help clients overcome ambivilance to change. Trust can be promoted by MI strategies such as accurate empathy and affirming clients' strengths (e.g., "It sure took courage to be so honest and open about the challenges you face"). Counselors can help clients overcome ambivalence by using the MI technique "amplified reflection" (exaggerating the client's resistance to change to promote change talk). For example, if clients say they do not want to share personal information about themselves with the group; the counselor can respond by saying, "You have decided that nothing positive can occur by sharing with the group?" This may encourage clients to modify their position by saying, "No, I didn't mean that. I just meant that it's hard for me to share information about myself." Young (2013) recommended that when counselors respond to clients with "amplified reflection," they speak in a manner that reflects sincerity and curiosity, not sarcasm.

Some authors have questioned whether group counseling actually has stages. Yalom (Forester-Miller, 1989) claimed that stages are merely a way of imposing a type of structure that does not actually exist in groups. Patterson (Vacc, 1989) also expressed a negative view of the stage model of group counseling. He contended that group counseling is a continuous process that does not have discrete stages (Vacc). In addition, Patterson believed that the stage model creates expectations for group members that can interfere with the normal developmental process of the group (Vacc). Additional research on this topic appears warranted.

Brief-Solution-Focused Group Counseling

As mentioned in other chapters, the trend in counseling is toward brief-solution-focused approaches. Group counseling has therefore been conceptualized within this framework. Coe and Zimpfer (1996) have applied the basic principles of brief counseling (described by de Shazer [1985, 1988] and Walter & Peller [1992]) to group counseling. Coe and Zimpfer contended that group counseling is particularly well suited to incorporate the major tenets of the brief model, which are solution focused and have a strengths perspective. For example, in group members can help identify situations in which one member does not have a problem with controlling anger. These "exceptions" to the anger problem can then be explored by the group to help the individual learn how to apply what works in certain situations to problem situations.

Brief-solution-focused group counseling models are being applied to specialty groups, such as in small-group debriefing for victims of violence or disaster (Juhnke & Osborne, 1997; Mitchell & Everly, 1993; Thompson, 1993). Critical-incident stress debriefing is an intensive 1- to 3-hour session that helps victims of violence and disaster process and debrief issues associated with their traumatic experience (Thompson). Groups like these have both experiential and didactic components, enabling participants to work through issues as well as obtain useful information regarding pertinent topics like posttraumatic stress disorder.

Juhnke and Osborne (1997) integrated critical-incident stress debriefing with solution-focused counseling techniques as an alternative method of counseling victims of violence. Their model is a structured program that extends over a 3-week period. It uses solution-focused techniques to promote positive change and recovery as quickly as possible. Some of the strategies involve identifying behaviors that promote change and using scaling questions to identify the degree of positive change between sessions.

Brief group counseling may not be appropriate for all clients. For example, the brief group counseling model would not be suited for individuals who need long-term supportive care (Couch, 1994). However, certain aspects of the brief model, such as its focus on a strengths perspective, appear to hold promise for all models of group counseling.

Dealing with Disruptive Group Members

There seems to be at least one difficult member in every group. Kottler (1994) noted that regardless of the screening procedures, difficult members end up in groups, creating challenges. The most difficult types of group members that Kottler has encountered are those who feel entitled, are manipulative, or have character disorders. Kottler contended that **disruptive group members** can benefit from honest and caring feedback from other group members and compassionate and firm interventions from group leaders. Group leaders also need to be open to possible contributions they are making to the difficulties group members are experiencing.

The following *Personal Note* provides an example of how I have worked with problematic group members.

A Personal Note

I have been challenged by difficult group members. When this occurs, I try to understand each group member as a unique individual. At the same time, I have found there are several typical problematic behaviors that present themselves. Individuals who engage in these behaviors are referred to as aggressors, obstructors, storytellers, and attention seekers.

Aggressors may be overt or covert in their aggressive behavior toward other group members or the leader. When this occurs, the leader should try not to become angry or threatened. The aggressor is often trying to create a conflict, so an angry reaction may only reinforce that behavior. An approach that may be more productive is to inform the aggressor firmly but kindly that group process is based on a philosophy of

(Continued)

(Continued)

encouragement and support. It may also be productive to explore and work through the aggressor's feelings.

Obstructors tend to be negative and obstruct the group process. They often find ways to sidetrack the issues being discussed and prevent the group from staying on task. This may involve a variety of disruptive behaviors, such as constantly trying to change the topic or complaining that nothing seems to be happening in the group. Obstructors often engage in their disruptive behavior as a means of gaining power and control. It is therefore important for the leader to avoid reacting with anger since that reaction may only create a power struggle. When the obstructor tries to change the topic, the leader might say, "No, let's not change the focus of our work. We need to spend more time with this so we can reach a meaningful conclusion."

Storytellers often like to monopolize the group by telling drawn-out stories about things that happened months ago. What they say usually holds little interest for the group because they typically have already resolved the issue or have no desire to do anything about it. When this occurs, the leader can ask what the storyteller is thinking and feeling at the moment. The leader can emphasize that it is important to try to stay in the here and now so the group can have something concrete to work on.

Attention seekers find different ways to draw attention to themselves. Since their goal is typically to gain attention, the leader must be careful not to reinforce the behavior. Two strategies can be used in working with attention seekers. The leader should first attempt to channel the attention seeker's need for attention in a positive direction by asking for assistance when possible. When that fails, the leader should ask the attention seeker to refrain from the behavior that is creating a problem. For example, if the behavior is making frequent, inappropriate jokes, the leader might say, "Turning a serious issue into a joke does not allow the group to work on issues realistically."

Common Mistakes of Group Leaders

The following are common mistakes group leaders make in therapy groups (Jacobs et al., 2012):

- *Attempting to conduct therapy without a contract.* It is important to ensure that a member wants help with a particular problem by directly inquiring whether the member would like assistance. Assuming a member wants help may waste the group's valuable time on someone who is not ready to make a commitment to work on his or her problem.

- *Spending too much time on one person.* Group time can be dominated by difficult group members or by members who are interesting and attractive and are eager for assistance during *each* session. Group leaders have an ethical responsibility to ensure that all members have an opportunity to participate.

- *Spending too little time with one person.* Group leaders can spend too little time with a member during the problem-solving process in an attempt to give everyone a chance to talk. While it is important to ensure that all members are encouraged to participate, this does not mean they all need to talk. Problem solving requires that one member be the focus of attention for a sufficient period of time.

- *Letting members rescue each other.* There can be a tendency for group members to rescue other members when they sense pain or sorrow. Emotional rescuing is not productive in any form of counseling because it communicates sympathy. Group leaders should instead encourage members to convey support, concern, and empathy.

- *Letting the session turn into advice giving.* Premature advice giving can be particularly prevalent when group members attempt to offer help to other members during problem solving. Premature advice giving is not productive in any counseling, including group counseling. When this occurs, the leader could suggest that members take more time to use listening skills to gain a better understanding of the problem before attempting to solve it.

Qualities of Effective Group Leaders

Perhaps the most important factor in effective group counseling is the personal qualities of the group leader. DeLucia-Waack (1999) addressed both the art and science of effective group leadership. The art of group leadership involves moving out of one's comfort zone to experience new and varied types of group experiences. Personal growth and renewal can be generated by ongoing self-reflection in terms of identifying strengths and weaknesses in group facilitation. DeLucia-Waack also spoke to the science of group leadership by suggesting that group counselors should function as "N of 1" researchers engaged in ongoing evaluation and development of group skills, techniques, and competencies.

Several others have attempted to describe the qualities of effective group leaders. Effective group counselors are in tune with the group process (Ohlsen, 1970). They can then make the necessary changes to ensure positive therapeutic movement. Personal qualities associated with effective group leadership include presence, personal power, courage, willingness to confront oneself, self-awareness, sincerity, authenticity, a sense of identity, belief in the group process, enthusiasm, inventiveness, stamina, creativity, and commitment to self-care (Corey, 2016). The group leader sets the emotional climate for the group (Yalom & Lieberman, 1971). When the leader acts in an autocratic, confrontational, or emotionally distant fashion, the group experience may actually do more harm than good to members. A leader with moderate amounts of executive function and emotional stimulation and high amounts of caring and meaning attribution contributes to improvements in group members. Taken collectively, the literature suggests that the qualities of effective group leaders are having a positive presence, which can instill trust and enthusiasm; being sensitive to the group process and capable of making adjustments as necessary; setting a positive and encouraging therapeutic climate; and seeking out new group experiences as opportunities to grow and develop.

ETHICAL-LEGAL ISSUES RELATING TO GROUP COUNSELING

The ASGW's *Best Practices Guidelines* were revised in 2007 (Thomas & Pender, 2008). Thomas and Pender noted that the ASGW endorsed the code of ethics of its parent organization, the American Counseling Association (which have since been updated, in 2014). The *Best Practices Guidelines* provide clarification regarding the practice of group work in terms of professional standards and ethical conduct and address professional issues relating to planning, performing, and processing groups. Highlights from the ASGW *Best Practices Guidelines* regarding planning, performing, and processing are as follows (Thomas & Pender).

PLANNING Group workers are able to utilize the ACA code of ethics; the ASGW Diversity Competencies, the Association for Multicultural Counseling and Development (AMCD) Multicultural Competencies and Standards, and other pertinent guidelines regarding professional standards and practice. Group workers engage in professional practice that is consistent with their training and competence. In addition, group workers screen prospective members to ensure that they are appropriate for group experiences, provide informed consent, and engage in professional development.

PERFORMING Group workers utilize appropriate skills and interventions to promote positive growth and development for group members. Group workers are sensitive to issues of diversity and attempt to develop the awareness, knowledge, and skills necessary to address issues of diversity. Group workers are engaged in ongoing evaluation of their own strengths and weaknesses and the efficacy of the groups they lead. Group workers also utilize ethical decision-making models in their group work.

PROCESSING Group workers process group issues such as the dynamics among group members within the group (with group members) and outside the group (with supervisors, coleaders, and other colleagues) as necessary. Group workers attempt to synthesize theory and practice to enhance the efficacy of group work. Group workers also evaluate group experiences to assist in program development. Follow-up services are utilized to assess whether group members need additional services.

Among the several legal issues relating to group counseling identified by Paradise and Kirby (1990) are extra precautions to be taken regarding confidentiality. It is especially important to clarify the limits to confidentiality and privileged communication for members during pregroup orientation or the first session. Counselors can be sued for negligence if they have given the impression that confidentiality is guaranteed.

In addition, group counselors should have all members sign a contract requiring confidentiality and stating that breach of confidentiality will result in the member being dropped from the group (Paradise & Kirby).

MULTICULTURAL ISSUES Corey, Williams, and Moline (1995) emphasized the importance of recognizing multicultural issues in group counseling and provided several guidelines for addressing diversity issues in groups. Group leaders must be respectful and sensitive to multicultural issues such as sexual orientation, age, gender, socioeconomic status, race, and ethnicity in groups. For example, group leaders need to be aware of sociocultural forces such as racism that may be playing a role in group members' functioning. In addition, leaders must be aware of their own biases and prejudices and work through them so they do not have an adverse effect on the group process.

LEGAL ISSUES IN GROUP COUNSELING An overview of legal issues in group counseling is provided by Corey et al. (1995), who noted that the best way to avoid malpractice suits is to practice within the boundaries of one's competency and to practice in a *reasonable, ordinary, and prudent* manner. In addition, they suggested that group counselors (1) understand state laws and how they affect confidentiality and privileged communication, (2) use written contracts with members to ensure informed consent, (3) secure permission from legal guardians when working with minors, and (4) ensure the rights and safety of group members.

Legal problems in group counseling can also arise from the counselor's duty to protect. As noted in Chapter 2, the *Tarasoff* litigation (*Tarasoff v. Board of Regents of the University of California*, 1974, 1976) mandated that counselors have a legal responsibility to warn anyone who is the target of a serious threat. The incidence of verbal abuse and subsequent casualties is higher in group counseling than in individual counseling because of the intensity of group work and interaction between members (Corey, Corey, Callanan, & Russell, 1982). Paradise and Kirby (1990) therefore suggested that group counselors screen out potentially dangerous clients and continuously monitor clients to ensure their physical and psychological safety.

Diversity Issues

Populations being served in group counseling are becoming more diverse (Horne, 1996). Group counseling paradigms are expanding to accommodate these diverse populations and settings. Counselors need to be aware of how cultural diversity can affect group dynamics (McRae, 1994). For example, individuals with similar worldviews can form coalitions or alliances within the group. These alliances can evolve between or within races. Counselors should avoid stereotyping group members along racial lines and attempt to understand members as individuals functioning within a group environment (McRae).

There are both challenges and opportunities in multicultural group counseling (Johnson, Torres, Coleman, & Smith, 1995). Challenges can evolve from prejudice, difficulty communicating, misunderstandings, and fear between group members. These types of challenges can impede or enhance group growth. When problems arise, they should be dealt with directly in the group (Johnson et al.). Within this context, the group process can be used to help members develop new levels of communication, understanding, trust, and sensitivity with other cultural groups (Johnson et al.). Opportunities also present themselves in terms of how diverse individuals in groups can broaden the perspective for problem solving and decision making.

Feminist group therapy is one example of how diversity issues can be infused into group work. Rittenhouse (1997) noted that the feminist perspective could be useful in survivor groups to help women recover from sexual trauma or other adverse life experiences. Rittenhouse contended that the key to achieving success in feminist group counseling is to create an egalitarian relationship among the group members themselves and between the members and the leader. In addition, fostering equality and empowerment can be important in encouraging members to take an active role in their recovery and in overcoming oppressive forces that have impeded their development.

A second major principle is to help members look beyond intrapsychic causality and explore problems from an ecological perspective. This process can help members shift from internalizing and self-blaming to exploring sociocultural and political forces, such as oppression in family roles and the workplace. It does not imply a shift in blame from self to others but an attempt to identify how members can "reinvent their world" in a more gender-sensitive and meaningful manner. This process of discovery can involve activities such as understanding the self in more gender-accurate terms, like those found in Carol Gilligan's (1982) work on female moral development. The group format is ideal for the discussion of such material since it allows for experiential processing of ideas and concepts.

DeLucia-Waack (2000) noted that group counseling must reflect a life span perspective, using different models and procedures depending on clients' age and developmental status. For instance, children tend to need extensive structure to maintain attention and concentration. Group counseling interventions must also be appropriate in terms of cognitive and psychosocial development. Models have been developed to specifically address concerns of children and adolescents, such as depression (Sommers-Flanagan, Barrett-Hakanson, Clarke, & Sommers-Flanagan, 2000), eating disorders (Daigneault, 2000), and psychosocial development through empathic skill enhancement (Akos, 2000).

Diversity issues are not restricted to those of gender or culture; they can include other attributes, such as disability. Corey et al. (2015) noted that "people with chronic medical, physical, and mental disabilities represent the largest minority and disadvantaged group in the United States" (p. 132). Unfortunately, this large group of individuals has historically been systematically excluded from many opportunities, including group counseling, because of attitudinal and environmental barriers (Patterson, McKenzie, & Jenkins, 1995). The Americans with Disabilities Act of 1990 established rights for those with disabilities to be included in the mainstream of society (Brown, 1995).

Specialists in group work are beginning to make progress in breaking down the barriers that people with disabilities face in participating in group work (Horne, 1995). Group counselors must sensitize themselves to the needs of individuals with disabilities (Patterson et al., 1995). Counselors must practice disability etiquette by treating all people as people first and foremost, regardless of disability status, and adjusting the group process, for example, by ensuring that a person with a hearing impairment can see the speaker's lips. It is also the responsibility of the leader to address attitudinal and environmental barriers that could impede the growth of the member with a disability and have an adverse effect on the group process.

Diversity in all its forms creates unique opportunities and challenges. In 2007, the ASGW responded to these challenges by identifying the qualities of diversity-competent group workers, including having the awareness, knowledge, and skills necessary to address the unique and emerging needs of clients in a multicultural society (Thomas & Pender, 2008).

SUMMARY

The art and science of group counseling add a dynamic and interesting dimension to the counseling process. Counselors as artists can adjust counseling approaches to the unique and emerging needs of diverse clients in a group setting. Counselors as scientists can engage in pregroup screening to ensure that prospective group members are appropriate for group work and can incorporate appropriate structure into the group process, such as ensuring that group members have personal counseling goals and that the group functions from a clear theoretical perspective.

Professional helpers are routinely involved in group work in their counseling practice and in all types of settings, including schools, hospitals, agencies, and private practice. Group counseling can be the only form of counseling intervention, such as in parent education or in groups like Alcoholics Anonymous. Groups can also be an important adjunct to other counseling processes, especially individual counseling, whose clients can try out what they have learned in individual counseling within the context of a group.

PERSONAL EXPLORATION

1. What issues do you feel are important in terms of group dynamics?

2. How would you assess your group leadership skills, and how can you work toward improving them?

3. What aspects of group work make you uncomfortable, and how might you address these issues?

4. How could group counseling be useful to you as a potential counseling client?

5. How can coleaders be useful in group counseling?

6. What are some of the types of groups that you find interesting?

7. How does problem solving take place in a group?

8. What are some common mistakes of group leaders?

9. What are common types of disruptive group members, and what has been your experience with these types of individuals?

10. What are qualities of effective group leaders? Do you have some of these qualities?

LEARNING ACTIVITIES

1. You may wish to view a documentary film on what takes place in group counseling called *Journey Into Self*. It is an old classic in the field that has Carl Rogers as one of the group leaders. Perhaps your professor would be able to arrange for you to see this film or another one.

2. You may wish to participate in a group experience (e.g., university counseling centers offer different types of group experiences).

WEBSITES

Franklin, D. J. (2010). *Group therapy.* Retrieved from http://psychologyinfo.com/treatment/group_therapy.html. *Presents a description of group therapy.*

Weinberg, H. (2000). *Group psychotherapy: An introduction.* Retrieved from http://www.grouppsychotherapy.com/intro.htm. *Presents an elementary introduction to group psychotherapy.*

Wood, D. (2009). *Group therapy for adolescents: Clinical paper.* Retrieved from http://mental-health-matters.com/group-therapy-for-adolescents-clinical-paper/. *Presents a clinical article on adolescent group counseling strategies with information on Gartner's group process theory.*

CHAPTER 13

Career Counseling

The Art and Science of Career Counseling

A fairly recent trend in career counseling is the integration of career theory and practice. These two dimensions of career counseling correspond to the art and science dimensions of counseling, with career theory representing the science and practice reflecting the art. Krumboltz (1996) has provided a rationale for the integration of career theory and practice in noting that the reason career theories have been largely ignored is practitioners' focus on career development and not on intervention strategies. Theories have provided little practical information on what career counselors can *do* during the counseling process.

The work of theorists like Holland, Super, and Krumboltz, however, has helped to integrate theory and practice (Herr, 1996). One obvious example is the assessment instruments developed by Holland (Vocational Preference Inventory; 1985b), Super (Career Development Inventory; 1970), and Krumboltz (Career Beliefs Inventory; 1994). Several other individuals have contributed as well (e.g., Chartrand, 1996; Harmon, 1996; Holland, 1996; Savickas, 1996). Savickas developed a framework that can be used to link career theories to practice. His model, an adaptation of "Wagner's (1971) theory of structural analysis of personality to the domain of vocational psychology" (Savickas, 1996, p. 196) is comprehensive, including six types of career services: occupational placement, vocational guidance, career counseling, career education, career therapy, and position coaching (Savickas). Although progress had being made in combining theory with practice, Savickas and Walsh (1996) contended that more work needed to be done to bridge the gap.

The integration of traditional career counseling with personal counseling is another trend that reflects the art and science of career counseling. Traditional career counseling has relied to a

Chapter Overview

Career counseling is a challenging and evolving specialty that helps individuals with career planning and decision making throughout the life span. Highlights of this chapter include the following

- **The art and science of career counseling**

- **The evolution of career counseling**

- **Theoretical foundations in terms of career development and decision making**

- **Treatment issues, including personal counseling versus career counseling, assessment instruments, intervention strategies, and the process of career counseling**

- **Special issues, including career counseling for women and computer-assisted career counseling**

- **Diversity issues in career counseling**

large extent on assessment instruments, such as interest inventories, which can be used with or without computer assistance. These instruments, which represent the science dimension, provide objective information that can enhance the counseling process. The art of career counseling involves the attempt to interface objective information with the subjective, ever changing world of the client. Central to this process is the art of addressing personal issues and problems that may arise during the counseling process. Career issues are thus not viewed as separate and isolated but as interrelated with the person's overall psychosocial functioning.

Evolution of Career Counseling

The world of work, like human society, has changed dramatically over the centuries. Our early ancestors had limited opportunities and choices regarding work (Axelson, 1999). What people did was primarily restricted to preserving their survival. Today, people work for many reasons that go beyond obtaining money for food and shelter. Some work to enhance their self-esteem, others have a goal of independence, some want to help people, and others work to experience power and control. As people's needs change over the life span, so too does the type of work they find rewarding, which in turn may account for the career changes that can occur throughout one's life.

Career counseling has become a means of assisting individuals in developing career-planning and decision-making skills to facilitate career choice. Over the years, it has gone by several different names, including *occupational counseling, vocational guidance,* and *vocational counseling.* These names tend to convey a narrower focus than does *career counseling*, since they emphasize the importance of obtaining occupational information for selecting a particular career. Career counseling is a more comprehensive concept with a strong theoretical foundation based on the various career development theories. *Career counseling* can be defined as "a series of general and specific interventions throughout the life span, dealing with such concerns as self-understanding; broadening one's horizons; work selection, challenge, satisfaction, and other interpersonal phenomena; and lifestyle issues, such as balancing work, family, and leisure" (Engels, Minor, Sampson, & Splete, 1995, p. 134).

Career counseling, as with all counseling specialties, must be based on general counseling competencies (Engels et al., 1995). Career counseling is practiced by professional counselors in schools and agencies. Some counselors incorporate career counseling into their repertoire of helping skills to assist clients in exploring career issues and personal problems. Counselors can also specialize in this field and identify themselves as career counselors or career development professionals. In 1952, the American Counseling Association recognized the special skills and professional interests associated with career counseling by creating a special division called the National Career Development Association (NCDA). The NCDA took an active role in establishing career counseling credentials, which resulted in career counseling becoming the first specialty designation offered by the National Board of Certified Counselors. Requirements for certification include

- becoming certified by the National Board of Certified Counselors (see requirements in Chapter 2);

- earning a graduate degree in counseling or a related profession;

- working at least part-time in career counseling for 3 years following graduate study; and

- passing the National Career Counselor Examination.

In the 21st century, the world of work is in a constant state of flux, creating opportunities and challenges. Some of the defining features of the present work environment are downsizing and a lack of job security, reduced opportunities for lifetime employment within the same industry, and increased global competition and expanding global marketplaces (Stoltz-Loike, 1996). The modern workplace is a "joint venture between the employer with problems to be solved and tasks to be done, and the employees who have the skills to sell and needs to be met" (Feller, 1995, p. 158). Individuals who develop these skills will be successful. Factors critical to this skill development are broad-based, flexible skills; educational credentials that promote lifelong learning; adaptability; and problem-solving skills (Stoltz-Loike).

Theoretical Foundations

There are several theories of career development and career decision making. These theories describe how career development occurs over the life span and what is entailed in the process of career choice and decision making.

Career Development Theories

Career development theories relate to how career issues develop over the life span. This section reviews three prominent career development theories—those of Donald Super, John Holland, and Ann Roe—and the influence of family of origin on career development.

SUPER'S THEORY Super (1990) described his theory as "a loosely unified set of theories dealing with specific aspects of career development, taken from developmental, differential, social, personality, and phenomenological psychology" (p. 199). **Super's theory** emphasizes the role of self-concept in career development and contends that how individuals define themselves has a major effect on their career choices (Super, 1957, 1980, 2002). For example, a person who has a self-image of being a strong, hard worker may be attracted to a physical job like auto mechanic. Super's (1957) theory can be considered developmental because he suggested there are five stages of career development, each with corresponding developmental tasks: growth, exploration, establishment, maintenance, and decline. An overview of these stages follows.

The *growth stage* spans from birth to 14 years of age. The self-concept develops as the individual identifies with significant others. Developmental tasks during the growth stage include gaining self-understanding and obtaining an overall understanding of the world of work. The growth stage has three substages. The *fantasy* substage occurs from age 4 to 10 and involves the child role-playing various fantasies regarding the world of work (e.g., playing doctor or nurse). The *interest* substage extends from age 11 to 12. During this period, a child's likes and dislikes have a major impact on career aspirations. The third substage is *capacity,* which takes place from age 13 to 14. The capacity substage is characterized by a more realistic view of the world of work as individuals consider their abilities and job requirements.

Super's second stage is the *exploration stage,* which spans from 14 to 24 years of age. This is a period of self-examination in relation to the world of work. During this time, the individual also begins to directly experience work by involvement in part-time jobs. Developmental tasks associated with the exploration stage include crystallizing, specifying, and implementing a career preference. The exploration stage has three substages. The *tentative* substage extends from age 15 to 17 and involves identifying appropriate fields of work. The *transition* substage begins at age 18 and continues to age 21. During this substage, the individual may pursue special educational or vocational training related to a field of work or enter directly into the job market. The third substage is referred to as *trial–little commitment* and ranges from age 22 to 24. During this period, the individual usually begins a first job. The commitment is usually tentative as the person decides whether the career choice was appropriate.

The third major stage is the *establishment stage,* spanning from 24 to 44 years of age, when individuals have identified an appropriate field of work to which they want to make a long-term commitment. The key developmental task involves consolidation and advancement. Two substages are associated with the establishment stage. First is *trial commitment and stabilization,* which occurs from age 25 to 30, when the individual either settles down with a particular occupation or becomes dissatisfied and begins to explore other occupational possibilities. *Advancement,* the second substage, extends from age 31 to 44. This is typically a time for stabilization, during which seniority is acquired. It also tends to be a very creative, productive period.

Super's fourth stage is the *maintenance stage,* which spans from 44 to 64 years of age. This is a time for the individual to enjoy the security of seniority while attempting to maintain status as a current and productive professional. The major developmental task is preservation of achieved status.

The final stage in Super's model is the *decline stage,* which begins at age 64. During this stage, the individual adjusts to retirement as well as declining mental and physical skills and abilities. The key developmental tasks are deceleration, disengagement, and retirement. The two substages in the decline state are, first, *deceleration,* which occurs between 60 and 65 years of age. This is a time when the individual begins to adjust to impending retirement, perhaps pursuing part-time jobs as a transition from full-time work. *Retirement* is the second substage and usually begins at age 61 or later. During this time, the individual may continue some part-time work or discontinue work and devote time to leisure activities.

Super (1980, 2002) referred to his theory as a life span, "life space" approach to career development, adding role theory to the five-stage model to create a model composed of multiple-role careers. According to this theory, "career is defined as the combination and sequence of roles played by a person during the course of a lifetime" (Super, 1980, p. 282). These roles vary as a person proceeds through the life span and include such possibilities as student, worker, husband, wife, and parent (Super, 1980).

Many research studies have tested various aspects of Super's theory. Osipow (1996) concluded that most of the literature has provided support for Super's model, and Savickas (1994) recognized Super's impact on career counseling in a special issue of *The Career Development Quarterly,* which highlighted Super's contributions to career theory and practice. For example, Savickas noted that Super helped shift the field from a focus on occupational choice to career development and extended vocational guidance into career counseling. It is not surprising that Super's work has generated a wide range of research activity on topics such as the role of the self-concept in career development (Betz, 1994), work values (Zytowski, 1994), and career adaptability (Goodman, 1994).

Super's theory appears to have pointed the way to some current trends, such as recognizing the contextual nature of career decision making (Phillips & Blustein, 1994). For example, Super noted that career decision making takes place within the broad context of economic, cultural, family, peer, and historic issues (Phillips & Blustein). Super's description of the role of the self-concept in decision making provides valuable information on the subjective-phenomenological dimension of career counseling (Jepsen, 1996). Since Super's death, his theory has continued to evolve and be redefined (Swanson & Gore, 2000). For example, Savickas (1997) suggested that Super's concept of career maturity be replaced with the concept of career adaptability to reflect an individual's need to adjust to such changing forces in the work world as increasing diversity, global marketing, downsizing, and the influence of technology.

HOLLAND'S THEORY Holland's (1973, 1985a, 1996, 1997) theory suggests that career choice is an attempt to obtain a satisfactory fit between the person and the environment. Job satisfaction results when there is a congruence of personality type and work environment (Holland, 1996). **Holland's theory** has had several practical applications in terms of career-counseling instruments, such as Holland's (1985b) Vocational Preference Inventory and Holland's (1994) Self-Directed Search (Weinrach & Srebalus, 2002).

The following four assumptions are the basis of Holland's theory (1973, 1985a, 1996, 1997):

1. *People tend to be characterized by one of six personality types.*
   Holland (1973) originally believed that people could be categorized into six personality types. He later expanded this conception of

personality types to include the possibility of subtypes or patterns that would provide further differentiation of a person's personality characteristic (Holland, 1985a). The original six personality types are as follows:

- *Realistic* individuals take a logical, matter-of-fact approach to life.

- *Investigative* people use an investigative, analytical approach to problem solving.

- *Social* individuals tend to be social, cooperative, and people oriented.

- *Artistic* people tend to be sensitive, creative, spontaneous, and nonconforming.

- *Conventional* individuals are conforming and inhibited, and they have a preference for structured situations.

- *Enterprising* individuals tend to take an extroverted, aggressive approach to problem solving.

2. **There are six kinds of environments that correspond with the six personality types (realistic, investigative, artistic, social, enterprising, and conventional).** Most environments attract workers with corresponding personality types. For example, artistic people work in places such as the theater. A congruent person-environment fit tends to promote job satisfaction.

3. **People seek out work environments that enable them to use their skills, express their values, and enter into agreeable roles.** People are motivated to work in settings that have complementary personality structures.

4. **The interaction of the environment and personality determines behavior.** An individual's behavior, such as his or her career choice and achievement, is determined by the nature of the person-environment fit.

Walsh and Srsic (1995) reported that Holland's theory continues to generate a substantial amount of research into investigating constructs such as personality types (Holland, Johnston, & Asama, 1994) and person-environment fit (Thompson, Flynn, & Griffith, 1994). Studies support the theory that people do well in their careers when there is a good fit between their personality type and the environment. In addition, evidence suggests that people experience dissatisfaction, poor job performance, and disruption in their career path when there is incongruence between their personality type and environmental fit (Holland, 1996).

Holland's theory has generated more research activity than any other (Swanson & Gore, 2000). A literature review of some of these studies concluded that Holland's congruence hypothesis relating to the person-environment fit has received the most empirical support (Fitzgerald & Rounds, 1989). In addition, Bullock-Yowell, Peterson, Wright, Reardon, and Mohn (2011) found that self-efficacy should be considered when using Holland's Self-Directed Search to identify career interests. Holland's most recent revision of his theory (Holland, 1997) has generated another extended period of research investigation (Swanson & Gore, 2000).

ROE'S THEORY The major principles of **Roe's theory** evolved from Maslowian and psychoanalytic theory (Roe, 1956; Roe & Lunneborg, 2002). Simply stated, Roe contended that unmet needs in childhood can have a major influence on career choice in adulthood. In addition, her theory suggests that people can fulfill all basic and higher-order needs associated with Maslow's hierarchy in their careers: needs related to physiology, safety, love and belonging, self-esteem, and self-actualization.

Roe (1956) identified three types of parent-child relationships that could foster need satisfaction in particular careers. An overview of these relationships follows (Osipow, 1996):

1. *Overprotective or excessively demanding parents.* Parents who are overly protective or make excessive demands tend to satisfy physiological needs, but they may be less prone to gratify psychological needs such as love and self-esteem. These parents foster dependency within their children since gratification of psychological needs is contingent on children engaging in socially desirable or high-achieving behaviors. Their children grow into adults with an excessive need for recognition and approval. As a result, they may choose highly visible occupations—politics or a branch of the performing arts like acting.

2. *Rejecting parents.* These parents either neglect or reject their children. Their children tend to have many unfulfilled needs and may become suspicious or untrusting of others. They may therefore select careers where their needs can be met in activities that involve working with things (such as computers) rather than people.

3. *Accepting parents.* These parents tend to be very loving toward their children, and they engage in unconditional love rather than conditional love. Their children's basic and higher-order needs are therefore met, promoting a sense of autonomy and independence in the children as they grow into adulthood. Since these children tend to feel secure with themselves, they may choose a profession like teaching or medicine in which they can assist others in moving toward their own self-realization.

Roe's theory is almost impossible to test empirically because of the subjective nature of the constructs on which the theory is based (Osipow, 1990). Additional refinement of the theory and empirical investigation of its principles appear warranted.

FAMILY OF ORIGIN AND CAREER DEVELOPMENT As noted earlier, Roe (1956) was perhaps the first to investigate the relationship between family-of-origin issues and career development. She contended that the nature of the parent-child relationship can play an important role in career development. Later, Vondracek, Lerner, and Schulenberg (1986) suggested that career development is a dynamic process influenced by relational, developmental, and contextual forces and proposed a systemic model that recognizes the role family dynamics play in career development. They stated, "Perhaps the most important way in which roles and role expectations link the family microsystem and children's career development entails the roles children learn in the context of the family setting" (Vondracek et al., p. 53). Vondracek et al. have stimulated a wide body of research activity. Whiston and Keller (2004) summarized this literature as follows:

> Across the life span, both family structure variables (e.g., parent's occupations) and family process variables (e.g., warmth, support, attachment, autonomy) were found to influence a host of career constructs; however, the process by which families influence career development is complex and is affected by many contextual factors such as race, gender, and age. (p. 493)

Career Decision-Making Theories

Career decision-making theories are another theoretical foundation for career counseling. These theories provide "guidelines for collection, processing, and utilization of information in order to improve decision making" (Gati, 1990a, p. 508). Several theories have been developed on career decision making, This section provides an overview of decision-making theories based on cognitive-dissonance theory, social-learning theory, and a multiple-career decision-making theory.

COGNITIVE-DISSONANCE THEORY Hilton (1962) was one of the first to suggest that career decision making is based on the theory of cognitive dissonance. Cognitive dissonance occurs when an individual has two incompatible cognitions (Festinger, 1957). For example, an individual may contend, "I don't like my job, and it has low pay." The person may then attempt to remove the dissonance by changing one of the cognitions or by aiding dissonance-reducing cognitions, saying, "I like my job even though it does not pay well." The following are implications of **cognitive-dissonance theory** for career counseling (Osipow, 1996):

- *It is important for counselors to identify factors that can increase occupational dissonance.* For example, a person might have an interest in an occupation with limited opportunities, perhaps wanting to be a professor in a field that has few academic positions available. If the dissonance cannot be resolved, the counselor might advise the client to avoid that occupation.

- *Counselors should develop strategies to deal with dissonance.* This can involve a career counselor introducing "counter-dissonance agents." For example, the counselor might tell a premedical student who lacks the aptitude for medical study that being a physician involves working long hours, resulting in little time for family life.

- *Counselors can help clients avoid making a premature choice.* One way to accomplish this is by noting that modifying a choice in the future may cause excessive dissonance. This in turn can interfere with making a more appropriate choice in the future. For example, a person with a strong need for being perceived as having clear goals and objectives may decide to pursue a career as a computer analyst. After several courses on the topic, the person might discover an aversion to computers and want to consider other occupations. This would create dissonance with the need to be perceived as "having clear goals and objectives." To avoid such perceptions and reduce dissonance, this individual may then decide to continue working in an undesirable career.

The following *Personal Note* provides an example of how I overcame cognitive dissonance in my career choice and decision making.

A Personal Note

I entered college as a predental major. I had wanted to be a dentist because my father was a dentist. As part of my predental studies, I had to take a lot of chemistry and biology courses, which I hated and for which I had limited ability. This created dissonance, since I thought I wanted to be a dentist but discovered I did not have the aptitude to do so.

I soon found myself changing my attitude toward becoming a dentist. Before I knew it, I began to think, "I don't want to be a dentist." I soon began to think of a lot of good reasons for not wanting to be a dentist, including not wanting to bend over and stick my hands in people's mouths all day. At this point, I had begun to resolve my dissonance by creating a new attitude. I was able to conclude, "I don't want to be a dentist, and I don't have the ability to become one." During my next semester, I took a psychology course and quickly became interested in the subject. I also discovered that I had the aptitude to become a psychologist.

SOCIAL-LEARNING THEORY Krumboltz's (1979, 1996) and Mitchell and Krumboltz's (2002) career decision-making model is based on Bandura's (1977) **social-learning theory**, which contends that learning experiences from observation, modeling, and imitation play a key role in occupational selection. According to the model, career choice is influenced by the following factors (Krumboltz, 1979):

- Genetic endowment places limits on career choice.

- Environmental factors, such as the economy and educational requirements, determine occupational choice to some degree.

- Learning experiences (e.g., observational learning, social modeling, and behavioral reinforcement for pursuing intellectual endeavors) influence one's interest and aspirations.

- Task-approach skills, such as work habits and interpersonal skills, affect one's ability to be successful in a particular occupation.

Cognitive-behavioral theory has also been incorporated into this model (Mitchell & Krumboltz, 2002), in that clients' cognitions and behaviors are seen as influencing career decision making. The importance of cognitive-behavioral strategies in career counseling has also received empirical support, which has demonstrated that cognitive-behavioral approaches contribute to appropriate career decisions and reduce anxiety regarding career decisions (Mitchell & Krumboltz, 1987).

Krumboltz (1996) has attempted to integrate his theory of career decision making into a theory of career counseling. The overall goal of his model "is to facilitate the learning of skills, interests, beliefs, values, work habits, and personal qualities that enable each client to create a satisfying life within a constantly changing work environment" (Krumboltz, 1996, p. 61). Krumboltz (1994) developed the Career Beliefs Inventory (CBI) as a tool that counselors can use during the early phases of counseling to help clients develop cognitions and behaviors that enhance career progress by helping them identify beliefs and assumptions that can impede career decision making. Swanson and Gore (2000) noted that Krumboltz has made great progress in integrating career theory and career practice into a theory of career counseling, but they also stress the need for empirical validation of Krumboltz's social-learning theory of career decision making.

Social cognitive career theory (SCCT), developed by Lent, Brown, and Hackett (1994), was based on Bandura's social cognitive theory relating to career interest, choice making, and performance and persistence in educational and vocational endeavors (1986, 1997). Lent and Brown (2013) expanded SCCT to address the influence of satisfaction, well-being, and self-management on career behaviors necessary to adapt to career challenges across the life span.

SCCT has been utilized in a variety of research studies relating to a wide range of psychological factors. For example, Wright, Perrone-McGovern, Boo, and White (2014) investigated the relationship between SCCT and attachment, career barriers, social support, academic self-efficacy, and career decision self-efficacy. Results of the study showed more securely attached individuals perceive higher levels of social supports and fewer career barriers. In addition, individuals who perceive higher levels of social support report higher levels of self-efficacy relating to career and academic decisions. Fitzgerald, Chronister, Forrest, and Brown (2014) conducted a study of adult male inmates that examined the effects of employment-focused brief group counseling (based on SCCT) on employment-related attitudes and behaviors. Results of the study showed that the SCCT group intervention had a positive effect on variables associated with preparing inmates for reentry into the community in terms of career search self-efficacy, problem solving, and hopefulness.

MULTIPLE CAREER DECISION-MAKING THEORY Gati (1986) and Gati and Tikotzki (1989) contended that all career decision-making theories can be described in terms of three major models, thus putting forward **multiple career decision-making theory**. These models are prescriptive in nature, using logic and rational approaches to identify the best way to make career decisions (Sharf, 2001). Gati and Tikotzki; Carson and Mowsesian (1990); Gati (1990a, 1990b); and Gati, Fassa, and Houminer (1995) have provided detailed descriptions and analyses of these models, which, reduced to their most basic elements, can be summarized as follows:

- *Expected utility model.* This model suggests making separate evaluations of the advantages and disadvantages of various occupations and comparing them to other occupational alternatives. The individual then chooses the occupation with the highest overall value.

- *Sequential elimination model.* This model involves identifying attributes of an ideal occupation (e.g., working outdoors) and ranking the attributes in terms of importance. Minimal levels of acceptability regarding these criteria are established. Occupations are evaluated on the basis of the criteria and sequentially eliminated if they do not meet the acceptable levels.

- *Conjunctive model.* In this model, occupational alternatives are considered only when they meet basic occupational requirements, such as a minimal salary level.

Gati (1986) suggested that no single model of career development is superior to another. The models, instead, should be empirically investigated to determine the conditions most appropriate for their use.

Treatment Issues

Several important treatment issues are involved in career counseling, and this section provides an overview of them, including personal counseling versus career counseling, assessment instruments, the process of career counseling, and intervention strategies.

Personal Counseling Versus Career Counseling

Career counseling appears to generate less interest among counseling professionals than does personal counseling (Birk & Brooks, 1986; Spengler, Blustein, & Strohmer, 1990; Watkins, Lopez, Campbell, & Himmell, 1986; Watkins, Schneider, Cox, & Reinberg, 1987). In a survey of 300 members of the Division of Counseling Psychology of the APA on attitudes toward various counseling activities, personal counseling was ranked as the most important activity, whereas career counseling was ranked 10th (Birk & Brooks). Another survey of members of the Division of Counseling Psychology of the APA showed that members in private practice spend 59.2% of their time conducting psychotherapy and only 3.5% of their time conducting career counseling, and that counseling psychologists are minimally engaged in career counseling and view it as an uninteresting and unattractive alternative to personal counseling (Watkins et al., 1986). An apparent treatment bias in favor of personal counseling is not surprising. Counselors who prefer personal counseling over career counseling engage in diagnostic and treatment overshadowing (Spengler et al.); that is, issues related to personal counseling overshadow the importance of diagnostic and treatment issues related to career counseling. Other studies have shown that vocational problems receive a poorer prognosis and less counselor empathy than personal problems (Hill, Tanney, & Leonard, 1977) and fewer of the core conditions and affective and exploratory responses (Melnick, 1975).

The literature suggests career counseling and personal counseling need not necessarily be thought of in dichotomous terms. Several authors have contended that career counseling should be integrated into nonvocational treatment approaches (Blustein, 1987; Blustein & Spengler, 1995; Richardson, 1996): "Separating work issues from other psychosocial concerns creates an artificial distinction between aspects of life that are clearly interrelated" (Blustein, p. 794). The manner in which a person relates to career issues involves coping strategies similar to those used for other life concerns (Blustein). Blustein and Spengler's comprehensive model integrates personal counseling with career counseling. It incorporates a number of recent counseling trends, such as social constructivism and problem-oriented brief psychotherapy. Richardson has suggested that an important first step in overcoming the personal counseling–career counseling split is to change the name of career counseling to "counseling/psychotherapy and work, jobs, and careers." By placing counseling and psychotherapy first, the role that counseling and psychotherapy theories can play in career development is acknowledged and may also encourage more counselors and psychotherapists to address career issues (Richardson).

Blustein's (1987) guidelines for integrating career counseling with psychotherapy recommend that counselors take a first step of obtaining a detailed work history during the intake process to assist in diagnosis. The next step is to gain a comprehensive understanding of career development and career decision-making theories to broaden one's understanding of human behavior. Counselors can select career theories that are compatible with their theories of personal counseling. For example, Super's (1990) theory of career development with its emphasis on the self could supplement Rogers's (1951) person-centered approach. As another example, Krumboltz's (1996) social-learning theory might be used in conjunction with the cognitive-behavioral approach. Blustein also noted that it is important to integrate career counseling with personal counseling in cases that involve substance abuse problems, since clients with these problems often have trouble with work and personal issues.

Others have attempted to integrate career counseling with personal counseling. Raskin (1987) integrated career counseling with interpersonally oriented counseling, Yost and Corbishley (1987) took a cognitive-behavioral perspective on career counseling, and Gysbers and Moore (1987) described career counseling within a broad framework that includes marriage and family counseling and cognitive psychology. This trend toward integration may promote more interest in career counseling so that these vital client issues and concerns will receive the attention they deserve.

Some individuals may have difficulty with career decision making even though they have had ample opportunity to obtain information regarding their interests, aptitude, the world of work, and so forth (Larson, Busby, Wilson, Medora, & Allgood, 1994). In these instances, Larson et al. suggested that there may be psychological blocks associated with problematic behaviors, cognitions, or feelings (e.g., fear of success or failure and fear of change). These psychological blocks can, in turn, contribute to problems within the personality structure such as low self-esteem, lack of self-awareness, external locus of control, and anxiety, which can undermine the career decision-making process (Larson et al.). Larson et al. noted that the Career Decision Diagnostic Assessment (CDDA) instrument (Bansberg & Sklare, 1986) can be used as a screening device to identify potential psychological blocks to alert counselors that more intense personal counseling may be required to help these clients overcome impasses to the career counseling process. Kjos (1995) provided suggestions for career-focused interventions and treatment planning for individuals who are in need of personality restructuring.

Assessment Instruments

Historically, career counseling has emphasized the assessment of interests, abilities, and personality traits (Phillips, Cairo, Blustein, & Myers, 1988). By increasing self-understanding and providing information on careers and educational programs, these assessment procedures play a vital role in career planning and decision making. An overview of the standardized instruments used in career counseling to assess aptitude, achievement, personality, values, and career maturity follows (Drummond, 2000; Zunker, 2002):

- *Aptitude.* Aptitude tests provide a measure of a particular skill or the ability to acquire a skill. Aptitude tests can be used by career counselors to predict a person's success in career/education training. Examples of aptitude tests are the General Aptitude Test Battery (GATB), the Differential Aptitude Test (DAT), the Flanagan Aptitude Classification Tests (FACT), and the Armed Services Vocational Aptitude Battery (ASVAB). (See Zunker [2002] for information regarding these instruments.)

- *Achievement.* Achievement tests assess current level of functioning regarding abilities such as reading, arithmetic, and language usage. Career counselors use achievement tests to determine academic strengths and weaknesses to assist with educational and career planning and placement. The three major types of achievement tests are diagnostic, broad survey, and subject area tests. Diagnostic tests can be used to determine whether the individual has the essential skills and competencies to be successful in an educational program. Survey tests can provide a general assessment of fundamental skills and competencies. Subject area tests are designed to assess functioning in specific subjects, such as chemistry and biology. Examples of achievement tests are the Wide Range Achievement Tests (a diagnostic test), the National Assessment of Education Progress (NAEP; a survey test), and the College Board Achievement Tests (subject area tests).

- *Interests.* Perhaps more than any other assessment instruments, interest inventories have been associated with career counseling. Interest inventories are used to assess personal and career interests to facilitate education/career planning and placement. Many of these interest inventories can provide useful information regarding the person-environmental fit discussed by Holland (1994). Examples of interest inventories are the Self-Directed Search (Holland), the Strong Interest Inventory (Harmon, Hansen, Borgen, & Hammer, 1994), and the series of Kuder interest inventories based on the Kuder General Interest Survey (Kuder, 1964; e.g., the Kuder Occupational Interest Survey [Zytowski, 1985]).

- *Values.* Values inventories have emerged in the past 25 years to assess the interface between personal values and the world of work. Midlife career changes that correspond to radical lifestyle changes demonstrate the potent influence that values can have on career choice. Congruence between values and career choice is considered an important component in career success and satisfaction. Examples of values inventories are the Work Values Inventory (WVI; Super, 1970), the Study of Values, the Survey of Interpersonal Values, the Survey of Personal Values, and the Values Scale. (See Zunker [2002] for current information regarding these instruments.)

- *Personality.* Career development theorists such as Roe and Super recognized the importance of considering personality in career counseling. Roe's (1956) theory suggests that early personality development within the context of the family influences career direction. Super's (2002) theory is based on the relationship between self-concept and career development. However, even though the relationship between personality and career choice has been established, career counseling has made limited use of personality inventories. A more meaningful use of these inventories in career counseling may come about as personal counseling is increasingly integrated with career counseling. Some of the personality instruments that are used in career counseling are the California Test of Personality, the Edwards Personal Preference Schedule (EPPS), the Guilford-Zimmerman Temperament Survey, the Minnesota Counseling Inventory, the Sixteen Personality Factor (16PF), Temperament and Values Inventory, and the Myers-Briggs Type Indicator.

Career assessment should take into account diversity issues like culture and disabilities. Several interest inventories have been evaluated to determine whether they are valid for ethnic minorities. A literature review of studies investigating the validity of the Strong Interest Inventory (Hansen & Campbell, 1985) for African American clients found little evidence of validity for these clients (Carter & Swanson, 1990). These findings are particularly significant because this instrument is the one most frequently used in college counseling centers (Zytowski & Warman, 1982). However, the Strong-Campbell Interest Inventory (Hansen & Campbell, 1985) has adequate criterion validity for Native American college students (Haviland & Hansen, 1987). Additional research on the cross-cultural use of interest inventories appears warranted.

Levinson (1994) has addressed career assessment issues for students with disabilities. A number of programs and initiatives have been implemented in an effort to meet their special needs. One need is transition planning. According to the 1990 Individuals with Disabilities Education Act (Public Law 94-142), schools are required to formulate transition plans for students with disabilities by the time they reach the age of 16. The overall goal of transition planning is to assist students in making a successful adjustment from school to work and to facilitate effective community living. Contemporary career assessment for students with disabilities is typically structured in three levels. Level 1 begins in elementary school and is focused on building self-awareness. During this time, students explore needs, interests, values, and careers and receive assistance in developing decision-making skills. Level 2 starts in middle or junior high school. Its aim is to assist students in making tentative career choices based on assessment of interests, aptitudes, career maturity, and work habits. Level 3 begins when students reach high school. During this time, assessment can involve a wide range of activities relating to career planning and decision making, such as refinement of issues associated with career choice and assistance with postsecondary education, training, employment, and community living.

Central to the task of counseling students with disabilities is treating them as people who have more in common with others than they have differences. It is also important to be aware of the special needs and requirements associated with their disabilities to facilitate the self-realization that comes about when they achieve their full career potential.

The Process of Career Counseling

Frank Parsons (1909) was one of the first to identify stages of career counseling. He described his three-stage approach as follows. To make an appropriate career decision, the person needs

> (1) a clear understanding of aptitudes, abilities, interests, ambitions, resources, limitations, and their causes; (2) a knowledge of the requirements and conditions of success, advantages and disadvantages, compensations, opportunities, and prospects in different lines of work; and (3) true reasoning on the relations of these two groups of facts. (p. 5)

Salomone (1988) has added two stages to Parsons's (1909) three-stage model. These additional stages focus on interventions that counselors can use after a client makes a career decision. The first stage is helping the client implement educational and career decisions. This might involve helping the client with job-seeking skills and assisting with job placement. The second stage is helping the newly employed individual adjust to the new job. This might involve helping the client deal effectively with job stress, fear of failure, or other barriers to a successful job placement. Salomone (1988) suggested that counselors do not necessarily have to proceed through these stages sequentially but can instead work in several stages simultaneously. He also noted that many counseling strategies are available for helping clients move through these stages, including establishing a positive counseling relationship; helping clients assess their abilities and aptitudes regarding work, including promoting self-assessment; providing information about careers and the world of work; and offering assistance with career placement.

Another model of career counseling, that of Gysbers, Heppner, and Johnson (1998), is similar to the six-stage model of counseling described in Chapter 3. In this model, the working alliance is at the center of the career-counseling process, emphasizing the importance of maintaining a positive relationship throughout the counseling process. The first stage, the *opening stage,* provides an opportunity to establish a working alliance and to work through possible obstacles to career counseling, such as client resistance. Career and personal issues may be addressed at any time throughout the process. Other stages of this model include gathering client information, understanding and hypothesizing client behavior, developing career goals and plans of action, evaluating results, and closing the relationship. The number and order of stages used in career counseling vary according to the unique and emerging needs of clients.

Intervention Strategies

The wide range of intervention strategies used in career counseling includes strategies associated with career planning and decision making, assisting with vocational adjustment, and helping clients overcome personal problems. Career counseling can also take place in a variety of formats, including individual, group, self-help, and computer-assisted programs.

A large body of research evaluating the various forms of career interventions has been summarized in several reviews (Brown & Ryan Krane, 2000; Morrow, Mullen, & McElvoy, 1990). One study shows that it is important to consider client characteristics when formulating treatment strategies (Kivlighan & Shapiro, 1987) and that the clients most likely to benefit from self-help career counseling are rated as realistic, conventional, and investigative on the Vocational Identity Scale of Holland's Vocational Situation (Holland, Daieger, & Power, 1980). Several meta-analyses of career counseling have provided support for the efficacy of career counseling; two of them have received considerable attention in the literature (Oliver & Spokane, 1983, 1988), and both support the efficacy of career counseling. Oliver and Spokane's (1988) review analyzed 58 studies published between 1950 and 1982 in an attempt to gain a more precise understanding of the variables associated with efficacy in terms of types of intervention, client characteristics, and outcome measures. Results of the study show differences in type and intensity of intervention. Individual career counseling produced the most gain per hour of any intervention strategy. Group career counseling and workshops were the least effective intervention per hour of treatment. The study also shows that intensity of intervention is important. Efficacy improved with increased length of sessions and number of sessions.

More recent, meta-analyses of career-counseling outcomes provide additional support for the overall efficacy of career counseling (Ryan, 1999; Whiston, Sexton, & Lasoff, 1998). The Whiston et al. (1998) analysis, based on 47 studies published between 1983 and 1995, showed that career interventions are effective "but how and why they work and for whom they are most (and least) effective is unknown" (Brown & Ryan Krane, 2000, p. 743). Ryan's meta-analysis, based on 62 studies, not only provides support for the overall efficacy of career counseling but also has implications for enhancing the process of career counseling. Five critical components are associated with brief (four- to five-session) group career interventions (Ryan). As summarized by Brown and Ryan Krane, these interventions are as follows:

1. *Have clients write down information* on their career goals and their plans for implementation. Also, engage them in written exercises designed to gain accurate information on careers.

2. *Information on the world of work* emphasizes the importance of ensuring that clients have up-to-date, accurate information on careers, including educational requirements, rewards, and potential challenges associated with different career paths.

3. *Modeling* involves exposing clients to individuals who have been successful in a career to demonstrate how to proceed with career planning and decision making.

4. *Attention to building support* suggests that clients can benefit from a culturally similar support system that can teach the necessary skills to successfully overcome environmental barriers such as racism.

5. *Individualized interpretation and feedback* ensures that clients receive accurate and relevant information regarding self-appraisal, career choice, and decision making.

Savickas (2012) developed Life Design, a model for career interventions that can be used to help individuals adapt to career challenges in the 21st century (e.g., adjusting to multiple job changes throughout life without losing a sense of self or identity). Life Design represents a paradigm shift in career interventions empahsizing "identity rather than personality, adaptability rather than maturity, intentionality rather than decidedness, and stories rather than scores" (Savickas, 2012, p. 14). Life Design is based on career construction counseling (Savickas, 2011) and narrative-constructivist career interventions. In this process, clients construct stories about the self, identity, and careers (e.g., a client struggling with identity issues following job loss). Next, counselors help clients deconstruct stories to address self-limiting horizons (such as racism in the workplace) and reconstruct stories to create a life portrait that can be used to promote meangingful career transitions.

Brown and Ryan Krane (2000) identified three areas for future research on career counseling: (1) further scientific investigation of the five critical components for career counseling identified by Ryan (1999); (2) the development of career interventions for working with clients having difficulty with career choice; (3) how career-counseling interventions can be modified to address diversity issues such as culture, gender, and sexual orientation.

Special Issues

This section covers two special issues in career counseling: career counseling for women and computer-assisted career counseling.

Career Counseling for Women

A major criticism of career counseling is that the majority of its theories and approaches have been based on the study of men and are therefore not sensitive to the issues of women (Brooks, 2002). Several theories have therefore attempted to make career counseling more responsive to women's needs. Two theories and their implications for career counseling for women are reviewed in this section.

SELF-EFFICACY THEORY Self-efficacy, as described in Chapter 9, is the belief in one's ability to successfully perform a particular behavior (Bandura, 1986, 1989). Self-efficacy concerns which behaviors will be initiated, the amount of effort that will be exerted, and how long the behavior will continue in the face of difficult circumstances (Luzzo, 1996). The application of self-efficacy to careers can be traced to the work of Hackett and Betz (1981) and Betz and Hackett (1986). In this context, it can be broadly viewed in terms of its relationship to the various behaviors associated with career choice and adjustment (Lent & Hackett, 1987).

The literature has provided support for career self-efficacy theories in terms of the interrelationship among career interests, self-efficacy, and desirable outcomes (Swanson & Gore, 2000).

Self-efficacy theory has particular relevance to career counseling for women (Hackett & Betz, 1981). A central factor is that women and men acquire different efficacy expectations owing to differential gender-role experiences and limited access to efficacy information (Lent & Hackett, 1987). This in turn can contribute to limiting the positions women hold in the labor force (Brooks, 2002). The career aspirations of women may be restricted by the perception that they lack the necessary job-related skills associated with male-dominated professions and that pursuing those professions may be in conflict with home and family responsibilities (Bonett, 1994). One study identifying gender differences in self-efficacy and career behavior (described by Morrow et al., 1990) found that men report equal levels of self-efficacy in male- and female-dominated occupations, whereas women have higher self-efficacy perceptions in female-dominated fields than in male-dominated ones (Matsui, Ikeda, & Ohnishi, 1989). A second study (also described by Morrow et al.) showed that women have lower self-efficacy perceptions than men in mathematical activities, although mathematical accomplishments are equivalent for men and women with similar preparatory backgrounds (Lapan, Boggs, & Morrill, 1989).

The primary use of self-efficacy theory in career counseling for women could be to broaden career options for women and facilitate the pursuit of those options (Brooks, 2002). Several counseling strategies can be used to promote these outcomes (Brooks), including cognitive strategies to help clients view their abilities more realistically; reattribution training to enable clients to attribute success to internal rather than external causes (Fosterling, 1980); the use of incremental graded success experiences (Lent & Hackett, 1987); vicarious learning, which can be promoted by arranging experiences for clients to "shadow" successful career women; and desensitization procedures to reduce anxiety that relates to career choice and performance.

Current trends in career self-efficacy research (Watkins & Subich, 1995) include integrating career self-efficacy with **social-cognitive career theory** (e.g., Lent, Brown, & Hackett, 1994, 2000) and the role of self-efficacy in work and nonwork settings as a coping mechanism (Matsui & Onglatco, 1992). One conclusion is that career self-efficacy is a robust, but as yet not fully realized, theoretical construct (Watkins & Subich, 1995). The social-cognitive aspects of career theory, which suggest that people will pursue career aspirations associated with perceived self-efficacy, environmental support, minimal environmental obstacles, and desirable outcome expectations (Lent et al., 1994), have also attracted considerable attention.

GOTTFREDSON'S THEORY Gottfredson's (1981, 1996) theory of occupational operations, one of the major vocational theories to emerge in the 1980s (Hesketh, Elmslie, & Kaldor, 1990), applies to both men and women (Brooks, 2002). **Gottfredson's theory** is important to career counseling for women because it explains how compromise takes place in vocational decision making, identifies factors associated with social identity, and explores the difficulties that women face entering nontraditional careers (Hesketh et al.). The following major principles are associated with Gottfredson's model (Brooks, 2002):

- People differentiate occupations in terms of sex type (job preferences relating to gender), work level, and field of work.

- People determine the appropriateness of an occupation in terms of their self-concept.

- Self-concept factors that have vocational relevance include gender, social class, intelligence, values, interests, and abilities.

- Vocationally relevant self-concept factors emerge in the following developmental sequence. From age 3 to 5, individuals understand the concept of being an adult; from age 6 to 8, they develop the concept of gender; from age 9 to 13, they understand the abstract concepts of social class and intelligence; and beginning at age 14, they refine their attitudes, values, traits, and interests.

- People reject occupations on the basis of self-concept as they proceed through the developmental stages.

- The reasons for rejecting occupations have the following hierarchy. Individuals reject occupations when they are not suitable—first in terms of gender, second for social class and ability reasons, and third on the basis of interests and values.

- Occupational preferences result from compatibility between job and self-concept and from judgments about job accessibility.

- Compromise in job choice follows a predictable pattern. People will first sacrifice their interests; then prestige; and finally sex type, or job preferences related to gender.

Gottfredson's (1981, 1996) theory has stimulated a wide range of research activity. Although Brooks (2002) has identified several studies that provide general support for Gottfredson's (1981) model (Henderson, Hesketh, & Tuffin, 1988; Holt, 1989; Taylor & Pryor, 1985), two more recent studies do not support Gottfredson's theory regarding the predictable nature of compromise in job choice. Leung and Plake (1990) found that prestige and not sex type is the most important factor in job choice. Hesketh et al. (1990) further challenged Gottfredson's (1981) position regarding the process of compromise. Results of their study suggest that interests incorporate attributes of prestige and sex type and are therefore the most important factor in job choice and compromise. In a review of the literature on Gottfredson's theory, Swanson (1992) and Watkins and Subich (1995) suggested that the theory needs to be modified in terms of the role of compromise in career decision making. They concluded that compromise appears to be a complex factor in career decision making, varying according to gender, sex-role attitudes, and interests. However, Swanson and Gore (2000) viewed Gottfredson's theory as useful in understanding vocational behavior regarding the role of compromise in career choice and decision making, although they noted that his theoretical constructs are difficult to test and lack empirical validation.

Gottfredson's theory has several implications for career counseling for women (Brooks, 2002). First, Gottfredson's model suggests that clients may experience indecision when they are unaware of the effects of sex type, prestige, and interests on career choice and compromise. Counselors can assist these clients by helping them clarify their vocational priorities in terms of these factors. Second, clients may need assistance in identifying occupations that are acceptable in terms of their self-concept. Third, clients may have aspirations that are incongruent with their abilities or interests. In these instances, counselors can evaluate the client's aspirations to determine whether they are associated with self-defeating processes, such as trying to live up to other people's standards.

Computer-Assisted Career Counseling

Computer-assisted career counseling (CACC) has become important in the delivery of career counseling in North America (Sampson, 1994). Although most clients can benefit from CACC, clients with stable goals gain the most in vocational identity as the result of using CACC (Kivlighan, Johnston, Hogan, & Mauer, 1994). Several factors have contributed to the increased use of CACC (Sampson): lower hardware costs; improved hardware and software capabilities, such as color graphics and more comprehensive and diversified programs; and increased expertise of counselors and other professional helpers in using CACC. Increasingly widespread availability of the Internet has also played a role.

Several authors have commented on the importance of including direct counseling services with computerized career counseling. The problems that could occur when computerized career counseling is used without direct counselor contact include use by inappropriate clients, clients not understanding the purpose or operation of the system, and clients not being able to integrate their computerized counseling experience into their decision-making process (Sampson, Shahnasarian, & Reardon, 1987). In addition, ethical standards require information orientation prior to and following administration of tests, including those given through computer-assisted career-counseling programs (Johnston, Buescher, & Heppner, 1988). Direct counseling also enhances the effectiveness of subsequent computer-assisted program use (Dungy, 1984). Thus, CACC can be viewed as an adjunct to direct career counseling. It provides a useful starting point for clients to gain information with which to narrow down their career choice (Sampson, 1994). Counselors must monitor the client's use of CACC by engaging in an ongoing dialogue with the client and assisting with the integration and interpretation of information to foster appropriate decision making (Gati, 1994).

Numerous computerized career programs are currently available. Heppner and Johnston (1985), Maze (1984), and Zunker (2002) have provided a description and comparative analysis of the major programs. Table 13.1 includes the computer-assisted career programs described by Zunker and some of the most current programs available.

Selecting from the wide variety of computer-assisted career programs can be overwhelming. Following are guidelines for selecting the most appropriate program (Maze, 1984):

- *Obtain staff input.* Perform a needs assessment with the staff, identifying areas that could be improved by computerized programs.

- *Obtain relevant information about the programs under consideration.* Evaluate each program in terms of cost, software packages, hardware requirements, and user population.

- *Arrange for demonstrations of software programs.* If possible, preview all software before purchasing a program.

- *Evaluate samples of the system's output.* Review sample printouts produced from each module or component of the system before deciding on a program.

- *Determine the total cost of the system.* Calculate the total cost of each software and hardware system under consideration.

- *Determine the cost per user.* Calculate the maximum, minimum, and average estimates for potential users to determine the cost-effectiveness of the system.

- *Determine one-time charges and ongoing charges.* Examples of one-time charges are the cost of a printer and a telephone adapter. Ongoing charges include the costs of renewing software packages and maintaining equipment. There may also be ongoing expenses associated with mainframe or centralized systems.

Diversity Issues in Career Counseling

As in other areas of counseling, diversity issues concerning differences in age, gender, culture, sexual orientation, socioeconomic status, race, ethnicity, and spirituality are becoming increasingly important in career counseling. There are no comprehensive models of career development for ethnic and racial minorities (Hackett & Byars, 1996). Practitioners must therefore take care when extrapolating from theory to practice and infuse awareness of culturally sensitive issues when appropriate. Education and

Table 13.1 Computerized Career Programs

Program Name	Publisher and Year	Program Overview	Special Features	Role of Counselor Client
Computerized Career Assessment and Planning Program (CCAPP)	Cambridge Career, 1989 (updated every 2 years)	Assists with career assessment, selecting alternatives, career planning, and career exploration.	Provides information on over 1,200 occupations, a list of college majors or vocational courses relating to career interest, and an individual career plan and a job-hunting plan.	Some aspects can be used independently by clients, but counselors explain how a counselor can use the program to assist the client.
C-LECT	Chronicle Guidance, 1991 (updated annually)	Assists with career awareness, exploration, decision making, and educational planning.	Connects 14 school subjects with over 700 occupations, describes 717 occupations, has five self-assessment options, provides information on financial aid, and answers questions on specific colleges and universities.	Can be used with minimal counselor assistance.
Choices	Human Resources Development—Canada, 1997	Assists with self-knowledge and assessment, career exploration, planning, and decision making.	Matches interests with careers, identifies schools that have programs and majors associated with career choice, and provides information on schools.	Can be used with minimal counselor assistance.

(Continued)

Table 13.1 (Continued)

Program Name	Publisher and Year	Program Overview	Special Features	Role of Counselor Client
DISCOVER	The American College Testing Program, Version 4.3, 1990	Assists with career choice and decision-making skills; enhances the general adjustment of the client.	Provides opportunities to take interest, ability, and value inventories, producing scores that are used to conduct job searches and search for college majors or programs of study; provides information regarding various occupational fields and educational institutions.	Can be used in conjunction with career planning, curriculums, or workshops.
The Guidance and Information System (GIS)	Riverside, Houghton Mifflin, 1991	Provides information on 1,200 primary occupations and 3,000 related occupations; grouped according to the US Office of Educational Occupational Clusters and the Dictionary of Occupational Titles (DOT)	Provides accessibility through a telephone and teletypewriter or display terminal that receives signals and prints or displays copy.	Not designed to be the sole source of career and educational information but can be a meaningful tool for the career counselor.

socioeconomic status are critical variables in the utility of career-counseling theories for minorities (Arbona, 1996). Although career-counseling theories can be useful cross-culturally with individuals who are progressing educationally or with those who are middle or upper class, theories that emphasize career choice appear to have less utility for individuals who live in poverty and/or are school dropouts (Arbona). In these instances, a more appropriate approach may be to foster cognitive, academic, and social emotional development (Arbona).

Additional cultural considerations in career counseling relate to Asian Americans and other ethnic minorities (Leong & Chou, 1994). Identity development, acculturation, and assimilation are key variables that can affect perceived prejudice, stress, and educational and career aspirations and expectations. For example, Asian Americans who rate low on acculturation and assimilation tend to score high on perceived prejudice and stress. Issues of prejudice and stress should therefore be monitored and addressed as potential barriers to career counseling. Of all minorities, Asian Americans also tend to suffer the highest degree of career stereotyping and segregation. The tendency is to perceive Asians as having skills in the fields of science and mathematics but not in careers that emphasize language and interpersonal relations. It is therefore not surprising that they are underrepresented in careers like law and overrepresented in science and engineering. Acculturation and assimilation levels may be important intervening variables. Individuals who have low levels of acculturation appear to be more vulnerable to the adverse effects of stereotyping and segregation than are people who are more assimilated into mainstream society. Movement toward assimilation and acculturation may promote a corresponding stage of identity development that rejects stereotypical views of career choice and decision making.

Asian Americans, African Americans, and Hispanics all experience potential career barriers relating to educational and career aspirations and expectations. There tends to be a greater discrepancy than for Whites between educational and career aspirations and the degree to which these individuals expect to achieve their goals, owing in part to perceived discrimination against minorities. Career counselors must therefore be cognizant of these perceptions and associated issues, such as motivation and discouragement. In addition, counselors can take a proactive role in helping clients overcome discriminatory practices that are having adverse effects on clients.

Women's career development has received the most attention in the career-counseling literature and continues to be the leading topic in scholarly investigation (Swanson & Gore, 2000). Issues of gender permeate all aspects of career development, including the complex interaction of personal/family life and the world of work (Swanson & Gore). As a result, these issues are perhaps more important in career counseling than in other specialty areas of counseling, owing in part to a long history of sexual discrimination in the workforce and practices of sex-role stereotyping, with its adverse consequences on career choice and decision making. Self-efficacy theory and Gottfredson's theory, described earlier in this chapter, can be useful in addressing women's career issues. For example, one of the most important issues that career counselors should address when working with African American women is how experiences of racism have an impact on their self-efficacy expectations (Hackett & Byars, 1996).

Age is another important consideration. Career counseling has historically focused on helping high school–age students with the process of career choice and decision making. In a world of rapidly changing technology and in an era when people are living longer, it is becoming increasingly common for individuals to change careers numerous times over their life span. Career counseling is therefore broadening its base to include a life span perspective. The concept of *career* needs to be redefined in order to encourage a developmental perspective in career counseling (Watts, 1996). The old concept of *career* as a progression up a hierarchical ladder within a profession or organization is obsolete (Watts). A more realistic concept of *career* is that it is a subjective experience and a lifelong progression in learning and work (Watts). This definition recognizes that people are ultimately responsible for defining their existence in terms of the world of work and the focus of their experience is on what they have learned and what they have contributed in their work. Seligman (1994) provided additional information regarding the theory, research, and practice of career counseling across the life span (childhood, adolescence, early adulthood, middle adulthood, and late adulthood). For example, self-esteem enhancement and career education can be important components of career counseling with children, and postretirement issues of work and leisure can become a focus in career counseling during late adulthood (Seligman).

Issues of sexual orientation represent another example of diversity in career counseling. It is especially important for career counselors to be aware of the special career issues of LGBTQ individuals. Sexual orientation and degree of openness about sexuality can influence the type of job and work environment one chooses (Chung, 1995). Unfortunately, theories regarding the career development of LGBTQ individuals have been slow to appear (Chung), although several researchers have attempted to fill the void; for examples, see Fassinger's (1995) study on lesbian identity in the workplace and Prince's (1995) study of the career development of gay men. Fassinger's research describes how lesbian identity development and theoretical constructs of the vocational psychology of women can be integrated with the vocational issues of lesbians, providing useful information that can help sensitize counselors to lesbian issues. For example, lesbians do not usually rely on men for financial support and therefore tend to seek employment that makes them more financially independent than their heterosexual female counterparts.

One means of addressing diversity and multicultural issues is the recommendation to incorporate social justice principles into vocational development and career counseling through the Emancipatory Communitarian Approach (Blustein, McWhirter, & Perry, 2005). Socially and economically disadvantaged individuals often have little choice or control over the world of work and few, if any, opportunities regarding career choice and decision making (Blustein et al.). This disparity is believed to be due in part to the inequities associated with the privileged prospering at the expense of disadvantaged individuals. Some believe that vocational psychologists and others in the career-counseling field should engage in social justice activities (Blustein et al.). According to the view, the primary goal of social justice is to "understand and transform mechanisms that perpetuate oppression, maintain privilege, and preserve social inequities" (Blustein et al. p. 143). Social justice, therefore, must be focused on observable results and not just social/political rhetoric (Blustein et al.).

Evans (2008) has provided an example of how multicultural counseling competencies could be applied to counseling specialities. Using the 31 multicultural competencies identified by Arredondo et al. (1996), she applied them to career counseling in terms of the counselors' awareness of their cultural values and biases, awareness of the worldview of clients, and multiculturally sensitive interventions.

SUMMARY

Several trends are emerging in career counseling, including the use of computer technology. The chapter describes popular career software and provides information that can aid in its selection. This chapter also provides an overview of diversity issues in career counseling, especially issues concerning women, as well as other factors that must be carefully considered in career counseling—age, culture, race, ethnicity, sexual orientation, and socioeconomic status.

PERSONAL EXPLORATION

1. How do you view the concept of career across your life span?

2. What do you believe are potential obstacles to your career growth?

3. How important is your career relative to other parts of your life, such as your personal relationships, social life, and family life?

4. Could you relate any of the career theories to your own career development, and if so, how?

5. What are your thoughts regarding interest inventories?

6. What experiences have you had regarding career counseling?

7. What are your career plans, and what do you believe are the challenges associated with reaching your goals?

8. What do you think about retirement? When should someone start to do retirement planning?

9. What are your thoughts about self-efficacy theory in career counseling?

10. What is cognitive-dissonance theory, and how might you apply it to everyday life situations?

LEARNING ACTIVITIES

1. Consider exploring career issues with a career counselor (e.g., university counseling centers can be a good source of assistance).

2. Read a book that can help you explore career issues (e.g., the best-selling book *What Color Is Your Parachute?*).

WEBSITES

SimilarMinds.com. (n.d.). *Personality tests.* Retrieved from http://similarminds.com/personality_tests.html. *Provides free online personality tests and assessment tools used by some career counselors.*

National Career Development Association. (2009). Retrieved from http://associationdatabase.com/aws/NCDA/pt/sp/Home_Page.

School Counseling

The Art and Science of School Counseling

It is an art to try to reach a reluctant or resistant student who has problems with drugs, gang involvement, and family. School counselors work closely with community agencies and organizations and consult with parents, teachers, and staff to provide services to students facing these and other problems. The art of school counseling lies in being sensitive to individual differences and embracing diversity as an opportunity to expand educational horizons. Flexibility and creativity are also necessary. Counselors can adjust their counseling approach by using innovative strategies such as play therapy (Campbell, 1993), music therapy (Newcomb, 1994), and sand play (Carmichael, 1994).

There is also an objective-scientific dimension to school counseling. Action research can be used to promote data-driven practice, accountability, and schoolwide goals such as enhanced student achievement and social justice (Dahir & Stone, 2009). A meta-analysis of school counseling research suggests that school counseling activities (such as individual counseling and group counseling) play an important role in enhancing students' academic and personal development (Borders & Drury, 1992). The more naturalistic approach of qualitative research offers a practical alternative to the more traditional statistical hypothesis testing associated with quantitative research. The use of the semistructured interview, for example, is an emerging trend in school counseling (Baker, 1995).

Research has an essential role in the future of school counseling. A school counselor's expertise in nine problem areas that students commonly face—self-esteem, eating disorders, child and adolescent suicide, depression, teenage pregnancy, drug abuse, physical and sexual abuse, stress, and divorced parents—is critical because these problems are roadblocks to children's psychosocial development (Capuzzi, 1988).

Chapter Overview

This chapter provides an overview of the issues relating to school counseling. Highlights of the chapter include the following:

- **The art and science of school counseling**

- **A comprehensive developmental model for guidance and counseling**

- **The role and function of school counselors**

- **Special skills and problems, including counseling exceptional students**

- **Trends in school counseling**

A Comprehensive Developmental Model for School Counseling

Developmental school counseling represents a shift from remediation and crisis intervention to learning and development (Paisley & DeAngelis-Peace, 1995). In the comprehensive developmental model (Paisley & Benshoff, 1996; Paisley & Borders, 1995; Paisley & DeAngelis-Peace), the term *comprehensive* refers to the notion that school counseling programs should function as an integral part of a K–12 program, not as separate entities. The *developmental* focus suggests that school counseling programs should be organized from a life span perspective: "The developmental program is proactive and preventive, helping students acquire the knowledge, skills, self-awareness, and attitudes necessary for successful mastery of normal developmental tasks" (Paisley & DeAngelis-Peace, p. 87). Some of the states that have comprehensive, K–12 developmental guidance programs are Arkansas, Illinois, Iowa, Missouri, New Hampshire, North Carolina, Ohio, Oklahoma, and Wisconsin (Bergin, Miller, Bergin, & Koch, 1990).

Two individuals who have played key roles in formulating comprehensive, developmental school counseling models are Robert Myrick and Norman Gysbers. In his model, Myrick (1987) identified a number of goals and objectives for counseling that focus on personal and social development, decision making and problem solving, career education, and educational planning. Gysbers (2004) suggested that a comprehensive guidance and counseling program should be implemented for Grades K–12 and provide school counselors with an opportunity to communicate accountability. Gysbers's program has three elements: content, an organizational framework, and resources (Gysbers, 2004; Gysbers & Henderson, 2012). The first element, *content,* relates to the mission statement and provides a rationale for school counseling and assumptions on which the program is based. The second element, *an organizational framework,* has the following four program components:

- *Individual planning.* Assisting students (in conjunction with parents) in carrying out their academic, career, and personal plans

- *Guidance curriculum.* Structured activities such as classroom presentations on time management

- *Responsive services.* Individual and small-group counseling, consultation, and referral

- *System support.* Using system support to organize and administer the program

The third element concerns whether or not a program has the necessary *resources.* According to Gysbers, a comprehensive guidance and counseling program requires adequate finances, personnel, and political support.

Gysbers developed his program in 75 schools in Missouri between 1984 and 1988; thus it is referred to as the *Missouri model* (Good, Fischer, Johnston, & Heppner, 1994). Gysbers estimated that the Missouri model is being used in some form in approximately 30 states in the United States. Gysbers also played an influential role in developing the recent National Model of School Counseling (ASCA, 2003, 2005, 2012), which incorporated an organizational framework of individual planning, guidance curriculum, response services, and systems support and included an emphasis on program accountability.

Neukrug, Barr, Hoffman, and Kaplan (1993) set forth a developmental school counseling and guidance model that has been supported by the **American School Counseling Association** (ASCA). School counselors can use this simple yet flexible model to address the special needs of the students they serve. The model, which is grounded in developmental theory, encourages counselors to implement interventions consistent with students' developmental tasks. It is a proactive model "whose primary emphasis is fostering the learning and growth of all students, with a secondary emphasis on assisting individual students with the resolution of special problems and concerns" (Neukrug et al., p. 358).

There has been only a limited amount of research on the effectiveness of these programs. A study by Bergin et al. (1990) evaluated a developmental guidance model called *Building Skills for Tomorrow* (Oklahoma State Department of Education, 1988) that was being implemented in a rural school district. The study found that the program elicited positive responses from parents, teachers, and community leaders. Additional support for the comprehensive, developmental school counseling model came from a survey of the attitudes of students, teachers, and parents toward the Missouri Comprehensive Guidance Program (Hughey, Gysbers, & Starr, 1993). Results indicated that school counselors were perceived as caring individuals whom students could freely go to for assistance in career and college planning and individual and group counseling. In addition, students, parents, and teachers believed that schools should hire additional school counselors.

School counselors have had difficulty implementing comprehensive programs because they do not clearly understand the concept and have difficulty translating these ideas into practice (Paisley & Borders, 1995). The knowledge and skills necessary to implement these programs include being well grounded in developmental theory (including understanding how change occurs); being familiar with programs such as peer-helping programs, which have successfully fostered development; and being aware of emerging strategies, such as person-to-environment fit (Paisley & Benshoff, 1996; Paisley & DeAngelis-Peace, 1995). Skills include using developmental theory in assessment to determine appropriate interventions and consulting with parents and teachers. Other skills include using dilemma discussions to help students explore difficult situations and the reasoning they use in making their choices (Paisley & Benshoff).

Technology could play an important role in implementing developmental school counseling (Casey, 1995). Casey contended that modern technology must be integrated into all aspects of the school counseling program, including individual counseling, small- and large-group counseling, and consultation. Casey provided examples of how technologies like interactive CD-ROMs and the Internet can be used with students of different ages. For example, a possible technology strategy with 10-year-olds is to develop a technology club, since fostering friendships is an important priority for students at this age.

A Developmental Perspective

The developmental perspective, which is central to the comprehensive, developmental school counseling model, represents a shift from the clinical role to the role of promoting prevention (Gysbers & Henderson, 1988). In this role, counselors work closely with teachers to promote developmental guidance and counseling as an integral aspect of the overall school program. The goals of developmental school counseling can never be fully realized unless teachers become active in offering guidance activities in the classroom (Myrick, 1987).

Several individuals have incorporated the developmental perspective into their counseling approach (e.g., Blocher's 1974 and 1987 work on developmental counseling and Ivey's 1986 developmental therapy). These theories suggest that counselors should first identify a client's developmental level and then implement an approach that addresses the needs for that level. **Developmental counseling** approaches incorporate various theories of development. Ivey (1986) emphasized Piaget's (1955) theory of cognitive development, whereas Blocher (1974, 1987) focused on Havighurst's (1972) concept of developmental tasks and Erikson's (1963) psychosocial theory. As noted elsewhere, developmental theories have also become increasingly sensitive to diversity issues as exemplified by Carol Gilligan's (1982) work on gender and moral development.

Blocher's (1974) model suggested that certain developmental tasks are associated with each stage of development. Clients must master coping skills to meet the challenges of these tasks to successfully move forward to the next developmental task. Blocher (1974) contended that counseling goals and strategies can be developed to help individuals master the necessary coping skills as they proceed through the life span.

According to Blocher (1974, 1987), elementary school students face the developmental tasks of industry and initiative. These tasks can be facilitated by establishing counseling goals that help students implement activities on their own and feel competent when competing with peers. Counselors can promote industry and initiative by helping students value themselves and feel a sense of control over their environment. Counseling strategies (such as consultation, individual counseling, and group counseling) that foster self-concept development and encouragement can be used to facilitate achievement of these counseling goals.

Blocher's (1974, 1987) theory can also be applied to middle school students. The main developmental task during these years is identity formation. Counseling goals can be developed to assist with this task, such as helping students enhance their self-awareness and clarify their values. The counselor can use consultation, individual counseling, and group counseling to address these issues as well as other problems that require attention.

The primary developmental task for high school students is intimacy. This task requires developing the skills necessary to establish close, trusting relationships with siblings, peers, parents, and others. The counseling goals associated with this task include promoting students' concern and interest in others and enhancing interpersonal relationship skills. Consultation, individual counseling, and group counseling that focus on social-skills training can be particularly useful as strategies to promote interpersonal effectiveness.

An overview of these developmental tasks, counseling goals, and associated counseling strategies according to Blocher's model is provided in Table 14.1. These tasks and their associated counseling goals and strategies can be useful in providing a focus for counseling services. At the same time, counselors should not limit their programs to these tasks and strategies. A comprehensive, developmental school counseling program should address a wide array of issues that concern school-age children, such as divorced parents, drug and alcohol abuse, and teenage pregnancy.

Table 14.1 Developmental Tasks, Goals, and Counseling Strategies

Age Level	Developmental Tasks	Counseling Goals	Counseling Strategies
Elementary school	Industry and initiative	To foster independence and autonomy	Consultation and individual and group counseling to promote self-concept development; encouragement strategies to help students believe in their capabilities and implement activities on their own; self-control interventions for students whose impulse control interferes with their ability to complete tasks
Middle school	Identity formation	To help students gain a clear understanding of who they are as individuals	Consultation and individual and group counseling to promote self-awareness and value clarification
High school	Intimacy	To promote social interest and interpersonal effectiveness	Consultation and individual, group, and family counseling to promote social interest and compassion for others; group counseling to foster interpersonal effectiveness; career counseling to relate to the world of work

Role and Function of School Counselors

One of the most controversial issues in school counseling has been the role and function of school counselors. The controversy has centered on the difficulties that school counselors have faced in trying to establish a clear professional identity (Paisley & Borders, 1995) and what steps should be taken to overcome these problems. One way to make a clear statement about the role and function of school counselors is to describe the main mission of school counseling in terms of enhancement of learning. Ultimately, all school counseling activities should maximize learning potential in students. For example, self-concept and school achievement have been shown to have a positive correlation (Hamachek, 1995). Therefore, a counselor who enhances a student's self-concept will contribute to the student's learning potential.

This section addresses the central issues associated with the school counselor's role and function, such as counseling from a historical perspective; the current ASCA role statement (1990); and the role and function of school counselors working in elementary, middle, and high schools and in rural schools.

A Historical Perspective

A historical perspective can be useful for understanding how the school counselor's role and function have evolved. Gysbers's (1988) description and observations on the history of school counseling have been incorporated into the following overview.

School counseling as a specialty began to develop in the period from 1909 to 1920. Its origins can be traced to the pioneering work of Frank Parsons (1909), who provided vocational guidance services in schools. During the 1920s, this emphasis shifted from vocational guidance to assistance with personal adjustment.

In the 1930s, there was an attempt to differentiate guidance from vocational guidance. The term *guidance* was broadly defined as assisting individuals who have problems adjusting to any aspect of life, including issues involving health or family and friends as well as work. *Vocational guidance* was more narrowly defined as helping people with choice, preparation, placement, and advancement in a vocation. During this period, school counselors also began to use more formal terms such as *counseling, assessment, information, placement,* and *follow-up* to describe what occurred in the helping process.

The initial impact of Carl Rogers's views of counseling was felt in the 1940s. Rogers's *Counseling and Psychotherapy* (1942) had a dramatic effect on the role and function of the school counselor. His person-centered approach provided a theoretical framework for individual counseling and resulted in school counselors adopting an overall clinical emphasis. Rogers's work continues to have a major impact on contemporary school counselors as they attempt to assist students with an ever increasing array of personal problems.

During the 1950s, support for school counselors increased with the passage of the National Defense Education Act (Public Law 85-864). This act allocated funds to colleges and universities for training students to become secondary school counselors.

In the 1960s, the focus shifted from guidance to promote adjustment to developmental guidance. Developmental guidance stresses the importance of understanding and working with students from a developmental perspective. It also places greater emphasis on preventing problems than on merely helping students adjust to their existing problems. School counselors continue to utilize the developmental perspective.

In the 1970s, the developmental perspective expanded to include a comprehensive K–12 developmental guidance model. This period also saw a national effort to integrate career education into the overall school program, an effort met with resistance from some teachers and administrators because they believed it took valuable time away from necessary academic endeavors. The integration of career education into the public schools therefore had limited success. This decade also saw the passage of the Education for All Handicapped Children Act (Public Law 94-142) in 1975. As a result of this act, the role of school counselors was expanded to include coordinating the testing and placement of exceptional students and assisting with the development and implementation of their individual education programs. The 1970s also introduced the use of personal computers in test scoring, scheduling, and career counseling and the beginning of group counseling in guidance and counseling programs.

During the 1980s, career guidance received renewed federal support. The Carl D. Perkins Vocational Education Act was passed in 1984 in response to the belief that public schools were not preparing students adequately to obtain employment or continue postsecondary education. Several states have used these funds to develop K–12 counseling and guidance programs. To qualify for these funds, states must provide opportunities for students to acquire job skills. The 1980s also witnessed a growing awareness of the importance of multicultural issues in counseling. School counselors began to modify their counseling approaches to include a multicultural perspective.

The 1980s was also a time of changes in the fabric of society that dramatically affected school-age children. During this period, school counselors witnessed substantial increases in divorce, suicide, drug and alcohol abuse, teenage pregnancy, and eating disorders. As a result, school counselors invested increasing amounts of energy in implementing prevention and treatment programs to address these complex issues. Examples include drug prevention and awareness programs, group counseling for children of alcoholics and children of divorce, parent education, and family counseling. At the same time, financially conscious educational systems began to scrutinize the effectiveness of school counseling and, as a result, placed greater emphasis on counselor accountability.

School counseling in the 1990s faced many opportunities and challenges. Counselors continued to deal with an ongoing array of social problems that students faced, such as drug use, violence in the schools, teenage pregnancy, and dropping out of school. Diversity issues were also emphasized as counselors conceptualized their role and function.

Numerous challenges and opportunities face school counselors in the 21st century. One central challenge relates to job security for school counselors, which has been undermined by economic factors such as downsizing and hiring part-time employees to provide school counseling (Paisley & Borders, 1995). The school-based mental-health movement is one example of how external funding is being used to bring people from different disciplines into the helping profession to provide counseling services in schools.

Some of the current influences that are reshaping the school-counseling profession include the reform movement associated with the Transforming School Counseling Initiative (Erford, House, & Martin, 2003) and the Education Trust (The Education Trust, 2002). These are also beginning to reshape the school counseling profession. For example, school counselors are being encouraged to establish school-community partnerships for the delivery of counseling services.

Another collaborative idea is to partner school counselors with counseling psychologists. These counseling specialties appear to be good candidates for collaboration since they both have roots in career counseling and human development and promote client strengths over deficits (Romano & Kachgal, 2004). Counseling psychologists can offer supervision and research skills for school-community partnerships, and in turn their professional identity can be enriched by the association with school counselors. School counseling's developmental/preventative perspective can be a welcome alternative for counseling psychologists, who have seen a recent emphasis on remediation in clinical work (Kenny, Waldo, Warter, & Barton, 2002). The as yet underutilized partnership of school counseling and counseling psychology therefore appears to warrant further investigation (Romano & Kachgal).

The American School Counselor Association (ASCA) has also played a role in the current redefinition of school counseling. The ASCA National Standards for School Counseling Programs (Campbell & Dahir, 1997) and the ASCA National Model (ASCA, 2003, 2005, 2012) provide a framework for developing and implementing school counseling programs. The ASCA (2010) also has an ethical code (Ethical Standards for School Counselors) that provides guidelines for professional practice.

Increased federal legislation (especially regarding students with exceptionalities) and other legal considerations are also having a major impact on education and the role and function of school counselors in the 21st century. For example, school counselors must be aware of legislation such as Section 504 of the Rehabilitation Act and the Individuals with Disabilities Education Act (IDEA) to ensure that issues of disability are considered in the educational process, including the manner in which students are disciplined. In addition, the Health Insurance Portability and Accountability Act (HIPAA) privacy rule provides safeguards regarding the security and privacy of individually identifiable health information. The No Child Left Behind Act of 2001 (NCLB, 2002) established schoolwide achievement standards for students, expectations regarding yearly progress, and strategies for overcoming barriers to learning.

The Current ASCA Role Statement, Definition, Standards, and National Model

ASCA revised its 1981 role statement in 1990. A significant change was the absence of the earlier differentiation among the roles and functions of counselors working in elementary, middle, and high schools. Instead, the statement identified five interventions that apply to all school counselors to promote a clearer and more concise understanding of the overall role and function of school counselors. The five basic interventions common to all school counselors identified in the statement are individual counseling; small-group counseling, which involves five to eight students; large-group guidance, which includes nine or more students, such as in a classroom; consultation; and coordination of the counseling program.

The revised ASCA role statement recognized and supported the comprehensive developmental guidance and counseling model. In this regard, school counselors should adjust the counseling approach to the developmental levels of students as they progress through the educational system. The aim of school counseling is to promote educational, social, career, and personal development so that students can become responsible, productive citizens. In addition, the ASCA recommends that the ratio between counselors and students should be 1:250 and that school counselors should spend 70% of their time providing direct services to students (Lum, 1999).

In 1997, the ASCA adopted a new definition of school counseling:

> Counseling is a process of helping people by assisting them in making decisions and changing behavior. School counselors work with all students, school staff, families, and members of the community as an integral part of the education program. School counseling programs promote school success through a focus on academic achievement, prevention and intervention activities, advocacy and social/emotional and career development.

This definition of school counseling is consistent with the comprehensive, developmental school counseling movement, which is focused on preventing problems and maximizing the learning potential of all students.

Campbell and Dahir (1997) assisted the ASCA in establishing national standards that could be incorporated in a comprehensive K–12 school counseling program. The national standards identified student competencies in three general areas: academic, career, and personal/social development. An example of a personal/social standard would be "Students will acquire the attitudes, knowledge, and interpersonal skills to help them understand and respect self and others" (Campbell & Dahir, p. 17). The ASCA suggested that these national standards be conceptualized as content standards for students (i.e., things they should know and be able to do in school). More recently, the ASCA (2003, 2005, 2012) established the ASCA National Model, which provides a framework for developing and implementing a comprehensive K–12 school counseling program. The ASCA National Model incorporates principles and recommendations from the ASCA national standards (Campbell & Dahir), the Education Trust (2002), and the Transforming School Counseling Initiative (Erford et al., 2003; Romano & Kachgal, 2004).

The National Model helped clarify the role of the school counselor and provided a framework and set of components that could be used to standardize all school counseling programs (ASCA, 2012). Four themes emerged from the ASCA National Model: leadership, advocacy, collaboration, and systemic change. Implementation of these themes promotes a shift in the role of the school counselor from an emphasis on providing direct services to a limited number of students with serious problems to working systemically to promote positive outcomes for all students (e.g., enhancing the school climate and school/community relationships). In addition, school counselors are encouraged to engage in leadership, advocacy, and collaboration to address barriers to learning so that all students can be successful and benefit from programs. For example, school counselors are encouraged to collaborate with counseling psychologists to create prevention programs.

The ASCA National Model also recommends that school counseling programs be based on four central elements: foundation, management, delivery, and accountability.

- *Foundation.* The foundation of the school counseling program is based on the academic, career, and personal/social needs of the students.

- *Management.* Management "provides organizational assessment and tools designed to manage a school counseling program" (ASCA, 2012, p. 41).

- *Delivery.* Delivery "focuses on the method of implementing the school counseling program to students" (ASCA, p. 83).

- *Accountability.* Accountability is a data-driven process that answers the question "How are students different as a result of the program?" (ASCA, p. 99).

The ASCA National Model represents the zeitgeist of the school counseling field. School districts can use it as a framework to develop and implement a comprehensive K–12 school counseling program.

Scarborough and Culbreth (2008) found that school counselors preferred to practice in a manner consistent with the ASCA comprehensive, developmental school counseling model and were more successful when they

- believed tasks led to specific outcomes;

- had organizational support;

- were committed to the National Model for School Counseling; and

- had sufficient experience to implement school counseling interventions.

Scarborough and Culbreth (2008) also found that elementary school counselors were the most successful in practicing in a manner consistent with the comprehensive, school counseling model (high school counselors were least successful in this regard). The authors suggested that elementary school counselors may be more successful because the comprehensive, developmental model is emphasized more in elementary schools than in high schools. Additional research on the ASCA National Model will be necessary to evaluate its effect on promoting student competencies and educational success.

Role and Function by Grade Level and Setting

The literature provides extensive information about the specific goals and strategies school counselors can use to work with students at various levels and in various settings. For example, Hardesty and Dillard (1994) surveyed 369 school counselors in terms of the activities they perform at elementary, middle, and high schools. Results of the survey showed that elementary school counselors focus on consulting with teachers, staff, and parents and engage in small- and large-group guidance programs with a preventative focus (e.g., drug prevention). Middle school counselors direct their efforts toward a variety of tasks such as personal counseling, conflict resolution, and scheduling students' classes. High school counselors' priorities include assisting with college or trade school admission (including help with scholarships and financial aid), career counseling, and scheduling and other administrative tasks.

Whiston, Tai, Rahardja, and Eder (2011) conducted a meta-analytic review of school counseling interventions. Results of the study provided evidence of the overall efficacy of K–12 school counseling interventions, especially in terms of helping students solve problems and reducing disciplinary infractions. Unfortunately, the research did not identify specific interventions that promoted these positive outcomes.

More specific information regarding the role and function of elementary, middle, and high school counselors follows.

ELEMENTARY SCHOOL COUNSELING Elementary school typically includes students from kindergarten through fifth grade. Elementary school counseling emphasizes prevention (Muro, 1981). In this regard, counselors spend a large percentage of their time consulting with teachers and parents to promote the child's mental health and leading group guidance activities (such as self-concept development).

Several studies have attempted to describe the role and function of elementary school counselors. A survey of how 130 elementary school counselors perceive their current role and their ideal role revealed three interesting observations (Morse & Russell, 1988). First, three of the top five functions listed as actual roles involved consultation. Second, these counselors ranked the function of helping teachers understand students' needs first as an ideal role, but it was ranked only fourth among functions they currently perform. Third, four of the top five ideal roles indicated that counselors want to engage more in group counseling, including activities such as social-skills training.

The results of this study emphasize the importance of elementary school counselors obtaining skills in consultation and group counseling.

A survey of how 313 teachers perceived the role and function of elementary school counselors showed that teachers view elementary school counselors as functioning primarily in the dual role of helper and consultant (Ginter, Scalise, & Presse, 1990). The helper role entails activities such as individual and group counseling, assessment, interpreting tests, and conducting guidance activities. The consultant role involves providing technical advice and expertise to school staff and parents. The authors of the study concluded that there appears to be congruence between how teachers and elementary school counselors view their role and function.

Another study surveyed teachers, principals, and parents to determine their views regarding the role and function of elementary school counselors (Miller, 1989). Elementary school counselors were believed to fulfill 28 functions related to six tasks: developmental or career guidance, consulting, counseling, evaluation and assessment, guidance program development, and coordination and management. Results of the survey show that teachers, principals, and parents strongly endorse these six tasks as relevant functions for elementary school counselors. The researcher believes the study provided grassroots support for a developmental model of elementary school guidance and counseling. Collectively, all of the studies cited here recognize the importance of the developmental model of counseling and the necessity for elementary school counselors to develop skills in direct services, such as group counseling.

Trice-Black, Bailey, and Riechel (2013) suggested that elementary school counselors can use play therapy to address the social-emotional needs of students. They provided guidelines for how play therapy can be incorporated into a comprehensive developmental school counseling program. The following *Personal Note* speaks to why I have found elementary school counseling very rewarding.

A Personal Note

I enjoyed working as an elementary school counselor. I liked the diversity of activities, which included play therapy, counseling, consulting, and working with parents. I also found children fun and exciting to work with because they are so open, spontaneous, and interested in exploring the world around them.

When I work with children, I feel a sense of optimism that real and lasting changes can be made. Their problems have usually not yet become well-established facets of their personality. I firmly believe that early intervention can prevent children's problems from blossoming into major mental disorders and can prevent them from becoming school dropouts. I often think that more of the educational and mental health budget should be invested in elementary school counseling. In the long run, I think it would be the most effective approach.

MIDDLE SCHOOL COUNSELING The middle school phenomenon is relatively recent. This level of schooling typically provides educational opportunities to students from Grades 6 through 8. The concept evolved from the junior high educational system, which encompassed Grades 7 through 9, and it represents an attempt to group students together as they make their transition from childhood to adolescence.

The literature shows that the role and function of the middle school counselor are just beginning to be formulated. A study that compared the ideal role of middle school counselors as perceived by counselors and principals showed essential agreement between them (Bonebrake & Borgers, 1984). Both groups ranked individual counseling first in importance. Other tasks ranked high by both groups include consultation, coordination of student assessment, interpretation of tests, and evaluation of guidance programs, suggesting that middle school counseling is similar to elementary school counseling in terms of the emphasis on consultation and direct services. One difference is that middle school counseling appears to emphasize individual counseling, whereas elementary school counseling stresses the importance of group counseling.

Conflict resolution skills are important for all students. Middle school students seem to be particularly prone to problems with interpersonal conflict, such as jealous reactions within peer groups. Conflict resolution strategies can be used with couples, small groups, or a classroom. Dysinger (1993) provided goals and objectives for conflict resolution for middle school students that are summarized as follows. The overall goal is for the participants to create a win-win experience based on understanding one another, accepting disagreements, and working toward resolution—not establishing who is right and wrong. The actual process of conflict management can involve tasks such as helping students to (a) separate the problem from the person, (b) enhance their tolerance for individual differences, (c) create insight into how relationships deteriorate, (d) learn how to respond to conflict sensitively rather than react abrasively, and (e) become aware of choices and options.

One method of conflict resolution that can be used in a classroom is the inside-outside fishbowl, an Adlerian-based approach that attempts to foster encouragement and mutual respect among students (Nelson, Thomas, & Pierce, 1995). In this process, a facilitator works with a small group of students in a time-limited, focused discussion on a topic of concern, while the rest of the class listens and provides feedback at the end of the discussion. The fishbowl approach can create opportunities for gaining a broad perspective on understanding and resolving conflicts. As in all group work, issues regarding confidentiality and informed consent must be addressed.

SECONDARY SCHOOL COUNSELING The origins of secondary school counseling can be traced to the vocational guidance movement that began in the early 1900s. Since that time, secondary school counseling has been closely identified with vocational and career guidance and counseling. The role and function of secondary school counselors have centered on assisting students in making the transition from public school to postsecondary education, acquiring vocational training, and entering the world of work.

Secondary school counselors tend to be assigned numerous clerical tasks, including scheduling and administrative functions such as assisting with disciplinary programs. The result has been a loss of clear mission (Aubrey, 1982) and a "role mutation" that has seriously damaged the professional image of school counselors (Peer, 1985). Hutchinson, Barrick, and Groves (1986) provided evidence of the role mutation phenomenon cited by Peer in a study that compared actual and ideal functions of secondary school counselors. According to the study, counselors believe they should ideally provide the traditional counseling activities of personal, academic, and group counseling. In actual practice, however, scheduling takes up more time than any other activity except personal counseling. The study concluded that counselors are performing noncounseling activities at the expense of more important functions such as group counseling, career and life planning, and providing classroom guidance. This observation was supported by a study noting that scheduling of students appears to take a higher priority than do the critical functions of promoting developmental guidance and counseling (Tennyson, Miller, Skovholt, & Williams, 1989).

When high school counselors do engage in direct counseling services, they are often unable to invest the necessary time and energy because of large numbers of students and conflicting role demands. Rowe (1989) surveyed the type and extent of involvement that high school counselors have with high school students. He found that counselors had sessions with 80% of the students who went to college. The primary purpose of this contact was to assist with college plans. Unfortunately, counselors averaged only two sessions with each student, for a total of 15 minutes. The students received the largest number of contacts—approximately five—regarding college planning from parents and friends. Results of this study suggest that high school counselors are not providing sufficient information about college planning, even though it is the main topic they are addressing with high school students (Rowe).

RURAL SCHOOL COUNSELING The role and function of school counseling vary not only according to educational level but also in terms of rural versus urban settings. Rural counselors have fewer referral sources and must therefore rely on their own resources and become jacks-of-all-trades (Sutton & Southworth, 1990). This can contribute to rural counselors experiencing more job-related stress than do urban school counselors (Sutton & Southworth). At the same time, they feel more freedom, strength, optimism, and happiness than urban counselors (Sutton & Southworth). In addition, rural school counselors tend to have more positive relationships with their principals than do urban counselors (Sutton & Southworth), which may be the result of rural counselors having more contact and involvement with their principals (McIntire, Marion, & Quaglia, 1990).

McIntire et al. (1990) noted that 40% of rural counselors do not work with other counselors and must therefore develop their own support systems, They also suggest that for counselors to be successful in rural settings, they must be aware of the special needs and circumstances of the community and become actively involved in the community.

More recently, Morrissette (2000) conducted research on rural school counseling that supports earlier research by McIntire et al. (1990) and Sutton and Southworth (1990). Morrissette found that rural school counseling is characterized by the following:

- A lack of personal privacy and anonymity, thus minimizing personal space and freedom

- Feelings of isolation (e.g., not having other school counselors with whom to formulate a distinct professional identity)

- A lack of community resources, requiring school counselors to be generalists and handle a wide range of problems

- Continuity of relationships with students that enable school counselors to get to know their students and their families over a long period of time

Students in rural schools face special challenges in terms of postsecondary education (Rubisch, 1995). Three interrelated problems are academic runoff, low self-esteem, and low career expectations. *Academic runoff* involves the brightest students leaving the rural community and not returning, thereby reducing the number of role models and mentors available to other students; this, in turn, can have an adverse effect on those students' self-esteem and career expectations. Rural school counselors can play a pivotal role in enhancing students' career aspirations by exposing them to postsecondary educational alternatives in junior and middle school, including field trips to college campuses (Rubisch).

Special Skills and Problems

This section discusses the special skills and problems associated with school counseling. These include consultation, counseling exceptional students, and some of the special problems that students face: drug abuse, teenage pregnancy, divorced or single parents, and dropping out of school.

Consultation

Dougherty (1995) defines *consultation* as "a process in which a human service professional assists a consultee with a work-related (or caretaking-related) problem with a client system, with the goal of helping both the consultee and the client system in some specified way" (p. 9). The individual who functions as a consultee varies according to the situation and may be a parent or teacher who has requested assistance on how to provide effective discipline for a child so the child can function better at home or school.

The four stages of consultation are summarized as follows (Dougherty, 1995):

Stage 1: *Entry.* Consultation begins with the consultant formulating a relationship with the consultee, determining the nature of the problem, and formulating a contract regarding the nature and scope of the consultation activities.

Stage 2: *Diagnosis.* Diagnosis involves making an assessment of the problem and determining possible goals and objectives.

Stage 3: *Implementation.* Once a diagnosis is made, an action plan can be formulated, implemented, and evaluated.

Stage 4: *Disengagement.* When the goals and objectives have been met, consultation processes can allow for a natural process of disengagement or "winding down" of services.

Dougherty (1995) also identified the following three models of consultation:

1. ***Organizational consultation*** conceptualizes the problem and directs interventions from a systems or organizational perspective.

2. ***Mental health consultation*** conceptualizes the problem and directs interventions with the goal of enhancing the mental health of individuals within the organizational structure.

3. ***Behavioral consultation*** takes a behavioral perspective (such as social-learning theory) toward conceptualizing problems and implementing interventions.

These three models are interrelated, and all consultation, to some degree, utilizes all three perspectives (i.e., it focuses on behaviors and the overall system to enhance mental health; Dougherty, 1995).

SCHOOL CONSULTATION Consultation, one of the primary functions of school counselors, involves providing assistance to teachers, parents, and administrators (Hall & Lin, 1994). Hall and Lin developed an integrative model of **school consultation** based on Dougherty's (1995) four-stage model (entry, diagnosis, implementation, and disengagement). These authors addressed some special considerations in school consultation, such as potential confusion in terms of role expectations since the consultant and consultee will typically know each other and work in the same building (e.g., counselor-teacher or counselor-administrator). In these instances, they recommend that expectations be made clear during the entry phase of consultation and that empathy, genuineness, respect, and concreteness be used to facilitate this process.

The following *Personal Note* is an example of how a school counselor conceptualized consultation in her problem-solving model.

A Personal Note

While I was teaching a school counseling course, I asked my wife, Laura (an elementary school counselor), if she had any material that would illustrate what school counselors do. She smiled and showed me a flowchart she had recently developed that describes what happens when a child is referred for counseling services. The flowchart (shown in Figure 14.1) provides a description of how she addresses problems that are presented by students in her school. The flowchart also communicates to staff, teachers, and parents what procedures she utilizes in the referral process. In addition, the flowchart is a required part of the Baldridge accountability program utilized in her school (all staff/teachers are required to develop flowcharts to depict tasks they perform).

Laura said that her flowchart was not meant to be a blueprint for how school counselors should address problems. She also noted that she did not apply the flowchart in a rigid fashion but modified it to address special issues as necessary.

In addition, the flowchart illustrates the role of consultation in the school counseling process. Consultation encourages ongoing communication and input from stakeholders and may be unique in school counseling because it occurs so often, interfacing with many aspects of the counseling process. Many consultations are informal interactions, such as a teacher "running a problem by" the school counselor for informal input.

The flowchart also illustrates other aspects of the school counseling process, such as obtaining informed consent from parents/guardians and how referral to a specialist may be required as part of the problem-solving process.

Consultation is especially important in elementary school counseling (Hall & Lin, 1994). To a large degree, the use of consultation in elementary school can be traced to the pioneering work of Don Dinkmeyer and Jon Carlson, who demonstrated how Adlerian principles can be used effectively in consulting with teachers, administrators, and parents (Dinkmeyer & Carlson, 1973). Dinkmeyer (1971, 1973) developed a collaborative model of consultation called the "C group," which can be used with groups of parents and teachers. It was designed to create a communication channel to discuss such issues as how to deal with children's misbehavior. It was called the C group model because the forces that operate within the group begin with the letter C: collaboration, consultation, clarification, confrontation, communication, concern, caring, confidentiality, change, and cohesion. Opportunities exist for school counselors to provide consultation services at all levels of public schools. Griggs (1988) suggested that school counselors should expand their consultation role to become facilitators of learning. Ferris (1988) noted that consultation is needed to provide safe, secure, and positive learning environments.

Results of a survey of school counselors on the merits of parent education as a consultative service show wide support for parent education (Ritchie & Partin, 1994). Although 84% of the counselors surveyed recognized the need for parenting

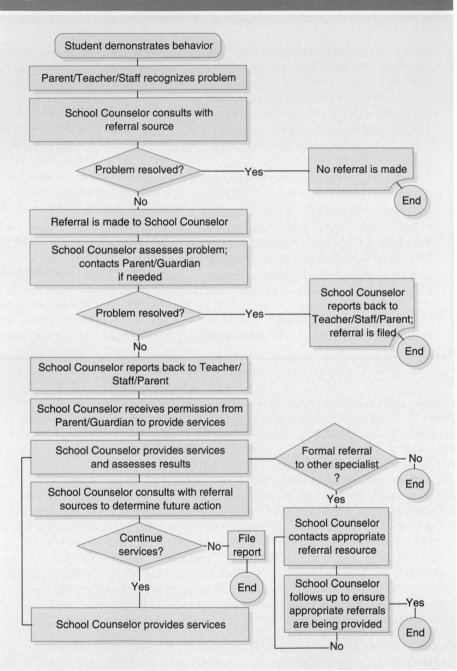

Figure 14.1   Referral and Consultation Flowchart

consultation, only half offered training and had an interest in providing this service. There appeared to be a gender and grade-level bias, with more female elementary school counselors expressing interest and involvement in parent education. Perhaps counselor educators need to focus more on this form of school consultation.

The following *Personal Note* describes why I have found consultation in schools rewarding.

A Personal Note

Some of my most rewarding experiences over the years have involved consultation with teachers, parents, and staff, including the use of parent education concepts. It is really exciting to see these individuals gain skills and confidence that they can use to overcome problems and enhance their life experiences. I see consultation as having the goal of educating for empowerment. In this process, I attempt to share information and strategies in a manner that can be easily understood and applied. I begin with sharing tools for understanding problems (such as why children misbehave) because I believe that understanding is always a prerequisite to change. In addition, I contend that understanding can foster connection, which in turn can lead to caring and compassion between people. And the caring and empathy between people can often be an important first step toward overcoming problems.

Tools for accomplishing change can then be explored in relation to the client's concerns. This, as in all phases of consultation, must be a highly individualized process that takes into consideration issues of diversity and the client's phenomenological perspective. I believe that for consultation to be successful, it must have meaning in terms of the client's worldview and be integrated into the client's internal frame of reference. The outcome of consultation is therefore clients achieving a heightened state of self-efficacy regarding the development of skills to understand and solve problems.

Counseling Exceptional Students

Glenn (1998) estimated that between 10% and 12% (40 to 50 million) of school-age children in the United States have some recognizable exceptionality. Issues that relate to counseling **exceptional students** have had a major impact on school counseling. An exceptional student can be defined as an individual whose physical or behavioral condition deviates from the norm in a manner such that special services are required to meet the individual's needs (Hardman, Drew, Egan, & Wolf, 2002). The following is an overview of legislative acts and guidelines concerning the counseling of exceptional students.

LEGISLATIVE ACTS Several federal laws deal with the identification and education of exceptional students. Key legislation includes the Education of All

Handicapped Children Act, the Americans with Disabilities Act, Section 504 of the Rehabilitation Act, and IDEA legislation, which are briefly described here.

The passage of the Education for All Handicapped Children Act (Public Law 94-142) in 1975 and the Americans with Disabilities Act (Public Law 101-306) in 1990 had a major impact on education reform and school counseling. Public Law 94-142 provided for public education within the least restrictive environment for all students with disabilities. This law has had a dramatic effect on the role of the school counselor (Cole, 1988). In many schools, the counselor has become the case manager for exceptional students, a role that requires counselors to devote enormous amounts of time to coordination activities, such as handling paperwork, attending meetings, and placing students (Cole). Counselors have also become more involved in providing counseling services to disabled students and their families.

The Americans with Disabilities Act's goal is to ensure civil rights protection to people who have disabilities (Helwig & Holicky, 1994). This landmark legislation prohibits discrimination in employment, public services (including education), transportation, and telecommunication (Parette & Hourcade, 1995). Parette and Hourcade went on to note that physical, policy, and procedural barriers can contribute to discrimination against individuals with disabilities. This includes not having equal access to all public places, such as a lack of wheelchair ramps providing access to schools and libraries.

Section 504 and IDEA legislation have also had a major impact on educational reform. These laws have redefined educational policies and procedures, creating enormous opportunities and challenges for educators. In 1990, Public Law 94-142 was renamed the Individuals with Disabilities Education Act (IDEA). IDEA legislation is updated every 3 to 5 years and covers the policies and procedures regarding the assessment, placement, education, and discipline of students with disabilities. IDEA guidelines are used to qualify students for special education services in terms of their physical, intellectual, or emotional disabilities. Once students have been placed in special education services, individual education programs (IEPs) are developed according to their special needs. IDEA legislation also ensures that disciplinary procedures take into consideration students' disabilities and avoid penalizing students for misbehavior that is the result of a disability. When possible, schools must first attempt to adjust students' IEPs to remediate problems associated with misbehavior.

Section 504 of the Rehabilitation Act of 1973 provides additional assistance to disabled students. Students who do not meet the full criteria for disability according to IDEA may still be considered disabled if they have physical or mental impairments that substantially limit their ability to learn and function at school. These students are not classified as special education students. Examples of 504 disabilities are medical conditions like a broken arm or being HIV positive. Included are students who have attention-deficit hyperactivity disorder (ADHD) but do not qualify for special education. Students who fulfill the criteria of 504 are entitled to special accommodations for their disabilities. For example, a student with a broken leg can be given extra time to get to class. Other 504 modifications and special considerations include enhanced physical access to school facilities, individualization of the educational program, and ongoing assessment and reevaluation as a prerequisite to educational placement. As is the case with IDEA, 504 requires disciplinary action to take into consideration students' disabilities. For example, common disciplinary actions such as suspension would probably not be appropriate if the student's misbehavior was due to the disability.

School counselors can play an important role in educational reform by ensuring that federal guidelines are applied in a manner that maximizes the learning potential of all disabled students. IDEA and 504 legislation offer both opportunities and challenges. Opportunities arise in the establishment of policies and procedures that encourage consideration of diversity issues associated with disabilities. Attempts to individualize educational programs help identify special needs and conditions that may undermine the learning process. Individualization of rules and policies can be a very taxing process for educators, however. Special challenges include legislative restrictions on discipline, which may impede attempts to reduce student violence and aggression. School counselors can play an important role in educational reform by ensuring that federal guidelines are applied in a manner that maximizes the learning potential of all disabled students. School counselors may wish to take a leadership role in terms of emerging legislative acts such as amendments to Section 504 and IDEA. Appropriate implementation of these laws is a high priority in school districts to ensure appropriate dissemination of available federal and state funding, avoid lawsuits and time-consuming legal action, and promote safeguards and educational opportunities for students.

Other legislation that has strongly affected the public schools includes the No Child Left Behind Act of 2001 (NCLB, 2002). This act has had a major impact on how schools are run through its special emphasis on accountability in educational achievement. NCLB monitors progress toward educational goals for all students, including students with exceptionalities, thus creating challenges for educators working with students with special needs. The Health Insurance Portability and Accountability Act (HIPAA) of 1996 and the HIPAA Privacy Rule of 2003 (Code of Federal Regulations, Title 45, Part 164) have broad implications for how health care information is communicated. HIPAA required the US Department of Health and Human Services to create a series of rules to safeguard health-related information. HIPAA legislation affects school health care workers, such as nurses, psychologists, and physiotherapists, because it deals with confidentiality and the release of health-related information to a third party.

Implementing the various federal mandates is an extremely complex process requiring various legal-ethical decision-making skills. School counselors can play a role in facilitating programs such as NCLB and Section 504 to ensure that all students (regardless of their disability) have access to equal educational opportunities. Compliance with these legislative acts creates opportunities for school counselors to perform highly specialized and essential services. Doing so can go a long way to dispel the notion that school counselors lack specialized, essential skills and are therefore soon to become obsolete.

GUIDELINES FOR COUNSELING EXCEPTIONAL STUDENTS School counselors should be familiar with the needs and services associated with different types of disabilities (Helwig & Holicky, 1994) and therefore aware of the special issues connected to counseling exceptional students.

Perhaps the most basic guideline is to understand that these individuals are more similar to those without disabilities than they are different (McDowell, Coven, & Eash, 1979). Exceptional students should therefore be treated as unique individuals first and people with special needs second. This attitude can help counselors become sensitive to individual differences and avoid stereotyping clients. A second guideline is to be aware of the common problems that exceptional students face. Students with exceptionalities often lack social skills and have problems with interpersonal relationships (Ciechalski & Schmidt, 1995). Students with physical abnormalities may be particularly prone to interpersonal difficulties (Goldberg, 1974). Social-skills training has a positive effect on their relationships, and the benefits can be enhanced by involvement with students who are not in special education (Ciechalski & Schmidt). Students with exceptionalities also tend to have problems with self-concept, body image, frustration, and dependency (Rotatori, Banbury, & Sisterhen, 1986).

Students with disabilities tend to suffer self-concept problems as a result of a history of frustration and failure (Bello, 1989). These failure-oriented experiences can contribute to irrational beliefs such as "I am not able to do schoolwork," "People think I'm dumb," and "In order to be successful, I must be able to do as well as people without disabilities" (Bello). Cognitive approaches can therefore play a key role in helping students overcome a failure orientation and improve their self-concept (Bello).

Parents of students with physical abnormalities tend to discourage them from exploring their bodies, contributing to a sense of denial (McDowell et al., 1979). Rotatori et al. (1986) therefore recommended that these students be encouraged to explore their bodies and accept their particular disabling condition. They also suggested that exceptional students can become frustrated when they do not feel they can measure up to expectations, undermining their self-confidence. Frustration can lead to behavioral problems like aggression (Talkington & Riley, 1971), sarcasm and cynicism (McDowell et al.), and stubbornness (Clarizio & McCoy, 1983). Counseling strategies can be directed at resolving frustration by providing a means for venting the negative emotions and fostering competency skills that prevent frustration (Rotatori et al.).

It is not uncommon for parents and teachers to foster dependency in an exceptional student because they believe the individual is incapable of functioning independently. Overdependent students can lack motivation and experience academic difficulties. They can also be easily influenced by peer pressure to engage in inappropriate behavior (Rotatori et al.1986). Counseling strategies should be directed at helping these students feel capable, maximizing their self-confidence and promoting self-reliance.

A third guideline for counseling exceptional students is to be aware of the special needs and counseling strategies associated with the various types of exceptionality.

For example, students with intellectual disabilities tend to experience social and emotional problems associated with rigid behavior. Behavior therapy has been proven effective at teaching self-help skills, enhancing social skills, and eliminating inappropriate behavior. Table 14.2 incorporates information from Rotatori, Gerber, Litton, and Fox (1986) and Parette and Hourcade (1995) to describe the special needs, counseling goals, and associated counseling strategies for nine categories of exceptionality. The following *Personal Note* describes how pet therapy can be used with exceptional students.

A Personal Note

I have found that pet therapy is an excellent tool for working with clients of all ages, especially with students with exceptionalities. Pet therapy involves using animals like dogs, cats, birds, fish, and horses to help individuals overcome various kinds of physical and emotional problems. I first learned of pet therapy from Dr. Herman Salk, the brother of Dr. Jonas Salk, who developed the polio vaccine. I met Herman when I worked on the Navajo Indian reservation. He was a veterinarian and had used pet therapy in a wide variety of settings. I was inspired by the passion he had for animals and his method of using pet therapy to overcome communication barriers, foster positive relationships, and enhance social interest.

Over the years, I have used pet therapy in a wide variety of settings—in nursing homes, schools, mental health clinics, and hospitals. My research on pet therapy has shown that it can promote physical and mental health (Nystul, Emmons, & Cockrell, 1992). For example, hospitalized patients tend to have a higher survival rate and faster recovery if they have a pet to go home to. Pet therapy has also been used to help individuals overcome shyness, aid in self-confidence, and provide a means of working through emotional disorders.

Pet therapy appears to be particularly useful in counseling exceptional students. Pets, such as seeing-eye dogs for the visually impaired, can provide meaningful stimulation and facilitation of sensory modalities. Pets can also be useful with seriously emotionally disturbed students. For example, caring for a pet can help a student overcome problems with anger management. Counselors may also bring a pet to a counseling session to overcome resistance and to enhance the counseling relationship. A friend of mine used to bring her parrot to work with her. The parrot was very friendly and would talk to her clients. As you can imagine, she was very popular and always had an abundant supply of students who wanted to see her. Naturally, some schools may have a policy against bringing pets to school.

I once was treating a suicidal student. With the approval of her parents, I was able to have her pick out a pet at the local animal shelter and adopt it. I explained to the student that she would be saving a life instead of taking a life. This seemed to bring meaning to her life, and the suicidal ideations soon subsided. I have been amazed by the profound effects that pets have on people. I encourage you to explore this exciting dimension of the counseling process.

Table 14.2 Counseling Exceptional Children

Disorder	Special Needs or Problems	Counseling Goals	Counseling Strategies
Students with intellectual disabilities (Litton, 1986; Parette & Hourcade, 1995)	High incidence of social-emotional problems due to rigid behavior; restricted life experience; problems perceiving personal and social situations	Improve social adaptation; enhance self-help skills; increase awareness of self and others; assist with development of interpersonal relations skills; promote a positive self-image.	Behavior therapy to teach self-help skills, enhance social skills, and eliminate inappropriate behavior. Be clear and concise when communicating, limit the number of directions, communicate respect, provide positive feedback when possible.
Students with learning disabilities (Gerber, 1986)	Poor self-concept and self-esteem; tendency to be rejected by peers; lack of self-appraisal skills; fear of failure; test anxiety; lack of motivation	Enhance self-esteem and self-concept; promote effective social skills; help overcome fear of failure; promote a positive attitude toward the learning process.	Self-concept programs, interpersonal relations training, and cognitive behavioral approaches to overcome a fear of failure
Students with mild behavioral disorders (Raiche, Fox, & Rotatori, 1986; Parette & Hourcade 1995)	Problems with impulse control, aggression, and defiance; emotional problems; hyperactivity; academic problems	Increase tolerance for frustration and self-restraint; help overcome academic difficulties; improve interpersonal relations skills.	Cognitive-behavioral techniques to teach anger control, play therapy and group counseling to assist with social-emotional problems, interpersonal relations training to enhance social skills. When a student misbehaves, don't overreact. Also, ask concrete, direct questions.

Disorder	Special Needs or Problems	Counseling Goals	Counseling Strategies
Students with speech or language disorders (Kelley & Rotatori, 1986)	Interpersonal problems resulting from exclusion, overprotection, and ridicule; educational difficulties; self-esteem problems; anxiety	Help develop coping mechanisms to deal effectively with negative remarks of peers; help broaden and adapt communication skills to various settings; improve interpersonal relations skills; enhance self-concept and self-esteem; overcome educational difficulties.	Cognitive-behavioral approaches to deal effectively with negative remarks; self-concept programs; and communication development in small groups
Students with hearing impairments (Sisterhen & Rotatori, 1986; Parette & Hourcade, 1995)	Language difficulties, including problems with articulation and voice quality, vocabulary, syntax, and grammar; social-emotional problems such as social isolation, emotional immaturity, behavioral problems, difficulty with interpersonal relations; identity problems	Assist with identity formation; encourage independence; help develop appropriate social skills (e.g., reduce tendencies to appear physically aggressive).	Behavioral counseling strategies that incorporate social modeling (particularly effective since children who are deaf tend to follow examples set by significant others); guidance programs that focus on self-concept development to promote identity formation. Speak directly to the student and look toward the student (not at an interpreter) to make it clear that your communication is directed at the student. Also, speak slowly and clearly and emphasize nonverbal communication such as facial expressions and gestures.

(Continued)

Table 14.2 (Continued)

Disorder	Special Needs or Problems	Counseling Goals	Counseling Strategies
Students with visual impairments (Heinze & Rotatori, 1986)	Low self-confidence; low self-concept; self-criticism; social isolation	Increase self-confidence; improve self-image; reduce tendencies toward self-criticism and social isolation.	Assertiveness training to increase self-confidence; cognitive-behavioral approaches to reduce tendencies toward self-criticism; interpersonal relations training to increase social interest. Introduce yourself before you begin talking and cue the student when a discussion is about to end and you are going to leave. Offer assistance if the student looks confused. If necessary, provide assistance that meets the student's needs.
Students with physical disabilities (Griffin, Sexton, Gerber, & Rotatori, 1986; Parette & Hourcade, 1995)	Problems vary according to disability type: Some need assistance with basic functioning such as eating, personal hygiene, and locomotion; others need assistance in establishing intimate relationships (including sexuality) or dealing with ridicule.	Help identify personal strengths to overcome physical disabilities; encourage students to become involved in self-advocacy to foster a sense of self-control over their life.	Adlerian counseling to identify strengths to overcome weaknesses; existential approaches to discover personal meaning in life; sex education and sex therapy to deal with sexuality issues. Sit when talking with someone in a wheelchair to maintain appropriate eye contact (that is, avoid talking down to the student).

Disorder	Special Needs or Problems	Counseling Goals	Counseling Strategies
Students with health impairments (Griffin, Gerber, & Rotatori, 1986)	Health problems such as leukemia, diabetes, asthma, or a seizure disorder that can interfere with academic functioning or psychosocial development	Alleviate anxiety, depression, and bodily discomfort; maximize bodily functioning; assist with academic difficulties.	Cognitive-behavioral strategies for anxiety and depression; stress management techniques and an exercise program to maximize bodily functioning; family therapy to help with familial factors associated with a seriously ill individual
Students identified as gifted (Kaufmann, Castellanos, & Rotatori, 1986)	Difficulties with peer relations due to being singled out as the "brain of the class"; lack of motivation and underachievement when not challenged	Increase awareness of self and others; enhance problem-solving and decision-making skills; clarify values and personal aspirations; maximize intellectual potential.	Appropriate classroom placement to ensure adequate academic challenge; career counseling (including the use of a mentor) to encourage pursuing personal goals and aspirations; personal counseling to increase awareness of self in relation to others
Students who have been abused (Kennell & Rotatori, 1986)	Multitude of problems such as dependency, anger, depression, anxiety, self-blame, withdrawal, low self-esteem, interpersonal relations, and educational problems	Improve self-image; promote positive interpersonal relations skills; assist with anger control; alleviate anxiety and depression; help overcome educational difficulties.	Counseling strategies that focus on helping students realize that they were not responsible for what happened, that the abuse was wrong, and that it will stop; self-concept development programs; cognitive-behavioral approaches to promote anger control and alleviate depression.

Source: Adapted from *Counseling Exceptional Students*, 1986, A.F. Rotatori, P.L. Gerber, F.W. Litton, & R.A. Fox (Eds.), Copyright 1986 by Human Science Press.

Special Problems

Students do not have to be exceptional to encounter problems in school. All face increasingly diverse problems and challenges as they progress through the school years. McWhirter, McWhirter, McWhirter, and McWhirter (1994) have identified the "five Cs of Competency" that are associated with students doing well in life: critical school competencies (including basic academic skills), the concept of self and self-esteem, communication skills, coping skills, and a sense of control. Students who lack these qualities are at high risk for self-destructive behaviors like school violence, mental health problems, substance abuse, teenage pregnancy, and dropping out (McWhirter et al.). An overview of these and other problems and challenges follows.

SCHOOL VIOLENCE **School violence**, such as fighting, bullying, and fatal shootings, is on the increase. A nationwide survey of 15,000 students in the year 2000 showed that 37% of middle school boys and 43% of high school boys believed that it is OK "to hit or threaten a person that makes me angry" (Josephson Institute of Ethics, 2001). In addition, the survey showed that 75% of male students and 68% of female students had in the past year hit someone who made them angry. Perhaps of more concern is the fact that 11% of middle school students and 14% of high school students had taken a weapon to school in the past year, and 31% of middle school boys and 60% of high school boys said they could get a gun if they wanted to. With the high incidence of aggression and violence in schools, it is not surprising that 39% of middle school students and 36% of high school students reported that they did not feel safe in school.

A number of factors are believed to contribute to school violence. For example, Popkin (2000) emphasized the role of the media (television, music, video games, and the Internet) in promoting youth violence, claiming that up to 15% of violence can be directly related to violence in the media. Other factors associated with youth violence include family dysfunction and societal values that promote getting even over social interest (Popkin). Positive parenting programs and spirituality that promotes forgiveness over revenge can play an important role in overcoming youth violence (Popkin).

Bullying has been receiving considerable attention as a possible factor associated with school violence. Bullying can be defined as teasing, harassing, or taking advantage of someone less powerful and can take many forms (e.g., physical, verbal, social, or cyberbullying (Phillips & Cornell, 2012). Bullying is widespread, with 41% of respondents to a survey claiming they have been picked on in school (Labi, 2001). Bullying has been linked to fostering a negative school climate and to school violence, including suicide and homicide. For example, the US Secret Service found that 37% of school shootings involved a shooter who at one time had felt bullied or threatened or had been the victim of violence (Labi, 2001). In addition, individuals who engage in bullying have a 4 times greater risk than others of engaging in criminal behavior by the time they reach early adulthood (Spivak & Prothrow-Stith, 2001).

A number of schools have implemented programs to address the problem of bullying, which can be summarized as follows (Labi, 2001; Lazar, 2001):

- School climates need to be changed so that students do not feel it is appropriate to bully. For example, parents and students can sign a contract at the beginning of the school year agreeing that students should not be teased or harassed because of their appearance, gender, race, performance, and so forth.

- Skill improvement in areas such as problem solving, conflict resolution, moral-ethical decision making, and character building as well as assertiveness training can help prevent aggression and bullying before it starts.

- Students, teachers, administrators, staff, and parents need to agree not to tolerate bullying and to report it when it occurs.

- Training on bullying intervention is necessary.

Phillips and Cornell (2012) noted that victims of bullying are often reluctant to seek help, and school staff are often unaware of victims of bullying. They suggested that school counselors obtain input from peers regarding who is being bullied and have follow-up interviews with potential victims to provide necessary support. School counselors can implement antibullying programs to ensure that bullying behavior does not continue, thereby promoting positive school climates and safer schools. They can also utilize a variety of interventions such as psychoeducational drama with the victims of bullying (to empower) and bullies themselves (to overcome bullying tendencies; Beale & Scott, 2001).

School counselors can also promote safe schools by working with other school personnel, such as school psychologists, to identify students who are at a high risk for engaging in violent acts. Hawkins et al. (2000) identified a list of potential risk factors associated with youth violence that can be especially useful in assessing students' threats to harm other students:

- Having a mental disorder (especially substance abuse), participating in antisocial behavior, and having deviant beliefs

- Being in a victim role (such as having been abused or bullied)

- Being socially isolated and lacking social ties

- Having low levels of parental involvement

- Having a history of violence and aggression (especially early onset)

- Experiencing high levels of exposure to crime and delinquency at school, at home, or in the neighborhood

- Experiencing academic failure, truancy, and lack of bonding to school

- Having ready access to firearms

Individuals with psychosis are considered to have a higher risk for violent behavior (Cornell & Sheras, 2006). This is especially true for psychotic individuals with paranoid delusions. In these instances, a person may contend that violence is justified because others are out to get them or are evil and must be killed (Cornell & Sheras). Psychotic individuals who also suffer from mania are at additional risk of violence because they tend to have excessive energy, which can undermine their ability to control their behavior (Schwartz, 2008).

Several violence prevention programs have been developed to address school violence. One comprehensive school-based violence prevention training model focuses on providing training on violence prevention to administrators, counselors, and teachers (D'Andrea, 2004). Topics covered in this model include identifying early warning signs of violence and developing and implementing intervention strategies associated with violence prevention.

Smith and Sandhu (2004) recommended taking a proactive approach to violence prevention by focusing on building connections. The overall goal of this approach is to enhance the well-being and optimal development of students. These authors contended that violence prevention is directly related to the students' ability to connect with their school and peer group. Developmental tasks associated with violence prevention include the following:

- Secure attachment with family

- Awareness of self and others

- Emotional literacy (e.g., understanding and expressing emotions)

- Self-regulation (e.g., anger management and impulse control)

- Resiliency (e.g., ability to handle stress)

Burrow-Sanchez, Call, Zheng, and Drew (2011) found that school counselors can play an important role in preventing online victimization of students. Results of the study suggested that school counseling could have a positive impact on preventing online victimization by assessing for student risk factors (e.g., a preference for online relationships, unsafe online behavior, and lack of coping mechanisms) and working with parents to promote positive parent-child communication, ongoing supervision, and limits and rules regarding online use.

As schools continue to investigate ways to make their environment safe, school counselors can play an important role in preventing violence and promoting a positive school climate by implementing antibullying programs, identifying students at high risk for violence, training staff and others in violence prevention, helping students make meaningful connections, and initiating other innovative programs and activities.

MENTAL HEALTH PROBLEMS DeKruyf, Auger, and Trice-Black (2013) and Baskin and Slaten (2014) suggested that school counselors should expand their role to provide mental health services to the large number of students who have mental health problems. DeKruyf et al. noted that 13% to 20% of children struggle with a mental disorder such as ADHD, disruptive mood dysregulation disorder, or oppositional defiant disorder, with less than 20% receiving mental health services. DeKruyf et al. and Baskin and Slaten reported that students with mental disorders were at risk for academic, social-emotional, and behavioral problems and had higher dropout rates, with half of all school dropouts having a mental disorder.

Erickson and Abel (2013) identified demographic trends corresponding to high school students' symptoms of depression, suicidal attempts, and deaths. They noted that approximately 26.1% of high school students report feelings of sadness and despair on a daily basis for several weeks at a time, 6.3% of students attempt suicide, and 12% of deaths of youth ages 10–24 result from suicide. Erickson and Abel provided information on how high school counselors can take a leadership role in screening for depression and promoting suicide awareness.

DeKruyf et al. (2013) recommended that school counselors have a conjoint professional identity, perceiving themselves as educational leaders helping students overcome barriers to learning and as mental health professionals providing mental health services to students. These authors contended the change is necessary to address the unmet mental health needs of students, maintain the role of providing direct counseling services to students (which they are in danger of losing), and avoid being displaced by other mental health professionals. Baskin and Slaten (2014) identified the competencies necessary for school counselors to provide mental health services to students. Slaten and Baskin (2014) developed a framework that could be used by counselor educators to promote these competencies in school counseling training programs.

Carlson and Kees (2013) provided research results that suggested school counselors were confident they could provide mental health services to students. School counselors did report some concern about working with students who had *DSM* mental disorders but believed they could work collaboratively with other mental health professionals to address these issues. Gruman, Marston, and Koon (2013) described how a rural high school counseling program was able to make data-driven programatic changes associated with role constraints to address the mental health needs of students. Gruman et al. noted that over a 6-year period, the school counseling program was transformed through "a school-wide advisory program, a new technology infrastructure, and partnerships with community agencies . . . leading to a more effective response to the mental health needs of students" (p. 334).

SUBSTANCE USE AND ABUSE In this discussion, the term *substance use* refers to alcohol; cigarettes; and illicit drugs like cocaine, marijuana, or heroin. Substance use among students in the United States continues to increase. For example, Putman (2007) reported that approximately 23% of youth between ages 12 and 18 have a serious problem with alcohol and 37.5% of high school seniors engage in heavy drinking. The cost of substance abuse to society has been estimated in billions of dollars, and the psychological cost in terms of human suffering is incalculable (Mason, 1996). In addition, Putman (2007) noted that accidental death was the leading cause of death for adolescents, with 40% of these deaths resulting from alcohol-related automobile accidents.

A survey conducted in 2000 (Josephson Institute of Ethics, 2001) provides information on drug and alcohol use among middle and high school students. This survey reported that 24% of middle school students and 66% of high school students believe they can get drugs if they want to, 14% of middle school students and 37% of high school students had used illegal drugs during the previous year, and 7% of middle school students and 16% of high school students had been drunk at school within the previous year. Many students initiate substance use during the middle school years (Hubbard, Brownlee, & Anderson, 1988). Recent research reveals that students who begin drinking before the age of 15 have significantly higher risk for problems than those who start drinking after age 15 (Kluger, 2001). Early drinkers, as compared to those who start drinking after age 15, have 5 times the risk of developing alcohol dependence, 10 times the risk of being involved in a fight while drinking, 7 times the risk of being in a car accident, and 12 times the risk of being seriously injured. There are clearly more reasons than ever for school counselors to develop interventions that prevent experimentation with alcohol and other substances while in elementary and middle school.

Some factors associated with substance use and abuse are related to limited educational pursuits and early marriages (Newcomb & Bentler, 1988). Polydrug use (the use of many drugs) among teenagers is associated with later difficulty as young adults in role acquisition (e.g., having a spouse or employer). Heavy use of so-called hard drugs is associated with loneliness, diminishing social support, psychoticism, and suicidal tendencies. Newcomb and Bentler (1989) studied the etiology, or cause, of substance use and abuse. They noted that *use* is prompted most by peer influence, whereas *abuse* stems from internal psychological distress. They also identified risk factors associated with substance use and abuse, including a personal history of drug use, use by peers, a lower socioeconomic level, family dysfunction, a family history of abuse, poor school performance, low self-esteem, disdain for the law, need for excitement, stressful life events, and anxiety and depression.

Ethnicity can also be associated with increased risk of substance abuse. Shi, Steen, and Weiss (2013) noted that Hispanic youth had significantly higher rates of substance use than did adolescents of other ethnic groups. In addition, Hispanic youth had fewer protective factors associated with substance use (e.g., friends who don't drink and a positive attitude toward school). Children of alcoholics (COA) are at particularly high risk for developing drug and alcohol problems (Vail-Smith, Knight, & White, 1995). A substantial number of elementary school students are COA and require special help (Vail-Smith et al.). Some of the problems associated with COA include negative emotions such as anger (Clair & Genest, 1987), low self-esteem (Werner, 1986), and an external locus of control (Werner). Elementary school counselors are in a particularly good position to provide services to COA, including fostering resiliency skills to help these students cope with family dysfunction (Vail-Smith et al.). Group counseling that focuses on the special problems of COA can be beneficial for this population (Brake, 1988).

Substance abuse prevention programs have received much attention in the literature. One meta-analysis of these studies found that none of the existing preventive programs had any appreciable effect on reducing substance use or abuse (Bangert-Drowns, 1988). Another study suggested that programs focusing on increasing knowledge about drugs and alcohol are not effective in reducing use or abuse. On the positive side, Tobler (1986) found that peer programs that included assertiveness, especially refusal skills, and social-skills training proved the most effective in preventing abuse (Tobler). Several programs are available for promoting assertiveness and social skills. Children Are People (Lerner & Naiditch, 1985) is a program that can be used at the elementary school level, and the SMART program (Pearson, Lunday, Rohrbach, & Whitney, 1985) is designed to be used at the middle school level. For teens who have substance abuse problems, the most effective programs are those that promote alternative activities, such as camping and sports; enhance confidence and social competence; and provide broadening experiences (Tobler).

TEENAGE PREGNANCY The National Campaign to Prevent Teen and Unplanned Pregnancy (2012, 2013) noted that in 2008, the rate of pregnancy among girls and women aged 15–19 years was 67.8 per 1,000, and in 2010 the teen pregnancy ratio had dropped to 34.2 per 1,000. Although the rates of teenage pregnancy appear to be declining in the United States, this country has historically had higher rates than other industrialized nations (twice as high as in the United Kingdom and 15 times the rate in Japan; Maynard, 1996).

The cost of teenage pregnancy to the individual and society can be enormous. Maynard (1996) estimated the cost to society from lost wages and social services to be between $13 billion and $19 billion a year. The costs to teenage mothers and their children include a tendency to have low-birth-weight and premature babies; higher rates of dropping out of school and lower high school graduation rates for teenage mothers and their children; higher rates of abuse and neglect; and lower lifelong earnings for both teenage mothers and their children (Maynard). Allen, El-Beshti, and Guin (2014) also noted that teenage mothers often lack the necessary life skills and postsecondary education to transition successfully into adulthood, resulting in difficulty entering the workforce and economic hardship. These authors provided an overview of a teen parent program based on Adlerian psychology that integrates parenting, life skills, relationship education, and educational attainment; such a program can be used to promote a positive learning environment for adolescent parents and their children.

Preventive programs can address the special problems associated with teenage pregnancy, and the most promising of these programs are contraceptive and family-planning services (Furstenberg, Brooks-Gunn, & Chase-Lansdale, 1989). Other preventive programs that focus on sex education or on attempting to change attitudes toward early sexual involvement have had limited success (Furstenberg et al.). One such program is a social inoculation program that involves group work with female adolescents (Berger & Thompson, 2000). The groups utilize role-play and discussion and focus on helping individuals learn how to resist pressure to have sex. Social inoculation has been shown to be useful, especially for individuals who are not already sexually active. Several programs that are implemented after a teenager becomes pregnant have had success. Prenatal programs promote healthy babies for teens (Brooks-Gunn, McCormick, & Heagerty, 1988; Brooks-Gunn et al., 1989). Parent-education programs have enhanced parenting skills as well as the development of the child (Clewell, Brooks-Gunn, & Benasich, 1989). Research on the effects of parent education using the PREP for Effective Family Living program (Dinkmeyer, McKay, Dinkmeyer, Dinkmeyer, & Carlson, 1985) in small groups with pregnant teenagers found that the PREP program increases teenagers' self-concept and fosters democratic parenting attitudes (Emmons & Nystul, 1994). The most useful approaches to working with pregnant teenagers include group counseling to provide necessary peer support; parent education after delivery of the baby; and creative, imaginative prenatal class presentations that encourage the active involvement of participants (MacGregor & Newlon, 1987).

DIVORCED OR SINGLE PARENTS Harris (2013) noted that the United States has higher rates of single-parent homes than do other developed nations. High divorce rates, fewer marriages, and more couples having children out of wedlock—all trends expected to continue—result in only 40% percent of children being reared by both biological parents until they reach 18 years of age (Berger & Thompson, 2000; Harris). Research has tended to focus on the effects of divorce on mothers' parenting (e.g., divorce tends to have an adverse effect on single mothers' parenting due to financial hardship; Nystul & Devall, 2010). However, recent research focused on single fathers' parenting skills has revealed that single parenthood tends to have a positive effect on fathers' parenting (e.g., single fathers were rated as effective as single mothers and more effective than married fathers; Nystul & Devall).

School counselors can help students overcome some of the adverse outcomes associated with divorce and single-parent homes (Frieman, 1993). Active, positive involvement in child rearing by both biological parents can minimize the adverse consequences of divorce. Involving the father can be a special challenge, since fathers tend to have lower levels of parental involvement than mothers before the divorce (Frieman). Group work with divorced men can be useful to help them become more involved in their children's lives (Frieman). Topics that may be especially relevant in these groups are common problems of fathers, parenting skills, developmental issues, dealing with negative emotions of anger and jealousy, and information on child care.

The effects of divorce vary according to the age of the child (Robson, 2002). Children up to 5 years of age tend to regress by developing feeding and toileting problems. Children from age 6 to 8 initially use denial to cope and later remain hopeful that their parents will get back together. From age 9 to 11, children typically react with shock, surprise, denial, and disbelief. In addition, these children can experience conflicts in loyalty to their parents, often viewing one parent as good and the other as bad. Adolescents from 13 to 18 years of age appear to be at increased risk of mental health problems and a negative view of their future, their parents, and their environment. Adolescent females also tend to engage in early heterosexual behavior.

Group counseling has been found effective in dealing with the special issues associated with divorce, such as alleviating guilt and dealing with anger and feelings of abandonment. Many different kinds of divorce groups have emerged (Bowker, 1982; Hammond, 1981). These groups tend to focus on easing children's level of stress and enhancing their self-esteem. Hammond's program is typical of these group approaches. Its structured format includes a multimedia presentation and exercises providing information on divorce as well as opportunities to process feelings. Burke and DeStreek (1989) have found empirical support for Hammond's approach in terms of enhanced self-concept. Additional research on these groups appears warranted.

DROPPING OUT OF SCHOOL Eggen and Kauchak (1994) estimated that 25% or more of the high school class of 2001 would not finish high school. The percentage of school dropouts is even higher for some minority groups (e.g., Native American students have the highest rate at 35.5%; Garrett, 1995). Students who are at a high risk for dropping out of school are referred to as *at-risk students*. Common characteristics of at-risk students include low socioeconomic status, transience, being minority, being male, having English as a second language, and being from divorced families (Eggen & Kauchak). Males have a higher risk of dropping out of school than females; other at-risk characteristics include a history of previous failures, drug abuse, academic and behavioral problems, poor school attendance, and boredom (Bearden, Spencer, & Moracco, 1989). Students who are at risk not only have a higher tendency to drop out of school but also tend to have other problems, such as substance abuse, delinquency, low self-esteem, and low motivation and underachievement in school (Eggen & Kauchak).

An increasing amount of research is focusing on identifying resiliency characteristics that can help students become less vulnerable to academic failure (e.g., Alva, 1991; Arellano & Padilla, 1996; Zimmerman & Arunkumar, 1994). School counselors can attempt to foster resiliency characteristics to maximize academic achievement in students. Arellano and Padilla identified personal and environmental factors that promote academic success in Latino students. These include parental support and encouragement; role models and mentors; ethnicity as a source of support, pride, and strength; the drive to succeed; and an optimistic outlook. The research of Gonzalez, Borders, Hines, Villalba, and Henderson (2013) provides evidence of the importance of parental involvement, noting that for Latino immigrant students, parental involvement promotes academic success as indicated by grades, motivation, attitude toward school, and participation in advanced classes.

Several counseling strategies can address the school dropout phenomenon. Preventive programs can provide special counseling services for students who are at risk for dropping out of school. (Gibson, 1989). Florida's Dade County Public Schools (1985) use peer counseling, academic support, and help with educational deficiencies. The Los Angeles Unified School District (1985) employs counseling, special tutoring, and vocational assistance. Ruben (1989) has recommended that preventive efforts should be geared to the elementary level by providing classroom guidance programs like Gerler and Anderson's (1986) Success in Schools.

Trends in School Counseling

The field of school counseling appears to be at a crossroads. School counselors are needed more than ever as students experience a complex array of personal and social problems. Yet concerns persist that school counseling cannot deal effectively with these challenges.

Sandhu and Portes (1995) contended that school counseling was in deep trouble as a profession, even in danger of becoming obsolete. The fundamental problem facing school counseling is that it tends to be perceived as a nonessential ancillary service requiring no specific expertise to perform. Sandhu and Portes believed that it was essential for school counselors to become proactive rather than reactive in their roles, priorities, and activities and described a proactive model of school counseling that could help move this profession from a peripheral to a central position in educational reform.

The College Entrance Examination Board (1987) also concluded that the school counseling profession was in trouble and in need of change. Its report recommended (a) making better use of the school counselor's special skills rather than imposing clerical tasks such as scheduling, (b) increasing support for federal programs that assist disadvantaged students, (c) placing more emphasis on counseling programs at the elementary and middle school level to prevent problems from becoming more serious, and (d) promoting greater involvement of parents in the school counseling program.

The key to future success of school counseling lies in its ability to adjust to the times, promote school improvement, and bridge the gap between opportunity and achievement so that no students are left behind (Dahir, 2009). Clark and Breman (2009) recommended that school counselors use an inclusion model by providing counseling services within the classroom. Advantages of the inclusion model include minimizing the amount of instruction missed, addressing behavioral and emotional concerns within the student's classroom, and promoting a positive learning environment. In the view of Portman (2009), school counselors of the future will be increasingly involved in cultural mediation. In this role, school counselors will "engage in prevention, intervention, and/ or remediation activities that facilitate communication and understanding between culturally diverse human systems (e.g., school, family, community, and federal and state agencies) that aid the educational progress of all students" (p. 23).

Welch and McCarroll (1993) made additional suggestions as to how school counselors can come to be perceived as vital to their school and community. These authors recommended that school counselors become more involved in the family and community by providing family counseling and becoming community resource specialists to link students with services that meet their needs. They also recommended a shift in emphasis from individual counseling to group work and suggested that counselors adopt a systems perspective in conceptualizing the overall functioning of the school. McMahon, Mason, Daluga-Guenther, and Ruiz (2014) provided support for this position suggesting that school counselors utilize an ecological model of school counseling to promote the social justice, advocacy, and systemic change necessary for students' success.

As noted earlier, school counselors can also seek out additional training in areas such as school law and administration to take a leadership role in implementing the provisions of legislation like Section 504, IDEA, and NCLB. School counselors would thus expand their role in providing specialized and essential services (e.g., interface between discipline and legal mandates and development of behavior management plans).

Russo and Kassera (1989) noted that school counselors have been unsuccessful in clearly communicating the importance of their services. They suggested that school counselors establish a comprehensive, ongoing accountability program and use Wiggins's (1985) accountability program, which includes setting goals, assessing needs, setting priorities, evaluating outcomes, and reporting results. Green (1988) suggested image-building activities for school counselors to help them be accepted as practitioners with specialized knowledge and establish professional autonomy. Green identified the following activities that could be used to promote a sense of professionalism for school counselors:

- Conduct a survey among colleagues to determine how they perceive the role of the school counselor. This type of peer review is a necessary component of professional behavior.

- Compile a list of professional activities undertaken over the previous 3 years. Determine whether these activities have promoted a professional image, required the special skills of a counselor or simply duplicated services offered by other professionals, and educated others on the complexity of the counselor's role.

- Provide programs for parents on topics such as parent education, drug abuse, and student achievement.

- Publish a newsletter describing activities of the school counseling program as well as issues that interest students, teachers, and parents.

- Become active in conducting research and writing articles for publication in professional journals.

- Become involved in professional organizations.

- Schedule special consultation days for parents and staff to assist with special needs.

- Provide inservice training to teachers.

- Sponsor a community seminar on a topical issue (e.g., teenage pregnancy).

Kaplan and Geoffroy (1990) and Thomas (1989) recommended that school counselors take a more active role in educational reforms. They suggested that school counselors can play an important role in promoting a positive school climate by encouraging a success orientation in the school, fostering the self-esteem of teachers and students, and helping to integrate cognitive and affective dimensions into the educational process.

Counselor educators can also play a role in moving the field of school counseling forward. Sweeney (1988) noted that school counseling has been deemphasized in most counselor education programs. The current focus appears to be on coursework and skills required by agency counselors, not school counseling. According to Sweeney, counselor educators have also neglected research on school counseling. For example, the number of articles published in *Counselor Education and Supervision* on the role and function of school counseling had steadily declined. Thirty-nine articles appeared on this topic from 1961 to 1968 but none from 1980 to 1988. Besides helping school counselors formulate a professional identity, counselor educators can place more emphasis on the educational needs of students interested in school counseling.

All of these studies collectively suggest that school counseling is a profession at risk and in need of dramatic changes. Briefly, school counselors should do the following:

- Become proactive in their roles, priorities, and activities.

- Use a family-systemic perspective to become more involved in the family and community.

- Assume leadership responsibilities for coordinating and acting as a liaison for legislative programs such as Section 504, IDEA, and NCLB.

- Clarify their role and function by encouraging others to focus on counselors' special skills and not on clerical tasks such as scheduling.

- Incorporate image-building activities and an ongoing accountability program.

- Encourage parents to involve themselves more in their children's counseling programs.

- Advocate greater emphasis on elementary and middle school counseling.

- Become more actively involved in the school reform movement.

- Promote research efforts on special problems such as suicide and depression.

- Convince counselor educators to place more emphasis on school counseling.

An increasing amount of attention is being paid to diversity issues, solution-focused counseling, and technology in the school counseling literature. An overview of these topics follows.

Diversity Issues

School counselors must consider diversity issues such as age, gender, culture, sexual orientation, socioeconomic status, race, ethnicity, and spiritualtity in all aspects of counseling because all facets of society are becoming increasingly multicultural. It is therefore imperative for school counselors to develop the necessary awareness, knowledge, and skills to work with students in a multicultural society. The recently revised American Counseling Association (2014) *Code of Ethics and Standards of Practice* advocates that counselors acquire and maintain the necessary multicultural competencies to practice. However, school counselors generally are in need of additional training in this area (Hobson & Kanitz, 1996). Because sensitivity to multicultural issues in schools is necessary to maximize learning, school counselors should engage in activities that improve the school climate by overcoming adverse stereotyping and promoting an acceptance and integration of students' cultures in the overall school curriculum (Whitledge, 1994). Promoting multicultural social justice goals is an important intervention school counselors can use to foster students' success (Bemak & Chung, 2008b). These authors contended that school counselors undermine their ability to function as effective advocates for students when they have an overriding need to be perceived positively by others.

To address this potential problem, Bemak and Chung (2008b) introduced the term *Nice Counselor Syndrome* (NCS). Bemak and Chung defined NCS as the desire for school counselors to be perceived (at any cost) as nice individuals who get along well with others, are problem solvers and mediators, and promote harmony in their school. Bemak and Chung suggested that when school counselors engage in the NCS, they may avoid activities that result in being perceived negatively by their colleagues, such as engaging in the conflict associated with promoting social justice and advocacy. Instead, school counselors engaged in the NCS attempt to maintain the status quo and harmony in the schools. Bemak and Chung contended that when this occurs, school counselors are not in a position to promote advocacy and social justice. They recommended that counselors instead adopt strategies that promote advocacy and social justice, such as maintaining a professional posture, not taking things personally, taking risks, and addressing conflict when necessary.

Advocating for social justice is clearly an important part of the role and function of school counselors. The following *Personal Note* explores whether school counselors can be perceived as nice people and successfully advocate for social justice.

A Personal Note

Bemak's and Chung's article (2008b) relating to multicultural/social justice and Nice Counselor Syndrome (NCS) raises an important issue: Can a school counselor be perceived as a nice person and still promote social justice? My experiences as a school counselor and school psychologist have shown me that being perceived positively by others (e.g., as a team player who gets along well with others and is a good problem solver and mediator) can promote the trust and support necessary to advocate successfully for students.

I would agree with Bemak and Chung that when school counselors have an overriding goal to be liked by others, they will not be able to do a good job promoting social justice. It seems that the key issue here is the importance of not putting one's needs before those of the students. When this occurs, counselors will not be able to do any aspect of their job effectively (including promoting social justice).

Spirituality and religion are other diversity issues that school counselors face. Counseling services provided to Christian fundamentalist families, for example, require special consideration (Miller, 1995). These families tend to respond to a counselor's referrals with fear and apprehension because they think their religious beliefs will not be considered in the counseling process. Counselors can overcome these tendencies by acknowledging the clients' manner of conceptualizing problems and solutions. For example, it is common for Christian fundamentalists to attribute problems of misbehavior to problems with religion (e.g., not spending enough time studying the Bible; Miller). When this occurs, school counselors should recognize the role that church practices may play in overcoming the student's problems and make every effort to listen to their clients' stories in an accepting and nonjudgmental manner. As trust develops, counselors will be in a better position to facilitate the construction of new stories that reflect a movement toward problem resolution and enhanced meaning.

Another important religious issue in school counseling concerns non-Christians. One study found that non-Christian fourth to sixth graders experienced more negative perceptions of themselves and their classroom's social environment than did Christian students during the month of December, with 20% to 30% of the non-Christian students experiencing negative emotions during that month because of classroom parties and holiday breaks focused on Christmas (Ribak-Rosenthal & Russell, 1994). School counselors could strive to create a positive school climate that recognizes religious diversity in the schools (Ribak-Rosenthal & Russell). For example, they could encourage referring to the school break in December as a holiday vacation and not

Christmas vacation and create opportunities to recognize other religious holidays and festivities in small- and large-group guidance and counseling activities.

Sexual orientation represents another important diversity issue, with approximately 10% of students having LGBTQ preferences. Unfortunately, sexual orientation has received so little attention in schools that it can be considered "a blind spot in the school mirror" (Marinoble, 1998). In fact, sexual orientation is often avoided altogether in all aspects of school functioning, from the curriculum to school policies and even in the selection of guest speakers (Marinoble). It is not surprising that exclusionary practices such as these contribute to gays and lesbians often feeling like "invisible people" (Ritter & O'Neill, 1995). Some of the special challenges and opportunities that LGBTQ students pose for school counselors involve helping these students overcome difficulties associated with being LGBTQ in a heterosexual/homophobic world. (Marinoble). They commonly experience identity conflict, feelings of isolation and stigmatization, peer-relation problems, and family disruptions. Identity conflicts can be due in part to the schools' fundamental orientation to the world in heterosexual terms (Marinoble). Even when the existence of homosexuality is acknowledged, the associations tend to be negative and derogatory, which can contribute to LGBTQ students struggling to define themselves as unique and positive individuals against a tide of negativity.

The isolation and stigmatization, peer-relation problems, and family conflicts that many LGBTQ youth experience can contribute to serious mental health problems. For example, suicide accounts for most of the deaths of LGBTQ adolescents, occurring at a rate 2 to 3 times that of heterosexual teens (Marinoble, 1998). Also, because LGBTQ individuals may have limited access to organized religion, they can experience spiritual difficulties (Ritter & O'Neill, 1995), which can compound mental health problems by denying them a source of strength and support during times of need (Miranti & Burke, 1995).

School counselors are in an ideal position to take a proactive role in assisting gay and lesbian students with their special problems and fostering their optimal development. Some of the possible interventions suggested by Cooley (1998), Fontaine (1998), Marinoble (1998), Muller and Hartman (1998), and Ritter and O'Neill (1995) are as follows:

- Promote a school climate (in terms of the curriculum and school policy) that is sensitive to and values diversity in sexual orientation.

- Ensure that *all* students have an opportunity to develop a positive self-image, self-acceptance, and personal identity.

- When appropriate, assist students in the process of "coming out" (sharing their sexual orientation with friends and family).

- Utilize individual and group counseling to help gay and lesbian students overcome negative feelings such as isolation and despair.

- Monitor students who are at a high risk for suicide and ensure treatment as necessary.

- Assist students with spiritual needs to promote inner strength and support necessary for problem resolution and movement toward optimal development.

Implementing these interventions may create serious challenges for school counselors. Schools tend to reflect the culture in which they are created. Successful implementation may therefore require strength and courage to fight the negative forces of homophobia, racism, stereotyping, discrimination, and prejudice. If schools truly exist to educate *all* students, then school counselors have an opportunity to advocate for the reforms necessary to address these important issues.

School counselors must have the necessary multicultural and sexual orientation competencies to address these challenges. A study by Bidell (2012), showed that students working on their master's degree in school counseling self-reported significantly lower levels of multicultural and sexual orientation competencies than their community/agency student counterparts. It appears that school counselors may need additional training to promote these competencies so they can effectively advocate for students.

Bryan, Day-Vines, Griffin, and Thomas (2012) noted that disparities regarding race and gender are predictive variables for disciplinary referrals and suspension rates even when risk factors such as socioeconomic status are considered. Bryan et al. cited past research that showed African American and Latino students are twice as likely to be suspended from school as White students. Bryan et al. also investigated racial and gender disparity relating to 10th-grade math and English teachers' disciplinary referrals to school counselors and found that a disproportional number of African American students were referred to school counselors. Gender was also a factor, with Englilsh teachers referring a disproportional number of African American and multiracial female students to school counselors. Bryan et al. recommended that school counselors utlilize advocacy strategies to address issues of racial and gender disparity regarding discipline practices.

Brief-Solution-Focused Counseling

Brief-solution-focused models of counseling continue to receive attention in the literature as an innovative alternative to standard approaches to school counseling (Bonnington, 1993; Bruce, 1995; LaFountain, Garner, & Eliason, 1996; Murphy, 1994). The advantages that brief-solution-focused counseling has for school counselors over more traditional counseling methods can be summarized as follows (Murphy):

1. It is a strengths approach that focuses on what works and exceptions to problem situations and therefore promotes collaborative relationships among students, parents, teachers, and staff.

2. It is time limited, focusing on the present and future rather than lengthy excursions into past history.

3. Its goal of small, concrete changes (such as increased class attendance and conflict resolution) is more realistic than more ambitious goals such as personality change.

4. It recognizes the importance of students being aware of the need for change as a prerequisite for change.

Bruce (1995) and Murphy (1994) have described the tasks associated with brief-solution-focused counseling in schools. Collectively, they suggested that school counselors first establish a positive counseling relationship, which is, of course, important regardless of the approach being used. Second, school counselors must assess the problem in concrete, behavioral terms and identify exceptions to the problem (i.e., examples of when the problem does not occur). Third, school counselors must identify a short-term goal that the student can successfully achieve. Fourth, they must elaborate on what worked in the past (the exceptions to the problem identified in step 2) and use this information to develop a new approach for the student. Fifth, they must evaluate the new approach with methods such as the scaling technique (On a 1–10 scale, with 1 being the worst and 10 being the best, how would you rate the situation now?) and make changes in the new approach as necessary. And sixth, they must empower students to use the brief-solution-focused method to deal with future problems.

Only a limited amount of research has evaluated the efficacy of brief-solution-focused counseling. Littrell, Malia, and Vanderwood (1995) found brief-solution-focused counseling (one session with high school students) to be as effective as brief-problem-focused counseling in terms of decreasing the degree of undesired feelings, but brief-solution-focused counseling took less time. Nevertheless, brief-solution-focused and other forms of brief counseling do appear to offer much to school counselors continually faced with large numbers of students to whom they must provide counseling services.

The following *Personal Note* describes a brief-solution-focused model of counseling I developed.

A Personal Note

I have developed a simple three-phase model of brief-solution-focused counseling based on the Adlerian principle of encouragement. Each phase has two steps. Although the model is particularly well suited for school counseling, it can also be used in other settings. An overview of these three phases follows.

(Continued)

(Continued)

Phase 1: Celebrating Success

The counselor identifies what is working, exceptions to the problem, strengths, good news, and so forth. I associate "celebrating success" with taking a mental picture of something a student has said or done. Together (with the student's permission), the student and counselor share the success with a significant other such as a parent, teacher, or school principal.

Phase 2: Application of Strengths

The counselor and student explore how a student's strengths can be used to address counseling goals (successes celebrated in phase 1 can be important strengths). For instance, a student who has had trouble finishing schoolwork may realize that it is important to listen to the teacher.

Phase 3: Creating Hope and Encouragement

In the final phase, the counselor promotes hope and encouragement by creating a connection between effort and success: "When you work hard, good things will happen." The "incomplete sentence" technique can be used to foster student ownership of the encouragement message (i.e., let the student say the last half of the sentence: "Good things will happen _____"). Encouragement fosters self-efficacy (a can-do spirit) and promotes a self-fulfilling prophecy of success.

Use of Technology

The challenges that technology offers include the inherent difficulty of trying to keep up with the ever increasing pace of change (e.g., the computer you just purchased, for example, is already out-of-date). But it creates opportunities as well to perform the job of school counseling better and more efficiently.

The wave of the future for state-of-the-art delivery of counseling programs to students includes technologies like multimedia authoring (the use of at least two media simultaneously—image processing, graphics production, sound editing, and three-dimensional modeling; Gerler, 1995). The possibilities for the use of technology in school counseling are limitless. For example, students could use CD-ROMs, the Internet, and other technologies to take an active role in their counseling by exploring topics like career exploration, drug and alcohol abuse, and prejudice (Casey, 1995).

A growing number of school counselors are finding that the Internet can be an excellent tool for communicating with other school counselors on issues ranging from counseling theory to day-to-day challenges (Gerler, 1995). Counselor educators have also expanded their use of technology in schools. For example, email can be a useful tool in supervising student interns; with it, information can be sent immediately and directly to a supervisor without having to wait for a weekly supervision meeting or playing telephone tag (Myrick & Sabella, 1995). Email supervision also helps students become more succinct in describing what is going on with a particular case and contributes to an enhanced focus in counselor supervision (Myrick & Sabella).

SUMMARY

School counseling is a dynamic and challenging field within the counseling profession. It can best be understood within the context of a comprehensive, K–12 developmental model. In 1990, the ASCA supported this model in a revised role statement, suggesting that school counselors engage in individual counseling, small-group counseling, large-group guidance, consultation, and coordination activities. More recently ASCA (2003, 2005, 2012) has established national standards and the **National Model for school counseling**. These initiatives could frame a new zeitgeist for the school counseling profession.

The role of consultation and guidelines for counseling exceptional students and students with the problems of drug abuse, teenage pregnancy, divorced or single parents, and dropping out of school are receiving increasing attention from school counselors.

The profession of school counseling appears to be at a crossroads. Several studies have suggested that changes are needed for the field to successfully move forward as a profession. Some of these changes include becoming more proactive and enhancing family-community involvement; taking leadership responsibility for legislative programs such as Section 504, IDEA, HIPAA, and NCLB; increasing direct services and reducing clerical activities; and engaging in image-building activities. In addition, school counselors need to be cognizant of emerging trends, such as incorporating a multicultural perspective, using brief-solution-focused counseling, and making effective use of technology. The ASCA National Model suggests that school counselors should establish a broader base to leverage leadership, advocacy, teaming/collaboration, and systemic change to ensure that all students have opportunities for success in school.

PERSONAL EXPLORATION

1. What do you believe are the challenges and opportunities in the field of school counseling?

2. What do you think are the major challenges facing children/adolescents today, and how might you address them if you were a school counselor?

3. If you were a school counselor, what grades would you want to work with (elementary, middle, or high school), and why would those grades appeal to you?

4. How do you think public school education can be improved, and what should the school counselor's role be in this process?

5. Do you believe school counselors should do more to address students' mental health problems?

6. What were your experiences with school counseling, both positive and negative?

7. What can be done to address the problems associated with teenage pregnancies?

8. What can school counselors do to prevent students from dropping out of school?

9. What are your views regarding students who have exceptionalities such as emotional or behavioral problems?

10. What are some of the special challenges faced by students who have sexual orientation issues such as identifying as LGBTQ?

LEARNING ACTIVITIES

1. What would you do if you became aware of a student who was being bullied?

2. If you were a school counselor, what type of activities would you do to promote a positive school climate?

WEBSITES

American School Counselor Association. (2010). *Ethical standards for school counselors.* http://www .schoolcounselor.org/asca/media/asca/Resource Center/Legal and Ethical Issues/Sample Documents/ EthicalStandards2010.pdf.

American School Counselor Association. (2015). Retrieved from http://www.schoolcounselor.org. *The official national site for the American School Counselor Association.*

Mental Health Counseling

The Art and Science of Mental Health Counseling

Mental health counseling is both an art and science. It is an art for mental health counselors to adjust to the demands of health care reform (such as managed care) and continue to provide high-quality mental health services. One of the challenges associated with this process is to maintain the philosophical core of mental health counseling (the developmental/preventative perspective) while continuing to be perceived as a viable provider for managed-care organizations, which tend to focus on symptom relief. In addition, it is an art for mental health counseling to make appropriate changes in its philosophical and theoretical orientation in response to current trends like postmodernism and issues relating to diversity.

Mental health counselors must strive to develop innovative, creative methods to address the challenges of the population that they serve (e.g., clients with mental disorders such as serious depression, schizophrenia, and substance abuse) and do so through the personal characteristics of patience, humbleness, kindness, and compassion. Clearly, for mental health counselors to be effective, they must become emotionally affected by their clients and the counseling process.

To be as effective as possible, however, the emotionally charged art of counseling must be balanced by a scientific perspective. Counselors can become overly enmeshed in their clients' lives, which can obscure boundaries and undermine the professional objectivity that is essential. Numerous objective practices can contribute to the science of counseling, for example, assessment instruments, psychological tests, and the clinical interview. Qualitative and quantitative research strategies can also be useful in promoting the scientific perspective in mental health

Chapter Overview

This chapter is an overview of mental health counseling. Highlights of the chapter include the following:

- **The art and science of mental health counseling**

- **Professional issues for mental health counselors, including professional organizations and certification**

- **The role and function of the mental health counselor, including direct and indirect intervention strategies**

- **Categories of mental health services: "problems of living" and mental disorders**

- **Suicidal clients**

- **Substance abuse counseling**

- **Gerontological counseling**

- **Trends and perspectives**

counseling. These assessment and research methodologies can help the mental health counselor stand back and evaluate what is going on in the counseling process, provide new direction for innovations in theory and practice, and determine the efficacy of the mental health services being offered.

Professional Issues

Mental health counseling is both a profession undertaken by mental health counselors and an amorphous job role performed by various members of the helping profession, such as counselors, psychologists, psychiatrists, psychiatric nurses, and social workers. Mental health counselors can be defined as individuals whose "primary affiliation and theoretical basis is counseling and not psychiatry, psychology, or social work" (Palmo, 1986, p. 41). The profession of mental health counselor is the fastest-growing segment of the mental health field (Dingman, 1988), with 57% of mental health agencies having a mental health counselor (Burtnett, 1986). Mental health counselors handle some of the most difficult cases, including crisis intervention (Ivey, 1989), and have therefore become an integral part of the mental health delivery system.

In 1976, the American Association for Counseling and Development (AACD)—now called the American Counseling Association (ACA)—created a special division called the **American Mental Health Counselors Association** (AMHCA). By 1985, the AMHCA had become the largest division of the AACD. In 1998, the AMHCA separated from the ACA (although it continues to be an ACA division) to promote the professional status of mental health counselors (Colangelo, 2009).

Since its inception, the AMHCA has embarked on numerous activities that have contributed to the professional identity of the mental health counselor. Its most important contributions include creating a code of ethics for mental health counselors, which was revised in 2010; publishing the *Journal of Mental Health Counseling,* which provides information regarding the theory, research, and practice of mental health counseling; spearheading a movement for mental health counselor licensure in all states; and establishing national standards for mental health counselor training.

By 2004, there were approximately 80,000 licensed mental health counselors (also called licensed professional counselors and clinical mental health counselors). Since 2009, all states and the District of Columbia, Guam, and Puerto Rico have had licensure laws for mental health counselors. In 1988, national preparation standards were established for mental health counselors to ensure adequate professional training and recognition in the health care delivery system (e.g., the eligibility of mental health counseling for third-party insurance reimbursement and participation in managed care; Smith & Robinson, 1995). The national clinical standards for mental health counselors are as follows. Individuals must graduate from a program that is accredited by the Council for Accreditation of Counseling and Related Educational Programs (CACREP) or has CACREP equivalency, have 3,000 hours of experience in the mental health field, have 100 hours of face-to-face supervision, adhere to the AMHCA standards of clinical practice and code of ethics, pass a national clinical exam, have work samples of counseling successfully reviewed (e.g., videotapes), and fulfill state licensure requirements (Smith & Robinson).

Mental health counselors work in a variety of settings, including private practice, community mental health centers, hospitals, alcohol and drug centers, social service agencies, and business and industry (Brooks & Gerstein, 1990). During the 1980s, there was an apparent shift in work settings for mental health counselors (Hershenson & Power, 1987). For example, in 1978, the highest percentage (39%) of AMHCA members worked in community mental health centers; 18% worked in private practice; and the remainder worked in a variety of other settings, including college counseling centers and as college teachers (Weikel & Taylor, 1979). In 1985, 22% of AMHCA members worked in private practice, 13% in private counseling centers; 13% in colleges and universities; only 11% in community mental health centers; and the rest in other settings, such as rehabilitation agencies and state and local government (Weikel, 1985). The trend toward private practice becoming the dominant work setting for AMHCA members continued in the 1990s (Brooks & Gerstein).

Several other studies have shown that a high percentage of mental health counselors work in substance abuse centers (Hosie, West, & MacKey, 1988; Richardson & Bradley, 1985). The largest percentage of professionals working in substance abuse centers hold a master's degree in counseling or a Master of Social Work (MSW) degree (Hosie et al.). In addition, mental health counselors are more likely to be program directors than are individuals from other disciplines (Hosie et al.).

It is imperative that mental health counseling continues to evolve in a manner that corresponds appropriately to the changing needs and challenges of society. Mental health counselors must continue to receive training in the diagnosis and treatment of mental disorders, and this training should emphasize a developmental/preventative perspective. It is also suggested that specialty skills (such as marriage and family counseling) can enhance the standing of mental health counselors within the health care community (Smith & Robinson, 1995). In an era of rapid change within the health care system, mental health counseling appears to be poised to receive greater acceptance and recognition. In this regard, mental health counseling appears to be a cost-effective alternative to other mental health delivery systems and therefore very attractive to managed-care organizations.

The Role and Function of Mental Health Counselors

Mental health counselors perform most of the same tasks as other mental health practitioners, such as marriage and family counselors, social workers, and psychologists (Nicholas, Gerstein, & Keller, 1988), including psychoeducational services, clinical or direct services, supervision, administration, program development, and consultation. Two tasks that mental health counselors do not tend to engage in are program evaluation and research, which are often performed by doctoral-level counselors and psychologists (Nicholas et al.).

Although mental health practitioners serve similar functions, their treatment philosophies vary from those of other practitioners (Brooks & Gerstein, 1990). Mental health counselors typically adopt a psychoeducational, developmental, and psychopathological point of view; marriage and family therapists use a systemic orientation; psychologists rely on a psychopathological frame of reference; and social workers adhere to a sociological perspective (Brooks & Gerstein). Mental health disciplines are also differentiated according to philosophical orientation: mental health counselors define themselves primarily within a developmental perspective, whereas psychologists adhere to a medical/therapeutic model and social workers focus on the environment (Ivey, 1989). According to Ginter (1996), the three philosophical pillars of mental health counseling are that counseling is contextually an interpersonal medium, it recognizes the importance of both prevention and remediation, and it has a developmental perspective.

There is a debate raging within the mental health profession regarding the validity of the developmental-preventative model versus the medical model, which emphasizes diagnosis and treatment (Messina, 1999). The developmental-preventative model can be traced to graduate training programs in mental health counseling. Messina suggested that the developmental-preventative legacy may be an inhibiting factor for the mental health profession. Clearly, managed care rewards clinicians who embrace the medical model. Mental health counselors who do not adhere to the medical model may be at a disadvantage in their ability to compete with psychologists and social workers, who promote their ability to diagnose and treat mental disorders. However, it would seem to be in the best interest of the managed care industry and mental health counselors to strike a balance between prevention and treatment. For example, managed care has emphasized symptom relief over comprehensive treatment of disorders, but tertiary prevention involves providing comprehensive treatment programs for disorders such as depression, thereby preventing future problems. Ongoing research and evaluation will be necessary to shape the identity of mental health counselors in the ever-changing landscape of mental health services.

Kelly (1996) looked to the future in terms of the role and function of mental health counselors. He suggested that mental health counselors are attempting to address three broad, interrelated challenges. First, mental health counselors are faced with asserting their right to be mental health service providers in a health care environment of shrinking resources. This challenge can be met only with continued support for mental health counseling licensure and recognition and its utilization by managed-care providers. A second challenge is to communicate accountability by documenting client improvement. Research and evaluation will play a key role in this process. And third, mental health counselors must effectively adjust to changes in the mental health field in terms of technology, diversity, and health care reform. The evolution and refinement of mental health counseling will enable this profession to continue to be a viable service in the mental health delivery system.

Direct Intervention Strategies

Central to the role and function of mental health counselors is providing direct and indirect intervention strategies. Mental health counselors provide direct counseling services to clients with a wide range of mental disorders (West, Hosie, & MacKey, 1988). This section addresses two commonly used direct intervention strategies: counseling and crisis intervention.

COUNSELING STRATEGIES Mental health counselors use a wide range of direct counseling strategies, such as individual counseling, group counseling, marriage and family counseling, and substance abuse counseling (NeJedlo, Arredondo, & Benjamin, 1985; Spruill & Fong, 1990; West et al., 1988). In addition, a shift in emphasis appears to have taken place in mental health counseling from preventive approaches to the direct counseling services of individual, group, and family counseling (Spruill & Fong).

CRISIS INTERVENTION SERVICES Mental health counselors also provide crisis intervention services (Ivey, 1989; West et al.,1988). **Crisis intervention** is not the same as counseling, even though it is a helping strategy (George & Cristiani, 1995). Its focus is more narrow and superficial, its goals are more modest, and it has a briefer duration than counseling. The following is a four-step model for crisis intervention.

The first step is to determine whether the client is in crisis. To determine whether crisis intervention is necessary, the counselor must decide whether the client is experiencing a personal crisis. A **crisis** has been defined as

> the perception or experiencing of an event or situation as an intolerable difficulty that exceeds the person's current resources and coping mechanisms. Unless the person obtains relief, the crisis has the potential to cause severe affective, behavioral, and cognitive malfunctioning up to the pont of instigating injurious or lethal behavior to oneself or others. (James & Gilliland, 2013, p. 8)

James and Gilliland (2013) and Puryear (1979) identified the following factors associated with a crisis:

1. The symptoms of stress result in psychological and physiological discomfort.

2. The client feels intense emotions such as feelings of inadequacy, helplessness, anxiety, panic, or agitation.

3. The client is more concerned with gaining relief from the symptom than with the problem that precipitated the symptom.

4. The client has a reduced ability to function efficiently.

5. The crisis is normally time limited but may develop into recurring long-term mental health problems.

6. Crises tend to be complex and difficult to resolve.

7. Crises represent both danger and opportunity for positive change.

The counselor should use listening skills during the initial phase of crisis intervention to gain a phenomenological understanding of the client (James & Gilliand, 2013). This can help the counselor determine whether the client is truly experiencing a crisis and enable the counselor to establish rapport and communicate support to the client.

The second step in crisis intervention involves assessment, using two separate procedures. First, the counselor must assess the severity of the crisis in terms of the potential for serious harm to the client or others. The primary goal of crisis intervention is to avoid a catastrophe in which someone would be seriously injured (James & Gilliand, 2013). The second assessment procedure involves determining whether the client is mentally able to take an active role in resolving the crisis situation. A useful tool in this process is a mental status exam (Othmer & Othmer, 1989), which can help determine whether the client is oriented to person, place, and time; free of hallucinations; and capable of coherent thinking. When a client does not appear to be capable of realistic decision making, the counselor may need to take a more active role in the crisis intervention process.

The third step in the crisis intervention model involves action. During a crisis, some form of action will usually be required to restore equilibrium to the client. Providing rest can be an important part of this process. For example, if the client is acutely suicidal, the counselor may work with family members to arrange for the client to be hospitalized. Once the client receives rest and equilibrium has been restored, counseling strategies can be implemented. The counselor can attempt to identify the precipitating factors associated with the crisis and help the client overcome these problems in the future.

The fourth and final step entails follow-up. Clients can have delayed reactions to a crisis, which may occur weeks or even months after the precipitating event (Cavanaugh, 1982). It is therefore important to arrange for appropriate follow-up counseling services.

The following *Personal Note* illustrates crisis intervention.

A Personal Note

Mary arrived at an outpatient mental health clinic where I was a psychologist and said that she was having trouble sleeping and wanted sleeping pills. She appeared agitated and tearful, and she spoke in monotone. It soon became clear that there was much more on her mind than her trouble with sleeping. She began to talk about an affair that her husband was having. She went on to say that because of her "religious beliefs," it was necessary for her to kill her three children and herself. Mary reasoned that since her husband had an affair, he had lost his right to have any more contact with his family.

I asked Mary what religion would want her to kill herself and her children. At this point, she seemed to ramble on incoherently. A brief mental status examination showed her to be oriented to person and place—she knew who and where she was—but not to time—she didn't know the day, month, or year. There was no evidence of hallucinations but some possibility of a delusion since she described herself as the "savior" of the family. She intended to kill herself and her children to "save" them all from the sins of her husband.

I then explored the seriousness of her suicidal and homicidal threat. I discovered that she had a gun and planned to use it. Since Mary had a plan and a method of carrying it through, I saw this as a crisis that required immediate action. I became very concerned about the safety of Mary and her children and decided that it would be best if Mary were hospitalized so that she could receive mental health treatment and be protected from hurting herself or her children.

I emphasized to Mary that I wanted her to be hospitalized for her safety and the safety of her children. Since there was no mental health legal code on the Indian reservation where I was working, I could not insist that she be hospitalized. Fortunately, Mary agreed to be admitted to the hospital for a couple of days. For the first two days, Mary slept around the clock, only getting up occasionally for water. After she rested, she said she felt much better. Although Mary was still very angry with her husband, she realized that killing herself and her children would accomplish nothing. Before Mary was discharged from the hospital, she made an appointment with me for individual and marriage counseling.

Indirect Intervention Strategies

Hershenson and Power (1987) have identified six indirect activities associated with the mental health counselor's role and function. These can be considered indirect intervention strategies because they are an indirect form of treatment. An overview of these activities follows.

PREVENTION Prevention represents the inverse of coping with a crisis (Barclay, 1984). **Prevention** can be defined as a helping strategy used to avoid or minimize a potential problem (Gladding, 2001). Prevention of mental disorders and the promotion of mental health have been an integral part of the community mental health movement (Matus & Neuhring, 1979). An example of a preventive focus is the recent emphasis on "wellness" in the counseling literature. Meyers (2014b, p. 33) noted that "the essence of wellness is the integration of mind, body, and spirit" to promote holistic health, and healthy lifestyles and prevent the development of illness.

Hershenson and Power (1987) identified three types of prevention: primary, secondary, and tertiary.

1. *Primary prevention* evolved from the public health model. It refers to strengthening the resistance of a particular population and offsetting of harmful influences before they can make an impact (Caplan, 1964). Primary prevention takes place before a problem

has manifested itself or when its symptoms are barely noticeable (Gilbert, 1982). It reduces the number of individuals requiring mental health services and is therefore an important aspect of any comprehensive human services program (Shaw & Goodyear, 1984). Unfortunately, primary prevention has historically taken a backseat to other strategies because resources are instead applied to people with existing problems.

2. *Secondary prevention* involves programs that attempt to identify individuals who are at risk for developing certain problems and then prescribe remedial activities to prevent those problems from occurring (McMurty, 1985). For example, there has been some interest in working with children of alcoholics to prevent them from becoming alcoholics.

3. *Tertiary prevention* attempts to avert further consequences of a problem that has already manifested itself (Hershenson & Power, 1987). The present mental health system puts most of its efforts into tertiary prevention, focusing on alleviating existing mental health problems.

Hage et al. (2007) have established 15 best-practice prevention guidelines that can be used by practitioners, researchers, and counselor educators. They noted that all 15 of the guidelines relate to one or more of the following principles:

- Stopping a problem before it occurs

- Delaying when a problem occurs

- Reducing the effects of a problem

- Strengthening attitudes, knowledge, and behaviors that promote physical and emotional well-being

- Promoting public policies that foster physical, social, and emotional well-being

Hage et al.'s (2007) 15 guidelines are comprehensive and clearly stated. Furthermore, they incorporate a multicultural/social justice perspective and provide standards that can be used to move the profession forward in terms of providing prevention services. These guidelines can be summarized as follows:

1. Prevention is associated with proactive interventions that reduce or eliminate risk factors and potential problems before they occur.

2. Preventive interventions should be based on theory and supported by empirically validated research.

3. Prevention initiatives should be culturally sensitive and have input from the target populations they serve.

4. Prevention interventions recognize that psychological distress is associated with both individual and contextual/systemic factors that undermine human growth and development.

5. Preventive strategies aim to reduce risk and increase strengths and protective factors across the life span.

6. Prevention recognizes the role of research in promoting the science of prevention (e.g., identifying social injustice associated with racism).

7. Prevention requires competencies in different research methodologies.

8. Prevention research recognizes the importance of environmental context to formulating appropriate prevention strategies (e.g., going beyond the individual and including a social-ecological perspective).

9. Prevention research considers ethical issues, including recognition of the potential negative impact of prevention interventions.

10. Prevention researchers consider the social justice implications of research findings (e.g., victims being blamed for their problems).

11. Prevention education and training promote knowledge, skills, and scholarship associated with prevention research and practice.

12. Prevention education and training include a focus on developing awareness, knowledge, and skills associated with prevention.

13. Prevention is associated with designing, promoting, and supporting systemic initiatives that reduce psychological distress and disability.

14. Prevention is associated with designing, promoting, and supporting institutional change to reduce psychological distress and promote well-being.

15. Prevention is directed at social-political advocacy that promotes health and well-being for a broad base of people (e.g., HIV-AIDS prevention).

Although prevention is clearly a recognized intervention in mental health counseling, it has not been adequately integrated into the training process or practice of mental health counselors (Kiselica & Look, 1993). The disparity between philosophy and practice may be due in part to a lack of insight into the "what and how" of prevention. Apparently, mental health educators and providers lack a clear understanding of what prevention is and how a clinician can engage in this endeavor. In addition, mental health trainees appear to be more interested in remedial interventions, such as psychotherapy, than prevention. Kiselica and Look suggested that counselor educators should make a renewed effort to emphasize prevention and provide adequate training on it. They further urged mental health counselors to work together to make primary prevention the principal mode of intervention in counseling. In addition, these authors recommended that increased effort be directed at pursuing grant money for prevention and journals, such as the *Journal of Mental Health Counseling*, make articles on prevention a higher priority.

ADVOCACY Advocacy is another indirect intervention strategy used by mental health counselors. **Advocacy** means to plead the cause of another person and follow through with action in support of that cause (Myers, Sweeney, & White, 2002). "A mental health counselor-advocate is one who is the client's supporter, the advisor, the champion, and if need be, the client's representative in dealing with the court, the police, the social agency, and other organizations that affect one's well-being" (Hershenson & Power, 1987, p. 246). Counselors should also advocate for the profession of counseling and for counselors (Myers et al.). In this way, advocacy can advance the cause of counseling so that more individuals can benefit from counseling services. Advocacy is an action-oriented form of intervention in which the counselor does something for the client. This can have a positive impact on the counseling relationship in that the client may perceive the counselor as someone who can get things done. Mental health counselors can function as advocates in many ways, such as working with a human services department to ensure that clients receive benefits to which they are entitled.

Hershenson and Power (1987) have identified the following advocacy skills as important to mental health counselors:

- *Timing.* Counselors must decide when to be an advocate and when to let the client take the initiative. As a basic rule, counselors should intervene when it becomes clear that the system is not working for the client or even appears to be working against the client.

- *Support.* Counselors must have the support of the system to be capable of working effectively with that system. In this vein, it is important for counselors not to alienate themselves from coworkers. Counselors are more successful when they work in a cooperative manner and avoid being perceived as blindly fighting for a cause that may sometimes be at cross-purposes with the interests of their colleagues.

- *Compromise.* To maintain support from the system, counselors should be flexible and willing to compromise. A give-and-take approach can also yield creative solutions to complex problems.

- *Communication.* Several communication skills can be useful in the role of advocate. It is important to be able to listen and communicate an understanding of different points of view regarding the client. Using these skills can promote a cooperative approach. Another communication skill that may be necessary is assertiveness. Occasionally, mental health counselors need to take an assertive position to obtain the desired results. Naturally, this must be done in a tactful, caring fashion to be effective.

CONSULTING Since the passage of the Community Mental Health Act in 1963, consultation has been an important aspect of the mental health worker's role and function (Kurpius, 1978). The act noted that consultation services were to become an essential part of community mental health programs of the future (Hershenson & Power, 1987). This legislation was viewed as an attempt to broaden mental health services to include more developmental and preventive approaches (Kurpius).

Caplan (1970) provided the following definition of **mental health consultation**:

> A process of interaction between two professional persons—the consultant, who is a specialist, and the consultee, who invokes the consultant's help in regard to a current work problem with which he is having some difficulty and which he has decided is within the other's area of specialized competence. (p. 19)

Caplan's definition of mental health consultation has been broadened to include a professional consulting with a layperson, such as a counselor consulting with a parent (Hansen, Himes, & Meier, 1990). In addition, consultation can involve working with individuals, couples, groups, families, organizations, and larger systems such as communities (Brown, 1993).

Brown (1993) observed that although consultation holds an important role in the overall philosophy of counseling, it does not appear to be a high priority for counselor educators or counselors. Brown made several recommendations about how to increase the role that consultation plays in all aspects of the counseling profession, including mental health counseling. First, more effort needs to be made to integrate consultation into the counselor education curriculum in terms of coursework and fieldwork experiences (e.g., counseling and consultation should both be considered during treatment planning). Second, licensing and accreditation boards should ensure that individuals and programs show evidence of appropriate consultation skills and activities.

The lack of attention paid to consultation appears to parallel the underutilization of preventative services by mental health counselors (Albee & Ryan-Finn, 1993). It therefore seems imperative that prevention and consultation be linked so that counselors can gain a better understanding of how to promote prevention through consultation. Clearly, the interrelationship of theory, research, and practice regarding these concepts requires further development.

MEDIATION Mediation is one of the newest roles of mental health counselors. Many states now offer mediation services to assist individuals who are going through a divorce (Hershenson & Power, 1987). *Mediation* has been defined as the "facilitation of an agreement between two or more disputing parties by an agreed-upon third party" (Witty, 1980, p. 4). It has the following components: Each party agrees to utilize the services of a mediator, the outcome is an agreement made by the disputants themselves, conflict resolution is cooperative instead of competitive, the focus is on "where we go from here" as opposed to on fault-finding, self-disclosure and empathy are promoted in place of deception and intimidation, decisions are self-imposed instead of imposed by others, and creative alternatives are promoted rather than win-or-lose positions (Kessler, 1979; Koopman, 1985).

Kessler (1979) described the actual process of mediation as being one of structured decision making that usually lasts one to three sessions. Hershenson and Power (1987) identified the following three steps that a mental health counselor could use to structure the mediation process:

1. The counselor initially provides the necessary structure by establishing a cooperative tone, setting the rules, obtaining a commitment to the process, and providing an overview of what is to come (Kessler).

2. In this strategic and planning phase, the mediator obtains an overview of the conflict by reviewing all pertinent information. Toward the end of this step, the mediator can begin to develop a specific plan of action with the disputants.

3. The third step is the problem-solving phase, in which the mediator works with the disputants to help them reach a specific agreement. The mediator may use a variety of tactics during this process, including negotiation, creative problem solving, joining meetings, and private caucuses. The final agreement is usually written out by the disputants so they will have a permanent record of the mediation process.

MENTORING Mentoring is another relatively new role for mental health counselors. *Mentoring* has been defined as a process in which a trusted and experienced individual takes a direct interest in the development and education of a younger, less experienced individual (Krupp, 1982). Numerous studies have shown that mentoring has a positive impact on the mentor, the less experienced individual, and the organization involved (Lynch, 1980; Valliant, 1977). Several guidelines for establishing a mentoring relationship include voluntary participation, minimal rules and maximum freedom, shared and negotiated expectations between the mentor and the less experienced individual, and rewards for the mentor's efforts (Farren, Gray, & Kaye, 1984).

EDUCATION The mental health counselor can also function as an educator, a role that may involve indirect and direct intervention strategies. Education is often an important factor in both types of strategies described in this section, as shown in the following examples:

- Counseling can help a client learn how to become more autonomous.

- Crisis intervention may teach a client how to avoid future crises.

- Prevention often occurs through programs that emphasize an educational component, such as parent education.

- Advocacy can teach a client how to be assertive without alienating others.

- Consultation may involve inservice training programs that teach special skills, such as how to avoid burnout.

- Mediation can help a client learn how to resolve conflicts in a cooperative fashion.

- Mentoring provides opportunities for a less experienced individual to learn from a more experienced person.

Categories of Mental Health Services

The majority of mental health services are directed at helping clients who are dealing with problems of living or who have mental disorders. This section provides an overview of the clinical issues associated with these two categories of problems.

Problems of Living

Problems of living have been defined as "aberrations and/or natural rough spots as one moves through the course of the life span development" (Hershenson & Power, 1987, p. 87). Typical problems of living that clients face include relationship difficulties, such as marital problems; lack of meaning in life, such as not feeling valued at work; and problems associated with stress, such as psychosomatic illness. Although mental disorders may contribute to problems of living, a client can experience these problems without having a recognized mental disorder.

Counseling is the primary treatment strategy used to help clients deal with problems of living. It can help clients deal with specific problems, prevent future problems, and cope with stress. Since problems of living typically do not involve mental disorders, the use of psychoactive drugs is usually not part of the treatment program.

Mental Disorders

A *mental disorder* can be broadly defined as a dysfunctional behavioral or psychological pattern associated with distress or disability (American Psychiatric Association, 2013). In 1984, the National Institute of Mental Health conducted an in-depth study of mental health problems in the United States ("Mental Disorders," 1984). The study estimated that 40 million people in the United States experience mental health problems at any given time. More specifically it found that

- 1 in 5 adults suffered from a recognized mental disorder.

- the three most common disorders in order of incidence were anxiety, substance abuse, and depression.

- only 1 out of 5 people with a mental disorder had sought professional help. Those who did tended to seek help from someone at their church or from a family physician.

- women tended to suffer from phobias and depression, whereas men tended to have problems with alcohol and drugs and antisocial behavior.

- the rate of incidence of mental problems was higher for those under 45.

- college graduates tended to be less prone to mental disorders than were those who had not graduated from college.

The results of this survey suggest that a large percentage of Americans suffer from mental disorders. Another important implication is that when people experience mental problems, they tend not to utilize mental health services. Instead, they often turn to other professionals, such as physicians or members of the clergy. A challenge for mental health counselors has been to overcome the stigma often associated with mental health services so that individuals will seek help when they need it.

TREATING MENTAL DISORDERS Treatment approaches for mental disorders include the use of psychoactive drugs and counseling. Psychoactive drugs are used by psychiatrists primarily to treat psychosis, depression, and acute anxiety reactions. It is important to note that these medications do not cure a person of a mental disorder. They are used primarily to treat underlying brain chemistry dysfunctions and provide symptom relief, such as alleviating depression or anxiety. There are potential dangers, such as the possibility of clients becoming dependent on these medications, especially in the case of tranquilizers to treat anxiety. There can also be serious side effects, such as tardive dyskinesia, an irreversible neurological disorder that can result from the prolonged use of antipsychotic medications.

Although psychoactive medications can have drawbacks and inherent dangers, their benefits usually outweigh the risks. For example, a client who has schizophrenia who does not receive medication may be overwhelmed by threatening hallucinations, dangerous delusions, or a disruptive thought disorder. Although medication cannot remove these symptoms entirely, it can usually control them to the degree that the client can function in society. Antidepressant medications can also be an important aspect of a treatment program for severely depressed clients, who may require medication to be able to work and engage in daily activities. Medication can also be very useful in treating a severe anxiety reaction since it can reduce anxiety to a point where the client can cope.

Counseling can also play a vital role in the overall treatment program for mental disorders (see Chapter 9 on cognitive-behavioral approaches). Counseling may not be indicated until a client has been medically stabilized by the psychoactive medication. A client can be considered *medically stable* when the symptoms associated with the mental disorder have been reduced to the extent that the client is capable of actively engaging in the counseling process.

Counseling is often used to treat mental disorders that do not require medication. The counseling strategies used will vary according to the unique needs of the client and the clinical indicators associated with the particular mental disorder.

The following *Personal Note* describes some of the things I have learned about the treatment of mental disorders.

A Personal Note

Over the years, I have learned many important lessons from clients who had mental disorders. Several clients have said something in particular that I have never forgotten. As I reflect on these cases, their comments symbolize lessons that I learned from them. I will describe five of these cases, giving the client's statement, a brief description of the situation, and the lesson I learned from each person.

Client's Statement:

"Someone said pull my eyes out and I did."

Description of Client's Situation:

The client who made this statement was a 25-year-old male who was in jail for theft. A psychiatrist had been asked to make an evaluation because the client was acting strangely. The psychiatrist made a provisional diagnosis of schizophrenia and arranged to have the client admitted to a psychiatric hospital.

The client was not given any antipsychotic medication and was to be transferred to the

(Continued)

(Continued)

hospital the next day. That night, he began to hallucinate that he was hearing voices. A "voice" told him to take his eye out, and he did. Then a "voice" said to take the other eye out, and he took it out as well. He was standing and holding his two eyes when a jailer walked by and saw with horror what had happened. The client was immediately taken to a hospital and provided treatment. At the hospital, the client was diagnosed as schizophrenic. I met this man while I was at the hospital checking on several clients. He told me about the voices he had heard, asking him to take his eyes out when he was in jail.

What I Learned:

I learned that clients who are actively hallucinating can do serious harm to themselves. Antipsychotic medications must therefore be considered to help control the hallucinations and other psychotic symptoms.

Client's Statement:

"Would you like to see the picture I painted?"

Description of Client's Situation:

The client was a 23-year-old woman who had a long history of severe depression. I had been providing counseling for the client for about 1 year. Although she had weekly appointments, she often missed them. I was actually surprised when she did make an appointment because she always seemed so disoriented.

One day, the client walked into the counseling center and said she wanted to see me. She told me she had painted a self-portrait and asked if I would like to see it. I could not believe my eyes. She had painted the most beautiful painting I had ever seen!

What I Learned:

This client taught me never to "write off " a client. Regardless of how incapacitated I may think some clients are, I will always remember that they are still capable of doing fantastic things with their lives.

Client's Statement:

"There were spiders crawling all over my face and voices telling me I was going to die. I was terrified!"

Description of Client's Situation:

This was a 54-year-old female who had been an alcoholic for 26 years. The client had been on a drinking binge for 2 weeks and then experienced alcohol hallucinosis, in which she saw and felt spiders crawling on her face and heard terrifying voices. The client came to the counseling center the next day and said she would never drink again. I provided weekly counseling services for her over the next year. During that time, the client did not drink. She later moved to another city.

What I Learned:

I discovered that the prognosis for overcoming alcoholism is good when the client decides that the costs outweigh the rewards of use. During the first few sessions, it became clear to me that this client had decided that drinking was just not worth it anymore.

Client's Statement:

"We just caught on fire."

Description of Client's Situation:

The client who made this statement was one of two brothers who had caught on fire when they were sniffing gasoline. Both had a history of inhalant abuse spanning a 5-year period. I had been seeing them in counseling for 2 years prior to their accident with gasoline. During the time I had worked with them, they had been hospitalized on numerous occasions for treatment of acute lead poisoning. On one occasion, one of the brothers had become psychotic during 8:00 a.m. rush-hour traffic, jumping out of a moving car and running down the street pounding on other cars.

What I Learned:

I learned several things from this case and similar cases involving inhalant dependency. First, I found that these individuals have a very difficult time attempting to overcome their dependency. My success rate has been very low with this population: Only 1 out of 5 stopped using inhalants while I worked with them.

I soon discovered that lead poisoning can produce serious side effects. For example, both of the brothers I worked with showed significant intellectual impairment. Their overall IQ scores on the Wechsler Adult Intelligence Scale dropped 15 and 20 points over a 12-month interval while they were using inhalants. I also discovered that gasoline sniffing can make a person psychotic. In addition, I learned that lead poisoning is very difficult to treat. I found out that when an individual inhales lead, the lead is absorbed into the bones as well as other parts of the body. Unfortunately, the lead tends to remain in the bones, gradually releasing lead into the body over a period of time, even if active abuse has stopped.

Client's Statement:

"I got my meat, my flour, and my Jesus."

Description of Client's Situation:

This was the statement of a 45-year-old woman who had been suffering from chronic schizophrenia for 20 years. A residential program had just opened for people who were chronically mentally ill and who had no relatives to assist them. I asked the client whether she would like to be admitted into the program, and she said, "Yes." Getting the client admitted was a very long and drawn-out process. It involved filling out numerous forms and dealing with other seemingly endless aspects of the bureaucracy. I was finally told that my client could get into the program. I couldn't wait to tell her the good news.

When I told her she was accepted, she looked puzzled. She then smiled and told me that she didn't want to go. She said, "I got my meat, my flour, and my Jesus." When I asked her what she meant, she said she had plenty of meat to eat and flour to make bread. Then she turned on her portable radio and played a religious station featuring a preacher giving a high-powered sermon. She pointed to the radio, smiled, and said, "That's my Jesus."

What I Learned:

I learned that freedom is essential to human dignity. Whenever possible, people need to have freedom of choice and be able to act on those choices. My job as a counselor was simply to help create choices. When I did create choices for this client, it seemed to bring more meaning to her existence—an existence that she already had.

Strategies for Suicidal Clients

Mental health services must continually adapt to the changes in society. Three types of clients requiring increased efforts from mental health counselors and other members of the helping profession are suicidal clients, clients with substance abuse problems, and gerontological clients. To illustrate the contemporary issues and skills associated with mental health counseling, this section provides an overview of suicide, and the next two sections will cover substance abuse and gerontological counseling.

The rate of suicides per 100,000 people has increased over the past 40 years and has now leveled off. In 1950, there were 4.2 suicides per 100,000; in 1974, 10.9; in 1984, 12.8; 1996, 11.65; and 2009, 12.0 (American Association of Suicidology, 2012; NIMH, 1999; Shneidman, 1984). Suicide rates are high across all levels of society. Among girls, the gifted have the highest rate of suicide nationally and are therefore considered to be at especially high risk (Taylor, 1979).

Capuzzi and Nystul (1986) provided a comprehensive overview of suicide—causes, myths, and treatment strategies. The remainder of this section is adapted from that work.

Causes

Shneidman (1984) identified four theoretical perspectives for understanding the motivation for attempting suicide: sociological, psychodynamic, psychological, and constitutional or biochemical.

SOCIOLOGICAL Durkheim (1897) described sociological reasons for suicide that seem to have withstood the test of time. These reasons can be categorized as *egoistic,* when a person lacks a sense of belonging and therefore lacks a sense of purpose; *altruistic,* when a person is willing to die for a particular cause (e.g., Japanese kamikaze pilots); *anomic,* when a person believes his or her relationship with society has been shattered (e.g., after being fired from a job or experiencing racial oppression); and *fatalistic,* when a person feels society does not offer any hope for a better future (e.g., someone who feels trapped in poverty).

PSYCHODYNAMIC Freud (1933) emphasized the role of unconscious forces in personality dynamics. He believed that all people have an unconscious death wish that could contribute to suicidal behavior.

PSYCHOLOGICAL Shneidman (1976) provided a psychological perspective on suicide, suggesting that it is associated with the following psychological conditions: *acute perturbation,* when a person is in a heightened state of unhappiness; *heightened inimicality,* when a person has negative thoughts and feelings toward the self, such as self-hate and guilt; *constriction of intellectual focus,* when a person experiences a tunneling of thought processes, resulting in an inability to see viable options; and *cessation,* when a person believes that suicide will make his or her suffering stop.

CONSTITUTIONAL OR BIOCHEMICAL The medical model suggests a link between depression and suicide and views depression as having an organic basis. In this model, therefore, suicide can be prevented by using psychoactive medication to restore an individual's biochemical balance.

Myths About Suicide

Numerous myths are associated with suicide. The following are some of the myths and the facts that contradict them, as provided by Capuzzi and Nystul (1986) and James and Gilliand (2013):

- *Suicide is committed only by people with severe psychological problems.* Studies have shown that most individuals who commit suicide had not been diagnosed with a psychological disorder (Shneidman, Farberow, & Litman, 1976).

- *Suicide usually occurs without warning.* In fact, most suicides are preceded by warning signs. The nature of the warning signs may be a sudden change of behavior, self-destructive behavior, verbal threats of suicide, talk of hopelessness and despair, and depression.

- *People who are suicidal will always be prone to suicide.* In truth, most people who become suicidal do not remain in that state forever. They may be struggling through a temporary personal crisis. Once they work through the crisis, they may never be suicidal again.

- *Discussing suicide may cause the client to want to carry out the act.* The opposite is actually true. Talking with a caring person can often prevent suicide.

- *When a person has attempted suicide and pulls back from it, the danger is over.* Actually, the greatest period of danger is usually during the upswing period, when the person becomes energized following a severe depression and has the energy to commit suicide.

Treatment Strategies

Capuzzi and Nystul (1986), Westefeld et al. (2000), Wong, Maffini, and Shin (2014), and Rogers and Russell (2014) provided an overview of treatment issues relating to suicide such as prevention, assessment, suicide risk factors, crisis intervention, postcrisis counseling, postintervention, and rational suicide.

PREVENTION Three types of prevention were described earlier in this chapter (primary, secondary, and tertiary). All three can be related to suicide. Primary prevention focuses on individuals before they become suicidal, such as when an elementary school counselor makes classroom presentations on dealing with stress. In secondary prevention, the counselor attempts to recognize people who are at risk for suicide and provide the necessary assistance before their problems get worse. Tertiary prevention involves assisting people who are currently suicidal. For example, crisis intervention services like telephone hotlines have been used to prevent individuals from committing suicide (Lester, 1993).

Wong et al. (2014) suggested that clinicians utilize culturally relevant suicide prevention interventions, because risk factors and protective factors vary across cultures. "*Cultural relevance* refers to interventions that incorporate the cultural practices, beliefs, values, norms, and customs that form the core of a community" (Wong et al., p. 32). Wong et al. recommended that clinicians incorporate an ecological perspective in suicide prevention that extends beyond traditional psychotherapy and includes consultation, training, advocacy, and community outreach (e.g., promoting life skills training in high schools).

ASSESSMENT Assessment of potential suicidal behavior should be a comprehensive process involving standardized and nonstandardized assessment procedures and the clinical interview discussed in Chapter 4. Westefeld et al. (2000) identified assessment tools that have been developed to specifically assess suicide. Some of these assessment tools are the Suicide Ideation Scale (Rudd, 1989), designed primarily for college students; the Reasons for Living Inventory (Linehan, Goodstein, Nielsen, & Chiles, 1983), based on Victor Frankl's (1959) existential theory; and the Fairy Tales Test (Orbach, Feshbach, Carlson, Glaubman, & Gross, 1983), which can be used with children.

Granello (2010a) provided 12 core principles that can be used to guide the process of suicide risk assessment. These 12 principles have been summarized as follows. Suicide risk assessment is unique for each person and is done in a cultural context. It is a process that is ongoing, complicated, and challenging and can be considered a form of treatment. Consultation and documentation are high priorities during suidide assessment. In addition, practitioners use clinical judgement, take threats seriously, when in doubt emphasize safety, and identify underlying messages associated with the suicidal ideations (e.g., a cry for help or attempt to control one's fate).

SUICIDE RISK FACTORS A number of empirically identified risk factors are associated with suicide (James & Gilliand, 2013; Westefeld et al., 2000; Wong et al., 2014):

Mental Disorders Several mental disorders have been associated with suicide, including depression, substance abuse, psychotic disorders, and personality disorders (especially borderline). Suicide, for example, can be an escape response to the sadness of depression. Wong et al. (2014) reported that depression is a poor predictor of suicide for Black American adolescents and adults as compared to their White

American counterparts. Impaired family relations is a more accurate predictor of suicide for Black American adolescents and adults (Wong et al.).

Loss   Loss can be a factor in any suicide. The breakup of a relationship or a divorce can trigger a suicide attempt. Multiple issues of loss can characterize the late adult stage: unwanted retirement, chronic illnesses and pain, and death of loved ones. Loss for seniors can, therefore, result in suicidal tendencies associated with lack of purpose and meaning, pain and suffering, and social-emotional isolation.

History   A history of past suicide attempts indicates a high risk for suicide. Suicide risk also increases if there is past family history of suicide, because it can be perceived by family members as a way of coping with mental problems such as depression. Another historical factor that may be associated with suicide is the contagion factor (i.e., being exposed to suicide may cause a person to be more prone to engaging in suicide).

Diversity Issues   Rogers and Russell (2014) noted that potential barriers to suicide assessment can occur when cultural factors are not considered (e.g., some cultures contend that discussing suicidal thoughts is shameful and taboo). Diversity factors like age, gender, culture, and sexual orientation can be associated with increased risk of suicide. Adolescents and adults over age 65 are at a higher risk of suicide than the general population. Gender statistics indicate that women *attempt* suicide at a much higher rate than men, although, surprisingly, men actually commit suicide 4.5 times more often than women. It is not clear what accounts for this discrepancy. Some have hypothesized that fatal suicides for women are often incorrectly reported as accidental deaths (Westefeld et al., 2000). Culture also plays a role in suicide. Native Americans have the highest suicide rates in the United States, estimated to be 1.6 to 4.2 times higher than the national average. Wong et al. (2014) noted that although Native American adolescents and young adults have the highest suicide rate of any cultural group, Native American seniors (ages 65–85) had lower rates of suicide in 2007 (7.58 per 100,000 individuals) than did White American seniors (16.08 per 100,000 individuals). The increased risk for suicide of Native American adolescents and young adults can be related to high rates of alcoholism and difficulty with acculturation and identity development. Sexual orientation has also been related to increased risk for suicide. This is especially true during adolescence, when gays and lesbians are 2 to 3 times more likely to die from suicide than are their heterosexual counterparts. A lack of public acceptance or tolerance of homosexual orientations can undermine identity development when adolescents need understanding and acceptance the most.

MMPI   MMPI does not stand for the commonly used personality inventory described in Chapter 4. Rather, MMPI is an acronym for *means, motive, plan*, and *intent* and can be used to identify risk factors associated with suicide.

The following *Personal Note* provides an example of how I used the MMPI to assess for suicide.

A Personal Note

Anne was a 32-year-old teacher who sought mental health services for depression and insomnia. Anne told me that she wanted to kill herself because her mom had recently died and she could no longer go on living. As I assessed her suicidal tendencies, Anne reported she had a bottle of sleeping pills that she planned to take (means and plan). The intensity and sincerity of her tone of voice suggested that she really did plan to do this (intent). Anne went on to justify killing herself by noting that her mom had been her best friend and she felt she had nothing to live for (motive). On the basis of the MMPI, clinical interview, and other input, I determined that Anne was a very high risk for suicide and arranged to have her hospitalized.

CRISIS INTERVENTION The section on crisis intervention services earlier in this chapter provides guidelines for crisis intervention in terms of potential suicide. As was noted, the aim of crisis intervention is to take the necessary steps to avoid a catastrophe in which the client is seriously hurt.

Crisis intervention strategies used with suicidal clients include contracts, assistance from relatives, medication, counseling, and hospitalization. Suicide contracts, which are commonly used to prevent suicide, involve having clients sign a no-harm contract promising not to kill themselves and to let the counselor, a family member, or another concerned adult know if they become suicidal. No-harm contracts must be used in conjuction with other interventions (Hyldahl & Richardson, 2011). Family members can play an integral role in suicide intervention by providing social-emotional support to clients, monitoring clients for suicidal ideations, and helping clients obtain professional help as needed. Other suicide interventions include medication to treat mental disorders such as depression. Counseling involves encouraging ventilation to defuse the crisis and to promote psychological equilibrium. Hospitalization provides the safest means of preventing suicide and should be considered for acutely suicidal individuals.

Providing mental health services to a suicidal client can be a very challenging experience. Granello (2010b) provided a seven-step model that can be used to address suicide ideations. The seven steps are summarized as follows.

- Assess the degree of lethality to determine what is necessary to promote safety.

- Establish a positive therapeutic relationship.

- Encourage clients to tell their story regarding why they are considering suicide.

- Help clients manage their feelings.

- Promote alternatives, hope, social support, and resilience.

- Create an action-safety plan to address factors associated with suicidal ideations.

- Ensure appropriate follow-up care.

POSTCRISIS COUNSELING Postcrisis counseling can be conducted when an individual is no longer at high risk. It can help determine underlying reasons the client was suicidal and foster coping mechanisms to prevent future psychological problems. Dialectic behavior therapy (Linehan, Armstrong, Suarez, Allmon, & Heard, 1991), which was specifically designed to treat clients who have a history of suicidal ideations, is directed at teaching skills associated with suicide prevention, such as emotional regulation, interpersonal effectiveness, and distress tolerance. Beck's (1986) cognitive therapy can also be a valuable approach to helping clients who have had a history of suicidal ideations (Tyrer et al., 1999).

POSTINTERVENTION Postintervention involves providing mental health assistance to bereaved individuals, families, and communities. The American Association of Suicidology (1990) identified the following postintervention strategies for suicide:

- Planning how schools and community agencies respond to suicide

- Providing opportunities to work through emotions such as grief, anger, and guilt associated with survivors of suicide

- Taking necessary steps to prevent contagion suicide (such as avoidance of glamorizing the suicide)

- Providing debriefing counseling for mental health staff involved

The following *Personal Note* provides additional insight into the suicide phenomenon.

A Personal Note

When I was the psychologist for an Indian reservation, I provided mental health counseling to more than 100 clients who had attempted suicide. Most of these clients were female adolescents who had tried to kill themselves by taking large amounts of pills they found in a medicine cabinet.

The thing that surprised me about these clients was that nearly all of them truly seemed to

(Continued)

(Continued)

want to die. They did not appear simply to be making a cry for help. Several nearly died when their hearts stopped. Each time, fortunately, the medical team was able to bring the client back from the grip of death. When these young women regained consciousness, however, almost all of them immediately said something that expressed their disappointment that they had not died.

As I explored their reasons for wanting to die, the majority seemed to believe that life had nothing to offer them. They had reached a dead end, with nowhere to go. They felt that if they did try to continue living, things would probably just get worse. There were feelings of futility and sorrow in their words and tone of voice. Their desire for life seemed to be gone, and in its place had grown a sense of apathy.

I would often use nontraditional approaches to counseling to help these clients overcome their preoccupation with suicide, death, and dying. For example, I might meet with them under a tree to awaken them to the beauty and innocence of life. During a session, we might stop and take time to hear a bird sing. Focusing on the wonder of nature helped clients shift from the negativity associated with their suicidal ideation and open their eyes to the simple, basic splendor of life that only nature can portray. The focus of counseling with these clients was to help them discover some personal meaning in life. Together, we worked to cultivate dreams and develop the means to turn those dreams into reality, a process that required intensive individual counseling and psychotherapy. In addition, I often utilized couples counseling and family therapy as an important facet of the overall treatment program.

RATIONAL SUICIDE **Rational suicide**, also referred to as *hastened death* and *assisted suicide,* may be the most controversial issue in suicidology. Rational suicide relates to a rational choice to hasten the end of one's life. Hastened death can be requested in instances of terminal illness or insufferable pain.

Oregon's Death with Dignity Act of 1999 (Oregon Act), as amended from the 1994 Oregon Act, has played a major role in the evolution of rational suicide. The Oregon Act legalizes physician-assisted suicide in Oregon. It includes conditions that must be met for physicians to participate in assisted suicide. For example, physicians must refer patients to state-licensed psychologists or psychiatrists if the patient appears to have a psychological or psychiatric condition such as depression that impairs judgment (Cohen, 2001). Care of the dying in Oregon appears to have improved since the Death with Dignity Act, which may represent a "wake-up call" to physicians to do a better job assisting individuals to prepare and move toward the end of their lives (Lee & Tolle, 1996). There appears to be an increasing interest in legislation similar to Oregon's Death with Dignity Act, as Vermont and Washington State allow assisted suicide, and Montana allows it if a court order is obtained. Rational suicide involves health care workers, such as psychologists, in promoting the psychological means of achieving a death with dignity and meaning. The American Psychological Association's (1997) position on rational suicide is as follows:

The American Psychological Association does not advocate for or against assisted suicide. What psychologists do support is high quality end-of-life care and informed end-of-life decisions based on the correct assessment of the patient's mental capacity, social support systems, and degree of self-determination. (p. 1)

The APA provides guidelines regarding the role of mental health workers in rational suicide. These activities include providing support to the patient and family, ensuring that patients receive proper diagnosis and treatment for mental disorders, and assisting in determining whether patients' decisions regarding hastened death are rational.

Although rational suicide appears to offer a death with dignity and meaning, it involves numerous moral, religious, ethical, and legal issues, which have yet to be addressed. Additional research and evaluation are necessary to determine the implications for the role of mental health workers in rational suicide.

Substance Abuse Counseling

Substance abuse counseling is a specialty directed at the prevention and treatment of problems associated with alcohol and other substances. Substance abuse has become a major health problem in the United States as well as in many other countries. Alcoholism has been considered to be the third most prevalent US public health problem (Pattison & Kaufman, 1982). Among some cultures, such as Native American, alcoholism ranks first among all health problems (Herring, 1994). Illicit drug use is also widespread in American society, including among children and adolescents, as discussed in Chapter 11. A 1982 survey estimated that 32 million Americans smoked marijuana at least once a year, and 20 million used it once a month; over 12 million used cocaine once a year; and several million used a variety of drugs, such as tranquilizers and stimulants, without medical supervision (Polich, Ellickson, Reuter, & Kahan, 1984).

The result of the high prevalence of alcohol and drug use (not counting tobacco) is that approximately 40% of hospital admissions and 25% of deaths a year in the United States are related to substance abuse, costing society in excess of $300 billion a year, in addition to human suffering and losses in productivity (American Psychiatric Association, 1995). Approximately half of all highway fatalities involve alcohol, one third of all new AIDS cases are related to intravenous drug use, and 7.5% to 15% of pregnant women had recently used a drug (not counting alcohol) just prior to their first prenatal exam (American Psychiatric Association).

Substance abuse permeates all levels of society: Approximately one fifth of all Americans have a problem with alcohol or drug abuse at some time in their lives, and one third of all psychiatric patients have alcohol or drug abuse problems (Frances, 1988). Counselors can therefore expect to have to deal with problems relating to drug abuse regardless of the counseling setting in which they work.

This section provides an overview of substance abuse counseling, with information relating to diagnosis, special treatment issues, counseling goals, treatment strategies, and prevention of relapses. Since alcoholism is the most prevalent of these problems, particular attention is devoted to that issue.

Diagnosis

The *DSM-5* (American Psychiatric Association, 2013) recognizes 10 classes of drugs that are included in substance-related disorders (e.g., alcohol, cannabis, hallucinogens, and opioids). The substance-related disorders are made up of two separate groups: substance use disorders and substance-induced disorders. A *substance use disorder* is characterized by a "pathological pattern of behaviors related to the use of the substance" resulting in significant problems for the individual (American Psychiatric Association, p. 483). *Substance-induced disorders* include "intoxication, withdrawal, and other substance/medication-induced mental disorders (e.g., substance-induced psychotic disorder, substance-induced depressive disorder"; American Psychiatric Association, p. 485).

Questionnaires can be part of the diagnostic process of determining whether a person is an alcoholic or has another substance abuse problem. One commonly used questionnaire is the Michigan Alcohol Screening Test (Selzer, 1971), which has 24 questions that require yes-or-no answers from the respondent.

There are some drawbacks to using the *DSM* system of diagnosis or a questionnaire to label a person as a substance abuser (e.g., alcohol use disorder), because these systems tend to have either-or definitions of alcoholism in that they provide a result that a client either is or is not an alcoholic. This type of definition could result in a counselor not providing needed services to a client with a borderline problem. Pattison and Kaufman (1982) rejected the either-or perspective and instead conceptualized alcoholism as a multivariant syndrome, which suggests that no two alcoholics are alike and that they manifest multiple patterns of dysfunctional use, varying personalities, numerous possibilities for adverse consequences, and various prognoses. Each individual thus requires a different type of treatment.

The multivariant position suggests that substance abuse should be thought of in terms of a continuum that begins with nonuse and can progress to moderate nonproblematic use use, heavy nonproblematic use, heavy use with moderate problems, heavy use with serious problems, and then dependence with life and health problems (Lewis, Dana, & Blevins, 2011). The continuum model does not imply that people who develop problems will always move steadily along the continuum from left to right (Lewis et al.). The relationship to the continuum will vary from individual to individual. Some will stay at the same spot; others will move to the right, signifying more serious problems; and some will develop less severe problems, moving to the left on the continuum.

Counselors can estimate the place where a person is functioning on the continuum by determining the number of problems the person has experienced in relation to substance abuse (Lewis et al., 2011). Valliant's (1983) Problem-Drinking Scale can identify problems relating to drinking, including work-related problems, such as excessive tardiness or sick leave or being fired from work; family problems, such as complaints from family members or marital problems; legal problems, such as alcohol-related arrests; and health problems, such as medical disorders, blackouts, and tremors.

Special Treatment Issues

Most of the counseling theories and strategies described in this text can be applied to substance abuse counseling. At the same time, there are some special issues involved in working with this population. Lewis et al. (2011) provided the following guidelines for substance abuse counseling:

- Conceptualize substance abuse problems on a continuum from nonproblematic to problematic rather than in dichotomous, either-or terms.

- Use evidence-based practices.

- Maintain a respectful-positive approach.

- Recognize that advocacy is an important role for the counselor.

- Utilize a multicultural perspective recognizing the needs of diverse client populations.

- Provide an individualized treatment program in terms of goals, methods, and plans for change.

- Incorporate a multidimensional treatment program that includes social and environmental aspects associated with long-term recovery.

These guidelines provide a general theoretical framework for working with substance abuse clients. There are also some unique counseling goals and treatment strategies associated with substance abuse counseling.

Counseling Goals

Considerable debate exists in the literature as to whether the primary goal of alcohol abuse counseling should be abstinence or controlled drinking (Fisher, 1982; Marlatt, 1983; Sobell & Sobell, 1984). Proponents of abstinence align themselves with the disease model of alcoholism, contending that alcoholism is a chronic and progressive disease and that abstinence is therefore the only solution. Alcoholics Anonymous (AA) and Narcotics Anonymous (NA) are among the proponents of this position. Supporters of controlled drinking, on the other hand, view alcoholism from a behavioral perspective, believing that it results from maladaptive learning.

Miller and Munoz (1982) noted that controlled drinking will be appropriate only for approximately 15% of all alcohol abusers and that certain conditions should preclude any consideration of controlled drinking as a treatment goal. These include clients who have a medical problem, such as a disease of the gastrointestinal system (e.g., liver disease), heart disease, or other conditions that may be made worse by drinking; who are pregnant or trying to become pregnant; who tend to lose control of their behavior when they drink; who have been physically addicted to alcohol; who take medication that is dangerous when combined with alcohol, such as antidepressants or tranquilizers; or who are currently abstaining successfully, particularly if there is a family history of alcoholism or a personal history of serious drinking problems.

Counselors who want to consider controlled drinking as a goal for a client should first receive specialized training. One approach that has received considerable attention, reporting a success rate between 60% and 80%, is behavioral self-control training (Miller, 1980). This program is educationally oriented and can be used in an outpatient setting. It involves a variety of behavioral techniques, including training the client to identify environmental cues that increase the frequency of drinking, to monitor drinking consumption, and to use self-reinforcement to control drinking rates.

Aside from the issue of abstinence versus controlled drinking, there are other, more specific goals that counselors should address when developing a comprehensive treatment program. Lewis et al. (2011) noted that substance abuse tends to be associated with social, psychological, family, and economic problems. With respect to the relationship of these problems to substance abuse, the authors identified the following goals that counselors could attempt to help clients with:

- Resolve legal problems.
- Attain stability in marriage and family.
- Establish and meet educational and career goals.
- Improve interpersonal and social skills.
- Enhance physical fitness and health.
- Develop effective coping mechanisms to deal with stress.
- Learn how to recognize and express feelings.
- Develop effective problem-solving and decision-making skills.
- Establish a social support system.
- Develop positive self-esteem and self-efficacy.
- Deal effectively with psychological issues such as anxiety and depression.
- Create recreational and social outlets.
- Adapt to challenges at work or school.

Treatment Strategies

Treatment approaches in substance abuse counseling vary according to the counselor's theoretical orientation as well as the goals established by the counselor and client. The following is an overview of some commonly used approaches.

THE MINNESOTA MODEL The Minnesota model has been one of the most widely used forms of treatment for substance abuse. According to James and Gilliand (2013), there are two phases to the Minnesota model. The first phase involves assembling a comprehensive treatment team to evaluate and provide initial treatment pertaining to the client's unique needs. The second phase typically involves an intensive, 28-day inpatient hospitalization directed at all aspects of the client's substance abuse problem (e.g., education, recovery, and relapse prevention). In an era of managed care, a 28-day hospitalization is in most instances not a realistic component of a treatment plan. Most managed-care organizations are shifting to an emphasis on outpatient substance abuse treatment programs.

THE ALCOHOLICS ANONYMOUS (AA) MODEL Since its founding in 1935, AA has grown into the most popular organization for the treatment of alcoholism and other substance abuse problems (Lê, Ingvarson, & Page, 1995). AA incorporates the disease model of alcoholism and is based on a 12-step program, which has a strong religious context. One of the strengths of AA is that it is run by individuals who have themselves struggled with substance dependence. In addition, it can be a place where people feel acceptance, hope, and encouragement. It is also a highly accessible model, with outlets available in almost every major city in the world.

There has been some concern that the efficacy of AA has not been established by empirical research and that its religiously oriented steps, such as admitting powerlessness, are inconsistent with counseling theory and practice are of some concern (Bristow-Braitman, 1995; Lê et al., 1995). Bristow-Braitman suggested that cognitive-behavioral counseling could be used to help reframe some AA concepts to make them more compatible with traditional counseling approaches. Nevertheless, professional counselors may benefit from a deeper understanding of AA to become more sensitive to the spiritual aspects of counseling and be more supportive of their clients who are attending AA.

THE MEDICAL MODEL This approach also adheres to the disease model of alcoholism. Researchers are investigating the role of physiological factors (including brain function) in the etiology and treatment of substance abuse disorders (Ruden & Byalick, 1997). A number of neurotransmitters may be important in the addiction process (Lewis, et al., 2011). For example, dopamine is believed to influence learning, motor activity, reward, and reinforcement and has been associated with commonly used drugs like cocaine, marijuana, and nicotine (Lewis et al.). The dopamine hypothesis of addiction suggests that dopamine plays a key role in addiction by sending pleasure signals to the brain when it is stimulated by drugs such as cocaine (Volkow et al., 1997).

Medical treatments for substance abuse problems include Antabuse (disulfiram) and methadone (Ruden & Byalick, 1997). Antabuse is a form of aversive therapy that can be taken to prevent relapse in alcoholism. A person will experience anxiety, vomiting, nausea, and palpitations within minutes if alcohol is consumed. Methadone maintenance can be used to block the withdrawal symptoms associated with heroin addiction, while avoiding its euphoric effects. Detoxification centers can also be important in the treatment of substance abuse problems. The detoxification process allows patients to overcome potentially life-threatening withdrawal effects of alcohol and other drugs under medical supervision.

COGNITIVE-BEHAVIORAL THERAPIES A number of research studies that have focused on the role of cognitive-behavioral therapies in the acquisition of skills necessary to overcome alcohol abuse and dependence have confirmed that cognitive-behavioral therapies are effective treatments for substance abuse (especially alcohol-related problems) (American Psychiatric Association, 1995). Some of these cognitive-behavioral skills are self-control, interpersonal functioning, self-efficacy, alternative coping mechanisms, and relapse prevention.

BEHAVIORAL THERAPIES Two of the more common behavioral approaches used in substance abuse counseling are operant conditioning, used to reward behaviors associated with abstaining and punish those involved in substance abuse, and systematic desensitization and aversion training, which countercondition clients' drug cravings (American Psychiatric Association, 1995).

INDIVIDUAL PSYCHODYNAMIC/INTERPERSONAL THERAPIES The American Psychiatric Association (1995) has provided some support for psychodynamic and interpersonal therapies in substance abuse counseling. The association noted that psychodynamic psychotherapy appears to help prevent relapse and newer, short-term forms of psychodynamic therapy (such as supportive-expressive therapy and interpersonal psychotherapy) have demonstrated efficacy in substance abuse counseling (American Psychiatric Association). These newer approaches focus on formulating supportive counseling relationships in which clients can learn the social skills necessary to overcome negative patterns of interpersonal functioning, which in turn decreases problems with substance abuse (Ruden & Byalick, 1997).

GROUP THERAPIES Lewis et al. (2011) suggested that group counseling has many advantages over other methods of substance abuse counseling. For example, it can provide an opportunity for group members to offer support and encouragement, generate problem-solving strategies, learn how to apply new skills such as assertiveness, and, when necessary, break through denial or other processes that interfere with recovery from substance abuse problems.

FAMILY THERAPY James and Gilliand (2013) contended that it is critical to involve the family in the treatment of substance abuse. Family therapy recognizes that the behavior of each family member must be understood from the perspective of the family system. Drinking or the use of other drugs is therefore not an isolated event but an action that affects the overall functioning of the family.

The family therapy literature has provided numerous insights into the systemic nature of family behavior. For example, the concepts *enabling* and *codependency* imply that two individuals (one with a substance abuse problem such as drinking) could be dependent on maintaining an adversarial relationship regarding the abuse. In this situation it is common for the drinker and the concerned family member to both gain secondary gains from their codependency, thereby enabling the drinker to continue drinking (i.e., drinkers feel they have an excuse to drink when they "get griped at," and concerned family members get sympathy from others for having to put up with the drinking).

Family therapy can also be used to overcome one of the most difficult barriers to treatment in substance abuse counseling: denial. It is very common for individuals to deny problems with alcohol or other drugs and resist treatment even when the problem is having a serious adverse effect on their health, family, social life, and work. When this occurs, Johnson's (1986) family-intervention model can be used to help a family confront a family member with the realities of his or her substance abuse problem. This approach involves training family members to communicate in a clear, caring, and direct manner their concerns regarding how the substance abuse is affecting the individual and the family as a whole. The family-intervention model can be a powerful tool in overcoming denial and motivating the individual to seek help (James & Gilliand, 2013).

Stages of Change

Helping clients successfully engage in the change process is perhaps the most difficult, yet important, aspect of counseling. Unfortunately, little was known about how the change process works. This bleak situation has been addressed by the pioneering work of Prochaska, DiClemente, and associates on how the change process relates to overcoming addictive behaviors (Prochaska, 1984; Prochaska, DiClemente, & Norcross, 1992). Their transtheoretical model of change is based on the idea that both the cessation of problematic behaviors and the acquisition of healthier behaviors involve five stages of change: precontemplation, contemplation, preparation, action, and maintenance (Prochaska et al.). The following is an overview of these five stages of change and the implications they have for developing intervention strategies.

- *Precontemplation.* During the first stage, clients have no serious plans to engage in the change process. Resistance and denial are common reactions in the precontemplation stage.

- *Contemplation.* The second stage is characterized by clients being aware that they have a problem and are thinking about making changes but have not quite reached the point of making a commitment to do something. During the contemplation stage, clients seriously consider resolving their problems. They tend to weigh the pros and cons associated with potential changes to help with decision making.

- *Preparation.* At the preparation stage, clients have unsuccessfully taken some action during the past year and plan to try to work on their problem during the next 30 days.

- *Action.* Clients have reached the action stage when they have made the necessary changes in their lives to successfully address a particular problem (e.g., they have stopped drinking for 1 day to 6 months).

- *Maintenance.* The maintenance stage is characterized by clients attempting to prevent relapse and to stabilize their gains. In substance abuse counseling, maintenance extends from 6 months to the rest of the client's life.

Change is like the tide. It moves forward and backward as clients progress and relapse. Since clients tend to relapse, it is common to regress to earlier stages in the change process (Prochaska et al., 1992). Fortunately, people tend to learn from their mistakes, using what they learn to be more successful as they work their way back through the stages of change. One of the most important implications of the change model is the need to identify where clients are in terms of the change process and match their position with the appropriate form of intervention. For example, some evidence suggests that during the precontemplation and contemplation stages, experiential, cognitive, and psychoanalytic approaches are the most effective, whereas during the action and maintenance stages, existential and behavioral theories have the strongest efficacy (Prochaska et al.).

Prevention of Relapses

A comprehensive treatment program for substance abuse should include strategies to prevent or deal with a client's relapse, or uncontrolled return to drug or alcohol use. The potential for relapse is a serious problem in substance abuse counseling. Some estimates suggest that 90% of all clients have a relapse within 4 years following treatment (Polich, Armor, & Braiker, 1981).

Several factors have been related to substance abuse relapse. Differences in the outcome of a substance abuse treatment program are related to the presence or absence of a mental disorder in addition to the substance abuse disorder (Svanum & McAdoo, 1989). Clients with no additional disorders tend to avoid relapse as long as they comply with after-care treatment, especially an exercise program; have a satisfactory job; and have an adequate living arrangement (Svanum & McAdoo). Clients with multiple mental disorders are more prone to relapse if their emotional disturbance continues after participation in a substance abuse program. Other factors such as exercise, work, or living conditions do not appear to be related to relapse for these clients. Since a substantial minority of substance abuse clients suffer from psychopathology, such as anxiety and depression (Mirin, Weiss, Michael, & Griffin, 1988), substance abuse programs should include careful screening and treatment for these disorders as part of relapse prevention.

A second factor related to substance abuse relapse is the lifestyle imbalance that can result from certain life events. The types of events that precipitate a relapse are negative emotional states (35%), interpersonal conflicts (16%), and social pressures (20%; Cummings, Gordon, & Marlatt, 1980). Lewis et al. (2011) incorporated Marlatt and Gordon's (1985) model of relapse into the following description of how relapse can occur. A lifestyle imbalance can occur when a client experiences a particular problem, such as a setback at work or a relationship problem. The imbalance may cause the client to feel the need for immediate stress release, and the client may rationalize taking a drink by thinking, "I deserve a drink, with all that I'm going through." At this point, the client may deny having a problem with alcohol and make apparently irrelevant decisions (AIDs). Lacking the necessary coping skills, the client will experience a decrease in self-efficacy, feeling unable to cope with the situation. This in turn will result in a slip—beginning to drink—creating an abstinence violation effect (AVE). The AVE further undermines the client's self-efficacy, reducing self-confidence. The client may think, "I'm just a hopeless drunk." Such negative thinking can create a self-fulfilling prophecy, leading to an increased probability of relapse. In this model, the key to preventing a relapse is to teach effective coping skills, such as stress management, that can increase self-efficacy and decrease the probability of relapse.

Gerontological Counseling

Medical advances and a drop in birth rates have resulted in a dramatic increase in the proportion of seniors throughout the world (Yen, 2009). Evidence of this global shift in demographics includes the following (Yen):

- Seniors currently comprise 8% of the 6.8 billion people in the world.

- Germany, Italy, Japan, and Monaco have the highest percentage of seniors (20% of their general populations).

- Since 2000, the percentage of seniors has increased by 23% to 516 million people (twice the growth rate of the general population).

- By 2050, 1 in 6 people in the world will be 65 or older (triple what they are now).

Baby boomers (individuals born between 1946 and 1964) account for the new wave of seniors in the United States (Maples & Abney, 2006). In 2006, 76 million US baby boomers were beginning to reach age 60 (approximately 40% of the adult population). Maples and Abney suggested these individulals would soon be in need of **gerontological counseling** services, from preretirement to end-of-life counseling.

Gerontological counseling represents an emerging specialty within the counseling profession. This section will address gerontological counseling from the perspective of successful aging, developmental issues, and counseling strategies.

Successful Aging

Sixty-five can be considered the chronological age when old age begins, and old age can be thought of as having three periods—young-old (65–74), old-old (75–84), and oldest-old (over 84)—each marked by distinct changes that occur throughout the aging process (Hooyman & Kiyak, 2005).

A major aim of gerontological counseling is to promote successful aging in older adults, including making successful transitions, overcoming stereotypes associated with ageism, encouraging personal strengths, and promoting lifestyle factors associated with longevity. Ponzo (1992) defined successful aging as "staying vital longer by reaching for and emphasizing the positive aspects of life, of seeing what is possible, instead of what is typical or expected" (p. 210).

Successful aging can involve adjusting to life transitions (such as from work to retirement), which can be thought of as turning points that occur between periods of stability within one's life (Goodman, Schlossberb, & Anderson, 2006). Transitions often require a person to journey into the unknown, take risks, adapt, and cope with fears. They can therefore be challenging times in one's life, often experienced as a crisis. Transitions can also create opportunities for personal discovery, renewal, and transcendence to heightened levels of existence.

Another challenge associated with successful aging can be the ageism associated with sexuality and definitions of beauty. Ageism comprises stereotypes regarding old age that contribute to negative attitudes (prejudice) and actions (discrimination; Hooyman & Kiyak, 2005). For example, sexual expression in older people can be met with prejudice (e.g., older people are asexual beings) and discrimination (e.g., restrictions regarding privacy in residential facilities). Women can face special challenges from ageism, especially as they transition into midlife and old age. It is not uncommon for women to struggle with self-esteem, anxiety, and depression associated with body image issues that result from unrealistic/unhealthy media messages (Saucier, 2004). Gerontological counselors can use feminist therapy, social justice/advocacy strategies, and other approaches to help older adults address issues associated with ageism.

Functional aging recognizes that definitions of aging vary according to the individual and the culture (Hooyman & Kiyak, 2005). Gerontological researchers like Hooyman and Kiyak and Maples and Abney (2006) have identified a number of personal strengths associated with successful aging, which have been incorporated into the following:

- Maintaining a positive attitude, or optimism, to promote a self-fulfilling prophecy of success

- Self-empowerment and self-efficacy to help seniors recognize the control they have over the aging process (e.g., engaging in healthy lifestyle habits)

- Creativity and wisdom to successfully navigate life's transitions

- Resiliency and self-esteem to provide strengths for overcoming adversity such as negativism associated with ageism

Buettner (2008) has researched "blue zones" associated with longevity (geographic regions where people live to 100 years or more), among them Loma Linda, California; Nicoya Peninsula, Costa Rica; Sardinia, Italy; and Okinawa, Japan. Through in-depth interviews with centenarians from these regions, Buettner and his colleagues identified nine key factors associated with longevity and successful aging (Blue Zones, 2015):

- Move naturally, as part of your daily routine.

- Have a sense of purpose in life.

- Avoid stress and find ways to relieve it.

- Avoid overeating (stop when 80% full).

- Eat a diet rich in vegetables and light on meat.

- Drink alcohol in moderation.

- Utilize a spiritual/belief system.

- Make family life a priority.

- Maintain a social network that supports a healthy lifestyle.

Developmental Issues

Gerontological counseling requires an understanding of human growth and development from the womb to the tomb. This section is a brief overview of some of the issues associated with physical, cognitive, and social and personality development of late adulthood.

PHYSICAL DEVELOPMENT By early adulthood, most physical growth and maturation has occurred (Feldman, 2008). Senescence (the natural decline of all physical functions) follows this period of growth and plays a major role in the aging process. Physical ailments, restrictions in mobility, and problems with vision and hearing can be early signs of senescence. Older adults can also have increased risk of disease, such as cancer, due to reduced functioning of the immune system. And they can suffer from other chronic conditions, like arthritis and osteoporosis (thinning of bones); the latter affects approximately 25% of women over 60 (Feldman).

Fortunately, the process of senescence can be offset by healthy lifestyle habits like regular exercise, good diet, and refraining from smoking. Regular exercise is especially important for older adults because it can enhance physical, cognitive, and social emotional functioning. Fitness programs that address the special needs of older adults can include weight lifting for bone and muscle strength, aerobics (running, walking, or swimming) for cardiovascular conditioning, tai chi for balance, and yoga for flexibility of movement.

COGNITIVE DEVELOPMENT Cognition is associated with intelligence, memory, and learning. Hooyman and Kiyak's (2005) overview of cognition in older adults states that in most instances, intellectual functioning remains relatively consistent throughout old age. This is especially true for crystallized intelligence (verbal tasks), with some decline experienced in terms of fluid intelligence (performance tasks). Problems with performance tasks may be related to noncognitive functions associated with perceptual, motor, and sensory skills, which tend to decline in old age. Cognition can be dramatically undermined by dementia associated with Alzheimer's disease and other medical conditions. Gerontological counselors can provide support to individuals stricken by these disorders and to their families.

Learning and memory are interrelated. Although difficulty with memory can be a common problem with older adults (e.g., trying to remember the name of something), intellectual stimulation and memory aids can enhance recall and promote learning. Learning is a lifelong endeavor. Healthy lifestyle habits, including regular exercise, can play an important role in promoting learning throughout the life span.

Wisdom can be defined as "expert knowledge in the practical aspects of life" (Feldman, 2008, p. 610). Wisdom is believed to be associated with contemplation, knowledge, and reflection on life experiences. Although research regarding wisdom is a relatively new science, several preliminary findings are beginning to emerge (Feldman). Older adults appear to be "wise thinkers" in terms of having superior skills in problem solving and analyzing complex situations from a number of perspectives. Older adults also appear to have more sophisticated skills in terms of "theory of mind"—being able to make accurate inferences about the mental states of others—because they are able to draw on past experiences in understanding the subtle nuances of human behavior.

SOCIAL AND PERSONALITY DEVELOPMENT Psychosocial factors are relatively stable through adulthood (Feldman, 2008), including a number of personal qualities that impact daily functioning, such as self-concept, self-confidence, affection, openness, agreeableness, conscientiousness, extroversion, and neuroticism. Well-being and happiness also tend to be relatively stable throughout the life span. Happiness is to a large degree associated with how well people are able to meet their basic needs—love, belonging, and self-esteem. External rewards like money and possessions do not appear to play a significant role in a person's happiness (Feldman).

Erikson (1963) suggested that the final stage of psychosocial developmental is ego integrity (having a sense of wholeness and completeness with life) versus despair. Older adults who are unable to derive meaning from life can feel regret and become prone to depression and suicide. The American Psychological Association (2014) noted that life review and reminiscence therapy can be used to help older adults integrate life experiences. Depression is the most common mental disorder in older adults (Hooyman & Kiyak, 2005). It can be associated with the following risk factors: female, unmarried, financial problems, multiple medical conditions, lack of social support, and family history of depression (Hooyman & Kikak). Men can also be at risk for depression and suicide, especially when cut off from their emotional support system (as in divorce or death of a spouse). Gerontological counselors can address mental disorders like depression in older adults through cognitive-behavioral counseling, life review and reminiscence therapy, managing medication issues, and monitoring for possible suicide (APA; Meyers, 2014a).

Briggs, Magnus, Lassiter, Patterson, and Smith (2011) noted that alcohol and drug abuse among adults 50 and over will triple by 2020 and that mental health practitioners need to be aware of the special needs of older adults regarding substance abuse assessment and treatment. These authors reported that substance abuse problems are often not recognized in older adults, because older adults tend to deny these problems due to feelings of shame and failure and concerns of loss of independence. Briggs et al. suggested that older adults with substance abuse problems require a multifaceted approach that is empathic and caring and not confrontational, addresses the special needs of older adults, and includes family support. In addition, they noted that older adults with substance abuse problems tend to repond positively to self-help groups and brief group counseling that includes cognitive behavioral strategies (e.g., motivational interviewing and brief advice).

Counseling Strategies

Gerontological counseling has come of age; it represents an important emerging counseling specialty (Maples & Abney, 2006; Meyers, 2014a). Meyers suggested that gerontological counselors address special issues of aging, such as dealing with loss and concerns regarding autonomy and independence. Chatters and Zalaquett (2013) recommended that gerontological counseling be comprehensive and strength based, emphasizing the positive aspects of aging and assisting clients to make life changes to promote successful aging. In addition, the APA (2014) identified the following positive aspects of aging on social/emotional development that may be addressed in counseling:

- Use of wisdom and life experiences to cope with challenges such as dealing with loss

- Enhanced plasticity of personality (ability to adapt and adjust to life circumstances)

- Making the most of their remaining years by developing emotionally meaningful goals and positive social networks necessary to achieve these goals

Although psychotherapy can be very effective with older adults, they often find it difficult to seek out mental health services because of misconceptions about counseling and psychotherapy (Hooyman & Kiyak, 2005). The APA (2014) and Meyers (2014a) suggested that generontological counselors incorporate a narrative perspective (e.g., life review and reminiscence therapy) to overcome the negative stigma many older adults have about mental health services and promote cultural sensitivity (e.g., exploring cultural belief systems and indigenous healing practices). Many other existing counseling theories, such as existential therapy, can also be adapted to gerontological counseling. The following *Personal Note* is an example of gerontological counseling.

A Personal Note

A mental health counseling student ("Tonya"), working as an intern in a hospital setting for her master's degree, was asked to provide counseling to a women in her 70s, "Maria," who was in the hospital for a medical condition. Maria's doctor had become concerned about possible depression and referred her to Tonya, who was in her early 20s. Maria said there was no way she was going to talk with a young girl. What could Tonya possibly know about her life or life in general?

Instead of arguing with Maria, Tonya simply "went with the resistance" and did not try to talk Maria into "counseling." She suggested instead that they "just talk." Before they knew it, Maria was telling Tonya about her three children (now grown up with families of their own); her deceased husband, whom she missed very much; and general uncertainty about life.

Tonya said her hour visiting with Maria was over before she knew it. The next week when Tonya returned to see Maria, the nursing staff said Maria had been driving them crazy asking when Tonya was coming back to see her. As the "just talking" evolved into counseling, Tonya was able to help Maria gain insight into her life. Although Maria said she wished she had said and done some things differently, overall she felt happy with her life. During supervision, Tonya commented on how the movement of therapy overlapped with Erikson's final stage of psychosocial development (ego integrity versus despair) and how existential therapy could help clients derive meaning from their lives.

LEGAL/ETHICAL ISSUES AND CLINICAL CHALLENGES Legal/ethical issues and clinical challenges should be considered when providing counseling and psychological services to clients with end-of-life (EOL) issues. The recently revised American Counseling Association's (ACA, 2014) code of ethics addresses EOL issues associated with confidentiality as follows. Counselors who become aware of clients wanting to hasten their deaths have the option of maintaining confidentiality depending on applicable laws and the circumstances of the situation. In these instances, the counselor should consult with professionals, including legal experts, to determine appropriate action regarding confidentiality.

The ACA (2014) code of ethics also provides information on a number of other topics that can impact clients with EOL issues, including client welfare and professional competency:

- *Client welfare.* The primary responsibility of counselors is to promote the dignity and welfare of the client.

- *Professional competency.* Counselors should practice only within the realm of their competence or obtain additional education, training, and supervision necessary to perform these tasks. Counselors who do not have or are unable to obtain the competencies necessary to assist clients should work with clients to obtain appropriate referral sources.

Werth and Crow (2009) identified particular clinical challenges associated with counseling EOL clients. They noted that correct diagnosis and treatment of mental disorders is an important aspect of EOL care. For example, grief is a common emotional response to death and dying. When necessary, counselors can assist dying individuals and their loved ones with the grieving process. Addressing spiritual/religious issues can be an important part of this process. Counselors can engage in other interventions associated with EOL care, such as facilitating meaningful communication between the dying person and family members.

Guidelines for Gerontological Counseling

Older adults face a number of challenges associated with successful aging. The overall aim of gerontological counseling is to promote successful aging in terms of adjusting to transitions; overcoming stereotypes associated with ageism; fostering personal strengths; encouraging lifestyle factors associated with longevity; promoting optimal physical, cognitive, social, and personality development; and coping successfully with EOL issues.

The following guidelines for gerontolological counseling incorporated information from APA (2014) and Meyers (2014a):

1. Obtain accurate knowledge about adult development and aging, including an awareness of positive aspects of aging such as the enhanced plasticity of personality (the ability to adapt and adjust to life circumstances).

2. Utilize culturally sensitive interventions, such as life review and reminiscence therapy, to overcome negative stigmas of mental health services, integrate life experiences, explore cultural beliefs systems, and identify indigenous healing practices.

3. Establish counseling goals and strategies to address the special needs of older adults, such as using creative arts in individual and group counseling to awaken social interest and overcome isolation and loneliness.

4. Utilize social justice/advocacy strategies with older adults to combat negative societal forces like ageism, prejudice, and discrimination.

5. Utilize cognitive-behavioral therapy and other approaches to promote personal strengths associated with successful aging (e.g., self-empowerment, positive attitude and optimism, and resiliency).

6. Promote lifestyle factors associated with longevity, including exercise, proper diet, meaning in life, social-family relationships, and reduced levels of stress.

7. Be cognizant of the role that spirituality and religion can play in the lives of seniors, especially when faced with EOL issues.

8. Promote preventative strategies, such as screening for possible medical and mental health issues (e.g., depression and dementia), that may require further evaluation and treatment.

9. Be aware of ethical codes and legal issues that may impact counseling of older adults (e.g., EOL care and elder abuse and neglect).

10. Be enriched by the wisdom of older adults. They have much to teach us about life.

Trends and Perspectives

Several trends have affected all aspects of the counseling profession, including mental health counseling. This section reviews mental health counseling trends and perspectives relating to postmodernism, the Internet, ecosystemic issues, diversity issues, and issues relating to managed care.

Postmodernism

Postmodernism is a force that is reshaping the manner in which mental health counseling is conceptualized and practiced (see the special 1994 issue of *Journal of Mental Health Counseling, 16*(1), on constructivist and ecosystemic views; D'Andrea, 2000; Gutterman, 1996). Postmodernism can be understood by contrasting its key concepts with those of modernism. Modernists view the "self" as autonomous and independent. It therefore follows from a modernist perspective that problems like depression are caused by internal struggles (e.g., intrapsychic conflicts). The modernist view of the world is objective, and it has a fixed understanding of knowledge and reality. Modernist research methodology tends to be quantitative, focusing on testing observable, measurable hypotheses. The assessment of clients' problems is based on cause-and-effect relationships with a focus on content over process (e.g., irrational and dysfunctional thinking causes depression and must therefore be analyzed in terms of its content). Goal setting and interventions are generated by mutual agreement between the counselor and client and are reflected in the major modernist counseling theories and approaches.

Postmodern thought takes a broader view of the self to include interpersonal, systemic, and sociocultural forces. Psychological problems, knowledge, and reality are viewed subjectively from a phenomenological perspective and are understood within the context in which they are presented (the sociocultural milieu). Assessment of clients' problems emphasizes process over content, with a focus on relational/contextual perspectives. Goal setting and intervention strategies often involve exploring clients' narratives and stories and working together to co-construct new stories that generate personal meaning. Postmodernist research and evaluation methods tend to be qualitative, whereby the counselor and client function as co-investigators interested in discovering patterns of meaning that can generate insight and understanding. Table 15.1 summarizes the major concepts that differentiate modern from postmodern perspectives. The following *Personal Note* is an example of how I engaged in a postmodern approach to counseling.

A Personal Note

I was a psychologist providing in-patient care in a hospital. My client was a 25-year-old Navajo woman, Martha, whose mother had died 2 months earlier. She was admitted to the hospital by an emergency room doctor who had diagnosed major depression with psychotic features. The ER doctor used traditional diagnostic procedures that are by their nature grounded in modernism (e.g., a fixed-objective view of reality). The doctor gave Martha the diagnosis "with psychotic features" because she had concluded that Martha was hearing voices and had lost contact with reality (she was conversing with her deceased mother). The ER doctor agreed to hold off on prescribing antipsychotic medication for Martha's voices until I could do a psychological consult.

At the time I saw Martha, I had been working on the Navajo reservation for 2 years as a psychologist with the Indian Health Service. By this time, I had become sensitized to some of the unique aspects of the Navajo culture, such as the role of medicine men in promoting mental health and healing. I was also aware of how attitudes, customs, and values shaped my clients' views of reality. I was, therefore, very open to Martha's story when she shared that she regularly conversed with her deceased mother. She asked me if I believed her when she said she often talked with her mother. I responded that it did not matter what *I* believed; it only mattered what made sense *to her.*

I worked with Martha, assisting her with her depression and grief, over a period of 2 weeks. With the support of her family, Martha was able to move on and let go of her sadness. In time, her story became one of hope and optimism versus one of sadness, despair, and loss. I believe that my relationship with her and the resulting therapeutic alliance was fostered by my openness to her experience. Clinical experiences such as this have made me aware of the importance of maintaining a postmodern phenomenological perspective in counseling.

Table 15.1   Comparison of Modern and Postmodern Views

	Modern Views	Postmodern Views
View of the self	Autonomous, independent self	Relational/contextual self
View of knowledge and reality	Fixed-objective concept of knowledge and reality	Phenomenological perspective; subjective/relative concept of knowledge and reality
Assessment of client's problems	Etiology of problems is intrapsychic, with a focus on cause-effect and content (e.g., how cognitions affect emotions).	Etiology of problems emphasizes process over content and is focused on relational/contextual perspectives.
Goal setting and interventions	Goals are mutually agreed on between counselor and client, as reflected in the major counseling theories.	Goals and interventions evolve from exploring client's narratives resulting in co-construction of new stories that generate personal meaning.
Research strategies	Quantitative research methodology	Qualitative research methodology

Mental Health Counseling, the Internet, and Technology-Assisted Counseling

The use of the Internet and other forms of technology-assisted counseling appear to be increasing (Sude, 2013).

Gutterman and Kirk (1999) identified Internet tools and resources that can be helpful to mental health counselors:

- *Email* can be used in a variety of ways, including for communication among practitioners and provision of mental health counseling services. Internet counseling has advantages and disadvantages. Advantages include easy access (e.g., clients can log on whenever they have time and are not restricted in terms of travel); disadvantages include difficulty in reviewing a counselor's credentials, the limited opportunity to develop a personal relationship between counselor and client, and reduced control over confidentiality. The National Board for Certified Counselors (NBCC) Standards for the Ethical Practice of Web Counseling (1997) was created to address potential ethical-legal issues relating to Internet counseling.

- *Chat rooms* are especially popular as a self-help group format to provide opportunities for two or more clients to share mental health information with each other in a manner that is not restricted by time or distance.

- *Websites* can disseminate information regarding mental health services. The American Counseling Association established its website in 1996 (http://www.counseling.org).

- *Search engines* can help clients and counselors locate information on the Internet. Mental Health Net (http://www.mentalhelp.net) had over 93,000 mental health listings as of 1999.

- *Web rings* have been created to facilitate interdisciplinary communication between laypeople and professionals.

- *Online communities* provide opportunities for individuals to visit sites that feature interactive services. Visitors are encouraged to visit often and get to know other users with common interests. There are a number of online communities developed for mental health professionals, such as Behavior Online: The Mental Health and Behavior Science Meeting Place (http://www.behavior.net).

- *Scholarly publications and professional newsletters* can be accessed through the Internet.

- *Education and training opportunities* are available on the Internet. Most professional organizations offer continuing education opportunities on the Internet, and many universities utilize the Internet for distance education programs, which in some instances include graduate coursework in mental health counseling.

The Internet is an active versus passive form of communication whereby all voices can be heard and can ultimately influence any field of endeavor, with the result that the knowledge base for various professions, including mental health counseling, is now more fluid and diversified. Mental health professionals are using the Internet to address all aspects of professional activity from theory to research to practice. Gutterman and Kirk (1999), for example, used the Internet to solicit feedback regarding the development of an article subsequently published in the *Journal of Mental Health Counseling*. The possibilities seem limitless regarding the impact of the Internet not only on shaping professions like mental health counseling but on influencing all other aspects of human existence.

Sude (2013) noted that there has been an increased use of cell phones and other mobile devices by mental health practitioners to create communication options with their clients. For example, text messaging (which can include videos and pictures) can been used to schedule appointments and provide other administrative services and to give clients support and assistance with interventions (Sude). Warren (2012) noted that mobile mind mapping provides clients with visual aids they can use to assess information as an adjunct to therapy. Warren suggested that mobile mind-mapping applications (such as SimpleMind and Thinking Space) have been used in rational-emotive behavior therapy (e.g., clients use apps to download a list of rational responses they can utilize when they experience an adverse event).

Although technology-assisted counseling can be useful for scheduling and other counseling-related tasks, there are ethical and clinical concerns regarding these emerging technologies. For example, Sude (2013) identified ethical and clinical concerns relating to text messaging such as confidentiality and problems with service delivery (e.g., difficulty establishing rapport outside of a face-to-face relationship and responding appropriately to crises). Professional organizations, such as the American Counseling Association and the Mental Health Counseling Association, have addressed ethical issues relating to technology-assisted counseling in their ethical codes. Clearly, mental health practitioners need appropriate training and competencies regarding the use of technology-assisted counseling.

Ecosystemic Mental Health Counseling

Sherrard and Amatea (1994) defined **ecosystemic mental health counseling** as an approach that "enlarges the field of inquiry and intervention from the individual to the couple, the family, and the larger sociocultural contexts that constitute the individual's environment" (p. 3). This approach appears to be an attempt to incorporate the major concepts of postmodernism into a new conceptualization of the role and function of the mental health counselor. Ecosystemic mental health counseling acknowledges the vital role that narrative psychology and counseling as storytelling play in the counseling process (Becvar & Becvar, 1994). The role of the mental health counselor is directed at exploring the linguistic and language systems of the client, resulting in a shift from managing lives to managing conversations (Daniels & White, 1994).

Postmodern thought offers an opportunity for effective integration of theoretical positions in mental health counseling. Fong and Lease (1994), for example, suggested that the ecosystemic perspective effectively translates systemic concepts (widely used in marriage and family counseling) into individual and group mental health counseling. Rigazio-DiGilio (1994) addressed the need to integrate theories of development into counseling theories and provided an in-depth description of how Piaget's theory of cognitive development can be integrated into ecosystemic mental health counseling. Gutterman (1996) noted that solution-focused counseling was derived from current trends in brief counseling and postmodernism/social constructionism and that solution-focused counseling provides a theoretical framework that can crystallize and bring into focus the unique professional identity of mental health counselors.

Postmodern trends such as ecosystemic mental health counseling are exciting new dimensions of mental health counseling. They appear to offer considerable promise for new paradigms in conceptualizing the counseling process. Postmodern trends can help create treatment programs that are more comprehensive and holistic in nature and that encourage awareness of and sensitivity to issues of diversity, such as sociocultural forces and gender. Future research activities will need to be directed at the efficacy of postmodern trends as they are integrated into the role and function of mental health counselors.

Diversity Issues

Mental health counseling is attempting to embrace all aspects of diversity—age, gender, culture, sexual orientation, socioeconomic status, race, ethnicity, and spirituality—so that counselors can sensitively and effectively provide mental health services to clients. Kohn-Wood and Hooper (2014) and Locke (1993) recommended that mental health counselors increase their efforts to respond to the immense challenges that diversity issues pose in the delivery of mental health services. Mental health counselors can address these challenges by promoting culturally sensitive competencies regarding assessment, diagnosis, and treatment and advocating for sociopolitical policy change relating to access, utilization of services, and service delivery (Kohn-Wood & Hooper). Kohn-Wood and Hooper also suggested that multidisciplinary teams (e.g., mental health specialists working directly with primary care practictioners) could be utilized to promote multicultural competency in health care settings.

The following personal note provides an example of mental health practitioners working collaboratively with primary care physicians and other health care workers.

A Personal Note

As a professor at New Mexico State University, I was the coordinator for the CACREP-accredited mental health counseling program and oversaw the master's degree practicum and internship programs. One of the most noteworthy clinical placements involved our master's and doctoral students working directly with primary care physicians who were residents in family medicine. Our students provided consulting (from a multicultural perspective) to the medical staff regarding possible mental health issues and psychological factors that could promote health and wellness. It was especially rewarding when the physicians reported that our students were perceived to be an intregal part of their treatment team.

This outstanding clinical placement was made possible by a training grant by Dr. Eve Adams, an associate professor in our department. I believe this innovative clinical placement worked because it was a mutually beneficial experience bringing together expertise in psychological and physical health. Collaboratively, these professionals were able to promote mental health and wellness from a holistic perspective.

The Patient-Centered Culturally Sensitive Health Care Model (PC-CSHC) was developed in an attempt to incorporate a culturally sensitive perspective into the treatment of low-income, racially diverse patients (Tucker et al., 2007). Training health care staff and patients in the PC-CSHC Model has a positive effect on the health care physical environment, enhances the behaviors and attitudes of health care staff and patients, and promotes positive health care outcomes in patients (Tucker et al.). Staff are encouraged to display attitudes and behaviors that are culturally sensitive (including modifying health care environments to make patients more comfortable), and patients are empowered to engage in healthy lifestyle behaviors.

The Multi-Level Model of Psychotherapy, Social Justice, and Human Rights (MLM) addresses mental health issues of immigrants from a multicultural/social justice perspective (Bemak & Chung, 2008a). The MLM appears to be an example of culturally sensitive interventions that may be adapted to other multicultural populations. Its five levels are as follows:

> *Level 1: Mental health education.* Psychoeducational interventions are used to help orient immigrant clients to counseling and mental health services.

> *Level 2: Individual, group, and family counseling.* Counselors are encouraged to adapt traditional counseling strategies to the unique needs of clients from a multicultural perspective.

> *Level 3: Cultural empowerment.* Social justice, advocacy, and other interventions are used to help immigrant clients achieve bicultural status (e.g., transition into the mainstream of society while maintaining cultural heritage as desired).

> *Level 4: Integrating of traditional and Western healing.* Counselors communicate a respect for traditional and Western forms of healing.

> *Level 5: Addressing social justice and human rights issues.* Counselors work with immigrant clients to ensure equal opportunity and access to community resources.

Cultural issues are critical in all phases of counseling. Substance abuse counseling, for example, illustrates the importance of cultural issues in mental health counseling. Acculturation, sources of stress, and beliefs and attitudes regarding substance use are important cultural factors that contribute to the development and treatment of substance abuse (Terrell, 1993). In terms of the stress experienced during the acculturation process and as a result of conflicting cultural values regarding substance use, acculturation can play a role in the development of substance abuse. An example can be seen in the stress experienced by Native Americans who move from a reservation to an urban area. Beliefs and attitudes regarding substance abuse can also play a role in treatment. For example, African Americans may resist investing themselves in substance abuse treatment that adheres to the medical model, contending that substance abuse is not a disease but a condition based on personal choice (Terrell).

Gender is another important diversity consideration in mental health counseling. Most treatment modalities for substance abuse counseling have been based on a male model of alcoholism (McDonough & Russell, 1994). Research is beginning to suggest that women alcoholics have special needs relating to relationship expectations, development issues, and societal stigma. For example, some Hispanic females feel a strong cultural sanction against alcohol use, which could make it difficult for them to admit to a problem and seek help from mental health services (Terrell, 1993). The relationship of gender and depression is another diversity issue. An international review of the literature on the prevalence of depression in males and females shows that women have higher rates of depression compared to men (2:1); women also suffer from more serious, profound depression at higher rates (the ratio of women to men with major depression is between 3:1 and 4:1), while rates of bipolar (manic/depressive) disorders appear to be similar for men and women (Culberston, 1997). Several factors could contribute to the different rates of major depression for women and men (Culberston). Women tend to seek out mental health services more than men, and there is some indication that men tend to "self-medicate" with alcohol and other drugs to deal with problems such as depression. Biological differences in men and women and sociopolitical forces, such as child care demands and less economic support, could also contribute to higher rates of depression in women than in men.

Clients with disabilities are an often neglected but important population that requires careful attention from mental health counselors (Helwig & Holicky, 1994). Clients with physical disabilities, such as spinal cord injuries, are prone to substance abuse problems (Helwig & Holicky). Although approximately half of these individuals have symptomatology associated with substance abuse, rehabilitation counseling tends to focus on helping the client adjust to the disability rather than on recognizing and treating the substance abuse. Helwig and Holicky suggested that substance abuse problems should be addressed first to facilitate clients' ability to deal with the challenges of their disability.

Spirituality (which may or not include religion) is now being addressed in the diversity literature (Bishop, 1995). Conceptualized as a developmental construct endemic to all people that is directed at addressing questions basic to one's existence (Ingersoll, 1995), spirituality has been supported in recent research for the positive role that it and religion can play in mental and physical health (Koenig, 1997; Richards & Bergin, 1997; Witmer & Sweeney, 1995). People turn to spiritual values as an important source of strength and support in times of great need (Miranti & Burke, 1995), a tendency that becomes stronger especially as people get older. A number of other factors make spirituality a particularly attractive dimension of the counseling process, including the following (Richards & Bergin):

- It fosters a secure sense of identity that promotes resiliency and helps alleviate stress and anxiety.

- It provides a sense of purpose and meaning to all phases of life, including death.

- It encourages positive feelings and thoughts like hope, healing, optimism, and forgiveness.

- It provides a support system through such activities as church involvement.

- It fosters processes like prayer and meditation that promote healing through activities such as communion with a "higher power."

- It encourages healthy lifestyles.

Managed Care

Managed care is here to stay, along with its advantages and limitations (Lawless, Ginter, & Kelly, 1999). Some of the advantages include the control of the costs of mental health services and establishment of standards of practice to ensure quality. Constraints are time limits for treatment of disorders, overuse of medication in treatment programs, and reduced access to inpatient treatment. **Managed care** is essentially an attempt by health organizations to control medical costs (Pipal, 1995). Its overall aim is to help clients achieve their premorbid levels of functioning and to obtain symptom relief; managed care has little interest in developmental or preventive enhancement (Pipal).

Mental health counselors and other health care professionals have had to become providers to managed-care organizations in order to access clients' insurance programs, which are still evolving under the health care reform movement. Two facets of managed care that have directly affected the delivery of mental health services are an emphasis on diagnosis and a preference for time-limited, solution-focused sessions. Mental health counselors (and other practitioners) therefore often feel under pressure to conform to managed care's expectations in order to remain approved providers. This can produce behaviors that are clearly ethical violations (Bachrach, 1995; Pipal, 1995), such as making improper diagnoses to gain authorization for services, not ensuring clients' confidentiality through communication with managed-care personnel, providing inadequate services owing to restriction on the number of sessions (usually fewer than six), and providing services beyond the scope of one's practice.

Some suggest that the advent of managed care requires changes in the counseling process and mental health delivery system (Wagner & Gartner, 1996). Therapists need to function as coaches or teachers and act as catalysts for change (Wagner & Gartner). In this mode, clients learn skills from a variety of individuals and practice what they learn in their everyday life experiences. The working-through phase of counseling therefore occurs outside of counseling. In addition, counseling becomes more of an open-ended process involving intermittent or episodic care (Wagner & Gartner). The therapist and client together work within the constraints of managed care to address the client's needs as efficiently as possible (e.g., the client may sign up for a certain number of sessions to treat a substance abuse problem and attempt to seek other assistance at a later date). One facet of counseling that does not seem to need to change is the nature of the therapeutic alliance: It is essential for counselors to maintain a positive counseling relationship as advocated by Carl Rogers and others (Wagner & Gartner).

Managed care poses many challenges to the mental health counselor and other health practitioners. In an era of increasing pressures for cost containment, it is becoming difficult to provide services that are consistent with the basic standards of practice and that are in the client's best interests. Former surgeon general C. Everett Koop voiced this concern when he noted that too much emphasis has been put on the economic/political pressures of health care with too little attention paid to the ethical imperatives for health care reform (Bachrach, 1995).

SUMMARY

Mental health counseling is both an amorphous job role performed by various members of the helping profession and an emerging profession for individuals who identify themselves as mental health counselors. Professional issues relating to mental health counselors include professional affiliation and certification requirements.

The role and function of mental health counselors are to provide direct and indirect counseling services to clients who have either problems of living or mental disorders. Mental health counselors can provide specialized services to a wide range of clients, including suicidal clients, clients with substance abuse problems, and gerontological clients.

PERSONAL EXPLORATION

1. What do you think are the major challenges and opportunities associated with mental health counseling, and would you consider entering this profession?

2. What do you believe are the key issues associated with substance abuse, and how should mental health counselors address these issues?

3. How can the concept of stages of change be useful in treating substance abuse and other mental health problems?

4. What is your opinion of rational (or physician-assisted) suicide?

5. How would you feel about working with older adults?

6. What do you think is the most important thing to do in a crisis?

7. How can mental health counselors engage in social advocacy?

8. What are the warning signs of suicide, and what would you do if you became aware of someone having these signs?

9. What are your views on providing mental health counseling via the Internet or using other forms of technology to provide mental health counseling?

10. What are some physical, cognitive, and social-emotional changes that occur with aging?

LEARNING ACTIVITIES

1. Apply some of the guidelines for gerontological counseling in your interactions with seniors.

2. How could you apply the factors associated with successful aging in your life?

WEBSITES

American Mental Health Counselors Association. (2010). *AMHCA code of ethics.* http://www.amhca.org/?page=codeofethics.

Counselor-License. (2015). *Mental health counselor.* http://www.counselor-license.com/careers/mental-health-counselor.html. *Provides information on what a mental health counselor does and credentialing of mental health counselors.*

ProCon.org. (2014). *State-by-state guide to physician-assisted suicide.* http://euthanasia.procon.org/view.resource.php?resourceID=000132. *Provides information on laws and court rulings in states that have assisted-suicide laws and on penalties for performing assisted suicide in those states that do not permit it.*

GLOSSARY

Acculturation (p. 204): The degree to which one adapts to the customs and values of the host culture.

Achievement tests (p. 113): Tests that provide information regarding what a person has learned.

Action research (p. 146): Action research is conducted collaboratively with participants (e.g., practitioners or clients) in a real-world setting with the aim of providing research that has a beneficial impact on the lives of participants in the study.

Adlerian family counseling (p. 346): Adlerian family counseling incorporates Adler's psychological constructs (e.g., social interest, the family constellation, and teleological movement) and Dreikurs's parent education principles (e.g., the four goals of misbehavior, encouragement, and natural and logical consequences).

Adolescence (p. 362): Adolescence can be considered a separate stage of development characterized by the onset of puberty and Erickson's developmental task of identity versus identity confusion (the ability to establish a clear sense of personal identity).

Advocacy (p. 516): Pleading the cause of another person and following through with action in support of that cause.

American Mental Health Counselors Association (AMNCA) (p. 508): The AMHCA is a professional organization that engages in numerous activities that have contributed to the mental health profession (e.g., with respect to professional identity, licensure, third-party insurance, and advocacy for individuals with mental health disorders).

American School Counseling Association (ASCA) (p. 463): The ASCA has played a key role in the current redefinition of school counseling through a number of initiatives (e.g., the National Model for school counseling) that have helped clarify the role of the school counselor and have provided a framework and set of components that could be used to standardize all school counseling programs.

Applied research (p. 146): Research that takes place in a field setting and is therefore reflective of people in their natural habitat.

Aptitude tests (p. 114): Tests that provide information on a person's potential for success.

Archetypes (p. 238): A Jungian concept that suggests there are separate systems within the personality (e.g., the shadow, which represents the dark side of the personality, and the anima and animus, which suggest people have both a feminine and masculine dimension to their personality).

Art of counseling (p. 3): The subjective dimension to counseling characterized by creative/flexible strategies that enable the counselor to enter into an authentic meaningful relationship with the client.

Art therapy (p. 266): Art therapy typically uses color analysis and spontaneous drawings.

Assessment (p. 107): Counselors use a wide range of techniques and processes to obtain an overall understanding of a client.

Attachment theory (p. 372): A study of the relationship between the parent-child emotional bond and the child's psychosocial development over the life span.

Basic research (p. 146): Research conducted under controlled conditions, often in a university setting with university students as participants in the study.

Behavior therapy (p. 280): Behavior therapy incorporates the principles from learning theories; is grounded in the scientific method; focuses on overt, observable behavior; and views psychopathology primarily in behavioral terms.

Bibliotherapy (p. 271): Books or another form of literature is read to promote particular counseling outcomes.

Brief-solution-focused counseling (p. 7): An approach to counseling based on strengths, solutions, and exceptions to the problem.

Brief-solution-focused group counseling (p. 424): The application of solution-focused counseling, which emphasizes strengths and exceptions to the problem, to specialty groups, such as in small-group debriefing for victims of violence or disaster.

Case studies (single-subject designs) (p. 149): Research that involves the intensive study of one individual or a group of individuals, which may incorporate principles of experimental design to evaluate outcomes objectively.

Certification (p. 39): Recognition of practitioners' professional competence authorizing the use of a title adapted by the profession (e.g., certified mental health counselor).

Classic psychological theories (of Freud, Adler, and Jung) (p. 212): The theories of Freud, Adler, and Jung are considered the classic theories because they all provide a well-developed theory of personality that can be used to understand the dynamics of behavior.

Client welfare (p. 44): Client welfare relates to what is in the best interest of the client.

Clinical interview (p. 130): The clinical interview provides a structure for assimilating information pertaining to assessment and diagnosis.

Cognitive-behavioral theories (p. 280): Cognitive-behavioral theories emphasize the role of cognition and/or behavior in psychological functioning and well-being.

Cognitive-dissonance theory (p. 440): Cognitive-dissonance theory suggests that career decision making can be influenced by conflicting cognitions (e.g., a person would like to be a teacher, but the job does not pay well) and that career counseling can address these conflicting cognitions.

Coleader (p. 421): Groups often have two leaders, one who focuses on group goals and another who

facilitates achievement of individual goals of group members.

Collective unconscious (p. 237): One of the most controversial concepts of Jung's theory, the collective unconscious suggests that people are born with memory traces inherited from their ancestral past.

Common factors (p. 171): The common-factor approach attempts to identify counseling strategies shared by different schools of psychotherapy that are curative and associated with positive therapeutic outcomes (e.g., a positive therapeutic relationship is believed to be especially important).

Computer-assisted career counseling (p. 453): The use of computers to directly or indirectly assist individuals with issues associated with career counseling (e.g., career assessment, career decision making, and educational planning).

Confidentiality (p. 45): Confidentiality is a process whereby the counselor does not disclose client information unless it is absolutely necessary (e.g., to address client issues relating to harm to self or others).

Conflict resolution (p. 384): Counseling strategies, which can be preventative or remedial, that can be used to teach youth how to resolve interpersonal conflict.

Congruence (p. 70): Behaving in a manner that is consistent with how one feels.

Conscious–unconscious continuum (p. 216): The continuum between conscious and unconscious processes that includes the unconscious proper (memory traces that a person is not aware of), preconscious (material a person is almost aware of), and conscious (material that a person is aware of).

Core conditions (p. 68): Counselor-offered conditions (e.g., empathy, congruence, and unconditional positive regard) that are believed to facilitate positive outcomes in counseling.

Correlational studies (p. 147): Research strategies that can be used to determine whether two factors are related (e.g., examining the relationship between exercise and mental health).

Counseling (p. 2): Use of therapeutic strategies (which primarily relate to conscious processes) to help clients address personal concerns and mental health issues; promote coping mechanisms, optimal development, health, and wellness; and prevent future problems or concerns.

Counseling and neuroscience (p. 33): The science of counseling and neuroscience explores the neurobiological basis of behavior and how professional counselors can expand their role to include a neuroscience perspective for the diagnosis and treatment of mental disorders.

Creative arts therapy (CAT) (p. 260): Creative arts therapy promotes psychological and physiological wellness through the use of creative modalities such as art, music, dance, or drama. CAT procedures vary according to the theoretical orientation of the practitioner.

Creative self (p. 225): At the heart of Adler's theory of personality, the creative self is the nucleus from which all movement occurs.

Crisis (p. 511): A crisis can be understood as an event that is perceived as overwhelming and that exceeds a person's ability to cope effectively.

Crisis intervention (p. 511): Taking the action necessary to prevent harm to self or others.

Cybercounseling (p. 29): Counseling via the Internet (e.g., client submits up to 200 words to counselor and counselor responds within 3 days).

Dance therapy (p. 269): Dance therapy involves spontaneous or structured dance experiences to improve motor skills and interpersonal relationships; facilitate expression of moods, attitudes, and ideas; and stimulate, energize, and relax the body.

Defense mechanisms (p. 215): Defense mechanisms (such as projection and reaction formation) are unconscious processes that occur when the ego feels threatened by an endopsychic conflict.

Developmental counseling (p. 464): Developmental counseling was developed by Blocher, who suggested that clients must master coping skills associated with developmental tasks so they can move forward in their development.

Developmental psychopathology (p. 367): The study of how mental disorders can evolve over the life span (e.g., children diagnosed with a conduct disorder in childhood may be diagnosed with an antisocial personality disorder during adolescence or adulthood).

Developmental school counseling (p. 462): Developmental school counseling is a preventative approach that promotes the knowledge, skills, self-awareness, and attitudes necessary to promote learning and mastery of developmental tasks.

Diagnosis (p. 120): The clinical process of determining whether a person meets the criteria for a recognized mental disorder as defined in diagnostic manuals such as the *DSM-5*.

Disruptive group members (p. 425): Group members who engage in behaviors that undermine group process and the ability for group members to address their issues. For example, the storyteller is someone who likes to monopolize the group by telling drawn-out stories that have little relevance to the "here and now" focus of the group.

Diversity issues (p. 168): Variables such as age, gender, culture, ethnicity, socioeconomic status, spirituality, and sexual orientation that are addressed within the context of multicultural counseling.

Drama therapy (p. 268): Drama therapy is based on spontaneous role-play and includes a variety of procedures such as movement, mime, and use of puppets.

DSM-5 (p. 123): A classification systems for all recognized mental disorders, published by the American Psychiatric Association in 2013.

Dual relationships (p. 47): Dual relationships are multiple relationships between the counselor and client that may undermine the counselor's ability to promote client welfare.

Ecosytemic mental health counseling (p. 550): Ecosystemic mental health counseling recognizes the importance of considering environmental factors that extend beyond the individual (e.g., couples, families, and the larger sociocultural context) throughout all phases of the counseling process.

Ego-analytic position (p. 222): Ego-analytic theory, based on ego psychology and object-relations theory, emphasizing the role of the ego, self, and objects (e.g., people) as primary organizing forces in personality functioning.

Emotional intelligence (p. 374): A study of the role that social emotions play in psychological functioning (e.g., the ability to accurately perceive emotions and respond to them appropriately).

Empathy (p. 69): The counselor communicates care and understanding to a client in a manner that fosters emotional support and encourages the client's self-exploration.

Endopsychic conflicts (p. 215): A conflict within the psyche that results from the interaction of the three parts of the personality (the id, ego, and superego), with each part of personality trying to dominate personality functioning.

Ethical-legal decision making (p. 43): Ethical-legal decision making relates to consideration of ethical-legal issues when deciding a course of action regarding clinical practice (e.g., determining what is in the best interest of clients) and when facing challenging clinical issues (e.g., how to address client issues of harm to self or others).

Evidenced-based treatment (p. 25): Empirically supported interventions for specific diagnostic conditions.

Exceptional students (p. 479): Exceptional students are individuals who have a cognitive, social-emotional, physical, or other condition that deviates from the norm in a manner that special services are required to meet the individual's needs.

Existential therapy (p. 256): Existential therapy involves exploring issues that relate to human existence (e.g., uniqueness of the individual, meaning in life, freedom and responsibility, and being and nonbeing).

Experiential family counseling (p. 345): Experiential family counseling incorporates humanistic and existential schools of counseling and contends that if family members can be freed to move toward self-actualization, the family will function effectively.

Experiential theories (p. 247): Experiential theories focus on what the client is experiencing during the counseling process.

Experimental methods (quantitative research) (p. 148): Research that evaluates a particular treatment under controlled conditions to determine whether a cause and effect relationship exists.

Factors that predict divorce (341): Factors identified by research that appear to be associated with divorce, including criticism, contempt, defensiveness, and emotional withdrawal during conflict.

Family constellation (p. 336): Factors associated with a person's family of origin (e.g., birth order and relationship between family members) that Adler believed play an important role in the development of the lifestyle.

Family life cycle (p. 360): The family life cycle is a model for understanding how a family proceeds through time and can be used in counseling to identify developmental tasks that can be addressed by a counselor.

Feminist therapy (p. 311): Feminist therapy promotes equality between the sexes and seeks to overcome oppressive forces, such as marginalization of women, that can undermine self-actualizing tendencies.

Functional family system (p. 330): The functional family system is characterized by a number of characteristics such as sharing feelings, social interest, adaptability, boundary clarity, acceptance of individual differences, cooperation, nonadversarial problem solving, a sense of humor, and coping skills.

Gerontological counseling (p. 539): Gerontological counseling involves promoting successful aging in older adults, including making successful transitions, overcoming stereotypes associated with ageism, encouraging personal strengths, and promoting lifestyle factors associated with longevity.

Gestalt therapy (p. 253): Gestalt therapy can be used to help clients move from dependence to independence and toward being aware and centered in the present.

Gottfredson's theory (p. 451): A vocational theory (which has special relevance to career counseling with women) that explains how compromise takes place in vocational decision making, identifies factors associated with social identity, and explores the difficulties that women face entering nontraditional careers.

Group goals and individual goals (p. 416): Groups have group goals (e.g., create a safe environment for group members) and individual goals (e.g., group members work on personal issues).

Guidance/psychoeducational groups (p. 417): Groups that provide information and learning opportunities associated with topics such as parent education and strategies that promote wellness.

Holland's theory (p. 437): Holland's theory suggests that career choice is an attempt to obtain a satisfactory fit between the person and the environment.

Identity development (p. 202): Identity development involves clarifying, integrating, and enhancing one's sense of self.

Impaired counselor (p. 32): Counselor experiences personal issues (which may include symptoms of burnout) that undermine the counselor's ability to function appropriately in the clinical or work setting.

Informed consent (p. 44): Informed consent involves the counselor providing clients with information before they start counseling (e.g., discussing what counseling is and the limits to confidentiality) and determining whether a client wants to engage in counseling (consents).

Interpersonal perspective (p. 221): The interpersonal perspective recognizes the effect of early life experiences (e.g., degree of attachment between parent and child) on the quality of interpersonal relationships later in life.

Large-scale review (meta-analysis) (p. 148): Research that reviews many published studies by using sophisticated statistical analysis to overcome methodological problems that can occur when numerous studies are grouped together for analysis.

LGBTQ (p. 185): LGBTQ is an acronym that is used to refer to individuals who may be lesbian, gay, bisexual, or transgender or may be questioning their sexual orientation.

Licensure (p. 39): Authorizes an individual to use a title adopted by the profession to practice independently. Licensure is regulated by states and usually requires a higher level of education and training than certification.

Lifestyle (p. 227): A central concept within Adler's theory that refers to a person's basic orientation to life.

Longitudinal studies (p. 148): Research that evaluates a particular group of subjects over an extended period of time (e.g., determining the effects of attending a Head Start program on K–12 dropout rates).

Managed care (p. 554): Managed care is an attempt by health providers to control medical costs (including of mental health care) with a primary aim of helping clients achieve their premorbid levels of functioning and obtain symptom relief.

Marital assessment (p. 339): Marital assessment involves assessing the situation, the system, each spouse, and the suitability of the couple for marriage counseling.

Mental disorder (p. 123): Psychological disturbance identified in diagnostic manuals such as the *DSM-5* resulting in distress that undermines functioning in social, occupational, or other activities.

Mental health consultation (p. 517): An interaction between the consultant (someone with expertise pertaining to a particular problem) and the consultee (a professional or layperson) who has asked for assistance to address a particular difficulty or area of concern.

Mindfulness (p. 319): Mindfulness incorporates principles from Eastern philosophies and meditation and can be described as an awareness that results from being focused in the present moment and reacting nonjudgmentally to experiences as they occur moment by moment.

Multicultural competency (p. 197): Counselor's attitudes and beliefs, knowledge, and skills associated with awareness of values and biases, worldview of clients, and multiculturally sensitive interventions.

Multicultural counseling (p. 181): Two or more individuals with different perspectives on their social environment are engaged in a helping relationship.

Multimodality creative arts therapy (CAT) (p. 271): Multimodality CAT involves using the full range of CAT modalities to facilitate involvement in creative expression.

Multiple career decision-making theory (p. 443): Multiple career decision-making theory contends that all career decision-making theories can be described in terms of three major models (expected utility, sequential elimination, and conjunctive) that are prescriptive in nature, using logic and rational approaches to identify the best way to make career decisions.

Music therapy (p. 261): Music therapy consists of using a musical experience to enhance and facilitate counseling goals.

National Model for school counseling (p. 505): The National Model for school counseling, developed by the American School Counseling Association, clarifies the role of the school counselor and provides a framework for developing and implementing a comprehensive K–12 school counseling program.

Neuropsychological tests (p. 115): Tests that evaluate the relationship among cerebral functioning, cognition, behavior, and psychological strengths and weaknesses.

Nonstandardized measures (p. 113): Assessment procedures that were not developed using a standardized norm group (e.g., observation and behavioral assessment) that can be used to generate subjective information and provide a flexible approach to assessment that can be easily modified to accommodate individual differences.

Optimal development (p. 369): A view of human development that focuses on positive, healthy development as opposed to a pathological view of development.

Personality tests (p. 114): Tests that provide information regarding personality dynamics.

Person-centered therapy (p. 250): Person-centered therapy is characterized by trust in the inherent self-actualizing tendencies of people and the role of the self and the client's internal frame of reference in personality dynamics.

Play therapy (p. 380): Play therapy involves the use of play media such as puppets, art, and music to foster growth and provide psychological healing.

Positive psychology (p. 26): Use of strengths and positive emotions such as happiness, hope, flow, and forgiveness to promote health and well-being.

Postmodernism (p. 7): A subjective view of knowledge and reality that recognizes the role that contextual factors (e.g., social, political, and culture) play in defining personal meaning in life.

Prejudice (p. 191): Prejudice involves thinking negatively about others without sufficient reason.

Prevention (p. 513): Using helping strategies to avoid or minimize potential problems.

Primary listening skills (p. 81): Listening skills such as open ended statements, reflection of feeling, paraphrasing, minimal encouragers, and summarizing can be used to obtain a phenomenological understanding of the client.

Privileged communication (p. 51): Privileged communication relates to state-mandated legal rights of clients to wave confidentiality in situations that qualify as "privileged" (e.g., doctor-patient relationship).

Problematic counselor (p. 32): Counselor exhibits behaviors that are unacceptable, such as inappropriate interpersonal behavior during academic training or clinical practice.

Problematic-impaired counseling students (p. 32): Inappropriate behavior or personal issues (such as emotional distress) that may undermine a student's ability to function appropriately in an academic or clinical setting.

Problems of living (p. 519): A difficulty or challenge experienced by a person as he or she progresses through the natural course of life.

Psychodynamic family counseling (p. 345): Psychodynamic family counseling recognizes the role of interpersonal and intrapersonal forces in family functioning (e.g., how intrapsychic conflicts within individual family members can contribute to family relationship difficulties).

Psychology of use (p. 226): An Adlerian construct that suggests all behavior has a purpose or use.

Psychosexual stages of development (p. 217): An aspect of Freudian theory that emphasizes the role of sexuality in personality development and stipulates a pregenital period (oral, anal, and phallic stages) and latency period.

Psychosocial development (p. 367): Erik Erikson's theory identified stages of psychosocial development across the life span (e.g., trust versus mistrust, birth to 1.5 years; identity versus role confusion, adolescence; and ego-integrity versus despair, late adulthood).

Psychotherapy (p. 3): Use of therapeutic strategies (associated with conscious and unconscious processes) to help clients overcome mental disorders or problems of living.

Qualitative methods (naturalistic approach) (p. 149): Research that attempts to understand people and events in their natural settings, often using nonstandardized measures such as interviews and observations.

Racial microaggressions (p. 193): A more subtle form of racism taking the form of brief, commonplace indignities such as negative racial slights or insults directed at the target person.

Racism (p. 192): Racism involves portraying a particular group as inferior to justify exploitation and other acts of injustice.

Rational suicide (p. 530): Also referred to as *hastened death* or *assisted suicide*, a rational choice to hasten the end of one's life (e.g., terminally ill individuals seeking assistance to end their life).

Rational-emotive behavior therapy (REBT) (p. 289): The basic premise of REBT is that emotional disturbance results from illogical or irrational thought processes.

Reaching in–reaching out model (p. 388): A counseling approach for children and adolescents that involves reaching into the client's world (the world that makes sense to and is of value to the child/adolescent) and then helping the child/adolescent learn skills necessary to reach out to the world of others (e.g., enhanced social interest and social skills).

Reality therapy (p. 306): The primary aim of reality therapy is to help clients develop a success identity through responsible action and use control theory to help clients meet their needs in a manner that does not interfere with the rights of others.

Reliability (p. 108): Reliability is a measure of the consistency of test scores on different occasions, with equivalent test items, or under variable test conditions.

Resiliency (p. 371): Characteristics that have been identified as buffering an individual from stress (e.g., positive self-concept, optimistic outlook, good interpersonal skills, good problem solving and decision-making skills, a well-developed sense of personal autonomy, and environmental support).

Roe's theory (p. 439): Roe's theory, which evolved from Maslowian and psychodynamic theories, contends that unmet needs in childhood can have a major influence on career choice in adulthood (e.g., selecting a career that will fulfill unmet needs).

Role flexibility (p. 413): Clients in group counseling can function both as helpers and helpees, whereas clients in individual counseling can only maintain the helpee role.

School consultation (p. 476): School consultation is a primary function of school counselors that involves assisting parents, teachers, or staff to achieve goals identified during the consultative process (e.g., developing disciplinary strategies to promote on-task behavior).

School violence (p. 488): School violence such as fighting, bullying, and fatal shootings is increasing, requiring comprehensive school-based violence prevention programs.

Science of counseling (p. 3): The objective dimension to counseling that recognizes the interrelationship among theory, research, and practice and the importance of utilizing objective-measureable strategies throughout the counseling process (e.g., use of psychological testing in assessment and evidenced-based practice to treat mental disorders).

Secondary listening skills (p. 81): Listening skills such as structuring, normalizing, and probing can be used to facilitate the counseling process (e.g., structuring clarifies the role of the counselor and client, normalizing helps clients realize that what they are experiencing is a normal reaction to life events, and probing can provide counselors with important information regarding safety issues and other clinical concerns).

Self-efficacy theory (p. 451): Based on Albert Bandura's theory of self-efficacy (the belief in one's ability to perform a particular behavior), self-efficacy theory has particular relevance to career counseling for women (e.g., by helping to promote a self-fulfilling prophesy of success).

Self-transcendence (p. 258): Self-transcendence involves moving beyond the subject-object relationship, resulting in an ontological at-oneness (e.g., a counselor directly experiencies a client's innermost feelings by directly encountering them via creative arts therapy).

Sexual orientation (p. 185): Sexual orientation refers to the complex set of behaviors, attitudes, and lifestyle factors associated with choosing a sexual partner.

Skills-based marriage counseling (p. 338): Skills-based marriage counseling is a psycho-educational approach that provides the couple with opportunities to learn skills that can promote a functional family system.

Social influence model (p. 72): When the counselor is perceived as expert, attractive, and trustworthy, clients will tend to be motivated to increase their involvement in the counseling process.

Social interest (p. 227): An Adlerian concept that suggests people are motivated to seek out involvement with others.

Social-cognitive career theory (SCCT) (p. 451): Based on Bandura's social-cognitive theory, SCCT addresses issues associated with career decision making (e.g., career interest, choice making, performance and persistence, satisfaction, well-being, and self-management).

Social-learning theory (p. 441): This theory by Albert Bandura contends that learning from observation, modeling, and imitation play a key role in occupational selection (e.g., a child grows up observing parents who are doctors and decides to become a doctor).

Stages in group counseling (p. 422):
Groups tend to progress through stages: the initial, transition, working, and final stage. These stages can be used to understand group process and group dynamics.

Standardized measures (p. 113): Assessment instruments that have been developed using a standardized norm group to provide objective information regarding a client.

Stereotyping (p. 187): A rigid preconception about all individuals associated with a particular group relating to race, gender, religion, or other aspects of diversity.

Strategic family counseling (p. 346): Strategic family counseling focuses on resolving the presenting problems directly, with little attempt to provide insight from past events.

Structural family counseling (p. 346): The goal of structural family counseling is to clarify boundaries between family members, increase flexibility of family interactions, and modify dysfunctional structures.

Substance abuse counseling (p. 531): A specialty directed at the prevention and treatment of problems associated with alcohol and other substances.

Super's theory (p. 435): Super's theory emphasizes the role of self-concept in career development and contends that how individuals define themselves has a major effect on their career choices.

Survey research (p. 147): Research that describes a variable in terms of its frequency in a population (e.g., which counseling approaches are used most often by counselors).

Systems theory (p. 329): Systems theory is based on the principle of circular causality (e.g., actions caused by one family member influence the actions of all other family members, affecting the functioning of the family system, including the person who was responsible for the initial action).

Teleological movement (p. 225): A construct from Adler's theory of personality that suggests all behavior involves movement and is purposeful and goal directed.

Test bias (p. 111): Factors such as cultural differences that can undermine the fairness of the test (e.g., a test that was normed on one culture is used with individuals from another culture).

Transactional analysis (TA) (p. 298): Transactional analysis is a psychoeducational approach in which clients learn how to understand and enhance the patterns of their communication with others and make positive decisions regarding their lives.

Transference (p. 219): Transference is a process in which the client projects thoughts or feelings onto the analyst that are associated with unresolved conflict from childhood.

Treatment planning (p. 132): A conceptual model that can be used to address treatment issues as necessary to help clients overcome dysfunctional states.

Unconditional positive regard (p. 70): Counselor's acceptance and regard for the client as an individual worthy of respect, while not necessarily accepting the client's behavior.

Universality (p. 413): Clients discover that other group members have similar concerns, fears, and problems, and this knowledge helps clients keep their problems in perspective.

Validity (p. 108): The degree that a test measures what it purports to measure (i.e., how well it fulfills its intended function).

Vicarious learning (p. 413): Group counseling offers opportunities for members to learn from observing other group members as they explore their concerns.

Worldview (p. 201): Assumptions and perceptions regarding the world that extend beyond the culture of a given ethnic group.

REFERENCES

Achenback, T. M., & Edelbrock, C. S. (1983). *Manual for the child behavior checklist and revised child behavior profile.* Burlington, VT: University of Vermont, Department of Psychiatry.

Ackerman, N. W. (1937). The family as a social and emotional unit. *Bulletin of the Kansas Mental Hygiene Society, 12*(2).

Ackerman, N. W. (1956). Interlocking pathology in family relationships. In S. Radó & G. Daniels (Eds.), *Changing conceptions of psychoanalytical medicine* (pp. 135–150). New York, NY: Grune & Stratton.

Ackerman, N. W. (1966). *Treating the troubled family.* New York, NY: Basic Books.

Ackerman, N. W. (1970). *Family therapy in transition.* Boston, MA: Little, Brown.

Adams, J. H. (1997). *Perspectives of the oldest-old concerning resilience across the life span.* Unpublished doctoral dissertation, New Mexico State University, Las Cruces, NM.

Addington, J. (1992). Separation groups. *Journal for Specialists in Group Work, 17,* 20–28.

Adler, A. (1930). *The education of children.* South Bend, IN: Gateway Editions.

Adler, A. (1964). *Social interest: A challenge to mankind.* New York, NY: Capricorn Books. (Original work published 1929.)

Adler, A. (1969). *The practice and theory of individual psychology.* Patterson, NJ: Littlefield, Adams.

Adler, K. (1972). Techniques that shorten psychotherapy. *Journal of Individual Psychology, 28,* 155–168.

Adler, R. B., Proctor, R. F., & Towne, N. (2005). *Looking out/looking in* (11th ed.). Belmont, CA: Thompson & Wadsworth.

Aiello, T. J. (1979). Short-term group therapy of the hospitalized psychotic. In P. Olsen & H. Grayson (Eds.), *Short-term approaches to psychotherapy* (pp. 101–123.). New York, NY: Human Sciences Press.

Ainsworth, M. D. S. (1989). Attachments beyond infancy. *American Psychologist, 44,* 709–716.

Ainsworth, M. D. S. (1991). Attachment and other affectional bonds across the life cycle. In C. M. Parkes, J. Stevenson-Hinde, & P. Marris (Eds.), *Attachment across the life cycle* (pp. 33–51). New York, NY: Tavistock/Routledge.

Ainsworth, M. D. S., Blehar, M. C., Waters, E., & Wall, S. (1978). *Patterns of attachment: A psychological study of the strange situation.* Hillsdale, NJ: Lawrence Erlbaum.

Ainsworth, M. D. S., & Bowlby, J. (1991). An ethological approach to personality development. *American Psychologist, 46,* 333–341.

Akos, P. (2000). Building empathic skills in elementary school children through group work. *Journal for Specialists in Group Work, 25,* 214–223.

Albee, G. W., & Ryan-Finn, K. D. (1993). An overview of primary prevention. *Journal of Counseling and Development, 72*(2), 115–123.

Alberto, P. A., & Troutman, A. D. (2006). *Applied behavior analysis for teachers* (7th ed.). Upper Saddle River, NJ: Pearson Education.

Al-Darmaki, F., & Kivlighan, D. M., Jr. (1993). Congruence in client-counselor expectations for relationship and the working alliance. *Journal of Counseling Psychology, 40*(4), 379–384.

Allen, J., & Allen, B. (1989). Stroking: Biological underpinnings and direct observations. *Transactional Analysis Journal, 19,* 26–31.

Allan, J., & Brown, K. (1993). Jungian play therapy in elementary school. *Elementary School Guidance and Counseling, 28*(1), 30–41.

Allen, K., El-Beshti, R., & Guin, A. (2014). An integrative Adlerian approach to creating a teen parenting program. *The Journal of Individual Psychology, 70,* 6–20.

Allen, S. F., & Stoltenberg, C. D. (1995). Psychological separation of older adolescents and young adults from their parents: An investigation of gender differences. *Journal of Counseling and Development, 73*(5), 542–546.

Allport, G. W. (1954). *The nature of prejudice.* Cambridge, MA: Addison-Wesley.

Allport, G. W., & Ross, J. M. (1967). Personal religious orientation and prejudice. *Journal of Personality and Social Psychology, 5,* 432–443.

Alper, J. (1986, May). Depression at an early age. *Science, 86,* 44–50.

Altmann, E. O., & Gotlib, I. H. (1988). The social behavior of depressed children: An observational study. *Journal of Abnormal Child Psychology, 16,* 29–44.

Alva, S. A. (1991). Academic invulnerability among Mexican-American students: The importance of protective resources and appraisals. *Hispanic Journal of Behavioral Sciences, 13*(1), 18–34.

American Association for Marriage and Family Therapy (AAMFT). (2015). *AAMFT code of ethical principles for marriage and family therapists.* Alexandria, VA: Author. Retrieved from http://www.aamft.org/imis15/Documents/Legal%20Ethics/AAMFT-code-of-ethics.pdf.

American Association of Suicidology. (1990). *Suicide postvention guidelines: Suggestions for dealing with the aftermath of suicide in the schools.* Denver, CO: Author.

American Counseling Association (ACA). (2014). *2014 ACA code of ethics.* Alexandria, VA: Author.

American Mental Health Counselors Association (AMHCA). (2010). *Code of Ethics.* (2010). *Code of ethics of the American Mental Health Counselors Association.* Alexandria, VA: Author.

American Psychiatric Association. (1980). *Diagnostic and statistical manual of mental disorders* (3rd ed.). Washington, DC: Author.

American Psychiatric Association. (1987). *Diagnostic and statistical manual of mental disorders* (3rd ed. rev.). Washington, DC: Author.

American Psychiatric Association. (1995). Practice guidelines for the treatment of patients with substance use disorders: Alcohol, cocaine, opioids. *American Journal of Psychiatry (Supplement), 152*(11), 3–59.

American Psychiatric Association. (2000). *Diagnostic and statistical manual of mental disorders fourth edition–text revision (DSM-IV-TR).* Washington, DC: Author.

American Psychiatric Association (2013). *Diagnostic statistical manual of mental disorders* (5th ed). Washington, DC: Author.

American Psychiatric Association. (1994). *Diagnostic and statistical manual of mental disorders* (4th ed.). Washington DC: Author.

American Psychological Association (APA). (1997, July). *Terminal illness and hastened death requests: The important role of the mental health professional* [Brochure]. Washington, DC: Author. (Reprinted as *Professional psychology: Research and practice, 28*, 544–547, by R. K. Farberman, 1997.)

American Psychological Association (APA). (2002). *Multicultural guidelines on education and training, research, practice and organizational development for psychologists.* Washington, DC: Author.

American Psychological Association (APA). (2010). *Ethical principles of psychologists and code of conduct.* Washington, DC: Author.

American Psychological Association. (2014). Guidelines for psychological practice with older adults. *American Psychologist, 60* (1), 34–65.

American School Counselor Association (ASCA). (1990). *American School Counselor Association role statement.* Alexandria, VA: Author.

American School Counselor Association (ASCA). (2003). *The ASCA National Model: A framework for school counseling programs.* Alexandria, VA: Author.

American School Counselor Association (ASCA). (2005). *American School Counselor Association National Model: A framework for school counseling programs* (2nd ed.). Alexandria, VA: Author.

American School Counselor Association (ASCA). (2010). *Ethical standards for school counselors.* Alexandria, VA: Author.

American School Counselor Association (ASCA). (2012). *The ASCA national model: A framework for school counseling programs* (3rd ed.). Alexandria, VA: Author.

Anastasi, A., & Urbina, S. (1997). *Psychological testing* (7th ed.). New York, NY: Macmillan.

Andersen, B., & Andersen, W. (1985). Client perceptions of counselors using positive and negative self-involving statements. *Journal of Counseling Psychology, 32,* 462–465.

Andersen, T. (1991). *The reflecting team: Dialogues and dialogues about the dialogues.* New York, NY: Norton.

Andersen, T. (1992). Reflections on reflecting with families. In S. McNamee & K. J. Gergen (Eds.), *Therapy as social construction* (pp. 54–68). Newbury Park, CA: SAGE.

Anderson, H., & Goolishian, H. (1992). The client is the expert: A not-knowing approach to therapy. In S. McNamee & K. J. Gergen (Eds.), *Therapy as social construction* (pp. 25–39). Newbury Park, CA: Sage.

Angle, S. S., & Goodyear, R. K. (1984). Perception of counselors' qualities: Impact of subjects' self-concepts, counselor gender, and counselor introductions. *Journal of Counseling Psychology, 31,* 576–579.

Ansbacher, H. L. (1989). Adlerian psychology: The tradition of brief psychotherapy. *Individual Psychology: The Journal of Adlerian Theory, Research, and Practice, 45*(1/2), 26–33.

Ansbacher, H. L., & Ansbacher, R. R. (Eds.). (1956). *The individual psychology of Alfred Adler.* New York, NY: Basic Books.

Ansbacher, H. L., & Ansbacher, R. R. (Eds.). (1964). *Superiority and social interest.* Evanston, IL: Northwestern University Press.

Ansell, C. A. (1987). *Ethical practices workbook.* Santa Monica, CA: Association for Advanced Training in the Behavioral Sciences.

Antony, M. M. (2014). Behavior therapy. In R. J. Corsini & D. Wedding (Eds.), *Current psychotherapies* (10th ed.; pp. 193–229). Belmont, CA: Brooks/Cole, Cengage Learning.

Appelbaum, P. S. (1993). Legal liability and managed care. *American Psychologist, 48*(3), 251–257.

Arbona, C. (1996). Career theory and practice in a multicultural context. In M. L. Savickas & W. B. Walsh (Eds.), *Handbook of career theory and practice* (pp. 45–54). Palo Alto, CA: Davies-Black.

Arellano, A. R., & Padilla, A. M. (1996). Academic invulnerability among a select group of Latino university students. *Hispanic Journal of Behavioral Sciences, 18*(4), 485–507.

Argyle, M. (1981). The contribution of social interaction research to social skills training. In J. D. Wine & M. D. Syme (Eds.), *Social competence* (pp. 261–286). New York, NY: Guilford.

Arlow, J. A. (2005). Psychoanalysis. In R. J. Corsini (Ed.), *Current psychoanalysis* (7th ed.; pp. 15–51). Itasca, IL: F. E. Peacock.

Arredondo, P., & Toporek, R. (2004). *Journal of Mental Health Counseling, 26,* 44–55.

Arredondo, P., Toporek, R., Brown, S., Jones, J., Locke, D. C., Sanchez, J., & Stadler, H. (1996). *Operationalization of the multicultural counseling competencies.* Alexandria, VA: Association for Multicultural Counseling and Development.

Arredondo, P., Tovar-Blank, Z .G., & Parham, T. A. (2008). Challenges and promises of becoming a culturally competent counselor in a sociopolitical era of change and empowerment. *Journal of Counseling and Development, 86*(3), 261–268.

Asarnow, J. R., & Calan, J. W. (1985). Boys with peer adjustment problems: Social cognitive processes. *Journal of Counseling and Clinical Psychology, 53,* 80–87.

Ascher, L. M. (1979). Paradoxical intention in the treatment of urinary retention. *Behavior Research and Therapy, 17,* 267–270.

Ascher, L. M., & Efran, J. S. (1978). The use of paradoxical intention in a behavioral program for sleep onset insomnia. *Journal of Consulting and Clinical Psychology, 46,* 547–550.

Ashby, J. S., Dickinson, W. L., Gnilka, P. B., & Noble, C. L. (2011). Hope as a mediator and moderator of multidimensional perfectionism and depression in middle school students. *Journal of Counseling and Development, 89,* 131–139.

Atkinson, D. R. (1993). Who speaks for cross-cultural counseling research? *The Counseling Psychologist, 21*(2), 218–224.

Atkinson, D. R., Morten, G., & Sue, D. W. (1998). *Counseling American minorities: A cross-cultural perspective* (5th ed.). Dubuque, IA: William C. Brown.

Atkinson, D. R., & Thompson, C. E. (1992). Racial, ethnic, and cultural variables in counseling. In S. D. Brown & R. W. Lent (Eds.), *Handbook of counseling psychology* (2nd ed.; pp. 349–382). New York, NY: John Wiley & Sons.

Aubrey, R. F. (1982). A house divided: Guidance and counseling in 20th-century America. *The Personnel and Guidance Journal, 61*(4), 198–204.

Avis, J. M. (1986). Feminist issues in family therapy. In F. P. Piercy, D. H. Sprenkle, & associates (Eds.), *Family therapy sourcebook* (pp. 213–242). New York, NY: Guilford Press.

Axelson, J. A. (1999). *Counseling and development in a multicultural society* (3rd ed.). Belmont, CA: Wadsworth.

Axline, V. M. (1964). *Dibs: In search of self.* Boston, MA: Houghton Mifflin.

Axline, V. M. (1974). *Play therapy.* New York, NY: Houghton Mifflin.

Ayllon, T., & Azrin, N. (1968). *The token economy: A motivation system for therapy and rehabilitation.* New York, NY: Appleton-Century-Crofts.

Bachrach, L. L. (1995). Managed care: I. Delimiting the concept. *Psychiatric Service, 46*(12), 1229–1230.

Baker, D. B., & Benjamin, L. T., Jr. (2000). The affirmation of the scientist-practitioner: A look back at Boulder. *American Psychologist, 55*(2), 241–247.

Baker, E. L. (1985). Psychoanalysis and psychoanalytic psychotherapy. In S. J. Lynn & J. P. Garske (Eds.), *Contemporary psychotherapies: Models and methods* (pp. 19–68). Columbus, OH: Merrill/Macmillan.

Baker, S. (1995). Qualitative research has a place in the school counseling literature. *The School Counselor, 42*(5), 339–340.

Ball, F. L. J., & Harassy, B. E. (1984). A survey of the problems and needs of homeless consumers of acute psychiatric services. *Hospital and Community Psychiatry, 35,* 917–921.

Ballou, M. (1996). MCT theory and women. In D. W. Sue, A. E. Ivey, & P. B. Pedersen (Eds.), *A theory of multicultural counseling and therapy* (pp. 236–246). Pacific Grove, CA: Brooks/Cole.

Bandler, R., & Grinder, J. (1975). *The structure of magic* (Vol. 1). Palo Alto, CA: Science and Behavior Books.

Bandura, A. (1974). Behavior theory and the models of man. *American Psychologist, 29,* 859–869.

Bandura, A. (1977). *Social learning theory.* Englewood Cliffs, NJ: Prentice-Hall.

Bandura, A. (1982). Self-efficacy mechanism in human agency. *American Psychologist, 37*(2), 122–167.

Bandura, A. (1986). *Social foundations of thought and action: A social cognition theory.* Englewood Cliffs, NJ: Prentice-Hall.

Bandura, A. (1989). Human agency in social cognitive theory. *American Psychologist, 44*(9), 1175–1184.

Bandura, A. (1997). *Self-efficacy: The exercise of control.* New York, NY: Freeman.

Bandura, A., Reese, L., & Adams, N. E. (1982). Microanalysis of actions and fear arousal as a function of differential levels of perceived self-efficacy. *Journal of Personality and Social Psychology, 43*(1), 5 21.

Bangert-Drowns, R. L. (1988). The effects of school-based substance abuse education: A meta-analysis. *Journal of Drug Education, 18,* 243–264.

Bansberg, B., & Sklare, J. (1986). *The career decision diagnostic assessment.* Monterey, CA: CTB/McGraw-Hill.

Barclay, J. R. (1984). Primary prevention and assessment. *The Personnel and Guidance Journal, 62*(8), 475–478.

Barlow, S. H., Burlingame, G. M., & Fuhriman, A. (2000). Therapeutic application of groups: From Pratt's "thought control classes" to modern group psychotherapy. *Group Dynamics: Theory, Research, and Practice, 4*(1), 115–134.

Barrett-Lennard, G. T. (1981). The empathy cycle: Refinement of a nuclear concept. *Journal of Counseling Psychology, 28,* 91–100.

Barrett-Lennard, G. T. (1997). The recovery of empathy— towards others and self. In A. C. Bohart & L. S. Greenberg (Eds.), *Empathy reconsidered: New directions in psychotherapy* (pp. 103–124). Washington, DC: American Psychological Association.

Barth, K., Nielson, G., Haver, B., Havik, O. E., Molstad, E., Rogge, H., & Statun, M. (1988). Comprehensive assessment of change in patients treated with short-term dynamic psychotherapy: An overview. *Psychotherapy Psychosomatic, 50,* 141–150.

Baruth, L. G., & Huber, C. H. (1985). *Counseling and psychotherapy: Theoretical analyses and skill application.* Columbus, OH: Merrill/Macmillan.

Baruth, L. G., & Manning, M. L. (1999). *Multicultural counseling and psychotherapy: A lifespan perspective* (2nd ed.). New York, NY: Macmillan.

Baruth, L. G., & Robinson, E. H. (1987). *An introduction to the counseling profession.* Englewood Cliffs, NJ: Prentice-Hall.

Baskin, T. W., & Slaten, C. D. (2014). Contextual school counseling approach: Linking contextual psychotherapy with the school environment. *The Counseling Psychologist, 42,* 73–96.

Beale, A. V., & Scott, P. C. (2001). Bullybusters: Using drama to empower students to take a stand against bullying behavior. *Professional School Counseling, 4*(4), 300–305.

Bearden, L. J., Spencer, W. A., & Moracco, J. C. (1989). A study of high school dropouts. *The School Counselor, 37,* 113–120.

Beck, A. T. (1986). Hopelessness as a predictor of eventual suicide. In J. J. Mann & M. Stanley (Eds.), *Psychobiology.* New York, NY: Academy of Sciences.

Beck, A. T. (1987). Cognitive therapy. In J. K. Zeig (Ed.), *The evolution of psychotherapy* (pp. 149–178). New York, NY: Brunner/Mazel.

Beck, A. T. (1991). Cognitive therapy: A 30-year retrospective. *American Psychologist, 46*(4), 368–375.

Beck, A. T. (1993). Cognitive therapy: Past, present, and future. *Journal of Consulting and Clinical Psychology, 61*(2), 194–198.

Beck, A. T. (1996). Cognitive therapy of personality disorders. In P. M. Salkovskis (Ed.), *Frontiers of cognitive therapy* (pp. 165–181). New York, NY: Guilford Press.

Beck, A. T., & Emery, G. (1985). *Anxiety disorders and phobias: A cognitive perspective.* New York, NY: Basic Books.

Beck, A. T., Rush, A., Shaw, B., & Emery, G. (1979). *Cognitive therapy of depression.* New York, NY: Guilford Press.

Beck, A. T., Sokol, L., Clark, D. A., Berchick, R., & Wright, F. (1992). A crossover study of focused cognitive therapy for panic disorder. *American Journal of Psychiatry, 149,* 778–783.

Beck, A. T., Steer, R. A., & Brown, G. K. (1996). *Manual for the Beck Depression Inventory* (2nd ed.). San Antonio, TX: Psychological Corporation.

Beck, A. T., & Weishaar, M. E. (1989). Cognitive therapy. In R. J. Corsini & D. Wedding (Eds.), *Current psychotherapies* (4th ed.; pp. 285–320). Itasca, IL: Peacock Club.

Beck, A., & Weishaar, E. (2011). Cognitive therapy. In R. J. Corsini & D. Wedding (Eds.), *Current* psychotherapies (9th ed.; pp. 257–287). Belmont, CA: Brooks/Cole, Cengage Learning.

Beck, A., & Weishaar, E. (2014). Cognitive therapy. In R. J. Corsini & D. Wedding (Eds.), *Current psychotherapies* (10th ed.; pp. 231–264). Belmont, CA: Brooks/Cole, Cengage Learning.

Beck, A., Wright, F. D., Newman, C. F., & Liese, B. (1993). *Cognitive therapy of substance abuse.* New York, NY: Guilford Press.

Becvar, R. J., & Becvar, D. S. (1994). The ecosystemic story: A story about stories. *Journal of Mental Health Counseling, 16*(1), 22–32.

Bednar, R. L., Bednar, S. C., Lambert, M. J., & Waite, D. R. (1991). *Psychotherapy with high-risk clients: Legal and professional standards.* Pacific Grove, CA: Brooks/Cole.

Bednar, R. L., Burlingame, G. M., & Masters, K. S. (1988). Systems of family treatment: Substance or semantics? *Annual Review of Psychology, 39,* 401–434.

Beers, C. (1908). *A mind that found itself.* New York, NY: Longman Green.

Belizaire, L. S., & Fuertes, J. N. (2011). Attachment, coping, acculturative stress, and quality of life among Haitian immigrants. *Journal of Counseling and Development*, 89, 89–97.

Bello, G. A. (1989). Counseling handicapped students: A cognitive approach. *The School Counselor, 36,* 298–304.

Bemak, F., & Chung, R. C.-Y. (2008a). Counseling and psychotherapy with refugees. In P. B. Pedersen, J. G. Draguns, W. J. Lonner, & J. E. Trimble (Eds.), *Counseling across cultures* (6th ed.; pp. 307–324). Thousand Oaks, CA: SAGe.

Bemak, F., Chung, R. C.-Y. (2008b). New professional roles and advocacy strategies for school counselors: A multicultural/social justice perspective to move beyond the nice counselor syndrome. *Journal of Counseling and Development, 86*(3), 372–382.

Berenson, B., & Mitchell, K. (1968). Therapeutic conditions for therapist-initiated confrontation. *Journal of Clinical Psychology, 24,* 363–364.

Berger, K. S., & Thompson, R. A. (2000). *The developing person through childhood and adolescence* (5th ed.). New York, NY: Worth.

Bergin, A. E. (1991). Values and religious issues in psychotherapy and mental health. *American Psychologist, 46,* 394–403.

Bergin, J. J., Miller, S. E., Bergin, J. W., & Koch, R. E. (1990). The effects of a comprehensive guidance model on a rural school's counseling program. *Elementary School Guidance & Counseling, 25*(1), 37–45.

Bergman, L. R., & Magnusson, D. (1997). A person-oriented approach in research on developmental psychopathology. *Development and Psychopathology, 9,* 291–319.

Berne, E. (1961). *Transactional analysis in psychotherapy.* New York, NY: Grove Press.

Berne, E. (1964). *Games people play.* New York, NY: Grove Press.

Bernstein, B. L., & Figioli, S. W. (1983). Gender and credibility introduction effects on perceived counselor characteristics. *Journal of Counseling Psychology, 30,* 506–513.

Berrigan, L. P., & Garfield, S. L. (1981). Relationships of missed psychotherapy appointments to premature termination and social class. *British Journal of Clinical Psychology, 20,* 239–242.

Berry, G. W., & Sipps, G. J. (1991). Interactive effects of counselor-client similarity and client self-esteem on termination type and number of sessions. *Journal of Counseling Psychology, 38*(2), 120–125.

Bertoia, J., & Allan, J. (1988). Counseling seriously ill children: Use of spontaneous drawings. *Elementary School Guidance and Counseling, 22*(3), 206–221.

Betz, N. E. (1994). Self-concept theory in career development and counseling. *Career Development Quarterly, 43*(1), 32–42.

Betz, N. E., & Hackett, G. (1986). Applications of self-efficacy theory to understanding career choice behavior. *Journal of Social and Clinical Psychology, 4,* 279–289.

Beutler, L. (1983). *Eclectic psychotherapy: A systematic approach.* New York, NY: Pergamon Press.

Beutler, L. E., Machado, P. P. P., & Neufeldt, S. A. (1994). Therapist variables. In A. E. Bergin & S. L. Garfield (Eds.), *Handbook of psychotherapy and behavior change* (4th ed.; pp. 229–269). New York, NY: John Wiley & Sons.

Beutler, L. E., Williams, R. E., Wakefield, P. J., & Entwistle, S. R. (1995). Bridging scientist and practitioner perspective in clinical psychology. *American Psychologist, 50*(12), 984–994.

Bidell, M. P. (2012). Examining school counseling students' multicultural and sexual orientation competencies through a cross-specialization comparision. *Journal of Counseling and Development*, 90, 200–207.

Bigler, E. D., & Ehrfurth, J. W. (1981). The continued inappropriate singular use of the Bender Visual Motor Gestalt Test. *Professional Psychology, 12,* 562–569.

Birk, J. M., & Brooks, L. (1986). Required skills and training needs of recent counseling psychology graduates. *Journal of Counseling Psychology, 33,* 320–325.

Bishop, D. R. (1995). Religious values as cross-cultural issues in counseling. In M. T. Burke & J. G. Miranti (Eds.), *Counseling: The spiritual dimension* (pp. 59–72). Alexandria, VA: American Counseling Association.

Bitter, J. R., & Corey, G. (1996). Family systems therapy. In G. Corey (Ed.), *Theory and practice of counseling and psychotherapy* (5th ed.; pp. 365–443). Pacific Grove, CA: Brooks/Cole.

Bitter, J. R., & Nicoll, W. G. (2004). Relational strategies: Two approaches to Adlerian brief therapy. *Journal of Individual Psychology, 60,* 42–66.

Black, J., & Underwood, J. (1998). Young, female, and gay: Lesbian students and the school environment. *Professional School Counseling, 1*(3), 15–20.

Blackburn, I. M., Bishop, S., Glen, A. I. M., Whalley, L. J., & Christie, J. E. (1981). The efficacy of cognitive therapy in depression: A treatment trial using cognitive therapy and pharmacotherapy, each alone and in combination. *British Journal of Psychiatry, 139,* 181–189.

Blackburn, I. M., Eunson, K. M., & Bishop, S. (1986). *A two-year naturalistic follow-up of depressed patients treated with cognitive therapy, pharmacotherapy, and a combination of both.* Unpublished manuscript, Royal Edinburgh Hospital, Scotland.

Blair, R. G. (2004). Helping older adolescents search for meaning in depression. *Journal of Mental Health Counseling, 26,* 333–348.

Blanco, P. J., & Ray, D. C. (2011). Play therapy in elementary schools: A best practice for improving academic achievement. *Journal of Counseling and Development, 89,* 235–243.

Blocher, D. H. (1974). *Developmental counseling* (2nd ed.). New York, NY: Ronald Press.

Blocher, D. H. (1987). *The professional counselor.* New York, NY: Macmillan.

Blue Zones. (2015). Power 9: Blue zones lessons [drop-down feature]. http://www.bluezones.com/live-longer/.

Blustein, D. L. (1987). Integrating career counseling and psychotherapy: A comprehensive treatment strategy. *Psychotherapy, 24,* 794–799.

Blustein, D. L., McWhirter, E. H., & Perry, J. C. (2005). An emancipatory communitarian approach to vocational development theory, research, and practice. *The Counseling Psychologist, 33*(2), 141–179.

Blustein, D. L., Prezioso, M. S., & Schultheiss, D. P. (1995). *The Counseling Psychologist, 23*(3), 416–432.

Blustein, D. L., & Spengler, P. M. (1995). Personal adjustment: Career counseling and psychotherapy. In W. B. Walsh & S. H. Osipow (Eds.), *Handbook of vocational psychology* (2nd ed.; pp. 295–329). Hillsdale, NJ: Erlbaum.

Boen, D. L. (1988). A practitioner looks at assessment in marital counseling. *Journal of Counseling and Development, 66*(10), 484–486.

Bonebrake, C. R., & Borgers, S. B. (1984). Counselor role as perceived by counselors and principals. *Elementary School Guidance & Counseling, 18*(3), 194–199.

Bonett, R. M. (1994). Marital status and sex: Impact on self-efficacy. *Journal of Counseling and Development, 73*(2), 187–190.

Bonner, H. (1959). *Group dynamics.* New York, NY: Ronald Press.

Bonnington, S. B. (1993). Solution-focused brief therapy: Helpful interventions for school counselors. *The School Counselor, 41*(2), 126–128.

Borders, D. L., & Drury, R. D. (1992). Comprehensive school counseling programs: A review for policy makers and practitioners. *Journal of Counseling and Development, 70*(4), 487–498.

Bordin, E. S. (1979). The generalizability of the psychoanalytic concept of the working alliance. *Psychotherapy: Theory, Research and Practice, 16,* 252–260.

Borg, W. B., & Gall, M. D. (1989). *Educational research: An introduction* (5th ed.). New York, NY: Longman.

Borys, D. S. (1994). Maintaining therapeutic boundaries: The motive is therapeutic effectiveness, not defensive practice. *Ethics and Behavior, 4,* 267–273.

Boswell, B. (1983). Adapted dance for mentally retarded children: An experimental study. *Dissertation Abstracts International, 43*(09), 2925.

Bowen, M. (1978). *Family therapy in clinical practice.* New York, NY: Jason Aronson.

Bowker, M. (1982). Children of divorce: Being in between. *Elementary School Guidance & Counseling, 17,* 126–130.

Bowlby, J. (1969/1982). *Attachment and loss: Vol I. Attachment.* London, UK: Tavistock.

Bowlby, J. (1973). *Attachment and loss: Vol. 2. Separation, anxiety and anger.* New York, NY: Basic.

Bowlby, J. (1988a). *A secure base: Parent-child attachments and healthy human development.* New York, NY: Basic Books.

Bowlby, J. (1988b). Developmental psychiatry comes of age. *American Journal of Psychiatry, 145,* 1–10.

Brabender, V. (1985). Time-limited inpatient group therapy: A developmental model. *International Journal of Group Psychotherapy, 35,* 373–390.

Brace, K. (1992). I and Thou in interpersonal psychotherapy. *The Humanistic Psychologist, 20*(1), 41–57.

Bradford, E., & Lyddon, W. J. (1994). Assessing adolescent and adult attachment: An update. *Journal of Counseling and Development, 73*(2), 215–219.

Brady, J. P. (1980). Some views on effective principles of psychotherapy. In M. Goldfried (Ed.), *Cognitive therapy and research, 4,* 271–306.

Brake, K. J. (1988). Counseling young children of alcoholics. *Elementary School Guidance & Counseling, 23,* 106–111.

Brammer, L. M. (1999). *The helping relationship: Process and skills* (7th ed.). Englewood Cliffs, NJ: Prentice-Hall.

Brammer, L. M. (2002). *The helping relationship: Process and skills* (8th ed.). Englewood Cliffs, NJ: Prentice-Hall.

Bray, D. W., Campbell, R. J., & Grant, D. L. (1974). *Formative years in business: A long-term AT&T study of managerial lives.* New York, NY: John Wiley & Sons.

Bredehoft, D. (1990). Self-esteem: A family affair. *Transactional Analysis Journal, 20,* 111–116.

Brennan, K. A., Shaver, P. R., & Tobey, A. N. (1991). Attachment styles, gender, and parental problem drinking. *Journal of Social and Personal Relationships, 8,* 451–466.

Briggs, W. P., Magnus, V. A., Lassiter, P., Patterson, A., & Smith, L. (2011). Substance use, misuse, and abuse among older adults: Implications for clinical mental health counselors. *Journal of Mental Health Counseling, 33,* 112–127.

Bristow-Braitman, A. (1995). Addiction recovery: 12-step programs and cognitive-behavioral psychology. *Journal of Counseling and Development, 73*(4), 414–418.

Brockman, M. P. (1987). Children and physical abuse. In A. Thomas & J. Grimes (Eds.), *Children's needs: Psychological perspectives* (pp. 418–427). Washington, DC: The National Association of School Psychologists.

Brooks, D. K., & Gerstein, L. H. (1990). Counselor credentialing and interprofessional collaboration. *Journal of Counseling and Development, 68,* 477–484.

Brooks, L. (2002). Recent developments in theory building. In D. Brown, L. Brooks, & Associates (Eds.), *Career choice and development* (4th ed.; pp. 364–394). San Francisco, CA: Jossey-Bass.

Brooks-Gunn, J., McCormick, M. C., Gunn, R. W., Shorter, T., Wallace, C. Y., & Heagerty, M. C. (1989). Outreach as casefindings: The process of locating low-income pregnant women. *Medical Care, 27*(2), 95–102.

Brooks-Gunn, J., McCormick, M. C., & Heagerty, M. C. (1988). Preventing infant mortality and morbidity: Developmental perspectives. *American Journal of Orthopsychiatry, 58,* 288–296.

Brown, B. M. (1995). The bill of rights for people with disabilities in group work. *Journal for Specialists in Group Work, 20*(2), 71–75.

Brown, D. (1993). Training consultants: A call to action. *Journal of Counseling and Development, 72*(2), 139–143.

Brown, D. (1997). Implications of cultural values for cross-cultural consultation with families. *Journal of Counseling and Development, 76*(1), 29–35.

Brown, D., & Brooks, L. (2002). Introduction to theories of career development and choice: Origins, evolution, and current approaches. In D. Brown & L. Brooks (Eds.), *Career choice and development* (4th ed.; pp. 3–23). San Francisco, CA: Jossey-Bass.

Brown, G. W., & Harris, T. (1978). *Social origins of depression.* London, UK: Tavistock.

Brown, K. S., & Parsons, R. D. (1998). Accurate identification of childhood aggression: A key to successful intervention. *Professional School Counseling, 2,* 135–140.

Brown, L. S. (1988). Feminist therapy with lesbians and gay men. In M. Dutton-Douglas & L. E. Walker (Eds.), *Feminist psychotherapies: Integration of therapeutic and feminist systems* (pp. 206–227). Norwood, NJ: Ablex.

Brown, L. S. (1997). The private practice of subversion: Psychology as tikkumolam. *American Psychologist, 52,* 449–462.

Brown, S. D., & Ryan Krane, N. E. (2000). Four (or five) sessions and a cloud of dust: Old assumptions and new observations about career counseling. In S. Brown & R. Lent (Eds.), *Handbook of counseling psychology* (3rd ed.; pp. 740–766). New York, NY: John Wiley.

Brownell, P. (2008). Practice-based evidence. In P. Brownell (Ed.) *Handbook for theory, research, and practice in Gestalt therapy* (pp. 90–103). Newcastle, UK: Cambridge Scholars.

Browning, C., Reynolds, A., & Dworkin, S. H. (1991). Affirmative psychotherapy with lesbian women. *The Counseling Psychologist, 19*(2), 177–196.

Bruce, M. A. (1995). Brief counseling: An effective model for change. *The School Counselor, 42*(5), 353–363.

Brunner, J. S. (1973). *Beyond the information given: Studies in the psychology of knowing.* New York, NY: Norton.

Bruscia, K. E. (1987). *Improvisational models of music therapy.* Springfield, IL: Charles C. Thomas.

Bryan, J., Day-Vines, N. L., Griffin, D., & Moore-Thomas, C. (2012). The disproportionality dilemma: Patterns of teacher referrals to school counselors for disruptive behvavior. *Journal of Counseling and Development, 90,* 177–190.

Buber, M. (1970). *I and thou* (W. Kaufmann, Trans.). New York, NY: Scribner's. (Original work published 1958.)

Buck, J. N. (1949). The H-T-P technique: A qualitative and scoring manual, part 2. *Journal of Clinical Psychology, 5,* 37–76.

Buettner, D. (2008, May & June). Living healthy to 100. *AARP Magazine,* 57–59, 88–89.

Bugental, J. (1976). *The search for existential identity.* San Francisco, CA: Jossey-Bass.

Bullock-Yowell, E., Peterson, G.W., Wright, L.K., Reardon, R.C., & Mohn, R.S. (2011). The contribution of self-efficacy in assessing interests using the self-directed search. *Journal of Counseling and Development, 89,* 470–478.

Burke, D. M., & DeStreek, L. V. (1989). Children of divorce: An application of Hammond's group counseling for children. *Elementary School Guidance & Counseling, 24,* 112–118.

Burlingame, G. M., & Fuhriman, A. (1990). Time-limited group therapy. *The Counseling Psychologist, 18*(1), 93–118.

Burrow-Sanchez, J. J., Call, M. E., Zheng, R., & Drew, C. J. (2011). How school counselors can help prevent online victimization. *Journal of Counseling and Development, 89,* 3–10.

Burtnett, F. E. (1986). *Staffing patterns in mental health agencies and organizations.* Unpublished report. Alexandria, VA: American Association for Counseling and Development.

Butler, A. C., Chapman, J. E., Forman, E. M., & Beck, A. T. (2006). The empirical status of cognitive-behavioral therapy: A review of meta-analysis. *Clinical Psychology Review, 26,* 17–31.

Butler, L., & Meichenbaum, D. (1981). The assessment of interpersonal problem solving skills. In P. C. Kendall & S. D. Hollen (Eds.), *Assessment strategies for cognitive behavioral interventions* (pp. 197–225). New York, NY: Academic Press.

Campbell, C. A. (1993). Play, the fabric of elementary school counseling programs. *Elementary School Guidance and Counseling, 28*(1), 10–16.

Campbell, C. A., & Dahir, C. A. (1997). *Sharing the vision: The national standards for school counseling programs.* Alexandria, VA: American School Counselor Association.

Campbell, T. J., & Patterson, J. M. (1995). The effectiveness of family interventions in the treatment of physical illness. *Journal of Marital and Family Therapy, 21,* 545–584.

Caplan, G. (1964). *Principles of preventive psychiatry.* New York, NY: Basic Books.

Caplan, G. (1970). *The theory and practice of mental health consultation.* New York, NY: Basic Books.

Capuzzi, D. (1988). Personal and social competency: Developing skills for the future. In G. R. Walz & J. C. Bleuer (Eds.), *Building strong school counseling programs.* Alexandria, VA: American Association for Counseling and Development.

Capuzzi, D., & Nystul, M. S. (1986). The suicidal adolescent. In L. B. Golden & D. Capuzzi (Eds.), *Helping families help children: Family interventions with school-related problems* (pp. 23–32). Springfield, IL: Charles C. Thomas.

Carkhuff, R. R. (1969). *Helping and human relations* (Vols. 1–2). New York, NY: Holt, Rinehart & Winston.

Carkhuff, R. R. (1971). *The development of human resources.* New York, NY: Holt, Rinehart & Winston.

Carlsen, M. B. (1995). Meaning-making and creative aging. In R. A. Neimeyer & M. J. Mahoney (Eds.), *Constructivism in psychotherapy.* Washington, DC: American Psychological Association.

Carlson, G. A., & Cantwell, D. P. (1979). A survey of depressive symptoms in a child and adolescent psychiatric population. *Journal of the American Academy of Child Psychiatry, 18,* 587–599.

Carlson, J. D., & Robey, P. A. (2011). An integrative Adlerian approach to family counseling. *The Journal of Individual Psychology, 67,* 232–244.

Carlson, J. F., Geisinger, K. F., & Jonson. J. L. (2014). *The nineteenth mental measurements yearbook.* Lincoln, NE: The Buros Center for Testing.

Carlson, L. A., & Kees, N. L. (2013). Mental health services in public schools: A preliminary study of school counselor perceptions. *Professional School Counseling, 16*(4), 211–221.

Carmichael, K. D. (1994). Sand play as an elementary school strategy. *Elementary School Guidance and Counseling, 28*(4), 302–307.

Carnelley, K. B., Pietromonaco, P. R., & Jaffe, K. (1994). Depression, working models of others, and relationship functioning. *Journal of Personality and Social Psychology, 66,* 127–140.

Carnes-Holt, K., & Bratton, S. C.(2014). The efficacy of child parent relationship therapy for adopted children with attachment disruptions. *Journal of Counseling and Development, 92,* 328–337.

Carr, J. E. (2005). Recommendations for reporting multiplebaseline designs across participants. *Behavioral Interventions, 20,* 219–224.

Carson, A., & Mowsesian, R. (1990). Some remarks on Gati's theory of career decision-making models. *Journal of Counseling Psychology, 37*(4), 502–507.

Carter, B., & McGoldrick, M. (1988). Overview: The changing family life cycle—A framework for family therapy. In B. Carter & M. McGoldrick (Eds.), *The changing family life cycle: A framework for family therapy* (2nd ed.; pp. 3–28). New York, NY: Allyn & Bacon.

Carter, R. T., & Swanson, J. L. (1990). The validity of the Strong Interest Inventory with black Americans: A review of the literature. *Journal of Vocational Behavior, 36,* 195–209.

Cartwright, B. Y., Daniels, J., & Zhang, S. (2008). Assessing multicultural competence: Perceived versus demonstrated performance. *Journal of Counseling and Development, 86*(3), 318–322.

Casas, J. M., & Pytluk, S. D. (1995). Hispanic identity development: Implications for research and practice. In J. G. Ponterotto, J. M. Casas, L. A. Suzuki, & C. M. Alexander (Eds.), *Handbook of multicultural counseling* (pp. 155–180). Thousand Oaks, CA: SAGE.

Casey, J. A. (1995). Developmental issues for school counselors using technology. *Elementary School Guidance and Counseling, 30*(1), 26–34.

Cashwell, C. S., Shcherbakova, J., & Cashwell, T. H. (2003). Effect of client and counselor ethnicity on preference for counselor disclosure. *Journal of Counseling and Development, 81,* 196–201.

Cashwell, C. S., & Vacc, N. A. (1996). Family functioning and risk behaviors: Influences on adolescent delinquency. *The School Counselor, 44*(2), 105–114.

Cass, V. C. (1979). Homosexual identity formation: A theoretical model. *Journal of Homosexuality, 4,* 219–235.

Cattell, R. B. (1949). *Culture-fair intelligence tests.* Champaign, IL: Institute for Personality and Ability Testing.

Cavanaugh, M. E. (1982). *The counseling experience.* Monterey, CA: Brooks/Cole.

Centers for Disease Control and Prevention (CDC). (2011). *International classification of diseases, ninth revision, clinical modification (ICD-9-CM).* Retrieved from http://www.cdc.gov/nchs/icd/icd9cm.htm.

Chae, M. H., & Foley, P. F. (2010). Relationship of ethnic identity, acculturation, and psychological well-being among Chinese, Japanese, and Korean Americans. *Journal of Counseling and Development, 88,* 466–476.

Chambers, W. J., Puig-Antich, J., & Tabrizi, M. A. (1978, October). *The ongoing development of the KiddieSADS (Schedule for Affective Disorders and Schizophrenia for School-Age Children).* Paper presented at the meeting of the American Academy of Child Psychiatry, San Diego, CA.

Chambless, D. L., & Gillis, M. M. (1993). Cognitive therapy of anxiety disorders. *Journal of Consulting and Clinical Psychology, 61,* 248–260.

Chao, R. C.-L. (2012). Racial/ethnic identity, gender-role attitudes, and multicultural counseling competence: The role of multicultural counseling training. *Journal of Counseling and Development, 90*(1), 35–44.

Chao, R. C.-L. (2013). Race/ethnicity and multicultural competence among school counselors: Multicultural training, racial/ethnic identity, and color-blind racial attitudes. *Journal of Counseling and Development, 91*(2), 140–151.

Charmaz, K. (2006). *Constructing grounded theory.* London, UK: SAGE.

Chartrand, J. M. (1996). Linking theory and practice: A sociocognitive interactional model for career counseling. In M. L. Savickas & W. B. Walsh (Eds.), *Handbook of career counseling theory and practice* (pp. 121–134). Palo Alto, CA: Davies-Black.

Chatters, S. S., & Zalaquett, C. (2013, June). Dispelling the myths of aging. *Counseling Today,* 46–51. Available at http://ct.counseling.org/2013/06/dispelling-the-myths-of-aging/.

Chesler, M. A. (1976). Contemporary sociological theories of racism. In P. A. Katz (Ed.), *Toward the elimination of racism* (pp. 21–72). New York, NY: Pergamon.

Chiles, A., Miller, M. L., & Cox, G. B. (1980). Depression in an adolescent delinquent population. *Archives of General Psychiatry, 37,* 1179–1184.

Choney, S. K., Berryhill-Paapke, E., & Robbins, R. R. (1995). The acculturation of American Indians: Developing frameworks for research and practice. In J. G. Ponterotto, J. M. Casas, L. A. Suzuki, & C. M. Alexander (Eds.), *Handbook of multicultural counseling* (pp. 73–92). Thousand Oaks, CA: SAGE.

Chu, L., & Powers, P. A. (1995). Synchrony in adolescence. *Adolescence, 30*(118), 453–461.

Chung, Y. B. (1995). Career decision making of lesbian, gay, and bisexual individuals. *Career Development Quarterly, 44*(2), 178–190.

Chwalisz, K. (2003). Evidence-based practice: A framework for twenty-first-century scientist-practitioner training. *The Counseling Psychologist, 31,* 497–528.

Cicchetti, D., Ackerman, B. P., & Izard, C. E. (1995). Emotions and emotion regulation in developmental psychopathology. *Development and Psychopathology, 7,* 1–10.

Ciechalski, J. C., & Schmidt, M. W. (1995). The effects of social skills training on students with exceptionalities. *Elementary School Guidance and Counseling, 29*(3), 217–222.

Claiborn, C. D. (1987). Science and practice: Reconsidering the Pepinskys. *Journal of Counseling and Development, 65*(6), 286–288.

Clair, D., & Genest, M. (1987). Variables associated with the adjustment of offspring of alcoholic fathers. *Journal of Studies on Alcohol, 48,* 345–356.

Clarizio, H. F., & McCoy, G. F. (1983). *Behavior disorders in children.* New York, NY: Harper & Row.

Clark, A. J. (1995). Projective techniques in the counseling process. *Journal of Counseling and Development, 73*(3), 311–316.

Clark, M. A., & Breman, J. C. (2009). School counselor inclusion: A collaborative model to provide academic and social-emotional support in the classroom setting. *Journal of Counseling and Development, 87*(1), 6–11.

Clarke, J., & Evans, E. (1973). Rhythmical intention as a method of treatment for cerebral-palsied patients. *Australia Journal of Physiotherapy, 19–20,* 57–64.

Clarke, K., & Breeberg, L. (1986). Differential effects of the Gestalt two chair intervention and problem solving in resolving decisional conflict. *Journal of Counseling Psychology, 33,* 48–53.

Clewell, B. C., Brooks-Gunn, J., & Benasich, A. A. (1989). Evaluating child-related outcomes of teenage parenting programs. *Family Relations, 38*(2), 201–209.

Cochran, J. L. (1996). Using play and art therapy to help culturally diverse students overcome barriers to school success. *The School Counselor, 43*(4), 287–298.

Coe, D. M., & Zimpfer, D. G. (1996). Infusing solution-oriented theory and techniques into group work. *Journal for Specialists in Group Work, 21*(1), 49–57.

Cohen, E. D. (1990). Confidentiality, counseling, and clients who have AIDS: Ethical foundations of a model rule. *Journal of Counseling and Development, 68,* 282–287.

Cohen, E. D. (2001). Permitted suicide: Model rules for mental health counseling. *Journal of Mental Health Counseling, 23*(4), 279–295.

Colangelo, J. J. (2009). The American Mental Health Counselors Association: Reflections on 30 historic years. *Journal of Counseling and Development, 87*(2), 234–240.

Cole, C. G. (1988). The school counselor: Image and impact, counselor role and function, 1960s to 1980s and beyond. In G. R. Walz & J. C. Bleuer (Eds.), *Research and counseling: Building strong school counseling programs* (pp. 127–150). Alexandria, VA: American Association for Counseling and Development.

Cole, I. (1982). Movement negotiations with an autistic child. *Arts in Psychotherapy, 9,* 49–53.

Cole, J. D., & Kupersmidt, J. B. (1983). A behavioral analysis of emerging social status in boys' groups. *Child Development, 54,* 1400–1416.

Cole, O. A., & Rehm, L. P. (1986). Family interaction patterns and childhood depression. *Journal of Abnormal Child Psychology, 14,* 297–314.

Coleman, S. (1985). *Failures in family therapy.* New York, NY: Guilford Press.

College Entrance Examination Board. (1987). *Keeping options open: Recommendations, final reports of the commission on precollege guidance and counseling.* New York, NY: Author.

Collins, B. G., & Collins, T. M. (1994). Child and adolescent mental health: Building a system of care. *Journal of Counseling and Development, 72*(3), 239–243.

Collins, N. L., & Miller, L. C. (1994). Self-disclosure and liking: A meta-analytic review. *Psychological Bulletin, 116*(3), 457–475.

Combs, A., Soper, D., Gooding, C., Benton, J., Dickman, J., & Usher, R. (1969). *Florida studies in the helping professions.* Gainesville: University of Florida Press.

Committee for Economic Development. (1991). *The unfinished agenda: A new vision for child development and education.* New York, NY: Author.

Congdon, D. (1987). *Professional issues.* Santa Monica, CA: Association for Advanced Training in Behavioral Sciences.

Constantine, M. G., & Ladany, N. (2000). Self-report multicultural counseling competence scales: Their relation to social desirability attitudes and multicultural case conceptualization ability. *Journal of Counseling Psychology, 47,* 155–164.

Mental health: Does therapy help? (1995, November). *Consumer Reports,* 734–739.

Cooley, J. J. (1998). Gay and lesbian adolescents: Presenting problems and the counselor's role. *Professional School Counseling, 1*(3), 30–34.

Cooper, J. O., Heron, T. E., & Heward, W. L. (2007). *Applied behavior analysis* (2nd ed.). Upper Saddle River, NJ: Prentice Hall.

Corey, G. (1982). *Theory and practice of counseling and psychotherapy* (2nd ed.). Pacific Grove, CA: Brooks/Cole.

Corey, G. (2013). *Theory and practice of counseling and psychotherapy* (9th ed.). Belmont, CA: Brooks/Cole, Cengage Learning.

Corey, G. (2016). *Theory and practice of group counseling* (9th ed.). Boston, Cengage Learning.

Corey, G., Corey, M., Callanan, P., & Russell, J. M. (1982). Ethical considerations in using group techniques. *Journal for Specialists in Group Work, 7,* 140–148.

Corey, G., Corey, M., Corey, C., & Callanan, P. (2015). *Issues and ethics in the helping professions* (9th ed.). Belmont, CA: Brooks/Cole, Cengage Learning.

Corey, G., Williams, G. T., & Moline, M. E. (1995). Ethical and legal issues in group counseling. *Ethics and Behavior, 5*(2), 161–183.

Corey, M. S., & Corey, G. (2016). *Becoming a helper* (7th ed.). Boston, MA: Cengage Learning.

Corey, M. S., Corey, G., & Corey, C. (2014), *Groups: Process and practice* (9th ed.). Belmont, CA: Brooks/Cole, Cengage Learning.

Cormier, L. S., & Hackney, H. (1993). *The professional counselor: A process guide to helping* (2nd ed.). Englewood Cliffs, NJ: Prentice-Hall.

Cormier, W. H., & Cormier, L. S. (1998). *Interviewing strategies for helpers* (4th ed.). Monterey, CA: Brooks/Cole.

Cornell, D. G., & Sheras, P. L. (2006). *Guidelines for responding to students' threats of violence.* Boston, MA: Sopris West Educational Services.

Corrigan, J. D., Dell, D. M., Lewis, K. N., & Schmidt, L. D. (1980). Counseling as a social influence process: A review [Monograph]. *Journal of Counseling Psychology, 27,* 395–441.

Corsini, R. J. (1977). Individual education. *Journal of Individual Psychology, 33,* 295–349.

Corsini, R. J. (1979). Individual education. In E. Ignas & R. J. Corsini (Eds.), *Alternate educational systems* (pp. 200–256). Itasca, IL: F. E. Peacock.

Corsini, R. J., & Wedding, D. (2000). *Current psychotherapies* (6th ed.). Itasca, IL: F. E. Peacock.

Costello, A. J., Edelbrock, C. S., Dulcan, M. K., & Kalas, R. (1984). *Testing of the NIMH Diagnostic Interview Schedule for Children (DISC) in a clinical population* (Contract No. DB-81-0027, final report to the Center for Epidemiological Studies, National Institute for Mental Health). Pittsburgh, PA: University of Pittsburgh.

Costello, A. J., Edelbrock, C., Kalas, R., Kessler, M. D., & Klaric, S. H. (1982). *The NIMH Diagnostic Interview Schedule for Children (DISC).* Unpublished interview schedule, Department of Psychiatry, University of Pittsburgh.

Cottone, R. R. (2001). A social constructivism model of ethical decision making in counseling. *Journal of Counseling and Development, 79*(1), 39–45.

Couch, R. D. (1994, February). Changes in the theory and practice of individual psychotherapy by the year 2003. *The Advocate, 6.*

Couch, R. D. (1995). Four steps for conducting a pregroup screening interview. *Journal for Specialists in Group Work, 20*(1), 18–25.

Couch, R. D., & Childers, J. H., Jr. (1989). A discussion of differences between group therapy and family therapy: Implications for counselor training and practice. *Journal for Specialists in Group Work, 14*(4), 226–231.

Council for Accreditation of Counseling and Related Educational Programs (CACREP). (2009). *2009 standards.* Alexandria, VA: Author.

Cox, O. C. (1959). *Caste, class, and race.* New York, NY: Monthly Review.

Craig, C. J. (2002). *Human development* (9th ed.). Englewood Cliffs, NJ: Prentice-Hall.

Cramer, D. (1994). Self-esteem and Rogers' core conditions in close friends: A latent variable path analysis of panel data. *Counseling Psychology Quarterly, 7*(3), 321–337.

Creswell, J. W., Hanson, W. E., Plano Clark, V. L., & Morales, A.

(2007). Qualitative research design. *The Counseling Psychologist, 35*(2), 236–264.

Crethar, H. C., Torres-Rivera, E., & Nash, S. (2008). In search of common threads: Linking multicultural, feminist, and social justice counseling paradigms. *Journal of Counseling & Development, 86*, 269–278.

Cripe, F. F. (1986). Rock music as therapy for children with attention deficit disorder: An exploratory study. *Journal of Music Therapy, 23*, 30–37.

Cronbach, L. J. (1984). *Essentials of psychological testing.* New York, NY: Harper & Row.

Cross, W. E., Jr. (1995). The psychology of nigrescence: Revising the Cross model. In J. G. Ponterotto, J. M. Casas, L. A. Suzuki, & C. M. Alexander (Eds.), *Handbook of multicultural counseling* (pp. 93–122). Thousand Oaks, CA: SAGE.

Culbertson, F. M. (1997). Depression and gender: An international review. *American Psychologist, 52*(1), 25–31.

Cummings, C., Gordon, J. R., & Marlatt, G. A. (1980). Relapse: Prevention and prediction. In W. R. Miller (Ed.), *The addictive behaviors* (pp. 291–321). New York, NY: Pergamon Press.

Cummings, N. A. (1990). The credentialing of professional psychologists and its implication for other mental health disciplines. *Journal of Counseling and Development, 68*, 485–490.

Curran, J., & Loganbell, C. R. (1985). Factors affecting the attractiveness of a group leader. *Journal of College Student Personnel, 24*, 250–255.

D'Andrea, M. (2000). Postmodernism, constructivism, and multiculturalism: Three forces reshaping and expanding

our thoughts about counseling. *Journal of Mental Health Counseling, 22*(1), 1–16.

D'Andrea, M. (2004). Comprehensive school-based violence prevention training: A developmental-ecological training model. *Journal of Counseling and Development, 82*, 277–286.

D'Andrea, M., & Foster Heckman, E. (2008a). Contributing to the ongoing evolution of the multicultural counseling movement: An introduction to the special issue. *Journal of Counseling and Development, 86*(3), 259–260.

D'Andrea, M., & Foster Heckman, E. (2008b). A 40-year review of multicultural counseling outcome research: Outlining a future research agenda for the multicultural counseling movement. *Journal of Counseling and Development, 86*(3), 372–382.

Dade County Public Schools. (1985). *Dropout prevention/reduction programs and activities.* Miami, FL: Author.

Dahir, C. A. (2009). School counseling in the 21st century: Where lies the future? *Journal of Counseling and Development, 87*(1), 3–5.

Dahir, C. A., & Stone, C. B. (2009). School counselor accountability: The path to social justice and systemic change. *Journal of Counseling and Development, 87*(1), 12–20.

Daigneault, S. D. (2000). Body talk: A school-based group intervention for working with disordered eating behaviors. *Journal for Specialists in Group Work, 25*, 191–213.

Daly, M., & Wilson, M. (1983). *Sex, evolution, and behavior* (2nd ed.). Boston, MA: Willard Grant Press.

Damon, L., & Waterman, J. (1986). Parallel group treatment of children and their mothers. In K. MacFarlane

& J. Waterman (Eds.), *Sexual abuse of young children.* New York, NY: Guilford Press.

Dana, R. H. (1993). *Multicultural assessment perspectives for professional psychology.* Boston, MA: Allyn & Bacon.

Daniels, M. H., & White, L. J. (1994). Revisiting Auerswald's conundrum—A response to Fong, Lease, and Lanning. *Journal of Mental Health Counseling, 16*(2), 217–225.

Danish, S. J., D'Augelli, A. R., & Brock, G. W. (1976). An evaluation of helping skill training: Effects on helpers' verbal responses. *Journal of Counseling Psychology, 23*, 259–266.

Davanloo, H. (1978). *Basic principles and techniques in short-term dynamic psychotherapy.* New York, NY: SP Medical and Scientific Books.

Davanloo, H. (1984). Intensive short-term dynamic psychotherapy In H. Kaplan and B. Sadock (Eds.), *Comprehensive textbook of psychiatry* (4th ed.; 1460–1467). Baltimore, MD: Williams & Wilkins.

Davis-Berman, J. (1988). Self-efficacy and depressive symptomatology in older adults: An exploratory study. *International Journal of Aging and Human Development, 27*(1), 35–43.

Day-Vines, N. L., Wood, S. M., Grothaus, T., Craigen, L., Holman, A., Dotson-Blake, K., & Douglass, M. J. (2007). Broaching the subjects of race, ethnicity, and culture during the counseling process. *Journal of Counseling and Development, 85*(4), 401–409.

de Shazer, S. (1985). *Key solutions in brief therapy.* New York, NY: Norton.

de Shazer, S. (1988). *Clues: Investigating solutions in brief therapy.* New York, NY: Norton.

de Shazer, S. (1991). *Putting difference to work.* New York, NY: Norton.

de Shazer, S. (1994). *Words were originally magic.* New York, NY: Norton.

DeHart, G., Sroufe, L. & Cooper, R. (2004). *Child development: Its nature and cause* (5th ed.). New York, NY: McGraw Hill.

DeKruyf, L., Auger, R. W., & Trice-Black, S. (2013). The role of school counselors in meeting student's mental health needs: Examining issues of professional identity. *Professional School Counseling, 16,* 271–282.

DeLucia-Waack, J. L. (1999). What makes an effective group leader? *Journal for Specialists in Group Work, 24,* 131–132.

DeLucia-Waack, J. L. (2000). Effective group work in the schools. *Journal for Specialists in Group Work, 25,* 131–132.

Denkowski, K. M., & Denkowski, G. C. (1982). Client-counselor confidentiality: An update. *Personnel and Guidance Journal, 60,* 371–375.

DePauw, M. E. (1986). Avoiding ethical relations: A timeline perspective for individual counseling. *Journal of Counseling and Development, 64*(5), 303–310.

Devine, D. A., & Fernald, P. S. (1973). Outcome effects of receiving a preferred, randomly assigned, or nonreferred therapy. *Journal of Consulting and Clinical Psychology, 41,* 104–107.

Digdon, N., & Gotlib, I. H. (1985). Developmental considerations in the study of childhood depression. *Developmental Review, 5,* 162–199.

Dingman, R. L. (Ed.). (1988). *Licensure for mental health counselors.* Huntington, WV: Marshall University Press.

Dinkmeyer, D. (1971). The "C" group: Integrating knowledge and experience to change behavior. *The Counseling Psychologist, 3,* 63–72.

Dinkmeyer, D. (1973). The parent "C" group. *Personnel and Guidance Journal, 52,* 4.

Dinkmeyer, D., & Carlson, J. (1973). *Consultation: Facilitating human potential and processes.* Columbus, OH: Merrill/Macmillan.

Dinkmeyer, D., & Carlson, J. (1984). *Time for a better marriage.* Circle Pines, MN: American Guidance Service.

Dinkmeyer, D., & Dinkmeyer, D., Jr. (1982). *Developing understanding of self and others, DUSO-1 and DUSO-2 revised.* Circle Pines, MN: American Guidance Service.

Dinkmeyer, D., & Dinkmeyer, D., Jr. (1985). Adlerian psychotherapy and counseling. In S. Lynn & J. P. Garske (Eds.), *Contemporary psychotherapies: Models and methods.* Columbus, OH: Merrill/Macmillan.

Dinkmeyer, D., & Dreikurs, R. (1963). *Encouraging children to learn: The encouragement process.* Englewood Cliffs, NJ: Prentice-Hall.

Dinkmeyer, D., & Losoncy, L. E. (1980). *The encouragement book: Becoming a positive person.* Englewood Cliffs, NJ: Prentice-Hall.

Dinkmeyer, D., & McKay, G., (1997). *Systemic Training for Effective Parenting (STEP): The parent's handbook* (4th ed.). Circle Pines, MN: American Guidance Service.

Dinkmeyer, D., McKay, G., & Dinkmeyer, D., Jr. (1997). *Parent's handbook: Systemic Training for Effective Parenting.* Circle Pines, MN: American Guidance Service.

Dinkmeyer, D., McKay, G., Dinkmeyer, D., Jr., Dinkmeyer, J. S., & Carlson, J. (1985). *PREP for effective family living: Student handbook.* Circle Pines, MN: American Guidance Service.

Dinkmeyer, D., Jr., & Sperry, L. (2000). *Counseling and psychotherapy: An integrated, individual psychological approach* (3rd ed.). Columbus, OH: Merrill/Macmillan.

Dixon, A. L., Scheidegger, C., & McWhirter, J. J. (2009). The adolescent mattering experience: Gender variations in perceived mattering, anxiety, and depression. *Journal of Counseling and Development, 87*(3), 302–310.

Dixon, D. N., & Glover, J. A. (1984). *Counseling: A problem solving approach.* New York, NY: John Wiley & Sons.

Dobson, K. S. (1989). A meta-analysis of the efficacy of cognitive therapy for depression. *Journal of Consulting and Clinical Psychology, 57*(3), 414–419.

Dodge, K. A. (1983). Behavioral antecedents of peer social station. *Child Development, 54,* 1386–1399.

Donne, J. (1952). Meditation XVII. In C. M. Coffin (Ed.), *The complete poetry and selected prose of John Donne.* New York, NY: Random House.

Dorn, F. J., & Day, B. J. (1985). Assessing change in self-concept: A social psychological approach. *American Mental Health Counselors Association Journal, 7,* 180–186.

Dougherty, A. M. (1995). *Consultation: Practice and perspectives in school and community settings* (2nd ed.). Pacific Grove, CA: Brooks/Cole.

Douglas, C. (2011). Analytical psychotherapy. In R. J. Corsini & D. Wedding (Eds), *Current psychotherapies* (9th ed.; pp. 104–136). Belmont, CA: Brooks/Cole, Cengage Learning.

Dowd, E. T., & Sanders, D. (1994). Resistance, reactance, and the difficult client. *Canadian Journal of Counseling, 28*(1), 13–24.

Dreikurs, R. (1949). The four goals of children's misbehavior. *Nervous Child, 6,* 3–11.

Dreikurs, R. (1971). *Social equality: The challenge of today.* Chicago, IL: Henry Regnery.

Dreikurs, R., Corsini, R. J., Lowe, R., & Sonstegard, M. (1959). *Adlerian family counseling.* Eugene: University of Oregon Press.

Dreikurs, R., & Soltz, V. (1964). *Children: The challenge.* New York, NY: Hawthorn Books.

Drummond, R. J. (2000). *Appraisal procedures for counselors and helping professionals* (4th ed.). Columbus, OH: Merrill.

Dryden, W. (1987). Theoretically consistent eclecticism: Humanizing a computer "addict." In J. C. Norcross (Ed.), *Casebook of eclectic psychotherapy* (pp. 221–237). New York, NY: Brunner/Mazel.

Duffey, T., & Somody, C. (2011). The role of relational-cultural theory in mental health counseling. *Journal of Mental Health Counseling, 33,* 223–242.

Dugger, S. M., & Francis, P. C. (2014). Surviving a lawsuit against a counseling program. Lessions learned from *Ward v. Wilbanks. Journal of Counseling and Development, 92,* 135–141.

Duncan, B. L., & Moynihan, D. W. (1994). Applying outcome research: Intentional utilization of the client's frame of reference. *Psychotherapy, 31,* 294–301.

Dungy, G. (1984). Computer-assisted guidance: Determining who is ready. *Journal of College Student Personnel, 25,* 539–546.

Dunn, R. L., & Schwebel, A. I. (1995). Meta-analytic review of marital therapy outcome research. *Journal of Family Psychology, 9*(1), 58–68.

Duran, L., Firehammer, J., & Gonzalez, J. (2008). Liberation psychology as the path toward healing cultural soul wounds. *Journal of Counseling and Development, 86*(3), 288–295.

Durkheim, E. (1897). *Suicide: A study in sociology.* Glencoe, IL: Free Press.

Durlak, J. A., Fuhrman, T., & Lampman, C. (1991). Effectiveness of cognitive-behavioral therapy for maladapting children: A meta-analysis. *Psychological Bulletin, 110,* 204–214.

Durrant, M. (1995). *Creative strategies for school problems: Solutions for psychologists and teachers.* New York, NY: Norton.

Dusay, J., & Dusay, K. M. (1989). Transactional analysis. In R. Corsini (Ed.), *Current psychotherapies* (4th ed.). Itasca, IL: F. E. Peacock.

Duvall, E. M. (1957). *Family development.* Philadelphia, PA: Lippincott.

Duvall, E.M. (1977) *Marriage and family development* (5th ed.). Philadelphia: Lippincott.

Dworetzky, J. P. (1996). *Introduction to child development* (6th ed.). New York, NY: ITP.

Dysinger, B. J. (1993). Conflict resolution for intermediate children. *The School Counselor, 40*(4), 301–308.

Ebert, B. (1978). The healthy family. *Family Therapy, 5*(3), 227–232.

Eccles, J. S., Midgley, C., Wigfield, A., Buchanan, C. M., Reuman, D., Flanagan, C., & Iver, D. M. (1993). Development during adolescence: The impact of stage environment fit on young adolescents' experiences in schools and families. *American Psychologist, 48,* 90–101.

Edelbrock, C., & Costello, A. J. (1988). Structured psychiatric interviews for children. In M. Rutter, A. H. Tuma, & I. S. Lann (Eds.), *Assessment and diagnosis in child psychopathology* (pp. 82–112). New York, NY: Guilford Press.

Edelson, M. (1994). Can psychotherapy research answer this psychotherapist's questions? In P. F. Tally, H. H. Strupp, & S. F. Butler (Eds.), *Psychotherapy research and practice: Bridging the gap.* New York, NY: Basic Books.

The Education Trust. (2002, December 12). *The Education Trust honors pioneers in school counseling reform* [press release]. Retrieved from http://edtrust.org/press_release/the-education-trust-honors-pioneers-in-school-counseling-reform/.

Egan, G. (2002). *The skilled helper: A model for systematic helping and interpersonal relating* (7th ed.). Monterey, CA: Brooks/Cole.

Eggen, P., & Kauchak, D. (1994). *Educational psychology: Classroom connections* (2nd ed.). Columbus, OH: Merrill.

Eidson, C. E., Jr. (1989). The effects of behavioral music therapy on the generalization of interpersonal skills from sessions to the classroom by emotionally handicapped middle school students. *Journal of Music Therapy, 26*(4), 206–221.

Elkaim, M. (1982). From the family approach to the sociopolitical approach. In F. Kaslow (Ed.), *The international book of family therapy* (pp. 331–357). New York, NY: Brunner/Mazel.

Elkin, I., Shea, M. T., Watkins, J. T., Imber, S. D., Sotsky, S. M., Collins, J. F., . . . Parloff, M. B. (1989). National Institute of Mental Health Treatment of Depression Collaborative Research Program: I. General effectiveness of treatments. *Archives of General Psychiatry, 46*(11), 971–982.

Elkind, D. (1984). *All grown up and no place to go.* Reading, MA: Addison-Wesley.

Elliott, D. S., Huizinga, D., & Ageton, S. S. (1985). *Explaining delinquency and drug use.* Beverly Hills, CA: SAGE.

Elliot, G. (1989). An interview with George M. Gazda. *Journal for Specialists in Group Work, 14*(3), 131–140.

Elliott, J. M. (1999). Feminist therapy. In C. Capuzzi & D. R. Gross (Eds.), *Counseling and psychotherapy: Theories and interventions* (2nd ed.; pp. 201–230). Columbus, OH: Merrill.

Elliott, R. (2002). The effectiveness of humanistic therapies: A meta-analysis. In D. J. Cain & J. Seeman (Eds.), *Humanistic psychotherapies: Handbook of research and practice* (pp. 57–81). Washington, DC: American Psychological Association.

Elliott, R., & Freire, E. (2008). Person-centered and experiential therapies are highly effective: Summary of the 2008 meta-analysis. *Person-Centered Quarterly, 45,* 1–3.

Elliott, R., & Freire, E. (2010). The effectiveness of person-centered and experienrtial therapies: A review of the meta-analyses. In M. Cooper, J. C. Watson, & D. Holldampf (Eds.), *Person-centered and experiential therapies work: A review of the research on counseling, psychotherapy, and related practices* (pp. 1–15). Ross-on-Wye, UK: PCCS Books.

Ellis, A. (1962). *Reason and emotion in psychotherapy.* New York, NY: Lyle Stuart.

Ellis, A. (1977). The basic clinical theory of rational-emotive therapy. In A. Ellis & R. Grieger (Eds.), *RET handbook of rational-emotive therapy* (pp. 3–34). New York, NY: Springer.

Ellis, A. (1986). Comments on Gloria. *Psychotherapy, 23,* 647–648.

Ellis, A. (1993, Summer). RET becomes REBT. *IRETletter, 1,* 4.

Ellis, A. (1994). *Reason and emotion in psychotherapy revised.* New York, NY: Carol.

Ellis, A. (1996). *Better, deeper and more enduring brief therapy.* New York, NY: Brunner/Mazel.

Ellis, A., & Ellis, D. J. (2014). Rational emotive behavior therapy. In R. J. Corsini & D. Wedding (Eds.), *Current psychotherapies* (10th ed.; pp. 151–191). Belmont, CA: Brooks/Cole, Cengage Learning.

Ellis, A., & Harper, R. (1975). *A new guide to rational living* (Rev. ed.). Hollywood, CA: Wilshire Books.

Ellis, P. L. (1982). Empathy: A factor in antisocial behavior. *Journal of Abnormal Child Psychology, 10,* 123–133.

Elman, N. S., & Forrest, L. (2004). Psychotherapy in the remediation of psychology trainees: Exploratory interviews with training directors. *Professional Psychology: Research and Practice, 35*(2), 123–130.

Emmelkamp, P. M. G. (1994). Behavior therapy with adults. In A. E. Bergin & S. L. Garfield, *Handbook of psychotherapy and behavior change* (4th ed.; pp. 379–427). New York, NY: John Wiley & Sons.

Emmons, R., & Nystul, M. S. (1994). The effects of a prenatal course including PREP for effective family living on self-esteem and parenting attitudes of adolescents: A brief report. *Adolescence, 29,* 935–938.

Engels, D. W., Minor, C. W., Sampson, J. P., & Splete, H. H. (1995). Career counseling specialty: History, development, and prospect. *Journal of Counseling and Development, 74*(2), 134–138.

England, L. W., & Thompson, C. L. (1988). Counseling child sexual abuse victims: Myths and realities. *Journal of Counseling and Development, 66,* 370–373.

Enns, C. Z. (1988). Dilemmas of power and equality in marital and family counseling: Proposals for a feminist perspective. *Journal of Counseling and Development, 67*(4), 242–248.

Enns, C. Z. (1993). Twenty years of counseling and therapy: From naming biases to implementing multifaceted practice. *The Counseling Psychologist, 21*(1), 3–87.

Epstein, E. S., & Loos, V. E. (1989). Some irreverent thoughts on the limits of family therapy: Towards a language-based explanation of human systems. *Journal of Family Psychology, 2*(4), 405–421.

Erford, B. T., Erford, B. M., Lattanzi, G., Weller, J., Schein, H., Wolf, E., . . . Peacock, E. (2011). Counseling outcomes from 1990 to 2008 for school-age youth with depression: A meta-analysis. *Journal of Counseling and Development, 89,* 439–457.

Erford, B. T., House, R., & Martin, P. (2013). Transforming the school counseling profession. In B. T. Erford (Ed.), *Transforming the school counseling profession* (pp. 1–20). Columbus, OH: Merrill.

Erford, B. T., Paul, L. E., Oncken, C., Kress, V. E., & Erford, M. R. (2014). Counseling outcomes for youth with oppositional behavior: A meta-analysis. *Journal of Counseling and Development, 92,* 13–25.

Eriksen, K., & Kress, V. E. (2008). Gender and diagnosis: Struggles and suggestions for counselors. *Journal of Counseling and Development, 86*(2), 152–162.

Erickson, A., & Abel, N. R. (2013). A high school counselor's leadership in providing school-wide screenings for depression and enhancing suicide awarenss. *Professional School Counseling, 16*, 283–289.

Erickson, M. (1954). Pseudo-orientation in time as a hypnotherapeutic procedure. *Journal of Clinical and Experimental Hypnosis, 2*, 261–283.

Erikson, E. H. (1950). *Childhood and society.* New York, NY: Norton.

Erikson, E. H. (1963). *Childhood and society* (2nd ed.). New York, NY: Norton.

Erikson, E. H. (1968). *Identity, youth, and crisis.* New York, NY: Norton.

Eron, J. B., & Lund, T. W. (1993). How problems evolve and dissolve: Integrating narrative and strategic concepts. *Family Process, 32*, 291–309.

Estés, C. P. (1992). *Women who run with the wolves.* New York, NY: Ballantine Books.

Estrada, A. U., & Pinsof, W. M. (1995). The effectiveness of family therapies for selected behavioral disorders of childhood. *Journal of Marital and Family Therapy, 21*, 403–440.

Evans, K. (2008). *Gaining cultural competence in career counseling.* Lahaska, PA: Lahaska Press.

Evans, K. M., Seem, S. R., & Kincade, E. A. (2005). In G. Corey (Ed.), *Case approach to counseling and psychotherapy* (6th ed.; pp. 212–246). Belmont, CA: Wadsworth.

Everett, C. A. (1990). The field of marital and family therapy. *Journal of Counseling and Development, 68*, 498–502.

Everstine, L., Everstine, D. S., Heymann, G. M., True, R. H., Frey, D. H., Johnson, H. G., & Seiden, R. H. (1980). Privacy and confidentiality in psychotherapy. *American Psychologist, 9*, 828–840.

Eysenck, H. J. (1965). The effects of psychotherapy. *Journal of Consulting Psychology, 16*, 319–324.

Fadiman, J., & Frager, R. (1976). *Personality and personal growth.* New York, NY: Harper & Row.

Farren, C., Gray, J. D., & Kaye, B. C. (1984). Mentoring: A boon to career development. *The Personnel and Guidance Journal, 61*, 20–24.

Fassinger, R. E. (1991). The hidden minority: Issues and challenges in working with lesbian women and gay men. *The Counseling Psychologist, 19*(2), 157–176.

Fassinger, R. E. (1995). From invisibility to integration: Lesbian identity in the workplace. *The Career Development Quarterly, 44*(2), 148–167.

Fassinger, R.E. (2005). Paradigms, praxis, problems, and promise: Grounded theory in counseling psychology research. *Journal of Counseling Psychology, 52*(2), 156–166.

Feist, J. (1985). *Theories of personality.* New York, NY: Holt, Rinehart & Winston.

Feldman, R. S. (2008). *Development across the life span* (5th ed.). Upper Saddle River, NJ: Pearson Prentice Hall.

Feller, R. W. (1995). Action planning for personal competitiveness in the "broken workplace." *Journal of Employment Counseling, 32*, 154–163.

Ferris, P. A. (1988). Future directions for elementary/middle school counseling. In G. R. Walz & J. C. Bleuer (Eds.), *Building strong school counseling programs* (pp. 181–188). Alexandria, VA: American Association for Counseling and Development.

Festinger, L. (1957). *A theory of cognitive dissonance.* Stanford, CA: Stanford University Press.

Field, T., Healy, B., Goldstein, S., Perry, S., Bendell, D., Schanberg, S., . . . Kuhn, C. (1988). Infants of depressed mothers show "depressed" behavior even with nondepressed adults. *Child Development, 59*, 1569–1579.

Finn, J. (2006). An exploratory study of email use of direct service workers. *Journal of Technology and Human Sciences, 24*, 1–20.

Fisch, R., Weakland, J. H., & Segal, L. (1982). *The tactics of change: Doing therapy briefly.* San Francisco, CA: Jossey-Bass.

Fischer, A. R., Jome, L. M., & Atkinson, D. R. (1998). Reconceptualizing multicultural counseling: Universal healing conditions in a culturally specific context. *The Counseling Psychologist, 26*, 525–588.

Fisher, B. L., & Sprenkle, D. H. (1978). Therapists' perceptions of healthy family functioning. *International Journal of Family Counseling, 19*(4) 9–18.

Fisher, K. (1982, November). Debate rages on 1973 Sonell study. *APA Monitor*, 8–9.

Fitzgerald, E. L., Chronister, K. M., Forrest, L., & Brown, L. (2014). OPTIONS for preparing inmates for community reentry: An employment preparation intervention. *The Counseling Psychologist, 41*, 990–1010.

Fitzgerald, L. F., & Rounds, J. B. (1989). Vocational behavior, 1988: A critical analysis. *Journal of Vocational Behavior, 35*, 105–163.

Fleshman, B., & Fryrear, J. L. (1981). *The arts in therapy.* Chicago, IL: Nelson-Hall.

Foa, E. B., Rothbaum, B. O., Riggs, D. S., & Murdock, T. B. (1991). Treatment of posttraumatic stress disorder in rape victims: A comparison between cognitive-behavioral procedures and counseling. *Journal of Consulting and Clinical Psychology, 59,* 715–723.

Fong, M. L., & Lease, S. H. (1994). Constructivist alternatives: The case for diversity and integration in mental health counseling. *Journal of Mental Health Counseling, 16*(1), 120–124.

Fontaine, J. H. (1998). Evidencing a need: School counselors' experiences with gay and lesbian students. *Professional School Counseling, 1*(3), 8–14.

Forester, J. R. (1977). What shall we do about credentialing? *Personnel and Guidance Journal, 55,* 573–576.

Forester-Miller, H. (1989). Dr. Irvin Yalom discusses group psychotherapy. *Journal for Specialists in Group Work, 14*(4), 196–201.

Forisha, B. L. (2001). Feminist psychotherapy. In R. J. Corsini (Ed.), *Handbook of innovative therapy* (2nd ed.; pp. 242–254). New York, NY: John Wiley & Sons.

Fosterling, F. (1980). Attributional aspects of cognitive behavior modification: A theoretical approach and suggestions for techniques. *Cognitive Therapy and Research, 24,* 27–37.

Foucault, M. (1980). *Power/knowledge: Selected interviews and other writings.* New York, NY: Pantheon Books.

Fowler, I. (1981). *Stages of faith.* San Francisco, CA: Harper & Row.

Framo, J. (1992). *Family of origin theory: An intergenerational approach.* New York, NY: Brunner/Mazel.

Framo, J. L. (1981). The integration of marital therapy with family of origin sessions. In A. Gurman & D. Kniskern (Eds.), *Handbook of family therapy.* New York, NY: Brunner/Mazel.

Frances, A. (2013). *DSM in philosophyland: Curiouser and curiouser.* In J. Paris & J. Phillips (Eds), *Making the DSM-5: Concepts and Controversies* (pp. 95–104). New York, NY: Springer.

Frances, R. J. (1988). Update on alcohol and drug disorder treatment. *Journal of Clinical Psychiatry, 49*(9), 13–17.

Frankl, V. (1959). *From death-camp to existentialism.* Boston, MA: Beacon.

Frankl, V. (1963). *Man's search for meaning.* New York, NY: Washington Square Press.

Frankl, V. (1967). *Psychotherapy and existentialism: Selected papers on logo therapy.* New York, NY: Simon & Schuster (Touchstone).

Frankl, V. (1971). *The doctor and the soul.* New York, NY: Bantam.

Frankl, V. (1978). *The unheard cry for meaning.* New York, NY: Simon & Schuster (Touchstone).

Frazier, S. H. (1985). Responding to the needs of the homeless mentally ill public. *Health Reports, 100,* 462–469.

Freeman, M. A. (1995). Behavioral at-risk contracting in a changing healthcare environment. In G. L. Zieman (Ed.), *The complete capitation handbook: How to design and implement at-risk contracts for behavioral healthcare* (pp. 11–27). Tiburon, CA: CentraLink Publications.

Freud, A. (1928). Introduction to the technique of child analysis. *Nervous and Mental Disease Monograph No. 48.* New York.

Freud, S. (1933). New introductory lectures on psychoanalyses. In J. Strachey (Ed. and Trans.), *The complete psychological works* (Vol. 22). New York, NY: Norton.

Freud, S. (1953). Fragment of an analysis of a case of hysteria. In J. Strachey (Ed.), *The standard edition of the complete psychological works of Sigmund Freud* (Vol. 7; pp. 3–122). London, UK: Hogarth.

Freud, S. (1965). *The interpretation of dreams* (J. Strachey, Trans.). New York, NY: Avon Books. (Original work published 1900)

Freud, S. (1969). *A general introduction to psycho-analysis* (Rev. ed., J. Riviere, Trans.). New York, NY: Simon & Schuster.

Friedan, B. (1963). *The feminine mystique.* New York, NY: Norton.

Friedlander, M. L., & Highlen, P. S. (1984). A spatial view of the interpersonal structure of family interviews: Similarities and differences across counselors. *Journal of Counseling Psychology, 31,* 477–487.

Friedlander, M. L., Highlen, P. S., & Lassiter, W. L. (1985). Content analytic comparison of four expert counselors' approach to family treatment: Ackerman, Bowen, Jackson, and Whitaker. *Journal of Counseling Psychology, 32*(2), 171–180.

Friedlander, M. L., & Tuason, M. T. (2000). Process and outcomes in couples and family therapy. In S. D. Brown & R. W. Lent (Eds.), *Handbook of counseling psychology* (3rd ed.; pp. 797–824). New York, NY: John Wiley & Sons.

Friedman, S. (1997). *Time-effective psychotherapy: Maximizing outcomes in an era of minimized resources.* Needham Heights, MA: Allyn & Bacon.

Frieman, B. B. (1993). Children of divorced parents: Action steps for the counselor to involve fathers. *Elementary School Guidance and Counseling, 28*(3), 197–205.

Fromm, E., Suzuki, D. T., & DeMartino, R. (1960). *Zen Buddhism and psychoanalysis*. New York, NY: Harper & Row.

Fuhriman, A., & Burlingame, G. M. (1990). Consistency of matter: A comparative analysis of individual and group process variables. *The Counseling Psychologist, 18*(1), 6–63.

Furstenberg, F. F., Jr., Brooks-Gunn, J., & Chase-Lansdale, L. (1989). *Unplanned parenthood: The social consequences of teenage childbearing*. New York, NY: Free Press.

Gabbard, G. O. (1994). Teetering on the precipice: A commentary on Lazarus's "How certain boundaries and ethics diminish therapeutic effectiveness." *Ethics and Behavior, 4*, 283–286.

Gall, M. D., Gall, J. P., & Borg, W. R. (2007). *Educational research: An introduction* (8th ed.). Boston, MA: Pearson Education.

Gardill, M. C., & Browder, D. M. (1995). Teaching stimulus classes to encourage independent purchasing by students with severe behavior disorders. *Education and Training in Mental Retardation and Developmental Disabilities, 30*, 254–269.

Garfield, J. C., Weiss, S. I., & Pollack, E. A. (1973). Effects of the child's social class on school counselors' decision-making. *Journal of Counseling Psychology, 20*, 166–168.

Garfield, S. L. (1983). *Clinical psychology. The study of personality and behavior* (2nd ed.). New York, NY: Aldine.

Garfield, S. L. (1994). Research on client variables in psychotherapy. In A. E. Bergin & S. L. Garfield (Eds.), *Handbook of psychotherapy and behavior change* (4th ed.; pp. 190–228). New York, NY: John Wiley & Sons.

Garfield, S. L., & Bergin, A. E. (1971). Therapeutic conditions

and outcome. *Journal of Abnormal Psychology, 77*, 108–114.

Garfield, S. L., & Bergin, A. E. (1994). Introduction and historical overview. In A. E. Bergin & S. L. Garfield (Eds.), *Handbook of psychotherapy and behavior change* (4th ed.; pp. 3–18). New York, NY: John Wiley & Sons.

Garland, A. F., & Zigler, E. (1993). Adolescent suicide prevention. *American Psychologist, 48*(2), 169–182.

Garrett, M. W. (1995). Between two worlds: Cultural discontinuity in the dropout of Native American youth. *The School Counselor, 42*(3), 186–195.

Garske, J. P., & Molteni, A. L. (1985). Brief psychodynamic psychotherapy: An integrative approach. In S. J. Lynn & J. P. Garske (Eds.), *Contemporary psychotherapies*. Columbus, OH: Merrill/Macmillan.

Gati, I. (1986). Making career decisions: A sequential elimination approach. *Journal of Counseling Psychology, 33*, 408–417.

Gati, I. (1990a). Interpreting and applying career decisionmaking models: Comments on Carson and Mowsesian. *Journal of Counseling Psychology, 32*(4), 508–514.

Gati, I. (1990b). Why, when, and how to take into account the uncertainty involved in career decisions. *Journal of Counseling Psychology, 37*(3), 277–280.

Gati, I. (1994). Computer-assisted career counseling: Dilemmas, problems, and possible solutions. *Journal of Counseling and Development, 73*(1), 51–56.

Gati, I., Fassa, N., & Houminer, D. (1995). Applying decision theory to career counseling practice: The sequential elimination approach. *Career Development Quarterly, 43*, 211–220.

Gati, I., & Tikotzki, Y. (1989). Strategies for collection and processing of occupational information in making career decisions. *Journal of Counseling Psychology, 35*(3), 430–439.

Gazda, G. M. (1989). *Group counseling: A developmental approach* (4th ed.). Boston, MA: Allyn & Bacon.

Gazda, G. M., Asbury, F., Blazer, F., Childress, W., & Walters, R. (1979). *Human relations development: A manual for educators*. Boston, MA: Allyn & Bacon.

Gelso, C. J., & Carter, J. A. (1985). The relationship in counseling and psychotherapy: Components, consequences, and theoretical antecedents. *The Counseling Psychologist, 13*, 155–243.

Gelso, C. J., & Fassinger, R. E. (1990). Counseling psychology: Theory and research on intervention. *American Review of Psychology, 41*, 355–386.

Gelso, C. J., & Fretz, B. R. (2001). *Counseling psychology* (2nd ed.). Orlando, FL: Holt, Rinehart & Winston.

Gelso, C.J., & Fretz, B.R. (1992). *Counseling psychology*. Orlando, FL: Holt, Rinehart & Winston.

Genia, V. (1994). Secular psychotherapists and religious clients: Professional considerations and recommendations. *Journal of Counseling and Development, 72*(4), 395–398.

George, R. L., & Cristiani, T. S. (1995). *Counseling: Theory and practice* (4th ed.). Englewood Cliffs, NJ: PrenticeHall.

Geoseffi, D. (1993). *On prejudice: A global perspective*. New York, NY: Doubleday.

Gerber, P. J. (1986). Counseling the learning disabled. In A. F. Rotatori, P. J. Gerber, F. W. Litton, & R. A. Fox (Eds.), *Counseling exceptional students*.

New York, NY: Human Sciences Press.

Gergen, K. (1982). *Toward transformation in social knowledge.* New York, NY: Springer-Verlag.

Gergen, K. (1994a). Exploring the postmodern. *American Psychologist, 49*(5), 412–416.

Gergen, K. (1994b). *Realities and relationships.* Cambridge, MA: Harvard University Press.

Gerler, E. R., & Anderson, R. F. (1986). The effects of classroom guidance on children's success in school. *Journal of Counseling and Development, 65,* 78–81.

Gerler, E. R., Jr. (1995). Advancing elementary and middle school counseling through computer technology. *Elementary School Guidance and Counseling, 30*(1), 8–15.

Germer, C. K. (2013). Mindfulness: What is it? What does it matter? In C. K. Germer, R. D. Siegel, & P. R. Fulton (Eds). *Mindfulness and psychotherapy* (2nd ed.; pp. 3–35). New York, NY: Guilford Press.

Gibbons, A. C. (1984). A program for noninstitutionalized, mature adults: A description. *Activities, Adaptation, and Aging, 6,* 71–80.

Gibbons, A. C. (1988). A review of literature for music development/ education and music therapy with the elderly. *Music Therapy Perspectives, 5,* 33–40.

Gibbs, N. (1995, October 2). The EQ factor. *Time,* 60–68.

Giblin, P., & Chan, J. (1995). A feminist perspective. *The Family Journal: Counseling and Therapy for Couples and Families, 3*(3), 234–238.

Gibran, K. (1965). *The prophet.* New York, NY: Alfred A. Knopf.

Gibson, R. L. (1977). *Counseling and annual guidance committee report.* Unpublished manuscript, North

Central Association of Colleges and Schools.

Gibson, R. L. (1989). Prevention and the elementary school counselor. *Elementary School Guidance & Counseling, 24,* 30–36.

Gilbert, L. A. (1992). Gender and counseling psychology: Current knowledge and directions for research and social action. In S. D. Brown & R. W. Lent (Eds.), *Handbook of counseling psychology* (2nd ed.; pp. 383–418). New York, NY: John Wiley & Sons.

Gilbert, L. A., & Scher, M. (1999). *Gender and sex in counseling and psychotherapy.* Needham Heights, MA: Allyn & Bacon.

Gilbert, N. (1982, July). Policy issues in primary prevention. *Social Work,* 293–296.

Gilligan, C. (1982). *In a different voice: Psychological theory and women's development.* Cambridge, MA: Harvard University Press.

Gilligan, C. (1987). Adolescent development reconsidered. In C. Irwin (Ed.), *Adolescent social behavior and health* (pp. 63–92). San Francisco, CA: Jossey-Bass.

Gilligan, C. (1990). Joining the resistance: Psychology, politics, girls, and women. *Michigan Quarterly Review, 29*(4), 501–536.

Gilligan, C. (1991). Women's psychological development: Implications for psychotherapy. *Women in Therapy, 11,* 5–31.

Gilligan, C. (1993). *In a different voice: Psychological theory and women's development* (2nd ed.). Cambridge, MA: Harvard University Press.

Ginter, E. J. (1988). Stagnation in eclecticism: The need to recommit to a journey. *Journal of Mental Health Counseling, 10,* 3–8.

Ginter, E. J. (1996). Three pillars of mental health counseling: Watch in what you step. *Journal of Mental Health Counseling, 18*(2), 99–107.

Ginter, E. J., Scalise, J. J., & Presse, N. (1990). The elementary school counselor's role: Perceptions of teachers. *The School Counselor, 38,* 19–23.

Gintner, G. G., & Poret, M. K. (1987). Factors associated with maintenance and relapse following self-management training. *Journal of Psychology, 122*(1), 79–87.

Gladding, S. T. (2001). *The counseling dictionary: Concise definitions of frequently used terms.* Upper Saddle River, NJ: Prentice-Hall.

Gladding, S. T. (2011). *The creative arts in counseling* (4th ed.). Alexandria, VA: American Counseling Association.

Gladstein, G. (1983). Understanding empathy: Integrating counseling, developmental and social psychology perspectives. *Journal of Counseling Psychology, 30,* 467–482.

Glaser, B. G., & Strauss, A. (1965). *Awareness of dying.* Chicago, IL: Aldine.

Glaser, B. G., & Strauss, A. (1967). *The discovery of grounded theory: Stategies for qualitative research.* Chicago, IL: Aldine.

Glasser, W. (1961). *Mental health or mental illness?* New York, NY: Harper & Row.

Glasser, W. (1965). *Reality therapy: A new approach to psychiatry.* New York, NY: Harper & Row.

Glasser, W. (1969). *Schools without failure.* New York, NY: Harper & Row.

Glasser, W. (1976). *Positive addiction.* New York, NY: Harper & Row.

Glasser, W. (1980). Reality therapy: An explanation of the steps of reality therapy. In N. Glasser (Ed.), *What are you doing? How people are helped through reality therapy* (pp. 48–59). New York, NY: Harper & Row.

Glasser, W. (1981). *Stations of the mind.* New York, NY: Harper & Row.

Glasser, W. (1984). *Take effective control of your life.* New York, NY: Harper & Row.

Glasser, W. (1985). *Control theory: A new explanation of how we control our lives.* New York, NY: Harper & Row.

Glasser, W. (1986). *Control theory in the classroom.* New York, NY: Harper & Row.

Glasser, W. (1989). Control theory in the practice of reality therapy. In N. Glasser (Ed.), *Control theory in the practice of reality therapy: Case studies* (pp. 1–15). New York, NY: Harper & Row.

Glasser, W. (1990). *The quality school.* New York, NY: Harper & Row.

Glasser, W. (1998). *Choice theory: A new psychology of personal freedom.* New York, NY: HarperCollins.

Glasser, W. (2000). *Counseling with choice theory: The new reality therapy.* New York, NY: Quill.

Glasser, W., & Glasser, C. (1999). *The language of choice theory.* New York, NY: HarperCollins.

Glasser, W., & Wubbolding, R. E. (1995). Reality therapy. In R. J. Corsini & D. Wedding (Eds.), *Current psychotherapies* (5th ed.; pp. 293–321). Itasca, IL: F. E. Peacock.

Glauser, A. S., & Bozarth, J. D. (2001). Person-centered counseling: The culture within. *Journal of Counseling and Development, 79*(2), 142–147.

Glenn, E. E. (1998). Counseling children and adolescents with disabilities. *Professional School Counseling, 2*(1), iii.

Glick, I., Clarkin, J., & Kessler, D. (1987). *Marital and family therapy* (3rd ed.). Orlando, FL: Grune & Stratton.

Glover, E. (1950). *Freud or Jung.* New York, NY: Norton.

Golann, S. (1987). On description of family therapy. *Family Process, 26,* 331–340.

Gold, C., Voracek, M., & Wigram, T. (2004). Effects of music therapy for children and adolescents with psychotherapy: A meta-analysis. *Journal of Child Psychology and Psychiatry, 45,* 1054–1063.

Goldberg, R. T. (1974). Adjustment of children with invisible and visible handicaps. *Journal of Counseling Psychology, 21,* 428–432.

Goldenberg, H., & Goldenberg, I. (2013). *Family therapy: An overview* (8th ed.). Belmont, CA: Brooks/Cole, Cengage Learning.

Goldfried, M. R., Greenberg, L. S., & Marmar, C. (1990). Individual psychotherapy: Process and outcome. *Annual Review of Psychology, 41,* 659–688.

Goldfried, M. R., & Wolfe, B. E. (1996). Psychotherapy practice and research: Repairing a strained alliance. *American Psychologist, 51*(10), 1007–1016.

Goldman, L. (1989). Moving counseling research into the 21st century. *The Counseling Psychologist, 17,* 81–85.

Goldman, L. (1990). Qualitative assessment. *The Counseling Psychologist, 18,* 205–213.

Goldman, S., & Beardslee, W. (1999). Suicide in children and adolescents. In D. Jacobs (Ed.), *The Harvard Medical School guide to assessment and intervention* (pp. 417–442). San Francisco, CA: Jossey-Bass.

Goldner, V. (1985). Feminism and family therapy. *Family Process, 24,* 31–47.

Goldstein, A. P. (1999). *Low-level aggression: First steps on the ladder to violence.* Champaign, IL: Research Press.

Goldston, S. E., Yager, J., Heinicke, C. M., & Pynoos, R. S. (Eds.). (1990). *Preventing mental health disturbances in childhood.* Washington, DC: American Psychiatric Press.

Goleman, D. (1997). *Emotional intelligence.* New York, NY: Bantam.

Gonzalez, L. M., Borders, L. D., Hines, E. M., Villalba, J. A., & Henderson, A. (2013). Parental involvement in children's education: Considerations for school counselors working with Latino immigrant families. *Professional School Counseling, 16,* 185–193.

Good, G. E., Fischer, A. R., Johnston, J. A., Jr., & Heppner, P. P. (1994). Norman C. Gysbers: A proponent of comprehensive school guidance programs. *Journal of Counseling and Development, 73*(2), 115–120.

Good, G. E., Gilbert, L. A., & Scher, M. (1990). Gender aware therapy: A synthesis of feminist therapy and knowledge about gender. *Journal of Counseling and Development, 68,* 376–380.

Gooding, P. R., & Glasgow, R. E. (1985). Self-efficacy and outcome expectations as predictors of controlling smoking status. *Cognitive Therapy and Research, 9,* 583–590.

Goodman, J. (1994). Career adaptability in adults: A construct whose time has come. *The Career Development Quarterly, 43*(1), 74–84.

Goodman, J., Schlossberg, M., & Anderson, M. L. (2006). *Counseling adults in transition: Linking practice with theory.* New York, NY: Springer.

Goodman, R. D., & Calderon, A. M. (2012). The use of mindfulness in trauma counseling. *Journal of Mental Health Counseling, 34*(3), 254–268.

Goodyear, R. K. (1990). Research on the effects of test interpretation: A review. *The Counseling Psychologist, 18*, 240–257.

Gordon, J., & Shontz, F. (1990). Representative case research: A way of knowing. *Journal of Counseling and Development, 69*, 62–66.

Gottfredson, L. S. (1981). Circumscription and compromise: A developmental theory of occupational aspirations. *Journal of Counseling Psychology Monograph, 28*, 545–579.

Gottfredson, L. S. (1996). Gottfredson's theory of circumscription and compromise. In D. Brown & L. Brooks (Eds.), *Career choice and development* (3rd ed.; pp. 179–232). San Francisco, CA: Jossey-Bass.

Gottman, J. M. (1994). *Why marriages succeed or fail.* New York, NY: Simon & Schuster.

Gottman, J. M., Coan, J., Carrere, S., & Swanson, C. (1998). Predicting marital happiness and stability from newlywed interactions. *Journal of Marriage and the Family, 60*(1), 5–22.

Gottman, J. M., & Notarius, C. I. (2000). Decade review: Observing marital interaction. *Journal of Marriage and the Family, 62*, 927–947.

Graham, M. A., Sauerheber, J. D., & Britzman, M. J. (2013). Choice theory and family counseling: A pragmatic, culturally sensitive approach. *The Family Journal: Counseling and Therapy for Couples and Families, 21*, 230–234.

Granello, D. H. (2010a). The process of suicide risk assessment: Twelve core principles. *Journal of Counseling and Development, 88*, 363–370.

Granello, D. H. (2010b). A suicide crisis intervention model with 25 practical strategies for implementation. *Journal of Mental Health Counseling, 32*, 218–235.

Grant, B. (1992). The moral nature of psychotherapy. In M. T. Burke & J. G. Miranti (Eds.), *Ethical and spiritual values in counseling* (pp. 27–36). Alexandria, VA: American Counseling Association.

Gray, L. A., & Harding, A. K. (1988). Confidentiality limits with clients who have the AIDS virus. *Journal of Counseling and Development, 66*(5), 219–223.

Green, R. L. (1988). Image-building activities for the elementary school counselor. *Elementary School Guidance & Counseling, 22*(3), 186–191.

Greenberg, L., Elliott, R., & Lietaer, G. (1994). Research on experiential psychotherapies. In A. E. Bergin & S. L. Garfield (Eds.), *Handbook of psychotherapy and behavior change* (4th ed.). New York, NY: John Wiley & Sons.

Greenberg, L. S., & Paivio, S. C. (1997). *Working with the emotions in psychotherapy.* New York, NY: Guilford Press.

Greenson, R. R. (1967). *Technique and practice of psychoanalysis.* New York, NY: International University Press.

Gregg, C. (1994). Group work with single fathers. *Journal for Specialists in Group Work, 19*, 95–101.

Griffin, H. C., Gerber, P. J., & Rotatori, A. F. (1986). Counseling the health impaired student. In A. F. Rotatori, P. J. Gerber, F. W. Litton, & R. A. Fox (Eds.), *Counseling exceptional students* (pp. 213–231). New York, NY: Human Sciences Press.

Griffin, H. C., Sexton, D., Gerber, P. J., & Rotatori, A. F. (1986). Counseling the physically handicapped child. In A. F. Rotatori, P. J. Gerber, F. W. Litton, & R. A. Fox (Eds.), *Counseling exceptional students* (pp. 197–212). New York, NY: Human Sciences Press.

Griggs, S. A. (1988). The counselor as facilitator of learning. In G. R. Walz & J. C. Bleuer (Eds.), *Building strong school counseling programs.* Alexandria, VA: American Association for Counseling and Development.

Gross, D. R., & Robinson, S. E. (1987). Ethics, violence, and counseling: Hear no evil, see no evil, speak no evil? *Journal of Counseling and Development, 65*(7), 340–344.

Gruman, D. H., Marston, T., & Koon, H. (2013). Bringing mental health needs into focus through school counseling program transformation. *Professional School Counseling, 16*, 333–341.

Guiffrida, D. A., Douthit, K. Z., Lynch, M. F., & Mackie, K. L. (2011). Publishing action research in counseling journals. *Journal of Counseling and Development, 89*, 282–287.

Guinan, J., & Foulds, M. (1970). Marathon groups: Facilitator of personal growth? *Journal of Consulting Psychology, 17*, 145–149.

Gumper, L. L., & Sprenkle, D. H. (1981). Privileged communication in therapy: Special problems for the family and couples therapist. *Family Process, 20*, 11–23.

Gunning, S., & Holmes, T. (1973). Dance therapy with psychotic children. *Archives of General Psychiatry, 28*, 707–713.

Gurman, A. S., & Kniskern, D. P. (1981). Family therapy outcome research: Knowns and unknowns.

In A. S. Gurman & D. P. Kniskern (Eds.), *Handbook of family therapy* (pp. 742–773). New York, NY: Brunner/Mazel.

Gushue, G. V., Constantine, M. D., & Sciarra, D. T. (2008). The influence of culture, self-reported multicultural counseling competence, and shifting standards of judgment on perceptions of family functioning of white family counselors. *Journal of Counseling and Development, 86*(1), 85–94.

Gutterman, J. T. (1996). Doing mental health counseling: A social constructionist re-vision. *Journal of Mental Health Counseling, 18*(3), 228–252.

Gutterman, J. T., & Kirk, M. A. (1999). Mental health counseling and the Internet. *Journal of Mental Health Counseling, 21*(4), 309–325.

Gysbers, N. C. (1988). Career guidance: A professional heritage and future challenge. In G. R. Walz & J. C. Bleuer (Eds.), *Building strong school counseling programs* (pp. 99–121). Alexandria, VA: American Association for Counseling and Development.

Gysbers, N. C. (2004). Counseling psychology and school psychology partnership: Overlooked? Underutilized? But needed! *The Counseling Psychologist, 32,* 235–244.

Gysbers, N. C., & Henderson, P. (1988). *Developing and managing your school guidance program.* Alexandria, VA: American Association for Counseling and Development.

Gysbers, N. C., & Henderson, P. (2012). *Developing and managing your school guidance and counseling program* (5th ed.). Alexandria, VA: American Counseling Association.

Gysbers, N. C., Heppner, M. J., & Johnson, J. A. (1998). *Career counseling: Process issues and techniques.* Needham Heights, MA: Allyn & Bacon.

Gysbers, N. C., & Moore, E. J. (1987). *Career counseling: Skills and techniques for practitioners.* Englewood Cliffs, NJ: Prentice-Hall.

Haase, J. E., Britt, T., Coward, D. D., Kline, N., & Penn, P. E. (1992). Simultaneous analysis of spiritual perspective, hope, acceptance and self-transcendence. *Images, 24*(2), 141–147.

Hackett, G., & Betz, N. E. (1981). A self-efficacy approach to the career development of women. *Journal of Vocational Behavior, 18,* 326–339.

Hackett, G., & Byars, A. M. (1996). Social cognitive theory and the career development of African American women. *Career Development Quarterly, 4*(4), 322–340.

Hackman, H. W., & Claiborn, C. D. (1982). An attributional approach to counselor attractiveness. *Journal of Counseling Psychology, 29,* 224–231.

Hage, S. M., Romano, J. L., Conyne, R. K., Kenny, M., Matthews, C., Schwartz, J. P., & Waldo, M. (2007). Best practice guidelines on prevention practice, research, training, and social advocacy for psychologists. *The Counseling Psychologist, 35*(4), 493–566.

Hale, S. (1990). Sitting on memory's lap. *The Arts in Psychotherapy, 17*(3), 269, 274.

Haley, J. (1963). *Strategies of psychotherapy.* New York, NY: Grune & Stratton.

Haley, J. (1971). Approaches to family therapy. In J. Haley (Ed.), *Changing families: A family therapy reader* (pp. 227–236). New York, NY: Grune & Stratton.

Haley, J. (1973). *Uncommon psychiatric techniques of Milton H. Erickson.* New York, NY: Norton.

Haley, J. (1976). *Problem-solving therapy.* San Francisco, CA: Jossey-Bass.

Haley, J. (1980). *Leaving home.* New York, NY: McGraw-Hill.

Haley, J. (1984). *Ordeal therapy: Unusual ways to change behavior.* San Francisco, CA: Jossey-Bass.

Haley, M., & Vazquez, J. (2009). Technology and counseling. In D. Capuzzi & D. R. Gross (Eds.). *Introduction to the counseling profession* (5th ed.; pp. 156–186).Upper Saddle River, NJ: Merrill, Pearson.

Haley-Banez, L., Brown, S., & Molina, B. (1998). *Association for specialists in group work: Principles for diversity-competent group workers.* Alexandria, VA: American Counseling Association.

Hall, A. S., & Lin, M. J. (1994). An integrative consultation framework: A practical tool for elementary school counselors. *Elementary School Guidance and Counseling, 29*(1), 16–27.

Hall, C. S. (1954). *A primer of Freudian psychology.* New York, NY: World.

Hall, C. S., & Lindzey, G. (1978). *Theories of personality* (3rd ed.). New York, NY: John Wiley & Sons.

Hall, G. S. (1904). *Adolescence.* New York, NY: Appleton.

Hamachek, D. (1995). Self-concept and school achievement: Interaction dynamics and a tool for assessing the self-concept component. *Journal of Counseling and Development, 73*(4), 419–425.

Hamann, E. E. (1994). Clinicians and diagnosis: Ethical concerns and clinician competence. *Journal of Counseling and Development, 72*(3), 259–260.

Hamilton, M. (1960). A rating scale for depression. *Journal of Neurology and Neuroscience, 23,* 56–62.

Hammen, C., & Rudolph, K. D. (2003). Childhood mood disorders. In E. R. Mash & R. A. Barkley (Eds.), *Child psychopathology* (pp. 233–278). New York, NY: Guilford Press.

Hammer, C., & Zupan, B. A. (1984). Self-schemas, depression, and the processing of personal information in children. *Journal of Experimental Child Psychology, 37,* 598–608.

Hammond, J. (1981). *Group counseling for children of divorce: A guide for the elementary school.* Ann Arbor, MI: Cranbrook.

Hammond, W. R., & Yung, B. (1993). Psychology's role in the public health response to assaultive violence among young African-American men. *American Psychologist, 48*(2), 142–154.

Hannon, K. (1996, May 13). Upset? Try cybertherapy. *U.S. News and World Report, 120,* 81–83.

Hansen, J. C., & Campbell, D. P. (1985). *Manual for the* SVIB-SCII (4th ed.). Palo Alto, CA: Consulting Psychologists Press.

Hansen, J. C., Himes, B. S., & Meier, S. (1990). *Consultation: Concepts and practices.* Englewood Cliffs, NJ: Prentice-Hall.

Hansen, J. T. (2002). Postmodern implications for theoretical integration of counseling approaches. *Journal of Counseling and Development, 80,* 315–321.

Hanson, W. E., Creswell, J. W., Plano Clark, V. L., Petska, K. S., & Creswell, J. D. (2005). Mixed methods research designs in counseling psychology. *Journal of Counseling Psychology, 52*(2), 224–236.

Hardesty, P. H., & Dillard, J. M. (1994). The role of elementary school counselors compared with their middle and secondary school counterparts. *Elementary School Guidance and Counseling, 29*(2), 83–91.

Hardman, M. L., Drew, C. J., Egan, M. W., & Wolf, B. (2002). *Human exceptionality* (7th ed.). Boston, MA: Allyn & Bacon.

Harmon, L. W. (1996). A moving target: The widening gap between theory and practice. In M. L. Savickas & W. B. Walsh (Eds.), *Handbook of career counseling theory and practice* (pp. 37–44). Palo Alto, CA: Davies-Black.

Harmon, L. W., Hansen, J. C., Borgen, F. H., & Hammer, A. L. (1994). *Strong Interest Inventory: Application and technical guide.* Palo Alto, CA: Consulting Psychologists Press.

Harrar, L. (Producer). (1984). *Make my people live: The crises in Indian health* [Television broadcast]. Boston, MA: Public Broadcasting System, NOVA.

Harris, A. H. S., Thoresen, C. E., & Lopez, S. J. (2007). Integrating positive psychology into counseling: Why and (when appropriate) how. *Journal of Counseling and Development, 85*(1), 3–13.

Harris, A. S. (1996). *Living with paradox: An introduction to Jungian psychology.* Pacific Grove, CA: Brooks/Cole.

Harris, D. E. (1963). *Children's drawings as measures of intellectual maturity: A revision and extension of the Goodenough Draw-A-Man Test.* San Diego, CA: Harcourt Brace Jovanovich.

Harris, H. L. (2013). Counseling single-parent multiracial families. *The Family Journal: Counseling and Therapy for Couples and Families, 21,* 386–395.

Harris, T. (1967). *I'm OK—You're OK.* New York, NY: Harper & Row.

Hart, S. N., & Brassard, M. R. (1987). A major threat to children's mental health: Psychological maltreatment. *American Psychologist, 42,* 160–165.

Havens, L. (1994). Some suggestions for making research more applicable to clinical practice. In P. F. Talley, H. H. Strupp, & S. F. Butler (Eds.), *Psychotherapy research and practice: Bridging the gap* (pp. 88–98). New York, NY: Basic Books.

Havighurst, R. J. (1972). *Developmental tasks and education* (3rd ed.). New York, NY: David McKay.

Haviland, M. G., & Hansen, J. C. (1987). Criterion validity of the Strong-Campbell Interest Inventory for American Indian college students. *Measurement and Evaluation in Counseling and Development, 19,* 196–201.

Hawkins, J. D., Herrenkohl, T. I., Farrington, D. P., Brewer, D., Catalano, R. F., Harachi, T. W., & Cothern, L. (2000). Predictors of youth violence. *Juvenile Justice Bulletin, 32,* 1–11.

Hayes, S. C., Follette, V. M., & Linehan, M. M. (2004). *Mindfulness and acceptance: Expanding the cognitive-behavioral tradition.* New York, NY: Guilford Press.

Hayes, S. C., Strosahl, K. D., & Wilson, K. G. (2012). *Acceptance and commitment therapy: The process and practice of mindful change* (2nd ed.). New York, NY: Guilford Press.

Hayes, S. G. (1995). Infusing diversity into family and couples counseling. *The Family Journal: Counseling and Therapy for Couples and Families, 3*(3), 231–233.

Hays, D. G., & Wood, C. (2011). Infusing qualitative traditions in counseling research designs. *Journal of Counseling and Development, 89*(3), 288–295.

Hazan, C., & Shaver, P. R. (1990). Love and work: An attachment-theoretical perspective. *Journal of Personality and Social Psychology, 59,* 270–280.

Hazelrigg, M. D., Cooper, H. M., & Borduin, C. M. (1987). Evaluating the effectiveness of family therapies: An integrative review and analysis. *Psychological Bulletin, 101*(3), 428–442.

Hazzard, A., King, H. E., & Webb, C. (1986). Group therapy with sexually abused adolescent girls. *American Journal of Psychotherapy, 40*(2), 213–223.

Heinlen, K. T., Welfel, E. R., Richmond, E. N., & Rak, C. F. (2003). The scope of Web-Counseling: A survey of services and compliance with NBCC Standards for the Ethical Practice of Web-Counseling. *Journal of Counseling and Development, 81,* 61–69.

Heinze, A., & Rotatori, A. F. (1986). Counseling the visually handicapped child. In A. F. Rotatori, P. J. Gerber, F. W. Litton, & R. A. Fox (Eds.), *Counseling exceptional students* (pp. 179–196). New York, NY: Human Sciences Press.

Helms, J. E. (1986). Expanding racial identity theory to cover the counseling process. *Journal of Counseling Psychology, 33,* 62–64.

Helms, J. E. (1989). At long last: Paradigms for cultural psychology research. *The Counseling Psychologist, 17,* 98–100.

Helms, J. E. (1995). An update of Helms's white and people of color racial identity models. In J. G. Ponterotto, J. M. Casas, L. A. Suzuki, & C. M. Alexander (Eds.), *Handbook of multicultural counseling* (pp. 181–198). Thousand Oaks, CA: SAGE.

Helwig, A. A., & Holicky, R. (1994). Substance abuse in persons with disabilities: Treatment considerations. *Journal of Counseling and Development, 72*(3), 227–233.

Henderson, S., Hesketh, B., & Tuffin, K. (1988). A test of Gottfredson's theory of circumscription. *Journal of Vocational Behavior, 32,* 37–48.

Henry, W. P., Strupp, H. H., Schacht, T. E., & Gaston, L. (1994). Psychodynamic approaches. In A. E. Bergin & S. L. Garfield (Eds.), *Handbook of psychotherapy and behavior change* (4th ed.; pp. 467–508). New York, NY: John Wiley & Sons.

Heppner, M. J., & Johnston, J. A. (1985). Computerized career guidance and information systems: Guidelines for selection. *Journal of College Students Personnel, 26,* 156–163.

Heppner, P. P., Casas, J. M., Carter, J., & Stone, G. L. (2000). The maturation counseling psychology: Multifaceted perspectives, 1978–1998. In S. D. Brown & R. W. Lent (Eds.), *Handbook of counseling psychology* (3rd ed.; pp. 3–49). New York, NY: John Wiley & Sons.

Heppner, P. P., & Claiborn, C. D. (1989). Social influence research in counseling: A review and critique [Monograph]. *Journal of Counseling Psychology, 36,* 365–387.

Heppner, P. P., & Dixon, D. N. (1981). A review of the interpersonal influence process in counseling. *Personnel and Guidance Journal, 59,* 542–550.

Heppner, P. P., & Heesacker, M. (1983). Perceived counselor characteristics, client expectations, and client satisfaction with counseling. *Journal of Counseling Psychology, 30,* 31–39.

Heppner, P. P., & Krauskopf, C. J. (1987). An information processing approach to personal problem solving. *The Counseling Psychologist, 15,* 371–447.

Heppner, P. P., & Petersen, C. H. (1982). The development and implications of a personal problem-solving inventory. *Journal of Counseling Psychology, 29,* 66–75.

Heppner, P. P., Rogers, M. E., & Lee, L. A. (1984). Carl Rogers: Reflections on his life. *Journal of Counseling and Development, 63,* 14–20.

Heppner, P. P., Witty, T. E., & Dixon, W. A. (2004). Problem-solving appraisal and human adjustment: A review of 20 years of research using the problem solving inventory. *The Counseling Psychologist, 32,* 344–428.

Herjanic, B., & Reich, W. (1982). Development of a structured psychiatric interview for children: Agreement between child and parent of individual symptoms. *Journal of Abnormal Child Psychology, 10,* 307–324.

Herlihy, B., & Sheeley, V. L. (1987). Privileged communication in selected helping professions: A comparison among statutes. *Journal of Counseling and Development, 65*(9), 479–483.

Herman, K. C. (1993). Reassessing predictors of therapist competence. *Journal of Counseling and Development, 72,* 29–32.

Herr, E. L. (1996). Toward the convergence of career theory and practice: Mythology, issues, and possibilities. In M. L. Savickas & W. B. Walsh (Eds.), *Handbook of career counseling theory and practice* (pp. 13–36). Palo Alto, CA: Davies-Black.

Herring, R. D. (1990). Nonverbal communication: A necessary component of cross-cultural counseling. *Journal of Multicultural Counseling and Development, 18*(4), 172–179.

Herring, R. D. (1994). Substance use among Native American Indian youth: A selected review of causality. *Journal of Counseling and Development, 72*(6), 578–584.

Herrington, B. S. (1979). Privilege denial in joint therapy. *Psychiatric News, 14*(1), 1–9.

Hershenson, D. B., & Power, P. W. (1987). *Mental health counseling.* New York, NY: Pergamon Press.

Hershenson, D. B., Power, P. W., & Waldo, M. (1996). *Community counseling: Contemporary theory and practice.* Needham Heights, MA: Allyn & Bacon.

Hertlein, K. M., Blumer, M. L. C., & Mihaloliakos, J. H. (2015). Marriage and family counselors' perceived ethical issues related to online therapy. *The Family Journal: Counseling and Therapy for Couples and Families, 23,* 5–12.

Hesketh, B., Elmslie, S., & Kaldor, W. (1990). Career compromises: An alternative account to Gottfredson's theory. *Journal of Counseling Psychology, 37*(1), 49–56.

Hill, C. E. (1992). An overview of four measures developed to test the Hill process model: Therapist intentions, therapist response modes, client reactions, and client behaviors. *Journal of Counseling and Development, 70,* 728–737.

Hill, C. E., & Corbett, M. M. (1993). A perspective on the history of process and outcome research in counseling psychology. *Journal of Counseling Psychology, 40*(1), 3–24.

Hill, C .E., Knox, S., Thompson, B. J., Williams, E. N., Hess, S. A., & Ladany, N. (2005). Consensual qualitative research: An update. *Journal of Counseling Psychology, 52,* 196–205.

Hill, C. E., Tanney, M. F., & Leonard, M. M. (1977). Counselor reactions to

female clients: Type of problem, age of client, and sex of counselor. *Journal of Counseling Psychology, 24,* 60–65.

Hill, C. E., Thompson, B. J., & Williams, E. N. (1997). A guide to conducting consensual qualitative research. *The Counseling Psychologist, 25*(4), 517–572.

Hilton, T. L. (1962). Career decision making. *Journal of Counseling Psychology, 9,* 291–298.

Hines, M. (1988). Similarities and differences in group and family therapy. *Journal for Specialists in Group Work, 13*(4), 173–179.

Hines, P. L., & Fields, T. H. (2002). Pregroup screening issues for school counselors. *Journal for Specialists in Group Work, 27,* 358–376.

Hipolito-Delgado, C. P. (April, 2014). Beyond cultural competence. *Counseling Today,* 50–55.

Hobson, S. M., & Kanitz, H. M. (1996). Multicultural counseling: An ethical issue for school counselors. *The School Counselor, 43*(4), 245–255.

Hoffmann, T., Dana, R., & Bolton, B. (1985). Measured acculturation and MMPI-168 performance of Native American adults. *Journal of Cross-Cultural Psychology, 16,* 243–256.

Hohenshil, T. H. (1996). Editorial: Role of assessment and diagnosis in counseling. *Journal of Counseling and Development, 75*(1), 64–67.

Holland, J. L. (1973). *Making vocational choices: A theory of careers.* Englewood Cliffs, NJ: Prentice-Hall.

Holland, J. L. (1985a). *Making vocational choices: A theory of vocational personalities and work environments* (2nd ed.). Englewood Cliffs, NJ: Prentice-Hall.

Holland, J. L. (1985b). *Manual for the Vocational Preference Inventory.* Odessa, FL: Psychological Assessment Resources.

Holland, J. L. (1994). *Self-directed search.* Odessa, FL: Psychological Assessment Resources.

Holland, J. L. (1996). Exploring careers with a typology: What we have learned and some new directions. *American Psychologist, 51*(4), 397–406.

Holland, J. L. (1997). *Making vocational choices: A theory of vocational personalities and work environments* (3rd ed.). Odessa, FL: Psychological Assessment Resources.

Holland, J. L., Daieger, D. C., & Power, P. G. (1980). Some diagnostic scales for research in decision making and personality: Identity information and barriers. *Journal of Personality and Social Psychology, 39,* 1191–1200.

Holland, J. L., Johnston, J. A., & Asama, N. F. (1994). More evidence for the relationship between Holland's personality types and personality variables. *Journal of Career Assessment, 2,* 331–340.

Hollingdale, R. J. (1978). *Twilight of the idols and the anti-Christ.* New York, NY: Penguin Books.

Hollon, S. D., & Beck, A. T. (1994). Cognitive and cognitive behavioral therapies. In A. E. Bergin & S. L. Garfield, *Handbook of psychotherapy and behavioral change* (4th ed.; pp. 428–466). New York, NY: John Wiley & Sons.

Hollon, S. D., DeRubeis, R. J., Evans, M. D., Wiemer, M. J., Garvey, M. J., Grove, W. M., & Tuason, V. B. (1992). Cognitive therapy and pharmacotherapy for depression: Singly and in combination. *Archives of General Psychiatry, 49,* 774–781.

Hollon, S. D., DeRubeis, R. J., Shelton, R. C., Amsterdam, J. D., Salomon, R. M., O'Reardon, J. P., . . . Gallop, R. (2005). Prevention of relapse following cognitive therapy vs. medication in moderate to severe depression. *Archives of General Psychiatry, 62,* 417–422.

Hollon, S. D., Evans, M. D., & DeRubeis, R. (1983). The cognitive-pharmacotherapy project: Study design, outcome, and clinical follow-up. Paper presented at the World Congress of Behavior Therapy, Washington, DC.

Holt, P. A. (1989). Differential effects of status and interest in the process of compromise. *Journal of Counseling Psychology, 36,* 42–47.

Homans, G. C. (1962). *Sentiments and activities.* New York, NY: The Free Press of Glencoe.

Honeyman, A. (1990). Perceptual changes in addicts as a consequence of reality therapy based on group treatment. *Journal of Reality Therapy, 9*(2), 53–59.

hooks, b. (1995). *Killing rage: Ending racism.* New York, NY: Henry Holt.

Hooyman, N. R. & Kiyak, H. A. (2005). *Social gerontology: A multidisciplinary perspective* (7th ed.). Boston, MA: Allyn & Bacon.

Horne, A. M. (1993). Editorial: Telling stories: The ecosystem model. *Journal for Specialists in Group Work, 18,* 98.

Horne, A. M. (1995). Changes and challenges in group work. *Journal for Specialists in Group Work, 20*(2), 67–68.

Horne, A. M. (1996). The changing world of group work. *Journal for Specialists in Group Work, 21*(1), 2–3.

Horne, A. M., & Ohlsen, M. M. (1982). Introduction: The family and family counseling. In M. Horne & M. M. Ohlsen (Eds.), *Family counseling and therapy.* Itasca, IL: F. E. Peacock.

Horst, E. A. (1995). Reexamining gender issues in Erikson's stages of identity and intimacy. *Journal of Counseling and Development, 73*(3), 271–278.

Hoshmand, L. L. S. (1989). Alternate research paradigms: A review and teaching proposal. *The Counseling Psychologist, 17,* 3–80.

Hoshmand, L. T. (1985). Phenomenological-based groups for developmentally disabled adults. *Journal of Counseling and Development, 64*(2), 147–148.

Hosie, T. W., West, J. D., & MacKey, J. A. (1988). Employment and roles of mental health counselors in substance-abuse centers. *Journal of Mental Health Counseling, 10*(3), 188–198.

Howard, G. S. (1991). Culture tales: A narrative approach to thinking, cross-cultural psychology, and psychotherapy. *American Psychologist, 46*(3), 187–197.

Huba, G. J., & Bentler, P. M. (1983). Causal models of the development of law abidance and its relationship to psychosocial factors and drug use. In W. S. Lauger & J. M. Day (Eds.), *Personality theory, moral development, and criminal behavior* (pp. 164–215). Lexington, MA: Lexington Books.

Hubbard, R. L., Brownlee, R. F., & Anderson, R. (1988). Initiation of alcohol and drug abuse in the middle school years. *Elementary School Guidance & Counseling, 23,* 118.

Hubble, M. A., Duncan, B. L., & Miller, S. D. (1999). *The heart and soul of change: What works in therapy.* Washington, DC: American Psychological Association.

Huebner, L. A. (1980). Interaction of student and campus. In E. Delworth, G. Hanson, & Associates (Eds.), *Student services: A handbook for the profession* (pp. 117–155). San Francisco, CA: Jossey-Bass.

Huey, W. (1986). Ethical concerns in school counseling. *Journal of Counseling and Development, 64*(5), 321–322.

Hughey, K. F., Gysbers, N. C., & Starr, M. (1993). Evaluating comprehensive school guidance programs. *The School Counselor, 41*(1), 31–35.

Humphrey, F. G. (1983). *Marital therapy.* Englewood Cliffs, NJ: Prentice-Hall.

Hutchinson, R. L., Barrick, A. L., & Groves, M. (1986). Functions of secondary school counselors in the public schools: Ideal and actual. *The School Counselor, 34*(2), 87–91.

Hyldahl, R. S., & Richardson, B. (2011). Key considerations for using no-harm contracts with clients who self-injure. *Journal of Counseling and Development, 89,* 121–127.

Ibrahim, F. A. (1991). Contribution of cultural world view to generic counseling and development. *Journal of Counseling and Development, 70*(1), 13–19.

Ibrahim, F. A. (1993). Existential world view theory: Transcultural counseling. In J. McFadden (Ed.), *Transactional counseling* (pp. 23–57). Alexandria, VA: American Counseling Association.

Ibrahim, F. A., & Kahn, H. (1984). *Scale to assess world views.* Unpublished manuscript, University of Connecticut, Storrs, CT.

Ibrahim, F. A., & Kahn, H. (1987). Assessment of world views. *Psychological Reports, 60,* 163–176.

Ingersoll, R. E. (1995). Spirituality, religion, and counseling: Dimensions and relationships. In M. T. Burke & J. G. Miranti (Eds.), *Counseling: The spiritual dimension* (pp. 5–18). Alexandria, VA: American Counseling Association.

Irwin, E. C. (1987). Drama: The play's the thing. *Elementary School Guidance and Counseling, 21*(4), 276–283.

Isenberg-Grzeda, C. (1988). Music therapy assessment: A reflection of professional identity. *Journal of Music Therapy, 25*(3), 156–169.

Ivey, A. (1971). *Microcounseling: Innovations in interviewing training.* Springfield, IL: Charles C. Thomas.

Ivey, A. (1986). *Developmental therapy: Theory and practice.* San Francisco, CA: Jossey-Bass.

Ivey, A. (1989). Mental health counseling: A developmental process and profession. *Journal of Mental Health Counseling, 11*(1), 26–35.

Ivey, A. (1996, June). The spirit and the challenge: Postmodernity or reality? *Counseling Today,* 33.

Ivey, A. E. , Ivey, M. B., & Zalaquett, C. P. (2010). *Intentional interviewing and counseling: Facilitating client development in a multicultural society* (7th ed.). Belmont, CA: Brooks/Cole, Cengage Learning.

Jacobs, E., Masson, R., Harvill, R., & Schimmel, C. (2012). *Group counseling: Strategies and skills* (7th ed.), Belmont, CA: Brooks/Cole, Cengage Learning.

James, M. R. (1988). Music therapy values clarification: A positive influence on perceived locus of control. *Journal of Music Therapy, 25*(4), 206–215.

James, R. K., & Gilliland, B. E. (2013). *Crisis intervention strategies* (7th ed.). Belmont, CA: Broosks/Cole.

Jepsen, D. A. (1996). Relationships between developmental career counseling theory and practice. In M. L. Savickas & W. B. Walsh (Eds.), *Handbook of career counseling theory and practice.* Palo Alto, CA: Davies-Black.

Jewell, D. A. (1989). Cultural and ethnic issues. In S. Wetzler & M. M. Katz (Eds.), *Contemporary approaches to psychological assessment* (pp. 299–309). New York, NY: Brunner/Mazel.

Johanson, G. (2006). A survey of mindfulness in psychotherapy. *Annals of the American Psychotherapy Association,* 15–24.

Johnson, A. C. (1995). Resiliency mechanisms in culturally diverse families. *The Family Journal: Counseling and Therapy for Couples and Families, 3*(4), 316–324.

Johnson, D. R. (1984a). Establishing the creative arts therapies as an independent profession. *The Arts in Psychotherapy,* 11, 209–212.

Johnson, D. R. (1984b). Perspectives, projects, and training facilities. *Journal of Mental Imagery, 7*(1), 105–109.

Johnson, E., Baker, S. B., Kapola, M., Kiselica, M. S., & Thompson, E. C., III. (1989). Counseling self-efficacy and counseling competency in prepracticum training. *Counselor Education and Supervision,* 28, 205–218.

Johnson, I. H., Torres, J. S., Coleman, V. D., & Smith, M. C. (1995). Issues and strategies in leading cultural diverse counseling groups. *Journal for Specialists in Group Work, 20*(3), 143–150.

Johnson, V. E. (1986). *Intervention: A professional guide.* Minneapolis, MN: Johnson Institute.

Johnson, W. B., & Campbell, C. D. (2004). Character and fitness requirements for professional psychologists: Training directors' perspectives. *Professional Psychology: Research and Practice, 35*(4), 405–411.

Johnston, J. A., Buescher, K. L., & Heppner, M. J. (1988). Computerized career information

and guidance systems: Caveat emptor. *Journal of Counseling and Development, 57*(1), 39–41.

Johnston, V. S., & Oliver-Rodriguez, J. C. (1997). Facial beauty and the late positive component of event-related potential. *Journal of Sex Research, 34*(2), 188–198.

Jones, A. S., & Gelso, C. J. (1988). Differential effects of style of interpretation: Another look. *Journal of Counseling Psychology, 35,* 363–369.

Jones, J. V., Jr. (1995). Constructivism and individual psychology: Common ground for dialogue. *Individual Psychology: The Journal of Adlerian Theory, Research, and Practice, 51*(3), 231–243.

Jongsma, A. E., & Petersen, L. M. (1995). *The complete psychotherapy treatment planner.* New York, NY: John Wiley & Sons.

Josephson Institute of Ethics. (2001). *Josephson Institute of Ethics report card on the ethics of American youth 2000. Report #1: Violence, guns, and alcohol.* Marina del Rey, CA: Author.

Jourard, S. M. (1958). *Personal adjustment: An approach through the study of healthy personality.* New York, NY: Macmillan.

Juhnke, G. A., & Osborne, W. L. (1997). The solution-focused debriefing group: An integrated postviolence group intervention for adults. *Journal for Specialists in Group Work, 22*(1), 66–76.

Jung, C. G. (1928). *Contributions to analytic psychology* (H. G. Baynes & C. Baynes, Trans.). New York, NY: Harcourt.

Jung, C. G. (1959). *The archetypes and the collective unconscious* (R. F. C. Hull, Trans.). New York, NY: Pantheon.

Kabat-Zinn, J. (2003). Mindfulness-based interventions in context:

Past, present, and future. *American Psychological Association, 10*(2), 144–156.

Kadushin, A., & Martin, J. A. (1981). *Child abuse: An interactional event.* New York, NY: Columbia University Press.

Kandel, D. B. (1973). Adolescent marijuana use: Role of parents and peers. *Science, 181,* 1067–1081.

Kanfer, F. H., & Busemeyer, J. R. (1982). The use of problem solving and decision making in behavior therapy. *Clinical Psychology Review, 2,* 239–266.

Kanfer, F. H., & Goldstein, A. P. (1986). Introduction. In F. H. Kanfer & A. P. Goldstein (Eds.), *Helping people change: A textbook of methods* (3rd ed.; pp. 1–18). New York, NY: Pergamon.

Kanner, L. (1962). *Child psychiatry* (3rd ed.). Springfield, IL: Charles C. Thomas.

Kaplan, D. M. (2014). Ethical implications of a critical legal case for the counseling profession. *Ward v. Wilbanks. Journal of Counseling and Development, 92,* 142–146.

Kaplan, D. M., & Gladding, S. T. (2011). A vision for the future of counseling: The 20/20 principles for unifying and strengthening the profession. *Journal of Counseling and Development, 89,* 367–372.

Kaplan, D. M., Tarvydas, V. M., & Gladding, S. T. (2014). 20/20: A vision for the future of counseling: The new consensus definition of counseling. *Journal of Counseling and Development, 92,* 366–372.

Kaplan, L. S., & Geoffroy, K. E. (1990). Enhancing the school climate: New opportunities for the counselor. *The School Counselor, 38,* 7–12.

Karlin, B. E., & Cross, G. (2014). From the laboratory to the therapy room: National dissemination and implementation of evidence-based psychotherapies in the U.S. Department of Veterans Affairs health care system. *American Psychologist, 69,* 19–33.

Kaufmann, F. A., Castellanos, Z. F., & Rotatori, A. F. (1986). Counseling the gifted child. In A. F. Rotatori, P. J. Gerber, F. W. Litton, & R. A. Fox (Eds.), *Counseling exceptional students.* New York, NY: Human Sciences Press.

Kaufmann, Y. (1989). Analytical psychotherapy. In R. J. Corsini (Ed.), *Current psychotherapies* (4th ed.; pp. 119–154). Itasca, IL: F. E. Peacock.

Kazdin, A. E. (1978). *History of behavior modification: Experimental foundations of contemporary research.* Baltimore, MD: University Park Press.

Kazdin, A. E. (1985). *Treatment of antisocial behavior in children and adolescents.* Homewood, IL: Dorsey Press.

Kazdin, A. E. (1987). Treatment of antisocial behavior in children: Current status and future directions. *Psychological Bulletin, 102,* 187–203.

Kazdin, A. E. (1988). Childhood depression. In E. J. Mash & L. Terdal (Eds.), *Behavioral assessment of childhood disorders* (2nd ed.; pp. 157–196). New York, NY: Guilford Press.

Kazdin, A. E. (1989). Developmental psychopathology: Current research, issues, and directions. *American Psychologist, 44*(2), 180–187.

Kazdin, A. E. (1993). Adolescent mental health: Prevention and treatment programs. *American Psychologist, 48*(2), 127–141.

Kazdin, A. E., Bass, D., Ayers, W. A., & Rodgers, A. (1990). Empirical and clinical focus of child and adolescent psychotherapy research. *Journal of Consulting and Clinical Psychology, 58,* 729–740.

Kazdin, A. E., Bass, D., Siegel, T., & Thomas, C. (1989). Cognitive-behavioral therapy and relationship therapy in the treatment of children referred for antisocial behavior. *Journal of Consulting and Clinical Psychology, 57*(4), 522–535.

Keeton, W. P. (1984). *Prosser and Keeton on the law of torts* (5th ed.). St. Paul, MN: West.

Kelley, R. H., & Rotatori, A. F. (1986). Counseling the language-disordered child. In A. F. Rotatori, P. J. Gerber, F. W. Litton, & R. A. Fox (Eds.), *Counseling exceptional students.* New York, NY: Human Sciences Press.

Kelly, K. R. (1996). Looking to the future: Professional identity, accountability, and change. *Journal of Mental Health Counseling, 18*(3), 195–199.

Kelly, K. R. (1999). Coda: A contextual perspective on the future of mental health counseling. *Journal of Mental Health Counseling, 21*(3), 302–307.

Kemp, C. G. (1971). Existential counseling. *The Counseling Psychologist, 2,* 2–28.

Kennell, S. E., & Rotatori, A. F. (1986). Counseling the abused child. In A. F. Rotatori, P. J. Gerber, F. W. Litton, & R. A. Fox (Eds.), *Counseling exceptional students.* New York, NY: Human Sciences Press.

Kenny, A. (1987). An arts activity approach: Counseling the gifted, creative, and talented. *The Gifted Child Today, 10*(3), 22–37.

Kenny, M. E., Waldo, M., Warter, E. H., & Barton, C. (2002). School-linked: Theory, science, and practice for enhancing the lives of children and youth. *The Counseling Psychologist, (30)*5, 726–748.

Kernberg, O. F. (1976). *Object-relations theory and clinical psychoanalysis.* New York, NY: Jason Aronson.

Kerwin, C., & Ponterotto, J. G. (1995). Biracial identity development: Theory and research. In J. G. Ponterotto, J. M. Casas, L. A. Suzuki, & C. M. Alexander (Eds.), *Handbook of multicultural counseling* (pp. 181–198). Thousand Oaks, CA: SAGE.

Kessler, S. (1979, November). Counselor as mediator. *The Personnel and Guidance Journal,* 194–197.

Kidder, L. H., Judd, C. M., & Smith, E. R. (1986). *Research methods in social relations.* New York, NY: Holt, Rinehart & Winston.

Kim, B. C. (1981). *New urban immigrants: The Korean community in New York.* Princeton, NJ: Princeton University Press.

Kim, B. S. K., Cartwright, B. Y., Asay, P. A., & D'Andrea, M. J. (2003). A revision of the Multicultural Awareness, Knowledge, and Skills Survey–Counselor Edition. *Measurement and Evaluation in Counseling and Development, 36,* 161–180.

Kim, B. S., Hill, C. E., Gelso, C. J., Goates, M. K., Asay, P. A., & Harbin, J. M. (2003). Counselor self-disclosure: East Asian American client adherence to Asian cultural values and counseling process. *Journal of Counseling Psychology, 50,* 324–332.

Kim, B. S., & Abreu, J. M. (2001). Acculturation measurement: Theory, current instruments, and future directions. In J. G. Ponterotto, J. M. Casas, L. A. Suzuki, and C. M. Alexander (Eds.), *Handbook of multicultural counseling* (2nd ed.; pp. 394–424). Thousand Oaks, CA: SAGE.

Kirk, M. A. (1997, January). Current perceptions of counseling and counselor education in cyberspace. *Counseling Today, 39,* 17–18.

Kiselica, M. S., & Look, C. (1993). Mental health counseling and prevention: Disparity between philosophy and practice? *Journal of Mental Health Counseling, 15*(1), 3–14.

Kitchener, K. S. (1984). Ethics in counseling psychology: Distinctions and directions. *Counseling Psychologist, 12,* 15–18.

Kitchener, K. S. (1985). Ethical principles and ethical decisions in student affairs. In H. J. Canon & R. D. Brown (Eds.), *Applied ethics: Tools for practitioners.* San Francisco, CA: Jossey-Bass.

Kitchener, K. S., & Anderson, S. K. (2000). Ethical issues in counseling psychology: Old themes—new problems. In S. D. Brown & R. W. Lent (Eds.), *Handbook of counseling psychology* (3rd ed.; pp. 50–82). New York, NY: John Wiley & Sons.

Kitchur, M., & Bell, R. (1989). Group psychotherapy with preadolescent sexual abuse victims: A literature review and description of an inner-city group. *International Journal of Group Psychotherapy, 39*(3), 285–310.

Kivlighan, D. M. (1990). Relation between counselors' use of intentions and clients' perception of working alliance. *Journal of Counseling Psychology, 37,* 27–32.

Kivlighan, D. M., Johnston, J. A., Hogan, R. S., & Mauer, E. (1994). Who benefits from computerized career counseling? *Journal of Counseling and Development, 27*(3), 289–292.

Kivlighan, D. M., Jr., & Shapiro, R. M. (1987). Holland type as a predictor of benefit from self-help career counseling. *Journal of Counseling Psychology, 34*(3), 326–329.

Kjos, D. (1995). Linking career counseling to personality disorders. *Journal of Counseling and Development, 73*(6), 592–597.

Klein, M. (1960). *The psychoanalysis of children.* New York, NY: Grove Press.

Klerman, G. L., & Weissman, M. M. (Eds.) (1993). *New applications of interpersonal psychotherapy.* Washington, DC: American Psychiatric Press.

Kluger, J. (2001, June 18). How to manage teen drinking (the smart way). *Time,* 42–44.

Knapp, S. (1980). A primer on malpractice for psychologists. *Professional Psychology, 11,* 606–612.

Knoff, H. M., & Prout, H. T. (1985). *The kinetic drawing system for family and school.* Los Angeles, CA: Western Psychological Services.

Kobak, R. R., & Hazan, C. (1991). Attachment in marriage: Effects of security and accuracy of working models. *Journal of Personality and Social Psychology, 60,* 861–869.

Koenig, H. G. (1997). *Is religion good for your health? The effects of religion on physical and mental health.* New York, NY: Haworth Press.

Kohlberg, L. (1963). Development of children's orientation towards a moral order: 1. Sequence in the development of moral thought. *Vita Humana, 6,* 11–33.

Kohlberg, L. (1973). Continuities in childhood and adult moral development revisited. In P. B. Baltes & K. W. Schaie (Eds.), *Life-span developmental psychology: Personality and socialization* (179–204). New York, NY: Academic Press.

Kohlberg, L. (1981). *The philosophy of moral development.* New York, NY: Harper & Row.

Kohn-Wood, L. P. & Hooper, L. M. (2014). Cultural competency, culturally tailored care, and the primary care setting: Possible solutions to reduce racial/ethnic disparities in mental health care. *Journal of Mental Health Counseling, 36,* 173–188.

Kohut, H. (1971). *The analysis of the self.* New York, NY: International University Press.

Kokotovic, A. M., & Tracey, T. J. (1990). Working alliance in the early phase of counseling. *Journal of Counseling Psychology, 37,* 16–21.

Koopman, E. J. (1985). The education and training of mediators. In S. Grebs (Ed.), *Divorce and family mediation.* Rockville, MD: Aspen Systems.

Kopp, S. B. (1971). *Guru: Metaphors from a psychotherapist.* Palo Alto, CA: Science and Behavior Books.

Koss, M. P., & Shiang, J. (1994). Research on brief psychotherapy. In A. E. Bergin & S. L. Garfield (Eds.), *Handbook of psychotherapy and behavior change* (4th ed.). New York, NY: John Wiley & Sons.

Kottler, J. A. (1994). Working with difficult group members. *Journal for Specialists in Group Work, 19*(1), 3–10.

Kottler, J. A. (2004). *Introduction to counseling: Voices from the field* (5th ed.). Pacific Grove, CA: Brooks/Cole, Thomson Learning.

Kottler, J. A., & Brown, R. W. (2000). *Introduction to therapeutic counseling: Voices from the field* (4th ed.). Monterey, CA: Brooks/Cole.

Kottler, J. A., & Brown, R. W. (2004). *Introduction to therapeutic counseling: Voices from the field* (5th ed.). Pacific Grove, CA: Thomson-Brooks/Cole.

Kottler, J. A., & Montgomery, M. J. (2011). *Theories of counseling and therapy: An experiential approach* (2nd ed.). Thousand Oaks, CA: SAGE.

Kottman, T. (2003). *Partners in play: An Adlerian approach to play therapy* (2nd ed.). Alexandria, VA: American Counseling Association.

Kottman, T., & Johnson, V. (1993). Adlerian play therapy: A tool for school counselors. *Elementary School Guidance and Counseling, 28*(1), 42–51.

Kottman, T., Lingg, M., & Tisdell, T. (1995). Gay and lesbian adolescents: Implications for Adlerian therapists. *Individual Psychology: The Journal of Adlerian Theory, Research, and Practice, 51*(2), 114–128.

Kovacs, L. (1988). Couple therapy: An integrated developmental and family system model. *Family Therapy, 15*(2), 133–155.

Kovacs, M. (1982). *The Interview Schedule for Children (ISC).* Unpublished interview schedule, Department of Psychiatry, University of Pittsburgh, Pennsylvania.

Kovacs, M. (1989). Affective disorders in children and adolescents. *American Psychologist, 44,* 209–215.

Kovacs, M. (2003). *Children's Depression Inventory: Technical manual update.* North Tonawanda, NY: Multi-Health Systems.

Kovacs, M., Palauskas, S., Gatsonis, C. A., & Richards, C. (1988). Depressive disorders in childhood: III. A longitudinal study of comorbidity with and risk for conduct disorders. *Journal of Affective Disorders, 15,* 205–217.

Kovacs, M., Rush, A. J., Beck, A. T., & Hollon, S. D. (1981). Depressed outpatients treated with cognitive therapy or pharmacotherapy. *Archives of General Psychiatry, 38,* 33–39.

Kramer, E. (1987). Sublimation and art therapy. In J. A. Rubin (Ed.), *Approaches to art therapy: Theory and technique.* New York, NY: Brunner/Mazel.

Krasner, M. (2004). Mindfulness-based interventions: A coming of age? *Family, Systems, & Health, 22*(2), 207–212.

Krause, A. M., & Haverkamp, B. E. (1996). Attachment in adult child–older parent relationships: Research, theory, and practice. *Journal of Counseling and Development, 75*(2), 83–92.

Kristeller, J. L., & Thomas Johnson, T., (2005). Cultivating loving kindness: A two-stage model of the effects of meditation on empathy, compassion, and altruism. *Zygon, 40,* 391–408.

Kroll, J., & Sheehan, W. (1989). Religious beliefs and practices among fifty-two psychiatric inpatients in Minnesota. *American Journal of Psychiatry, 67–72,* 146.

Krumboltz, J. D. (1979). A social learning theory of career decision making. In A. M. Mitchell, F. B. Jones, & J. D. Krumboltz (Eds.), *Social learning theory and career decision making.* Cranston, RI: Carroll.

Krumboltz, J. D. (1994). The Career Beliefs Inventory. *Journal of Counseling and Development, 72*(4), 424–428.

Krumboltz, J. D. (1996). A learning theory of career counseling. In M. L. Savickas & W. B. Walsh (Eds.), *Handbook of career counseling theory and practice* (pp. 55–80). Palo Alto, CA: Davies-Black.

Krupp, J. (1982). *Mentoring as a means to personal growth and improved school climate: A research report.* Colchester, CT: Project Rise.

Kuder, G. F. (1964). *Kuder general interest survey: Manual.* Chicago, IL: Science Research Associates.

Kupersmidt, J. B., & Patterson, C. J. (1991). Childhood peer rejection, aggression, withdrawal, and perceived competence as predictors of self-reported behavior problems in preadolescence. *Journal of Abnormal Child Psychology, 19*, 437–449.

Kurpius, D. (1978). Consultation theory and process: An integrated model. *Personnel and Guidance Journal, 56*, 335–378.

L'Abate, L. (1986). *Systematic family therapy.* New York, NY: Brunner/ Mazel.

Labi, N. (2001, April 2). Let bullies beware. *Time*, 46–47.

La Crosse, M. B. (1980). Perceived counselor social influence and counseling outcomes: Validity of the Counselor Rating Form. *Journal of Counseling Psychology, 27*, 320–327.

La Fromboise, T. D., & Dixon, D. N. (1981). American Indian perceptions of trustworthiness in a counseling interview. *Journal of Counseling Psychology, 28*, 135–139.

LaFountain, R. M., Garner, N. E., & Eliason, G. T. (1996). Solution-focused counseling groups: A key for school counselors. *The School Counselor, 43*(4), 256–267.

Lamb, D. H. (1985). A time-frame model of termination in psychotherapy. *Psychotherapy, 22*, 604–609.

Lamb, D. H., Catanzaro, S. J., & Moorman, A. S. (2004). A preliminary look at how psychologists identify, evaluate, and proceed when faced with possible multiple relationship dilemmas. *Professional Psychology: Research and Practice, 35*(3), 248–254.

Lambert, M. J. (1991). Introduction to psychotherapy research. In L. E. Beutler & M. Crago (Eds.), *Psychotherapy research. An international review of programmatic*

studies (pp. 1–11). Washington, DC: American Psychological Association.

Lambert, M. J. (2011). Psychotherapy research and its achievements. In J. C. Norcross, G. R. Vandenbos, & D. K. Freedheim (Eds.), *History of psychotherapy* (2nd ed.; pp. 299–332). Washington, DC: American Psychological Association.

Lambert, M. J., & Bergin, A. E. (1994). The effectiveness of psychotherapy. In A. E. Bergin & S. L. Garfield (Eds.), *Handbook of psychotherapy and behavior change* (4th ed.; pp. 143–189). New York, NY: John Wiley & Sons.

Lancaster, C., Lenz, A. S., Meadows, E., & Brown, K. C. (2013). Evaluation of a conflict resolution program for unban African American adolescent girls. *The Journal for Specialists in Group Work, 38*, 225–240.

Landreth, G. L. (1993). Child-centered play therapy. *Elementary School Guidance and Counseling, 28*(1), 17–29.

Landreth, G. L. (2012). *Play therapy: The art of the relationship* (3rd. ed.). New York, NY: Routledge.

Landreth, G. L., & Bratton, S. C. (2006). *Child Parent Relationship Therapy (CPRT): A 10-session filial therapy model.* New York, NY: Routledge.

Lang, M., & Tisher, M. (1978). *Children's Depression Scale.* Victoria, Australia: Australian Council for Educational Research.

Langs, R. (1985). *Madness and cure.* New York, NY: Newconcept Press.

Lapan, R. T., Boggs, K. R., & Morrill, W. H. (1989). Self-efficacy as a mediator of investigative and realistic general occupational themes on the Strong-Campbell Interest Inventory. *Journal of Counseling Psychology, 36*, 176–182.

Larson, J. H., Busby, D. M., Wilson, S., Medora, N., & Allgood, S. (1994). The multidimensional assessment of career decision problems: The career decision diagnostic assessment. *Journal of Counseling and Development, 72*(3), 323–328.

Lasseter, J., Privette, G., Brown, C. G., & Duer, J. (1989). Dance as treatment approach with a multi-disabled child: Implications for school counseling. *The School Counselor, 36*, 310–315.

Lawless, L. L., Ginter, E. J., & Kelly, R. R. (1999). Managed care: What mental health counselors need to know. *Journal of Mental Health Counseling, 21*(1), 50–65.

Lawrence, G., & Kurpius, R. (2000). Legal and ethical issues involved when counseling minors in nonschool settings. *Journal of Counseling and Development, 78*(2), 130–136.

Lawson, G., & Myers, J. E. (2011). Wellness, professional quality of life, and career-sustaining behaviors: What keeps us well? *Journal of Counseling and Development, 89*, 163–171.

Lazar, S. W. (2005). Mindfulness research. In C. K. Germer, R. D. Siegel, & P. R. Fulton (Eds.), *Mindfulness and psychotherapy* (pp. 220–240). New York, NY: Guilford Press.

Lazar, Z. (2001, February). Bullying: A serious business. *Child, 79*–84.

Lazarus, A. A. (1993). Tailoring the therapeutic relationship, or being an authentic chameleon. *Psychotherapy, 30*(3), 404–407.

Lazarus, A. A. (1997). *Brief but comprehensive psychotherapy.* New York, NY: Springer.

Lazarus, A. A. (1998). How do you like these boundaries? *The Clinical Psychologist, 51*, 22–25.

Lazarus, A. A. (2000). Multimodal therapy. In R. J. Corsini & D. Wedding (Eds.), *Current psychotherapies* (6th ed.; pp. 340–374). Itasca, IL: F. E. Peacock.

Lazarus, A. A. (2001). Not all "dual relationships" are taboo: Some tend to enhance treatment outcomes. *The National Psychologist, 10,* 16.

Lazarus, A. A., & Beutler, L. E. (1993). On technical eclecticism. *Journal of Counseling and Development, 71*(4), 381–385.

Lê, C., Ingvarson, E. P., & Page, R. C. (1995). Alcoholics Anonymous and the counseling profession: Philosophies in conflict. *Journal of Counseling and Development, 73*(6), 603–609.

Lebow, J. L., & Gurman, A. S. (1995). Research assessing couple and family therapy. *Annual Review of Psychology, 46,* 27–57.

Lee, C. (1982). Self-efficacy as a predictor of performance in competitive gymnastics. *Journal of Sports Psychology, 4,* 405–409.

Lee, C. C. (1991). Cultural dynamics. Their importance in multicultural counseling. In C. C. Lee & B. L. R. Richardson (Eds.), *Multicultural issues in counseling: New approaches to diversity.* Alexandria, VA: American Association for Counseling and Development.

Lee, C. C., Oh, M. Y., & Mountcastle, A. R. (1992). Indigenous models of helping in non-Western countries: Implications for multicultural counseling. *Journal of Multicultural Counseling and Development, 20,* 1–10.

Lee, D. (1984). Counseling and culture: Some issues. *Personnel and Guidance Journal, 62,* 592–597.

Lee, J. H., Nam, S. K., Kim, A-R., Kim, B., Lee, M. Y., & Lee, S. M. (2013). Reslience: A meta-analytic approach. *Journal of Counseling and Development, 91,* 269–279.

Lee, M. A., & Tolle, S. W. (1996). Oregon's assisted suicide vote: The silver lining. *Annals of Internal Medicine, 124,* 267–269.

Lee, S. D. (1968). *Social class bias in the diagnosis of mental illness.* Doctoral dissertation, University of Oklahoma. Ann Arbor, MI: University Microfilms No. 68-6959.

Lee, S. M., Cho, S. H., Kissinger, D., & Ogle, N. T. (2010). A typology of burnout in professional counselors. *Journal of Counseling and Development, 88,* 131–138.

Leichsenring, F., & Rabung, S. (2008). Effectiveness of long-term psychodynamic psychotherapy: A meta-analysis. *Journal of the American Medical Association, 300,* 1551–1565.

Lent, J., & Schwartz, R. C. (2012). The impact of work setting, demographic characteristics, and personality factors related to burnout among professional counselors. *Journal of Mental Health Counseling, 34,* 355–372.

Lent, R. W., & Brown, S. D. (2013). Social cognitive model of career self-management: Toward a unifying view of adaptive career behavior across the life span. *Journal of Counseling Psychology, 69,* 4, 557–568.

Lent, R. W., Brown, S. D., & Hackett, G. (1994). Toward a unifying social cognitive theory of career and academic interest, choice, and performance. *Journal of Vocational Behavior, 45,* 79–122.

Lent, R. W., Brown, S. D., & Hackett, G. (2000). Contextual supports and barriers to career choice: A social cognitive analysis. *Journal of Counseling andDevelopment, 47,* 36–49.

Lent, R. W., & Hackett, G. (1987). Career self-efficacy: Empirical status and future divisions. *Journal of Vocational Behavior, 30,* 347–382.

Lenz, A. S., Taylor, R., Fleming, M., & Serman, N. (2014). Effectiveness of dialectical behavior therapy for treating eating disorders. *Journal of Counseling and Development, 92,* 26–35.

Leppma, M. (2012). Loving-kindness meditation and counseling. *Journal of Mental Health Counseling, 34*(3), 197.

Leong, F. T. L., & Chou, E. L. (1994). The role of ethnic identity and acculturation in the vocational behavior of Asian Americans: An integrative review. *Journal of Vocational Behavior, 44,* 155–172.

Lerner, H. G. (1988). *Women in therapy.* New York, NY: Harper & Row.

Lerner, R., & Naiditch, B. (1985). *Children are people.* St. Paul, MN: Children Are People.

Leslie, R. (1991, July/August). Psychotherapist-patient privilege clarified. *The California Therapist,* 11–19.

Lester, D. (1993). The effectiveness of suicide prevention centers. *Suicide and Life-Threatening Behavior, 23,* 263–267.

Leung, S. A., & Plake, B. S. (1990). A choice dilemma approach for examining the relative importance of sex type and prestige preferences in the process of career choice compromise. *Journal of Counseling Psychology, 37*(4), 399–406.

LeVine, E., & Sallee, A. (1992). *Listen to our children: Clinical theory and practice* (2nd ed.). Dubuque, IA: Kendall/Hunt.

Levinson, E. M. (1994). Current vocational assessment models for students with disabilities. *Journal of Counseling and Development, 73*(1), 94–101.

Levitsky, A., & Simkin, J. S. (1972). Gestalt therapy. In L. N. Solomon &

B. Berzon (Eds.), *New perspectives on encounter groups* (pp. 245–253). San Francisco, CA: Jossey-Bass.

Levitt, E. E. (1957). The results of psychotherapy with children: An evaluation. *Journal of Consulting Psychology, 21,* 189–196.

Lewis, J. A., Dana. R. Q., & Blevins, G. A. (2011). *Substance abuse counseling: An individualized approach* (4th ed.). Belmont, CA: Brooks/Cole, Cengage Learning.

Lewis, S. Y. (1994). Cognitive-behavioral therapy. In L. Comas-Díaz & B. Greene (Eds.), *Women of color: Integrating ethnic and gender identities in psychotherapy* (pp. 223–238). New York, NY: Guilford Press.

Lewis, T. F., & Osborn, C. J. (2004). Solution-focused counseling and motivational interviewing: A consideration of confluence. *Journal of Counseling and Development, 82,* 38–48.

Liddle, H. (1982). On the problems of eclecticism: A call for epistemological clarification and human-scale theories. *Family Process, 21,* 243–250.

Lincoln, Y. S., & Guba, E. G. (1985). *Naturalistic inquiry.* Beverly Hills, CA: SAGE.

Linder, R. (1954). *The fifty-minute hour.* New York, NY: Bantam Books.

Lindquist, T. G., & Watkins, K. L. (2014). Modern approaches to modern challenges: A review of widely used parenting programs. *The Journal of Individual Psychology, 70,* 148–165.

Linehan, M. M. (1993). *Cognitive-behavioral treatment of borderline personality disorder.* New York, NY: Guilford Press.

Linehan, M., Armstrong, H., Suarez, A., Allmon, D., & Heard, H. (1991). Cognitive-behavioral treatment of chronically parasuicidal borderline patients. *Archives of General Psychiatry, 48,* 1060–1064.

Linehan, M. M., Comtois, K. A., Murray, A. M., Brown, M. Z., Gallop, R. J. Heard, H. L., & Lindenboim, N. (2006). Two-year randomized controlled trial and follow-up of dialectical behavior therapy vs. therapy by experts for suicide and borderline personality disorder. *Archives of General Psychiatry, 63,* 757–776.

Linehan, M., Goodstein, J., Nielsen, S., & Chiles, J. (1983). Reasons for staying alive when you are thinking of killing yourself: The Reasons for Living Inventory. *Journal of Consulting and Clinical Psychology, 51,* 276–286.

Litton, F. W. (1986). Counseling the mentally retarded clinic. In A. F. Rotatori, P. J. Gerber, F. W. Litton, & R. A. Fox (Eds.), *Counseling exceptional students* (pp. 78–98). New York, NY: Human Sciences Press.

Littrell, J. M., Caffrey, P., & Hopper, G. C. (1987). Counselor's reputation: An important precounseling variable for adolescents. *Journal of Counseling Psychology, 34,* 228–231.

Littrell, J. M., Malia, J. A., & Vanderwood, M. (1995). Single-session brief counseling in a high school. *Journal of Counseling and Development, 73,* 451–458.

Livneh, H., & Wright, P. E. (1999). Rational-emotive theory. In D. Capuzzi & D. R. Gross (Eds.), *Counseling and psychotherapy: Theories and interventions* (2nd ed.; pp. 325–350). Columbus, OH: Merrill.

Locke, D. C. (1993). Diversity in the practice of mental health counseling. *Journal of Mental Health Counseling, 15*(3), 228–231.

Loeber, R., & Schmaling, K. B. (1985). Empirical evidence for overt and covert patterns of antisocial conduct problems: A meta-analysis. *Journal of Abnormal Child Psychology, 13,* 337–352.

Lonner, W. J. (1985). Issues in testing and assessment in cross-cultural counseling. *The Counseling Psychologist, 13*(4), 599–614.

Lopez, F. G. (1995). Contemporary attachment theory: An introduction with implications for counseling psychology. *The Counseling Psychologist, 23*(3), 395–415.

Lopez, F. M., Jr. (1966). *Evaluating executive decision making.* New York, NY: American Management Association.

Los Angeles Unified School District. (1985). *Dropout prevention and recovery.* Los Angeles, CA: Author.

Lowe, R. N. (1982). Adlerian/Dreikursian family counseling. In A. M. Horne & M. M. Ohlsen (Eds.), *Family counseling and therapy.* Itasca, IL: F. E. Peacock.

Luborsky, E. B., O'Reilly-Landry, M., & Arlow, J. A. (2008). Psychoanalysis. In R. J. Corsini & D. Wedding (Eds.), *Current psychotherapies* (8th ed.; pp. 15–62). Itasca, IL: F. E. Peacock.

Lum, C. (1999). *A guide to state laws and regulations on professional school counseling.* Alexandria, VA: American Counseling Association.

Lundervold, D. A., & Belwood, M. F. (2000). The best kept secret in counseling: Single-case ($N = 1$) experimental designs. *Journal of Counseling and Development, 78*(1), 92–102.

Luzzo, D. A. (1996). A psychometric evaluation of the career decision-making self-efficacy scale. *Journal of Counseling and Development, 74*(3), 276–279.

Lyddon, W. J. (1995). Cognitive therapy and theories of knowing: A social constructionist view. *Journal* of Counseling and Development, 73, 579–585.

Lyddon, W. J., Bradford, E., & Nelson, J. P. (1993). Assessing adolescent and adult attachment: A review of current self-report measures. Journal of Counseling and Development, 71(4), 390–395.

Lynch, M. F. (2013). Attachment, autonomy, and emotional reliance: A multilevel model. Journal of Counseling and Development, 91, 301–312.

Lynch, S. (1980). The mentor link: Bridging education and employment. Journal of College Placement, 40, 44–47.

Lynn, S. J., & Frauman, D. (1985). Group psychotherapy. In S. J. Lynn & F. P. Garske (Eds.), Contemporary psychotherapies: Model and methods (pp. 419–458). Columbus, OH: Merrill/Macmillan.

Lynn, S. J., & Garske, J. P. (1985). Contemporary psychotherapies: Models and methods. Columbus, OH: Merrill/Macmillan.

Lyons, L. C., & Woods, P. J. (1991). The efficacy of rational-emotive therapy: A quantitative review of the outcome research. Clinical Psychology Review, 11, 357–369.

Mabe, A. R., & Rollin, S. A. (1986). The role of a code of ethical standards in counseling. Journal of Counseling and Development, 64(5), 294–297.

MacGregor, J., & Newlon, B. J. (1987). Description of a teenage pregnancy program. Journal of Counseling and Development, 65, 447.

Madanes, C. (1981). Strategic family therapy. San Francisco, CA: Jossey-Bass.

Madanes, C. (1984). Behind the one-way mirror: Advances in the practice of strategic therapy. San Francisco, CA: Jossey-Bass.

Mahoney, M. J. (1988). Constructive metatheory: 1. Basic features and historical foundations. International Journal of Personal Construct Psychology, 1, 1–35.

Mahoney, M. J. (1991). Human change processes: The scientific foundations of psychotherapy. New York, NY: Basic Books.

Mahoney, M. J. (1995a). Continuing evolution of cognitive sciences and psychotherapies. In R. A. Neimeyer & M. J. Mahoney (Eds.), Constructivism in psychotherapy (pp. 39–68). Washington, DC: American Psychological Association.

Mahoney, M. J. (Ed.). (1995b). Cognitive and constructive psychotherapies: Theory, research, and practice. New York, NY: Springer.

Mahoney, M. J., & Lyddon, W. J. (1988). Recent developments in cognitive approaches to counseling and psychotherapy. The Counseling Psychologist, 16(2), 190–234.

Mahrer, A. R. (1988). Discovery-oriented psychotherapy research: Rationale, aims, and methods. American Psychologist, 43, 694–702.

Makinson, R. A., & Young, J. S. (2012). Cognitive behavioral therapy and the treatment of posttraumatic stress disorder: Where counseling and neuroscience meet. Journal of Counseling & Development, 90, 131–140.

Makover, R. B. (1992). Training psychotherapists in hierarchical treatment planning. Journal of Psychotherapy Practice and Research, 1(4), 337–350.

Malan, D. (1976). The frontier of brief psychotherapy. New York, NY: Basic Books.

Malan, D. H. (1980). The most important development since the discovery of the unconscious. In H.

Davanloo (Ed.), Short-term dynamic psychotherapy. New York, NY: Aronson.

Maldonado, A. (1982). Terapia de conducta y depresion: Un analisis experimental de los modelos conductal y cognitivo [Cognitive and behavioral therapy for depression. Its efficacy and interaction with pharmacological treatment]. Revista de psicologia general y aplicada, 37(1), 31–56.

Maling, M. S., & Howard, K. I. (1994). From research to practice to research to. . . . In P. F. Talley, H. H. Strupp, & S. F. Butler (Eds.), Psychotherapy research and practice: Bridging the gap (pp. 247–253). New York, NY: Basic Books.

Mallen, M. J., Vogel, D. L., & Rochlen, A. D. (2005). The practical aspects of online counseling: Ethics, training, technology, and competency. The Counseling Psychologist, 33(6), 776–818.

Mallinckrodt, B., & Helms, J. E. (1986). Effect of disabled counselors' self-disclosure on clients' perceptions of the counselor. Journal of Counseling Psychology, 33, 343–348.

Maniacci, M. P. (1996). An introduction to brief therapy of the personality disorders. Individual Psychology: The Journal of Adlerian Theory, Research, and Practice, 52(2), 158–168.

Maniacci, M. P., Sackett-Maniacci, L., & Mosak, H. H. (2014). Adlerian psychotherapy. In D. Wedding & R. J. Corsini (Eds), Current psychotherapies (10th ed.; pp. 55–94). Belmont, CA: Brooks/Cole, Cengage Learning.

Mann, J. (1973). Time-limited psychotherapy. Cambridge, MA: Harvard University Press.

Mann, J. (1981). The core of time-limited psychotherapy: Time and central issue. In S. H. Budman (Ed.), *Forms of brief therapy*. New York, NY: Guilford Press.

Maples, M. F., & Abney, P. C. (2006). Baby boomers mature and gerontological counseling comes of age. *Journal of Counseling & Development, 84*, 3–9.

Mardirosian, K., McGuire, J. M., Abbott, D. W., & Blau, B. I. (1990). The effects of enhanced informal consent in a profile pregnancy counseling center. *Journal of Counseling and Development, 69*, 39–41.

Margolin, G. (1982). Ethical and legal considerations in marriage and family therapy. *American Psychologist, 7*, 788–801.

Marinoble, R. M. (1998). Homosexuality: A blind spot in the school mirror. *Professional School Counseling, 1*(3), 4–7.

Markham, A. N. (2004). Internet communication as a tool for qualitative research. In D. Silverman (Ed.), *Qualitative research: Theory, method, and practice* (3rd. ed.; pp. 95–124). Thousand Oaks, CA: SAGE.

Marlatt, G. A. (1983). The controlled drinking controversy: A commentary. *American Psychologist, 38*, 1097–1110.

Marlatt, G. A., & Gordon, J. R. (Eds.). (1985). *Relapse prevention*. New York, NY: Guilford Press.

Marmar, C. R., & Horowitz, M. J. (1988). Diagnosis and phase-oriented treatment of post-traumatic stress disorder. In J. F. Wilson, Z. Harel, & B. Kahana (Eds.), *Human adaptation to extreme stress: From the Holocaust to Viet Nam* (pp. 81–104). New York, NY: Plenum.

Marquis, A., Douthit, K. Z., & Elliot, A. J. (2011). Best practices: A critical yet inclusive vision for the counseling profession. *Journal*

of Counseling and Development, 89, 397–405.

Martin, D. G. (1989). *Counseling and therapy skills* (2nd ed.). Prospect Heights, IL: Therapy Press.

Marziali, E. (1984). Predictions of outcomes of brief psychotherapy from therapist interpretive interventions. *Archives of General Psychiatry, 41*, 301–304.

Maslow, A. H. (1968). *Toward the psychology of being* (2nd ed.). New York, NY: Van Nostrand Reinhold.

Mason, M. J. (1996). Evaluation of an alcohol and other drug use prevention training program for school counselors in a predominantly Mexican American school district. *The School Counselor, 43*(4), 308–316.

Matsui, T., Ikeda, H., & Ohnishi, R. (1989). Relations of sex-typed socializations to career self-efficacy expectations of college students. *Journal of Vocational Behavior, 35*, 1–16.

Matsui, T., & Onglatco, M.-L. (1992). Career self-efficacy as a moderator of the relation between occupational stress and strain. *Journal of Vocational Behavior, 41*, 79–88.

Matus, R., & Neuhring, E. M. (1979). Social workers in primary prevention: Action and ideology in mental health. *Community Mental Health Journal, 15*, 33–38.

May, R. (1953). *Man's search for himself*. New York, NY: Norton.

May, R. (1961). *Existential psychology*. New York, NY: Random House.

May, R. (1977). *The meaning of anxiety* (Rev. ed.). New York, NY: Norton.

May, R., & Yalom, I. (2005). Existential psychotherapy. In R. J. Corsini & D. Wedding (Eds.),

Current psychotherapies (7th ed.; pp. 269–298). Itasca, IL: F. E. Peacock.

May, T. M. (1990). An evolving relationship. *The Counseling Psychologist, 18*, 266–270.

Mayer, J. D. (1999, September). Emotional intelligence: Popular or scientific psychology? *APA Monitor, 50*.

Mayer, J. D. (2001). A field guide to emotional intelligence. In J. Ciarrochi, J. P. Forgas, & J. D. Mayer (Eds.), *Emotional intelligence in everyday life* (pp. 3–24). Philadelphia, PA: Psychology Press.

Mayer, J. D., Caruso, D. R., & Salovey, P. (1999). Emotional intelligence meets traditional standards for intelligence. *Intelligence, 27*(4), 267–298.

Mayer, J. D., Dipaolo, M. T., & Salovey, P. (1990). Perceiving affective content in ambiguous visual stimuli: A component of emotional intelligence. *Journal of Personality Assessment, 54*, 772–781.

Mayer, J. D., & Geher, G. (1996). Emotional intelligence and the identification of emotion. *Intelligence, 22*, 89–113.

Mayer, J. D., & Salovey, P. (1997). What is emotional intelligence? In P. Salovey and D. Sluyter (Eds.), *Emotional development and emotional intelligence: Implications for educators* (pp. 3–31). New York, NY: Basic Books.

Mayer, J. D., Salovey, P., & Caruso, D. R. (2000). Models of emotional intelligence. In R. J. Sternberg (Ed.), *Handbook of intelligence* (pp. 396–420). Cambridge, UK: Cambridge University Press.

Maynard, R. A. (1996). *Kids having kids: A Robin Hood Foundation special report on the costs of adolescent childbearing*. New York, NY: The Robin Hood Foundation.

Maze, M. (1984). How to select a computerized guidance system. *Journal of Counseling and Development, 63*(3), 158–162.

McAuley, E. (1985). Modeling and self-efficacy: A test of Bandura's model. *Journal of Sports Psychology, 7,* 283–295.

McBride, M. C., & Martin, G. E. (1990). A framework for eclecticism: The importance of theory to mental health counseling. *Journal of Mental Health Counseling, 12,* 495–505.

McCarthy, J., Downes, E. J., & Sherman, C. A. (2008). Looking back at adolescent depression. *Journal of Mental Health Counseling, 30*(1), 49–66.

McCarthy, P. R. (1982). Differential effects of counselor self-disclosure versus self-involving counselor statements across counselor-client gender pairings. *Journal of Counseling Psychology, 26,* 538–541.

McCrae, R. R., & Costa, P. T., Jr. (1989). Reinterpreting the Myers-Briggs Type Indicator from the perspective of the five-factor model of personality. *Journal of Personality, 57*(1), 17–40.

McDonough, R. L., & Russell, L. (1994). Alcoholism in women: A holistic, comprehensive care model. *Journal of Mental Health Counseling, 16*(4), 459–474.

McDowell, W., Coven, A., & Eash, V. (1979). The handicapped: Special needs and strategies for counseling. *Personnel and Guidance Journal, 58,* 228–232.

McFadden, J., & Brooks, D. K. (1983). *Counselor licensure action packet.* Alexandria, VA: American Association for Counseling and Development.

McGlothlin, J. M. (2003). Response to the mini special issue on technology and group work. *Journal for Specialists in Group Work, 28,* 42–47.

McIntire, M., Marion, S. F., & Quaglia, R. (1990). Rural school counselors: Their communities and schools. *The School Counselor, 37,* 166–172.

McKenzie, V. M. (1986). Ethnographic findings on West Indian–American clients. *Journal of Counseling and Development, 65,* 40–44.

McMahon, R. J., & Forehand, R. (1988). Conduct disorders. In E. J. Mash & L. G. Terdal (Eds.), *Behavioral assessment of childhood disorders* (2nd ed.; pp. 105–156). New York, NY: Guilford Press.

McMahon, H. G., Mason, E. C. M., Daluga-Guenther, N., & Ruiz, A. (2014). An ecological model of professional school counseling. *Journal of Counseling and Development, 92,* 159–171.

McMillan, J. H. (1984). Culture-fair tests. In R. Corsini (Ed.), *Encyclopedia of psychology* (pp. 335–336). New York, NY: John Wiley & Sons.

McMurty, S. C. (1985, January–February). Secondary prevention of child maltreatment: A review. *Social Work,* 42–46.

McNair, L. D. (1992). African American women in therapy: An Afrocentric and feminist synthesis. *Women and Therapy, 12*(1/2), 5–19.

McNeill, B. W., May, R. J., & Lee, V. E. (1987). Perceptions of counselor source characteristics and successful terminators. *Journal of Counseling Psychology, 34,* 86–89.

McNeilly, C. L., & Howard, K. I. (1991). The effects of psychotherapy: A reevaluation based on dosage. *Psychotherapy Research, 1,* 74–78.

McRae, M. B. (1994). Interracial group dynamics: A new perspective. *Journal for Specialists in Group Work, 19*(3), 168–174.

McRoberts, C., Burlingame, G. M., & Hoag, M. J. (1998). Comparative efficacy of individual and group psychotherapy: A meta-analytic perspective. *Group Dynamics: Theory, Research, and Practice (2)*2, 101–117.

McWhirter, E. H. (1994). *Counseling for empowerment.* Alexandria, VA: American Counseling Association.

McWhirter, J. J., McWhirter, B. T., McWhirter, A. M., & McWhirter, E. H. (1994). High- and low-risk characteristics of youth: The five Cs of competencies. *Elementary School Guidance and Counseling, 28*(3), 188–196.

Meany-Walen, K. K., Bratton, S., & Kottman, T. (2014). Adlerian play therapy: Effectivenes on disruptive behaviors of early elementary-aged children. *Journal of Counseling and Development, 92,* 47–56.

Meara, N. M., Schmidt, L. D., & Day, J. D. (1996). Principles and virtues: A foundation for ethical decisions, policies, and character. *The Counseling Psychologist, 24*(1), 4–77.

Meichenbaum, D. (1972). Cognitive modifications of testanxious college students. *Journal of Consulting and Clinical Psychology, 39,* 370–390.

Meichenbaum, D. (1977). *Cognitive-behavior modification: An integrative approach.* New York, NY: Plenum.

Meichenbaum, D. (1985). *Stress inoculation training.* New York, NY: Pergamon.

Meichenbaum, D. (1986). Cognitive behavior modification. In F. H. Kanfer & A. P. Goldstein (Eds.), *Helping people change: A textbook of methods* (pp. 346–380). New York, NY: Pergamon.

Meichenbaum, D., & Fitzpatrick, D. (1992). A constructivist narrative perspective on stress and coping: Stress inoculation applications. In L. Golderger & S. Breznitz (Eds.), *Handbook of stress* (pp. 706–723). New York, NY: Free Press.

Mellin, E. A., Hunt, B., & Nichols, L. M. (2011). Counselor professional identity: Findings and implications for counseling and interprofessional collaboration. *Journal of Counseling and Development, 89*, 140–147.

Melnick, R. R. (1975). Counseling responses as a function of method of problem presentation and type of problem. *Journal of Counseling Psychology, 22*, 108–112.

Melton, G. B. (1988). Ethical and legal issues in AIDS-related practice. *American Psychologist, 43*(11), 941–947.

Mendoza, R. H. (1989). An empirical scale to measure type and degree of acculturation in Mexican-American adolescents and adults. *Journal of Cross-Cultural Psychology, 20*, 372–385.

Mental disorders may affect 1 in 5. (1984, October 3). *Washington Post*, p. A1.

Mercer, J. R. (1977). *SOMPA: System of Multicultural Pluralistic Assessment.* New York, NY: Psychological Corp.

Merluzzi, T. V., & Brischetto, C. S. (1983). Breach of confidentiality and perceived trustworthiness of counselors. *Journal of Counseling Psychology, 30*, 245–251.

Merrill, C., & Andersen, S. (1993). A content analysis of person-centered expressive therapy outcomes. *The Humanistic Psychologist, 21*, 354–363.

Messina, J. J. (1999). What's next for the profession of mental health counseling? *Journal of Mental Health Counseling, 21*(3), 285–294.

Meyer, A. (1957). *Psychobiology: A science of man.* Springfield, IL: Charles C Thomas.

Meyers, L. (2014a). Ages and stages. *Counseling Today, 56*(9), 33–41.

Meyers, L. (2014b). In search of wellness. *Counseling Today 56*(10), 33–40.

Milich, R., & Dodge, K. A. (1984). Social information processing in child psychiatric population. *Journal of Abnormal Child Psychology, 12*, 471–490.

Miller, C. A., & Capuzzi, D. (1984). A review of transactional analysis outcome studies. *American Mental Health Counselors Association Journal, 6*(1), 30–41.

Miller, D. R. (1995). The school counselor and Christian fundamentalist families. *The School Counselor, 42*(4), 317–320.

Miller, G. D. (1989). What roles and functions do elementary school counselors have? *Elementary School Guidance and Counseling, 24*, 77–88.

Miller, G. M. (1982). Deriving meaning from standardized tests: Interpreting test results to clients. *Measurement and Evaluation in Guidance, 15*, 87–94.

Miller, J. B. (1976). *Toward a new psychology of women.* Boston, MA: Beacon Press.

Miller, J. B. (1987). *Toward a new psychology of women* (2nd ed.). Boston, MA: Houghton Mifflin.

Miller, J. B., & Stiver, I. P. (1995). *The healing connection: How women form connections in therapy and life.* Boston, MA: Beacon Press.

Miller, M. J., & Cochran, J. R. (1979). Evaluating the use of technology in reporting SCII results to students. *Measurement and Evaluation in Guidance, 12*, 166–173.

Miller, W. R. (1980). Treating the problem drinker. In W. R. Miller (Ed.), *The addictive behaviors:* *Treatment of alcoholism, drug abuse, smoking, and obesity.* New York, NY: Pergamon Press.

Miller, W. R., & Munoz, R. F. (1982). *How to control your drinking.* Albuquerque, NM: University of New Mexico Press.

Mills, J. A., Bauer, G. P., & Miars, R. D. (1989). Use of transference in short-term dynamic psychotherapy. *Psychotherapy, 26*(3), 112–119.

Milner, J. S. (1986). *The child abuse potential inventory: Manual* (Rev. ed.). Webster, NC: Psytec.

Minton, H. L., & McDonald, G. J. (1984). Homosexual identity formation as a developmental process. *Journal of Homosexuality, 9*, 91–104.

Minton, H. L., & Schneider, F. W. (1981). *Differential psychology.* Monterey, CA: Brooks/Cole.

Mintz, J., Luborsky, L., & Auerbach, A. (1971). Dimensions of psychotherapy: A factor-analytic study of ratings of psychotherapy sessions. *Journal of Consulting and Clinical Psychology, 36*, 106–120.

Minuchin, S. (1974). *Families and family therapy.* Cambridge, MA: Harvard University Press.

Minuchin, S. (1984). *Family kaleidoscope.* Cambridge, MA: Harvard University Press.

Mio, J. S., & Iwamasa, G. (1993). To do, or not to do: That is the question for white cross-cultural researchers. *The Counseling Psychologist, 21*(2), 197–212.

Miranti, J. G., & Burke, M. T. (1995). Spirituality: An integral component of the counseling process. In M. T. Burke & J. G. Miranti (Eds.), *Counseling: The spiritual dimension* (pp. 1–4).Alexandria, VA: American Counseling Association.

Mirin, S. M., Weiss, R. D., Michael, J., & Griffin, M. L. (1988).

Psychopathology in substance abusers: Diagnosis and treatment. *American Journal of Drug and Alcohol Abuse, 14*(2), 139–157.

Mischel, W., Shoda, Y., & Rodriguez, M. L. (1989). Delay of gratification in children. *Science, 244,* 933–938.

Mitchell, J. T., & Everly, G. S. (1993). *Critical incident stress debriefing: An operations manual for the prevention of traumatic stress among emergency services and disaster workers.* Ellicott City, MD: Chevron.

Mitchell, L. K., & Krumboltz, J. D. (1987). The effects of cognitive restructuring and decision-making training on career indecision. *Journal of Counseling and Development, 66,* 171–174.

Mitchell, L. K., & Krumboltz, J. D. (2002). Social learning approach to career decision making: Krumboltz's theory. In D. Brown, L. Brooks, & Associates (Eds.), *Career choice and development* (4th ed.). San Francisco, CA: Jossey-Bass.

Monahan, J. (1993). Limiting therapist exposure to Tarasoff liability: Guidelines for risk containment. *American Psychologist, 48*(3), 242–250.

Montes, S. (2013). The birth of the neuro-counselor? *Counseling Today, 56*(6), 32–40.

Moon, K. A. (2007). A client-centered review of Rogers with Gloria. *Journal of Counseling and Development, 85*(3), 277–285.

Moon, S. M., Dillon, D. R., & Sprenkle, D. H. (1990). Family therapy and qualitative research. *Journal of Marital and Family Therapy, 16*(4), 357–373.

Moreno, J. (1988). Multicultural music therapy: The world music connection. *Journal of Music Therapy, 25*(1), 17–27.

Moreno, J. L. (1946). *Psychodrama* (Vol. 1). Beacon, NY: Beacon House.

Morrissette, P. J. (2000). The experiences of the rural school counselor. *Professional School Counseling, 3*(3), 197–207.

Morrow, D., Worthington, E. L., & McCullough, M. E. (1993). Observers' perceptions of a counselor's treatment of a religious issue. *Journal of Counseling and Development, 71*(4), 452–456.

Morrow, P. C., Mullen, E. J., & McElvoy, J. C. (1990). Vocational behavior, 1989: The year in review. *Journal of Vocational Behavior, 37,* 121–195.

Morse, C. L., & Russell, T. (1988). How elementary counselors see their role: An empirical study. *Elementary School Guidance & Counseling, 23*(1), 44–62.

Mosak, H. (1991). Where have all the normal people gone? *Individual Psychology: The Journal of Adlerian Theory, Research, and Practice, 47*(4), 437–446.

Mosak, H., & Maniacci, M. (2011). Adlerian psychotherapy. In R. J. Corsini & D. Wedding (Eds), *Current psychotherapies* (9th ed.; pp. 63–103). Belmont, CA: Brooks/Cole, Cengage Learning.

Moss, J. M., Gibson, D. M., & Dollarhide, C. T. (2014). Professional identity development: A grounded theory of transformational tasks of counselors. *Journal of Counseling & Development, 92,* 3–12.

Moyerman, D. R., & Forman, B. D. (1992). Acculturation and adjustment: A meta-analytic study. *Hispanic Journal of Behavioral Sciences, 14,* 163–200.

Muller, B. E., & Erford, B. T. (2012). Choosing assessment instruments for depression outcome research with school-age youth. *Journal of*

Counseling and Development, 90, 208–220.

Muller, L. E., & Hartman, J. (1998). Group counseling for sexual minority youth. *Professional School Counseling, 1*(3), 38–41.

Muro, J. J. (1981). On target—on top. *Elementary School Guidance and Counseling, 15,* 307–314.

Murphy, G. E., Simons, A. D., Wetzel, R. D., & Lustman, P. J. (1983). Cognitive therapy and pharmacotherapy: Singly and together in the treatment of depression. *Archives of General Psychiatry, 41,* 33–41.

Murphy, J. J. (1994). Working with what works: A solution-focused approach to school behavior problems. *The School Counselor, 42*(1), 59–65.

Murray, T. L. (2009). The loss of client agency into the psyhopharmaceutical-industrail complex. *Journal of Mental Health Counseling, 31,* 283–308.

Murray, C. E. (2009). Diffusion of innovation theory: A bridge for the research-practice gap in counseling. *Journal of Counseling and Development, 87*(1), 108–116.

Myers, J. E., & Sweeney, T. J. (2004). The indivisible self: An evidence-based model of wellness. *Journal of Individual Psychology, 60,* 234–244.

Myers, J. E., & Sweeney, T. J. (2008). Wellness counseling: The evidence base for practice. *Journal of Counseling and Development, 86,* 482–493.

Myers, J. E., Sweeney, T. J., & White, V. E. (2002). Advocacy for counseling and counselors: A professional imperative. *Journal of Counseling and Development, 80,* 394–402.

Myers, J. E., Willse, J. T., & Villalba, J. A. (2011). Promoting self-esteem in adolescents: The influence of wellness factors. *Journal of Counseling and Development, 89,* 28–36.

Myers, J. E., & Young, J. S. (2012). Brain wave biofeedback: Benefits of integrating neurofeedback in counseling. *Journal of Counseling and Development, 90,* 20–28.

Meyers, L. (2014). In search of wellness. *Counseling Today, 56*(9), 32–40.

Myers, L. J. (1988). *Understanding an Afrocentric worldview: Introduction to optimal psychology.* Dubuque, IA: Kendall/Hunt.

Myers, L. J., Speight, S. L., Highlen, P. S., Cox, C. I., Reynolds, A. L., Adams, E. M., & Hanley, C. P. (1991). Identity development and worldview: Toward an optimal conceptualization. *Journal of Counseling and Development, 70*(1), 54–63.

Myrick, R. D. (1987). *Developmental guidance and counseling. A practical approach.* Minneapolis, MN: Educational Media.

Myrick, R. D., & Sabella, R. A. (1995). Cyberspace: New place for counselor supervision. *Elementary School Guidance and Counseling, 30*(1), 35–44.

Nadal, K. L., Griffin, K. E., Wong, Y., Hamit, S. & Rasmus, M. (2014). The impact of racial microaggressions on mental health: Counseling implications for clients of color. *Journal of Counseling & Development, 92,* 57–66.

Nafziger, J., & DeKruyf, L. (2013). Narrative counseling for professional school counselors. *Professional School Counseling, 16,* 290–302.

Nansel, T. R., Overpeck, M., Pilla, R. S., Ruan, W. J., Simons-Morton, B., & Scheidt, P. (2001). Bullying behaviors among US youth:

Prevalence and association with psychosocial adjustment. *JAMA, 285*(16), 2094–2100.

Nathan, P. E., & Harris, S. L. (1980). *Psychopathology and society* (2nd ed.). New York, NY: McGraw-Hill.

National Association of Social Workers. (2008). *Code of ethics.* Washington, DC: Author.

National Board for Certified Counselors (NBCC). (2012). *Code of ethics.* Retrieved from http://www .nbcc.org/Certification/Ethics

National Board for Certified Counselors (NBCC). (1997, December 1). *The practice of Internet counseling.* Retrieved from http:// www.cce-global.org/Assets/ethics/ internetCounseling.pdf

National Campaign to Prevent Teen and Unplanned Pregnancy. (2012). *Fast facts: Teen childbearing in the United States, 2010.* Retrieved from http://www. thenationalcampaign.org/resources/ pdfFastFacts-TeenChildbearing- Final2010BirthData.pdf

National Campaign to Prevent Teen and Unplanned Pregnancy. (2013). *Fast facts: Teen pregnancy in the United States.* Retrived from http://www.the nationalcampaign.org/resources/pdf/ FastFacts-TeenPregnancyinUS.pdf

National Institute of Mental Health (NIMH). (1999). *Suicide fact sheet.* Retrieved from http://www.nimh. nih.gov/suicideprevention/suifact. cfm (no longer available online)

Neimeyer, R. A., & Mahoney, M. J. (1995). *Constructivism in psychotherapy.* Washington, DC: American Psychological Association.

NeJedlo, R. J., Arredondo, P., & Benjamin, L. (1985). *Imagine: A visionary model for the counselors of tomorrow.* Alexandria, VA: Association for Counselor Education and Supervision.

Nelson, M. D., Thomas, J. V., & Pierce, K. A. (1995). Inside-outside: A classroom discussion model for conflict resolution. *The School Counselor, 42*(5), 399–404.

Nelson, M. L., & Holloway, E. L. (1990). Relation of gender to power and involvement in supervision. *Journal of Counseling Psychology, 37,* 473–481.

Nelson-Jones, R. (1992). *Group leadership: A training approach.* Pacific Grove, CA: Brooks/Cole.

Nergaard, M. O., & Silberschatz, G. (1989). The effects of shame, guilt, and the negative reaction in brief dynamic psychotherapy. *Psychotherapy, 26,* 330–337.

Neukrug, E. S., Barr, C. G., Hoffman, L. R., & Kaplan, L. S. (1993). Developmental counseling and guidance: A model for use in your school. *The School Counselor, 40*(5), 356–362.

Newcomb, M. D., & Bentler, P. M. (1988). *Consequences of adolescent drug use: Impact on the lives of young adults.* Newbury Park, CA: SAGE.

Newcomb, M. D., & Bentler, P. M. (1989). Substance use and abuse among children and teenagers. *American Psychologist, 44*(2), 242–248.

Newcomb, N. S. (1994). Music: A powerful resource for the elementary school counselor. *Elementary School Guidance and Counseling, 29*(2), 150–155.

Newmark, C. S. (1985). *Major psychological assessment instruments.* Boston, MA: Allyn & Bacon.

Nicholas, D., Gerstein, L., & Keller, K. (1988). Behavioral medicine and the mental health counselor. Roles and interdisciplinary collaboration. *Journal of Mental Health Counseling, 10,* 79–94.

Nichols, M. (1984). *Family therapy: Concepts and methods.* New York, NY: Gardner Press.

Nichols, M. (1987a). The individual in the system. *Family Therapy Networker, 11*(2), 33–38, 85.

Nichols, M. (1987b). *The self in the system: Expanding the limits of family therapy.* New York, NY: Brunner/Mazel.

Nichols, W. (1988). *Marital therapy: An integrative approach.* New York, NY: Brunner/Mazel.

Nichols, W. C., & Everett, C. A. (1986). *Systematic family therapy: An integrative approach.* New York, NY: Guilford Press.

Nicki, R. M., Remington, R. M., & MacDonald, G. A. (1984). Self-efficacy, nicotine fading/self-monitoring and cigarette-smoking behavior. *Behavior Research and Therapy, 22,* 477–485.

Nielsen, S. L., Smart, D. W., Isakson, R. L., Worthen, V. E., Gregersen, A. T., & Lambert, M. J. (2004). The *Consumer Reports* effective score: What did consumers report? *Journal of Counseling Psychology, 51,* 25–37.

Niemiec, R. M., Rashid, T., & Spinella, M. (2012). Strong mindfulness: Integrating mindfulness and character strengths. *Journal of Mental Health Counseling, 34*(3), 240–253.

Nietzel, M. T., Russell, R. L., Hemmings, K. A., & Gretter, M. L. (1987). The clinical significance of psychotherapy for unipolar depression: A meta-analytic approach to social comparison. *Journal of Consulting and Clinical Psychology, 55,* 156–161.

Nilsson, J. E., Schale, C. L., & Khamphakdy-Brown, S. (2011). Facilitating trainees' multicultural development and social justice advocacy through a refugee/immigrant mental health program. *Journal of Counseling and Development, 89,* 413–422.

No Child Left Behind Act of 2001 (NCLB), Pub. L. No. 107-110 (2002).

Norcross, J. C., & Beutler, L. E. (2014). Integrative psychotherapies. In D. Wedding & R. Corsini (Eds), *Current psychotherapies* (10th ed.; pp. 499–532). Belmont, CA: Brooks/Cole, Cengage Learning.

Norcross, J. C., & Hill, C. E. (2003). Empirically supported (therapy) relationships: ESRs. *The Register Report, 29,* 22–27.

Norcross, J. C., & Newman, C. F. (1992). Psychotherapy integration: Setting the context. In J. C. Norcross & M. R. Goldfried (Eds.), *Handbook of psychotherapy integration* (pp. 3–45). New York, NY: Basic Books.

Norcross, J. C., Prochaska, J. O., & Gallagher, K. M. (1989). Clinical psychologists in the 1980s: II. Theory research, and practice. *The Clinical Psychologist, 42,* 45–53.

Northcutt, N., & McCoy, D. (2004). *Interactive qualitative analysis.* Thousand Oaks, CA: SAGE.

Nykodym, N., Rund, W., & Liverpool, P. (1986). Quality circles: Will transactional analysis improve their effectiveness? *Transactional Analysis Journal, 16,* 182–187.

Nystul, M. S. (1976). Identification and movement within three levels of social interest. *Journal of Individual Psychology, 30,* 211–215.

Nystul, M. S. (1978a). Adler as a Sherlockian. *The Individual Psychologist, 15*(1), 41–45.

Nystul, M. S. (1978b). The use of creative arts therapy within Adlerian psychotherapy. *The Individual Psychologist, 15,* 11–18.

Nystul, M. S. (1979a). The courage to be imperfect: Now more than ever. *Individual Psychologist, 26,* 15–19.

Nystul, M. S. (1979b). Integrating current psychotherapies into Adlerian psychotherapy. *The Individual Psychologist, 16,* 23–29.

Nystul, M. S. (1979c). Three levels of a counseling relationship. *The School Counselor, 26,* 144–148.

Nystul, M. S. (1980a). Nystulian play therapy: Applications of Adlerian psychology. *Elementary School Guidance and Counseling, 15,* 22–30.

Nystul, M. S. (1980b). Systematic Training for Effective Parenting: STEP in Australia. *Australian Child and Family Welfare, 1–2,* 32–34.

Nystul, M. S. (1981). Avoiding roadblocks in counseling. *The Individual Psychologist, 18,* 21–28.

Nystul, M. S. (1982). Ten Adlerian parenting principles applied to the Navajos. *Individual Psychology: The Journal of Adlerian Theory, Research, and Practice, 38,* 183–198.

Nystul, M. S. (1984). Positive parenting leads to self-actualizing children. *Individual Psychology: The Journal of Adlerian Theory, Research, and Practice, 40,* 177–183.

Nystul, M. S. (1985a). An interview with Dr. Albert Ellis. *Individual Psychology: The Journal of Adlerian Theory, Research, and Practice, 41*(2), 243–254.

Nystul, M. S. (1985b). The use of motivation of modification techniques in Adlerian psychotherapy. *Individual Psychology: The Journal of Adlerian Theory, Research, and Practice, 44*(2), 199–209.

Nystul, M. S. (1986). Reaching in–reaching out: Counseling an autistic child. American *Mental Health Counselors Association Journal, 8,* 18–26.

Nystul, M. S. (1987a). Creative arts therapy and the existential encounter. *The Creative Child and Adult Quarterly, 12*(3), 243–249.

Nystul, M. S. (1987b). Strategies of parent-centered counseling of the young. *The Creative Child and Adult Quarterly, 12*(2), 103–111.

Nystul, M. S. (1988). An interview with Dr. Shulman. *Individual Psychology: The Journal of Adlerian Theory, Research, and Practice, 44*(2), 210–216.

Nystul, M. S. (1991). An interview with Jon Carlson. *Individual Psychology: The Journal of Adlerian Theory, Research, and Practice, 47*(4), 498–503.

Nystul, M. S. (1994a). Increasing the positive orientation to Adlerian psychotherapy: Redefining the concept of "basic mistakes." *Individual Psychology: The Journal of Adlerian Theory, Research, and Practice, 50*(3), 271–278.

Nystul, M. S. (1994b). The use of normalizing and structuring in the counseling process. *Counseling and Human Development, 26*(8), 11–12.

Nystul, M. S. (1995). A problem-solving approach to counseling: Integrating Adler's and Glasser's theories. *Elementary School Guidance and Counseling, 29*(4), 297–302.

Nystul, M. S. (1999). Problem-solving counseling: Integrating Adler's and Glasser's theories. In R. E. Watts & J. Carlson (Eds.), *Interventions and strategies in counseling and psychotherapy* (pp. 31–42). Philadelphia, PA: Accelerated Development.

Nystul, M. S. (2002a). Emotional balancing: A parenting technique to enhance parent-child relationships. In R. E. Watts (Ed.), *Techniques in marriage and family counseling* (Vol. 2; pp. 125–132). Alexandria, VA: American Counseling Association.

Nystul, M. S. (2002b). The role of parental emotions in parenting. *New Zealand Journal of Counseling, 23,* 29–39.

Nystul, M. S. (2010). Transcendental Meditation. In P. Rossi (Ed.), *The Corsini encyclopedia of psychology and behavioral sciences* (4th ed.; pp. 1795–1797). New York, NY: John Wiley & Sons.

Nystul, M. S., & Devall, E. L. (2010). Single parenthood. In I. B. Weiner & W. E. Craighead (Eds.), *The Corsini encyclopedia of psychology* (4th ed.; pp. 1599–1601). New York, NY: John Wiley and Sons.

Nystul, M. S., Emmons, R., & Cockrell, K. (1992). The use of pet therapy in counseling. *New Zealand Journal of Counseling, 14*(1), 32–35.

Nystul, M. S., & Garde, M. (1979). The self-concept of regular transcendental meditators, dropout meditators, and nonmeditators. *Journal of Psychology, 103,* 15–18.

Nystul, M. S., & Musynska, E. (1976). Adlerian treatment of a classical case of stuttering. *Journal of Individual Psychology, 32*(2), 194–202.

O'Brien, S. (1983). *Child pornography.* Dubuque, IA: Kendall/Hunt.

O'Connor, M. (1992). Psychotherapy with gay and lesbian adolescents. In S. Dworkin & F. Gutierrez (Eds.), *Counseling gay men and lesbians: Journey to the end of the rainbow.* Alexandria, VA: American Association for Counseling and Development.

O'Hanlon, W. H., & Weiner-Davis, M. (1989). *In search of solutions: A new direction in psychotherapy.* New York, NY: Norton.

Office of Strategic Services. (1948). *Assessment of men.* New York, NY: Holt, Rinehart & Winston.

Ohlsen, M. M. (1970). *Group counseling.* New York, NY: Holt, Rinehart & Winston.

Oklahoma State Department of Education. (1988). *Building skills for tomorrow: A developmental guidance model.* Oklahoma City, OK: State Board of Affairs.

Okun, B. F. (2002). *Effective helping interviewing and counseling techniques* (6th ed.). Monterey, CA: Brooks/Cole.

Oliver, L. W. (1977). Evaluating career counseling outcome for three modes of test interpretation. *Measurement and Evaluation in Guidance, 10,* 153–161.

Oliver, L. W., & Spokane, A. R. (1983). Research integration: Approaches, problems and recommendations for research reporting. *Journal of Counseling Psychology, 30,* 252–257.

Oliver, L. W., & Spokane, A. R. (1988). Career-intervention outcome: What contributes to clients' gain? *Journal of Counseling Psychology, 35*(4), 447–462.

Olson, D. H., & DeFrain, J. (1997). *Marriage and family: Diversity and strengths* (2nd ed.). Mountain View, CA: Mayfield Press.

Orbach, I., Feshbach, S., Carlson, G., Glaubman, H., & Gross, Y. (1983) Attraction and repulsion by life and death in suicidal and in normal children. *Journal of Consulting and Clinical Psychology, 51,* 661–670.

Orenchuk-Tomiuk, N., Matthey, G., & Christensen, C. P. (1990). The resolution model: A comprehensive treatment framework in sexual abuse. *Child Welfare, 69*(5), 417–431.

Orlando, D. E., & Howard, K. I. (1986). Process and outcome in psychotherapy. In S. L. Garfield & A. E. Bergin (Eds.), *Handbook of psychotherapy and behavior change.* New York, NY: John Wiley & Sons.

Orton, G. L. (1997). *Strategies for counseling with children and their parents.* Pacific Grove, CA: Brooks/Cole.

Osipow, S. H. (1990). Convergence in theories of career choice and development: Review and prospects. *Journal of Vocational Behavior, 36,* 122–131.

Osipow, S. H. (1996). *Theories of career development* (4th ed.). Englewood Cliffs, NJ: Prentice-Hall.

Othmer, E., & Othmer, S. C. (1989). *The clinical interview: Using DSM-III-R.* Washington, DC: American Psychiatric Press.

Page, B. J., Delmonico, D. L., Walsh, J., L'Amoreaux, N. A., Danninhirsh, C., Thompson, R. S., , , , Evans, A. D. (2000). Setting up on-line support groups using the Palace software. *Journal for Specialists in Group Work, 25,* 133–145.

Page, B. J., Jencius, M. J., Rehfuss, M. C., Foss, L. L., Dean, E. P., Petruzzi, M J , Sager, D. E. (2003). PalTalk online groups: Process and reflections on students' experience. *Journal for Specialists in Group Work, 28,* 35–41.

Paisley, P. O., & Benshoff, J. M. (1996). Applying developmental principles to practice: Training issues for the professional development of school counselors. *Elementary School Guidance and Counseling, 30*(3), 163–169.

Paisley, P. O., & Borders, D. L. (1995). School counseling: An emerging specialty. *Journal of Counseling and Development, 74*(2), 150–153.

Paisley, P. O., & DeAngelis-Peace, S. (1995). Developmental principles: A framework for school counseling programs. *Elementary School Guidance and Counseling, 30*(2), 85–93.

Paivio, S., & Greenberg, L. (1992). *Resolving unfinished business: A study of effects.* Paper presented at the annual meeting of the Society for Psychotherapy Research, Berkeley, CA.

Palmatier, L. L. (1990). Reality therapy and brief strategic interactional therapy. *Journal of Reality Therapy, 9*(2), 3–17.

Palmo, A. J. (1986). Professional identity of the mental health counselor. In A. J. Palmo & W. J. Weikel (Eds.), *Foundations of mental health counseling.* Springfield, IL: Charles C. Thomas.

Pan, Z., & Wu, X. (2008). A study on the effect of Systematic Training for Effective Parenting on improving the parent-child relation. *Chinese Journal of Clinical Psychology, 16,* 446–447

Paniagua, F. A. (1996). Cross-cultural guidelines in family therapy practice. *The Family Journal: Counseling and Therapy for Couples and Families, 4*(2), 127–138.

Papalia, D. E., Olds, S. W., & Feldman, R. D. (2007). *Human development* (10th ed). New York, NY: McGraw-Hill.

Paradise, L. V., Conway, B. S., & Zweig, J. (1986). Effects of expert and referent influence, physical attractiveness, and gender on perceptions of counselor attributes. *Journal of Counseling Psychology, 33,* 16–22.

Paradise, L. V., & Kirby, P. C. (1990). Legal issues in group work: Some perspectives on the legal liability of group counseling in private practice. *The Journal for Specialists in Group Work, 15*(2), 114–118.

Parette, H. P., & Hourcade, J. J. (1995). Disability etiquette and school counselors: A commonsense approach toward compliance with

the Americans with Disabilities Act. *The School Counselor, 52*(3), 224–233.

Paris, J. (2013a). The ideology behind *DSM-5.* In J. Paris & J. Phillips (Eds), *Making the DSM-5 concepts and controversies* (pp. 39–44). New York, NY: Springer.

Paris, J. (2013b). *The intelligent clinican's guide to DSM-5.* New York, NY: Oxford University Press.

Paris, J. (2013c). Preface. In J. Paris & J. Phillips (Eds). *Making the DSM-5: Concepts and controversies* (pp. v–vi). New York,NY: Springer.

Parker, S. (2011). Spirituality in counseling: A faith development perspectice. *Journal of Counseling and Development, 89,* 112–119.

Parr, G. D., & Ostrovsky, M. (1991). The role of moral development in deciding how to counsel children and adolescents. *The School Counselor, 39,* 14–19.

Parsons, F. (1909). *Choosing a vocation.* Boston, MA: Houghton Mifflin.

Passons, W. R. (1975). *Gestalt approaches in counseling.* New York, NY: Holt, Rinehart & Winston.

Pate, R. H., & Bondi, A. M. (1992). Religious beliefs and practice: An integral aspect of multicultural awareness. *Counselor Education and Supervision, 32*(2), 108–115.

Patterson, C. H. (1986). *Theories of counseling and psychology.* New York, NY: Harper & Row.

Patterson, C. H. (1992). Values in counseling and psychotherapy. In M. T. Burke & J. G. Miranti (Eds.), *Ethical and spiritual values in counseling* (pp. 107–120). Alexandria, VA: American Counseling Association.

Patterson, C. H. (1996). Multicultural counseling: From

diversity to universality. *Journal of Counseling and Development, 74*(3), 227–231.

Patterson, C. H. (2004). Do we need multicultural counseling competencies? *Journal of Mental Health Counseling, 26*, 67–73.

Patterson, G. R., DeBaryshe, R. D., & Ramsey, E. (1989). A developmental perspective on antisocial behavior. *American Psychologist, 44*(2), 329–335.

Patterson, J. B., McKenzie, B., & Jenkins, J. (1995). Creating accessible groups for individuals with disabilities. *Journal for Specialists in Group Work, 20*(2), 76–82.

Pattison, E. M., & Kaufman, E. (1982). The alcoholism syndrome: Definitions and models. In E. M. Pattison & E. Kaufman (Eds.), *Encyclopedic handbook of alcoholism* (pp. 3–30). New York, NY: Gardner Press.

Pavlov, I. P. (1906). The scientific investigation of the psychical faculties of processes in the higher animals. *Science, 24,* 613–619.

Pearson, J., Lunday, B., Rohrbach, L., & Whitney, D.(1985). *Project SMART: A social approach to drug abuse prevention.* Unpublished curriculum guide, University of Southern California, Health Behavior Research Institute, Los Angeles, CA.

Pedersen, P. (1987). Ten frequent assumptions of cultural bias in counseling. *Journal of Multicultural Counseling and Development, 15*(1), 16–24.

Pedersen, P. (1988). *A handbook for developing multicultural awareness.* Alexandria, VA: American Association for Counseling and Development.

Pedersen, P. (Ed.). (1991a). Multiculturalism as a fourth force in counseling [Special issue]. *Journal of Counseling and Development, 70.*

Pedersen, P. (1991b). Multiculturalism as a generic approach to counseling. *Journal of Counseling and Development, 70*(1), 6–12.

Pedersen, P. (1993). The multicultural dilemma of white cross-cultural researchers. *The Counseling Psychologist, 21*(2), 229–232.

Pedersen, P. (1997). The cultural context of the American Counseling Association Code of Ethics. *Journal of Counseling and Development, 76*(1), 23–28.

Peer, G. G. (1985). The status of secondary school guidance: A national survey. *The School Counselor, 32*(3), 181–189.

Peluso, P. R., Peluso, J. P., White, J. F., & Kern, R. (2004). A comparison of attachment theory and individual psychology: A review of the literature. *Journal of Counseling and Development, 82,* 139–145.

Penrose, L. S., & Raven, J. C. (1936). A new series of perceptual tasks: Preliminary communication. *British Journal of Medical Psychology, 16,* 97–104.

Pepinsky, H. B., & Pepinsky, P. N. (1954). *Counseling: Theory and practice.* New York, NY: Ronald Press.

Perls, F. (1969a). *Gestalt therapy verbatim.* Moab, UT: Real People Press.

Perls, F. (1969b). *In and out of the garbage pail.* Moab, UT: Real People Press.

Petersen, A. C., Compas, B. E., Brooks-Gunn, J., Stemmler, M., Ey, S., & Grant, K. E. (1993). Depression in adolescence. *American Psychologist, 48*(2), 155–168.

Peterson, D. R. (1995). The reflective educator. *American Psychologist, 50*(12), 975–983.

Peterson, D. R. (2000). Scientist-practitioner or scientific practitioner? *American Psychologist, 55*(2), 252–253.

Pettigrew, T. F., & Tropp, L. R. (2006). A meta-analytic test of inter-group contact theory. *Journal of Personality and Social Psychology, 90,* 751–783.

Phillips, S. D., & Blustein, D. L. (1994). Readiness for career choices: Planning, exploring, and deciding. *Career Development Quarterly, 63*–73.

Phillips, S. D., Cairo, P. C., Blustein, D. L., & Myers, R. A. (1988). Career development and behavior, 1987: A review. *Journal of Vocational Behavior, 33,* 119–184.

Phillips, V. I., & Cornell, D. G. (2012). Identifying victims of bullying: Use of counselor interviews to confirm peer nominations. *Professional School Counseling, 15,* 123–131.

Piaget, J. (1952). *The origins of intelligence in children* (M. Cook, Trans.). New York, NY: Norton.

Piaget, J. (1955). *The language and thought of the child.* New York, NY: New American Library. (Original work published 1923)

Piaget, J. (1965). *The moral judgment of the child* (M. Gabain, Trans.). New York, NY: Free Press. (Original work published 1936)

Pierre, J. M. (2013). Overdiagnosis, underdiagnosis, synthesis: A dialectic for psychiatry and the *DSM.* In J. Paris & J. Phillips (Eds), *Making the DSM-5: Concepts and controversies* (pp. 105–124). New York, NY: Springer.

Pickert, K. (2014, February 3). The art of being mindful. *Time, 183*(4), 40–48.

Pincus, H. A., Goodwin, F. K., Barchas, J. D., Cohen, D. J., Judd, L. L., Meltzer, H. Y., & Vaillant, G. E. (1989). The future of the science of psychiatry. In J. A. Talbott (Ed.), *Future directions for psychiatry* (pp. 75–106). Washington, DC: American Psychiatric Press.

Pipal, J. E. (1995). Managed care: Is it the corpse in the living room? An expose. *Psychotherapy, 32*(2), 323–332.

Pistole, M. C. (1993). Attachment relationships: Self-disclosure and trust. *Journal of Mental Health Counseling, 15,* 94–106.

Poidevant, J. M., & Lewis, H. A. (1995). Transactional Analysis theory. In D. Capuzzi and D. R. Gross (Eds.), *Counseling and psychotherapy: Theories and interventions* (pp. 297–324). Columbus, OH: Merrill.

Polansky, N., Chalmers, M., Buttenwieser, E., & Williams, D. (1981). *Damaged parents: An anatomy of child neglect.* Chicago, IL: University of Chicago Press.

Polich, J. M., Armor, D. M., & Braiker, H. B. (1981). *The course of alcoholism: Four years after treatment.* New York, NY: Wiley.

Polich, J. M., Ellickson, P. L., Reuter, P., & Kahan, J. P. (1984). *Strategies for controlling adolescent drug use.* Santa Monica, CA: Rand.

Polk, E. (1977). Dance therapy with special children. In K. Mason (Ed.), *Dance therapy: Focus on dance VII* (pp. 56–58). Washington, DC: American Alliance for Health, Physical Education, and Recreation.

Pomerantz, A. M. (2014). *Clinical psychology: Science, practice, and culture* (3rd ed.). Thousand Oaks, CA: SAGE.

Ponterotto, J. G. (2005). Qualitative research in counseling psychology: A primer on research paradigms and philosophy of science. *Journal of Counseling Psychology, 52*(2), 126–136.

Ponterotto, J. G., & Casas, J. M. (1991). *Handbook of racial/ ethnic minority counseling research.* Springfield, IL: Charles C. Thomas.

Ponzo, Z. (1992). Promoting successful aging: Problems, opportunities, and counseling guidelines. *Journal of Counseling and Development, 71,* 210–213.

Pope-Davis, D. B., & Ottavi, T. M. (1994). Examining the association between self-reported multicultural counseling competencies and demographic variables among counselors. *Journal of Counseling and Development, 72,* 651–654.

Pope-Davis, D. B., Toporek, R. L., Ortega-Villalobos, L., Ligiéro, D. P., Brittan-Powell, C. S., Liu, . . . Liang, C. T. H. (2002). Client perspectives of multicultural counseling competence: A qualitative examination. *The Counseling Psychologist, 30,* 355–393.

Popkin, M. H. (2000). Youth violence in our communities— And what we can do. *The Journal of Individual Psychology, 56*(4), 395–410.

Popkin, M. H. (2014). Active parenting: 30 years of video-based parent education. *The Journal of Individual Psychology, 70,* 166–176.

Portman, T. A. A. (2009). Faces of the future: School counselors as cultural mediators. *Journal of Counseling and Development, 87*(1), 21–27.

Post, P. B., Ceballos, P. L., & Penn. S. L. (2012). Collaborating with parents to establish behavioral goals in child-centered therapy. *The Family Journal: Counseling and Therapy for Couples and Families, 20,* 51–57.

Prince, J. P. (1995). Influences on the career development of gay men. *Career Development Quarterly, 44*(2), 148–167.

Prochaska, J. O. (1984). *Systems of psychotherapy: A transtheoretical analysis.* Chicago, IL: Dorsey Press.

Prochaska, J. O., DiClemente, C. C., & Norcross, J. C. (1992). In search of how people change: Applications to addictive behaviors. *American Psychologist, 47*(9), 1102–1114.

Prochaska, J. O., & Norcross, J. C. (2002). *Systems of psychotherapy: A transtheoretical analysis* (5th ed.). Pacific Grove, CA: Brooks/Cole.

Prochaska, J. O., & Norcross, J. C. (2010). *Systems of psychotherapy: A transtheoretical analysis* (7th ed.) Belmont, CA: Brooks/Cole Cengage Learning.

Proctor, G., & Napier, M. (2004). *Encountering feminism: Intersections between feminism and the person-centered approach.* Ross-on-Wye, UK: PCCS Books.

The Education for All Handicapped Children Act of 1975, Pub. L. 94-142, (1975).

Puig Antich, J., Perel, J. M., Lupatkins, W., Chambers, W. J., Tabrizi, M. A., King, J., . . . Stiller, R. L. (1987). Imipramine in prepubertal major depressive disorders. *Archives of General Psychiatry, 44,* 81–89.

Puryear, D. A. (1979). *Helping people in crisis.* San Francisco, CA: Jossey-Bass.

Putman, M. L. (1997). Crisis intervention with adolescents with learning disabilities. In J. Carlson & J. Lewis (Eds), *Counseling adolescents* (5th ed., pp. 61–104). Denver, CO: Love.

Putnam, M.L. (2007). Crisis intervention with adolescents with learning disabilities. In J. Carlson & J. Lewis (Eds.). *Counseling the adolescents: Individual, family, and school interventions* (5th Ed.) (pp.61-104). Denver, CO: Love Publishing Co.

Putman, S. E. (2009). The monsters in my head: Posttraumatic stress disorder and the child survivor of sexual abuse. *Journal of Counseling and Development, 87*(1), 80–89.

Quay, H. C., & Petersen, D. R. (1983). *Interim manual for the revised behavior problem checklist.* Unpublished manuscript, University of Miami.

Quintana, S. M., & Holahan, W. (1992). Termination in short-term counseling: Comparison of successful and unsuccessful cases. *Journal of Counseling Psychology, 39*(3), 299–305.

Radbill, S. X. (1980). Children in a world of violence: A history of child abuse. In C. H. Kempe & R. E. Helfer (Eds.), *The battered child* (3rd ed.; pp. 3–20). Chicago, IL: University of Chicago.

Raffa, H., Sypek, J., & Vogel, W. (1990). Commentary on reviews of "outcome" studies of family and marital psychotherapy. *Contemporary Family Therapy, 12*(1), 65–73.

Rahim, M. A. (1983). A measure of styles of handling interpersonal conflict. *Academy of Management Journal, 26*(2), 368–376.

Raiche, B. M., Fox, R., & Rotatori, A. F. (1986). Counseling the mildly behaviorally disordered child. In A. F. Rotatori, P. J. Gerber, F. W. Litton, & R. A. Fox (Eds.), *Counseling exceptional students* (pp. 123–143). New York, NY: Human Sciences Press.

Raimy, V. (1950). *Training in clinical psychology.* Englewood Cliffs, NJ: Prentice-Hall.

Rak, C. F., & Patterson, L. E. (1996). Promoting resilience in at-risk children. *Journal of Counseling and Development, 74*(4), 368–373.

Rapaport, D. (1958). The theory of ego autonomy: A generalization. *Bulletin of Menninger Clinic, 22,* 13–35.

Rapin, L. S., & Keel, L. (1998). *Association for specialists in group work: Best practice guidelines.* Alexandria, VA: American Counseling Association.

Raque-Bogdan, T. L., Torrey, C. L., Lewis, B. L., & Borges, N. J. (2012). Counseling health psychology: Assessing health psychology training within counseling psychology docotoral programs. *The Counseling Psychologist, 41,* 428–452.

Rashid, T., & Seligman, M. (2014). Positive psychotherapy. In R. J. Corsini & D. Wedding (Eds.), *Current psychotherapies* (10th ed.; pp. 461–498). Belmont, CA: Brooks/Cole, Cengage Learning.

Raskin, N. J., & Rogers, C. R. (2000). Person-centered therapy. In R. J. Corsini & D. Wedding (Eds.), *Current psychotherapies* (6th ed.; pp. 133–167). Itasca, IL: F. E. Peacock.

Raskin, N. J., & Rogers, C. R. (2005). Person-centered therapy. In R. J. Corsini & D. Wedding (Eds.), *Current psychotherapies* (7th ed.; pp. 133–167). Itasca, IL: F. E. Peacock.

Raskin, N., Rogers, C., & Witty, M. (2011). Client-centered therapy. In R. J. Corsini & D. Wedding (Eds.), *Current psychotherapies* (9th ed.; pp. 137–180). Belmont, CA: Brooks/Cole, Cengage Learning.

Raskin, N., Rogers, C., & Witty, M. (2014). Client-centered therapy. In R. J. Corsini & D. Wedding (Eds.), *Current psychotherapies* (10th ed.; pp. 95–150). Belmont, CA: Brooks/Cole, Cengage Learning.

Raskin, P. A., & Israel, A. C. (1981). Sex role imitation in children: Effects of sex of child, sex of model, and sex role appropriateness of modeled behavior. *Sex Roles, 7*(11), 1067–1077.

Raskin, P. M. (1987). *Vocational counseling: A guide for the practitioner.* New York, NY: Teachers College Press.

Rasmussen, P. R. (2014). The task, challenges, and obstacles of parenting. *The Journal of Individual Psychology, 70,* 90–113.

Rawlings, E. I. (1993). Reflections on "Twenty Years of Feminist Counseling and Therapy." *The Counseling Psychologist, 21*(1), 88–91.

Rawlins, M. E., Eberly, C. G., & Rawlins, L. D. (1991). Infusing counseling skills in test interpretation. *Counselor Education and Supervision, 31,* 109–120.

Read, H., Fordham, M., & Adler, G. (Eds.). (1953–1978). *Jung's collected works.* New York, NY: Pantheon.

Reams, R., & Friedrich, W. N. (1983). *Play therapy: A review of outcome research.* Seattle: University of Washington, Department of Psychology.

Reichenberg, L. W. (2014). *DSM-5 essentials: The savvy clinician's guide to the changes in criteria.* Hoboken, NJ: Wiley.

Reiner, S. M., Dobmeier, R. A., & Hernandez, T. J. (2013). Perceived impact of professional counselor identity: An exploratory study. *Journal of Counseling and Development, 91,* 174–183.

Reisetter, M., Korcuska, J. S., Yexley, M., Bonds, D., Nikels, H., & McHenry, W. (2004). Counselor educators and qualitative research: Affirming a research identity. *Counselor Education and Supervision, 44*(1), 2–16.

Remafedi, G. (1987). Homosexual youth: A challenge to contemporary society. *Journal of the American Medical Association, 258,* 222–225.

Remley, T. P. (1991). *Preparing for court appearances.* Alexandria, VA: American Association for Counseling and Development.

Remley, T. P., & Herlihy, B. (2014). *Ethical, legal, and professional issues in counseling* (4th ed.). Upper Saddle River, NJ: Merrill/Prentice Hall.

Reynolds, C. R. (1982). The problem of bias in psychological assessment. In C. R. Reynolds & T. B. Gutkin (Eds.), *The handbook of school psychology* (pp. 178–208). New York, NY: John Wiley & Sons.

Reynolds, M. (1976). Threats to confidentiality. *Social Work, 21,* 108–113.

Reynolds, W. M. (2002). *Reynolds Adolescent Depression Scale–second edition: Professional manual.* Odessa, FL: Psychological Assessment Resources.

Reynolds, W. M., & Coats, K. I. (1986). A comparison of cognitive-behavioral therapy and relocation training for the treatment of depression in adolescents. *Journal of Counseling and Clinical Psychology, 54,* 653–660.

Rhyne, J. (1987). Gestalt art therapy. In J. A. Rubin (Ed.), *Approaches to art therapy: Theory and technique* (pp. 167–187). New York, NY: Brunner/Mazel.

Ribak-Rosenthal, N., & Russell, T. T. (1994). Dealing with religious differences in December: A school counselor's role. *Elementary School Counseling and Guidance, 28*(4), 295–301.

Ricard, R. J., Lerma, E., & Heard, C. C. C. (2013). Piloting a dialectical behavioral therapy (DBT) infused skills group in a disciplinary alternative education program (DAEP). *The Journal for Specialists in Group Work, 38,* 285–306.

Rice, K. G. (1990). Attachment in adolescence: A narrative and meta-analytic review. *Journal of Youth and Adolescence, 19,* 511–536.

Rice, K. G., & Meyer, A. L. (1994). Preventing depression among young adolescents: Preliminary process results of a psycho-educational program. *Journal of Counseling and Development, 73*(2), 145–152.

Richards, K. C., Campenni, C. E., & Muse-Burke, J. L. (2010). Self-care and well-being in mental health professionals: The mediating effects of self-awareness and mindfulness. *Journal of Mental Health Counseling, 32,* 247–264.

Richards, P. S., & Bergin, A. E. (1997). *Strategy for counseling and psychotherapy.* Washington, DC: American Psychological Association.

Richards, P. S., & Bergin, A. E. (2004). A theistic spiritual strategy for psychotherapy. In P. S. Richards & A. E. Bergin (Eds.), *Casebook for a spiritual strategy in counseling and psychotherapy* (pp. 3–32). Washington, DC: American Psychological Association.

Richardson, B. K., & Bradley, L. J. (1985). *Community agency counseling: An emerging specialty in counselor education programs.* Alexandria, VA: American Association for Counseling and Development.

Richardson, M. S. (1996). From career counseling to counseling/psychotherapy and work, job, and career. In M. L. Savickas & W. B. Walsh (Eds.), *Handbook of career counseling theory and practice* (pp. 347–360). Palo Alto, CA: Davies-Black.

Richardson, T. Q., & Molinaro, K. L. (1996). White counselor self-awareness: A prerequisite for developing multicultural competence. *Journal of Counseling and Development, 74*(3), 238–242.

Ricks, M. H. (1985). The social transmission of parental behavior: Attachment across generations. *Monograph of the Society for Research on Child Development, 50,* 211–227.

Ridley, C. R., & Kleiner, A. J. (2003). Multicultural counseling competence: History, themes, and issues. In D. B. Pope-Davis, H. L. K. Coleman, W. M. Liu, & R.

L. Toporek (Eds.), *Handbook of multicultural competencies in counseling and psychology* (pp. 3–20), Thousand Oaks, CA: SAGE.

Ridley, C. R., Li, L. C., & Hill, C. L. (1998). Multicultural assessment: Reexamination, reconceptualization, and practical application. *The Counseling Psychologist, 26,* 827–910.

Ridley, C. R., Mendoza, D. W., & Kanitz, B. E. (1994). Multicultural training: Reexamination, operationalization, and integration. *The Counseling Psychologist, 22*(2), 227–289.

Rigazio-DiGilio, S. A. (1994). A co-constructive-developmental approach. *Journal of Mental Health Counseling, 16*(1), 43–74.

Rimm, D. C., & Cunningham, H. M. (1905). Behavior therapies. In S. J. Lynn & J. P. Garske (Eds.), *Contemporary psychotherapies.* Columbus, OH: Merrill/Macmillan.

Riordan, R. J., & Wilson, L. S. (1989). Bibliotherapy: Does it work? *Journal of Counseling and Development, 67,* 506–508.

Ritchie, M. H., & Partin, R. L. (1994). Parent education and consultation activities of school counselors. *The School Counselor, 41*(3), 165–170.

Rittenhouse, J. A. (1997). Feminist principles in survivors' groups: Out-of-group contact. *Journal for Specialists in Group Work, 22*(2), 111–119.

Ritter, K. Y., & O'Neill, C. W. (1995). Moving through loss: The spiritual journey of gay men and lesbian women. In M. T. Burke & J. G. Miranti (Eds.), *Counseling: The spiritual dimension* (pp. 127–141). Alexandria, VA: American Counseling Association.

Robbins, A. (1985). Working towards the establishment of creative arts therapies as an independent profession. *The Arts in Psychotherapy, 12,* 67–70.

Robins, L., Helzer, J. E., Croughan, J., & Ratcliff, K. S. (1981). National Institute of Mental Health diagnostic interview schedule: Its history, characteristics, and validity. *Archives of General Psychiatry, 38,* 381–389.

Robson, B. E. (2002). Changing family patterns: Developmental impacts on children. In J. Carlson & J. Lewis (Eds.), *Counseling the adolescent: Individual, family and school interventions* (4th ed.; pp. 261–278). Denver, CO: Love.

Roe, A. (1956). *The psychology of occupations.* New York, NY: Wiley.

Roe, A., & Lunneborg, P. W. (2002). Personality development and career choice. In D. Brown, L. Brooks, & Associates (Eds.), *Career choice and development* (4th ed.). San Francisco, CA: Jossey-Bass.

Rogers, C. (1939). *The clinical treatment of the problem child.* Boston, MA: Houghton Mifflin.

Rogers, C. (1942). *Counseling and psychotherapy.* Boston, MA: Houghton Mifflin.

Rogers, C. (1951). *Client-centered therapy.* Boston, MA: Houghton Mifflin.

Rogers, C. (1957). The necessary and sufficient condition of therapeutic personality change. *Journal of Consulting Psychology, 21,* 95–103.

Rogers, C. (1961). *On becoming a person.* Boston, MA: Houghton Mifflin.

Rogers, C. (1970). *On encounter groups.* New York, NY: Harper & Row.

Rogers, C. (1981). *A way of being.* Boston, MA: Houghton Mifflin.

Rogers, C., Gendlin, E. T., Kiesler, D. J., & Truax, C. B. (1967). *The therapeutic relationship and its impact: A study of psychotherapy with schizophrenics.* Madison: University of Wisconsin Press.

Rogers, C., & Wood, J. K. (1974). Client-centered theory: Carl R. Rogers. In A. Burton (Ed.), *Operational theories of personality* (pp. 211–258). New York, NY: Bruner/Mazel.

Rogers, F., & Sharapan, H. (1993). Play. *Elementary School Guidance and Counseling, 28*(1), 10–16.

Rogers, J. R., & Russell, E. J. (2014). A framework for bridging cultural barriers in suicide risk assessment: The role of compatibility heuristics. *The Counseling Psychologist, 42,* 55–72.

Roll, S. A., Crowley, M. A., & Rappl, L. E. (1985). Client perceptions of counselors' nonverbal behavior: A reevaluation. *Counselor Education and Supervision, 24,* 234–243.

Romano, J. L., & Kachgal, M. M. (2004). Counseling psychology and school counseling: An underutilized partnership. *The Counseling Psychologist, 32,* 184–215.

Rosen, C. S., Chow, H. C., Finney, J. F., Greenbaum, M. A., Moos, R. H., Sheikh, J. I., & Yesavage, J. (2004). VA practice patterns and practice guidelines for teating posttraumatic stress disorder. *Journal of Traumatic Stress, 17,* 213–222.

Rosenhan, D. L., & Seligman, M. E. P. (1995). *Abnormal psychology* (3rd ed.). New York, NY: Norton.

Rotatori, A. F., Banbury, M., & Sisterhen, D. (1986). Overview of counseling exceptional students. In A. F. Rotatori, P. J. Gerber, F. W. Litton, & R. A. Fox (Eds.), *Counseling exceptional students* (pp. 21–38). New York, NY: Human Sciences Press.

Rotatori, A. F., Gerber, P. J., Litton, F. W., & Fox, R. A. (Eds.). (1986). *Counseling exceptional students.* New York, NY: Human Sciences Press.

Roth, E. A. (1987). A behavioral approach to art therapy. In J. A. Rubin (Ed.), *Approaches to art therapy: Theory and technique.* New York, NY: Brunner/Mazel.

Rothenberg, P. S. (1995). *Race, class, and gender in the United States: An integrated study.* New York, NY: St. Martin's Press.

Rowe, F. A. (1989). College students' perceptions of high school counselors. *The School Counselor, 36,* 260–264.

Rowe, W., Behrens, J. T., & Leach, M. M. (1995). Racial/ethnic identity and racial consciousness: Looking back and looking forward. In J. G. Ponterotto, J. M. Casas, L. A. Suzuki, & C. M. Alexander (Eds.), *Handbook of multicultural counseling* (pp. 218–235). Thousand Oaks, CA: SAGE.

Ruben, A. M. (1989). Preventing school dropouts through classroom guidance. *Elementary School Guidance and Counseling, 24,* 21–29.

Rubin, J. A. (1987). Freudian psychoanalytic theory: Emphasis on uncovering and insight. In J. A. Rubin (Ed.), *Approaches to art therapy: Theory and technique.* New York, NY: Brunner/Mazel.

Rubisch, J. C. (1995). Promoting postsecondary education in rural schools. *The School Counselor, 42*(5), 404–409.

Rudd, M. D. (1989). The prevalence of suicidal ideation among college students. *Suicide and Life-Threatening Behavior, 19,* 173–183.

Ruden, R. A., & Byalick, M. (1997). *The craving brain: The biobalance approach to controlling addiction.* New York, NY: HarperCollins.

Rupert, P. A., & Baird, K. A. (2004). Managed care and the independent practice of psychology. *Professional Psychology: Research and Practice, 35*(2), 185–193.

Russell, R. L., & Lucariello, J. (1992). Narrative, yes; narrative ad infinitum, no! *American Psychologist, 47*(5), 671–672.

Russell, T., & Madsen, D. H. (1985). *Marriage counseling report user's guide.* Champaign, IL: Institute for Personality and Ability Testing.

Russo, T. J., & Kassera, W. (1989). A comprehensive needsassessment package for secondary school guidance programs. *The School Counselor, 36,* 265–269.

Rutter, M. (1996). Transitions and turning points in developmental psychopathology: As applied to the age span between childhood and mid-adulthood. *International Journal of Behavioral Development, 19*(3), 603–626.

Rutter, M., Dunn, J., Plomin, R., Simonoff, E., Pickles, A., Maughan, B., . . . Eaves, L. (1997). Integrating nature and nurture: Implications of person-environment correlations and interactions for developmental psychopathology. *Development and Psychopathology, 9,* 335–364.

Ryan, N. E. (1999). *Career counseling and career choice goal attainment.* Unpublished doctoral dissertation, Loyola University, Chicago.

Saayman, G. S., Faber, P. A., & Saayman, R. V. (1988). Archetypal factors revealed in the study of marital breakdown: A Jungian perspective. *Journal of Analytical Psychology, 33,* 253–276.

Sadler, J. Z. (2013). Considering the economy of *DSM* alternatives. In J. Paris & J. Phillips (Eds), *Making the DSM-5: Concepts and Controversies* (pp. 21–38). New York, NY: Springer.

Safran, J. D., & Kriss, A. (2014). Psychanalytic psychotherapies. In D. Wedding & R. J. Corsini (Eds), *Current psychotherapies* (10th ed.;

pp. 19–54). Belmont, CA: Brooks/Cole, Cengage Learning.

Sager, C. (1976). *Marriage contracts and couple therapy.* New York, NY: Brunner/Mazel.

Sakolske, D. H., & Janzen, H. L. (1987). Dependency. In A. Thomas & J. Grimes (Eds.), *Children's needs: Psychological perspectives* (pp. 157–166). Washington, DC: The National Association of School Psychologists.

Salkind, N. (1994). *Child development* (7th ed.). San Diego, CA: Harcourt Brace Jovanovich.

Salomone, P. R. (1988). Career counseling: Steps and stages beyond Parsons. *Career Development Quarterly, 36,* 218–221.

Salovey, P., & Mayer, J. D. (1990). Emotional intelligence. *Imagination, Cognition, and Personality, 9,* 185–211.

Sampson, J. P. (1990). Computer-assisted testing and the goals of counseling psychology. *The Counseling Psychologist, 18,* 227–239.

Sampson, J. P. (1994). Factors influencing the effective use of computer-assisted career guidance: The North American experience. *British Journal of Guidance and Counselling, 22*(1), 91–106.

Sampson, J. P., Jr., Shahnasarian, M., & Reardon, R. C. (1987). Computer-assisted career guidance: A national perspective on the use of DISCOVER and SIGI. *Journal of Counseling and Development, 65*(8), 416–419.

Samuels, A. (1985). *Jung and the post-Jungians.* London, UK: Routledge & Kegan Paul.

Samuels, A. (1989). Analysis and pluralism: The politics of psyche. *Journal of Analytical Psychology, 34,* 33–51.

Sandage, S. J., Crabtree, S., & Schweer, M. (2014). Differentiation of self and social justice:

Commitment mediated by hope. *Journal of Counseling & Development, 92,* 67–74.

Sandhu, D. S., & Aspy, C. B. (1997). *Counseling for prejudice prevention and reduction.* Alexandria, VA: American Counseling Association.

Sandhu, D. S., & Portes, P. R. (1995). The proactive model of school counseling. *International Journal for the Advancement of Counselling, 18,* 11–20.

Satir, V. M. (1983). *Conjoint family therapy* (3rd ed.). Palo Alto, CA: Science and Behavior Books.

Satir, V. M. (1988). *The new peoplemaking.* Palo Alto, CA: Science and Behavior Books.

Saucier, M. G. (2004). Midlife and beyond: Issues for aging women. *Journal of Counseling and Development, 82,* 420–425.

Savickas, M. L. (1994). A festschrift for Donald E. Super. *The Career Development Quarterly, 43*(1), 3.

Savickas, M. L. (1996). A framework for linking career theory and practice. In M. L. Savickas & W. B. Walsh (Eds.), *Handbook of career counseling theory and practice* (pp. 191–208). Palo Alto, CA: Davies-Black.

Savickas, M. L. (1997). Career adaptability: An integrative construct for life-span, life-space theory. *Career Development Quarterly, 45,* 247–259.

Savickas, M. L. (2011). *Career counseling.* Washington, DC: American Psychological Association.

Savickas, M. L. (2012). Life design: A paradigm for career intervention in the 21st century. *Journal of Counseling and Development, 90,* 13–19.

Savickas, M. L., & Walsh, W. B. (1996). Toward convergence between career theory and practice. In M. L. Savickas & W. B. Walsh

(Eds.), *Handbook of career counseling theory and practice* (pp. xi–xvi). Palo Alto, CA: Davies-Black.

Sayger, T. V., Horne, A. M., & Glaser, B. A. (1993). Marital satisfaction and social learning family therapy for child conduct problems: Generalization of treatment effects. *Journal of Marital and Family Therapy, 19,* 393–402.

Scarborough, J. L., & Culbreth, J. R. (2008). Examining discrepancies between actual and preferred practice of school counselors. *Journal of Counseling and Development, 86*(4), 446–459.

Scheel, M. J., Davis, C. K., & Henderson, J. D. (2012). Therapist use of client strengths: A qualitative study of positive processes. *The Counseling Psychologist, 41,* 392–427.

Schulte, J. M. (1992). The morality of influencing in counseling. In M. T. Burke & J. G. Miranti (Eds.), *Ethical and spiritual values in counseling* (pp. 107–120). Alexandria, VA: American Counseling Association.

Schultz, C., & Nystul, M. S. (1980). Mother-child interaction behavior as an outcome of theoretical models of parent group education. *Journal of Individual Psychology, 36,* 16–29.

Schultz, C., Nystul, M. S., & Law, H. (1980). Attitudinal outcomes of theoretical models of parent group education. *Journal of Individual Psychology, 37,* 107–112.

Schultz, W. C. (1977). *FIRO-B* (2nd ed.). Palo Alto, CA: Consulting Psychologists Press.

Schwartz, J. P., & Waldo, M. (2003). Interpersonal manifestations of lifestyle: Individual psychology integrated with interpersonal theory. *Journal of Mental Health Counseling, 25,* 101–111.

Schwartz, R. C. (2008). Psychosocial symptoms and poor insight as predictors of homicidality among clients with psychosis: Implications for counseling practice and research. *Journal of Counseling and Development, 86*(4), 471–481.

Scott, C. N., Kelly, F. D., & Tolbert, B. L. (1995). Realism, constructivism, and the individual psychology of Alfred Adler. *Individual Psychology: The Journal of Adlerian Theory, Research, and Practice, 51*(1), 5–20.

Segal, Z. V., Williams, M. G., & Teasdale, J. D. (2002). *Mindfulness-based cognitive therapy for depression.* New York, NY: Guilford Press.

Segal, Z. V., Williams, J. M., & Teasdale, J. D. (2013). *Mindfulness-based cognitive therapy for depression* (2nd ed.). New York, NY: Guilford Press

Seligman, L. (1986). The manuscript evaluation process used by AACD journals. *Journal of Counseling and Development, 65*(4), 189–192.

Seligman, L. (1994). *Developmental career counseling and assessment* (2nd. ed.). Thousand Oaks, CA: SAGE.

Seligman, L. (1998). *Selecting effective treatments: A comprehensive, systematic guide to treating adult mental disorders* (2nd ed.). San Francisco, CA: Jossey-Bass.

Seligman, L., & Reichenberg, L. W. (2012). *Selecting effective treatments: A comprehensive, systematic guide to treating mental disorders* (4th ed.). Hoboken, NJ: John Wiley & Sons.

Seligman, M. (1991). *Learned optimism.* New York, NY: Knopf.

Seligman, M. E. P. (1995). The effectiveness of psychotherapy: The *Consumer Reports* study. *American Psychologist, 50*(12), 965–974.

Selvini-Palazzoli, M. (1980). Why a long interval between sessions? The therapeutic control of the family-therapist suprasystem. In M. Andolfi & I. Zwerling (Eds.), *Dimensions of family therapy.* New York, NY: Guilford Press.

Selzer, M. L. (1971). Michigan alcoholism screening test: The quest for a new diagnostic instrument. *American Journal of Psychiatry, 127,* 1653–1658.

Senge, P. M. (1990). *The fifth discipline: The art and practice of the learning organization.* New York, NY: Doubleday/Currency.

Sexton, T. L., & Whiston, S. C. (1994). The status of the counseling relationship: An empirical review, theoretical implications and research directions. *The Counseling Psychologist, 22*(1), 6–78.

Shadish, W. R., Ragsdale, K., Glaser, R. R., & Montgomery, L. M. (1995). The efficacy and effectiveness of marital and family therapy: A perspective from meta-analysis. *Journal of Marital and Family Therapy, 21*(4), 345–360.

Shafranske, E. P. (Ed.). (1996). *Religion and clinical practice of psychology.* Washington, DC: American Psychological Association.

Shakespeare, W. (1938). Hamlet. In *The works of William Shakespeare: Gathered into one volume.* New York, NY: Oxford University Press. (Original work published 1603)

Shannon, J. W., & Woods, W. J. (1991). Affirmative psychotherapy for gay men. *The Counseling Psychologist, 19*(2), 197–215.

Sharf, R. S. (2001). *Applying career development theory to counseling* (3rd ed.). Pacific Grove, CA: Brooks/Cole.

Sharpley, C. F. (2007). So why aren't counselors reporting *n* = 1 research designs? *Journal of Counseling & Development, 85,* 349–356.

Shaver, P. R., & Brennan, K. A. (1992). Attachment styles and the "big five" personality traits: Their connections with each other and with romantic relationship outcomes. *Personality and Social Psychology Bulletin, 18,* 536–545.

Shaw, H. E., & Shaw, S. F. (2006). Critical ethical issues in online counseling: Assessing current practices with an ethical intent checklist. *Journal of Counseling and Development, 84*(1), 41–53.

Shaw, M. D., & Goodyear, R. K. (1984, April). Introduction to special issues on primary prevention. *The Personnel and Guidance Journal,* 444–445.

Shea, M. T., Pilkonis, P. A., Beckham, E., Collins, J. F., Elkin, I., Sotsky, S. M., & Docherty, J. P. (1990). Personality disorders and treatment outcome in the NIMH Treatment of Depression Collaborative Research Program. *American Journal of Psychiatry, 147,* 711–718.

Sherman, R., & Dinkmeyer, D. (1987). *Systems of family therapy: An Adlerian integration.* New York, NY: Brunner/Mazel.

Sherrard, P. A. D., & Amatea, E. S. (1994). Looking through the looking glass: A preview. *Journal of Mental Health Counseling, 16*(1), 3–5.

Sherrard, P. A. D., & Amatea, E. S. (2003). Ecosystem theory. In D. Capuzzi & D. R. Gross (Eds.), *Counseling and psychotherapy: Theories and interventions* (3rd ed.). Columbus, OH: Merrill.

Sherwood-Hawes, A. (1995). Nontraditional approaches to counseling and psychotherapy.

In D. Capuzzi & D. R. Douglas (Eds.), *Counseling and psychotherapy: Theories and interventions* (2nd ed.). Columbus, OH: Merrill.

Shi, Q., Steen, S., & Weiss, B. A. (2013). The impact of parental support and perception of school on Hispanic youth's substance use. *The Family Journal: Counseling and Therapy for Couples and Families, 21,* 425–434.

Shields, C. G. (1986). Critiquing the new epistemologies: Towards minimum requirements for scientific theory of family therapy. *Journal of Marital and Family Therapy, 12,* 359–372.

Shneidman, E. S. (1976). A psychological theory of suicide. *Psychiatric Annals, 6,* 51–66.

Shneidman, E.S. (1984). Suicide. In R. Corsini (Ed.), *Encyclopedia of psychology* (Vol.3) (pp. 383–386). New York, Wiley.

Shneidman, E. S., Farberow, N. L., & Litman, R. E. (1976). *The psychology of suicide.* New York, NY: Aronson.

Shoda, Y., Mischel, W., & Peake, P. K. (1990). Predicting adolescent cognitive and self-regulatory competencies from preschool delay of gratification: Identifying diagnostic conditions. *Developmental Psychology, 26,* 978–986.

Sholevar, G. (1985). Marital therapy. In H. Kaplan & B. Sadock (Eds.), *Comprehensive textbook of psychiatry IV* (Vol. 2; pp. 1443–1450). Baltimore, MD: Williams & Wilkins.

Shostrom, E. L. (Producer). (1965). *Three approaches to psychotherapy* [Film]. Orange, CA: Psychological Films.

Shulman, B. H. (1973). *Contributions to individual psychology.* Chicago, IL: Alfred Adler Institute.

Sifneos, P. (1979). *Short-term dynamic psychotherapy.* New York, NY: Plenum.

Sifneos, P. (1984). The current status of individual short-term dynamic psychotherapy and its future. *American Journal of Psychotherapy, 38*(4), 472–483.

Silver, R. A. (1987). A cognitive approach to art therapy. In J. A. Rubin (Ed.), *Approaches to art therapy: Theory and technique* (pp. 233–250). New York, NY: Brunner/Mazel.

Silverman, D. (2001). *Interpreting qualitative data: Methods for analyzing talk, text, and interaction* (2nd ed.). London, UK: SAGE.

Silverman, D. (2004). Who cares about 'experience'? Missing issues in qualitative research. In D. Silverman (Ed.), *Qualitative research: Theory, method, and practice* (3rd ed.; pp. 342–367). Thousand Oaks, CA: SAGE.

Silverman, D. (2011). *Interpreting qualitative data: A guide to the principles of qualitative research* (4th ed.). Thousand Oaks, CA: SAGE.

Simons, A. D., Murphy, G. E., Levine, J. L., & Wetzel, R. D. (1986). Cognitive therapy and pharmacotherapy: Sustained improvement over one year. *Archives of General Psychiatry, 43,* 43–48.

Simpson, J. A., Rholes, W. S., & Nelligan, J. S. (1992). Support-seeking and support-giving within couples in an anxiety-provoking situation: The role of attachment styles. *Journal of Personality and Social Psychology, 62,* 434–446.

Sin, N. L., & Lyubomirsky, S. (2009). Enhancing well-being and alleviating depressive symptoms with positive psychology interventions: A practice-friendly meta-analysis. *Journal of Clinical Psychology, 65,* 467–487.

Singh, A. A., Hays, D. G., & Watson, L. S. (2011). Strength in the face of adversity: Resilience strategies of transgender individuals. *Journal* of *Counseling and Development, 89,* 20–27.

Singh, A. A. &, Shelton, K. (2011). A content analysis of LGBTQ qualitative research in counseling: A ten-year review. *Journal of Counseling and Development, 89,* 217–226.

Sire, J. W. (1976). *The universe next door.* Downers, IL: Intervarsity.

Sisterhen, D., & Rotatori, A. F. (1986). Counseling the hearing-impaired child. In A. F. Rotatori, P. J. Gerber, F. W. Litton, & R. A. Fox (Eds.), *Counseling exceptional students* (pp. 162–178). New York, NY: Human Sciences Press.

Skinner, B. F. (1938). *The behavior of organisms.* New York, NY: Appleton-Century-Crofts.

Skinner, B. F. (1953). *Science and human behavior.* New York, NY: Macmillan.

Skinner, B. F. (1961). *Cumulative record.* New York, NY: Appleton-Century-Crofts.

Skinner, B. F. (1990). Can psychology be a science of mind? *American Psychologist, 45,* 1206–1210.

Sklare, G., Keener, R., & Mas, C. (1990). Preparing members for "here and now" group counseling. *Journal for Specialists in Group Work, 15*(3), 141–148.

Slaten, C. D., & Baskin, T. W. (2014). Contextual school counseling: A framework for training with implications for curriculum, supervision, practice, and future research. *The Counseling Psychologist, 42,* 97–123.

Sloane, B., Staples, F., Cristol, A., Yorkston, N., & Whipple, K. (1975). *Psychotherapy versus behavior therapy.* Cambridge, MA: Harvard University Press.

Smart, D. W., & Smart, J. F. (1997). *DSM-IV* and culturally sensitive diagnosis: Some observations for counselors. *Journal of Counseling and Development, 75*(5), 392–398.

Smart, J. F., & Smart, D. W. (1995). Acculturative stress: The experience of the Hispanic immigrant. *The Counseling Psychologist, 23*(1), 25–42.

Smith, D. C. (1993). Exploring the religious-spiritual needs of the dying. *Journal of Counseling and Values, 37,* 71–77.

Smith, D. C., & Sandu, D. S. (2004). Toward a positive perspective on violence prevention in schools: Building connections. *Journal of Counseling and Development, 82*(3), 287–293.

Smith, E. J. (2006). The strength-based counseling model. *The Counseling Psychologist, 34*(1), 13–79.

Smith, H. B., & Robinson, G. P. (1995). Mental health counseling: Past, present, and future. *Journal of Counseling and Development, 74*(2), 158–162.

Smith, L., Foley, P. F., & Chaney, M. P. (2008). Addressing classism, ableism, and heterosexism in counselor education. *Journal of Counseling and Development, 86*(3), 303–309.

Smith, M. B. (1994). Selfhood at risk: Postmodern perils and the perils of postmodernism. *American Psychologist, 49*(5), 405–411.

Smith, M. L., & Glass, G. J. (1977). Meta-analysis of psychotherapy outcome studies. *American Psychologist, 32,* 752–760.

Smith, M. L., Glass, G. V., & Miller, T. I. (1980). *The benefits of psychotherapy.* Baltimore. MD: Johns Hopkins University Press.

Smith, R. L. (1994). Directions in marriage and family graduate level training. *Counselor Education and Supervision, 34,* 180–183.

Smith, R. L., Carlson, J., Stevens-Smith, P., & Dennison, M. (1995). Marriage and family counseling. *Journal of Counseling and Development, 2*(74), 154–157.

Snell, W. E., Jr., Hampton, B. R., & McManus, P. (1992). The impact of counselor and participant gender on willingness to discuss relational topics: Development of the relationship disclosure scale. *Journal of Counseling and Development, 70,* 409–416.

Snodgrass, J. L., McCreight, D., & McFee, M. R. (2014). To whom shall I refer. *Counseling Today, 57*(6), 55–59.

Snyder, D. K. (1981). *Marital Satisfaction Inventory (MSI).* Los Angeles, CA: Western Psychological Services.

Snyder, J. J. (1977). Reinforcement analysis of interaction in problem and nonproblem families. *Journal of Abnormal Psychology, 86,* 528–535.

Sobell, M. B., & Sobell, L. C. (1984). The aftermath of heresy: A response to Pendery et al.'s (1982) critique of "Individualized Behavior Therapy for Alcoholics." *Behavior Research and Therapy, 22,* 413–447.

Solomon, J. (1996, May 20). Breaking the silence. *Newsweek,* 20–24.

Solomon, M. A. (1973). A developmental, conceptual premise for family therapy. *Family Process, 12,* 179–188.

Sommers-Flanagan, R., Barrett-Hakanson, T. B., Clarke, C., & Sommers-Flanagan, J. (2000). A psychoeducational school-based coping and social skills group for depressed students. *Journal for Specialists in Group Work, 25,* 170–190.

Sonstegard, M. A., Hagerman, H., & Bitter, J. (1975). Motivation modification: An Adlerian approach. *The Individual Psychologist, 12,* 17–22.

Sparks, R. W., & Deck, J. W. (1994). Melodic intonation therapy. In R. Chapey (Ed.), *Language intervention strategies in adult aphasia* (pp. 368–379). Baltimore, MD: Williams & Wilkins.

Spence, J. A. (2009). *Changes in perception of family environment and self-reported symptom status in adolescents whose parents participate in an Adlerian parent-training intervention.* Retrieved from ProQuest Digital Dissertations (AAT 3329198).

Spencer, G. (1977). Effectiveness of an introductory course in TA. *Transactional Analysis Journal, 7,* 346–349.

Spengler, P. M., Blustein, D. L., & Strohmer, D. C. (1990). Diagnostic and treatment overshadowing of vocational problems by personal problems. *Journal of Counseling Psychology, 37*(4), 372–381.

Sperry, L. (1987). ERIC: A cognitive map for guiding brief therapy and health care counseling. *Individual Psychology, 43*(2), 237–241.

Sperry, L. (1989a). Assessment in marital therapy: A couples-centered biopsychosocial approach. *Individual Psychology: The Journal of Adlerian Theory, Research, and Practice, 45,* 446–451.

Sperry, L. (1989b). Varieties of brief therapy: An introduction. *Individual Psychology: The Journal of Adlerian Theory, Research, and Practice, 45*(1/2), 1–2.

Sperry, L., & Carlson, J. (1991). *Marital therapy: Integrating theory and technique.* Denver, CO: Love.

Spiegelman, J. M. (1989). The one and the many: Jung and the post-Jungians. *Journal of Analytical Psychology, 34,* 53–71.

Spitz, R. (1946). Anaditic depression. *Psychoanalytic Study of the Child, 2,* 113–117.

Spivak, H., & Prothrow-Stith, D. (2001). The need to address bullying: An important component of violence prevention. *Journal of the American Medical Association, 285*(16), 2131–2132.

Spruill, D. A., & Fong, M. L. (1990). Defining the domain of mental health counseling: From identity confusion to consensus. *Journal of Mental Health Counseling, 12*(1), 12–23.

Sroufe, L. A. (1997). Psychopathology as an outcome of development. *Development and Psychopathology, 9,* 251–268.

Stabler, B. (1984). *Children's drawings.* Chapel Hill, NC: Health Science Consortium.

Stanard, R., & Hazler, R. (1995). Legal and ethical implications of HIV and duty to warn for counselors: Does *Tarasoff* apply? *Journal of Counseling and Development, 73*(4), 397–400.

Starker, S. (1988). Psychologists and self-help books: Attitudes and prescriptive practices of clinicians. *American Journal of Psychotherapy, 12,* 448–455.

Steenbarger, B. N. (1992). Toward science-practice integration in brief counseling and therapy. *The Counseling Psychologist, 20*(3), 403–450.

Stern, M., & Newland, L. M. (1994). Working with children: Providing a framework for the roles of counseling psychologist. *The Counseling Psychologist, 22*(3), 402–425.

Sternberg, R. J., Wagner, R. K., Williams, W. M., & Horvath, J. A. (1995). Testing common sense. *American Psychologist, 50*(11), 912–926.

Stile, S. W. (1993). *N = 1 handbook: Designs for inquiry in special education and related services.* Dubuque, IA: Kendall/Hunt.

Stinnet, N., & DeFrain, J. (1985). *Secrets of strong families.* Boston, MA: Little, Brown.

Stoltz, K. B., & Kern, R. M. (2007). Integrating lifestyle, the therapeutic process, and the stages of change. *The Journal of Individual Psychology, 63*(1), 32–47.

Stoltz-Loike, M. (1996). Annual review: Practice and research in career development and counseling—1995. *The Career Development Quarterly,* 99–140.

Strachey, J. (Ed. & Trans.). (1953–1974). *The standard edition of the complete psychological works of Sigmund Freud.* London, UK: Hogarth Press.

Strassberg, Z., Dodge, K. A., Pettit, G. S., & Bates, J. E. (1994). Spanking in the home and children's subsequent aggression toward kindergarten peers. *Development and Psychopathology, 6,* 445–462.

Straus, M. A., Gelles, R. J., & Steinmetz, S. (1980). *Behind closed doors: Violence in the American family.* Garden City, NY: Doubleday/Anchor.

Strober, M., Hanna, G., & McCracken, J. (1989). Bipolar illness. In C. Last & M. Hersens (Eds.), *Handbook of child psychiatric diagnosis.* New York, NY: Wiley.

Strohmer, D. C., & Biggs, D. A. (1983). Effects of counselor disability status on disabled subjects' perceptions of counselor attractiveness and expertness. *Journal of Counseling Psychology, 30,* 202–208.

Strong, S. R. (1968). Counseling: An interpersonal influence process. *Journal of Counseling Psychology, 15,* 215–224.

Strong, S. R., & Claiborn, C. D. (1982). *Change through interaction.* New York, NY: John Wiley & Sons.

Strupp, H. H. (1992). The future of psychodynamic psychotherapy. *Psychotherapy, 29*(1), 21–27.

Stuart, R. B. (1983). *Couples' pre-counseling inventory, counselor's guide.* Champaign, IL: Research Press.

Sude, M. E. (2013). Text messaging and private practice: Ethical challenges and guidelines for developing personal best practices. *Journal of Mental Health Counseling, 35*(3), 211–227.

Sue, D. W. (1978). World views and counseling. *The Personnel and Guidance Journal, 56,* 458–462.

Sue, D. W. (1981). *Counseling the culturally different: Theory and practice.* New York, NY: John Wiley & Sons.

Sue, D. W., Arredondo, P., & McDavis, R. J. (1992). Multicultural counseling competencies and standards: A call to the profession. *Journal of Counseling and Development, 70,* 477–486.

Sue, D. W., Bermier, T. E., Durran, A., Feinberg, L., Pedersen, P., Smith, E. T., & Vasquez-Nuttall, E. (1982). Position paper: Cross-cultural counseling competencies. *The Counseling Psychologist, 10*(2), 45–52.

Sue, D. W., Capodilupo, C. M., Torino, G. C., Bucceri, J. M., Holder, Nadal, K. L., & Esquilin, M. (2007). Racial microaggressions in everyday life: Implications for clinical practice. *American Psychologist, 62*(4), 271–286.

Sue, D. W., Ivey, A. E., & Pedersen, P. B. (2007). *A theory of multicultural counseling and therapy.* Pacific Grove, CA: Brooks/Cole. (Original work published 1996)

Sue, D. W., Nadal, K. L., Capodilupo, C. M., Lin, A. I., Torino, G. C., & Rivera, D. P. (2008). Racial microaggressions against

Black Americans: Implications for counseling. *Journal of Counseling and Development, 86*(3), 330–338.

Sue, D. W., & Sue, D. (1977). Barriers to effective crosscultural counseling. *Journal of Counseling Psychology, 24,* 420–429.

Sue, D. W., & Sue, D. (1999). *Counseling the culturally different* (3rd ed.). New York, NY: John Wiley & Sons.

Sue, S. (1988). Psychotherapeutic services for ethnic minorities. *American Psychologist, 43*(4), 301–308.

Suinn, R. M., Rickard-Figueroa, K., Lew, S., & Vigil, S. (1987). The Suinn-Lew Asian Self-Identity Acculturation Scale: An initial report. *Education and Psychological Measurement, 47,* 401–407.

Suit, J. L., & Paradise, L. V. (1985). Effects of metaphors and cognitive complexity on perceived counselor characteristics. *Journal of Counseling Psychology, 32,* 23–28.

Sullivan, H. S. (1968). *The interpersonal theory of psychiatry.* New York, NY: Norton.

Sundberg, N. D. (1977). *Assessment of persons.* Englewood Cliffs, NJ: Prentice-Hall.

Super, D. E. (1957). *The psychology of careers.* New York, NY: Harper & Row.

Super, D. E. (1970). *Work values inventory.* Boston, MA: Houghton Mifflin.

Super, D. E. (1980). A life-span, life-space approach to career development. *Journal of Vocational Behavior, 16,* 282–298.

Super, D. E. (1990). A life-span, life-space approach to career development. In D. Brown & L. Brooks (Eds.), *Career choice and development: Applying contemporary*

theories to practice (pp. 197–261). San Francisco, CA: Jossey-Bass.

Super, D. E. (2002). A life-span, life-space approach. In D. Brown, L. Brooks, & Associates (Eds.), *Career choice and development* (4th ed.). San Francisco, CA: Jossey-Bass.

Sutherland, J. (2011). Art therapy with families. *Journal of Individual Psychology. 67,* 292–304.

Sutton, J. M., Jr., & Southworth, R. S. (1990). The effect of the rural setting on school counselors. *The School Counselor, 37,* 173–178.

Svanum, S., & McAdoo, W. G. (1989). Predicting rapid relapse following treatment for chemical dependence: A matched subjects design. *Journal of Consulting and Clinical Psychology, 57,* 222–226.

Swan, G. E., & MacDonald, M. D. (1978). Behavior therapy in practice: A national survey of behavior therapists. *Behavior Therapy, 9,* 799–807.

Swanson, J. L. (1992). Vocational behavior, 1989–1991: Life-span career development and reciprocal interaction of work and nonwork. *Journal of Vocational Behavior, 41,* 101–161.

Swanson, J. L., & Gore, P. A. (2000). Advances in vocational psychology, theory, and research. In S. Brown & R. Lent (Eds.), *Handbook of counseling psychology* (3rd ed.; pp. 233–269). New York, NY: John Wiley.

Sweeney, T. J. (1988). Building strong school counseling programs: Implications for counselor preparation. In G. R. Walz & J. C. Bleuer (Eds.), *Building strong school counseling programs.* Alexandria, VA: American Association for Counseling and Development.

Szymanski, D. M., Kashubeck, S., & Meyer, J. (2008). Internalized heterosexism: A historical and theoretical overview. *The Counseling Psychologist, 36*, 510–524.

Takanishi, R. (1993). The opportunities of adolescence—research, interventions, and policy. *American Psychologist, 48*, 85–87.

Talbutt, L. C. (1986). The abused child. In L. B. Golden & D. Capuzzi (Eds.), *Helping families help children* (pp. 45–58). Springfield, IL: Charles C. Thomas.

Talerico, C. J. (1986). The expressive arts and creativity as a form of therapeutic experience in the field of mental health. *The Journal of Creative Behavior, 20*(4), 229–247.

Talkington, L. W., & Riley, J. B. (1971). Reduction diets and aggression in institutionalized mentally retarded patients. *American Journal of Mental Deficiency, 76*, 370–372.

Tanaka-Matsumi, J., & Higginbotham, H. N. (1994). Clinical application of behavior therapy across ethnic and cultural boundaries. *The Behavior Therapist, 17*(6), 123–126.

Tarasoff v. Board of Regents of the University of California, 13 Cal. 3d 177, 529 P.2d 553 (1974), vacated, 17 Cal. 3d 425, 551 P.2d 334 (1976).

Task Force on Promotion and Dissemination of Psychological Procedures. (1995). Training in and dissemination of empirically validated psychological treatments. *The Clinical Psychologist, 48*, 3–23.

Taylor, D. D., & Bratton, S. C. (2014). Developmentally appropriate practice: Adlerian play therapy with preschool children. *The Journal of Individual Psychology, 70*, 205–219.

Taylor, N. B., & Pryor, R. G. L. (1985). Exploring the process of compromise in career decision making. *Journal of Vocational Behavior, 27*, 171–190.

Taylor, R. (1979). *The gifted and the talented*. Englewood, CO: Educational Consultant Agency.

Taylor, R. M., & Morrison, L. P. (1984). *Taylor-Johnson temperament analysis manual*. Los Angeles, CA: Psychological Publications.

Taylor, S. E., & Brown, J. D. (1988). Illusion and well-being: A social psychological perspective on mental health. *Psychological Bulletin, 103*, 193–210.

Teasdale, J. D., Fennell, M. J. V., Hibbert, G. A., & Amies, P. L. (1984). Cognitive therapy for major depressive disorder in primary care. *British Journal of Psychiatry, 144*, 400–406.

Tennyson, W. W., Miller, G. D., Skovholt, T. G., & Williams, R. C. (1989). Secondary school counselors: What do they do? What is important? *The School Counselor, 36*, 253–259.

Terrell, M. D. (1993). Ethnocultural factors and substance abuse: Toward culturally sensitive treatment models. *Psychology of Addictive Behaviors, 7*(3), 162–167.

Teyber, E. (2000). *Interpersonal process in psychotherapy: A relational approach* (4th ed.). Pacific Grove, CA: Brooks/Cole.

Thomas, K. R., & Weinrach, S. G. (2004). Mental health counseling and the AMCD multicultural counseling competencies: A debate. *Journal of Mental Health Counseling, 26*(1), 41–43.

Thomas, M. D. (1989). The role of the secondary school counselor: The counselor in effective schools. *The School Counselor, 36*, 249–252.

Thomas, R. V., & Pender, D. A. (2008). Association for specialists in group work: Best practice guidelines 2007 revisions. *The Journal for Specialists in Group Work, 33*(2), 111–117.

Thompson, C. E., & Neville, H. A. (1999). Racism, mental health, and mental health practices. *The Counseling Psychologist, 27*(2), 155–223.

Thompson, C.L., & Rudolph, L.B. (2007). *Counseling children* (7th ed.). Pacific Grove, CA: Brooks/Cole.

Thompson, C., & Henderson, D. (2007). *Counseling children* (7th ed.). Belmont, CA: Thomson Brooks/Cole.

Thompson, J. M., Flynn, R. J., & Griffith, S. A. (1994). Congruence and coherence as predictors of congruent employment outcomes. *Career Development Quarterly, 42*, 271–281.

Thompson, L. W., Gallagher, D., & Breckenridge, J. S. (1987). Comparative effectiveness of psychotherapies for depressed elders. *Journal of Consulting and Clinical Psychology, 55*, 385–390.

Thompson, R. A. (1993). Posttraumatic stress and posttraumatic loss debriefing: Brief strategic intervention for survivors of sudden loss. *The School Counselor, 41*, 16–22.

Thompson, R. A. (1996). *Counseling techniques: Improving relationships with others, ourselves, our families, and our environment*. Washington, DC: Accelerated Development.

Thompson, R. A., & Wilcox, B. L. (1995). Child maltreatment research. *American Psychologist, 50*(9), 789–793.

Thorndike, E. L. (1920). Intelligence and its uses. *Harper's Magazine, 140*, 227–235.

Tobler, N. S. (1986). Meta-analysis of 143 adolescent drug prevention programs: Quantitative outcome results of program participants compared to a control or comparison group. *Journal of Drug Issues, 16,* 537–568.

Topper, M. D. (1985). Navajo "alcoholism": Drinking, alcohol abuse, and treatment in a changing cultural environment. In L. A. Bennett & G. M. Ames (Eds.), *The American experience with alcohol: Contrasting cultural perspectives* (pp. 227–251). New York, NY: Plenum Press.

Towberman, D. B. (1992). Client-counselor similarity and the client's perception of the treatment environment. *Journal of Offender Rehabilitation, 18*(1/2), 159–171.

Tremblay, R. E., LeBlanc, M., & Schwartzman, A. E. (1988). The predictive power of first-grade peer and teacher ratings of behavior: Sex differences in antisocial behavior and personality at adolescence. *Journal of Abnormal Child Psychology, 16,* 571–583.

Trevino, J. G. (1996). Worldview and change in crosscultural counseling. *The Counseling Psychologist, 24*(2), 198–215.

Trice-Black, S., Bailey, C. L., & Riechel, M. E. K. (2013). Play therapy in school counseling. *Professional School Counseling, 16,* 303–312.

Truax, C. B., & Carkhuff, R. R. (1967). *Toward effective counseling and psychotherapy.* Chicago, IL: Aldine.

Truax, C. B., & Mitchell, K. M. (1971). Research on certain therapist interpersonal skills in relation to process and outcome. In A. E. Bergin & S. L. Garfield (Eds.), *Handbook of psychotherapy and behavior change* (pp. 299–344). New York, NY: John Wiley & Sons.

Trzepacz, P. T., & Baker, R. (1993). *The psychiatric mental status examination.* New York, NY: Ford University Press.

Tucker, C. M., Ferdinand, L. A., Mirsu-Paun, A., Herman, K. C., Delgado-Romero, E., van den Bern, J. J., & Jones, J. D. (2007). The roles of counseling psychologist in reducing health disparities. *The Counseling Psychologist, 35*(5), 650–678.

Tucker, C. M., Herman, K. C., Ferdinand, L. A., Bailey, T. R., Lopez, M. T., Beato, C., Adams, D., & Cooper, L. L. (2007). Providing patient-centered culturally sensitive health care: A formative model. *The Counseling Psychologist, 35*(5), 679–705.

Tuma, J. M. (1989). Mental health services in children: The state of the art. *American Psychologist, 44*(2), 188–199.

Turner, R. M., & Ascher, L. M. (1979). Controlled comparison of progressive relaxation, stimulus control, and paradoxical intention therapies for insomnia. *Journal of Consulting and Clinical Psychology, 47,* 500–508.

Tyrer, K., Catalan, J., Schmidt, U., Davidson, K., Dent, J., Tata, P., . . . Thompson, S. (1999). Manual-assisted cognitive-behaviour therapy (MACT): A randomized controlled trial of a brief intervention with bibliotherapy in the treatment of recurrent self-harm. *Psychological Medicine, 29,* 19–25.

Tyson, J. A., & Wall, S. M. (1983). Effect of inconsistency between counselor verbal and nonverbal behavior on perceptions of counselor attributes. *Journal of Counseling Psychology, 30,* 433–437.

Umana-Taylor, A. J., O'Donnell, M., Knight, G. P., Roosa, M. W., Berkel, C., & Nair, R. (2014). Mexican-origin early adolescents' ethnic identity, and psychosocial functioning. *The Counseling Psychologist, 42,* 170–200.

Unger, R. (1989). Selection and composition criteria in group psychotherapy. *Journal for Specialists in Group Work, 14*(3), 151–157.

Usher, C. H. (1989). Recognizing cultural bias in counseling theory and practice: The case of Rogers. *Journal of Multicultural Counseling and Development, 17,* 62–71.

Utsey, S. O., Ponterotto, J. G., & Porter, J. S. (2008). Prejudice and racism, year 2008—Still going strong: Research on reducing prejudice with recommended methodological advances. *Journal of Counseling and Development, 86*(3), 339–347.

Vacc, N. A. (1989). Group counseling: C. H. Patterson—A personalized view. *Journal for Specialists in Group Work, 14*(1), 4–15.

Vacha-Haase, T., Davenport, D. S., & Kerewsky, S. D. (2004). Problematic students: Gatekeeping practices of academic professional psychology programs. *Professional Psychology: Research and Practice, 35*(2), 115–122.

Vail-Smith, K., Knight, S. M., & White, D. M. (1995). Children of substance abusers in the elementary school: A survey of counselor perceptions. *Elementary School Guidance and Counseling, 29*(3), 163–176.

Valliant, G. E. (1977). *Adaptation to life.* Boston, MA: Little, Brown.

Valliant, G. E. (1983). *The natural history of alcoholism.* Cambridge, MA: Harvard University Press.

Van Hoose, W. H. (1980). Ethics in counseling. *Counseling and Human Development, 13*(1), 1–12.

Van Slyck, M., Stern, M., & Zak-Place, J. (1996). Promoting optimal adolescent development through conflict resolution education, training, and practice: An innovative approach for counseling psychologists. *The Counseling Psychologist, 24*(3), 433–461.

VandenBos, G. R. (1996). Outcome assessment of psychotherapy. *American Psychologist, 51*(10), 1005–1006.

Vera, E. M., & Speight, S. L. (2003). Multicultural competence, social justice, and counseling psychology. *The Counseling Psychologist, 31*(3), 253–272.

Verdeli, H., & Weissman, M. M. (2014). Interpersonal psychotherapy. In D. Wedding & R. J. Corsini (Eds), *Current psychotherapies* (10th ed.; pp. 339–372). Belmont, CA: Brooks/Cole, Cengage Learning,

Vernon, A. (1995). Working with children, adolescents, and their parents: Practical application of developmental theory. *Counseling and Human Development, 27*(7), 1–12.

Vernon, P. E., & Parry, J. B. (1949). *Personnel selection in the British forces.* London, UK: University of London Press.

Vinson, M. L. (1995). Employing family therapy in group counseling with college students: Similarities and a technique employed in both. *Journal for Specialists in Group Work, 20*(4), 240–252.

Volkow, N. D., Wong, G. J., Fischman, M. W., Foltin, R. W., Fowler, J. S., Abumrad, N. N., . . . Shea C.E. (1997). Relationship between subjective effects of cocaine and dopamine transporter occupancy. *Nature, 386,* 827–833.

von Bertalanffy, L. V. (1968). *General systems theory: Foundations, development, application.* New York, NY: Braziller.

Vondracek, F. W., Lerner, R. M., & Schulenberg, J. M. (1986). *Career development: A life-span developmental approach.* Hillsdale, NJ: Lawrence Erlbaum.

Vontress, C. E. (1973). Counseling the racial and ethnic minorities. *Focus on Guidance, 5*(6), 1–10.

Vontress, C. E. (1988). An existential approach to crosscultural counseling. *Journal of Multicultural Counseling and Development, 16,* 73–83.

Wachtel, P. L. (1991). From eclecticism to synthesis: Towards a more seamless psychotherapeutic integration. *Journal of Psychotherapy Integration, 1*(1), 43–54.

Wadeson, H. (1980). *Art psychotherapy.* New York, NY: John Wiley & Sons.

Wagner, E. (1971). Structural analysis: A theory of personality based on projective techniques. *Journal of Personality Assessment, 35,* 422–435.

Wagner, J., & Gartner, C. G. (1996). *Psychiatric Services, 47*(1), 15–20.

Wagner, W. G. (1991). Counseling with children: An opportunity for tomorrow. *The Counseling Psychologist, 22*(3), 381–401.

Wagner, W. G. (1996). Optimal development in adolescence: What it is and how it can be encouraged. *The Counseling Psychologist, 24*(3), 360–399.

Wahler, R. G., & Dumas, J. E.(1987). Family factors in childhood psychopathology: Toward a coercion neglect model. In T. Jacob (Ed.), *Family interaction and psychopathology* (pp. 581–627). New York, NY: Plenum Press.

Wakefield, J. C. (1997). When is development disordered? Developmental psychopathology and the harmful dysfunction analysis of mental disorder. *Development and Psychopathology, 9,* 193–229.

Waldo, M., & Bauman, S. (1998). Regrouping the categorization of group work: A goals and process

(GAP) matrix for groups. *Journal for Specialists in Group Work, 23*(2), 215–224.

Waldo, M., Horne, A. M., & Kenny, M. E. (2009). Developing healthy family relationships. In M. E. Kenny, A. M. Horne, P. Orpinas, & L. E. Reece (Eds.), *Realizing social justice: The challenge of preventive interventions* (pp. 207–227). Washington, DC: American Psychological Association.

Walsh, W. B. (1990). Putting assessment in context. *The Counseling Psychologist, 18,* 262–265.

Walsh, W. B., & Srsic, C. (1995). Annual review: Vocational behavior and career development—1994. *Career Development Quarterly, 44*(2), 98–145.

Walter, J., & Peller, J. (1992). *Becoming solution-focused in brief therapy.* New York, NY: Brunner/Mazel.

Wampold, B. E., Lichtenberg, J. W., & Waehler, C. A. (2002). Principles of empirically supported interventions in counseling psychology. *The Counseling Psychologist, 30,* 197–217.

Ward v. Wilbanks, No. 09-CV-11237, Doc. 1 (E.D. Mich., Apr. 2, 2009). *Ward v. Wilbanks,* No. 10-2100, Doc. 006110869854 (6th Cir. Court of Appeals, Feb. 11, 2011).

Warren, J. M. (2012). Mobile mind mapping: Using mobile technology to enhance rational emotive behavior therapy. *Journal of Mental Health Counseling, 34,* 72–81.

Wartik, N. (2001, February). Bullying: A serious business. *Child,* 78–84.

Warwar, S., & Greenberg, L. S. (2000). Advances in theories of change and counseling. In S. D. Brown & R. W. Lent (Eds.), *Handbook of counseling psychology* (3rd ed.; pp. 571–600). New York, NY: Wiley & Sons.

Wastell, C. A. (1996). Feminist developmental theory: Implications for counseling. *Journal of Counseling and Development, 74*(6), 575–581.

Waterman, A. S. (2013). The humanistic psychology-positive psychology divide: Contrast in philosophical foundations. *American Psychologist, 68*, 124–133.

Watkins, C. E. (1993). Person-centered theory and the contemporary practice of psychological testing. *Counseling Psychology Quarterly, 6*(1), 59–67.

Watkins, C. E., & Campbell, V. L. (1990). Testing and assessment in counseling psychology. *The Counseling Psychologist, 18*, 189–197.

Watkins, C. E., Jr., Lopez, F. G., Campbell, V. L., & Himmell, C. D. (1986). Contemporary counseling psychology: Results of a national survey. *Journal of Counseling Psychology, 33*, 301–309.

Watkins, C. E., Jr., Schneider, L. J., Cox, J. R. H., & Reinberg, J. A. (1987). Clinical psychology and counseling psychology: On similarities and differences revisited. *Professional Psychology: Research and Practice, 18*, 530–535.

Watkins, C. E., Jr., & Subich, L. M. (1995). Annual review, 1992–1994: Career development, reciprocal work/non-work interaction, and women's workforce participation. *Journal of Vocational Behavior, 47*, 109–163.

Watkins, E. (1984). The individual psychology of Alfred Adler: Towards an Adlerian vocational theory. *Journal of Vocational Behavior, 24*, 27–48.

Watts, A. G. (1996). Toward a policy for lifelong career development: A transatlantic perspective. *Career Development Quarterly, 45*(1), 41–53.

Watts, R. E. (1993, Spring). Developing a personal theory of counseling: A brief guide for students. *Texas Counseling Association Journal,* 103–104.

Watts, R. E. (2000). Entering the new millennium: Is individual psychology still relevant? *Journal of Individual Psychology, 56*, 21–30.

Watts, R. E., & Pietrzak, D. (2000). Adlerian "encouragement" and the therapeutic process of solution-focused brief therapy. *Journal of Counseling and Development, 78*, 442–447.

Watts, R. E., Trusty, J., & Lim, M. (1996). Characteristics of healthy families as a model of systemic social interest. *Canadian Journal of Adlerian Psychology, 26*(1), 1–12.

Watzlawick, P., Weakland, J. H., & Fisch, R. (1974). *Change: Principles of problem formation and problem resolution.* New York, NY: Norton.

Webster-Stratton, C. (1990). Long-term follow-up with young conduct problem children: From preschool to grade school. *Journal of Clinical Child Psychology, 19*, 144–149.

Weighill, V. E., Hodge, J., & Peck, D. F. (1983). Keeping appointments with clinical psychologists. *British Journal of Clinical Psychology, 22*, 143–144.

Weikel, W. J. (1985). The American Mental Health Counselors Association. *Journal of Counseling and Development, 63*, 457–460.

Weikel, W. J., & Taylor, S. S. (1979). AMHCA: Membership profile and five journal preferences. *AMHCA Journal, 1*, 89–94.

Weinberg, R. S., Hughes, H. H., Critelli, J. W., England, R., & Jackson, A. (1984). Effects of pre-existing and manipulated self-efficacy on weight loss in a self-control program. *Journal of Research in Personality, 18*, 352–358.

Weiner, I. B. (1992). *Psychological disturbance in adolescence.* New York, NY: Wiley.

Weinhold, B. K. (2007). Uncovering the hidden causes of bullying and school violence. In J. Carlson and J. Lewis (Eds.), *Counseling the adolescent* (5th ed.; pp. 185–217). Denver, CO: Love.

Weinrach, S. G. (1988). Cognitive therapist: A dialogue with Aaron Beck. *Journal of Counseling and Development, 67*(3), 159–164.

Weinrach, S. G. (1995). Rational emotive behavior therapy: A tough-minded therapy for a tender-minded profession. *Journal of Counseling and Development, 73*(3), 296–300.

Weinrach, S. G., & Srebalus, D. J. (2002). Holland's theory of careers. In D. Brown, L. Brooks, & Associates (Eds.), *Career choice and development* (4th ed.). San Francisco, CA: Jossey-Bass.

Weinrach, S. G., & Thomas, K. R. (2002). A critical analysis of the multicultural counseling competencies: Implications for the practice of mental health counseling. *Journal of Mental Health Counseling, 24*, 20–35.

Weinrach, S. G., & Thomas K. R. (2004). The AMCD multicultural counseling competencies: A critically flawed initiative. *Journal of Mental Health Counseling, 26*, 81–93.

Weissberg, R. P., Caplan, M., & Harwood, R. L. (1991). Promoting competent young people in competence-enhancing environments: A systems-based perspective on primary prevention. *Journal of Consulting and Clinical Psychology, 59*, 830–841.

Weisz, J. R., Weiss, B., & Donenberg, G. R. (1992). The lab versus the clinic: Effects of child and adolescent psychotherapy. *American Psychologist, 47*(12), 1578–1585.

Welch, I. D., & McCarroll, L. (1993). The future role of school counselors. *The School Counselor, 41*(1), 48–53.

Welfel, E. R. (2013). *Ethics in counseling and psychotherapy: Standards, research, and emerging issues* (5th ed.). Belmont, CA: Brooks/Cole, Cengage Learning.

Wells, N. F., & Stevens, T. (1984). Music as a stimulus for creative fantasy in group psychotherapy with young adolescents. *The Arts in Psychotherapy, 11*, 71–76.

Werner, E. E. (1986). Resident offspring of alcoholics: A longitudinal study from birth to age 18. *Journal of Studies on Alcoholism, 47*, 34–41.

Werner, E. E. (1992). The children of Kauai: Resiliency and recovery in adolescence and adulthood. *Journal of Adolescent Health, 13*, 262–268.

Werner, E. E., & Smith, R. S. (1982). *Vulnerable but not invincible: A longitudinal study of resilient children and youth.* New York, NY: McGraw-Hill.

Werner, E. E., & Smith, R. S. (1992). *Overcoming the odds: High risk children from birth to adulthood.* Ithaca, NY: Cornell University Press.

Werth, J. L., Jr., & Crow, L. (2009). End of life care: An overview for professional counselors. *Journal of Counseling and Development, 87*(2), 194–202.

West, J. D., Hosie, T. W., & Mackey, J. A. (1988). The counselor's role in mental health: An evaluation. *Counselor Education and Supervision, 27*, 233–239.

Westefeld, J. S., Range, L. M., Rogers, J. R., Maples, M. R., Bromley, J. L. & Alcorn, J. (2000). Suicide: An overview. *The Counseling Psychologist, 28*, 445–510.

Wester, K. L., & Borders, D. (2014). Research competencies in counseling: A Delphi study. *Journal of Counseling and Development, 92*, 447–458.

Westgate, C. E. (1996). Spiritual wellness and depression. *Journal of Counseling and Development, 75*(1), 26–35.

Westwood, M. J., & Ishiyama, F. I. (1990). The communication process as a critical intervention for client change in cross-cultural counseling. *Journal of Multicultural Counseling and Development, 18*(4), 163–171.

Whiston, S. C., & Keller, B. K. (2004). The influence of family of origin on career development: A review and analysis. *The Counseling Psychologist, 32*(4), 493–568.

Whiston, S. C., & Li, P. (2011). Meta-analysis: A systematic method for synthesizing counseling research. *Journal of Counseling and Development, 89*, 273–281.

Whiston, S. C., Sexton, T. L., & Lasoff, D. L. (1998). Career-intervention outcome: A replication and extension of Oliver and Spokane (1988). *Journal of Counseling Psychology, 45*, 150–165.

Whiston, S. C., Tai, L. W., Rahardja, D., & Eder, K. (2011). School counseling outcome: A meta-analytic examination of interventions. *Journal of Counseling and Development, 89*, 37–55.

Whitaker, C. A. (1976). The hindrance of theory in clinical work. In P. J. Guerin Jr. (Ed.), *Family therapy: Theory and practice* (pp. 154–164). New York, NY: Gardner Press.

Whitaker, C. A. (1977). Process techniques of family therapy. *Interaction, 1*, 4–19.

Whitaker, C. A., & Bumberry, W. M. (1988). *Dancing with the family: A symbolic-experiential approach.* New York, NY: Brunner/Mazel.

Whitaker, C. A., & Keith, D. V. (1981). Symbolic-experiential family therapy. In A. S. Gurman & D. P. Kniskern (Eds.), *Handbook of family therapy* (pp. 187–225). New York, NY: Brunner/Mazel.

White, J. A., & Allers, C. T. (1994). Play therapy with abused children: A review of the literature. *Journal of Counseling and Development, 72*(4), 390–394.

White, M., & Epston, D. (1990). *Narrative means to therapeutic ends.* New York, NY: Norton.

Whitledge, J. (1994). Cross-cultural counseling: Implications for school counselors in enhancing student learning. *The School Counselor, 41*(5), 314–318.

Wickman, S. A., & Campbell, C. (2003). An analysis of how Carl Rogers enacted client-centered conversations with Gloria. *Journal of Counseling and Development, 81*, 178–184.

Wickman, S. A., Daniels, M. H., White, L. J., & Fesmire, S. A. (1999). A "primer" in conceptual metaphor for counselors. *Journal of Counseling and Development, 77*(4), 389–394.

Wiggins, J. D. (1985). Six steps towards counseling program accountability. *NASSP Bulletin, 69*(485), 28–31.

Wiggins-Frame, M. (1998). The ethics of counseling via the Internet. *The Family Journal: Counseling and Therapy for Couples and Families, 5*(4), 328–330.

Wilcoxon, S. A. (1985). Healthy family functioning: The other side of family pathology. *Journal of Counseling and Development, 63*, 495–499.

Wilcoxon, S. A., Remley, T. P., & Gladding, S. T. (2012). *Ethical, legal,* and professional issues in the practice of marriage and family therapy (5th ed.). Upper Saddle River, NJ: Pearson Education.

Wilkerson, C. D. (1967). The effects of four methods of test score presentation to eighth-grade students. *Dissertation Abstracts International*, 1318A.

Wilkinson, W. K., & McNeil, K. (1996). *Research for the helping professions*. Pacific Grove, CA: Brooks/Cole.

Wilson, G. T. (2011). Behavior therapy. In R. J. Corsini & D. Wedding (Eds.), *Current psychotherapies* (9th ed.; pp. 219–256). Belmont, CA: Brooks/Cole, Cengage Learning.

Wilson, G. T., & Fairburn, C. G. (1993). Cognitive treatments for eating disorders. *Journal of Consulting and Clinical Psychology, 61,* 261–269.

Wilson, J. Q., & Hernstein, R. J. (1985). *Crime and human nature.* New York, NY: Simon & Schuster.

Wilson, L. (1987). Symbolism and art therapy: Theory and clinical practice. In J. A. Rubin (Ed.), *Approaches to art therapy: Theory and technique.* New York, NY: Brunner/Mazel.

Wilson, R. E., Rapin, L. S., & Haley-Banez, L. (2000). *Association for Specialists in Group Work: Professional standards for the training of group workers.* Alexandria, VA: American Counseling Association.

Winslade, J. M., & Monk, G. D. (2007). *Narrative counseling in schools: Powerful and brief* (2nd ed.). Thousand Oaks, CA: Corwin.

Wislocki, A. (1981). Movement is their medium: Dance movement methods in special education. *Milieu Therapy, 1,* 49–54.

Wisner, B. L., & Norton, C. L. (2013). Capitalizing on behavioral

and emotional strengths of alternative high school students through group counseling to promote mindfulness skills. *The Journal for Specialists in Group Work, 38,* 207–224.

Witmer, J. M., & Sweeney, T. J. (1995). A holistic model for wellness and prevention over the life span. In M. T. Burke & J. G. Miranti (Eds.), *Counseling: The spiritual dimension* (pp. 19–40). Alexandria, VA: American Counseling Association.

Witty, C. (1980). *Mediation and society: Conflict management in Lebanon.* New York, NY: Academic.

Wogan, M., & Norcross, J. C. (1985). Dimensions of therapeutic skills and techniques: Empirical identification, therapist correlates, and predictive utility. *Psychotherapy, 22,* 63–74.

Wolf, C. P., Thompson, I. A., Thompson, E. S., & Smith-Adcock, S. (2014). Refresh your mind, rejuvenate your body, renew your spirit: A pilot wellness program for counselor education. *The Journal of Individual Psychology, 70,* 57–75.

Wolfe, D. A. (1988). Child abuse and neglect. In E. J. Mash & L. G. Terdal (Eds.), *Behavioral assessment of childhood disorders* (2nd ed.; pp. 627–679). New York, NY: Guilford Press.

Wolpe, J. (1958). *Psychotherapy by reciprocal inhibition.* Stanford, CA: Stanford University Press.

Wolpe, J. (1973). *The practice of behavior therapy* (2nd ed.). New York, NY: Pergamon Press.

Wolter-Gustafson, C. (2004). Towards convergence: Client-centered and feminist assumptions about epistemology and power. In G. Proctor & M. B. Napier (Eds.), *Encountering feminism: Intersections between feminism and the person-centered approach* (pp.97–115). Ross-on-Wye, UK: PCCS Books.

Wong, Y. J., Maffini, C. S., & Shin, M. (2014). The racial-cultural framework for addressing suicide-related outcomes in communities of color. *The Counseling Psychologist, 42,* 13–54.

Woody, R. H., Hansen, J. C., & Rossberg, R. H. (1989). *Counseling psychology: Strategies and services.* Pacific Grove, CA: Brooks/Cole.

Worthington, E. L., Jr. (1989). Religious faith across the life span: Implications for counseling and research. *The Counseling Psychologist, 17,* 555–612.

Wright, R. (1994). *The moral animal: The new science of evolutionary psychology.* New York, NY: Pantheon Books.

Wright, S. L., Perrone-McGovern, K. M., Boo, J. N., & White, A. V. (2014). Influential factors in academic and career self-efficacy: Attachment, supports, and career barriers. *Journal of Counseling & Development, 92,* 36–46.

Wubbolding, R. (1986). *Reality therapy training.* Cincinnati, OH: Center for Reality Therapy.

Wubbolding, R. (1990). *Expanding reality therapy: Group counseling and multicultural dimensions.* Cincinnati, OH: Real World.

Wubbolding, R. (2000). *Reality therapy for the 21st century.* Philadelphia, PA: Taylor and Francis.

Wubbolding, R. (2003). Reality therapy theory. In D. Capuzzi & D. R. Douglas (Eds.), *Counseling and psychotherapy: Theories and interventions* (3rd ed.; pp. 252–282). Columbus, OH: Merrill.

Wubbolding, R. E. (2010). *Reality therapy.* Washington, DC: American Psychological Association.

Yager, J. (1989). A futuristic view of psychiatry. In J. Yager (Ed.),

The future of psychiatry as a medical specialty (pp. 135–156). Washington, DC: American Psychiatric Press.

Yalom, I. D. (1980). *Existenital psychotherapy*. New York, NY: Basic Books.

Yalom, I. D. (1995). *The theory and practice of group psychotherapy* (4th ed.). New York, NY: Basic Books.

Yalom, I. D., & Lieberman, M. (1971). A study of encounter group casualties. *Archives of General Psychiatry, 25,* 16–30.

Yalom, I. & Leszcz, M. (2005). *The theory and practice of group psychotherapy* (5th ed.). New York, NY: Basic Books.

Yen, H. (2009, June 24). Graying nations will face struggles. *Albuquerque Journal*, p. A4.

Yontef, G., & Jacobs, L. (2008). Gestalt therapy. In R. J. Corsini & D. Wedding (Eds.), *Current psychotherapies* (8th ed.; pp. 328–365). Belmont, CA.: Thomson Brooks/Cole.

Yontef, G., & Jacobs, L. (2014). Gestalt therapy. In D. Wedding & R. J. Corsini (Eds.), *Current psychotherapies* (10th ed.; pp. 299–338). Belmont, CA: Brooks/Cole, Cengage Learning.

Yontef, G. M., & Simkin, J. S.(1989). Gestalt therapy. In R. J. Corsini (Ed.), *Current psychotherapies* (4th ed.; pp. 323–361). Itasca, IL: F. E. Peacock.

Yost, E., & Corbishley, M. (1987). *Career counseling: A psychological approach*. San Francisco, CA: Jossey-Bass.

Young, M. E. (1992). *Counseling methods and techniques: An eclectic approach*. Columbus, OH: Merrill.

Young, T. L. (2013). Using motivational interviewing within the early stages of group development. *The Journal for Specialists in Group Work, 38,* 169–181.

Young, T. L., Winburn, A., & Hagedorn, W. B. (2013). The effects of training in motivational interviewing on client adherence: A controlled study. *Journal of Mental Health Counseling, 35,* 142–153.

Younggren, J. N., & Gottlieb, M. C. (2004). Managing risk when contemplating multiple relationships. *Professional Psychology: Research and Practice, 35,* 255–260.

Zaccaria, J. S., & Moses, J. A. (1968). *Facilitating human development through reading: The use of bibliotherapy through teaching and counseling*. Champaign, IL: Stipes.

Zajonc, R. B., & Mullally, P. R. (1997). Birth order: Reconciling conflicting effects. *American Psychologist, 52*(7), 685–699.

Zalaquett, C. P., Fuerth, K. M., Stein, C., Ivey, A. E., & Ivey, M. B.(2008). Reframing the *DSM-IV-TR* from a multicultural/social justice perspective. *Journal of Counseling and Development, 86*(3), 364–371.

Zerin, M. (1988). An application of the drama triangle to family therapy. *Transactional Analysis Journal, 18,* 94–101.

Zimmerman, M. A., & Arunkumar, R. (1994). Resiliency research: Implications for schools and policy. *Social policy report: Society for research in child development, 8*(4), 1–17.

Zinnbauer, B. J., & Pargament, K. I. (2000). Working with the sacred: Four approaches to religious and spiritual issues in counseling. *Journal of Counseling and Development, 78*(2), 162–171.

Zunker, V. G. (2002). *Career counseling: Applied concepts of life planning* (6th ed.). Monterey, CA: Brooks/Cole.

Zytowski, D. G. (1985). *Kuder Occupational Interest Survey Form DD Manual supplement*. Chicago, IL: Science Research Associates.

Zytowski, D. G. (1994). A Super contribution to vocational theory: Work values. *Career Development Quarterly, 43*(1), 25–31.

Zytowski, D. G., & Warman, R. E. (1982). The changing use of tests in counseling. *Measurement and Evaluation in Guidance, 15,* 147–152.

INDEX

theory of counseling and
psychotherapy, 239–240
theory of personality and,
237–239
Analytic stage, 240
Anastasi, A., 107, 108, 111, 113
Andersen, Tom, 344 (table)
Anderson, Harlene, 350–351
Anima, 238
Animus, 238
Ansbacher, H. L., 225
Ansbacher, R. R., 225
Ansell, C. A., 390
Antabuse, 536
Anthropology, 178
Antisocial behavior, 402–406
Antony, M. M., 284
Anxiety
cognitive model of, 295
existential therapy and, 257
Appearance, client, 131
Appelbaum, P. S., 52
Apple, 23
Applied research, 146
Appraisal of problem solving
skills, 77
Aptitude tests, 114, 445
Arbitrary inference, 295
Archetypes, 238
Arellano, A. R., 495
Aristotle, 18, 360
Arlow, J. A., 219
Armed Services Vocational
Aptitude Battery
(ASVAB), 445
Arredondo, P., 201, 459
Art and science
of assessment and
diagnosis, 106
of career counseling,
433–434
of child and adolescent
counseling, 360–361
of classic theories, 211–212
of cognitive-behavioral
counseling, 279–280
of counseling and
psychotherapy, 3–6
of counseling process, 66
of developing a personal
approach to multicultural
counseling, 168–169
of ethical-legal issues, 42–43

of experiential counseling,
246–247
of group counseling, 410
of marriage and family
counseling, 326–327
of mental health counseling,
507–508
of research and evaluation, 141
of school counseling, 461
Artistic ability of counselor, 12
Art therapy, 266–268
Ashby, J. S., 398
Asian Americans/Asians, 187
acculturation theory and, 204
individualism and, 189
Assertiveness training, 287
Assessment
administration and
interpretation
of tests in, 109–110
antisocial behavior, 403
art and science of, 106
behavioral, 118
career counseling, 445–447
child abuse and neglect, 391
child and adolescent, 376–379
child and adolescent suicide
risk, 401
clinical interview and, 130–132
defined, 107
depression in children and
adolescents, 396–398
diversity and postmodern issues
in, 136–139
of divorce, 341–342
environmental/ecological,
118–120
evaluation of tests in, 107–109
interrelatedness with
diagnosis, 107
marital, 339–342
stage of counseling process,
74, 94–95
suicide risk, 526
test bias in, 110–112
treatment planning and, 132–136
types of tests in, 113–119
See also Diagnosis
Assessment of Men, 107
Assimilative integration, 170
Association for Multicultural
Counseling and
Development, 411

Association for Specialists in Group
Work (ASGW), 411
Atkinson, D. R., 163, 184, 195
At-risk students, 495
Attachment theory,
370 (table), 372–374
Attention deficit hyperactivity
disorder (ADHD), 127 (box),
397, 400, 403
Attitude, client, 131
Autonomic physiological
behavior, 117
Avis, Judith, 351
Avoidant attachment, 373
Axline, Virginia, 381
Ayllon, T., 288
Azrin, N., 288

Baker, E. L., 222
Balance, emotional, 88
Bandura, Albert, 77, 281 (table),
283, 286, 441
Barth, K., 224
Baruth, L. G., 44, 116
Basic research, 146
Beck, Aaron, 19, 87, 281 (table),
283, 294, 295, 296, 297, 316
Beck Depression Inventory, 397
Beers, Clifford, 20
Behavioral assessment, 118
Behavior change as counseling
goal, 75
Behavior therapy, 280–288
brief counseling
perspective, 316
diversity issues, 317
for substance abuse, 536
Being and nonbeing in existential
therapy, 257–258
Belizaire, L. S., 204
Bemak, F., 499
Benton Visual Retention Test, 115
Bergin, J. J., 463
Bergin, J. W., 463
Berne, Eric, 282 (table), 298, 303
Berry, G. W., 195
Bertoia, J., 267
Beutler, L. E., 3, 12
Bias, test, 110–112, 190–191
Bibliotherapy, 179, 270–271
feminist therapy and, 315
Bidell, M. P., 502
Bigler, E. D., 115

having difficulty differentiating
between normal and
abnormal, 102
having excessive desire
to help, 101
having excessive need to be
liked, 101
marriage, child, and
family, 16 (table)
mental health, 16 (table)
overlooking physical or medical
issues, 97–98
pastoral, 16 (table)
perfectionist tendencies in, 99
process for becoming, 36–37
professional ethics, 11
as professional helpers,
15, 16–17 (table)
professional identity, 21–22
professional involvement, 42
school, 17 (table), 43
self-assessment by, 172–173
sensitivity to individual
differences, 180
supervision of, 32
taking things to personally, 102
unrealistic expectations of,
99–100
using inappropriate phrases,
100–101
values, 53–55
wanting to rescue clients from
their unhappiness, 98
Countertransference, 219, 221
Couples counseling, 328
Couples Precounseling Inventory
(SCPI), 340
Courage, 14
Cox, O. C., 192
Cramer, D., 252
Creative arts therapy (CAT),
247, 260
art therapy, 266–268
bibliotherapy, 179, 270–271
brief counseling, 276
dance therapy, 269–270
drama therapy, 268–269
multimodality, 271–274
music therapy, 261–266
professional issues, 260–261
Creative self, 225
Crethar, H. C., 200
Cripe, F. F., 265

Crisis intervention services,
511–513, 528–529
Criterion-related validity, 108
Critical incident technique, 118
Cross-cultural counseling, 182
Cross transactions, 300, 302 (figure)
Cultural encapsulation, 190
Culture, 181
Cybercounseling, 29–30
ethical issues relating to, 56–58
group, 418
mental health, 547–550

Dahir, C. A., 469
Dance therapy, 269–270
D'andrea, M., 24, 63, 163,
201, 322
Daniels, J., 163
Danish, S. J., 71
Darwin, Charles, 18, 362, 375
Data analysis, 151, 153
Databases, 31
Data gathering, 151, 152
Davanloo, H., 223
Day-Vines, N. L., 103, 502
Death with Dignity Act, 530
Decatastrophizing, 296
Decentering, 296
Decision making
ethical-legal, 58–60
promotion as counseling goal, 73
Deconstruction, 90
Deep relaxation, 287
Defense mechanisms, 215–216
DeKruyf, L., 490–491
Delucia-Waack, J. L., 427, 430
Denkowski, K. M., 45
DePauw, M. E., 53
Dependence on linear thinking, 189
Depression
child and adolescent counseling
for, 396–400
cognitive triad of, 295
Dereflection, 259
Desensitization, systematic, 287–288
De Shazer, Steve, 93, 95, 351
Developmental psychology,
173, 363–364
cognitive theories, 364–366
Developmental psychopathology,
365 (table), 367–368
Developmental school counseling,
462–465

Devine, D. A., 76
Diagnosis
art and science of, 106
categorical versus dimensional
approaches to, 125–127
clinical interview and, 130–132
diversity and postmodern issues
in, 136–139
historical perspective of,
120–122
interrelatedness with
assessment, 107
mental status exam and,
131–132
treatment planning and,
132–136
uses of, 122–123
See also Assessment
Diagnostic and Statistical Manual of
Mental Disorders, Fifth Edition
(DSM-5), 28, 112, 123, 367
changes in, 124
controversies, 127–129
on depression, 397
diversity and, 136–137
elements of diagnosis, 125
historical perspective, 120–122
nonaxial system, 124
on substance abuse, 532
WHO-ICD-CM and, 124
Diagnostic Interview for Children
and Adolescents, 378
Diagnostic Interview Schedule for
Children, 379
Dialectical behavior therapy (DBT),
319, 321–322
Dibs: In Search of Self, 381
Dichotomous thinking, 295
Dickinson, W. L., 398
Differential Aptitude Test, 114
Differential Aptitude
Test (DAT), 445
Dinkmeyer, Don, 85, 225, 229,
230, 233, 338,
348, 382, 387, 477
Discovery-oriented psychotherapy
research, 152–153
Discussion groups, 418
Disorganized/disoriented
attachment, 373
Disruptive group members,
425–426
Dissonance, 203

Distal events in child abuse and neglect, 392
Diversity issues, 63–64, 168, 182
  in assessment and diagnosis, 136–139
  in career counseling, 454–459
  in child and adolescent counseling, 407–408
  in classic theories, 242–243
  cognitive-behavioral counseling and, 317–319
  complexity of women's lives and, 313
  experiential counseling, 276–277
  gender and, 184–185
  in group counseling, 429–431
  intrapsychic perspective, 185
  in marriage and family counseling, 356–357
  in mental health counseling, 551–554
  in research and evaluation, 162–163
  school counseling and, 499–502
  sexual orientation, 185–187
  social class, 184
  See also Multicultural counseling
Divorce
  assessment of risk of, 341–342
  children of, 494–495
Dixon, A. L., 399
Dixon, D. N., 77
DO A CLIENT MAP, 133, 134 (table)
Dobson, K. S., 297
Donne, John, 226
Dougherty, A. M., 475–476
Drama therapy, 268–269
Draw-a-Person and House-Tree-Person tests, 115
Drawings in child and adolescent assessment, 376–377, 378 (figure)
Dream analysis, 220
  in Adlerian psychotherapy, 230–231
Dreikurs, Rudolph, 232–233, 243, 344 (table), 346, 368, 382
Drew, C. J., 490
Dual relationships, 47–50
  in marriage and family therapy, 355

Duffey, T., 313
Dugger, S. M., 54
Duncan, B. L., 275
Dunn, R. L., 358
Durkheim, E., 524
Durrant, M., 93, 94
Dusay, J., 299
Duty to disclose, 52
Duty to warn, 55, 58
Duvall, E. M., 335–336
Dworkin, S. H., 186
Dysinger, B. J., 385, 473

E-coaching, 30
Ecosystemic mental health counseling, 550
Ecosystems theory, 334
Educational Testing Service (ETS), 108
Education for All Handicapped Children Act, 467, 479–480
Education of professional counselors, 37–38
  certification and licensure and, 38–41
  continuing, 41
Education Trust, 468
Edwards Personal Preference Schedule (EPPS), 447
Egan, G, 69
Eggen, P., 495
Ego
  Freud on, 214–215
  Jung on, 237–238
  states in transactional analysis, 300
Ego-analytic theory, 222
Egogram, 300, 301 (figure)
Ehrfurth, J. W., 115
Eidson, C. E., Jr., 265
Eigenwelt, 258
Eight-stage model for developing personal approach to counseling, 172–181
El-Beshti, R., 493
Electra complex, 218
Electromyography (EMG), 32
Elementary school counseling, 471–472
ELIZA, 31
Elkind, David, 364, 365 (table)
Elliott, J. M., 311, 316
Elliott, R., 275

Ellis, Albert, 19, 232, 281 (table), 289, 290, 292, 316, 322
  See also Rational emotive behavior therapy (REBT)
Elman, N. S., 32
Email counseling, 29
Emmelkamp, P. M. G., 288
Emotional balance, 88
Emotional balancing, 87
Emotional disengagement, 87–88
Emotional enmeshment, 88
Emotional intelligence, 370 (table), 374–376
Emotional Intelligence, 375
Emotional stability of counselors, 13
Emotive techniques in rational emotive behavior therapy, 293
Empathy, 13
  as core condition for relationship building, 68 (table), 69–70
  in person-centered therapy, 250
Empirically supported treatments (EST), 25
Employer assistance programs (EAPs), 24
Empty-chair technique, 255
Encapsulation, cultural, 190
Encouragement, 12
  in Adlerian family counseling, 347
  in Adlerian psychotherapy, 230
Encouragers, minimal, 82
Endopsychic conflicts, 215
Engagement, 419
Enns, Carolyn, 282 (table), 311, 314, 351
Entwistle, S. R., 3
Environmental/ecological assessment, 118–120, 208
Epston, David, 351
Erford, B. T., 384, 403, 405
Erickson, A., 491
Erickson, Milton, 93
Erikson, Erik, 75, 222, 365 (table), 407, 464, 542
Estes, C. P., 237
Ethical-legal issues, 11
  art and science of, 42–43
  clinical examples, 61–63
  codes and standards of practice, 44–50

Mental health counselors, 16 (table)
role and function of, 509–519
Mental health movement, 20
Mental health or Mental Illness?, 306, 308
Mental health services, managed, 24–25
Mental Measurement Yearbook, 107
Mental status exams, 131–132
Mentoring in mental health counseling, 518
Mercer, J. R., 111–112
Merrill, C., 252
Mesmer, Anton, 18
Meta-analysis, 148
Metaphors, 91–92
Meyer, Adolph, 120, 298
Meyers, L., 26, 513, 543, 545
Michigan Alcohol Screening Test, 532
Microaggressions, racial, 193–194
Microassaults, 194
Microinsults, 194
Microinvalidations, 194
Middle school counseling, 473
Mid-spaced clients, 180
Miller, C. A., 305–306
Miller, G. M., 109
Miller, Jean Baker, 312
Miller, S. E., 463
Miller, W. R., 534
Mills, J. A., 223
Mindfulness-based approaches, 22–23, 279
cognitive-behavioral counseling, 319–320
research on, 321–322
Mindfulness-based cognitive therapy (MBCT), 320
Mindfulness-based stress reduction (MBSR), 320
Mind mapping, 30
Mind of a Child, The, 362
Mind That Found Itself, A, 20
Minimal encouragers, 82
Minimization of one's worth, 231
Minnesota Counseling Inventory, 447
Minnesota model, 535
Minnesota Multiphasic Personality Inventory (MMPI), 110, 114, 401

Minority, 182
Minors, online counseling of, 58
Minuchin, Salvador, 87, 343 (table)
Miranti, J. G., 104
Mischel, W., 375
Misconceptions of normal behavior, 188
Misrepresentations of life's demands, 231
Mitchell, L. K., 441
Mitwelt, 258
Mixed-methods research designs, 23–24, 154–155
Modeling, participant, 286–287
Mohn, R. S., 439
Molstad, E., 224
Monahan, J., 50
Montes, S., 33
Mood and affect, client, 131
Moon, K. A., 251–252
Moore-Thomas, C., 502
Moral development, theory of, 365 (table), 366–367
Moralizing, avoidance of, 85
Moreno, J., 268
Moreno, J. L., 411
Morrissette, P. J., 475
Morten, G., 184
Mosak, H., 229
Moss, J. M., 36
Motivational interviewing (MI), 96
Muller, L. E., 501
Multicultural Assessment Procedure (MAP), 112
Multicultural competency, 197
debate over, 200–201
social justice and, 197–200
Multicultural counseling and therapy (MCT), 24, 103–104
acculturation theory and, 204
art and science of developing a personal approach to, 168–169
communication problems in, 188
counseling viewed as white, middle-class activity and, 183–184
defined, 182
developing a personal approach to, 169–172
efficacy of, 195–196

eight-stage model for developing personal approach to, 172–181
etic-emic model, 205–206
evaluating counseling theories and, 204–206
faulty assumptions in, 188–190
gender and, 184–185
guidelines for, 207–209
identity development and, 202–204
intrapsychic perspective and, 185
potential challenges in, 183–196
prejudice and, 191–192
racism and, 192–193
sexual orientation and, 185–187
social class and, 184
stereotyping and, 187
suggestions for incorporating multicultural perspective in, 197–209
terms and concepts, 181–182
test bias and, 190–191
theoretical perspectives for, 182–183
Usher's model and, 205
worldview and, 201–202
See also Diversity issues
Multicultural Knowledge Skills Survey-Counselor Edition Revised (MAKSS-CE-R), 163
Multicultural psychology, 173
Multidimensional model of prejudice prevention and reduction (MMPPR), 191
Multi-Level Model of Psychotherapy, Social Justice, and Human Rights (MLM), 552
Multimodality creative arts therapy, 271–274
Multimodal therapy (MMT), 134–135, 170
Multiple-baseline designs, 159–160
Multiple career decision-making theory, 443
Murphy, J. J., 503
Murray, T. L., 25, 128
Music therapy, 261–266
Mutual-sharing groups, 418
Myers, J. E., 26, 33, 34
Myers, L. J., 202, 203